say yes
to everything

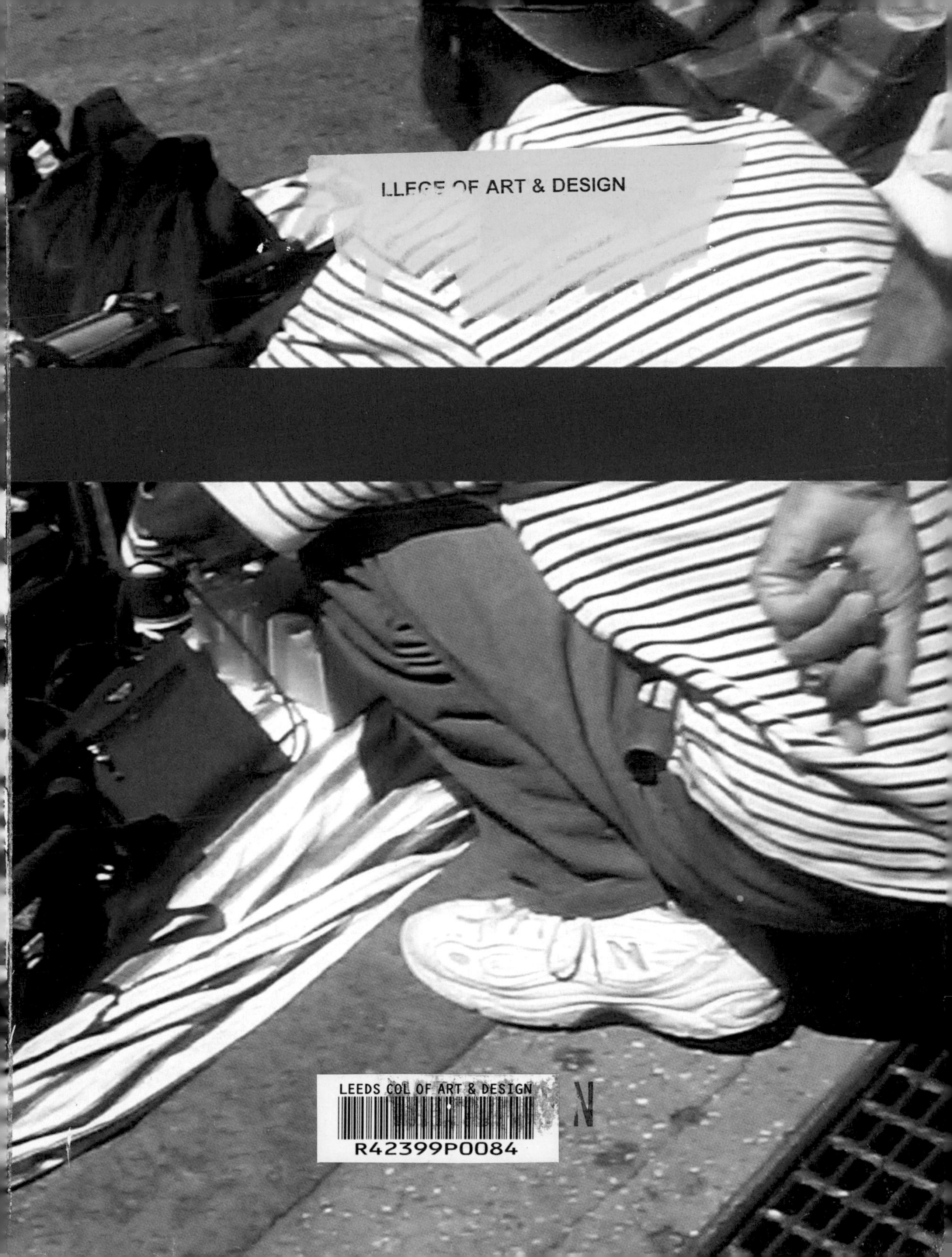

www.holland.com
Federal Government of the Netherlands official website: www.government.nl
Prime Minister of the Netherlands official website: www.jpbalkenende.nl
holland welcomes the new eu members

UNITY AND FAITH
LAGOS · CENTER OF

For more information on Nigeria visit: www.nigeriatourism.net
www.nigeria.gov.ng

EXCELLENCE

PY
NG

no alarms

no surprises

I'm not sure if this is a book or a magazine.

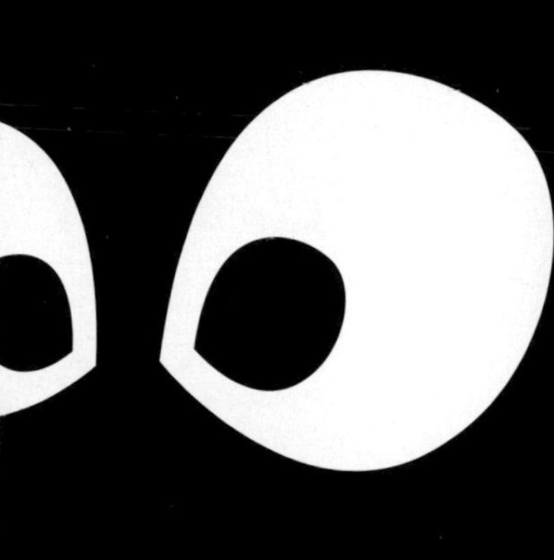
Actually, I find the tension between the two super-interesting.

contents

USA

OMA USA

AMO

M.A.

S.A.

U.K.
SPAIN
FRANCE
ITALY
GERMANY
GREECE
SCANDINAVIA
ARABIA
RUSSIA
INDIA
ASIA
S.E. ASIA
JAPAN

OMA EUR

AFRICA

TASCHEN
KÖLN LONDON LOS ANGELES MADRID PARIS TOKYO

contents

Editor's letter

Content is a product of the moment.

Inspired by the ceaseless fluctuations of the early 21st century, it bears the marks of globalism and the market, ideological siblings that, over the past twenty years, have undercut the stability of contemporary life.

This book is born of that instability. It is not timeless; it's almost out of date already. It uses volatility as a license to be immediate, informal, blunt; it embraces instability as a new source of freedom.

Content is a follow-up to *SMLXL*, an inventory of seven years of OMA's tireless labor. In many ways it is structured according to what its predecessor is not - dense, cheap, disposable.... The relentless internal logic that propelled *SMLXL* is here counteracted by the incorporation of critical, external voices. Subjects are not arranged according to size, but by geographical proximity: the trajectory moves ever eastward, beginning in San Francisco, ending in Tokyo.

Content is dominated by a single theme – "Go East" – at once a response to 9-11's mounting wreckage and an acknowledgment of the eastward momentum that has, through AMO's political involvement with the EU and an increasing density of Chinese projects, redirected the office's energy. It is an attempt to illustrate the architect's ambiguous relations with the forces of globalization, an account of seven years spent scouring the earth - not as business traveler or backpacker, but as a vagabond - roving, searching for an opportunity to realize the visions that make remaining at home torturous. *Content* is, beyond all, a tribute to what are perhaps OMA-AMO's greatest virtues - its courage, its dogged, almost existential pursuit of discomfort, its commitment to engaging the world by inviting itself to places where it has no authority, places where it doesn't "belong."

Brendan McGetrick

contents

Triumph of Realization

Rem Koolhaas: Editor-in-Chief
Brendan McGetrick: Editor
&&& **: Simon Brown, Jon Link:** Art Directors

Jason Long: Associate Editor
Jennifer Sigler: Lifestyle Editor
Penelope Dean: Society Editor
Bill Millard: Editor-at-Large
Matthew Murphy: Copy Editor
Maja Borchers: Advertising Coordinator

Thanks to:
All of OMA-AMO past and present for your help and inspiration.

Cover Illustration

Kenneth Tin-Kin Hung:
www.tinkin.com

Contributors

(in order of appearance)
***Archis*/Ole Bouman, Bill Millard, Margaret Arbanas, Shumon Basar, Eyal Weizman, R. E. Somol, Theo Deutinger, Michael Rock, Lucia Allais, Dan Wood, Hans Werlemann, Joshua Ramus, Ari Marcopoulos, Hans-Ulrich Obrist, Ellen Grimes, Richard Barnes, Fenna Haakma Wagenaar, Luis Fernández-Galiano, Shohei Shigematsu, Beatriz Colomina, Ole Scheeren, Jeffrey Inaba, Ademide Adelusi-Adeluyi, Jan Knikker, Scott Lash, Aryan Mulder, Charlie Koolhaas, Philippe Ruault, Nicolas Firket, Markus Schaefer, Nanne de Ru, Michael Hardt, Jeff Preiss, Olga Aleksakova, Reinier de Graaf, Anastassia Smirnova, Kayoko Ota, Irma Boom, Rene Daalder**

Images provided by 

Corbis

First published 2004 by TASCHEN GmbH
Hohenzollernring 53, D–50672 Köln
www.taschen.com

Printed in Germany
ISBN 3–8228–3070–4

AMOMA

PARTNERS
Rem Koolhaas, Ole Scheeren, Ellen van Loon, Joshua Ramus (NY)

DIRECTORS
David Gorin, Reiner de Graaf, Floris Alkemade

PROJECT ARCHITECTS
Adekunle Adeyemi, Olga Aleksakova, Anu Leinonen, Charles Berman, David Chacon, Eric Chang (NY), Meghan Corwin (NY), Fernando Donis, Chris van Duijn, Erez Ella, Adrianne Fisher, Mark von Hof-Zogrotzki (NY), Michelle Howard, Jeffrey Johnson (NY), Rob de Maat, Paz Martin, Roberto Otero, Shohei Shigematsu, Hiromasa Shirai, Dongmei Yao

AMO
Ademide Adelusi-Adeluyi,Theo Deutinger, Nicolas Firket, Emilie Gomart, Kayoko Ota, Nanne de Ru

ARCHITECTS
Gabriela Bojalil, Catarina Canas, Bart Cardinaal, Kees van Casteren, Holly Chacon, Jin Chong, Stephane Derveaux, Vincent van Duin, Keren Engelman, Gaspard Estourgie, Jeremy Godenir, Selva Gurdogan, Christoph Helmus, Olaf Hitz, Christopher James, Alex de Jong, Abhijit Kapade, Michel van der Kar, Joao Leal Bravo da Costa, Peter Lee, Alexey Levchuk, Mee Michelle Liu, Xiaodong Liu, Fabienne Louyot, Cristina Murphy, Daan Ooievaar, Monica Pacheco, Shade Rahbaran, Nuno Rosado, Andre Schmidt, Torsten Schroder, Manuel Shvartzberg, Isabel da Silva, Michael Smith, Alexander Sverdlov, Gregers Thomsen, Johan de Wachter, Camia Young, Dirk Zschunke

PUBLIC RELATIONS
Chantal Defesche, Talitha van Dijk, Rebecca Ehn, Joosje van Geest, Jan Knikker, Marcelle van Bokhoven

ADMINISTRATION
Monique Bernadina, Miranda Grit, Sharon Ullman (NY), Jolanda van der Reijden, Vanessa Saa Ordonez, Cees de Vries, Marije de Vries

SECRETARIAT
Sandra Bloemrijk, Marianne Kornaat, Kurt van der Ende, Mayyan Fan, Sylvie Londerman, Carolien van der Niet, Sonia Rijnhout, Nicolette Pot

IT
Rodger Kelly, Mat Schimmel, Kevin Sonneveld

contents

Architecture is a fuzzy amalgamation

of ancient knowledge and contemporary practice, an awkward way to look at the world and an inadequate medium to operate on it.

Any architectural project takes five years; no single enterprise - ambition, intention, need - remains unchanged in the contemporary maelstrom. Architecture is too slow. Yet, the word "architecture" is still pronounced with certain reverence (outside of the profession). It embodies the lingering hope - or the vague memory of a hope - that shape, form, coherence could be imposed on the violent surf of information that washes over us daily. Maybe, architecture doesn't have to be stupid after all. Liberated from the obligation to construct, it can become a way of thinking about anything - a discipline that represents relationships, proportions, connections, effects, the diagram of everything.

The random sequence of commissions on which each architect depends is the opposite of an agenda. The birth - shortly after *SMLXL* - of OMA's mirror image AMO enabled us to create knowledge independent of chance and to pursue our own interests in parallel to those of our clients.

Content documents a "split" - a *grand écart*, the fiendishly difficult moment, immobile, on the ground in classical ballet - the maximum stretch between two opposite forces, realization and speculation, performed by OMA and AMO. Because the relationship is fluid and unstable, it is presented as a magazine - a freeze frame of one particular moment. Like a magazine, it may be resurrected when there is more to report....

Rem Koolhaas

ACKNOWLEDGMENTS

This work has been deeply influenced by others:
Without communication and collaborations with: Lucia Allais, Edgar Cleyne, Beatriz Colomina, Catherine David, Chris Dercon, Okwui Enwezor, Rebecca Gomperts, Hou Hanru, Michael Hardt, Frederick Jameson, Sanford Kwinter, Scott Lash, Bruno Latour, Mark Leonard, Hans-Ulrich Obrist, Bob Somol, Sarah Whiting, Mark Wigley.... Without the participation of: Cecil Balmond and ARUP, Petra Blaisse and Inside Outside, Michael Rock and 2x4, Irma Boom, Michel Cova, Renz van Luxemburg.... Without architects Peter Eisenman, Herzog & de Meuron, Jeffrey Inaba, Qinyun Ma, Lars Spuybroek, Robert Venturi and Denise Scott Brown.... Without the demands of clients Chris Anderson, Maxwell Anderson, Patrizio Bertelli, Duc Boorsma, Edgar Bronfman, Pedro Burmeister, Willard Holmes, Madame Hong, Deborah Jacobs, Tom Krens, Li Xiao Ming, Mikhail Petrovsky, He Ping, Miuccia Prada, Si Newhouse, Romano Prodi, Donna Robertson, Xu Wei, Huan Yen.... Without the contributions of: Marc Heummer, Vincent de Rijk, Hans Werlemann.... Without the support of Madelon Vriesendorp and of Peter Rowe.... Without the globalized intelligence of AMOMA.... Without Dan Wood (AMOMA NY), Markus Schaefer (AMO), Jeffrey Johnson (IIT), no longer with us.... Without the curator Kayoko Ota.... Without the help of Margit Mayer, Ingrid Sischy, and Mathias Vriens....

there would be no

Content

contents

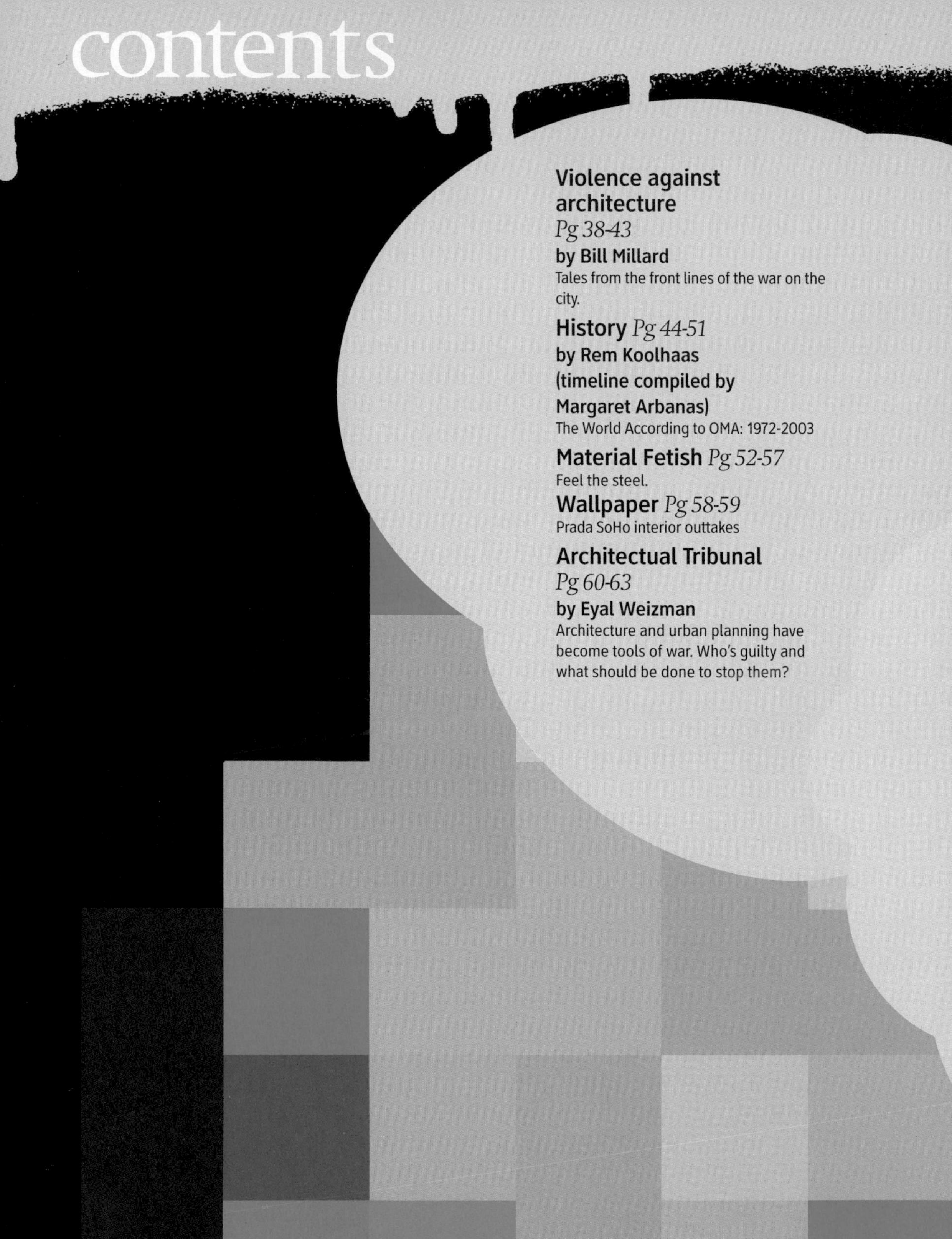

FOCKA F2

contents

contents

TOLET
TOLET
NO KIDS
NO BALLGAME

contents

MUSEUM

AMO

Event Sample Formats:

Event Sample Formats:

Event Sample Formats:

Event Sample Formats:

Event Sample Formats:

DON'T ASK WHAT CONTENT CAN DO FOR YOU

Small response: Intimate, Micro-scale Event

Average to Substantial response: Event of Moderate to Considerable Size

Massive to Mega-Scale Response: Major Discursive Break-through, Profound Social Change

ASK WHAT YOU CAN DO FOR CONTENT

Content

Archis is the most awkward architectural magazine at the moment, a kind of aggressive anti-*Domus* that tries to drag architecture from the Stone Age - where it is still firmly stuck, in spite of Catia® - into a more integrated, contemporary culture.... Content offered them space to launch a number of events - microscopic or monumental - whose nature will be entirely decided by its readers.

Just as architecture is full of concepts that are in danger of sinking under their own weight, so the debate about architecture is organized according to worn-out formulas: the conference, the lecture, the seminar, the workshop. Architecture seems to have been reduced to the mantra of academic exchange, far removed from realities in which architecture is not only a topic of discussion, but also a source of conflict. Archis, magazine for Architecture, City and Visual Culture, is therefore introducing a new form of debate. Events in which reflection and action coincide. In which spirit becomes architecture, with you as its bricks and mortar.
More info at **www.archis.org** or **Archis Magazine**

ARCHIS R.S.V.P. EVENTS are a series of actions that will be organized all over the world from December 2003 onwards. The form of each event is determined by the size of the response; in other words, you just respond to the content and your response helps us to determine the actual form of the event which might be anything from mass demonstration to free-running, from cruise to performance; from mega event to flash mob.

ARCHIS

Event Sample Formats: | Coffee break | Event Sample Formats: | Demonstration | Teach Inn

ARCHIS R.S.V.P. EVENTS

Response-based Events; A Quest for Ideas, Spirit and Action featuring You, Archis and AMO

EVENT NO. 01 OF 09

Berlin, January 17/18, 2004

SINGLE ISSUE SPACE

We are for ever talking about globalization and connectivity, but meanwhile we are busy dividing the world up into zones. Swamped by good intentions and other strategies of fear, the spatial interweave of programme and meaning is everywhere being picked apart into discrete areas named after their function. The thematization of space is leading to a spatial apartheid, a universal archipelago of 'scripted spaces' separated by hard boundaries and strict checkpoints. An event about monocultures.

If you are interested in the CONTENT, please reply to this page by fax, or email your response to rsvp@archis.org, giving your name, profession and number of reservations before December 22, 2003. We'll get back to you with details about the time, place and form of event in due course. More info at **www.archis.org** or **Archis Magazine**

PLEASE FILL IN THIS FIELD

I hereby make a reservation for RSVP event no. 01: SINGLE ISSUE SPACE
By making this reservation, I co-determine the size of the forthcoming event.

name: number of reservations:

e-mail address:

phone number:

profession:

fax +31 20 3203927 or e-mail rsvp@archis.org

ARCHIS R.S.V.P. EVENTS are a series of actions that will be organized all over the world from December 2003 onwards. The form of each event is determined by the size of the response; in other words, you just respond to the content and your response helps us to determine the actual form of the event which might be anything from mass demonstration to free-running, from cruise to performance; from mega event to flash mob.

Diner Pensant

Flash Mob

Casual Encounter

High Tea

Event Sample Formats:

ARCHIS R.S.V.P. EVENTS

Response-based Events; A Quest for Ideas, Spirit and Action featuring You, Archis and AMO

EVENT NO. 02 OF 09

Berlin, January 17/18, 2004

BANNING THE BANNERS

Most of what we say and write about architecture is determined by key concepts that appear to have outlived their meaning. The world is pinned down by formulas and clichés that allow for orderly debate, but which also limit our ability to renew our insights.

For example, everyone talks about architecture as if it is clear exactly what it is. Where it begins and where it ends. What you need to know and what not. What it is made of. An event about the regime of concepts.

If you are interested in the CONTENT, please reply to this page by fax, or email your response to rsvp@archis.org, giving your name, profession and number of reservations before December 22, 2003. We'll get back to you with details about the time, place and form of event in due course. More info at **www.archis.org** or **Archis Magazine**

PLEASE FILL IN THIS FIELD

I hereby make a reservation for RSVP event no. 02: BANNING THE BANNERS
By making this reservation, I co-determine the size of the forthcoming event.

name: number of reservations:

e-mail address:

phone number:

profession:

fax +31 20 3203927 or e-mail rsvp@archis.org

ARCHIS R.S.V.P. EVENTS are a series of actions that will be organized all over the world from December 2003 onwards. The form of each event is determined by the size of the response; in other words, you just respond to the content and your response helps us to determine the actual form of the event which might be anything from mass demonstration to free-running, from cruise to performance; from mega event to flash mob.

Cruise | Event Sample Formats: | Global Meditation | Electro Magnetic Synergy | Issue Dating

ARCHIS R.S.V.P. EVENTS

Response-based Events; A Quest for Ideas, Spirit and Action
featuring You, Archis and AMO

EVENT NO. 03 OF 09

Brussels, March, 2004

EUROPEAN IDENTITIES

Does Europe really exist? Does it correspond to the area that bears that name? Or is it a mental concept? Whatever one's answer, a different outer limit can be drawn for every definition and it is this vagueness that gives rise to the never-ending uncertainty surrounding European integration.

Perhaps the problem of expressing Europe by means of its architecture in Brussels, is the perfect example of the problem of Europe itself. An event about an old continent.

If you are interested in the CONTENT, please reply to this page by fax, or email your response to rsvp@archis.org, giving your name, profession and number of reservations before December 22 2003. We'll get back to you with details about the time, place and form of event in due course. More info at **www.archis.org** or **Archis Magazine**

PLEASE FILL IN THIS FIELD

I hereby make a reservation for RSVP event no. 04: EUROPEAN IDENTITIES
By making this reservation, I co-determine the size of the forthcoming event.

name: number of reservations:

e-mail address:

phone number:

profession:

fax +31 20 3203927 or e-mail rsvp@archis.org

ARCHIS R.S.V.P. EVENTS are a series of actions that will be organized all over the world from December 2003 onwards. The form of each event is determined by the size of the response; in other words, you just respond to the content and your response helps us to determine the actual form of the event which might be anything from mass demonstration to free-running, from cruise to performance; from mega event to flash mob.

Causerie | Free Running | Master Class | Web Course | Event Sample Formats:

ARCHIS R.S.V.P. EVENTS

Response-based Events; A Quest for Ideas, [illegible] nd Action
featuring You, Archis and AM[illegible]

EVENT NO. 04 OF 09

Athens/Istanbul, September, 2004

PERVERSION

It is not difficult to find evidence for the existence of a perverse age. Psychological self-absorption, internal wrangling, unquestioned wealth, pollution and depletion of natural resources, erosion of the public domain, a lack of historical awareness, pointless regulation, excessive policy making, cultural incest...

We ask whether this kind of lawlessness can be thought of as a liberating climate of true innovation.
An event about perversity as a liberating device.

If you are interested in the CONTENT, please reply to this page by fax, or email your response to rsvp@archis.org, giving your name, profession and number of reservations before May 15, 2004. We'll get back to you with details about the time, place and form of event in due course. More info at **www.archis.org** or **Archis Magazine**

PLEASE FILL IN THIS FIELD

I hereby make a reservation for RSVP event no. 05: PERVERSION
By making this reservation, I co-determine the size of the forthcoming event.

name: number of reservations:

e-mail address:

phone number:

profession:

fax +31 20 3203927 or e-mail rsvp@archis.org

ARCHIS R.S.V.P. EVENTS are a series of actions that will be organized all over the world from December 2003 onwards. The form of each event is determined by the size of the response; in other words, you just respond to the content and your response helps us to determine the actual form of the event which might be anything from mass demonstration to free-running, from cruise to performance; from mega event to flash mob.

Event Sample Formats: | Talk Show | Event Sample Formats: | Happening | Jam Session

ARCHIS R.S.V.P. EVENTS

Response-based Events; A Quest for Ideas, Spirit and Action
featuring You, Archis and AMO

EVENT NO. 05 OF 09

Amman, October, 2004

PARANOIA

New and old social antagonisms, between individuals and between civilizations, reorganize our spaces. The chorus of Angst is paramount. So, you'd better adapt to your environment. Brace yourself against the hazardous elements with an aesthetics of surveillance.

There is a job for design in a culture of fear. But do we need Paranoid Chic? Packaged and marketed, the aesthetics of surveillance participates in the fashion world, transforming a condition into a commodity? Do you like fear any more now?
An event about protecting your life and belongings.

If you are interested in the CONTENT, please reply to this page by fax, or email your response to rsvp@archis.org, giving your name, profession and number of reservations before June 15, 2004. We'll get back to you with details about the time, place and form of event in due course. More info at **www.archis.org** or **Archis Magazine**

PLEASE FILL IN THIS FIELD

I hereby make a reservation for RSVP event no. 06: PARANOIA
By making this reservation, I co-determine the size of the forthcoming event.

name: number of reservations:

e-mail address:

phone number:

profession:

fax +31 20 3203927 or e-mail rsvp@archis.org

ARCHIS R.S.V.P. EVENTS are a series of actions that will be organized all over the world from December 2003 onwards. The form of each event is determined by the size of the response; in other words, you just respond to the content and your response helps us to determine the actual form of the event which might be anything from mass demonstration to free-running, from cruise to performance; from mega event to flash mob

ILLUSTRATION SIMON BROWN

Violence against Architecture:

Quixote Comes of Age in Sarajevo

BY BILL MILLARD

Architects are necessarily concerned with construction, but construction is only half the story: almost everything that goes up also eventually comes down. Destruction, the other part of the life cycle of buildings, receives less attention than it probably deserves. Whether a structure falls through deliberate, often dramatic human effort or through the long, embarrassing grind of natural wear, its fall is as much a human decision as its rise. Why and how do we unbuild, after all the effort we've devoted to building?

Building is a drastic intervention not only in space but in the field of possible behavioral choices; it lights up segments of the Borgesian Garden of Forking Paths, guiding some decisions, making others possible, and foreclosing some options entirely. Buildings require peace, if not always stability, on the part of the people who inhabit and surround them; the civilized coexistence of humans and their well-planned, well-tended structures may in some senses be Earth's highest symbiosis. Yet buildings stand in the way of many types of change, from social restructurings to the wars people wage. To the extent that these struggles include the built environment as a target - sometimes a target in its own right, not an incidental victim of a general onslaught - the forms and purposes of our unbuilding offer a useful channel for interrogation into how societies function or fail.

URBICIDE, ACTIVE AND PASSIVE

The prototypical attack on built structures by a human being is Don Quixote tilting at windmills: absurd, futilitarian, self-parodying. The real event is less comical. Except for the occasional controlled and spectacular demolition, rapid violence against architecture is a wartime event. As forms of warfare evolve to express human purposefulness more precisely, and more darkly, the destruction of buildings is increasingly a specific strategic maneuver. Among the forms war, terror, and insurrection now take, including genocide and ethnocide, one may include deliberate assault on urban structures, or *urbicide*.

If war is the continuation of politics by other means, in Clausewitz's famous formulation, urbicide is the eruption of implicit struggle into the sphere of organized space. Forms of struggle don't all take the same pace. Energy can also be applied to a building slowly, through the subterfuges of politics or the erosions of neglect. Buildings and infrastructure can fall victim to more gradual forces, some involving human intent and some more careless than malicious. *Passive urbicide* is less dramatic but more insidious, and in some cases outright perverse, even if ostensibly benign - a city can be ruined through acts of construction as well. Urbicide doesn't always imply outright hatred of buildings and their occupants; arrogance and obliviousness often accomplish the same thing.

WAR AND THE CITY

Since the days of the garrisonlike city-state, warfare has expanded in scale, relocated in space, and observed an ever more elaborate division of labor. Cities are harder to defend and have even grown fatalistically indifferent toward defense, neglecting or repurposing their fortifications; the armories of Manhattan, by the later 20th century, had morphed into museums, convention sites, and office space. In the shadow of the ultimate urbicidal instrument, the atomic bomb, urban life, in the words of historian Martin Shaw, has become "post-military."[1] Polarization between urban and anti-urban worldviews, conversely, reaches its extreme in military cultures: warrior castes and guerrilla movements in nation after nation have defined themselves in terms of rustic purity, in contrast to the heterogeneity and hedonism found in urban centers. It is no accident that the dominant accent in the U.S. military is the Southern agrarian twang, or that special schools for officers (often pervaded by religious fundamentalism, hostile to coeducation, etc.) cluster in rural states. The antebellum-nostalgia-mongering Virginia Cavalier shares with the *Sendero Luminoso* peasant militant, the Wahhabi nomad, the *volkische* Nazi judeophobe, the Maoist cadre, the Khmer Rouge guerrilla, and the Serbian nationalist a predisposition to view cities and their residents as decadent, polluted, effeminate, and probably in need of some form of cleansing fire.

Among the forms war, terror, and insurrection now take, one may include deliberate assault on urban structures, or *urbicide*.

The bookburnings and genocides that distinguish fascist movements from history's less ideologically oriented belligerents are now accompanied by this new tactical category, consciously antihistorical and in a precise sense anticivil. It is said to have acquired its name from architect Bogdan Bogdanovitch, initially in Serbo-Croat (*Urbicid*),[2] in discussions of the deliberate destruction of Sarajevo, whose physical layout once maximized and embodied intercultural exchange: a hub-and-spoke structure with ethnic conclaves on the periphery joined in a central marketplace.[3]

By disturbing civic space, with its turbulent negotiations of identity borders, urbicide sharpens previously fluid definitions in a desperate attempt to erase difference, to reverse the interpenetrations through which difference can flourish. Urbicide, as a predisposition bordering on an ideology, is ultimately rooted in fear: dread of unpredictable interactions, unease at ways of life premised on constant change, outrage at the discovery that someone else has constructed, controlled, and publicly shared a set of resources that complicate the equation of identity and place. The practitioner of urbicide is often someone whose experience of physical space is inseparable from an experience of group solidarity: someone who has not traveled.

SLOW AND SMOKELESS BURNINGS

If wars and revolts are the heart attacks of the urban body, that body is susceptible to cancers as well. Our species also attacks its buildings through indolence and abandonment. Both private-sector and public-sector stewardship can fail here; the landlord who warehouses apartments, or consciously lets decay and vermin drive out low-paying tenants so as to replace them at a higher rent, has substantially the same effect on the built environment as the state that arranges market mechanisms too awkwardly to support incentives for preservation.[4] Either way, attention to the forms of entropy that plague any form of life tends to flag over time, as if the gradual pace of change in buildings implied that they could look after themselves. Admirers of buildings may find this form of passive urbicide even more painful than violence, since it prolongs the spectacle of once-admirable structures in decrepitude and decline.

Robert Frost's phrase "the slow smokeless burning of decay"[5] identifies an abandoned pile of wood, never assembled into a habitable structure or consumed as useful energy, slowly returning its molecules to the Earth through rot and oxidation, an emblem of inexorable entropic change regardless of human volition and decisions. Whether buildings burn rapidly or erode slowly, they are destined to abandon us when we fail to attend to them, or misunderstand them, or remain obtuse to their potential to civilize us.

NOTES

1. Shaw, Martin. "New wars of the city: 'urbicide' and 'genocide.'" Available online at *www.sussex.ac.uk/Users/hafa3/city.htm www.martinshaw.org/city.htm*.
2. Stephen Graham ("'Clean Territory': Urbicide in the West Bank," *openDemocracy*, August 7, 2002 *www.opendemocracy.net/debates/article-2-45-241.jsp)* attributes the term to both Bogdanovitch and U.S. urban historian Marshall Berman, who began using it in the 1980s in reference to the collapsing South Bronx, cloven by the aggressively urbicidal highway constructions of Robert Moses; see *All That Is Solid Melts into Air: the Experience of Modernity* (NY: Penguin, 1982) and "Falling Towers: City Life after Urbicide," in Dennis Crow, ed. *Geography and Identity: Living and Exploring Geopolitics of Identity* (Washington, DC: Maissoneuve, 1996). Berman himself, however (*http://eserver.org/clogic/4-2/monchinski_berman.html*), has described first encountering the term in Eric Darton, *Divided We Stand: A Biography of New York's World Trade Center* (NY: Basic Books, 1999), quoted from discussions of the WTC planning process in the 1960s, which accused the WTC itself of being an instrument of urbicide - in its erection and transformation of its neighborhood, *n.b.*, not its later destruction.
3. Cynthia Simmons, in "Urbicide and the Myth of Sarajevo" (*Partisan Review* 68 [Fall 2001]: 624-631), discusses the views of Bogdanovic, Dzevad Karahasan, Adam Seligman, and others, offering a nuanced view of the case of Sarajevan ethnic pluralism while still supporting the value of "true multiculturalism (a real knowledge of and respect for various cultures) and the city as its embodiment in order to avoid the chaos of nationalism and the periphery."
4. Even the World Bank now appears to recognize that both market failure and governmental failure are involved in urban infrastructural decline: see its report *Cities in Transition: A Strategic View of Urban and Local Government Issues* (2000) , available at *www.worldbank.org/html/fpd/urban//publicat/cities_in_transition.pdf.*
5. "The Wood-pile," from *North of Boston* (NY: Holt, 1917).

Urbicide: selected case studies

BY BILL MILLARD

Stari Most Mostar, Bosnia and Herzegovina

SITE: LOS ANGELES, CALIFORNIA, AND ENVIRONS
DATE: 1920's-1950's
CHARGE: URBICIDE BY SUBVERSION OF MASS TRANSIT

In 1938 General Motors, Standard Oil, and Firestone Tire & Rubber form a subsidiary, Pacific City Lines, to purchase and dismantle Californian urban streetcar lines, beginning in Stockton, Fresno, and San Jose; project extends to Los Angeles and 18 other cities by 1943. Similar activity by GM's holding companies has been under way in Portland, New York, and other cities since the 1920s, accelerating national transition from streetcars to buses. Assault on LA's 1,000-mile Pacific Electric Railway or "Big Red" line attracts particular attention: federal grand jury indicts GM, subsidiary National City Lines, and seven other firms for criminal conspiracy in 1947 over Big Red case, but with over 100 streetcar systems destroyed nationwide by 1950, urban mass transit is essentially dead in the U.S. and antitrust investigators can convict GM only of conspiring to monopolize sales of buses. GM is fined $5,000 in 1949, and its treasurer H. C. Grossman is personally fined $1. Federal Highway Acts of 1944, 1956, and 1968 realize a strategy

designed by GM's Alfred Sloan (chairman, 1923-1956) to suburbanize or "Los Angelize" the national landscape and economy through crippling of city infrastructure, replacement of trolleys by diesel buses, and direction of the vast majority of public funds from mass transit to highway construction. In later decades, amidst growing skepticism about automotive hegemony nationwide, renewed support for mass transit will become a pivotal component of Green activism, "New Urbanist" planning theory, slow-growth advocacy, and related movements. Los Angeles will open two light rail lines in 1990 and a small subway line in 1993, covering a total of 59 miles. Part of the light rail Blue Line between LA and Long Beach retraces a Pacific Electric interurban Red Car route.

SITE: SARAJEVO AND MOSTAR, FORMER YUGOSLAVIA
DATE: CA. 1990-1996...
CHARGE: URBICIDE BY TARGETING OF CIVIC INFRASTRUCTURE

Despite the enduring cliché "balkanization," cities in this region enjoy a high degree of intergroup harmony in centuries between Habsburg wars and World War I; as philosopher/historian Cynthia Simmons comments, "The modern stereotype of age-old Balkan hatreds is a post-World War I invention."[1] Tradition of pluralism, however, does not pervade entire region. Intervention by "Great Powers" and construction of artificial states creates new tensions and brings latent ones to foreground. Nazi support of Croatian nationalist-fascist (*Ustashe*) regime, which massacres Serbs in six figures during World War II, fuels lasting animosity, as does Serbian puppet fascist (*Chetnik*) regime. Death of Tito in 1980 and gradual dissolution of Communist Yugoslavian state removes one artificial source of stability; Bosnian Muslims, Kosovar Albanians, and other minorities are increasingly caught in vise between Serbian and Croatian nationalists. Serbian Orthodox Church joins Slobodan Milosevic's Serbian

Soldiers built an elaborate mechanism specifically to remove any physical evidence that a vibrant, hybrid culture had existed there.

Socialist Party [sic] and other groups in denouncing industrialization, migration to cities, intermarriage, low birth rates, decadence of educated classes, and other perceived threats to ethnic solidarity (title of influential book by Ilijas Bosnjovic, Sarajevo, 1990: *Demografska crna jama: Nova zamka industrijskog drustva*, or *The Demographic Black Hole: The New Trap of Industrialized Society*). Conditions degenerate into anarchy, "ethnic cleansing" (forced migration), military atrocities, and mass imprisonment, particularly of Muslims. Siege of Sarajevo begins in 1992; shelling continues until 1996. In a region where kinship is critical to self-definition, mass rape becomes a deliberate strategy for terrorizing populations. Ethnic-nationalist forces (largely Serbian and Croatian villagers) specifically attack Sarajevo's cultural monuments and infrastructure, bombing bridges, mosques, churches, synagogues, markets, museums, libraries, and cafes, as well as homes, in an attempt to eradicate the conditions of urbanity. One Croatian historian,[2] recounting the burning of the Vijecnica (the National Library of Bosnia and Herzegovina) and other structures, describes the former Yugoslav Army's systematic preparations to destroy both these institutions and the history they preserved: before the attack, soldiers built a complex series of tunnels, subterranean bunkers, storage spaces, and camouflaged elevators - an elaborate mechanism constructed specifically to remove and disperse any physical evidence that a vibrant hybrid culture comprising Catholics, Orthodox Christians, Muslims, and Jews had ever existed there.[3] Likewise, the Ottoman *Stari Most* (Old Bridge) that linked Mostar's Muslim east and Croatian west, defended against Serb forces by the Croatian Defense Council in 1992, sustained overwhelming bombardment in 1993 - by the same Croatian Defense Council. The notorious proclamation by an anonymous U.S. military press officer in Vietnam, "We had to destroy the village in order to save it," is subjected here to a bizarre *détournement*: "We had to save the bridge so that we could destroy it.

SITE: LAGOS, NIGERIA, AND ENVIRONS
DATE: 1956-PRESENT
CHARGE: URBICIDE BY GOVERNMENT LAND POLICY

Lagos after the 1970s undergoes the kind of explosive, irregular economic growth that perhaps only a petroleum-based economy can generate. Large oil reserves are discovered in 1956 in Oloibiri in the Niger River delta; Western petroleum firms move in immediately, welcomed by a series of governments, military and civilian. Manic development during the oil-price fluctuations of the 1970s attracts civil and social engineers bent on transforming space; Lagos rapidly sprouts Eurostyle bridges, highways, and office buildings that form vertiginous contrasts with traditional landscapes and folkways. Amid massive migration from the countryside–governmental and UN studies project Lagos to be the world's third largest city by 2015–inequalities of wealth become as stark as any in the world, need for housing vastly outstrips supply, rents and building-material costs skyrocket, and conflict over land rights and built resources becomes frequent and brutal. Housing demolition, usually but not exclusively by federal or state officials, becomes a recurrent weapon in land-rights battles. A typical experience is the forcible eviction in 1989-1990 of some 300,000 squatters in the shantytown of Maroko on Victoria Island, Lagos, a high-density settlement on land 1.5 m above sea level (and in close proximity to prosperous areas of Victoria >

By identifying urban space as part of the battleground, conflict has essentially weaponized the bulldozer, the crane, and even the architect's studio.

Island and Ikoyi, whose influential residents fear for their property values). Former military president Ibrahim Babangida visits Maroko in February 1989 with promises of rapid development; instead, on July 7, the state government announces that the coastal town is scheduled for mass demolition on seven days' notice. Promises of relocation for refugees are kept in roughly 3% of cases, invariably into slum conditions. Samuel Aiyeyemi, leader of the Maroko Evictees Committee, tells reporters of a circulating ambulance filled with empty coffins for the use of "anyone who cared to die." The demolition of Maroko, according to UN-HABITAT, is planned during 1987 as officials were taking part in the UN's International Year of Shelter for the Homeless.[5] A similar fate befalls 100 homes in Ala village, about 20 km east of Victoria Island, in August 1995, demolished by the miltary state government despite a court order to the contrary. No comprehensive land register exists to help settle ownership disputes between individuals and the government, or between family and village groups; repeated sales of the same plot of land to more than one buyer are common, exacerbating conflicts and increasing the prevalence of extralegal "resolutions" in the form of demolition. With each destructive incident adding to the numbers of unresettled refugees, the cycle of mass drift, illegal settlements, and repeated forcible relocation continues to spiral. Sometimes the cycle comes full circle: after a pipeline rupture and oil spill, Friends of the Earth reports an eight-day forcible eviction/demolition operation in November 2002, destroying 150 houses and shops and dislocating 5,000 settlers who had built on land claimed by Shell Oil – once again in Maroko.

SITE: JERUSALEM; WEST BANK AND GAZA SETTLEMENTS
DATE: 1990S-2000S
CHARGE: URBICIDE BY CYCLICAL CONSTRUCTION, RESTRICTION, AND DESTRUCTION

Perhaps, given global population-concentrating tendencies and group interspersal, the political and theo-ethnic clashes of the 21st century will increasingly, even inevitably feature an urbicidal component. The Israeli-Palestinian struggle includes among its infinite ramifications, entanglements, and impasses the explicitly urbicidal practices of both sides. Guerrilla tactics such as the Hamas signature - the suicide bombing in a public square, street, restaurant, or disco - are the obvious and well-publicized example: those who reject the entire Israeli presence in the region have identified the transformation of public urban space from unreflectively habitable to consciously hazardous as a key instrument in asymmetrical warfare, a means of amplifying their overmatched local power. The response from the Israeli military and political establishment has been equally hostile to urbanity, or at least to Palestinian urbanity. Along with constructing strikingly modern and comfortable settlements for Israeli civilians in the West Bank ("facts on the ground") and bulldozing critical infrastructural elements in Palestinian areas, the Israeli state maintains a series of highly restrictive building-permit laws effectively limiting Palestinian housing construction to small, primitive illegal structures. The urban conditions and ensuing quality of life that Israel wishes to protect for its own citizens thus remain unavailable to Arabs in the adjacent territories.[6] Existing buildings lacking the permits are regularly razed, and a new structure that ought to have ominous symbolic resonances for Israelis with roots in Central or Eastern Europe, a 217-mile wall (euphemized as a "security fence"), is under construction, with the aim of blocking at least some suicide attacks against Israeli cities, at the cost of

CORBIS

isolating Palestinian enclaves, worsening the conditions associated with resentment and terrorist recruitment, and violating international strictures against permanent construction in disputed territories. By identifying urban space and structure as part of the wider battleground, this conflict has essentially weaponized the bulldozer, the crane, and even the architect's studio.[7]

SITE: AYODHYA, INDIA
DATE: 1857; 1992; ONGOING
CHARGE: URBICIDE BY THEOLOGICAL DISPUTE

British Prime Minister Palmerston, in a letter to Lord Canning, Viceroy of India, regarding the end of Muslim rule after the British capture of Delhi, recommends, "Every civil building connected with Mahommedan tradition should be levelled to the ground without regard to antiquarian veneration or artistic predilection" (9 October 1857, Canning Papers). In subsequent eras Christian colonialsts would exercise no monopoly on tactical demolition in this contentiously religious region. In the 20th century, charging that Muslims had built their mosque Babri Masjid (1528) directly on the site of the Ram Janambhoomi, the sacred birthplace of the god Ram a.k.a. Rama, Hindus associated with a series of militant fundamentalist groups (the Bajrang Dal, Adam Sena, Rashtriya Swayamsevak Sangh, Bharatiya Janata Party, and Vishwa Hindu Parishad) attack the structure with the intention of razing it. This would finally be accomplished on the afternoon of 6 December 1992, when a mob of Hindu *karsevaks* storm and demolish the domes of the mosque, erecting a makeshift temple to Sri Rama in its place. The Babri Masjid Action Committee (a fundamentalist Muslim organization) and other Muslim commentators respond that Ram's birthplace is by no means certain, that thousands of Hindus venerate other sites as the birthplace, that archaeological evidence of a Ram Mandir temple destroyed in the construction of Babri Masjid is spurious, and that the Ram Janambhoomi movement is less interested in worship than in routing Muslims from territories that the two religions have shared for centuries. Litigation before the Allahabad High Court between the rival Hindu and Muslim groups is not expected to yield a clear resolution of the Ayodhya dispute, as both sides have carried out riotous reciprocal attacks on thousands of persons, homes, and rival shrines, with increased violence promised in the event of a verdict either way. Non-militant Hindu leaders have formed a Ramalaya Trust to construct a grand *mandir* lawfully at an alternate site. Building and demolition, however, remain key instruments in this polarized theo-political standoff. ■

NOTES

1. Simmons, C. "Urbicide and the myth of Sarajevo." *Partisan Review* 68 (2001): 624-631.
2. Lovrenovic, Ivan. "The Hatred of Memory: In Sarajevo, Burned Books and Murdered Pictures." *New York Times*, May 28, 1994; archived by the Bosnian Ingathering Manuscript Project at *www.kakarigi.net/manu/lovrenov.htm*.
3. The loyalty of prewar Sarajevans to cosmopolitanism, not to specific groups, could inspire resistance through strategic absurdism: "Sarajevo, [narrator Bill] Tribe explained, was not tribal: Serbs marry Croats, Croats Muslims. Before the war, the authorities had tried to get citizens to define themselves in a census, the better to split them up. Many refused, volunteering suitable Alice in Wonderland responses. Nationality: Lampshade; Religion: Tablecloth." — Allison Pearson, *The Independent* (London), on the film *Urbicide: A Sarajevo Diary* (dir. Dom Rotheroe, 1993), *www.frif.com/cat97/t-z/urbicide.html*.
4. Oghifo, Bennett. "Evicted Maroko Residents Chart Own Resettlement Programme." *This Day Online*, archived at *www.thisdayonline.com/archive/2003/07/01/20030701est02.html*.
5. *Strategies to Combat Homelessness*. Nairobi: UN Centre for Human Settlements (Habitat), 2000, p. 56, www.unhabitat.org/en/uploadcontent/publication/hs-599-00.pdf
6. Graham, *op.cit.*; Human Rights Watch, World Report 1999, "Israel, the Occupied West Bank, Gaza Strip, and Palestinian Authority Territories," *www.hrw.org/worldreport99/mideast/israel.html*.
7. For discussions by Eyal Weizman, Stephen Graham, Claire Moon, and others, including Paul Hilder's report on censorship of the Israeli contribution to the 2002 World Congress of Architecture in Berlin based on politically engaged material written for the group's catalogue "A Civilian Occupation," see *open Democracy*'s series "The Politics of Verticality," *www.opendemocracy.net/debates/issue-2-45.jsp*.

A Brief History of OMA by Rem Koolhaas

Prologue In 1966, I first heard of a brief mom
Soviet Union, 1923 - where the most intimate details of daily life became the legitimate subject of the architect's i
my late participation - to think of architecture not as form, but as organization, to influence the way lives are l
script writing. I went to America in 1972; the Twin Towers seemed Utopian insertions in Manhattan's skyline. It is n
'70s marked the beginning of the new financial/political twin regimes, **Liberalism and Globalization.** Lib
west, reduce the involvement of the state in favor of the market as the overriding mechanism for assigning structure an
value. For the architect, the market implies a definitive loss of identity and status. Since (s)he no longer works f
longer claim to work for the public good. All his work is at the service of the private. Globalization implies a new c
needs? No longer "planning," the architect has become essentially passive, someone waiting for a private impulse
"call" him. There are two kinds: those who demand an architecture that enables them to make money, and those who alre
to invest it in architecture. The vast majority of his knowledge is counterproductive to serve the first; the second s
him into a vicious circle: to get his money's worth, the client wants to "respect" the architect, but the essential ine
lationship erodes the respect. Architect and client are only truly united in their knowledge that the "Master" is a ph
the architect is only to produce "master" pieces. The Seagram building by Mies was perhaps one of the last moments wher
ty of architecture could make private ambitions "public." When we were invited by the grandson of the tycoon who had
commissioned Mies to emulate that effort less than 50 years later, the budget per square foot was one fifth of the I
earlier building. Had architecture suffered an 80% loss of (self) worth? Instead of being able to state and US Laun
represent an ideal, we were asked to represent a commercial intention, the merger of four businesses: liquor, film,
music, and Internet. The entity was so unstable that six months after its beginning, 20% of these C, a programming la
entities had disappeared. **Universal** became the first warning of a fundamental change in architecture, a progre
evaporation of a project's feasibility simply because the company was mutating as fast as a 442 m high Sears Tower
virus, at a pace that no architecture could hope to main- Quaker Oats, first commercial granola is introduced Nixor
tain. There was a conflict between the slowness of architecture and the Pascal programming language developed Presi
volatility of the market. Wattstax concert held in Los Angeles Coliseum commemorating seventh anniversary of the Watts
We were tempted to abandon the complexity of building to see if we could apply architectural thinking in its Deep Pur
pure form, without the superhuman effort that each realization implies. Soviet Prime Minister Brezhnev and Presiden
Perhaps we could become more Utopian without Stanley Kubrick makes "A Clockwork Orange" 1st mass produced video ga
the classical burden that architects carry on Palestinian terrorists attacked the Israeli team at the 1972 Summer Oly
their shoulders. **SMLXL** embodied a "grand ecart." It combined projects with other forms of Death of Jim Morrison Gam
reporting that were, for the moment, divorced from the production of archi- Mark Spitz wins 7 gold medals at Munich (
tecture. There was little hope that the two would meet. The "reporting" caused a big misunder- First Starbucks opens
Oil crisis: Arab-nations impose oil embargo on United States for its support of Israel during the October 6th Yom Kip
standing - colliding with architecture's fundamental(ist) moralism: be- Marlon Brando rejects Oscar because he objec
cause we are "good," we are not allowed to look at the "bad"; because we manage, we should not Exodus, or the Volu
engage the unmanageable. To be more systematic, **Harvard** Design school's Project on United States suspends the conve
the City offered a position of independence that enabled us to define an agenda - to document Greenpeace founded Cit
the combined effects of the market economy and globalization on the architectural David Bowie releases "Ziggy Stardust"
discipline and to speculate how it should be redefined. We also began partnerships within architec- Bretton-Woods pc
ture. Inspired by **Merger-Mania,** we arranged intensive collabora- Pablo Neruda awarded nobel prize for littera
tions, with our alleged fr□res enemies - Herzog & de Meuron, combining the Klaus Schwab founds the World Economic F
best in vertical planes with the most ingenious in horizontal plates - or sim- Charles Manson and three followers are
ply the most "architectural" and least "architectural," or Idi Amin overthrows President Milton Obote of Uganda and
even more simply the good and the bad. There is a blatant contradiction: architecture itself is per- Michael Hart sta
haps the profession where collaboration is most systematic, essential, and inevitable First word processor the "Wang 1
- and, admitted or not, the foundation of every office. But collaboration between offices upsets. With Herzog and de Me
planned to work as a team in the most literal sense: not to simply do a project together, but European manufacturers
to eventually create a new entity that would produce knowledge, a pool where our individual signatures, LIFE magazine
identities, etc. would be subsumed in a larger whole. As "authors" we could remain relatively small entities, but we w
of competencies. The density of the project we produced was too much for the client to stomach. The market economy has
ded the possibility of Utopia, partly for good reasons, but also at a loss. At the moment where most of the professio
Zero, we entered a competition to design the new headquarters of **CCTV.** We proposed a scheme of almost Utopian Mitter
purity - to integrate every element of TV making in a single entity. In any other commercial operation the studios
would be built in a cheap area outside the city, the administrators might go to the business district, the Sony's Port
creative people would go to the old or rehabilitated parts of town; they would never be together and would perpetually
sibility of creating a single, self-sustaining entity inspired us to merge two skyscrapers into a loop, representing R
interconnectedness and intelligence moving through all its components. An explicit ambition of the building was to tr
typology, to explode its increasingly vacuous nature, loss of program, and refuse the futile competition for height. I
the WTC, there was now a single, integrated loop, where two towers merge. **Epilogue** The initial attraction to/inspi
of architecture-triggered by Communism 40 years ago - consummated under Communism 40 years later

General Augusto Pinochet (backed by the US Central Intelligence Agency) leads a milit
time - the Constructivists in the President Ford distributes "Whip Inflation Now" - WIN - buttons "Coming Home", Jon Vo
on. I could not resist Sinclair releases Executive pocket calculator "Dog Day Afternoon" is released Egyptian President
ultimate form of Church of England and Vatican end a 400 year dispute Concorde supersonic airplane makes its first tra
that the John Boorman's "Deliverance" release South Africa voted out of UN for apartheid policies New York discoteque
tion would, in the Jordan expels the PLO to Lebanon Alaska okays private use of marijuana Gang of Four arrested in Chi
-Pakistan War - Bangladesh declared independent republic Erno Rubik applies for a Hungarian patent for the Magic Cube
blic entity, (s)he can no Yasser Arafat's PLO recognized as political representative Palestinians New York City experienc
: can you ever know what the Other Stanley Cubrick's "One Flew Over the Cuckoo's Nest" is released Amnesty International
mer Manson cult figure Lynette "Squeaky" Fromme attempts to kill President Ford in Sacramento 1st laser printer by Xero
e money and want The Rolling Stones become first band from the West to receive royalties from the Soviet Union Steven
ast and West Germany become members of the UN Portugal recognises the independence of Mozambique Electronic typewriter
of the re- John Le Carré's spy novel "Tinker, Tailor, Soldier, Spy" is published US passes legislation allowing independent p
e task of "Last Tango in Paris" by Bernardo Bertolucci Communists triumph in Vietnam, Laos and Cambodia Groucho Marx dies
gni- Allende nationalizes large mines in Chile Jaws and Nashville are released Jimmy Carter elected US president Muham
rk, Ireland and the United Kingdom join EC (Belgium, Germany, France, Italy, Luxembourg and The Netherlands) Charlie Cha
andi becomes Prime Minister of India First optical scanners used at checkout counters Cult leader Jim Jones and 910 fol
oneer II to explore outer planets Sara Jane Moore attempts to assassinate President Ford Konica introduces the point-and
nt Nixon becomes first U.S. President to visit Moscow Apple Computer is founded by Steve Jobs and Steve Wozniak Iranian
for the Unix operating system developed The Clash performs its first concert in London, England Deregulation comes to t
laygirl introduced Communists in Italy propose a Democratic-Communist Coalition, but Christian Democrats refuse 64 count
ago completed - the tallest building at the time Dutch colony of Surinam achieves independence Commodore and Tandy begi
China Benoit Mandelbrot discovers the Mandelbrot fractal set African bloc boycotts Montreal Olympics Carter drops the
d grants Richard Nixon a "full, free, and absolute pardon." Martin Scorsese's "Taxi Driver" released Welfare Palace Hotel,
"That's The Way (I Like It)" by KC & the Sunshine Band released Death of Mao Zedong; Mao succeeded by Deng Xiaoping The first
eases "Smoke on the Water" Arab oil embargo ends The Spanish Monarchy is restored Afghan president Muhammad Daoud is ov
sign a strategic arms limitation agreement NBC airs first program of "Saturday Night Live" "Saturday Night Fever" becomes
ng," becomes available Indonesian troops occupy East Timor New Welfare Island, Study, 1976 Aldo Moro assassinated by lef
WTC completed ATM patented North Vietnamese troops capture Saigon First G7 summit in France Louise Brown, the first t
ur takes over in China Roosevelt Island, Study, 1975 Birmingham Pub bombings by IRA The Sex Pistols' "God Save the Queer
United Nations adopts resolution that equates Zionism with racism Chiang Kai-shek dies Gaddafi declares a "people's r
ippur War begins Hotel Sphinx, Study, 1975 Bill Gates (age 19) and Paul Allen (age 21) found Microsoft The Story of The F
Pink Floyd releases "Dark Side of the Moon" News baron Rupert Murdoch acquires The New York Post Howard Hughes dies Du
he film industry's treatment of Indians in films In Italy, Communists win 35% of votes in election for the Chamber of De
Prisoners of Architecture, Study, 1972 Mysterious ailment dubbed "Legionnaire's Disease" kills 29 attending American L
ity of the dollar into gold Social Democrat Helmut Schmidt becomes West Germany Chancelor Deng Xiaoping launches "Four M
e Captive Globe, Study, 1972 An Air France airliner is hijacked by a joint German Baader-Meinhof/Popular Front for the L
recognizes East and West Germany as sovereign states President Nixon Resigns after Watergate affair The Ramones "Rocket
economic system ends Bloody Sunday in Ireland Abba has 3 UK number one hits - "Mamma Mia", "Fernando", and "Dancing Quee
ylon becomes independent Republic of Sri Lanka Black Sabbath Release "Sabbath Bloddy Sabbath" Baader-Meinhof Gang (leftist te
WEF)as a not-for-profit foundation Pablo Picasso dies 1975 Water Tower Place, the first vertical mall, Chicago Last of th
cted of murdering seven Juan Peron is re-elected president of Argentina Civil war breaks out in Angola Steven Spielberg
dictator British impose direct rule over Northern Ireland "The Man Who Fell to Earth" starring David Bowie is released ET
oject Gutenberg -online database Giscard's prime minister, Jacques Chirac, resigns after failing to "modernize" the Frer
troduced Valery Giscard d'Estaing becomes French president, succeding Georges Pompidou Richard Nixon sells memoirs for $2
e US secretary of state Henry Kissinger secretly visits China Barcode products appear in US King Faisal of Saudi Arabi
, Philips, AEG) introduce the video disc Civil war between Muslim and Christian forces begins in Lebanon George Lucas re
publication Henry Kissinger awarded the Nobel Peace Prize First drive-through McDonalds Patricia Hearst released on $1
are a factory Desktop computer introduced by HP First Apollo-Soyuz joint space mission by USSR and the US Centre Pompi
ely ero- Emperor Haile Selassie is deposed in Ethiopia by a military coup "No Woman No Cry" by Bob Marley and the Wai
bsessively focused on Ground "The Godfather Part II" becomes the first film sequel to win an Academy Award for Best Pictur
ecomes leader of the French Socialist Party "Blazing Saddles" is released Israel under Menachem Begin begins construction
e describes Ethernet, inspired by ALOHANET, in his doctoral thesis for Harvard Pol Pot comes to power in Cambodia Queen
a portable video recorder comes out Portugal overthrows dictatorship - Antonio de Spinola becomes President Czech intell
in about each other. The pos- Portugal grants independence to Mozambique, Angola and other colonies Floppy disk (5 1/4")
linson of BBN develops a program to send e-mail messages British ambassador to Irish Republic, Christopher Ewart Briggs,
sten the end of the skyscraper as a Foreign language film Oscar - "Amarcord", Italy Turkey invades Cyprus United States
of the two separate towers of India explodes first nuclear device CIA Factbook made available to the public Sony intro
McDonald's open in Japan, Germany, Australia, Guam, Holland and Panama Under the leadership of King Juan Carlos, Spain
27 August 03 US Completes Withdrawal from Vietnam Roman Polanski's "Chinatown" is released Pakistan's prime mi
Alexsandr Solzhenitsyn is deported by the U.S.S.R. to West Germany Spanish Dictator Franco Ba

ary coup in Chile Czeslaw Milosz awarded Nobel Prize literature French scientist Dr. Luc Montagnier discovers HIV One yea
ght and Jane Fonda win academy awards Mitterrand institutes a shortened work week, longer holidays, a strengthened soci
Anwar Sadat pays a surprise visit to Israel The first black Barbie (#1293) hits the shelves PLO leaves Lebanon and moves
nsatlantic flights European Monetary System established Mrs. Thatcher becomes UK Prime Minister IBM building completed To
Studio 54 opens Vietnamese troops invade Cambodia Ridley Scott's "Blade Runner" released Bundesbank intervenes to support DM a
a First person implanted with a Bionic Ear Second oil crisis Microsoft introduces the Microsoft mouse for $200 Enver Hox
First oil flows from Alaska pipeline Military coup in Turkey under Kenan Evren Deng Xiaoping tours Guangdong Horton Plaza
s 25-hour blackout allegedly caused by an electric storm Martha Stewart publishes her first book Windows 2.0, MS/OS 2 released
awarded Nobel Peace Prize MIT Media Lab founded by Nicholas Negroponte First US Cruise missiles arrive at Greenham Commo
introduced President Park Chung Hee of South Korea assassinated Mrs. Thatcher wins 2nd term as Britain's Prime Minister
iko is murdered while in police custody Andrew Lloyd-Webber's musical "Cats" opens in London First combined heart and liver tra
ntroduced Zulfikar Ali Bhutto executed First computer viruses created Mexican debt crisis Brunei Darussalam joins ASEAN
wer production in the energy electricity sector Prince Charles marries Lady Diana Spencer Chevron acquires Gulf in the
Full diplomatic relations between US and China established "Anti-Spiritual Pollution Campaign" starts in China Silicon m
ed Zia Ul-Haq becomes hard-line Muslim President of Pakistan "Rock The Casbah" released by the Clash UK privatizes Britis
lin dies Marxist Sandinistas overthrow Nicaraguan goevernment Spielberg's "ET" released De Brink, 1984 - 1988 Drought an
owers commit suicide in Guyana Rupert Murdoch's News Corporation is established The European Round Table of Industrials
-shoot, autofocus camera Saddam Hussein becomes president of Iraq Socialist government headed by Mario Soares in Portuga
evolution - Ayatollah Khomeini proclaims Islamic Republic "Under Pressure" released by David Bowie & Queen Trump Tower co
e U.S. airline industry Delirious New York, 1978 UK government's ownership share in North Sea oil and gas privatized S
ies boycot Moscow Olympic Games to protest the Soviet's invasion of Afghanistan "Super Freak" by Rick James released Rec
selling PC's Robert Mugabe leads first black government in Zimbabwe (Rhodesia) A Soviet fighter shoots down a Korean
ban on travel to Cuba 3M starts making Post-It notes OPEC pricing structure collapses "Hungry Like A Wolf" released by
Study, 1976 Clash releases "Train In Vain" Panopticon Prison, Competition, 1980 Massacre at Sabre and Shatilla "Girls J
book of "The Chronicles of Thomas Covenant" is Published Attempted assassination of Pope John Paul II Nintendo makes "Do
rthrown and killed in a coup China establishes four SEZ's in Guangdong First Asian Barbie introduced Israel Invades Leba
a best selling album Gdansk Shipyard Strike in Poland - Lech Walesa forms Solidarity Personal computer named Time's Man
tist Red Brigade terrorist Prime Minister Residence, Competition, 1979 Iraq- Iran War breaks out 'AutoCAD' released Palesti
st-tube baby, is born in Britain Military coup in Bolivia "Christiane F" a film by Uli Edel comes out Indira Ghandi assa
" reached number 2 Pacific Economic Cooperation Council (PECC) is established 5.5 million PCs have been sold Parc de la
evolution" Pink Floyd release "The Wall" US imposed economic sanctions on Poland as a reaction to martial law First
ool, Study, 1976 Female condom released Tanzanian troops invade Uganda and overthrow the regime of Idi Amin Diet Coke introdu
ch Parliament Competition, 1st, 1978 Soviets invade Afghanistan Reagan fires striking air traffic controllers Philippin
uties Iranian students seize US Embassy and take hostages "Pac-Man" released Cyanide in Tylenol capsules kills seven in Ch
gion convention Home satellite dish TV antennas become available Mitterrand was elected president in France "Mario Br
odernizations" and "Open Door Policy" Tito dies - Yugoslavia's six states begin to argue The term AIDS is used for the
iberation of Palestine terrorist group Aspartame - sugar substitute - introduced IJ-Plein Urban Planning, 1981 - 1992 "N
to Russia" released Ronald Reagan elected US President TGV goes into service in France Japan passes the US as the larg
n" Elvis Presley dies "Superman" the film released US Air force destroys Saddam Hussein's nuclear reactor near Baghdad "Th
rorist group) active in Germany Eruption of Mount St Helens (60 killed) 100 millionth Rubik's Cube sold Police Station, 19
14 Concordes manufactured Emoticons first used Boompjes Tower Slab, Competition, 1st, 1980 Michael Jackson releases s
makes "Close Encounters of the Third Kind" John Lennon killed Greece joins EU Britain regains the Falkland Islands (Malvin
(Basque seperatist group) becomes active in Spain The first compact disc (CD) players go on sale French Prime Minister
ch economy and society Hosts win the World Cup in Argentina Under Moscow directive, Polish government imposes martia law in a
million Mitternad launches nationalization of seven of the largest twenty industrial conglomerate companies in France Di
assassinated Home Depot's first store opens in US US shoots down two Libyan aircrafts Beginning of the Third World deb
leases "Star Wars" Between 1974 and 1981 France loses 700,000 industrial jobs Small pox is considered eradicated by the Wor
5 million bail McDonald's Happy Meal introduced Preferential Trade Area for Eastern and Southern Africa (PTA) establishec
dou completed "Video Killed the Radio Star" by Buggles is the first video to air on MTV US government dismisses it's ant
ers Camp David Agreement brokers peace between Israel and Egypt Severe race riots in Britain Christian Democrat Helmu
e Radical reorganization of Cambodia by cruel Pol-Pot regime CNN begins broadcasting Reagan Administration reestablishes
f West Bank The Green Revolution in India changes India from starving nation to an exporter of food David Bowie's "Let's
releases "We Are The Champions" IRA inmates at the Maze prison in Northern Ireland begin a hunger strike Adobe founded by
ectuals signed and published Charter 77 Francis Ford Coppol's Apocalypse Now released Ronald Reagan proposes the - 'Star
introduced UK announced its intention sell some of the government's shares in BA to the private sector "Flashdance" rel
killed by an IRA car-bomb Ben & Jerry's opens Green Party is formed in Germany Mexico starts to implant IMF's Structural
romises to return the Panama Canal to Panama by 2000 West Edmonton Mall opens in Canada - the world's largest shopping m
uces home Betamax video system Egypt's President Anwar Sadat is assassinated by Islamic fundamentalists Mrs. Thatcher de
dopts a liberal constitution Three Mile Island nuclear reactor incident in US Word "internet" used for the first time Gr
nister Zulfikar Ali Bhutto is overthrown in a military coup Mother Teresa awarded Nobel Peace Prize IMF imposes austerity
amonde dies Sony introduces the Walkman Greece votes in Socialist Andreas Papandreou Vietnam War Memorial built in Wash

e in the coal mines of the UK lost by the National Union of Miners Anti-Apartheid Act passed in the US Andy Warhol dies P
urity system and nationalized banks Uithof Masterplan, 1986 B-2 Stealth Bomber unveiled by US New Kids on The block relea
isia World Commission on Environment and Development issues defines the term sustainable development After 28 years, Be
leak in India kills 2,500 "Leisure Suite Larry" computer game released Terrorists kill nine tourists on Aegean cruise Eu
soaring dollar Prime Minister Olof Palme of Sweden assisinated Ville-Nouvelle Melun-Senart Competition, 1988 "The Simpsons"
- Albania gradually relaxes foreign relations Chinese troops suppress a nationalist uprising in Tibet Thousands killed
ned by Jon Jerde is opened to the public General Electric acquires NBC Yasser Arafat calls for a political solution to th
hina Agree on Hong Kong handover The US stock market crashes after hitting record high in August Russia withdraws from Afgha
se in Britain "Tetris" game released Byzantium, 1985-1991 Semiconductor created by Paul Chu APEC is established at its fi
Cameron's "Terminator" released Desmond Tutu elected archbishop in South Africa Prozac is introduced as an anti-depressar
performed Nevado del Ruiz volcano in Colombia claims 25,000 lives U2 releases "The Joshua Tree" Salman Rushdie's "The Satan
lished 1967) Bus Terminal, 1985-1988 US bombs Libyan military facilities Benazir Bhutto, first Islamic female prime minis
merger to date in US Yen begins sharp rise Nintendo releases Game Boy US and Canada sign GATT free trade agreement Davic
p developed European flag becomes the official emblem of the European Community Coastal Development Strategy starts in
ys First Domain names replace numbers Volkswagen group (VAG) buys SEAT A terrorist bomb planted in Pan-Am flight 103 exp
e in Ethiopia, Eritrea and Sudan EU network between departments/faculties across Europe - ERASMUS, started East German
created Chernobyl nuclear power station explodes, contaminating much of Europe Ecstasy becomes drug of choice Emperor H
elections Bob Geldof organizes Live Aid concerts Bijlmermeer Redevelopment, 1986 First Japanese Post-Script Printer Mo
Checkpoint Charlie Housing, 1984-1992 US and USSR sign INF treaty banning medium-range nuclear missiles Natural Gas We
Florida developed Reagan is sworn in for a second term Jorge Luis Borges dies McDonald's opens in the USSR George Bush
in the US "Papa Don't Preach" released by Madonna Spain and Portugal join European Economic Community Ayatollah Khomeini
s 747 with 269 passengers on board National Amusements buys Viacom for $3.4 billion Stephen Hawking's "A Brief History
uran US invades Grenada US becomes debtor nation Campaigning as a centrist, Mitterand re-elected as French President Ma
To Have Fun" released by Cyndi Lauper Black Monday, Dow falls record 508 points First driver's side air bag Czech Par
ng" Gorbachev becomes General Secretary of the Soviet Comunist Land-use reform starts in China TGB, Competition Ho
trian president Kurt Waldheim's service as Nazi army officer revealed Whitney Houston has her seventh consecutive Number
Year Villa DallÁva, 1984-1991 AOL launched Big Mac Index introduced Kunsthal, Rotterdam, 1987-1992 David Dinkins electe
beration Organization (PLO) terrorists hijack the Achille Lauro PSA is merged into USAir P. W. Botha quits as South Afr
ed by Sikhs - violence erupts in India Right-wing Jacques Chirac becomes French Prime Minister Piedmont is integrated int
e, Competition, 1982 "Sledgehammer" released by Peter Gabriel Iran-Contra Affair - arms for aid scandal General Augusto Pir
Publishing software developed by Aldus British Telecom privatized US advertising is permitted on Soviet TV ZKM, 1989 U
ael-Lebanon War ends A hole in the ozone layer above Antarctica is discovered Jim Jarmusch films "Down by Law Romanian uprisi
osition leader Benigno Aquino assassinated Capital Cities acquires ABC Shuttle Challenger Explodes Dalai Lama awarded Nob
PostScript (Adobe - John Warnock) developed Mrs. Thatcher wins 3rd term as Prime Minister 7.1 magnitude earthquake hits
mputer game features Mario's brother Luigi Haiti president Jean-Claude Duvalier flees to France CCP introduces Law of Tran
ime Plaza Accords imposed on Tokyo by U.S. Treasury Secretary Donald Regan Martin Scorsese's film "The Last Temptation of
cer" by William Gibson published Iraqi missiles kill 37 in attack on U.S. frigate Stark in Persian Gulf Deng Xiaoping re
tomaker Nestle meets with the organizers of consumer boycott of infant milk formula "Walk This Way" released by Run D.M.C.
fter" released Reagan and Gorbachev meet CBS acquires the Loews Corporation Furkablick, Furka Pass, 1988-1991 Lech Walesa
World Court rules U.S. broke international law in mining Nicaraguan waters Ruptured tanker Exxon Valdez sends 44 millior
'Thriller" Tamil separatist resurgence in Sri Lanka First Disney mall store opens in Glendale, California U.S. Appeals Co
er Argentinean occupation Cellular telephone system is launched in Britain "Sim City" Amiga Version released Airport City, Co
resigns and left-wing government collapses Palestinians in the occupied territories begin an intifada Tokyo stock marke
o stop Solidarity Akira Kurosawa's Ran released City Hall Competition - 1st, 1986 Ben Johnson fails a steroids test after setting a
d Tokyo opens Klaus Barbie, 73, Gestapo wartime chief in Lyon, sentenced to life by French court for war crimes Akihito
s Nederlands Dans Theater, 1984-1987 Marcos flees country and Corazon Aquino takes power in Philippines Romanian dictato
th Orginization First portable computer, "Osborne 1," introduced General Electric purchases RCA A Japanese busines
riginal "Jane Fonda Workout" released Patio Villa, 1985-1988 Students in Burma protest against military rule Nexus Worl
case against IBM First HIV antibody test Congress overrides Reagan veto of stiff sanctions against South Africa The Cuba
becomes West Germany's Chancellor UK's "Black Monday" "Adobe Illustrator" introduced Arab Maghreb Union (AMU) established
vel ban to Cuba Pro-Solidarity Father Jerzy Popieluzsko assassinated in Poland NAI, Competition, 1988 US Army general
hits Number One AT&T's monopoly of US market telephone market dismanteled First transatlantic fiber optic cable conne
rnock Churchillplein Office Tower, Competition, 1984 CDs outsell vinyl for the first time Mikhail S. Gorbachev named Soviet pr
nissile defense system Terry Gilliam's "Brazil" released Japanese corporations use their real estate holdings for stock ma
Privatization of British Gas Reagan re-elected as US President Starbucks purchased by Howard Shultz Kim Basinger buys Br
ent programs (SAP) Max Headroom - computer-animated live action figure - debuts U.S. Navy ship shoots down Iranian airli
eenpeace's Rainbow Warrior sunk by operatives of French intelligence (DGSE) Sea Terminal Competition, 1st, 1988 Vaclav H
o sell minor interests in public utilities to private businesses Kurt Waldheim cleared of war crimes during World War II
e's Rainbow Warrior protests against French nuclear testing in Polynesia British Airways privatized U.S. jury convicts O
es on debtor countries Optical fibres are first used to link mainframe computers Ceasefire ends the Iran-Iraq War Gazpro
DC The Uruguay Round - expands the notions of trade in services and intellectual property US invades Panama and overthro

ane blast kills Pakistani president Mohammad Zia ul-Haq Cardinal O'Connor asks Pope to excommunicate Madonna Aum Shinrik
se Hangin' Tough Gorbachev awarded Nobel Peace Prize Roh replaced by Kim Young-sam and his Democratic Liberal Party in S
lin Wall is open to West Hubble Space Telescope launched Bush and Yeltsin proclaim formal end to Cold War Nearly a mill
opean Monetary System (EMS) established Haitian troops seize president in uprising Viacom, Inc. acquires Paramount Comm
premiers on Fox TV India removes state control on corporations Benazir Bhutto returns to power in Pakistan Bali launches
in Tiananmen Square demonstartions William H. Webster retires as director of CIA Yeltsin's forces crush revolt in Russia
e Middle East conflict Berlage Institute founded French Usinor buys J & L Specialty Steel of US Republicans win the House
istan Venezuelan partial debt moratorium "Losing My Religion" released by R.E.M. Viacom acquires Blockbuster Video for $8
st Ministerial Meeting in Canberra Communist government of Albania resigns UN imposes sanctions on Libya TCI, Cox Enterp
t British Electric privatized Congrexpo, 1990-1994 Israeli Parliament approves Yitzhak Rabin's coalition government The
ic Verses" published Margaret Thatcher resigns; John Major becomes UK Prime Minister US passes banking deregulation bill; b
ter, elected in Pakistan Jiang Qing, widow of Mao, commits suicide Jussieu Library, Competition 1st, 1992 The Multilatera
Lynch's "Twin Peaks" makes its television debut U.S. forces leave Philippines, ending nearly a century of American milita
China South Africa frees Nelson Mandela, imprisoned 27 1/2 years U.S. begins airlift of supplies to besieged Bosnia towns
lodes over Lockerbie, Scotland Computer game "Lemmings" released First free general elections are held in Taiwan Salvatore
government opens its borders Guns 'n'Roses release "Appetite for Destruction" Robert Maxwell dies Quentin Tarantino's
rohito of Japan dead at 87 Symantec launches Norton AntiVirus Quebec votes to remain part of Canada The Central European
ntreal Massacre McDonalds opens in China Around 1300 computer viruses are in existence World Trade Center in New York is
llhead Decontrol Act in US La Baye d'Agadir, Competition 1st, 1990 UK and Italy exit ERM Hypo Theatiner-Zentrum, Comp
inaugurated as 41st U.S. president Warsaw Pact dissolved Russia deregulates domestic prices and liberates international
sentences Salmon Rushdie to death "Nothing Compares 2 U" released by Sinead O'Connor Channel Tunnel between Britain and
f Time" published Time, Inc. merges with Warner Gen. Noriega, former Panama leader sentenced to 40 years on drug charges in
onna releases "Like a Prayer" Civil war begins in the former Yugoslavia VW buys Skoda Disneyland-Paris opens China bre
liament ends Communists' dominant role 'Adobe Photoshop' released Zac Danton, Competition 1st, 1991 Maastricht Treaty comes
orable Mention, 1989 Alberto Fujimori elected President in Peru Four police officers acquitted in Los Angeles beating
One single U.S. suspends assistance to Haiti South African Parliament repeals apartheid laws Common Market for Eastern
first black NYC mayor U.S. planes shoot down two Libyan fighters over Mediterranean "Absolutely Fabulous" starts on BBC
ca's president '3D Studio' (AutoDesk) released Ethiopian Civil War ends - Eritrea becomes independent Violence erupts in
o USAir Mercosur - Southern Common Market (Argentina, Brazil, Paraguay, Uruguay) established ERM crisis on "Black Wedne
ochet allows democratic elections Japanese "bubble economy" bursts Democrat Bill Clinton defeats incumbent Republican Ge
S.-Soviet summit reaches accord on armaments Agreement is reached to establish the ASEAN Free-Trade Area - AFTA Zapatist
g overthrows Communist government World Wide Web debuts, popularizes Internet Cease-fire ends Persian Gulf War Siege of the Koresh
l Peace Prize ASEAN reaches agreement on creating the East Asian Economic Caucus - EAEC Point City/South City Study,
an Francis European directive calls for open access of networks to European trains Mall of America opens Rudolph Giulian
sfer of Land-use rights Last three U.S. hostages freed in Lebanon U.S. recognizes three former Yugoslav republics NAFTA
Christ" US-backed Violeta Barrios de Chamorro is elected president of Nicaragua Prince and Princess of Wales agree to s
signs from China's leadership Euralille, 1990-1994 East and West Germany reunited Los Angeles riots IRA announce uncond
featuring Aerosmith Peace accord ends an 11-year civil war in El Salvador The Spice Girls promote "girl power" Miami Pe
is elected president of Poland Iraqi troops invade Kuwait and seize petroleum reserves, setting off Persian Gulf War Wir
liters of oil into Alaska's water 'Adobe Premiere' released Lithuania , Latvia, and Estonia leave Soviet Union Dutch Ho
urt overturns Oliver North's Iran-Contra conviction Czechoslovak Parliament approves separation into two nations EU sing
mpetition 1st, 1989 Soviet Union breaks up after President Gorbachev's resignation Clinton agrees to compromise on milit
t had fallen 38% Big Dig - Boston Central Artery project begins construction Sheffield Steel merges with Avesta of Swede
ew world record in the 100 m at the Seoul Olympics Haiti elects leftist priest as president in first democratic election For
succeeds his father Hirohito as Emperor of Japan Banking regulators from 69 countries shut down the BCCI MTV Japan laun
Ceausescu and his wife are executed Bundesbank intervenes to support DM US troops arrive in Somalia on a humanitarian
sman buys a Van Gough for $82.5mn Death of Salvador Dalí Souterrain, 1990- 2004 UN expels Serbian-dominated Yugoslavia
Housing, 1989-1991 B. Yeltsin inaugurated as first freely elected president of Russian Republic "Enter the Wu-Tang" r
Museum of Arts and Culture in Miami is bombed for exhibiting work by artists living in Cuba Jean-Pierre Jeunet and Marc
(Algeria, Libya, Mauritania, Morocco, Tunisia) Lithuania, Estonia, and Latvia win independence MCI takes US$31 billion s
Colin R. Powell is first black chairman of Joint Chiefs of Staff Urban Design Forum, Masterplan, 1991 Fidel Castro lif
ts France, UK and US Museumpark, 1988-1994 Soviet troops leave Cuba The first free elections in Romania for 53 years Ed
esident Kodak releases the first photo CD The Church of England General Synod votes to allow women to be ordained into the priesthood
ket speculation Bush-Gorbachev summit negotiates strategic arms reduction treaty Mike Tyson is found guilty of rape Yug
aselton, Georgia for $20 million U.S. indicts two Libyans in 1988 bombing of Pan Am Flight 103 over Lockerbie Gazprom in
er in Persian Gulf Vietnam's economy experiences rapid growth U.S. declares war on Iraq - operation Desert Storm Iraq acce
avel is elected Czechoslovakia's president Roman Catholic Church officially rehabilitates Galileo Galilei U2 finishes up
Video Bus Stop, 1989 Milli Vanilli win Best New Artist Grammy (it is later revoked) Stedelijk Museum, 1992 Viacom buy
iver North in Iran-Contra affair Israel and Soviet Union resume relations after 24 years Civil war begins in Bosnia Prim
is set up under state control in Russia Gorbachev assumes emergency powers British Rail privatized Negotiations begin fo
s Manuel Noriega France agrees to sign 1968 treaty banning spread of atomic weapons 22 members of the UN Peace-keeping

ase sarin gas in Tokyo subway Korea joins OECD and opens up for foreign investment - GDP growth = 7% "Titanic", the most
ea Oliver Stone's "Natural Born Killers" released "Harry Potter" comes out in UK Andrew Cunanan murders fashion designer Giann
ple killed within a period of four months in Rwanda Bill Clinton re-elected as US President First Global Action Days org
ns in a 8.2 billion dollar deal IBM launches World Avenue, a Web shopping mall Lensvelt, 1997-2000 Naomi Klein's "No Lo
erBra Sprint, Deutsche Telekom and France Telecom form Global One joint venture "Half-Life" computer game released Haus um
ament Internet Explorer 1.0 released Kobe earthquake Schiphol Logistics, 1996 Value of worldwide mergers and acquisitio
resentatives for first time in 40 years Diana, Princess of Wales dies in Paris car crash ATTAC founded Gerhard Schroeder
n The McKinsey Global Institute - McKinsey's think tank - established China moves towards a socialist - market economy Th
nd Comcast join Sprint Luxor Theater Competition, 1996 452 m high Petronas Towers in Kuala Lumpur become the world's ta
ouse launches its website Grand Central Station undergoes $175 million renovation Netherlands Embassy Berlin, 1997-2000
king fees and ATM fees rise sharply Microsoft releases Internet Explorer IMF provided $36 billion-to Indonesia, Korea, a
ment on Investment (MAI) treaty initiated by OECD and WTO Hanoi New Town Master plan, Hanoi, 1997 Antitrust suit against
ence Russia's GDP has fallen 42% and industrial production 46% since 1992 Labour party, led by Tony Blair, wins general
ation agreement initialed between Morocco and the European Union Fela Anikulapo-Kuti dies of AIDS-related causes MAB Towe
reputed Mafia leader, arrested Zuid As Development, 1996 Cable Modems introduced IIT Campus Center, 1997-2003 Ford Mo
iction" released Stockholm Olympic Stadium, 1995 Telecommunication deregulation begins in Europe "Born Again" released
de Agreement (CEFTA)Nas releases "Illmatic" UK sterling hits record lows Scotish scientists produce first clone, Dolly the ewe
Nelson Mandela is elected as the president of post-apartheid South Africa MCI Communications acquires WorldCom for $30 b
, 1993 Amazon.com sells its first book Hyperbuilding Study, 1996 Steve Jobs returns to Apple Clinton signs Digital M
resident of Sri Lanka assassinated Jacques Chirac elected French President Japanese banks announce record losses for 1995
opens Kurt Cobain commits suicide Thomas Hamilton guns down 16 primary school children and their teacher in Dunblane, Sc
First episode of "Friends" airs O.J. Simpson murder trial Web TV introduced Taliban troops capture Kabul in Afghanistan
lear test moratorium House in Bordeaux, 1994-1998 Westinghouse/ CBS acquires Infinity Broadcasting Good Friday Agreement
ffect - EU single market starts Prime Minister Yitzhak Rabin asssasinated There are 5,600 coffeehouses in the US; ten ti
y King Westinghouse buys CBS for $5.4 billion MoMA, Competition, 1997 Devaluation of Thai Bhat marks beginning of A
rn Africa COMESA replaces PTA treaty from 1984 "Tomb Raider" released for Sony PlayStation General Motors' turnover is high
Havel elected as Czech president Vietnam joins ASEAN China agrees to a world ban on testing nuclear American Airlin
an estimated 800,000 people are massacred Oosteljke Hamdelskade, 1995 Celebration, Florida opens IBM closes World Ave
The New York Times publishes help-wanted ads on the Web General Motors' turnover is higher that the GNP of Denmark Secon
sh C3 Maas Towers Study, 1994 CNBC Asia launched Russian space station greets American Astronauts MAI is halted due to m
t begins in Chiapas, southern Mexico Breuninger Department Store, 1995 Kofi Annan named UN Secretary-General Sprint buys
d in Waco, Texas BMW buys Rover Yen hits all-time high The New York Times launches Web site Indonesian ruler General Suh
Mexican currency crisis New Seoul Intl. Airport Study, 1995 DVD format released Russia joins G7 in Denver, Colorado Go
d NYC mayor Uruguay Round agreements signed President Clinton signs Telecommunications Deregulation Act Airline deregul
American Free Trade Agreement ratified H-Project - I, 1995 - 2004 Deng Xiaoping dies Deep Blue computer defeats Kaspa
IMF approved its largest loan to date of $17.8 billion to Mexico Boris Yeltsin is re-elected Russian president Mexico-Ni
cease-fire - lasts until 1996 Serb massacre of 4,000 Muslims at Srebrenica Universal Headquarters, 1996 AT&T and Britis
g Arts Center, Competition, 1994 British Telecommunications buys MCI for $23 billion Thyssen and Krupp announce a $63 bi
azine launched First ad on WWW featuring Wired magazine Oklahoma City Bombing Korea becomes 3rd Asian Nation to join IMF
92-1995 The Serb siege of the Bosnian capital Sarajevo is lifted News Corp. buys New World Communications Group Inc. for
ket starts Place des Nations, 1994 Prime Minister Benazir Bhutto is fired by Pakistani President WTO gives final clearan
an on homosexuals WEF gets NGO status from UN Hypobank, 1995 Benjamin Netanyahu and Palestinian president Yasser Arafa
Bridge blown-up Mexico-Bolivia and Mexico-Costa Rica Free Trade Agreements Cuba starts its official web site De Rotterd
t time in history chain bookstores outsell independent stores in US Saddam Hussein expels all US members of the UN arms-inspe
e Gallery Competition, 1994 Civil servant strikes in France Palm Pilot introduced World Bank approves $1.5 billion st
Russian troops invade the breakaway republic of Chechnya 'tPaard 1995 Peoples' Global Action against "Free" Trade and
ff Bay Opera House Competition, 1994 Java inroducd by Sun Microsystems Bell Atlantic and NYNEX, merge; new Bell Atlant
by Wu-Tang Clan The FDA approves Procter & Gamble's controversial fat substitute, Olestra Puff Daddy releases "No Way Out"
s "Delicatessen" released Andrew Wiles publishes a general proof of Fermat's last theorem IMF and the World Bank launch
wireless service provider Nextel Communications Togok Towers Study, Seoul, 1996 Guggenheim Bilbao opens MCA Masterplan
rictions on those wanting to leave Cuba SAS, THAI, United and Lufthansa announce Star Alliance United States and Britain
m, 1992-1996 Shell attemts to sink the Brent Spar oil platform - Greenpeace protests National Library Competition, 1996
nd PLO reach accord in Oslo Janet Jackson becomes the highest-paid musician in history, with an $80-million record deal T
ederation breaks up Tupac Shakur shot five times during an apparent robbery Chassé Parking, 1996-2002 "You've Come A Long
is privatized McDonalds opens branch in Kuwait City Francois Mitterrand dies Asian Economic Crisis /South Korea, Indone
weapons monitoring Los Angeles earthquake Disney purchases Capital Cities/ABC for $19 billion CIA's 50th Anniversary Sa
year Zooropa tour Schauspielhaus Zurich, Competition, 1995 McDonald's become Disney's primary promotional partner in the r
buster and Paramount USAir posts is first profitable year since 1988 Vietnam's economy slows down GTE-Bell Atlantic me
ter Yitzhak Rabin awarded Nobel Peace Prize Harvard Project on the City, 1995 Bank of Tokyo acquired by Mitsubishi Bank
Trade Area of the Americas (FTAA) GPS satallite navigation system launched Value of worldwide mergers and acquisitions
illed in a battle with Somali rebels Extension to Zurich Airport, 1995 Russian troops attack Chechen rebels holding

expensive movie ever made (US$260 million) is released McDonalds switches to recyclable packaging under pressure from ch
i Versace The 1999 sales of GE, Wal-Mart, ExxonMobil, Ford Motor, and Daimler Chrysler are bigger than the GDPs of
anized by PGA during the 2nd WTO ministerial conference in Geneva The reality TV series Big Brother premiers in Netherlar
ogo" published Each year, the World Bank awards some 40,000 contracts to private firms BAM, 2000 There are 63,000 transna
die Schenkung, 1998 At G8 meeting the group G20 is formed $6 trillion in goods and services were exchanged worldwide The
ns reaches $3.4 trillion Scientists detect a 40% reduction in the average thickness of Arctic ice over the past 40 years
becomes German chancellor Casa da Musica, 1999-2003 France win Euro 2000 to add the their World Cup 98 victory Prada Sa
e US launches air strikes at alleged terroist facilities in Afghanistan and Sudan Love Bug virus infects 45 million comp
llest building AOL-Time Warner group has a revenue ($106 billion), comparable to India's GDP ($139 billion) ASEAN-China F
Asia-Pacific Economic Cooperation (APEC) forms representing 2.5 billion people and 47% France's Vivendi Universal finis
nd Thailand Columbine High School Shooting Y2K comes and goes and the feared computer anarchy is knowhere in site Globa
Microsoft starts United States transfers the Panama Canal to Panama Royal Dutch Shell's revenues are greater than Venezu
election in UK NATO air strikes on Serbia Microsoft gives the mouse an optical sensor Microsoft anti-trust judgment Pinaul
rs, 1998 SkyTeam Alliance formed by AeroMexico, Delta, Air France and Korean Air PGA demonstrations in Prague First feat
or Co. acquires Swedish-based Volvo Havas, 1999 Vivendi merges with Seagram "Doggy Style" released by Snoop Dogg First UK
by Notorious B.I.G. PGA demonstrations shut down Seattle J.P. Morgan and Chase merge JTC, 2000 Sogo collapse in Japan Le
American embassies in Kenya and in Tanzania are bombed Britney Spears releases "Baby One More Time" 40 million mobile wireless users
illion Document X, New Urbanism, 1997 Eurasian Economic Union (EAEU) formed by Russia, Belarus, Kazakhstan, Kyrgyz Stan
illennium Copyright Act Brian Jones and Bertrand Piccard make first non-stop balloon flight around world Whirlpool (U.S.)
-96 Citicorp bank acquisition by Travelers ($82.9 billion) Wenner House Study, Bahamas, 1999 Britain restores Northern Ir
otland Estimated 30-60 million people worldwide have Internet access Guggenheim, 2000 Eminem releases "The Marshall Mathe
ong-Do New Town Master plan, Inchon-Seoul, 1998 US passes Financial Services Modernization Act Ang Lee makes "Crouching
is reached in Northern Ireland Dozens of African immigrants are killed by Libyan mobs in the west of Libya Common Market
mes more than in 1991 Almere Block 6, 1998 BP and ARCO announce $55 billion merger The merger of Swiss Novartis and Briti
sian financial crisis A record total of $484 million worth of mergers were announced in Europe in the first half of 1999 Cord
er that the GNP of Denmark South Korean economy shrinks 5.8 percent, the biggest drop in 45 years Bluetooth lets compute
s, British Airways, Cathay Pacific, Canadian Airlines and Qantas form OneWorld alliance Mutations, 2000 First World So
ue AOL acquires Netscape **Schiphol City, 1998** The World Bank has a 65-70% failure rate of its projects in the poorest cour
d Stage Theater, 1998-2000 Euro becomes the common currency of 12 of the 15 EU member states **Prada IT, 2000** Whirlpool a
unting public pressure PGA Conference in Bangalore, India South Bank Masterplan, 1999 China enters WTO Worldcom declares
out TCI, Comcast Corporation and Cox Communications forming wireless joint venture Sprint PCS The first series of Ricky (
rto resigns Dr.Dre releases "2001" Cities on the move, 1999 Nine Inch Nails release their 2 disc opus "The Fragile" US and
gle search engine founded WTO meets in Seattle GUUAM, a military-political-economical-grouping, formed by Georgia, Azerb
tion begins in Europe Entire EU Commission resigns 30 Colours, 1999 Viacom/CBS merger Global Crossing declares bankruptc
ov in chess match Avesta Sheffield of Sweden and Finland's Outokumpu merge their stainless steel operations US officially
aragua Free Trade Agreement Russia launches a major offensive against separatist guerillas in Chechnya People's global a
h Telecom announce a $70 billion merger Zurich Stadium, 1999 A French cameraman captures shocking footage of a Palestini
llion merger Frank Sinatra dies of a heart attack **Prada Research, 1999** US airline industry loses $8 billion, inspite of
MOCA Rome Competition, 1999 Viacom acquires CBS for $40.6 billion "The Sims" come out - the best selling PC game of all t
$10.8 billion China regains sovereignty in Hong Kong Revolutionary United Front (RUF) takes more than 500 UN peacekeepe
ce for the US to impose trade sanctions on EU goods as compensation for losses in the "Banana War" Tyco declares bankru
sign a 'land-for-peace' agreement Radiohead release Kid A Wenner House, 2000 Google.com answers 100 million searches
m, Rotterdam - Completion, 1998-2006 Yugoslavian President Slobodan Milosevic is voted out of office Caltrans, 2001 Septe
ction team Air France becomes a publicly traded company, 50% still owned by the government Enron declares bankruptcy Zined
ructural adjustment loan to Russian Federation Astor Place Hotel, 2000 Japan and Singapore sign Free Trade Agreement F
the World Trade Organization (PGA) started Russian president Boris Yeltsin resigns Intra-EU duty-free abolished German (
c acquires GTE Daimler-Benz and Chrysler Merge to form Daimler Chrysler More than 58,000 computer viruses exist Jeffrey
Y2K House Study, Rotterdam, 1998 West Nile virus outbreak in US and Canada April 14 - DOW-Jones Industrial Average drops
he Initiative for the Heavily Indebted Poor Countries Philips, 1999 "Aquemini" released by Outkast Maytag (US) and Sanyo Elec
study, 1996 United States agrees to ease trade restrictions on Fidel Castro's Cuba Taschen House, 2000 On April 14th te
launch air strikes on targets in Iraq Google answers 3 million searches per day George W.Bush becomes US president Flick
Clinton-Lewinsky scandal unfolds Almere Terminal, 1999 First U.S.-Sub-Saharan African Trade and Economic Cooperation Fo
e international sex trade generates an estimated $7 billion in revenue for organized crime US-Jordan Free Trade Agreemen
Way, Baby" released by Fatboy Slim Seattle Public Library, 1999-2004 Europe blocks a proposed merger between US firms Gen
ia and Thailand/ Santa Cruz de Tenerife, Competition 1998 Pokemon fever grips the US Alejandro Gonzalez Iccarritu's
sung National University Museum - I , 1996 Larry and Andy Wachowski's "The Matrix" released Ford announces over 8,000 jo
estaurant J. K. Rowling's "Harry Potter and the Sorcerer's Stone" published Genoa/Isola Parodi, 2000 Israel's hard-line To
ger Steel jobs in EU have fallen from 870,000 in 1975 to 280,000 China's nine biggest airline merge into Air China, Chi
or $33.8 billion Exxon and Mobil merge in a $76 billion deal to from the world's largest oil company AOL merges with Time W
eaches $2.5 trillion Anti-impotence drug VIAGRA becomes available Kosovo peace deal 3/4 of all transnational corporations
to 100 hostages Almere Masterplan, 1998-2000 PGA demonstrations held at G8 meeting Elian Gonzalez returns to Cuba

sumers Media Building HK, 2002 A gas explosion in a Chinese mine claims the lives of 81 miners Sabena and Swissair decla
tries Mac OS X released Les Halles, 2003 Baghdad falls to US forces British police force accused of racist culture Prin
as Study, 2002 50 Cent releases Get Rich Or Die Tryin' FCC Telecom Deregulation Mahmoud Abbas resigns as Palestinian
orporations worldwide, with 690,000 foreign affiliates David Blunkett became the most senior British minister to publ
Iranian ambassador to UK arrested by British police over his alleged role in the bombing of a Jewish community centre i
is now formally available for depressed children Shanghai Study, 2003 Alias Wavefront receives Oscar for development of
isco, 2000 Hans Blix June 11th 2003 - "I had my detractors in Washington, there are bastards who spread things around
rldwide Conde Nast/AMO magazine, 2001 Kelly commits suicide after being named as the source of a BBC report which claime
de Agreement is signed Demonstrations during G8 summit BJBB, 2003 'Greeks accuse Blair of war crimes in Iraq' - The Guar
with a $12 billion loss Roman Polanski wins Best Director Oscar for the Pianist Rotterdam CS, 2003 "Bubba Ho Tep, star
ion industry sheds 400,000 jobs Ali Hassan al Majid, also known as Chemical Ali captured by Coalition forces Joy Peskin
ross Domestic Product Koningin Julianplein, 2002 Bomb attack at UN HQ in Baghdad kills at least 20 people China sends fi
Argentina's financial crisis worsens and peso-US$ link is finally broken; largest ever sovereign debt default announced
, "Attack of the Clones", produced entirely in digital format Virgin Atlantic offers to buy the Concords from BA for £1,
of foot-and-mouth disease in 20 year US tests Massive Ordnance Air Blast - MOAB bomb Bomb attack at Jordanian embassy
upin Gallery, 2001 Libyan government and lawyers representing families of Lockerbie bombing victims sign compensation
de Sierra Delta Concorde flew from Paris to New York for the last time Viacom president had offers to buy CNN from AOL Time
kistan Prada New York, 2000-2001 Turkey devaluates currency by 40% Frank Gehry's Maggie Centre completed in Dundee, Scotl
ulinex (France) form a joint venture Brussels Study, 2002 A Reuters TV cameraman was shot dead by American troops after
parliament Dutch politician Pim Fortuyn is murdered a week before national elections Singer Elliott Smith commits suicid
mazon reports first quarterly profit Shenzen building, 2003 Radiohead release their 6th album "Hail to the Thief" A.C.
Hidden Dragon" Concorde airplane crashes during takeoff EU Study, 2001 544.2 million people use Internet worldwide U.S. C
tern & Southern Africa Deltametropool, 2002 Maglev makes first trial run to Shanghai Kylie Minogue releaes hit sing
aZeneca is announced creating world's biggest agribusiness American Idol continues reality programming trend Scaramush S
gress Centre, 2001 Floods and landslides in south-central Sri Lanka George Bush calls on the world to set aside past di
erse via low power radio signals Harvard Planning Study, 2001 Ryan air is the only European airline to make a profit eve
um held in Porto Alegre, Brazil as a response to World Economic Forum Beijing Olympic Conference Center, 2003 Widesprea
rada Los Angeles, 2000-2004 World Bank Meeting - Pragu AOL Time Warner announces the biggest quarterly loss in corporat
erware Corp. form a strategic alliance Police in the Californian city of Oakland fire on anti-war protesters with rubber
tcy UN City, 2001 The Columbia Space Shuttle, on its 28th mission, breaks up upon reentry into Earth's atmosphere, killi
"The Office" is aired on the BBC for the first time Hermitage, 2003 In Algiers 2,000 people killed in an earthquake Arno
re sign free trade agreement (USSFTA) Samsung National University Museum II, 2002-2004 Mogwai release "Happy Songs fo Ha
Uzbekistan, Moldova and Ukraine Dutch and US authorities launch investigation into Ahold's accounting practices Hottest
ey Museum Extension Scheme A, 2001 Deutsche Telekom reported $ 28bn loss the largest corporate loss in Europe since the
ession Severe acute respiratory syndrome (SARS), a deadly form of pneumonia, detected in southern China and is responsi
PGA) Conference Media Building HK, 2002 Disneyland-Hong Kong starts construction Wired Guest Issue, 2003 Time magazine na
being shot by Israeli soldiers while his father desperately tries to shield him from the attack Britney Spears kisses Mad
ent $5 billion injection CCTV & TVCC, 2002 The Bush administration awards the Bechtel group of San Francisco the first m
dium Satellite network launched Zeche Zollverein Masterplan, 2002 Autostadt, 2003 The "Matrix Reloaded" and "Revolutions"
ge in Sierra Leone Museum Ludwig, 2001 Ruhr Study, 2002 Rowling's "Harry Potter and the Order of the Phoenix" becomes
reportedly reaches 250 million homes world wide Guangzhou Opera House, 2002 Euro-merchandise Form, 2003 David Beckam s
in nearly 40 different languages Vestbanen, 2002 Intensive 6 month search for Iraqi WMD fail to discover any trace of a
h Terrorist attacks on World Trade Centre and Pentagon The largest peace-time rallies in French history against far-righ
ane signs for Real Madrid from Juventus for 70 million euro becoming the world most expensive footballer Stirling Albion
ausplein, 2001 CEFTA countries establish free trade H -Project II, 2002-2004 G8 summit held in Switzerland Arus, 2003 Alan Gree
confirms that Eurozone's largest economy is in recession CBD Core, Beijing, 2003 Tony Blair suffers a heart attack, poo
Jailed for 4 years for perjury OTAN Siege Sociale (NATO), 2002 The EU's rapid reaction force is used for the first tim
points Mexico-EU Free Trade Agreement Napster shuts down Time names Albert Einstein the Person of the Century Outkast
iance agreement Barcelona Airport, 2001 Compaq Computer and HP merge Naples HST, 2003 Kmart files for Chapter 11 bankruptcy
y NASDAQ drops 350 points Introduction of Euro notes and coins American troops kill 7 Iraqi women and children at checkp
2001 MTV Philippines, MTV Thailand, and MTV Indonesia begin broadcasting Beijing Preservation Study, 2003 Global warming
largest peace-time rallies in French history against far-right Jean-Marie Le Pen held Ian Duncan Smith ousted as conse
sion LACMA, 2001 Wall Street suffers worst December since 1930s Ascott House, 2003 Hungarians vote to join the EU despit
ectric and Honeywell Peter Jackson's "Lord of the Rings: The Fellowship of the Ring" released ECB, 2003 Johnny Cash dies
nores Perros" released Whitney Museum Extension Scheme B, 2002 Michael Moore's "Stupid White Men" is published New York
intendo release their next generation games console The GameCube Peter Jackson's "Lord of the Rings: The Two Towers rele
nister, Rehavam Zeevi, is shot dead by gunmen in a Jerusalem hotel AOL-TimeWarner reports overall loss for 2002 of $98.
thern Airlines and China Eastern Airlines UN Security Council approves resolution backing US-led administration in Iraq a
the largest merger in corporate history 8 men die in the crowd during a Pearl Jam concert at the Roskilde Festival in Denmark
sed in North America, Western Europe and Japan FNWI, 2002 "Zelda Wind Waker" released for Gamecube using new 'toon shad
Airlines offers $1 special on seats booked online for September 11 - one way travel only Robin Cook resigns in protes

19

Material Fetish

After the last of them had left the site, I jumped the fence and climbed up three levels of scaffolding. High on the toxic fumes of modernity, I sank my arm elbow-deep into the wet concrete and waited.

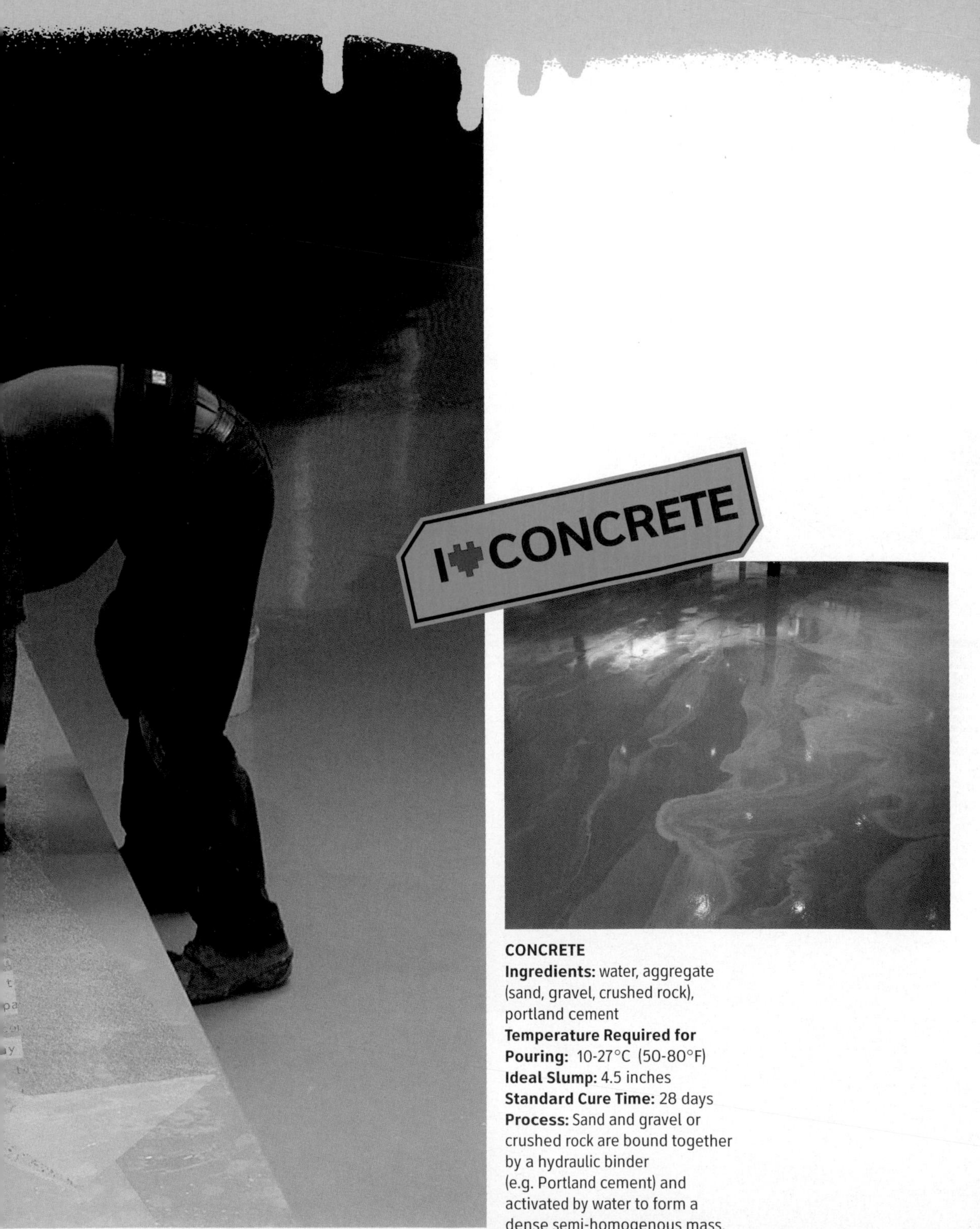

CONCRETE
Ingredients: water, aggregate (sand, gravel, crushed rock), portland cement
Temperature Required for Pouring: 10-27°C (50-80°F)
Ideal Slump: 4.5 inches
Standard Cure Time: 28 days
Process: Sand and gravel or crushed rock are bound together by a hydraulic binder (e.g. Portland cement) and activated by water to form a dense semi-homogenous mass.

PLYWOOD

Ingredients: wood veneer, protein based adhesive (water, dried blood, soya flour, lime, sodium silicate, caustic soda and a formaldehyde donor) or urea-formaldehyde or phenol-formaldehyde based adhesive (water, defoamers, extenders (wheat flour) and urea-formaldehyde resin)
Available Grades: Good Two Sides (G2S), Good One Side (G1S), Select-Tight Face (SEL TF)*, Select (SEL)*, Sheathing (SHG). *May be Cleaned and Sized (C&S)
Process: Layers of wood veneers are bonded by applying phenolic resin glue mix and polymerizing (curing or hardening) the glue in a "hot press." The hot press subjects panels to an approximate temperature of 150°C (300°F) and a pressure of about 1.4 MPa (200 psi), resulting in an inert water and boil-proof bond.

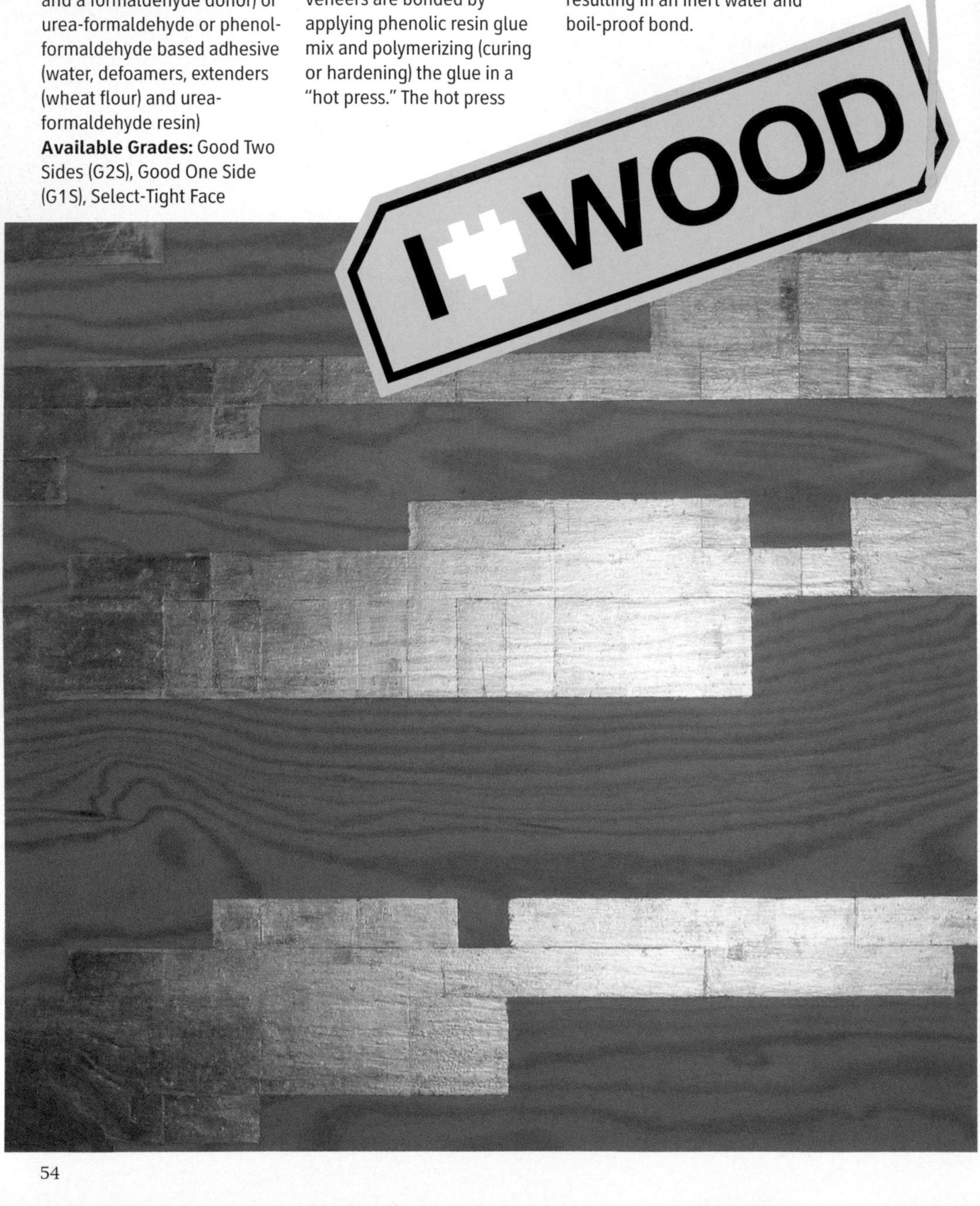

I ♥ WOOD

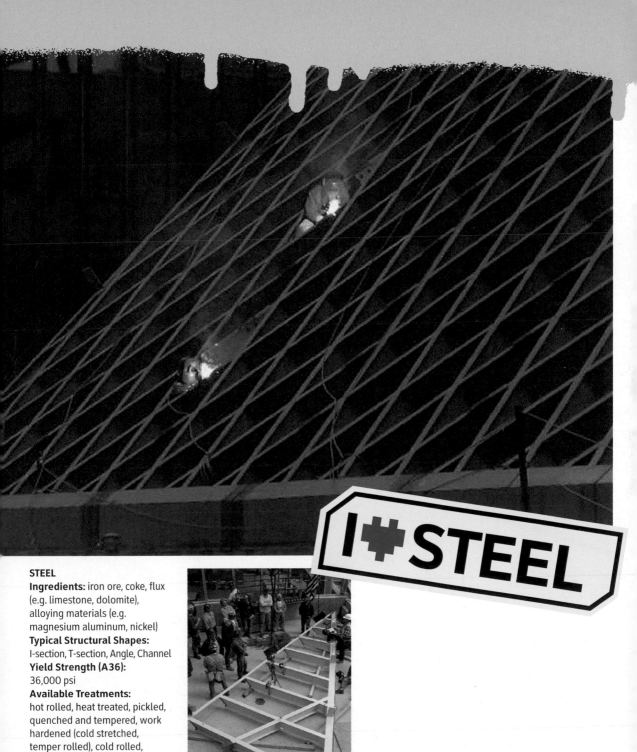

STEEL
Ingredients: iron ore, coke, flux (e.g. limestone, dolomite), alloying materials (e.g. magnesium aluminum, nickel)
Typical Structural Shapes: I-section, T-section, Angle, Channel
Yield Strength (A36): 36,000 psi
Available Treatments: hot rolled, heat treated, pickled, quenched and tempered, work hardened (cold stretched, temper rolled), cold rolled, heat treated, pickled, skinpassed, skinpassed on roughened rolls, bright annealed

I ♥ GLASS

GLASS

Ingredients: sand, soda, ash, limestone, dolomite, cullet

Process: The ingredients are melted in a furnace at 1500°C (2700°F). The mixture then flows onto a bath of molten tin in a continuous ribbon. The glass, which is highly viscous, and the tin, which is very fluid, do not mix. As a result, the contact surface between them is perfectly flat. After moving over the bath of molten tin, the glass has cooled sufficiently to pass to an annealing chamber - "the lehr." In the lehr, it is cooled under strict controls.

Typical Impact Velocity Causing Fracture:
30 ft/sec (Annealed)
60 ft/sec (Tempered)

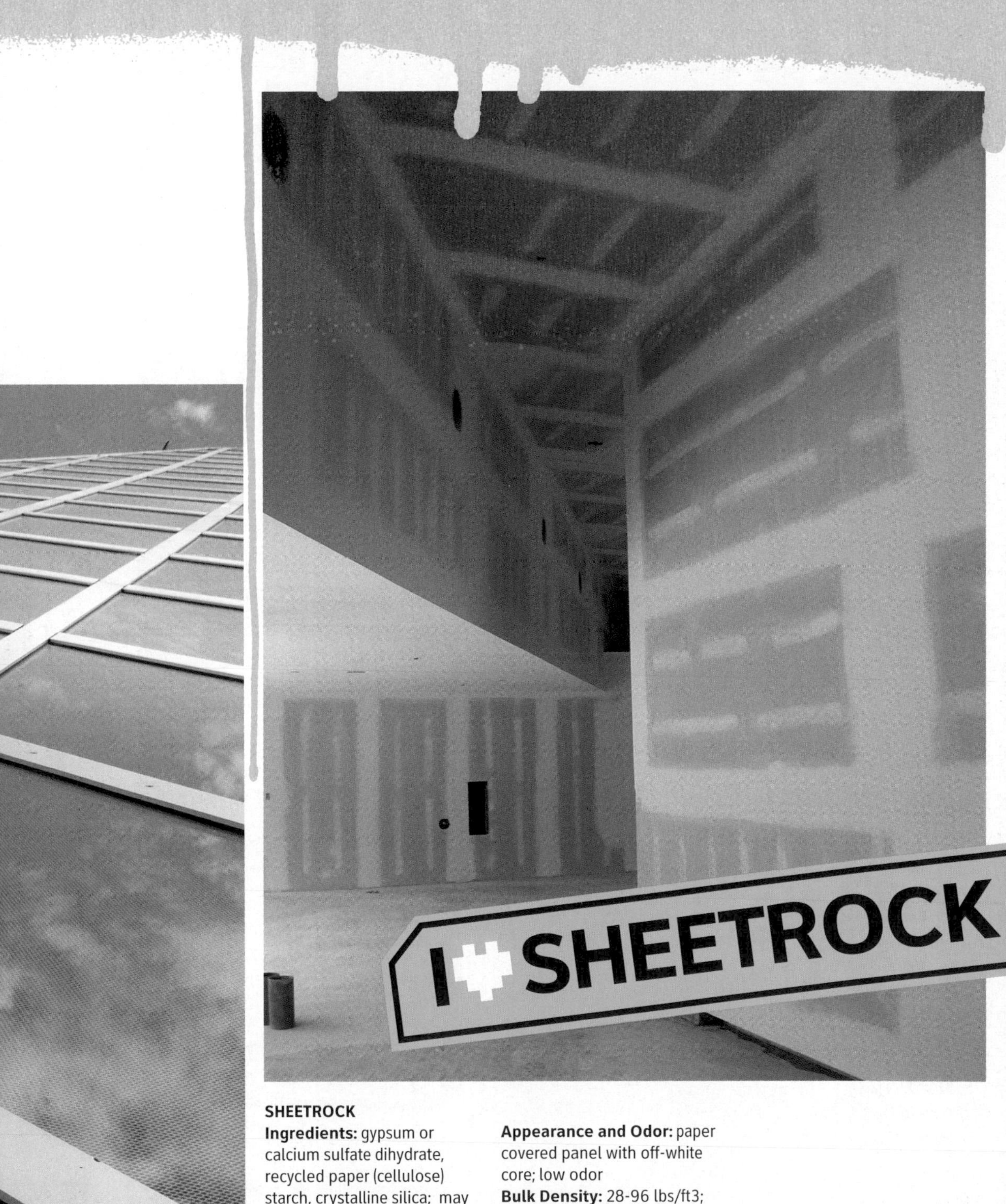

SHEETROCK

Ingredients: gypsum or calcium sulfate dihydrate, recycled paper (cellulose) starch, crystalline silica; may contain the following: fibrous glass (textile grade), boric acid, potassium sulfate

Appearance and Odor: paper covered panel with off-white core; low odor

Bulk Density: 28-96 lbs/ft3; varies with panel thickness

Solubility in Water: ~0.2% ■

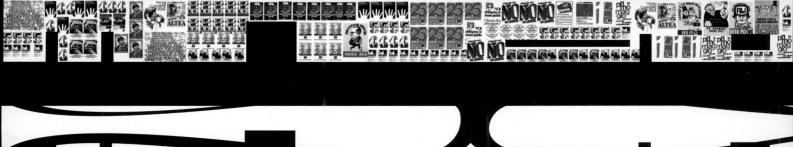

Wallpaper

PRADA WALLPAPER DESIGNED BY 2X4

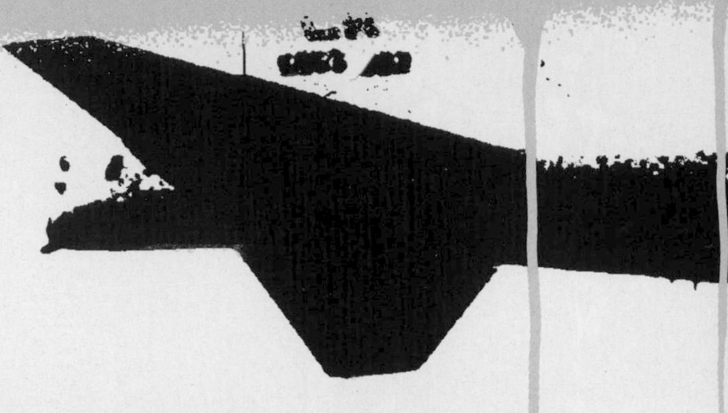

The Evil Architects Do

As urban planning becomes an increasingly common tool of military conflict, has the time come to add architecture to the list of war crimes?

BY EYAL WEIZMAN

The inauguration in the Hague of the International Criminal Court[1] announces the prospect of a Judiciary Utopia: under international jurisdiction, individuals can be charged for the most serious crimes of international concern, such as the crimes of apartheid and war.[2] At the basis of the court, the International Humanitarian Law is designed to address military personnel or politicians in executive positions.[3] But in the frictions of a rapidly developing and urbanizing world, human rights are increasingly violated by the organization of space. Just like the gun or the tank, mundane building matter is abused as a weapon with which crimes are committed.

The application of international law as the most severe method of architectural critique has never been more urgent. Crimes relating to the organization of the built environment, originating on computer screens and drafting tables, call for placing an architect/planner, for the first time, on the accused stand of an international tribunal.

International justice must bypass the legal system of states - usually complicit in such cases - and decide whether a particular planning practice deviated from the naturally aggressive character of planning and its "acceptable" level of "collateral damage" to qualify as a violation of international law. When an architect's design premeditatedly aims to cause material damage - as part of a large-scale policy of organized aggression - a war crime may have been committed. The evidence for these crimes are in the drawings - marked as lines on plans, maps, or their immediate real time replacement - aerial photographs.

The nature of the planning action concerned is twofold, including both acts of strategic form making: construction and destruction.

From the political/military point of view, the city is a social/physical obstacle that must be reorganized before it can be controlled. "Design by destruction" increasingly involves planners as military personnel reshaping the battleground to meet strategic objectives. As urban warfare gradually comes to resemble urban planning, armies have established research programs to study the complexities of cities and train their own urban practitioners. The effect is evident worldwide. The destruction in Bosnia of public facilities - mosques, cemeteries and public squares - followed a clear and old fashioned planner's logic: social order cannot be maintained without its shared functions (Article 8.3.b.ix). The manipulation of key infrastructure - roads, power, water and communication, such as in Baghdad - seeks to control an urban area by disrupting its various flows. Bombing campaigns rely on architects and planners to recommend buildings and infrastructure as potential targets in order to evaluate the urban effect of their removal. The destruction of monuments and heritage sites, such as in the bombing of Belgrade, seeks a psychological victory over "enslaving" architectural projects (Article 8.3.b.ix). The grid of roads, the width of an army bulldozer, that carved through the fabric of the refugee camp of Jenin and the "clearing out" of a large area at its center reveals another planners' specialty - the replacement of an existing circulation system with another - one more accessible to the occupying army and

therefore easier to control (Article 8,2.a.iv). Revealingly, the Israeli army employs architects and civil engineers as commanders of its military bulldozers.

These violations of the articles of war do not require an official declaration of war to qualify as such, however. The source of the term "urbicide" - the destruction of the condition of plurality that defines a city - did not originate in Belgrade, Mostar, Grozny, or Gaza but in the regenerations and "hygienic" practices of American urban planning, such as those described by Marshal Berman after the aggressive "clean up" of the Bronx.

Planning's pretence to facilitate the social and economic improvement of an abstract "public" has long been ignored, and physical development now largely manifests itself as the executive arm of a geopolitical strategic or market-driven agenda. Large scale development such as in the Pearl River Delta or the Three Gorges Dam in Yichang, China respond to political and market demands by displacing huge populations across national space (Article 7.2.d) and erasing their home villages. The design of a closely knit fabric of homes and infrastructure, such as in Sao Paulo, Mexico City, or California acts as a form of spatial exclusion - creating wedges that separate the habitat of a population of >

This section of the map of the West Bank marks the location, size and form of Jewish settlements (dark blue), the areas allocated for their expansion (light blues), Palestinian cities and villages (dark browns), and the projected path of the barrier (red line), now under construction, designed to pull them apart. Plans of Jewish settlements respond to regional master plans that state as one of their aims the bisection of Palestinian built fabric and circulation continuity.[6]

THE ROME STATUE OF THE INTERNATIONAL CRIMINAL COURT

Articles referred to above in relation to the transformation of the built environment.
(See the complete statue on: http://www.un.org/law/icc/statute/romefra.htm)

CRIMES AGAINST HUMANITY

Article 7.2.d
"Deportation or forcible transfer of population" means forced displacement of the persons concerned by expulsion or other coercive acts from the area in which they are lawfully present.

WAR CRIMES

Article 8.2.a.iv
Extensive destruction and appropriation of property, not justified by military necessity and carried out unlawfully and wantonly

Article 8.3.b.viii
The transfer, directly or indirectly, by the Occupying Power of parts of its own civilian population into the territory it occupies, or the deportation or transfer of all or parts of the population of the occupied territory within or outside this territory

Article 8.3.b.ix
Intentionally directing attacks against buildings dedicated to religion, education, art, science or charitable purposes, historic monuments, hospitals and places where the sick and wounded are collected, provided they are not military objectives

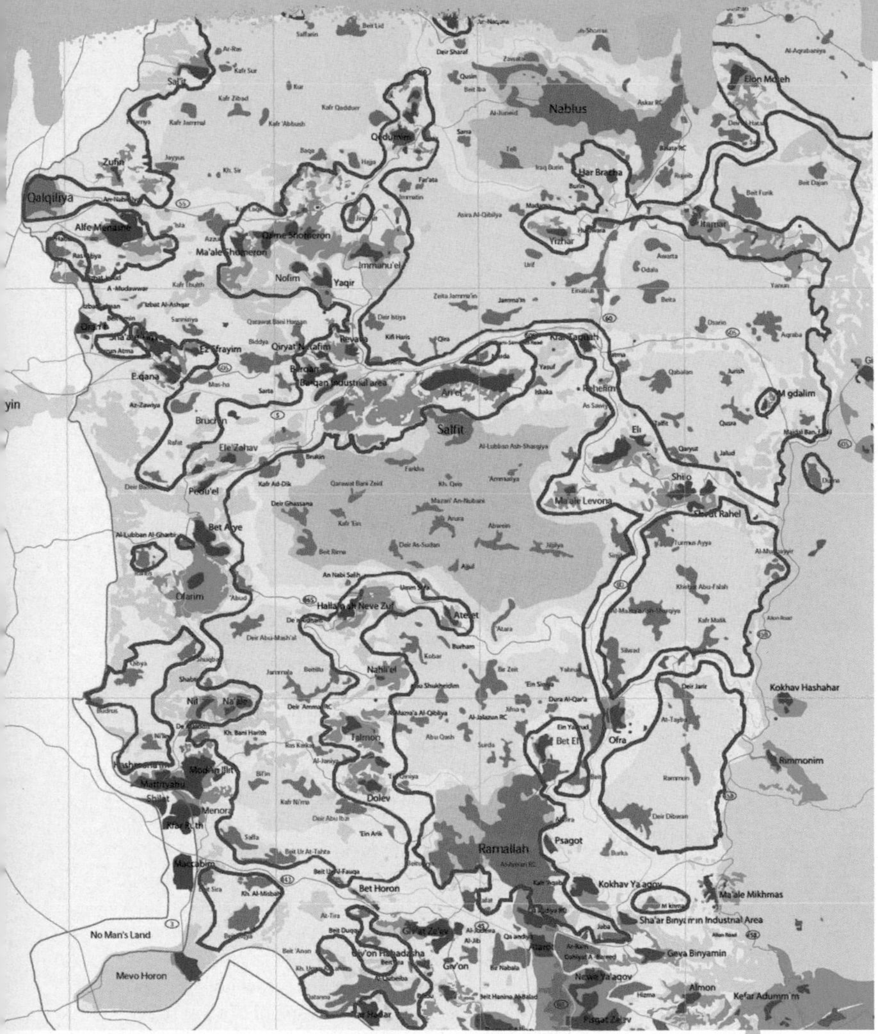

citizens marked as political "outsiders." Policies such as those guiding the official town planners of Jerusalem - to limit Palestinian population growth - are mostly achieved through spatial manipulations.[4] The form and layout of neighborhoods, the positioning of major roads, and the establishment of "no build" green spaces between and around Palestinian neighborhoods are meant to shrink the Palestinian habitat and its economic possibilities in order to generate the "quiet transfer" the authorities seek (Article 8.3.b.viii). It is only appropriate that the Israeli Attorney-General urged parliament to retreat from joining the ICC lest "every building (in the occupied territories) start to be considered a war crime," and Israeli planners, architects, constructors, suppliers, or residents in the settlement be indicted.[5]

The legal basis for indicting architects or planners already exists, but architecture and planning intersects with the strategies of contemporary conflicts

PHOTO: NIR KAFRI

Troops from the engineering corps of the IDF inspecting for places to place dynamite during a raid of Tul Qarem refugee camp

"Architecture and planning intersects with the strategies of contemporary conflicts in ways that the semantics of international law are still ill-equipped to describe."

in ways that the semantics of international law are still ill-equipped to describe. International Humanitarian Law is predicated on a obsolete distinction between civilians and combatants, trapped in a low intensity urban conflict that can no longer be understood according to its clear dialectics of war and peace. The removal of urban matter must not only be quantified as a statistical problem relating the number of buildings destroyed (Article 8.2.a.iv) nor be valued by their status as heritage sites (Article 8.3.b.ix) - but must be understood as an active form of design, having a cumulative effect on the creation of new spaces. Similarly, it is not enough to indict an architect for the very act of planning in occupied areas (Article 8.3.b.viii) or for participating in an aggressive state policy, but for the immediate consequences of his formal and organizational practice.

Architectural critics, previously limited to the professional and cultural domains, must take legal measures to meet the challenges of regulating a profession flirting with both utopia and crime. The legal accountability of architects and planners stands in direct relation to their newly acquired potency and sharpens the choice each must face: should a tempting commission be accepted even if the general policy it serves stands in breach of human and political rights? If its motivations and the possible consequences are destructive? Collaboration has always an alternative - refusal!

In an interview on CNN, former American president and Nobel Peace Prize laureate Jimmy Carter said that "the knowledge that the ICC functions... will repel those who are inclined to commit crimes." The first architect to face international tribunals will send a shiver down the spine of a complicit profession. ■

NOTES

1 The Statute outlining the creation of the International Criminal Court (ICC) was adopted at an international conference in Rome on 1998; the tribunal came into force on July 1st, 2002. The court can only hear cases that occur after this date.

2 Although the establishment of the ICC is a major boost, the prospect of international justice is still unclear. The ICC applies only to citizens of the states that ratified its constitution. As of May 2003, 90 countries had ratified it. Fearing international prosecution, the post-September 11 US administration withdrew its signature from membership in the ICC. The Israeli government under Ariel Sharon followed soon after. Russia, China, Libya and Yemen are amongst those not to have ratified. The problem of voluntary membership is that the states whose citizens engaged in war crimes would likely not join and will thus remain immune.

3 International humanitarian law (IHL), based on the four Geneva Conventions of 1949, is the body of rules which protects, limits, and prevents human suffering in times of armed conflict.

4 The official Jerusalem city policy aims to keep the Palestinian portion of the city's population at a constant 28%, although their rate of population growth is much higher than the Jewish-Israeli one.

5 Israeli Attorney-General Elyakim Rubinstein warned Israeli Law makers on the Knesset's (Israeli Parliament) Constitution, Law and Justice Committee in June 2002 about the possible legal consequences of the ICC. Allen Baker, then the legal adviser to the foreign office, put it in bolder terms: "Every person who is involved in decision making regarding the setting of citizens on occupied area may be arrested, from the prime minister down to the last citizen."

6 The planning of the settlements and of the barrier violates Palestinian political and human rights but also various articles of war crimes including Article 8.3.b.viii. (For the complete map of the West Bank and the analysis of various violations inscribed on it see "Land Grab" on www.btselem.org)

The Poisonous Mixture

Corruption infects all bodies, buildings, and standards. Can you maintain?

BY SHUMON BASAR ILLUSTRATIONS SIMON BROWN

The Deal

A dopey-looking architect is happily married to an improbably beautiful woman when a sudden recession strikes. In a fit of panic, they go to Las Vegas to try to save themselves. In a casino, the wife duly declines the advances of a suave, smoldering magnate. He persists, finally making an offer to the financially desperate couple: one million dollars to spend one night with the beautiful wife. After dismissing the outrageous proposal, the architect and his wife lie back in bed and, from the righteous silence hovering between them, the possibility of agreeing to the million dollars begins to seem not so obscene after all. What's "one night," they think, compared to the thousands of nights that their fortified, watertight marriage will indubitably contain. But once the deal is consumed, the very edifice of the marriage begins to fall apart, brick by brick, as the architect-husband becomes distraught with anxieties that his wife might actually have enjoyed the night she spent with "the client." Nothing, the architect realizes, will ever be the same.

The Detail

Woody Harrelson's character in the film *Indecent Proposal* suffers an ignoble fate because he didn't focus on the detail. He didn't understand how the torrid part - Robert Redford's plea for "just one night" - would relate to the fragile whole of his marriage. The good parable should teach us that one must not underestimate the latent dangers of imperfect detailing - that vigilance to detail should be second only to breathing for any self-respecting architect. "God is in the details," pronounced Germany's very own architectural St. Augustine, Mies van der Rohe, which probably came as a surprise to those who thought God had died and gone to heaven. Amen.

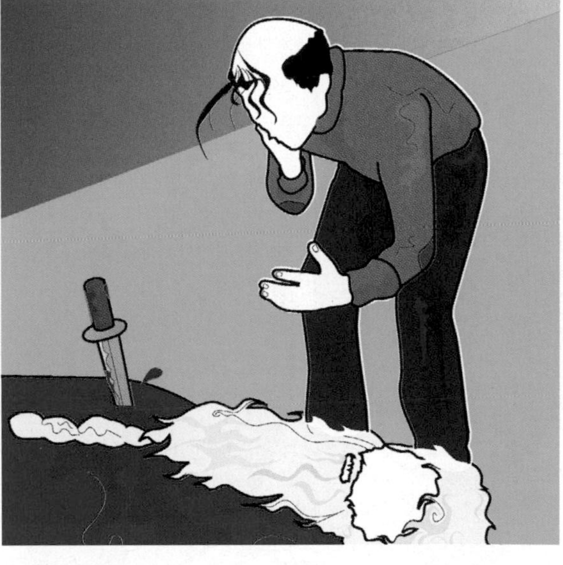

The Virtuous

Indecent Proposal was released the year I started my education in architecture. Very quickly, I felt the need to become au fait with the rules governing what is considered virtuous and what is sinful. Ever since Mies's unique brand of fastidious, materially terse architecture proliferated to become the DNA of the neutered world that surrounds us, architects have valorized, with religious ferment, the absolute gravitas of "detailing": that is, a strange fetishization of screws, joints, gaps, and junctions. In a further twist of obsessive perversity, the construction of the detail should be almost imperceptible and, above all, it should not show evidence of having been made by human hands. Along with wearing one's shirt with the top button closed (without a tie) and listening to freeform jazz while drafting, the (male) architect's pursuit of the controlled finish is a wayward, contagious infliction peculiarly at odds with the true unwieldy scale of architecture and the manifold, abstract dimensions in which it is situated.

The Battle

"Architecture is a poisonous mixture of power and impotence."[1] When I read this statement as a student, my idealism was violated in the way a child's world is slowly dismantled with the successive abduction of Santa Claus, Superman, and the Man in the Moon. "But surely," I protested, "if our concepts are bold enough, if our passion is hi-octane fueled, can't we achieve anything? Shouldn't we be able to achieve everything?" It's only when one begins to try to build something that one understands the second half of architecture's dialectical recipe. Like Hercules, or Bruce Willis in *Die Hard*, the architect must fight a veritable battle against ever-embittered combatants who seem to want to see him fail. There are building regulations, bored bureaucrats, economic vicissitudes, nefarious political climates, unspoken histories, indifferent construction industries, and the "public." And often, above all of these harbingers of impotence, the architect faces The Client in a relationship that can be as infernal or beautiful as any marriage. This litany is sometimes referred to as "external forces," implying that the nature of practice is the reciprocity between this "outer realm" and the "inner realm" - the seat of the architect's creativity and will. Understanding the character of architecture's "impotence" might, I thought a few years later, be the key to liberation: how to unlock idealist delusion and give way to practicable strategy.

The Schism

There are two piles of images on my desk. The first includes a series of diagrams and flow-charts showing how a firm, OMA, has recently been extending its operations and presence by affiliating itself with diverse companies and experts. The other pile is a series of close-up photographs of three buildings in Holland, revealing how various joints, gaps, surfaces, and apertures have held out over time.[2] Cracks, oxidation, deterioration, patination, a panel falling off here, dead flies: a mesmerizing smear of decay in color. Leafing through the two sets of images is like looking at two possible future outcomes of a single decisive present.

The Inevitable

The pictures of aging buildings are a Dorian Gray-like reminder of the inevitable perishability of everything. It might sound portentous to claim that it is the fear of death that both plagues and motivates architects. This would assume that buildings are physical personifications of their authors, estranged metonyms, or abandoned look-alikes. Any building is however marked by the mortality of its material assemblage. It can go wrong at any time, and might do so in public. The author is unable to hide from the unforeseen problems - the imperfections - of the creation. This may be why James Stirling never revisited his finished buildings: he claimed it was too much like visiting ex-loves. Perhaps going back is so terrifying because, if the building is the architect, any tectonic failures are tantamount to corporeal failures. It's like staring at your own expiry, and realizing that there is nothing you can do to stop it.

The Tactical

"The important thing is to be aware one exists"[3]

I organize the diagrams into a matrix on my table and behold a spray of acronyms - OMA, AMO, VPRO, 2x4, IDEO; proper names - Prada, Harvard, Ove Arup; and a miscellany of individuals, some of whose names I recognize and others I don't. In relation to the photos of decay, these diagrams seem to outline an exploratory search for external, abstract organization - abstract not in the sense of "not-there," but in the way that freedom is abstract. The various permutations of letters and names look like a desire to discover tactics - tactics of ensuring one's freedom. Having been taught that the only way architects can generate the conditions of their freedom is by building more and better, getting bigger commissions and ending up with a fat cigar and a helipad, the spidery networks of interlaced diversification that orbit OMA look insane, and therefore the right thing to be doing. I can't help but think that the inward-looking species of architect - frozen by its love for frozen things - seems doomed to D-list subjugation. These bubble diagrams on the other hand, linking Chinese TV broadcasting with notions of rethinking Europe, attest to an unbridled locomotive where Surrealistic juxtapositions begin to operate at the level of culture, economics, and language.

The Cure

It isn't just a question of accepting that there are waves, and agreeing to surf them. Imagine, like Leonardo da Vinci, that you can create weather, and with weather, the mother of all waves. It could strike anywhere (New York, China, Las Vegas, the Ruhr Valley, Portugal ...) so one has to appear as though one can and will be everywhere at once. Make friends with culture (that's where the money is), hang out with fashion (it works for Christina Aguilera), celebrate superficiality (it's today's depth), be brutal and soft (we want it both ways), see the treasure in Junk (there is no such thing as obsolescence), spawn tribute clones (it's the true measure of fame), ditch piety and ennoble promiscuity (when have the youth ever been wrong?) and most of all, realize that power isn't something worth believing in, you have to live it. From architecture's funeral pyre, a new Andrew Lloyd Webber musical could be born. The project of architecture, if it is to survive intact and potent, must transcend its former self: it has to wake up and realize that the true and only important task is the vigilant corruption of the chain of causality that begins with "client" and ends in "building." Appear self-aggrandizing? Accept Machiavellian tendencies? Dance like John Travolta? Sure. Just don't look inwards, look out. The most powerful effect of impotence is the desire to find the cure.

1 REM KOOLHAAS, LECTURE AT COLUMBIA UNIVERSITY, 1989.
2 NETHERLANDS DANCE THEATER, THE HAGUE; KUNSTHAL, ROTTERDAM; EDUCATORIUM, UTRECHT.
3 JEAN-LUC GODARD, PIERROT LE FOU (LONDON: LORRIMAR, 1969).

One man
Cannot a
Man's de

T

s hatred
ter another
stiny.

ENERGY BAR
Draws on advances in theory, mathematics, and computing

POWER MOVES
Fluidity, Asymmetry, Biomorphism, Structural Dynamics, Multiplicity

BLOB II

FIGH
ROU

ILLUSTRATION SIMON BROWN

ENERGY BAR
Draws on intuitive appeal of orthogonality

POWER MOVES
Rationality, Golden Mean, Universality, Exactitude

BOX II

T ON
ND II

„EIN GUTES
INTERIOR LÄSST
MENSCHEN
GUT AUSSEHEN."
Jasmin Grego vom Züricher Architekturbüro Grego & Smolenicky
AD
AD
AD
best of
GERMANY
AD ARCHITECTURAL DIGEST
MONATLICH AM KIOSK

Patent Office

The half-life of architecture's collective memory is now around six months. Ideas emerge, inspire, and are conveniently forgotten. Here, OMA stakes its claim for eternity.

UNIVERSAL MODERNIZATION PATENT [14]
"SOCIAL CONDENSER" (1982)

Patent Number: 3,818,150

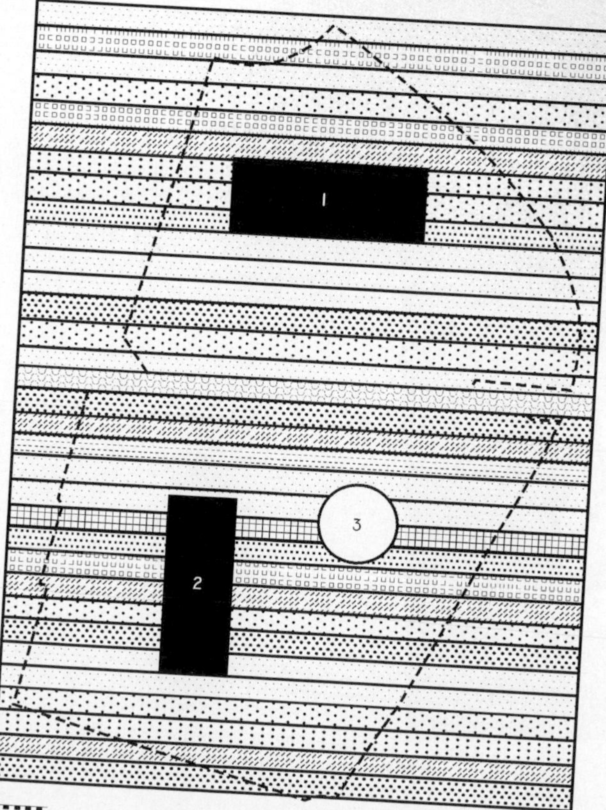

[21] Patent for: "Social Condenser"

(29) PROGRAMMATIC LAYERING UPON VACANT TERRAIN TO ENCOURAGE DYNAMIC COEXISTENCE OF ACTIVITIES AND TO GENERATE THROUGH THEIR INTERFERENCE, UNPRECENTED EVENTS.

(36) Inventor(s): **Rem Koolhaas, Elia Zenghelis**

Correspondence Address:
OMA
BOOMPJES 55
3011 XB ROTTERDAM
TEL: + 31(0) 10 411 1216

[42] **Initial Application of Concept: Parc de la Villette, Paris, FRANCE**

[54] **Filed:..........................1982**

(71) **ABSTRACT**

Take the section of the typical skyscraper and put it on its side; now declare each floor a different program; distribute recurrent obligations mathematically across the site in intervals dictated by need; design one (or more) symbolic elements (1,2,3) to acknowledge "eternal" human values. Instead of treating "park" as the opposite of the city - a programmatic non-entity, this approach demonstrates that the park can sustain program with superior ease.

UNIVERSAL MODERNIZATION PATENT [14]

"STRATEGY OF THE VOID I" (PLANNING) (1987)

Patent number: 5, 143,723

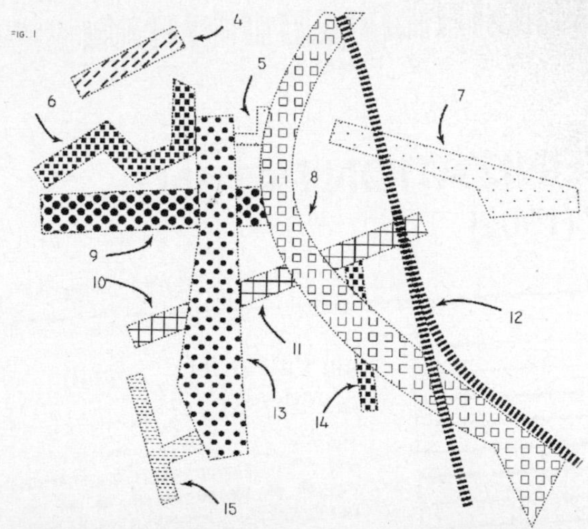

FIG. 2

1 KM

(21) **Patent for "Strategy of the Void I" (planning)**

(29) **METHOD FOR PLANNING CITY THROUGH MANIPULATION OF THE UNBUILT AND THE LEFT OUT.**

(36) Inventor(s): **Rem Koolhaas, Yves Brunier, Xaveer de Geyter, Mike Guyer.**

Correspondence Address:
**OMA,
BOOMPJES 55
3011 XB ROTTERDAM
TEL 31 (0)10 411 1216**

(42) **Initial Application: the new town of Melun-Senart, FRANCE**

[54] Filed:......................1987

(71) **ABSTRACT**

Given that practically all we build today is disappointing, we invest our hopes in the unbuilt as the last source of the sublime. If we deploy in the unbuilt (4-15) the powers formerly applied to the built, we can afford to treat the built as we formerly did nature, and take it for granted (16).

UNIVERSAL MODERNIZATION PATENT [14]

"TIMED ERASURES" (1991)

Patent Number: 7,675, 280

2005

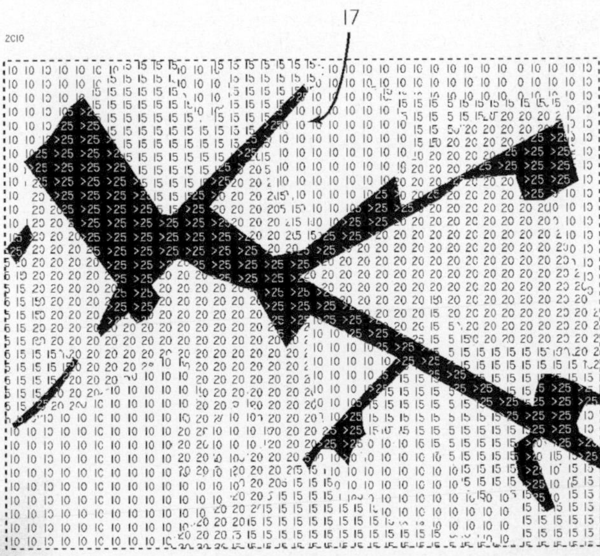

21) Patent for "Timed Erasures"

(29) METHOD OF PROSPECTIVE PRESERVATION BASED ON PREDICTED LIFESPANS OF URBAN FABRIC.

(36) Inventor(s): **Rem Koolhaas, Winy Maas**

Correspondence Address:
OMA
BOOMPJES 55
3011 XB ROTTERDAM HOLLAND
31 (0)10 411 1216

(42) InitialApplication of Concept: La Defense, Paris, FRANCE

(54) **Filed:....................1991**

(71) ABSTRACT

Adopting the hypothesis that - contrary to the Egyptians, the Greeks, the Romans, the Incas, the Goths, the Italians, the metabolists - all buildings constructed after 1950 contain an expiration date, the death of architecture equals, potentially, the rebirth of the city. A campaign of razing what is expired (17) could reveal, in every metropolis, vast amounts of redundant urban substance that , if removed, would offer central locations to ever new iterations of what the city can be.

UNIVERSAL MODERNIZATION PATENT [14]

"LOOP-TRICK" (1987)

Patent Number: 5, 241, 680

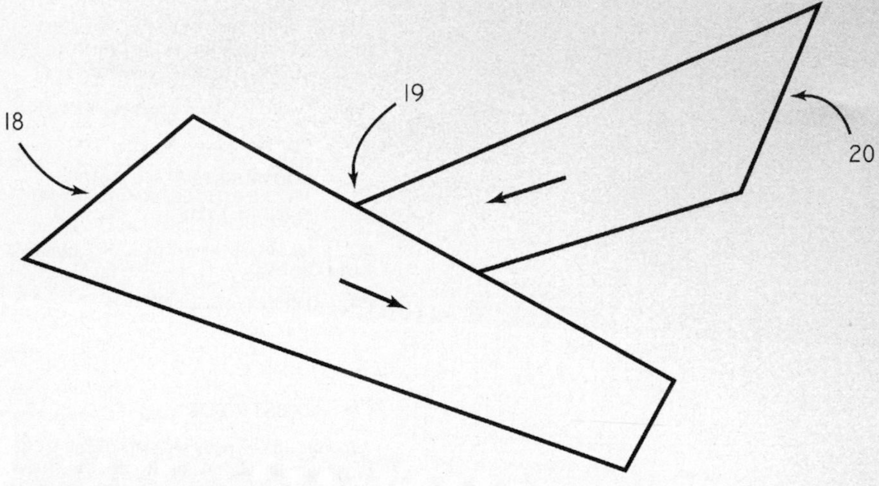

(21) **Patent for "Loop-Trick"**

(29) SYSTEM OF INTERSECTING RAMPS THAT DESTOYS THE STATUS OF THE INDIVIDUAL FLOOR

(36) Inventor(s): **Rem Koolhaas, Fuminori Hoshino**

Correspondence Address:
OMA
BOOMPJES 55
3011 XB ROTTERDAM
31 (0)10 4111216

(42) **Initial Application: Kunsthal, Rotterdam, THE NETHERLANDS**

(54) **Filed:......................1987**

(71) **ABSTRACT**

Introducing an X of intersecting floors (18, 20) in a two-story building creates a continuous surface that destroys the status of the individual floor, eliminates the notion of above and below (19).

UNIVERSAL MODERNIZATION PATENT [14]
"STRATEGY OF THE VOID II" (BUILDING) (1989)

Patent Number 6,345, 780

(21) Patent for "Strategy of the Void II" (building)

(29) METHOD FOR DEFINING A BUILDING THROUGH MANIPULATING ABSENCES OF BUILDING

(36) Inventor(s): **Rem Koolhaas, Art Zaaijer, Xaveer de Geyter, Georges Heintz, Heike Lohmann, Ron Steiner, Alex Wall**

Correspondence Address:
OMA
BOOMPJES 55
3011 XB ROTTERDAM
31 (0)10 411 1216

(42) Initial Application:
Très Grande Bibliothèque Paris, FRANCE

(54) Filed:....................1989

(71) ABSTRACT

Instead of laboriously creating difference and importance in a building that consists of repetitive accomodation and public space, the most communal spaces can be created more easily. Because it is harder to construct than to take away, the most important spaces in a building can be created by elimination (21-24) rather than addition - by scooping out forms from a solid block, like ice-cream.

FIG. 1

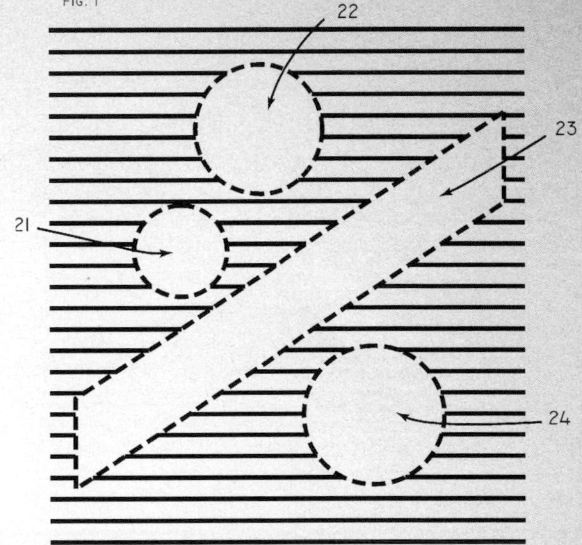

FIG. 2

10 M

UNIVERSAL MODERNIZATION PATENT [14]
"STACKED FREEDOMS" (1989)

Patent Number: 7,375, 230

(21) **Patent for: "Stacked Freedoms"**

(29) **SYSTEM OF VIERENDEEL BEAMS THAT ALLOWS FREE OCCUPANCY OF ALTERNATING FLOORS.**

(36) Inventors: **Rem Koolhaas, Cecil Balmond, Heike Lohmann, Georges Heintz, Alex Wall.**

Correspondence Address:
OMA,
BOOMPJES 55
3011 XB ROTTERDAM
31 10 411 1216

(42) **Initial Application: Center for Art and Media Technology, Karlsruhe, GERMANY**

54) Filed:....................1989

(71) **ABSTRACT**

Instead of accepting structural depth as a "lost" segment of the section, it can be expanded and turned into habitable floors (26-29). The increasingly inhibiting legacy of cumulative structure is transformed into a regime of alternating structural absence and presence.

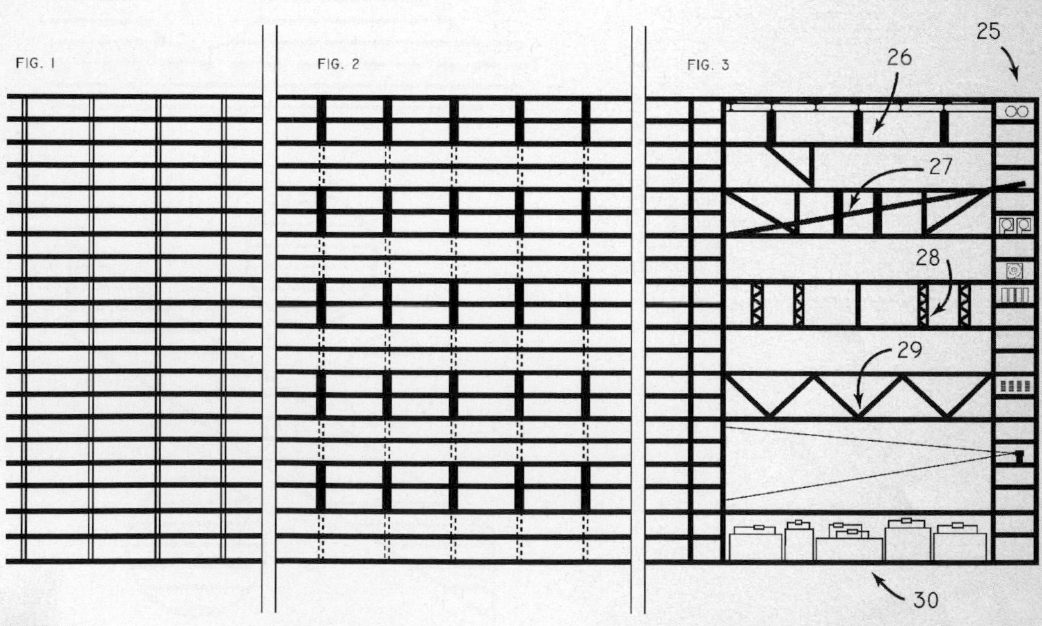

UNIVERSAL MODERNIZATION PATENT [14]

"INSIDE-OUT CITY" (1993)

Patent Number: 8,728, 220

FIG. 1

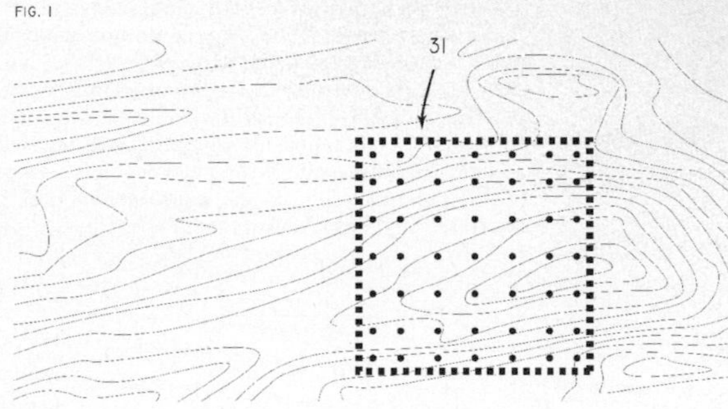

FIG. 2

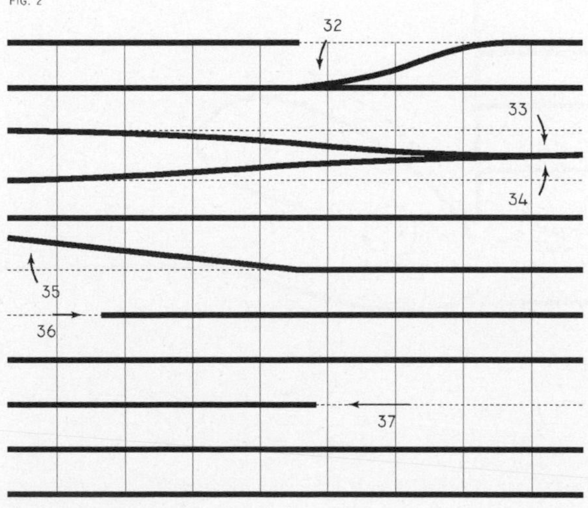

(21) **Patent for "Inside-out City"**

(29) FOLDING OF "STREET" TO GENERATE VERTICAL INTERIOR BOULEVARD THAT EXPOSES AND RELATES ALL PRO GRAMS IN A SINGLE SEQUENCE

(36) Inventors: **Rem Koolhaas, Christophe Cornubert, Xaveer de Geyter, Rene Heijne, Markus Rothlisberger, Yushi Uehara.**

Correspondence Address:

OMA
BOOMPJES 55
3011 XB ROTTERDAM
31 (0)10 411 1216

(42) Initial Application: Jussieu Libraries, Paris FRANCE

(54) Filed:...................... 1993

(71) **ABSTRACT**

Deforming the floor not in plan but in section (32-37) potentially turns the seemingly inevitable separation of different floors into a continuous experience, while ending at the same time the regimes of spatial orthogonality that have dominated architecture. Yet, by combining this new architecture with the traditional discipline of the structural grid, it can be imagined, supported, stacked instead of being condemned to a life as a blob; become communal instead of autarkic.

UNIVERSAL MODERNIZATION PATENT [14]

"DISCONNECT" (1994)

Patent Number: 9, 765, 233

(21) **Patent for: "Disconnect"**

(29) **METHOD OF DEFINING A THEATER BY STRICT SEPARATION OF ITS COMPONENTS**

(36) Inventor (s): **Rem Koolhaas**

Correspondence Address:
OMA, HEER BOKELWEG 149
3032 AD ROTTERDAM
TEL: + 31(0) 102438200

(42) **InitialApplication: Cardiff Bay Opera House, Cardiff WALES.**

(54) **Filed:.....................1994**

(71) **ABSTRACT**

The two parts that are usually combined in a theater into a single whole (stage and auditorium wrapped in public space) are separated (38, 39) to enable both to perform their designated tasks as efficiently as possible.The stage becomes a utilitarian illusion-factory; the auditorium a continuous consumption belt that begins as stairs (42), turns into foyer, becomes stalls, warps up (41) to meet the factory - the stage opening their only interface - and turns back on itself as ceiling, to end as balcony.

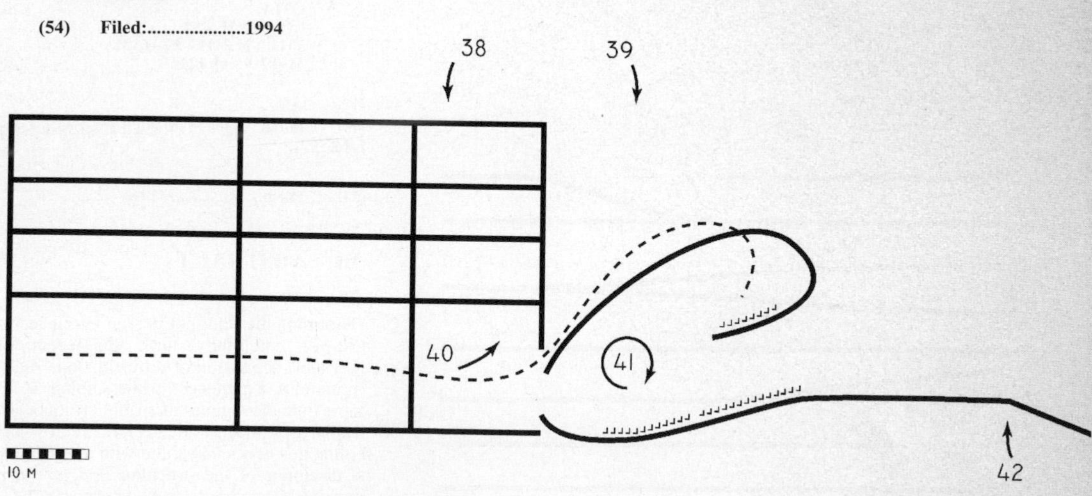

UNIVERSAL MODERNIZATION PATENT [14]

"EVERYWHERE AND NOWHERE" (1994)

Patent Number: 9,745, 214

(21) Patent for "Everywhere and Nowhere"

(29) SYSTEM FOR TRANSFORMING A TRANSPORTATION DEVICE INTO A ROOM TO CREATE A CHANGE-ABLE HOUSE

(36) Inventor(s): **Rem Koolhaas**

Correspondence Address:
OMA, HEER BOKELWEG 149
3032 AD ROTTERDAM
TEL: + 31(0) 102438200

(42) InitialApplication: Maison á Bordeaux, FRANCE

(54) Filed:....................1994

(71) ABSTRACT

By piercing a vertical shaft through a multilevel architecture and installing a moving platform that can engagewith any level (43, 44, 45), the stability of domestic architecture is overturned by an element of real instability that, as it offers new scenarios to inhabitants, also changes the architecture of the structure.

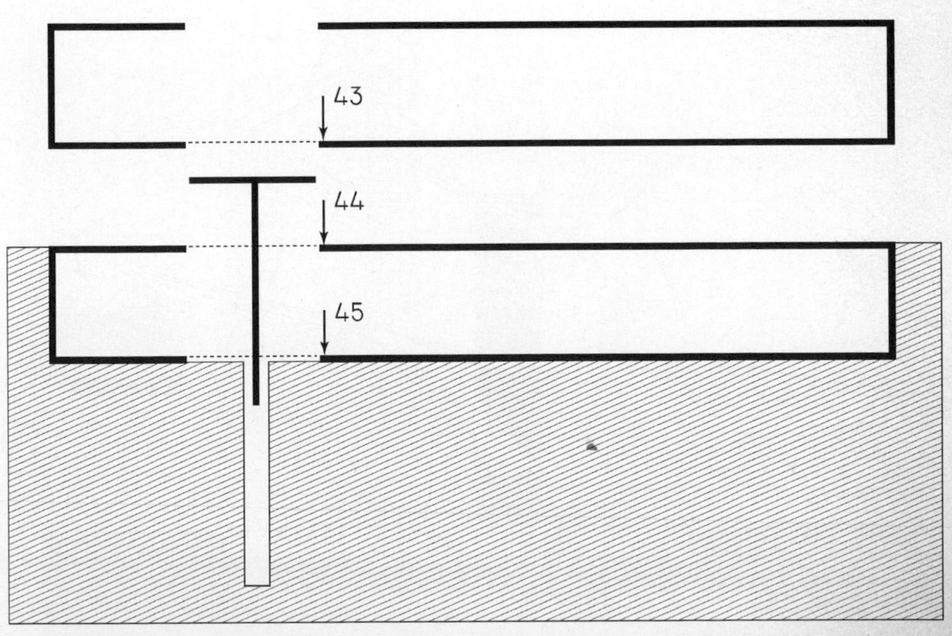

UNIVERSAL MODERNIZATION PATENT [14]
"VARIABLE-SPEED MUSEUM" (1995)

Patent Number: 10,365, 340

(21) **Patent for:"Variable-Speed Museum"**

(29) **USE OF MECHANICAL TRANSPORT TO MULTIPLY, DIVERSIFY, AND INDIVIDUALIZE MOVEMENT THROUGH A MUSEUM BUILDING .**

(36) Inventors: **Rem Koolhaas, Floris Alkemade.**

Correspondence Address:
OMA, HEER BOKELWEG 149
3032 AD ROTTERDAM
TEL: + 31(0) 102438200

(42) **Initial Application: The Tate Gallery, London, UK**

(54) **Filed:....................... 1995**

(71) **ABSTRACT**

The museum experience insists on a dictatorial parade on foot past artifacts that are supposed to trigger individual revelation. The simultaneous applications of many technologies of mechanical transport (47-53) vastly extends the repertoire of potential movement, multiplies the circumstances of the atavistic encounter in the museum, and transcends the type's century-old limitations.

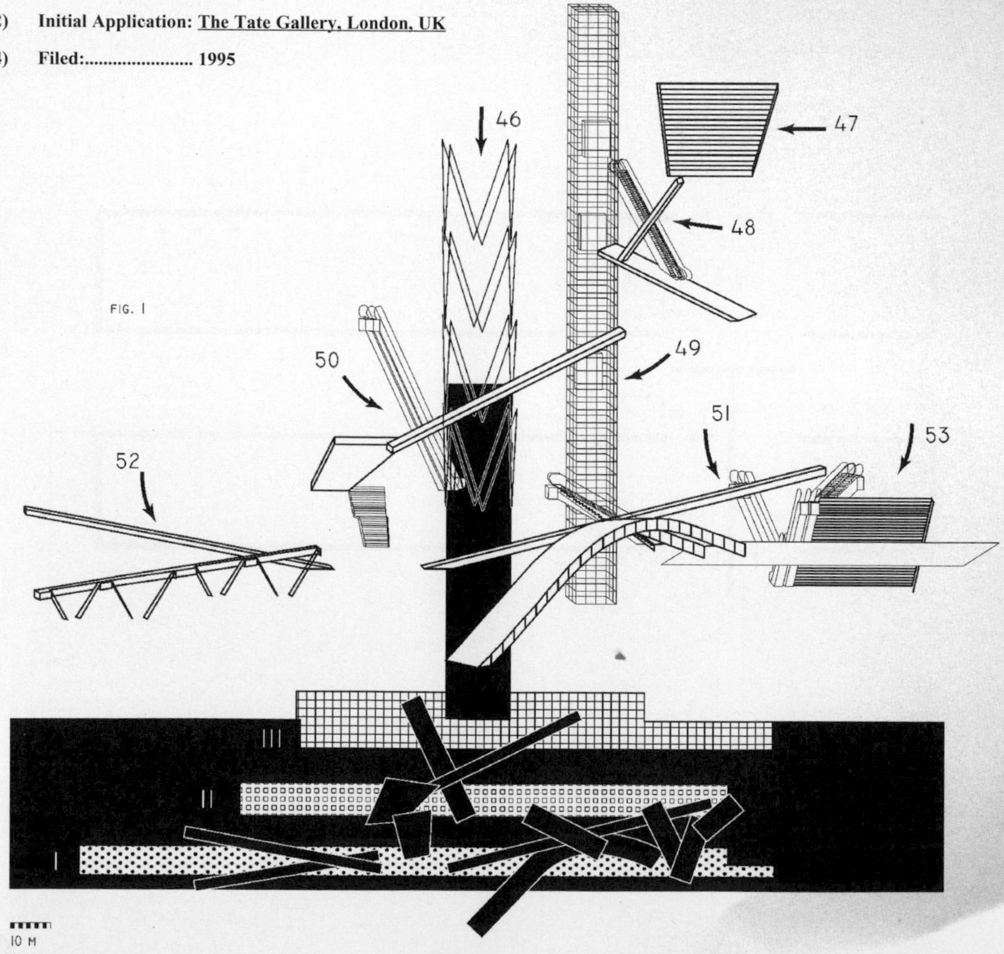

UNIVERSAL MODERNIZATION PATENT [14]

"INERTNESS MODIFIED" (1997)

Patent Number: 10,521, 230

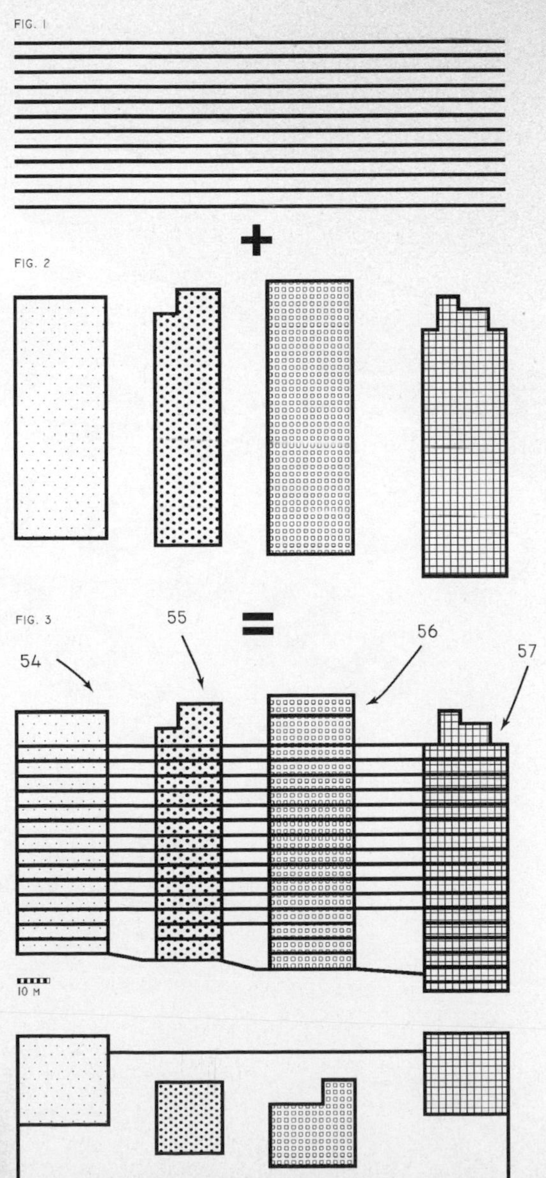

(21) **Patent for "Inertness Modified"**

(29) INTRODUCING SPECIFITY IN INDETERMINATE ACCOMODATIONS

(36) Inventor(s): **Dan Wood**

Correspondence Address:

OMA, HEER BOKELWEG 149
3032 AD ROTTERDAM
TEL: + 31(0) 102438200

(42) **Initial Application: Universal HQ, Burbank, California, USA**

(54) **Filed:.......................1997**

(71) **ABSTRACT**

Now that buildings have become vague accommodations to enable whoever to do whatever with anybody, in ways that do not preclude other uses in the imminent future, their universality may be modified by shafts of specificity (54-57) that create, at every horizontal section, identical moments of difference and uniqueness.

continued on p. 510

PATENT PENDING
Wooden mobile.

Banned words!

Time to chlorinate the meme pool

BY BILL MILLARD

A form of collective wisdom is encoded in etymologies; this is part of the reason people respond to puns. But on occasion, when the counterweight of shifting idiom and unreflective repetition separates a term from its history and erodes its resonances, that term gradually ceases to carry its own weight. Words ossify, decay, and perish as surely as organisms. Any sufficiently large dictionary recognizes their senescence and mortality: languages grow and mutate as any other complex system does, with the occasional nod to Darwin and a tip of the cap to the Reaper. What fails either to remain vibrant or to die off usefully can stand pruning. A language in which all words were immortal and none archaic would be not the upbeat chaos of the healthy city, recombinant and gleefully anarchic, but chaos in an older and murkier sense, that of the abyss (*Obs.*).

In the past OMA has proposed retirement for buildings that have failed to earn eternal life.[1] Not all do. Someone has to pull the occasional plug, if one can't rely on acts of gods for this (and verifiable acts of gods have been rather scarce of late). The same winnowing function applies to the language of building. Within the discourse of an alienated, circumscribed professional group, particularly one that habitually wrenches terms out of the vernacular, the meme pool can come to resemble the gene pools of certain mountain regions: the Melungeons near Sneedville, Tennessee, or the schizop prone Daghestanis of th Caucasus.[2] It is not fasci eugenics, just practical a unavoidable triage, to dr few lines here - and to ca wagon through the langu of architecture, crying "Br out your dead!"

Let the following antiglossary impeach a fe terms that have decayed t the point that they stagge zombielike and even pesti across the thoughtscape o the profession. Let their conviction and execution, o pardon, be a matter for broader jury-room debate than space allows here; but when a conviction stands, le justice be merciful and swift OMA now suggests the following collective memectomies:

03

12 Reasons to Get Back into Shape

BY R. E. SOMOL

Shape is **ILLICIT.** Since architects today only like to do things the hard way, or at least talk about doing things the hard way, shape has become the great taboo. It is the last thing one can be caught doing in public, a five-letter expletive of professional denigration. But it doesn't have to be that way. Architecture doesn't have to hurt.

Shape is **EASY.** At a moment when architecture stakes its claim to expertise on only undertaking the most self-consciously difficult and complicated of tasks, shape has been commoditized. It has become the special competence of no one and everyone, withdrawn as a protected property of architecture. At best, it ambivalently belongs to "design."

Shape is **EXPENDABLE.** Having officially refused all claims to shape, architectural culture nevertheless retains its rights to two related properties: form and mass. In the current climate, form is increasingly an elaboration of geometry that seeks legitimacy in terms of the discipline of architecture, while massing is an act of expression that achieves its value through the cult of the author. Contemplative and potentially critical, form is indebted to architecture as text (it is to be read), massing (with ambitions to the spectacle), to architecture as object-sculpture. Head and eye work, respectively.

Shape is **GRAPHIC.** Avoiding the rhetorical excess of geometric form or expressive mass, shape exhibits the immediacy of the graphic. And it this "graphic" nature of shape, in all its senses, that frees it from the obligation to represent architecture at work (whether the discipline or the signature oeuvre) and allows it to perform other tasks. Despite the arguments of its detractors, shape avoids the form/content opposition. It performs precisely because of its "defective" condition: crude, explicit, fast, material.

Shape is **ADAPTABLE.** Fully Latinized, form remains a classical problem (*forma* = beauty), and this extends to the more recent critique offered by the *informe*: forms can be beautiful or ugly (or some new hybrid), but they are always serious. Dismissible, shapes are simply cool or boring, and have a more vulgar, or at least vernacular, provenance. Form is essential, whereas shape adapts, it is made fit for a purpose, contingent. Regulated not by the articulation of geometry but by the seduction of contour, shape has a requisite degree of slack. Shape eliminates information, is often low resolution, and is in this sense a "cool" medium. It solicits (participation).

Shape is **FIT.** On the fringes of architectural production, one lineage of shape can be traced to the "calculated vagueness" produced by the atmospheric renderings of Hugh Ferris, faceted experiments in the evacuation of detail. Shape is a problem in the fitness of power (in Ferris's case, the fitness of the 1916 Zoning Law) rather than the intricacy of geometry. In shape is not *informe*.

Shape is **EMPTY** a relatively neglected territo within architecture, shape ha had a more energetic discus in art. While trying to save sh for (modernist) art, Michael Fr nevertheless reveals that sha generally involved with the contextual and situational. In critique of minimalism he observes that its investment in shape produces a pervasive eff of "hollowness." Shape is not simply an exterior condition. In Astor Place, this form of holey monumentality rises as a charc wedge shot through with multip entry points. A Hugh Ferris after drive-by.

Shape is **ARBITRARY.** While all architecture has an interior, the inside-out relationship has been configured quite differently in recent years. In that work motivated by an interest in form, the inside is a continuation of its outside disturbances, while with the massing school the inside is a straightforward (if blind) resolution independent from the exterior wrap. With shape, the arbitrary is rendered natural though its own violation by an independent interior. Here, hollowness is exposed (unlike massing), but this inside is inconsistent with its exterior treatment (unlike form). Thus, shape never appears as a definitive object itself, but at most is the residual for *other* objects. Porto, a Melnikov Worker's Club in reverse, appears as formwork for future construction, leftover packing material for an object that has been removed.

Shape is **INTENSIVE.** Typically, as size increases, volume exponentially outstrips surface area. The recent projects of OMA indulge an alternative mathematics, one where surface area appears to increase more rapidly than interior space, whether through voids, holes, perforations, or "captured" negative volumes. The twisted knot of CCTV operates as a minimalist frame for a monumental void, almost a case of "excision" as a graphic censorship technique, where that which is missing receives the greatest attention.

Shape is **BUOYANT.** The hollowness of shape also produces (and requires) an effect of buoyancy. While massive, the projects seem to be made of Styrofoam, sponge, or aero-gel, each supported on an impossibly small footprint. The Whitney, diced by seemingly arbitrary horizontal slots and vertical cuts, maintains a slightly bulging structural truss at its "waist" that somehow conjures the white, sequined jumpsuit of the late Elvis caught in mid-karate kick: a little less conversation a little more action please. Whereas form is conceived in the abstract, immaterial realm of the drawing or computer (and therefore avoids gravity as an issue until the moment of its construction), mass begins its life as a pile, and confirms gravitational pull through the horizontal spread at its base even if it tries to cover this fact with animated volumes and surfaces. By contrast, shape exists in the material world (unlike form), but refuses its limitations (unlike mass). In contrast to form or mass, *shape must float*.

Shape is **PROJECTIVE.** Rather than offering a critique of this world (the commentary of form) or a confirmation of it (the spectacle of mass), shape - in a genealogy that runs from Malevich's architectons to Superstudio's continuous monument to John Hejduk's cartoon-like characters from the various masques - is experienced more like a visitation from an alternative world. The OMA shape projects don't only operate with the graphic immediacy of logos, generating a new identity, but they are also holes in the skyline that reframe the city. One doesn't look *at* them so much as through them or from them. To radically paraphrase Carl Andre, a shape is a hole in a thing it is not.

Shape is **COOL.** Along with size, shape is evidence of the effect of entropy on architecture. Together, they conspire to "cool down" the discipline, as the properly hot articulation offered by *scale* and *form* are relaxed into a state of mere *size* (bigness) and *shape* (vagueness). If scale and form were always the privileged *representational* devices of the discipline, *size* and *shape* can now be understood as their performative doubles. In this regard, shape requires no special pleadings; it simply exists. An architectural bastard or no-name clone, shape has no need to point back to its paternity for justification. In a profession prone to confession, shape is never having to say you're sorry.

BIG

There is quantitative bigness, which might as well be translated simply "size," and there is Bigness, in which quantity generates novel qualities as well. Marketing has simultaneously placed the big tantalizingly within everyone's reach as the ultimate desideratum (getting more for your money, giving good weight) and devalued the big (Wendy's sandwich chain: "Biggie Size it!" - *it* being a bag of fries). Impressive Bigness needs rarity, theory,[3] menace, and a capital B, as in Brobdingnag. Pynchon[4] had the idea, along with the 18th-century capitalization habit to denote it, in offering the Badass (who is not necessarily big, but is always Big as well as Bad, a Beast susceptible only to Beauty) as the paradigmatic resistance-hero. As the theory of the Big advances to the point of delineating who and what is plausibly revolutionary, simple bigness must yield to complex Bigness.

COMMUNITY

One hesitates to take a Jacobin tone toward a term beloved of Jane Jacobs. Still, nostalgia is now inseparable from this one, and nostalgia carries the whiff of the grave (not to mention the occasional force of law). Actual communities can arise, function, recombine, and disperse without drawing attention to themselves through a reifying term. In the era when antimodernism has grown razor-sharp teeth and the rootless cosmopolitan must once again cast the occasional panicky glance over his shoulder toward the torch-bearing mob, the bandying of the C-word is too often the prelude to a mawkish insularity that would make Sinclair Lewis's Babbitt blanch: community standards as a pretext for banning art or restraining its exuberance, communitarianism as pretext for lockstep. It is troublesome when used as object, not only as subject; the group characterized from outside as a Community is about to be circumscribed. The collective of the future will have to master the art of self-defense through mobility, not the bulk of the mob but the mercurial tactics of the flash mob.

MASS

Thought-provoking Bigness does not have to be dense, any more than it has to be empty (the Fallacy of the Atrium). The point of experimentation with scale is not to ape the rural towns that claim fame as birthplaces of the World's Largest Rutabaga, Cucumber, or Eggplant (one suspects their farmers now cheat, anyway, with hormones from Monsanto) but to discover the unique properties and potentials of large urbanist scale, as the nanotechnologist on the opposite end of the continuum can build new materials because electrostatic properties and quantum-mechanical effects at the scale of a few nanometers differ from those at the micro-, mega-, or any other scale. Mass as a quantitative property without qualitative difference is dull, triumphalist, undifferentiated, overbearing, big rather than Big.

ZONE

The local political substitute, in the United States, for planning. Zoning - here the residences, there the engines of employment, there the transportation corridor, elsewhere the industries >

designated Light or Heavy - represents an apartheid of social functionalities, a failure to imagine interpenetration. To zone a space is to assume it has a limited capacity for change, and thus to limit its capacity for change: zoning is what John Searle would call a performative speech act, like "I pronounce you man and wife." I pronounce you lower-middle-class bedroom community. I pronounce you industrial park. I pronounce you retail. You, over there, I pronounce wholesale (discount, larger-scale in the name of frugality for holders of the membership card). Who am I to pronounce you?

CHAOS
If a butterfly flaps its wings incessantly, yet a few continents away no storm follows, the question is not so much "Does anyone hear?" as "Must everyone keep listening?"

RADICAL
Too rarely striking at any actual roots, the radicalism of *épater les bourgeois* is too often self-appointed, armchaired, frivolous. The radical departure is only half the journey; departures in the absence of fundamentally altered returns are easy, a racquet sport with the net down. A useful uprooting is completed in a replanting. An esthetic politics or political esthetic that gestures toward only its dissatisfactions, not its imagined and preferred solutions, is as self-referential as a confessional songwriter opening his diary, or his veins, over three or four chords. Confusing the rootless with the radical is a child's game.

PROGRAM
Whatever homologies exist between the design of physical structures conducive to imaginative forms of collective human life and the design of machine code conducive to, at best, imaginative (more often merely efficient) dances of information, there remains a key discrepancy that invalidates the programming metaphor. No architect cognizant of a simple fact - that human beings will enter, inhabit, leave, change, resist, and ultimately tolerate, hate, or love the built structure - will aim for the same degree of control that the coder seeks over units of information. Pixels and bits, the individuals within the antichaotic system of any program, have no particular options, and the system would fail if they did; a building's intelligent relation to its inhabitants is the exact converse. A building that metaphorically executes a program is executing other things as well.

SOCIETY
There is never only one of these. When anyone (particularly anyone official) claims to be acting in its name and protecting its interests, expect prevarications and euphemisms and Reasons of State, and consider reaching for your revolver. See "community."

BRUTAL
Originating not from any tropism toward thuggery or bent toward the bestial, but from the French phrase for rough concrete (*béton brut*), architectural brutalism has as much to do with textures as with scales, angles, or functionality. The coarse texture is more complex - carries more information -

12 Reasons to Get Back into Shape

BY R. E. SOMOL

Shape is **ILLICIT.** Since architects today only like to do things the hard way, or at least talk about doing things the hard way, shape has become the great taboo. It is the last thing one can be caught doing in public, a five-letter expletive of professional denigration. But it doesn't have to be that way. Architecture doesn't have to hurt.

Shape is **EASY.** At a moment when architecture stakes its claim to expertise on only undertaking the most self-consciously difficult and complicated of tasks, shape has been commoditized. It has become the special competence of no one and everyone, withdrawn as a protected property of architecture. At best, it ambivalently belongs to "design."

Shape is **EXPENDABLE.** Having officially refused all claims to shape, architectural culture nevertheless retains its rights to two related properties: form and mass. In the current climate, form is increasingly an elaboration of geometry that seeks legitimacy in terms of the discipline of architecture, while massing is an act of expression that achieves its value through the cult of the author. Contemplative and potentially critical, form is indebted to architecture as text (it is to be read), massing (with ambitions to the spectacle), to architecture as object-sculpture. Head and eye work, respectively.

Shape is **GRAPHIC.** Avoiding the rhetorical excess of geometric form or expressive mass, shape exhibits the immediacy of the graphic. And it this "graphic" nature of shape, in all its senses, that frees it from the obligation to represent architecture at work (whether the discipline or the signature oeuvre) and allows it to perform other tasks. Despite the arguments of its detractors, shape avoids the form/content opposition. It performs precisely because of its "defective" condition: crude, explicit, fast, material.

Shape is **ADAPTABLE.** Fully Latinized, form remains a classical problem (*forma* = beauty), and this extends to the more recent critique offered by the *informe*: forms can be beautiful or ugly (or some new hybrid), but they are always serious. Dismissible, shapes are simply cool or boring, and have a more vulgar, or at least vernacular, provenance. Form is essential, whereas shape adapts, it is made fit for a purpose, contingent. Regulated not by the articulation of geometry but by the seduction of contour, shape has a requisite degree of slack. Shape eliminates information, is often low resolution, and is in this sense a "cool" medium. It solicits (participation).

Shape is **FIT.** On the fringes of architectural production, one lineage of shape can be traced to the "calculated vagueness" produced by the atmospheric renderings of Hugh Ferris, faceted experiments in the evacuation of detail. Shape is a problem in the fitness of power (in Ferris's case, the fitness of the 1916 Zoning Law) rather than the intricacy of geometry. In shape is not *informe*.

Shape is **EMPT[Y]** a relatively neglected territo[ry] within architecture, shape ha[s] had a more energetic discuss[ion] in art. While trying to save sh[ape] for (modernist) art, Michael Fr[ied] nevertheless reveals that sha[pe is] generally involved with the contextual and situational. In hi[s] critique of minimalism he observes that its investment in shape produces a pervasive eff[ect] of "hollowness." Shape is not simply an exterior condition. In Astor Place, this form of holey monumentality rises as a charc[oal] wedge shot through with multip[le] entry points. A Hugh Ferris after drive-by.

Shape is **ARBITRARY.** While all architecture has an interior, the inside-out relationship has been configured quite differently in recent years. In that work motivated by an interest in form, the inside is a continuation of its outside disturbances, while with the massing school the inside is a straightforward (if blind) resolution independent from the exterior wrap. With shape, the arbitrary is rendered natural though its own violation by an independent interior. Here, hollowness is exposed (unlike massing), but this inside is inconsistent with its exterior treatment (unlike form). Thus, shape never appears as a definitive object itself, but at most is the residual for *other* objects. Porto, a Melnikov Worker's Club in reverse, appears as formwork for future construction, leftover packing material for an object that has been removed.

Shape is **INTENSIVE.** Typically, as size increases, volume exponentially outstrips surface area. The recent projects of OMA indulge an alternative mathematics, one where surface area appears to increase more rapidly than interior space, whether through voids, holes, perforations, or "captured" negative volumes. The twisted knot of CCTV operates as a minimalist frame for a monumental void, almost a case of "excision" as a graphic censorship technique, where that which is missing receives the greatest attention.

Shape is **BUOYANT.** The hollowness of shape also produces (and requires) an effect of buoyancy. While massive, the projects seem to be made of Styrofoam, sponge, or aero-gel, each supported on an impossibly small footprint. The Whitney, diced by seemingly arbitrary horizontal slots and vertical cuts, maintains a slightly bulging structural truss at its "waist" that somehow conjures the white, sequined jumpsuit of the late Elvis caught in mid-karate kick: a little less conversation a little more action please. Whereas form is conceived in the abstract, immaterial realm of the drawing or computer (and therefore avoids gravity as an issue until the moment of its construction), mass begins its life as a pile, and confirms gravitational pull through the horizontal spread at its base even if it tries to cover this fact with animated volumes and surfaces. By contrast, shape exists in the material world (unlike form), but refuses its limitations (unlike mass). In contrast to form or mass, *shape must float*.

Shape is **PROJECTIVE.** Rather than offering a critique of this world (the commentary of form) or a confirmation of it (the spectacle of mass), shape - in a genealogy that runs from Malevich's architectons to Superstudio's continuous monument to John Hejduk's cartoon-like characters from the various masques - is experienced more like a visitation from an alternative world. The OMA shape projects don't only operate with the graphic immediacy of logos, generating a new identity, but they are also holes in the skyline that reframe the city. One doesn't look *at* them so much as through them or from them. To radically paraphrase Carl Andre, a shape is a hole in a thing it is not.

Shape is **COOL.** Along with size, shape is evidence of the effect of entropy on architecture. Together, they conspire to "cool down" the discipline, as the properly hot articulation offered by *scale* and *form* are relaxed into a state of mere *size* (bigness) and *shape* (vagueness). If scale and form were always the privileged *representational* devices of the discipline, *size* and *shape* can now be understood as their performative doubles. In this regard, shape requires no special pleadings; it simply exists. An architectural bastard or no-name clone, shape has no need to point back to its paternity for justification. In a profession prone to confession, shape is never having to say you're sorry.

Banned words!

Time to chlorinate the meme pool

BY BILL MILLARD

A form of collective wisdom is encoded in etymologies; this is part of the reason people respond to puns. But on occasion, when the counterweight of shifting idiom and unreflective repetition separates a term from its history and erodes its resonances, that term gradually ceases to carry its own weight. Words ossify, decay, and perish as surely as organisms. Any sufficiently large dictionary recognizes their senescence and mortality: languages grow and mutate as any other complex system does, with the occasional nod to Darwin and a tip of the cap to the Reaper. What fails either to remain vibrant or to die off usefully can stand pruning. A language in which all words were immortal and none archaic would be not the upbeat chaos of the healthy city, recombinant and gleefully anarchic, but chaos in an older and murkier sense, that of the abyss (*Obs.*).

In the past OMA has proposed retirement for buildings that have failed to earn eternal life.[1] Not all do. Someone has to pull the occasional plug, if one can't rely on acts of gods for this (and verifiable acts of gods have been rather scarce of late). The same winnowing function applies to the language of building. Within the discourse of an alienated, circumscribed professional group, particularly one that habitually wrenches terms out of the vernacular, the meme pool can come to resemble the gene pools of certain mountain regions: the Melungeons near Sneedville, Tennessee, or the schizophrenia-prone Daghestanis of the Caucasus.[2] It is not fascistic eugenics, just practical and unavoidable triage, to draw a few lines here - and to carry a wagon through the language of architecture, crying "Bring out your dead!"

Let the following antiglossary impeach a few terms that have decayed to the point that they stagger, zombielike and even pestilent, across the thoughtscape of the profession. Let their conviction and execution, or pardon, be a matter for broader jury-room debate than space allows here; but when a conviction stands, let justice be merciful and swift. OMA now suggests the following collective memectomies:

BIG
There is quantitative bigness, which might as well be translated simply "size," and there is Bigness, in which quantity generates novel qualities as well. Marketing has simultaneously placed the big tantalizingly within everyone's reach as the ultimate desideratum (getting more for your money, giving good weight) and devalued the big (Wendy's sandwich chain: "Biggie Size it!" - *it* being a bag of fries). Impressive Bigness needs rarity, theory,[3] menace, and a capital B, as in Brobdingnag. Pynchon[4] had the idea, along with the 18th-century capitalization habit to denote it, in offering the Badass (who is not necessarily big, but is always Big as well as Bad, a Beast susceptible only to Beauty) as the paradigmatic resistance-hero. As the theory of the Big advances to the point of delineating who and what is plausibly revolutionary, simple bigness must yield to complex Bigness.

COMMUNITY
One hesitates to take a Jacobin tone toward a term beloved of Jane Jacobs. Still, nostalgia is now inseparable from this one, and nostalgia carries the whiff of the grave (not to mention the occasional force of law). Actual communities can arise, function, recombine, and disperse without drawing attention to themselves through a reifying term. In the era when antimodernism has grown razor-sharp teeth and the rootless cosmopolitan must once again cast the occasional panicky glance over his shoulder toward the torch-bearing mob, the bandying of the C-word is too often the prelude to a mawkish insularity that would make Sinclair Lewis's Babbitt blanch: community standards as a pretext for banning art or restraining its exuberance, communitarianism as pretext for lockstep. It is troublesome when used as object, not only as subject; the group characterized from outside as a Community is about to be circumscribed. The collective of the future will have to master the art of self-defense through mobility, not the bulk of the mob but the mercurial tactics of the flash mob.

MASS
Thought-provoking Bigness does not have to be dense, any more than it has to be empty (the Fallacy of the Atrium). The point of experimentation with scale is not to ape the rural towns that claim fame as birthplaces of the World's Largest Rutabaga, Cucumber, or Eggplant (one suspects their farmers now cheat, anyway, with hormones from Monsanto) but to discover the unique properties and potentials of large urbanist scale, as the nanotechnologist on the opposite end of the continuum can build new materials because electrostatic properties and quantum-mechanical effects at the scale of a few nanometers differ from those at the micro-, mega-, or any other scale. Mass as a quantitative property without qualitative difference is dull, triumphalist, undifferentiated, overbearing, big rather than Big.

ZONE
The local political substitute, in the United States, for planning. Zoning - here the residences, there the engines of employment, there the transportation corridor, elsewhere the industries >

designated Light or Heavy - represents an apartheid of social functionalities, a failure to imagine interpenetration. To zone a space is to assume it has a limited capacity for change, and thus to limit its capacity for change: zoning is what John Searle would call a performative speech act, like "I pronounce you man and wife." I pronounce you lower-middle-class bedroom community. I pronounce you industrial park. I pronounce you retail. You, over there, I pronounce wholesale (discount, larger-scale in the name of frugality for holders of the membership card). Who am I to pronounce you?

CHAOS
If a butterfly flaps its wings incessantly, yet a few continents away no storm follows, the question is not so much "Does anyone hear?" as "Must everyone keep listening?"

RADICAL
Too rarely striking at any actual roots, the radicalism of *épater les bourgeois* is too often self-appointed, armchaired, frivolous. The radical departure is only half the journey; departures in the absence of fundamentally altered returns are easy, a racquet sport with the net down. A useful uprooting is completed in a replanting. An esthetic politics or political esthetic that gestures toward only its dissatisfactions, not its imagined and preferred solutions, is as self-referential as a confessional songwriter opening his diary, or his veins, over three or four chords. Confusing the rootless with the radical is a child's game.

PROGRAM
Whatever homologies exist between the design of physical structures conducive to imaginative forms of collective human life and the design of machine code conducive to, at best, imaginative (more often merely efficient) dances of information, there remains a key discrepancy that invalidates the programming metaphor. No architect cognizant of a simple fact - that human beings will enter, inhabit, leave, change, resist, and ultimately tolerate, hate, or love the built structure - will aim for the same degree of control that the coder seeks over units of information. Pixels and bits, the individuals within the antichaotic system of any program, have no particular options, and the system would fail if they did; a building's intelligent relation to its inhabitants is the exact converse. A building that metaphorically executes a program is executing other things as well.

SOCIETY
There is never only one of these. When anyone (particularly anyone official) claims to be acting in its name and protecting its interests, expect prevarications and euphemisms and Reasons of State, and consider reaching for your revolver. See "community."

BRUTAL
Originating not from any tropism toward thuggery or bent toward the bestial, but from the French phrase for rough concrete (*béton brut*), architectural brutalism has as much to do with textures as with scales, angles, or functionality. The coarse texture is more complex - carries more information -

than the smooth; a simple vector-graphic program can recreate a graceful surface, but the patternless roughened surface is beyond mimesis. Like pure undifferentiated video noise (Gibson's famous "sky... the color of television, tuned to a dead channel"[5]), *béton brut* and similar textures are information theory's nightmare: infinite complexity with zero redundancy to support comprehension. Abrasion is ultimately a quantitative matter. The human body recoils from *béton brut* for the same reason it dreads insects or becomes annoyed with clusters of rowdy children: it does not like to be quantitatively overwhelmed.

The brutalist building indeed assaults the eye - it assumes that some eyes, some sensibilities, need assaulting - but in practice its force is sometimes a subtraction of energy, not an addition. Vast expanses of coarse gray material will deliver a shock, but it is the physical shock of a blow, not the electrical shock of a recognition. The street thug's brutality may take a sharp form as easily as a dull one (the knife, sir, or the truncheon? Choose your punishment!); the neo-Corbusian machine or Stalinistic Smithsonian prison-block invariably declines to sport with uncertainty.

ORNAMENT

Visual and tactile delights *qua* visual and tactile delights will be selected for budget-cutting every time, just as an underfunded school system inevitably removes arts and sports (in that order). The most striking feature of a building must now be the one that all the more mundane features require, the one whose subtraction would demolish the structure. Beauty that also solves problems is free to remain beauty.

And, finally:

CONTENT

If a building or building-idea or book has content, conveys content, disseminates content, then it is a container: in other words, it is close to nothing. It is certainly no organism, nothing with signs of life. It is defined by its empty capacity, like the massive nondescript atrium of the Hotel Interchangeable, the space designed to impress rather than to live and give life. Artists lost something when the market made them content providers. OMA offers its *Content* and its content under full and cognizant erasure.

We stress, again, that this list is an act of impeachment, not conviction: authority in language belongs to the open forum, not the self-appointed arbiters. And, having sounded an awakening bugle-blast, we're more than content to let reveille turn into jazz, step aside for someone else's solo, and let the cleansing jam session begin. ■

NOTES

1. "Tabula Rasa Revisited," *S,M,L,XL*, pp. 1090-1135.
2. Bulayeva KB, Leal SM, Pavlova TA, Kurbanov R, Coover S, Bulayev O, Byerley W. The ascertainment of multiplex schizophrenia pedigrees from Daghestan genetic isolates (Northern Caucasus, Russia). *Psychiatr Genet.* 2000 Jun;10(2):67-72.
3. "Bigness, or the Problem of Large," *S,M,L,XL*, pp. 494-516.
4. "Is It OK to Be a Luddite?" *New York Times Book Review*, Oct. 28, 1984: 1, 40-41. Here Pynchon anatomizes the recurrent desire for a revolutionary Badass, or "any countercritter Bad and Big enough, even in the most irresponsible of fictions, to begin to compare with what would happen in a nuclear war."
5. Gibson, William. *Neuromancer* (NY: Ace, 1984), p. 3.

Context

Snapshots of the world in transition...

Inhabitants (million)		Area (km²)		Density (inh/km²)		Birth rate (child/woman)		Population growth		Average age	
1 Tokaido	60	1 SanSan	130,260.0	1 Tokaido	1,320.0	1 Ganges Delta	4.6	1 Ganges Delta	2.30%	1 Eurocore	43
2 Boswash	39	2 Boswash	87,420.0	2 Sechon	1,190.0	2 SãoRio	2.3	2 SãoRio	1.50%	2 Tokaido	41
3 Eurocore	32	3 SãoRio	70,740.0	3 PRD	1,010.0	3 Boswash	2.0	3 PRD	1.40%	3 Boswash	37
4 SãoRio	30	4 Ganges Delta	62,700.0	4 Eurocore	750.0	4 SanSan	2.0	4 BTT	1.40%	4 SanSan	35
5 Ganges Delta	28	5 YRD	46,980.0	5 YRD	570.0	5 Sechon	2.0	5 SanSan	1.30%	5 PRD	34
6 YRD	28	6 Tokaido	45,240.0	6 BTT	510.0	6 YRD	1.8	6 YRD	1.30%	6 Sechon	32
7 SanSan	26	7 BTT	45,060.0	7 Boswash	450.0	7 PRD	1.8	7 Sechon	1.20%	7 YRD	32
8 BTT	23	8 Eurocore	42,720.0	8 Ganges Delta	440.0	8 BTT	1.8	8 Boswash	0.50%	8 BTT	30
9 PRD	21	9 PRD	20,760.0	9 SãoRio	420.0	9 Tokaido	1.4	9 Tokaido	0.40%	9 SãoRio	26
10 Sechon	20	10 Sechon	16,740.0	10 SanSan	200.0	10 Eurocore	1.3	10 Eurocore	-0.20%	10 Ganges Delta	21

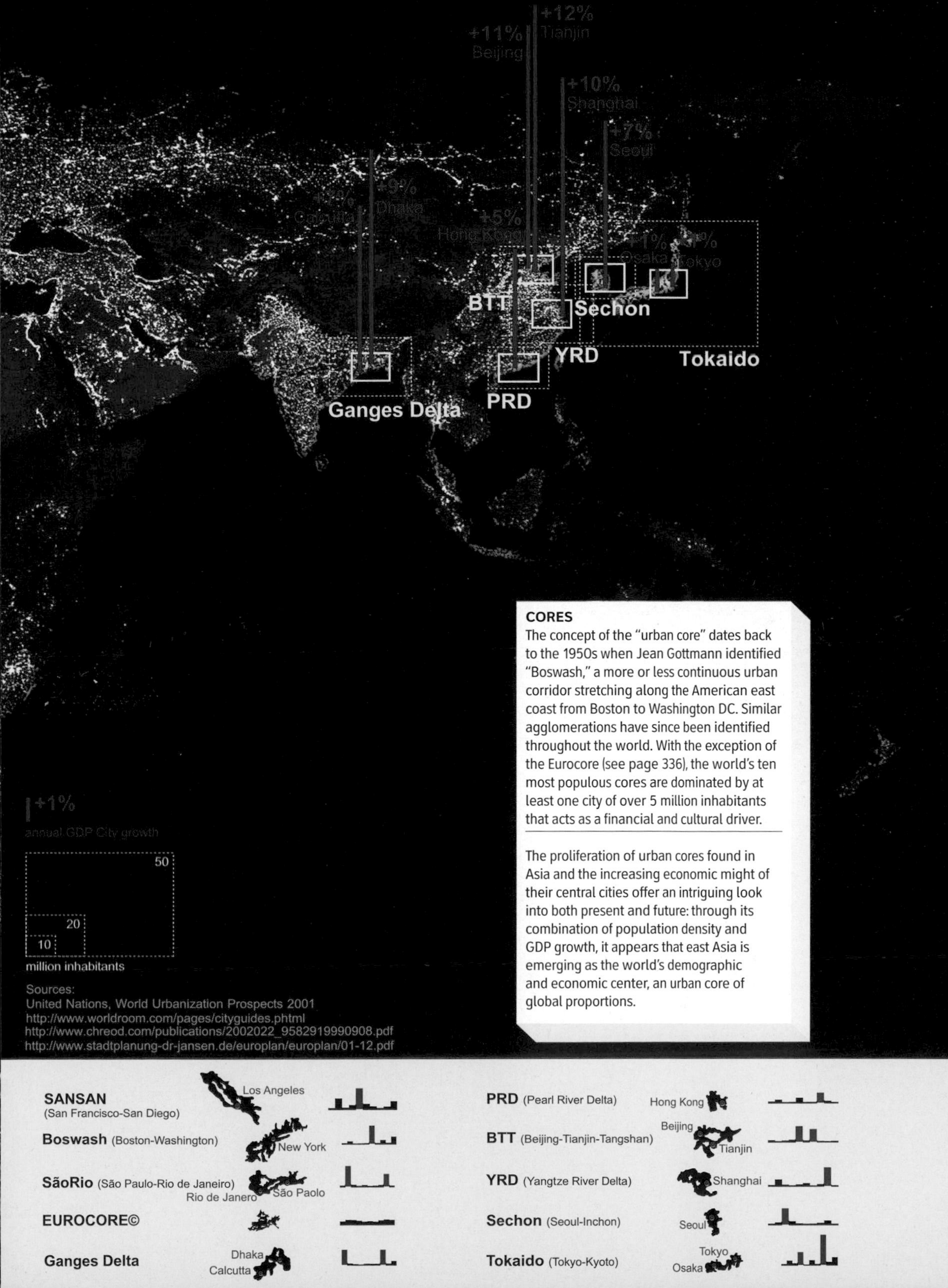

CORES

The concept of the "urban core" dates back to the 1950s when Jean Gottmann identified "Boswash," a more or less continuous urban corridor stretching along the American east coast from Boston to Washington DC. Similar agglomerations have since been identified throughout the world. With the exception of the Eurocore (see page 336), the world's ten most populous cores are dominated by at least one city of over 5 million inhabitants that acts as a financial and cultural driver.

The proliferation of urban cores found in Asia and the increasing economic might of their central cities offer an intriguing look into both present and future: through its combination of population density and GDP growth, it appears that east Asia is emerging as the world's demographic and economic center, an urban core of global proportions.

ADVENTURES IN GLOBALISM

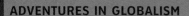

1 6,702 US military bases in 41 countries
SOURCE: WWW.DEFENSELINK.MIL/NEWS/JUN2003/BASESTRUCTURE2003.PDF

2 31,235 McDonalds outlets in 119 countries
SOURCE: WWW.MCDONALDS.COM

3 22 "Big Brother" series in 33 countries
SOURCE:BIGBROTHERWEB.NETFIRMS.COM /FOREIGN.HTM; WWW.ENDEMOL.COM

4 184 IKEA warehouses in 34 countries
SOURCE: WWW.IKEA.COM

5 37 Chinatowns in 13 countries
SOURCES:WWW.INDEXCHINA.COM/INDEX-ENGLISH/OVERSEA.HTML

6 306 astronauts, 124 cosmonauts, and 1 taikonaut in 41 countries
SOURCE: WWW.SPACEFACTS.DE

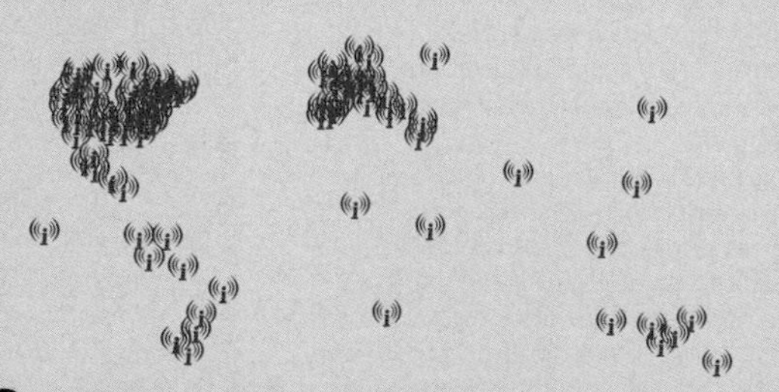

7 127 Indymedia centers in 45 countries
SOURCE: WWW.INDYMEDIA.ORG/

8 730 World Heritage Sites in 129 countries
SOURCE: WHC.UNESCO.ORG

1. The $48 billion increase in U.S. military spending in 2003 equals the annual GDP of the United Arab Emirates (the 68th richest nation on earth) for the same year.
2. While the number of McDonalds restaurants continued to grow between 2002-2003 in the US (+278) and Europe (+175), the number in South America grew by only one, and in South East Asia declined by 57.
3. Following the success of "Big Brother Africa," the show's first international version, a pan-Arab version, "Big Brother Middle East," is planned to air in 2004 on Bahrain-based Channel 2.
4. With 115 million copies printed, the IKEA catalogue now has a larger circulation than the Bible.
5. Approximately 35 million ethnic Chinese now reside in 144 countries.
6. With the safe return of "Taikonaut" Yang Liwei on 15 Oct. 2003, China became the third nation to send a man into space.
7. Indymedia, founded in 1999 for the purpose of providing grassroots coverage of the World Trade Organization (WTO) protests in Seattle via the World Wide Web, has emerged as the primary vehicle for organizing global political protests.
8. 35 out of the 730 monuments nominated for designation as World Heritage sites, are considered endangered by UNESCO.

COLUMN 1

COLUMN 2

Quality Control

International Standards Organisation guidelines (for products, services and systems)

< 10
10 - 100
100 - 1.000
1.000 - 10.000
> 10.000

< 3 %
3 - 5 %
5 - 7 %
7 - 10 %
> 10 %

GDP Growth

Suicide

males per 100.000

no data
<5
5-10
10-20
20-30
>30

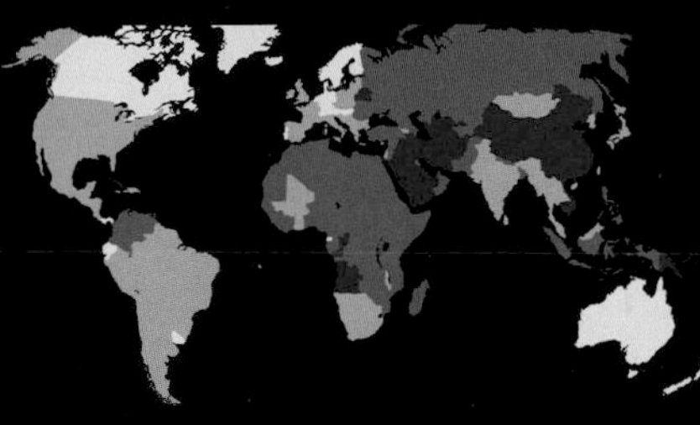

1
2 - 3
4 - 5
6 - 7

Repression

Civil & political liberties index by Freedom House (Higher is less free)

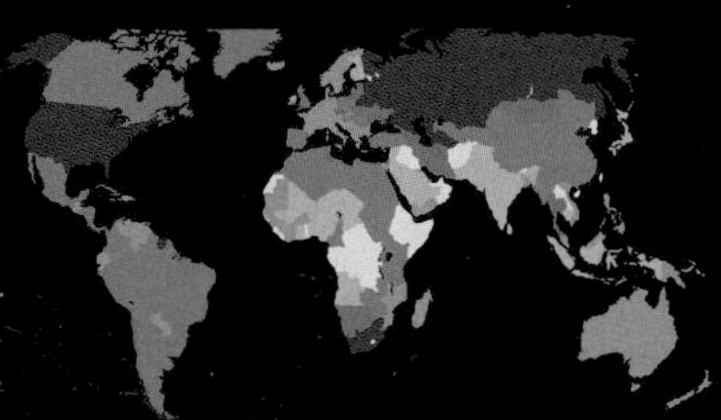

Prisoners

per 100.000 inhabitants

No data
25 - 50
50 - 100
100 - 200
200 - 400
400 - 800

No Data
< 10 %
10 - 30 %
30 - 50 %
> 50 %

Illiteracy

% of the population that is illiterate

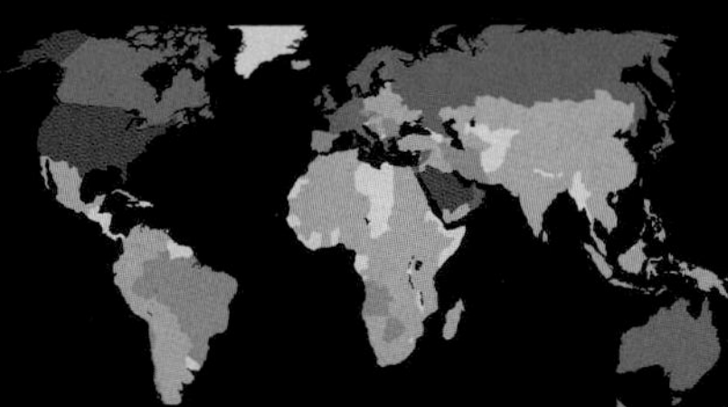

Military expenditure

$ per capita

No Data
0 -100
100 - 200
200 - 400
400 - 800
800 - 1600

> 35
31 - 35
26 - 30
21 - 25
< 20

Youth

Average age

A-Z WORLD

By imposing quantitative analyses according to almost any conceivable criteria - suicide, life expectancy, military expense - the world divides in two with disturbing consistency. One half, labeled here the A World, is "developed" - increasingly old, obsessed with security, its development carefully controlled by rules and regulations. The other, the Z World, is "developing" - young and vigorous, yet unstable and disordered. Certain nations, such as China and Russia, straddle both worlds, potentially providing windows to the advantages of both A and Z.

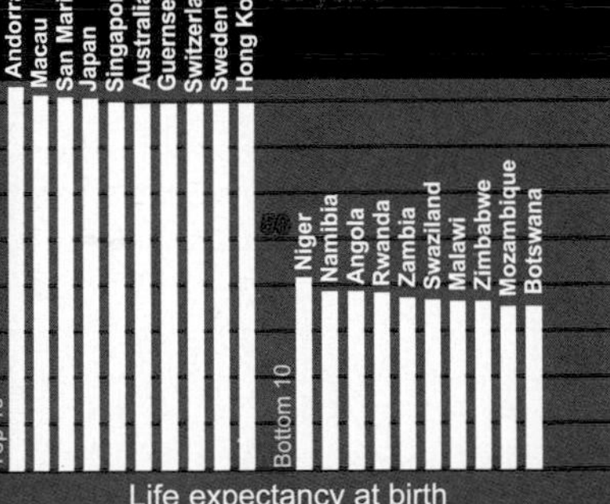

Life expectancy at birth

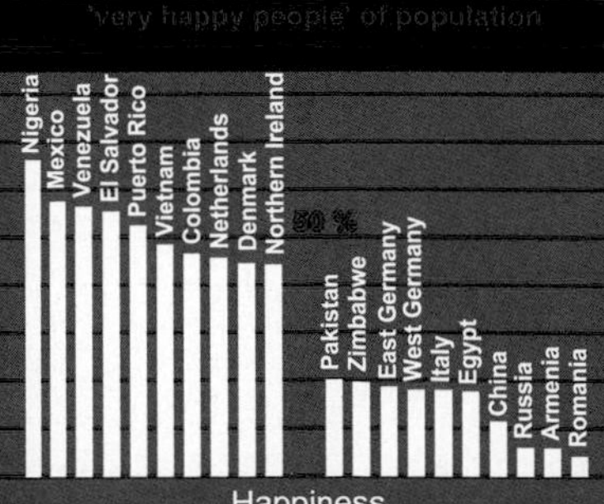

Happiness

Overlay Column 1
= A-World

Overlay Column 2
= Z-World

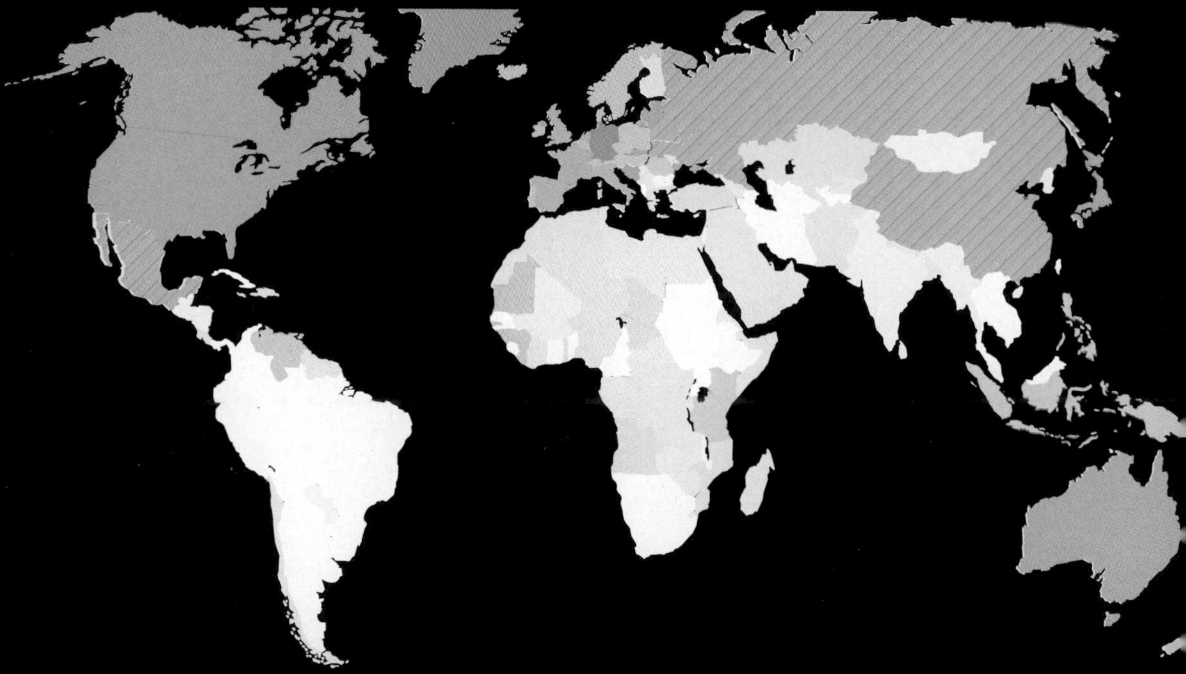

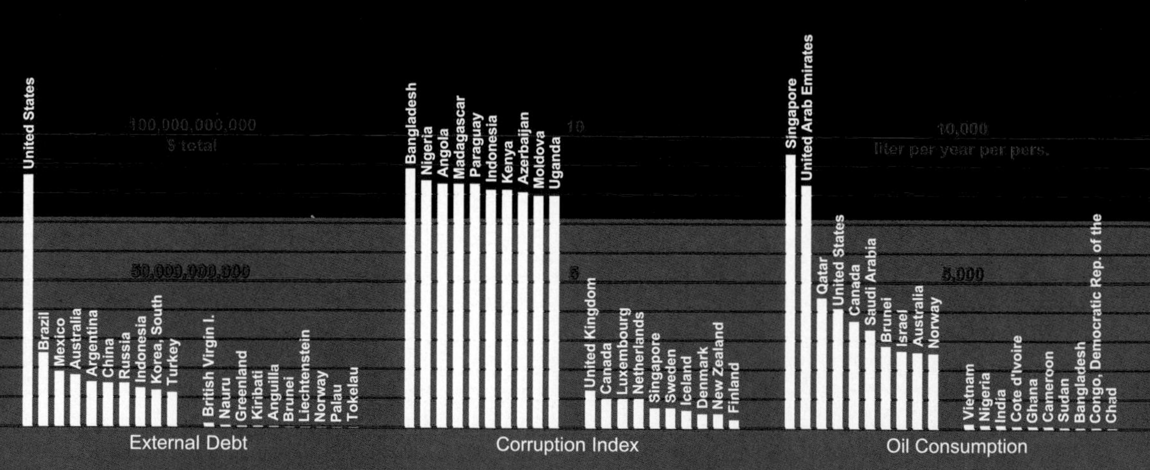

CHANGE IN PASSENGER AIR TRAFFIC

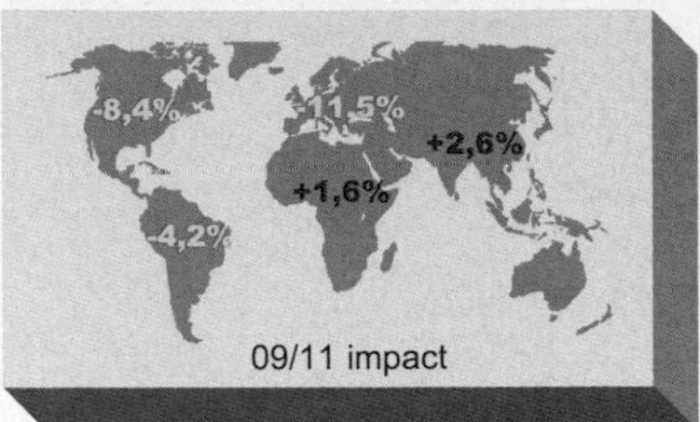

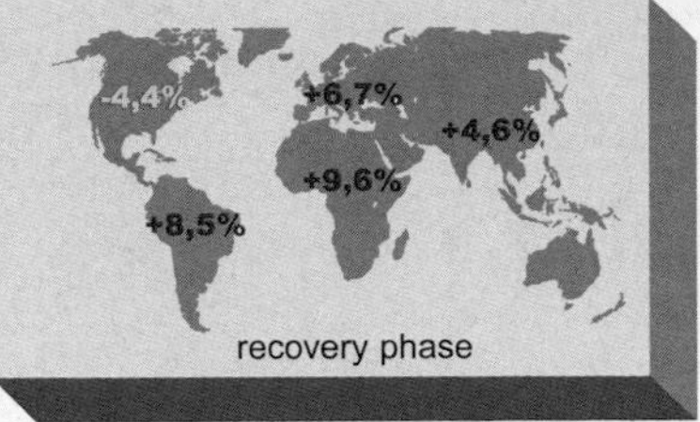

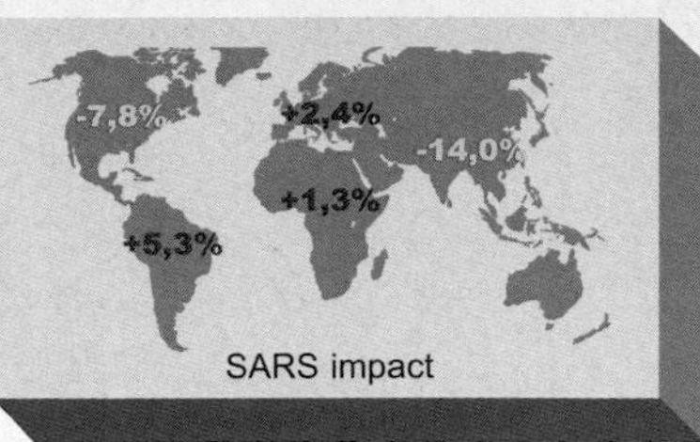

SOURCE: THE IMPACT OF 11 SEPTEMBER ON THE AVIATION INDUSTRY:
TRAFFIC, CAPACITY, EMPLOYMENT AND RESTRUCTURING
WWW.OAG.COM/ABOUT_OAG/COMPANY_INFO/PRESS_RELEASES/US/QUARTERLY0903UK.ASP

TRANSATLANTIC WANING, EURASIAN GAINING

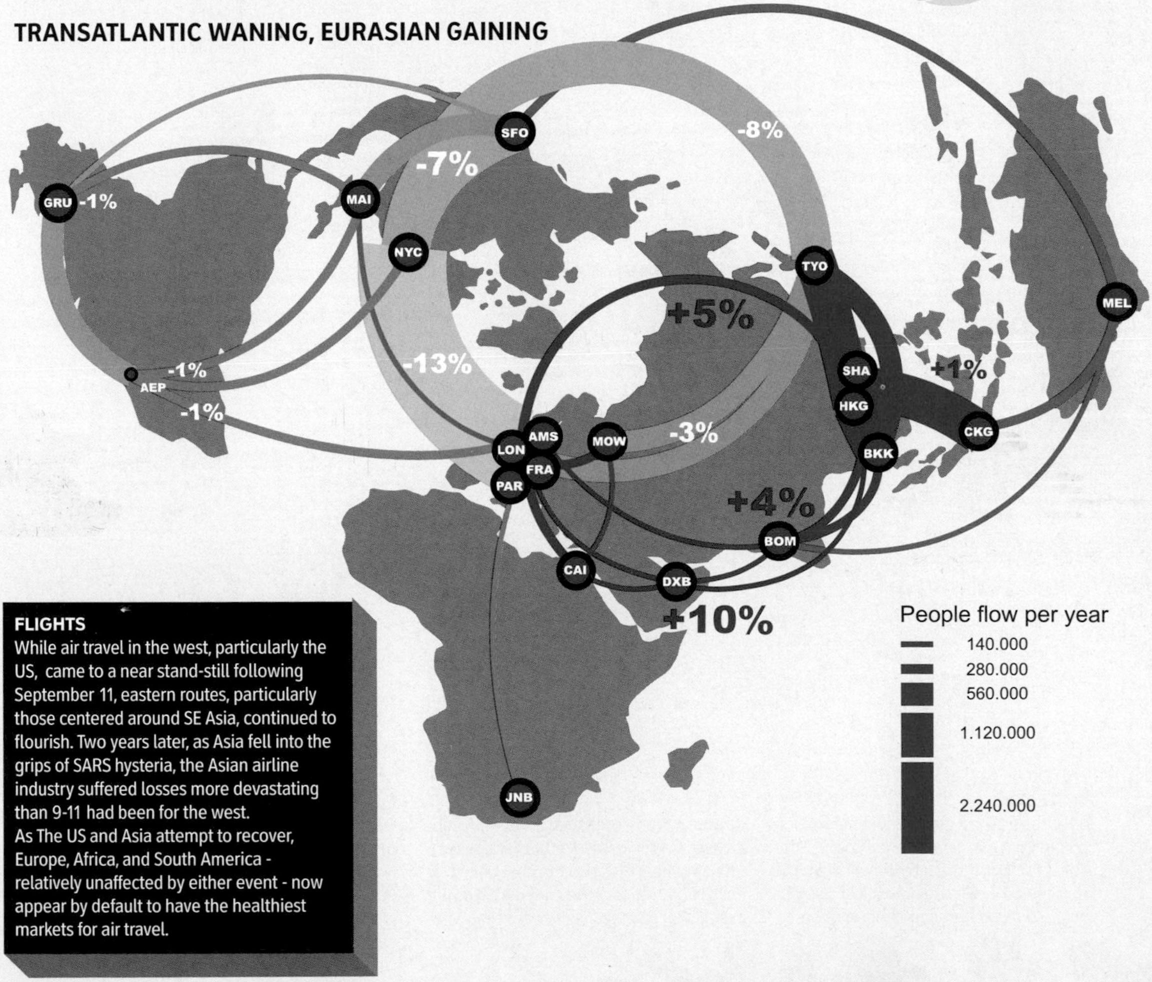

SFO -8% -7% GRU -1% MAI NYC TYO MEL +5% -13% SHA +1% HKG AEP -1% -1% AMS MOW -3% CKG LON BKK FRA PAR +4% BOM CAI DXB +10% JNB

People flow per year

- 140.000
- 280.000
- 560.000
- 1.120.000
- 2.240.000

FLIGHTS

While air travel in the west, particularly the US, came to a near stand-still following September 11, eastern routes, particularly those centered around SE Asia, continued to flourish. Two years later, as Asia fell into the grips of SARS hysteria, the Asian airline industry suffered losses more devastating than 9-11 had been for the west.
As The US and Asia attempt to recover, Europe, Africa, and South America - relatively unaffected by either event - now appear by default to have the healthiest markets for air travel.

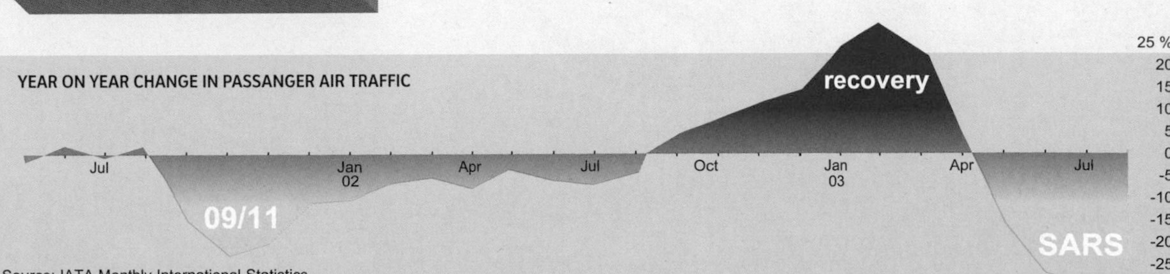

Source: IATA Monthly International Statistics

RIGHT WING THINK TANKS

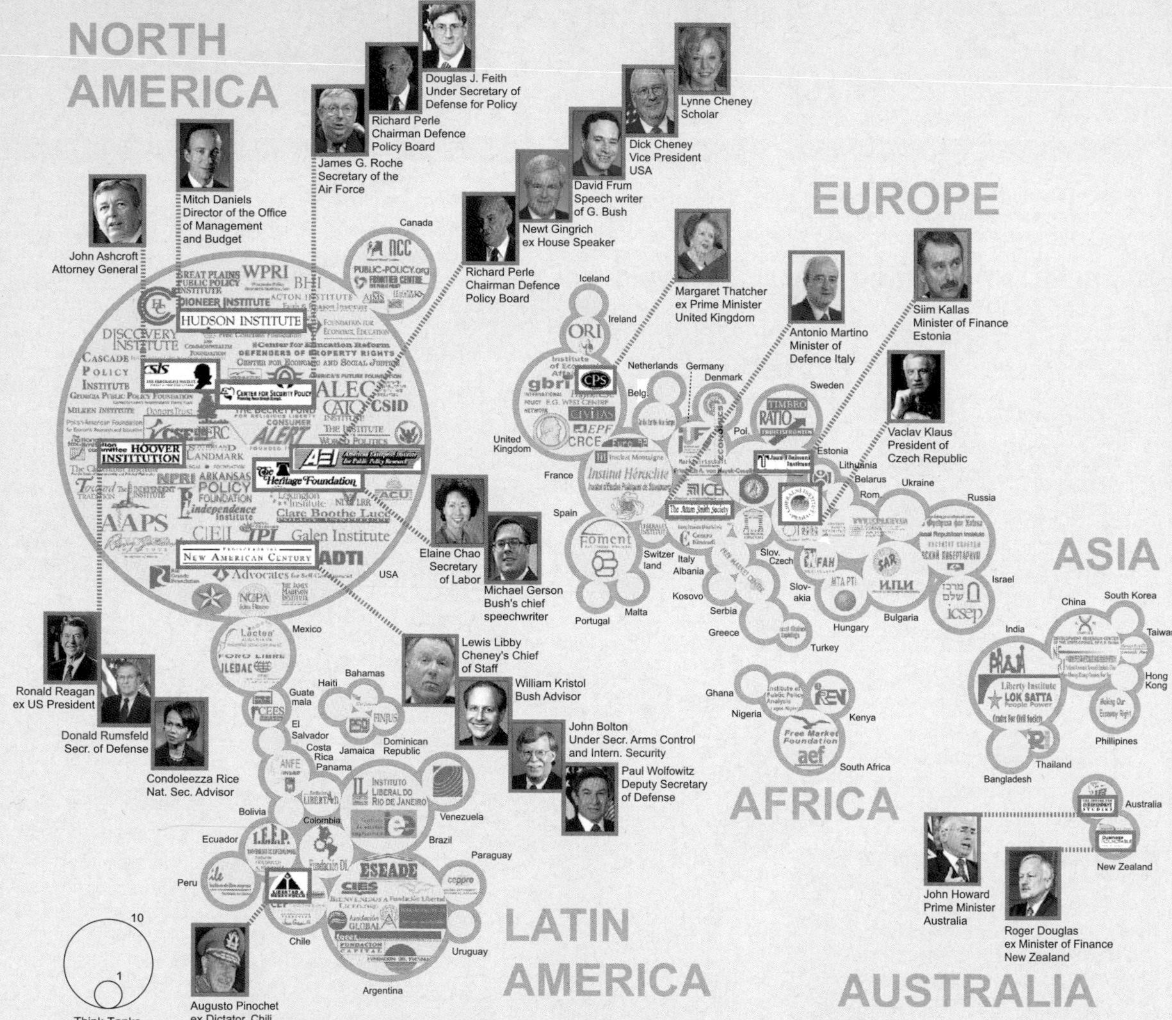

PROTEST

Today, the freshest political ideas are coming from two very different sources: the activist left and the establishment right. The left is fueled by a loose network of activist groups; their preferred method: massive demonstrations, organized largely through the Net. On 15 February 2003, groups like Attac, People's Global Action and United for Peace and Justice orchestrated F15, the first ever global protest against war in Iraq.

On the right, think tanks are a hub of activity. A new conservatism is flowing from a network of policy shops, where the free exchange of both business cards and ideas is transforming governments in America, Europe, and Asia.

LEFT WING ACTION TANKS

M16
May 16 1998
Geneva WTO Meeting
~ 10.000 people

Geneva

N30
November 30 1999
Seattle WTO Meeting
~ 40.000 people

A16
April 16 2000
IMF & World Bank
Meeting Washington DC
~ 50.000 people

J20
July 20-22 2001
G8 Summit,
Genoa, Italy
~ 280.000 people

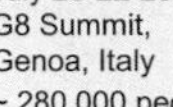

D20
December 20/21 2002
Global Day of Action
for Argentina
~ 500.000 people

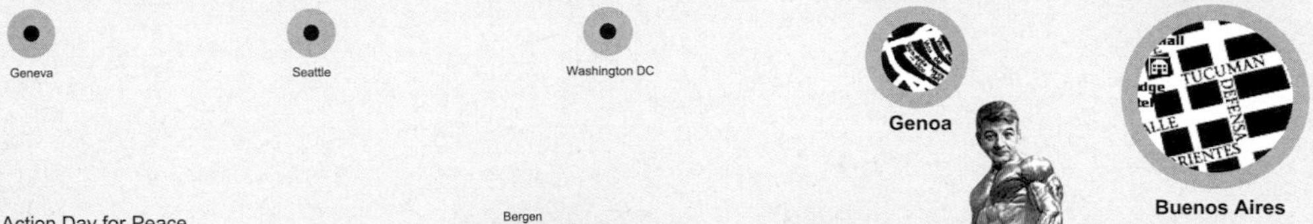

F15
Global Action Day for Peace
February 15 2003
~ 14.000.000 people

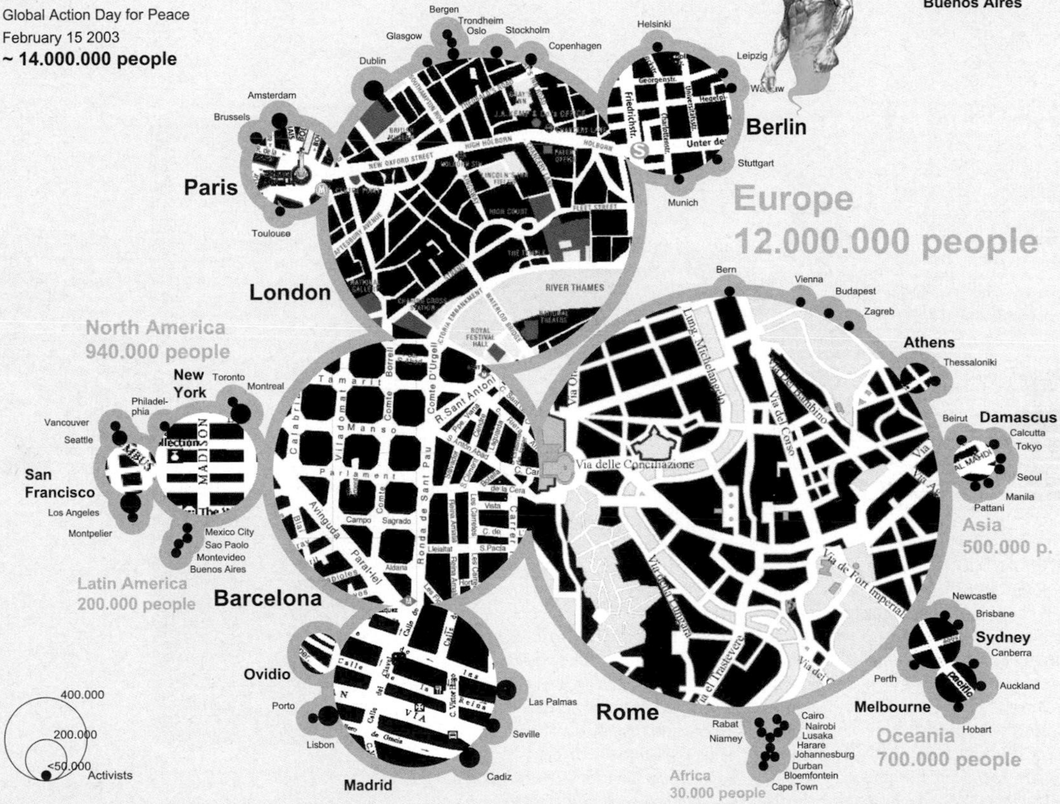

Europe
12.000.000 people

Bergen, Trondheim, Oslo, Stockholm, Glasgow, Copenhagen, Dublin, Helsinki, Leipzig, Warsaw, Amsterdam, Brussels, Paris, Toulouse, London, Berlin, Stuttgart, Munich, Bern, Vienna, Budapest, Zagreb, Athens, Thessaloniki, Barcelona, Rome, Ovidio, Porto, Lisbon, Madrid, Las Palmas, Seville, Cadiz

North America
940.000 people

New York, Toronto, Montreal, Philadelphia, Vancouver, Seattle, San Francisco, Los Angeles, Montpelier

Latin America
200.000 people

Mexico City, Sao Paolo, Montevideo, Buenos Aires

Asia
500.000 p.

Beirut, Damascus, Calcutta, Tokyo, Seoul, Manila, Pattani

Oceania
700.000 people

Newcastle, Brisbane, Sydney, Canberra, Auckland, Perth, Melbourne, Hobart

Africa
30.000 people

Rabat, Niamey, Cairo, Nairobi, Lusaka, Harare, Johannesburg, Durban, Bloemfontein, Cape Town

400.000
200.000
<50.000
Activists

AMO ATLAS

THEO DEUTINGER, DANIEL DENDRA, MAMMEN ESCORILHUELLA, REINIER DE GRAAF, NANNE DE RU, MARKUS SCHÄFER, MAX SCHWITALLA, SEBASTIAN THOMAS

Alaska (U.S.A.)

CANADA

UNITED STATES OF AMERICA

MEXICO

St. Pierre and Miquelon (Fr.)

Bermuda (U.K.)

BRAZIL

PARAGUAY

URUGUAY

Falkland Islands (U.K.) (Malvinas)

†613 Europe

†587 Far East

†356 Middle East

†27 Latin America

†1.511 Africa

3.094 refugee deaths while attempting to enter "Fortress Europe" between 1993-2003

SOURCE: WWW.UNITED.NON-FIT.NL/PDFS/LISTOFDEATHS.PDF

Leg 1: Flight IB77440 from Madrid to Lima.
Leg 2: Trip to Machu Picchu, the famous Lost City of the Incas.
Leg 3: Trip to Cuzco, former capital of the Inca empire.
Leg 4: Flight IB6651 from Lima to Madrid.

€ 4.100,-

Leg 1: Flight KL747 from Lima to Madrid.
Leg 2: Travel to La Rioja, Almeria, Valencia by car or train, seeking work as fruit picker in the vineyards, orange groves and horticultural centers.

ENTER AND EXIT "FORTRESS EUROPE"

The European Union is characterized by a paradox: a graying society with negligible space for economic growth, it is certain to face profound problems in maintaining its pension system in the future; at the same time, European politicians are encouraging the construction walls – both virtual and physical - to prevent the introduction of young, foreign labor. Exclusion is applied to all non-members of the Union with almost the same rigidity.

For the horrifying trips to the EU, immigrants pay a high price - sometimes the highest. Between 1993 and 2003, more than 3,094 refugees (including 600 Europeans) have died in the attempt to enter the European Union.

At the same time, for EU members seeking "adventure" in exotic locales travel has never been easier or cheaper.

1. Gibraltar Strait swimming competition

2. Suspected migrant found dead in the waters off the coast of Algeciras by Spanish police

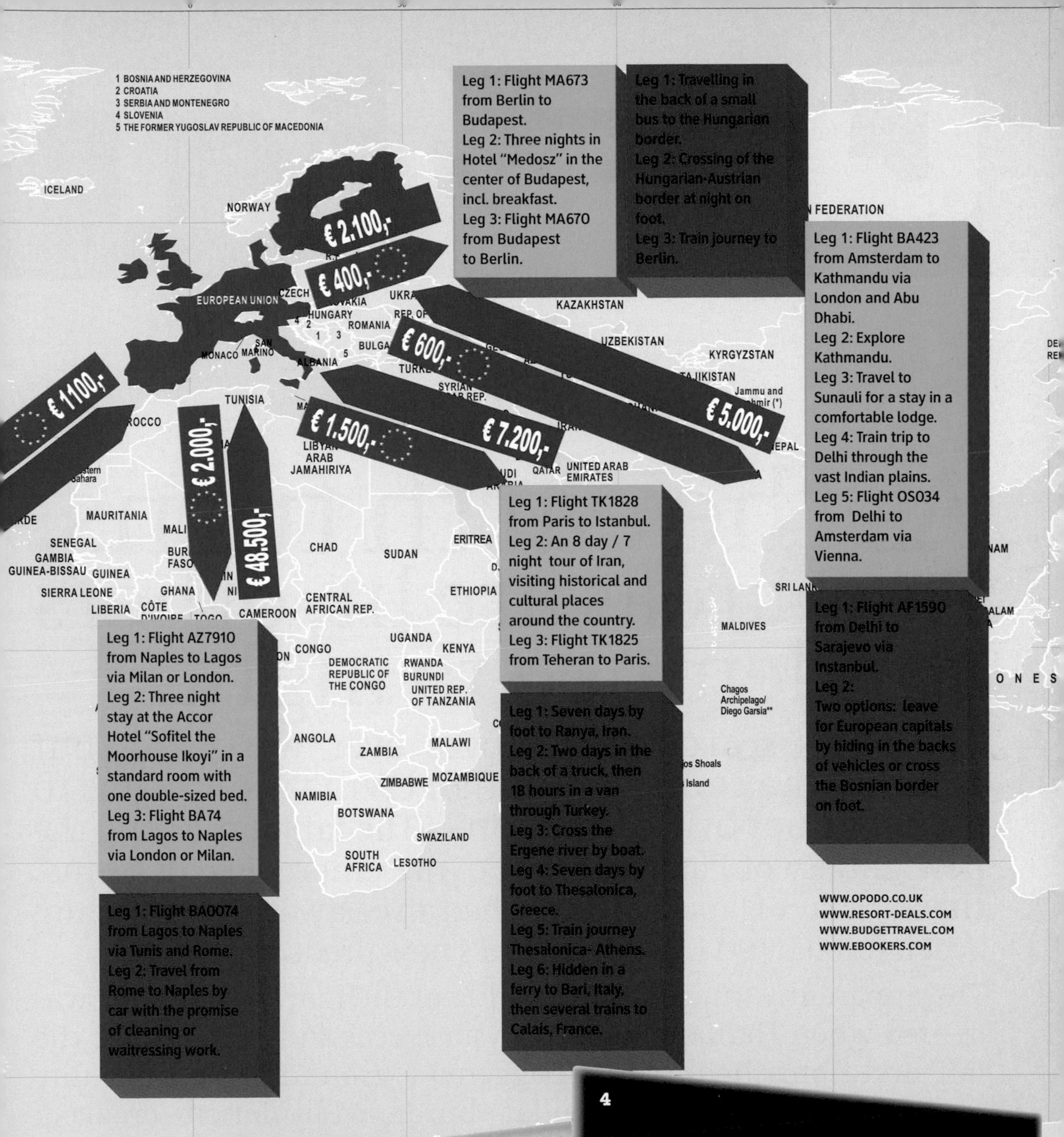

1 BOSNIA AND HERZEGOVINA
2 CROATIA
3 SERBIA AND MONTENEGRO
4 SLOVENIA
5 THE FORMER YUGOSLAV REPUBLIC OF MACEDONIA

€ 2.100,-

€ 400,-

€ 1100,-

€ 2.000,-

€ 48.500,-

€ 600,-

€ 1.500,-

€ 7.200,-

€ 5.000,-

Leg 1: Flight MA673 from Berlin to Budapest.
Leg 2: Three nights in Hotel "Medosz" in the center of Budapest, incl. breakfast.
Leg 3: Flight MA670 from Budapest to Berlin.

Leg 1: Travelling in the back of a small bus to the Hungarian border.
Leg 2: Crossing of the Hungarian-Austrian border at night on foot.
Leg 3: Train journey to Berlin.

Leg 1: Flight BA423 from Amsterdam to Kathmandu via London and Abu Dhabi.
Leg 2: Explore Kathmandu.
Leg 3: Travel to Sunauli for a stay in a comfortable lodge.
Leg 4: Train trip to Delhi through the vast Indian plains.
Leg 5: Flight OS034 from Delhi to Amsterdam via Vienna.

Leg 1: Flight AF1590 from Delhi to Sarajevo via Instanbul.
Leg 2:
Two options: leave for European capitals by hiding in the backs of vehicles or cross the Bosnian border on foot.

Leg 1: Flight TK1828 from Paris to Istanbul.
Leg 2: An 8 day / 7 night tour of Iran, visiting historical and cultural places around the country.
Leg 3: Flight TK1825 from Teheran to Paris.

Leg 1: Seven days by foot to Ranya, Iran.
Leg 2: Two days in the back of a truck, then 18 hours in a van through Turkey.
Leg 3: Cross the Ergene river by boat.
Leg 4: Seven days by foot to Thesalonica, Greece.
Leg 5: Train journey Thesalonica- Athens.
Leg 6: Hidden in a ferry to Bari, Italy, then several trains to Calais, France.

Leg 1: Flight AZ7910 from Naples to Lagos via Milan or London.
Leg 2: Three night stay at the Accor Hotel "Sofitel the Moorhouse Ikoyi" in a standard room with one double-sized bed.
Leg 3: Flight BA74 from Lagos to Naples via London or Milan.

Leg 1: Flight BA0074 from Lagos to Naples via Tunis and Rome.
Leg 2: Travel from Rome to Naples by car with the promise of cleaning or waitressing work.

WWW.OPODO.CO.UK
WWW.RESORT-DEALS.COM
WWW.BUDGETTRAVEL.COM
WWW.EBOOKERS.COM

3. Paris to Beijing classic transcontinental vintage car race

4. Refugees discovered hiding amongst cargo at the German Polish border of Görlitz

As the earth turns, new areas are lit, others condemned to night.

The sun's searchlight moves ever westward, but recently the course of human civilization seems to go in the opposite direction.... The fall of the wall, the new gravity of Eastern Europe, the emergence of China, the disarray of Japan, all launched an eastward momentum, accelerated by 9-11 and America's new preoccupations.

The apparently impregnable dogma of the market economy was dented when Thailand and Malaysia successfully challenged the IMF and flourished. Seattle triggered a groundswell of hostility against globalization. The dollar - burdened by deficit - croaked; the euro insinuated itself in its place.

The average age of the American board is now 70, the average decision maker in Europe 50; but in China the architect is surrounded by 30 year-olds on Promethean ozone.

Through its usual cocktail of design and default, the architect's compass follows.

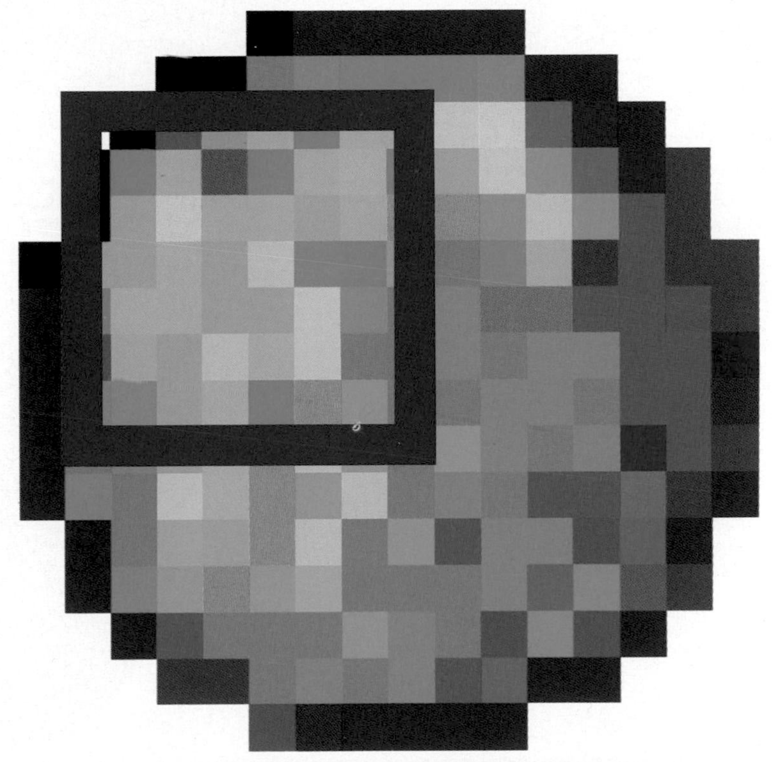

37°47'N 122°26' W

Cover Logic

In April 2001, Condé Nast asked AMO to look at *Wired*, post boom. Where to locate a new mission, how to position a magazine previously based on the relentless narcissism of Silicon Valley?

Wired ________ is History.

Fashion magazines adhere to a rigorous cover forumla – a focus-group-tested mélange of cleavage, airbrushed skin, and exclamation points. *Wired*'s strategy for techno-seduction generated its own cover logic, calibrated to a single mission: eulogize the old and herald the new. This formula served as an ever-renewable font of optimism for a monthly package perpetually promising the next big thing.

BY LUCIA ALLAIS AND MICHAEL ROCK

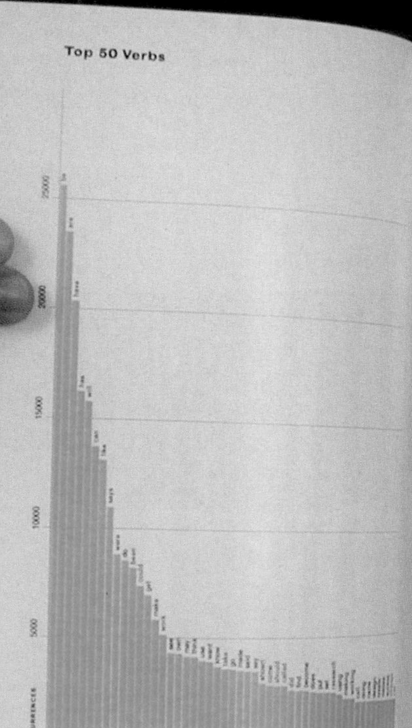
Top 50 Verbs
25000
20000
15000
10000
5000
OCCURRENCES

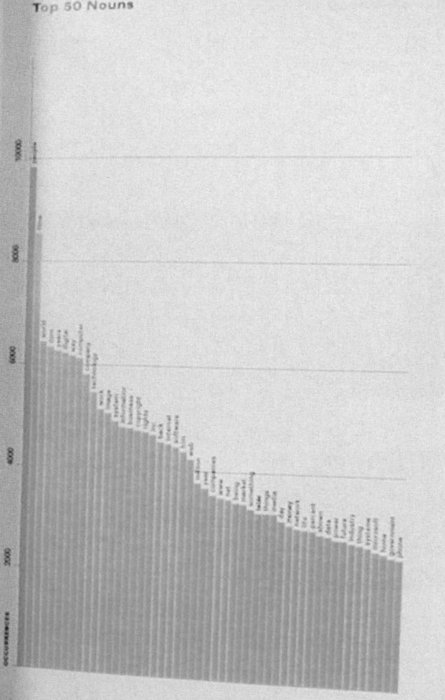
Top 50 Nouns
10000
8000
6000
4000
2000
OCCURRENCES

AMO + 2X4

In the beginning, the Word

The *Wired* Dictionary emerged out of a hunch: that a magazine's vocabulary can be as glossy as its paper stock. The simplest way to understand *Wired*'s message was to strip its language of grammar, catalog every word it had ever published and record the frequency of its use. The dictionary made apparent the invisible *fin-de-siècle* lexicon that *Wired* both chronicled and helped produce.

new people could now most first
even world years digital .com
computer way me over these our make company
technology wired work after image system
information business 1
copyright rights inc internet software
him still see very own going web
she well reserved down while think
may around such that's her use
want those every million 0.

Wired's 50 most frequently-used words revealed its ambition with poetic accuracy.

Perpetual Revolution

And so tracing *Wired*'s history was no longer a matter of following shifts in ownership, tracking world events, or chronicling editorial regimes. We found that a simple and consistent rhythm punctuated *Wired*'s seven years of existence: on average, *Wired* proclaimed a revolution every three months. A new future generated before other futures had time to be verified.

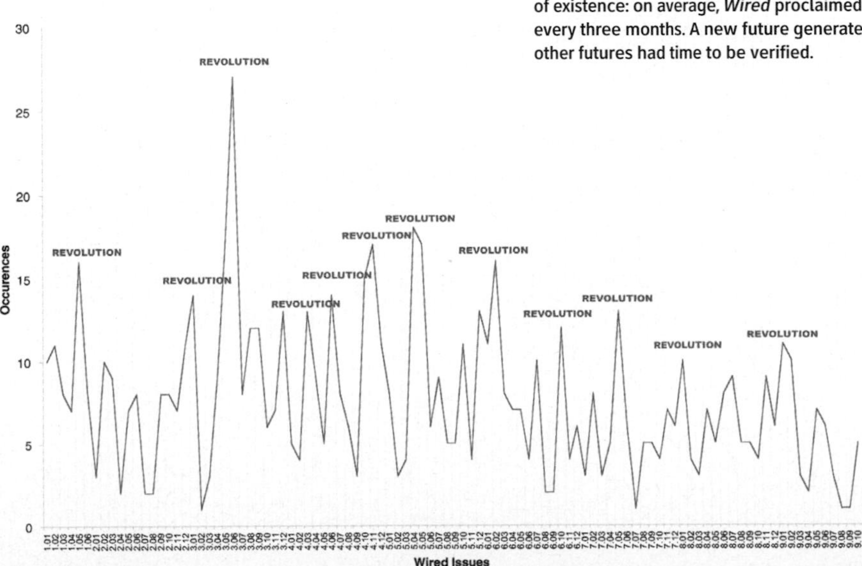

Then: Optimism

We're facing 25 years of prosperity, freedom, and a better environment for the whole world.
You got a problem with that?

Peter Schwartz and Peter Leyden, in "The Long Boom: A History of the Future." *Wired* 5.07 (July 1997)

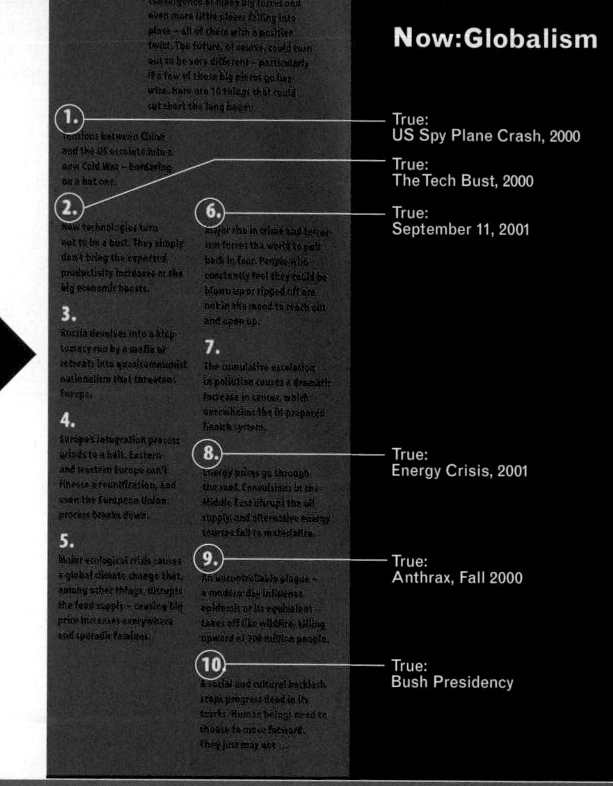

convergence of many big forces and even more little pieces falling into place – all of them with a positive twist. The future, of course, could turn out to be very different – particularly if a few of these big pieces go haywire. Here are 10 things that could cut short the long boom:

1. Tensions between China and the US escalate into a new Cold War – bordering on a hot one.

2. New technologies turn out to be a bust. They simply don't bring the expected productivity increases or the big economic boosts.

3. Russia devolves into a kleptocracy run by a mafia or retreats into quasicommunist nationalism that threatens Europe.

4. Europe's integration process grinds to a halt. Eastern and western Europe can't finesse a reunification, and even the European Union process breaks down.

5. Major ecological crisis causes a global climate change that, among other things, disrupts the food supply – causing big price increases everywhere and sporadic famines.

6. Major rise in crime and terrorism forces the world to pull back in fear. People who constantly feel they could be blown up or ripped off are not in the mood to reach out and open up.

7. The cumulative escalation in pollution causes a dramatic increase in cancer, which overwhelms the ill-prepared health system.

8. Energy prices go through the roof. Convulsions in the Middle East disrupt the oil supply, and alternative energy sources fail to materialize.

9. An uncontrollable plague – a modern-day influenza epidemic or its equivalent – takes off like wildfire, killing upward of 300 million people.

10. A social and cultural backlash stops progress dead in its tracks. Human beings need to choose to move forward. They just may not ...

What happens to a magazine that proclaims prophecies if only its worst-case scenarios come true?

Can you make a magazine out of pessimism?

>> *Wired* captured a moment of historical change with iconic perfection - the advent of the internet, the triumph of the market economy, the optimism for a technologically enhanced world, and the promise of a digitally-fueled political revolution: all found their voice in *Wired*'s alchemy of four distinct audiences. The geeks that ruled the '90s can be classified into 4 typologies, and *Wired* consistently identified the fronts on which all could unite.

If the optimism that fueled a revolution dissolves, what happens to the flag carrier?

During the boom, the genius of *Wired* was to create a vehicle where four typologies of geek could overlap.

Then: Synergy

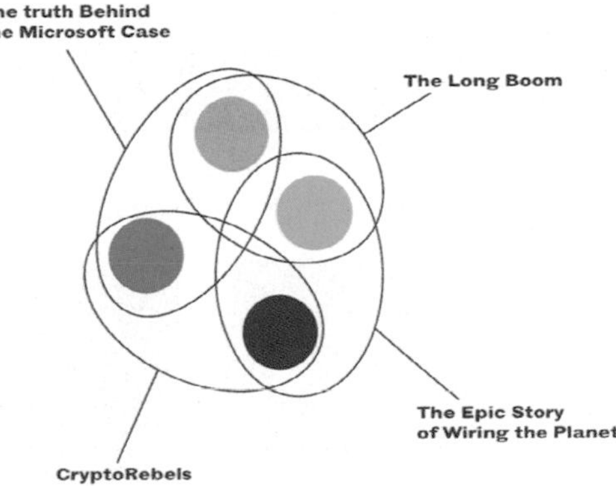

Geek Typologies

● **Pragmatist** a.k.a Venture Capitalist
Looking for: The Next Big Thing
Methodology: Follow the Money
Probable Location: Silicon Valley, Sites of Global Development
Wired Figurehead: Gary Wolf
Favorite Wired Pages: Fetish, Wired Index.
Timeframe of future: "_________, as soon as the tech economy recovers."

● **Idealist** a.k.a Hippie
Looking for: Peace, love and understanding
Methodology: Sustainability
Probable Location: Washington State, India
Wired Figurehead: Steward Brand, Kevin Kelly
Favorite Wired Pages: Netizen
Timeframe for the future: "_________, before it's too late."

● **Technocrat** a.k.a Organization Man
Looking for: A job in the Military / Industrial Complex
Methodology: "Applied Research"
Probable Location: A-World Capital City
Wired Figurehead: Nicholas Negroponte
Favorite Wired Pages: Infoporn
Time frame for the future: "___________ is already happening."

● **Nihilist** a.k.a Cyberpunk
Looking for: Outlaw
Methodology: Hacking
Probable Location: Genoa / wherever the WTO is
Wired Figurehead: William Gibson
Favorite Wired Pages: Geek Page
Time frame for the future: Fuck the future.

Now: Cacaphony

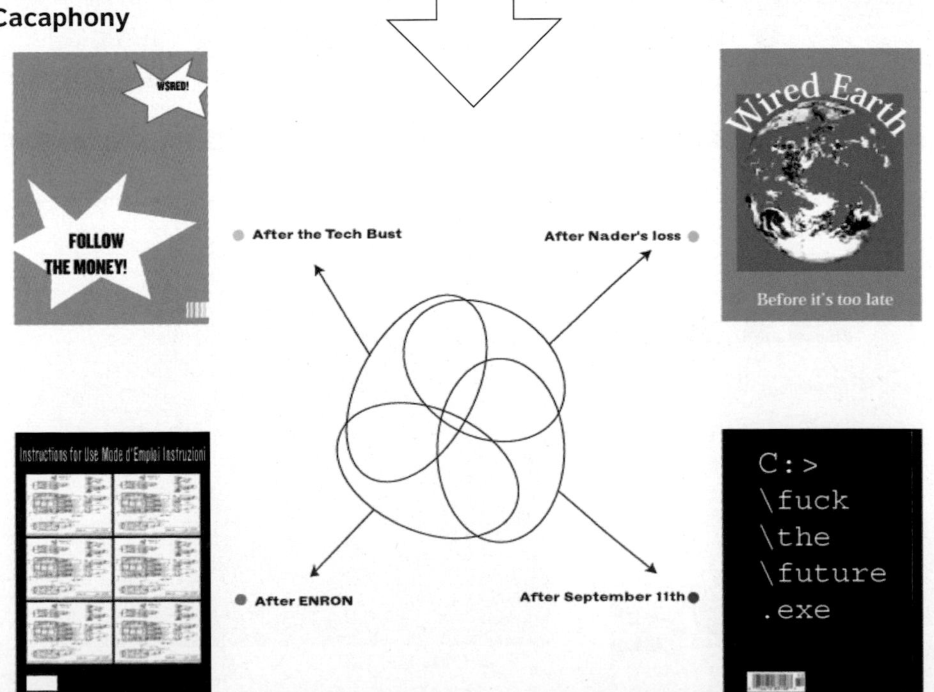

If not technology what; if not America where?

World Agenda

How can NEW continue to be *Wired's* favorite word when the cycle of newness has changed? How can *Wired's* rhythmic consistency help calibrate its agenda to the apparently chaotic field of events that seems to regulate the world? Can NEW and GLOBAL combine to create unexpected adjacencies?

Art

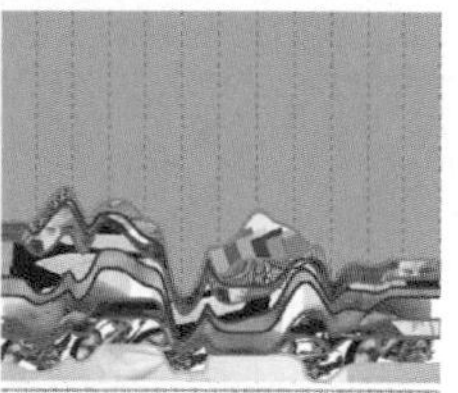

Entertainment

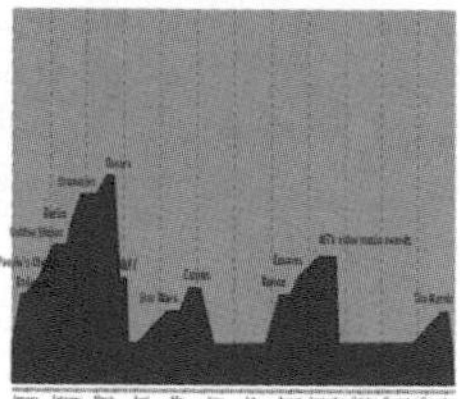

Technology

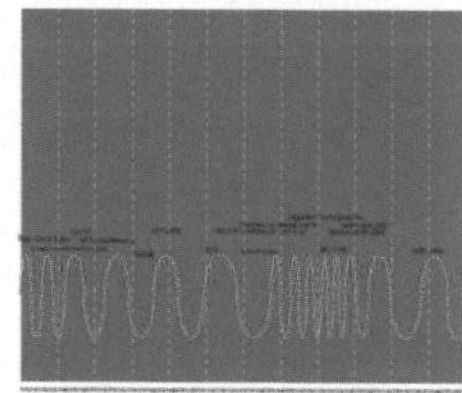

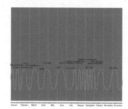

Academia & Literati

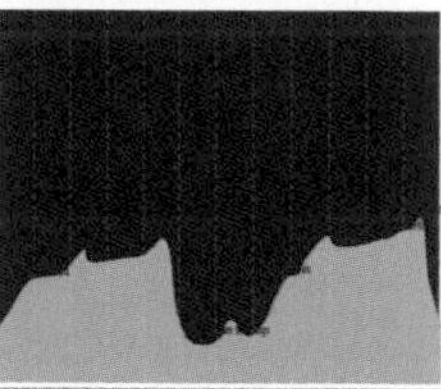

Global Politics

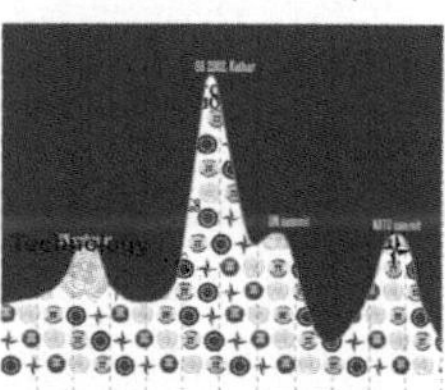

National Elections

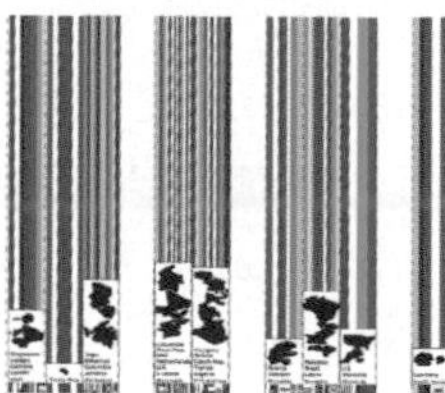

International Sports

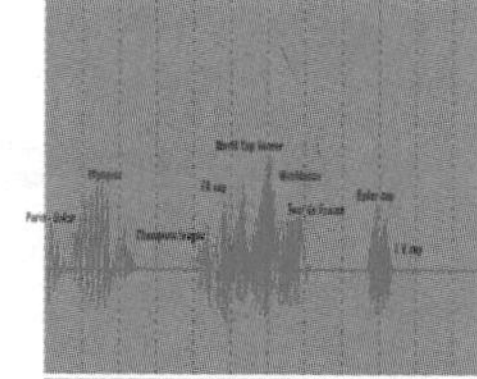

Religion

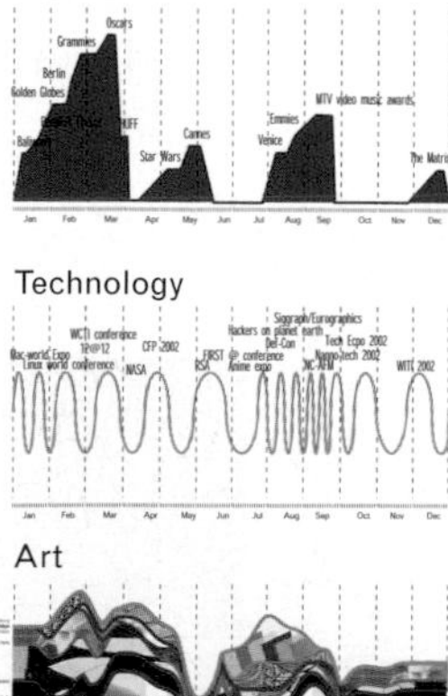

Special Entertainment Issue

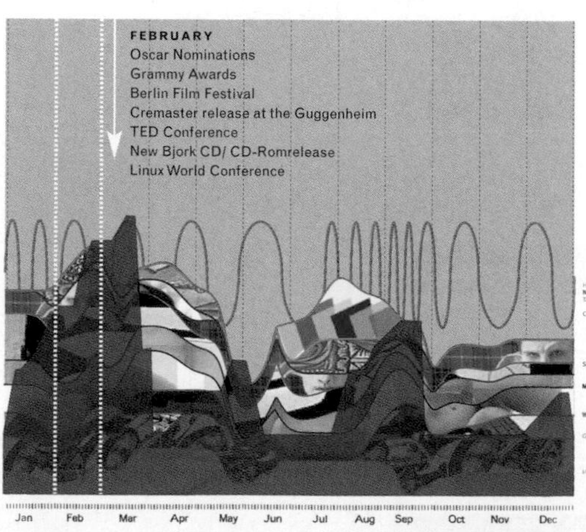

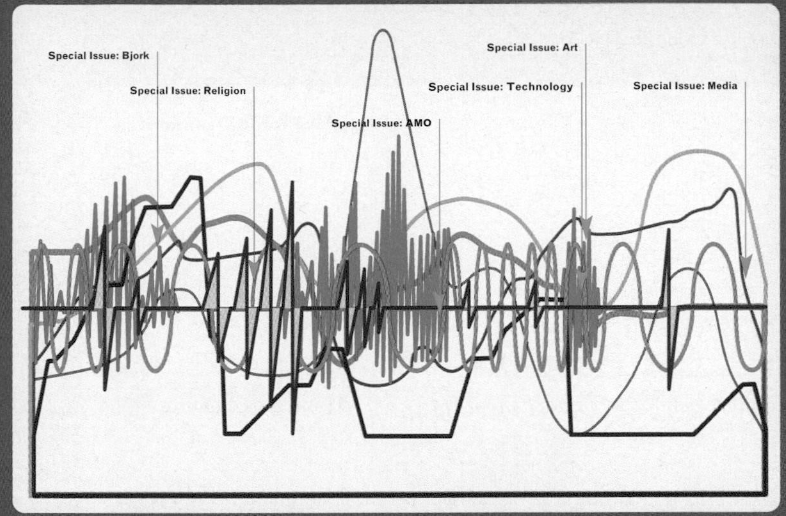

In the face of economic, political, and cultural turmoil, *Wired* could abandon its claims of certainty and invite guest editors - instead of a revolution every three months, a guest editor every season.

BWJIORREKD
guest edited by
bjork
and
matthew barney

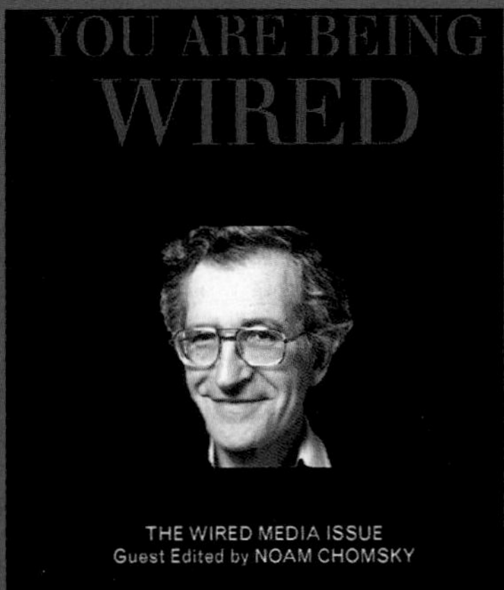

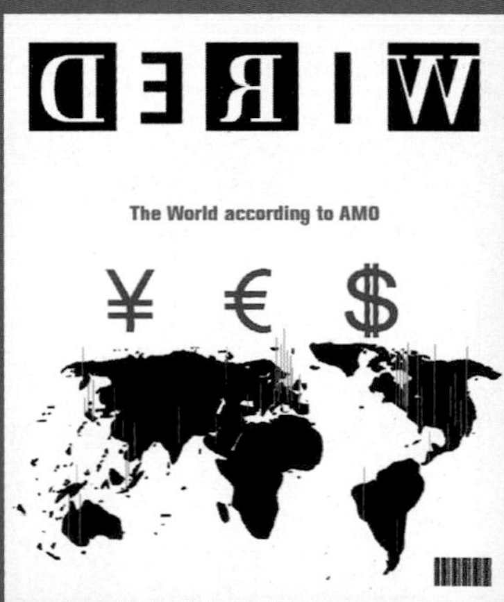

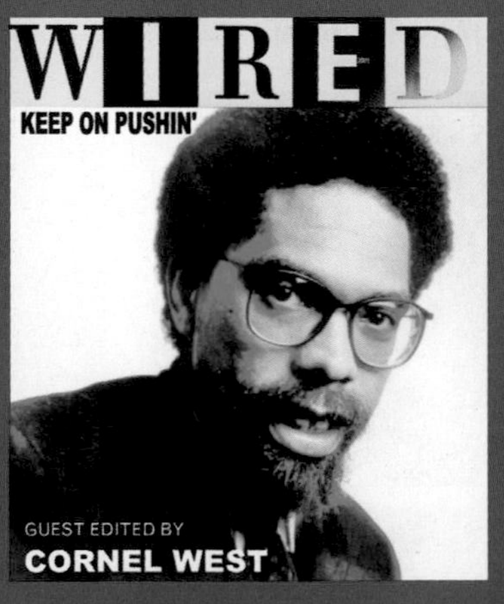

WIRED
KEEP ON PUSHIN'
GUEST EDITED BY
CORNEL WEST

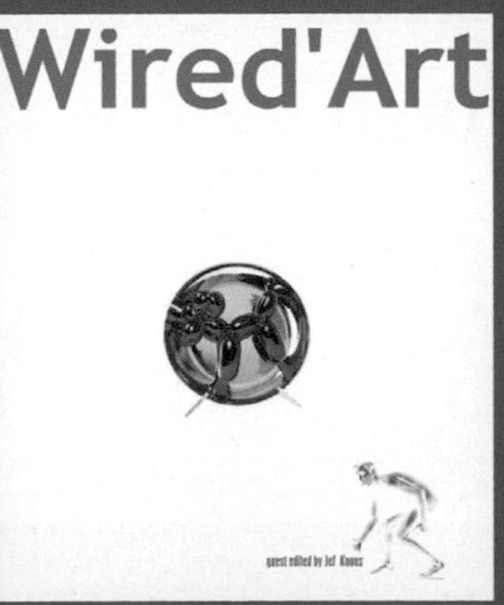

World
THE WORLD ISSUE
GUEST EDITED BY KOFI ANNAN

Demographics

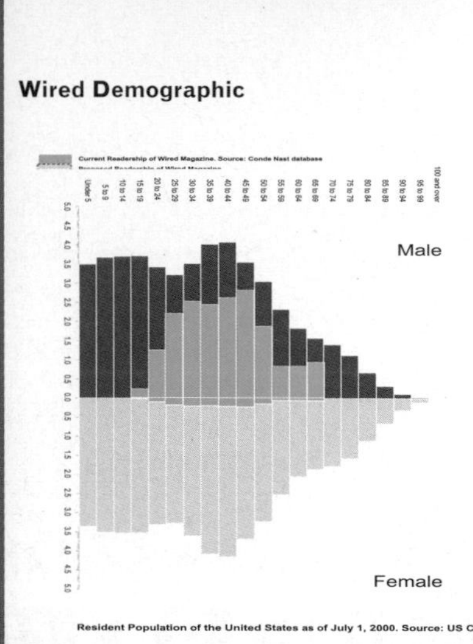

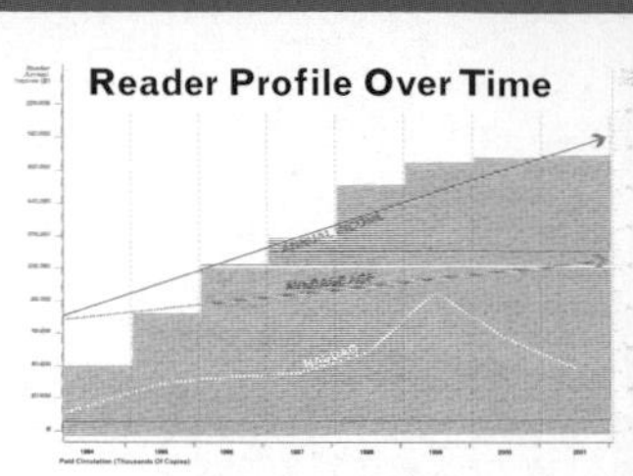

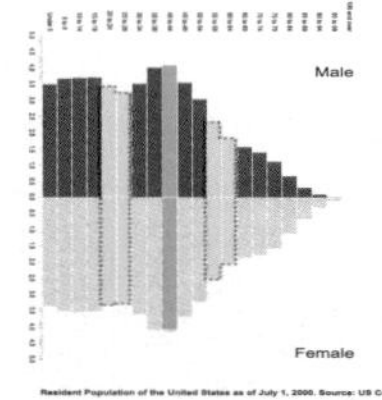

Wired's readership aged in perfect synchrony with the magazine - what if *Wired* staged an Oedipal confrontaton between two generations and their respective revolutionary ideals? Isn't it time to reveal who is a sell-out and who isn't?

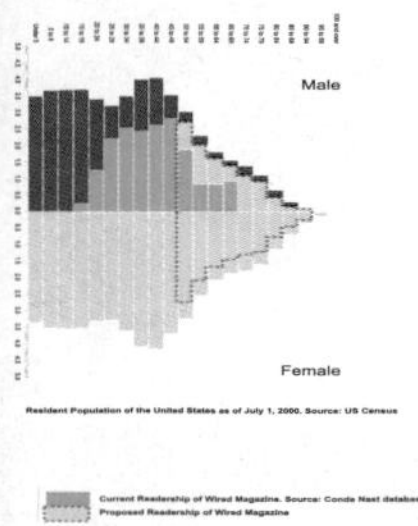

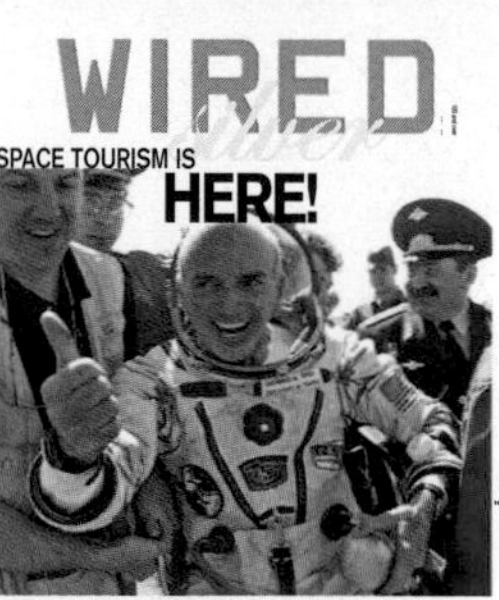

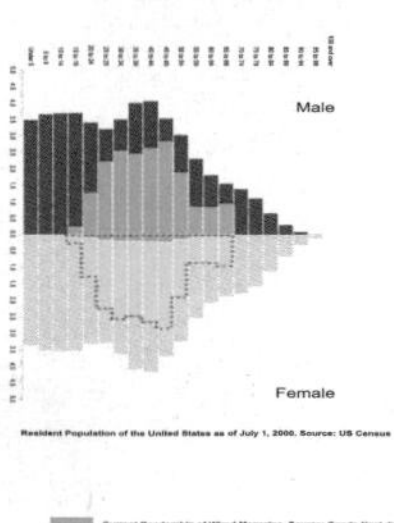

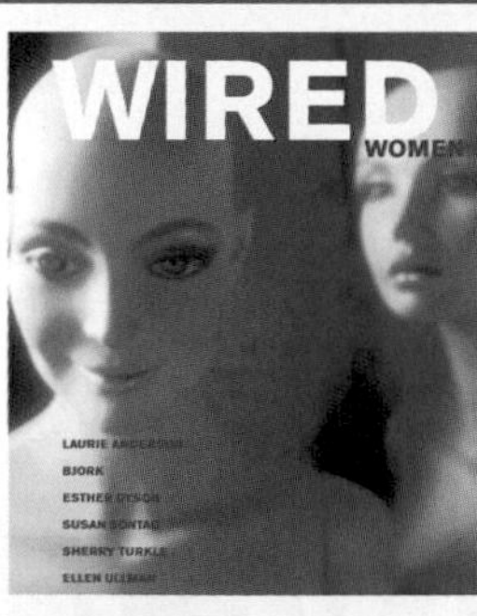

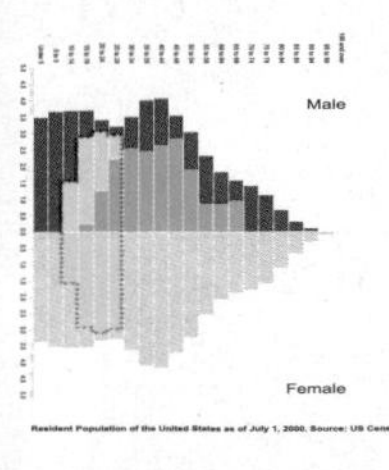

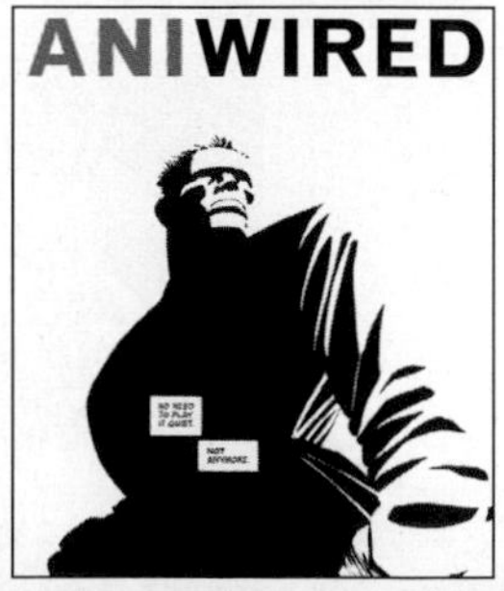

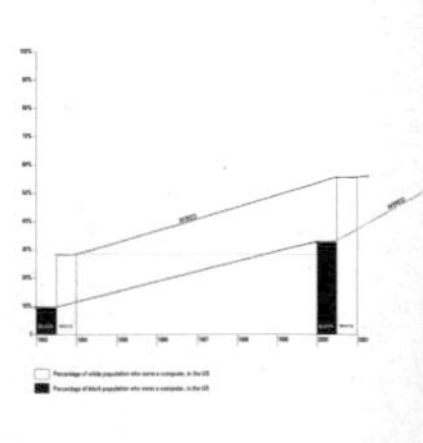

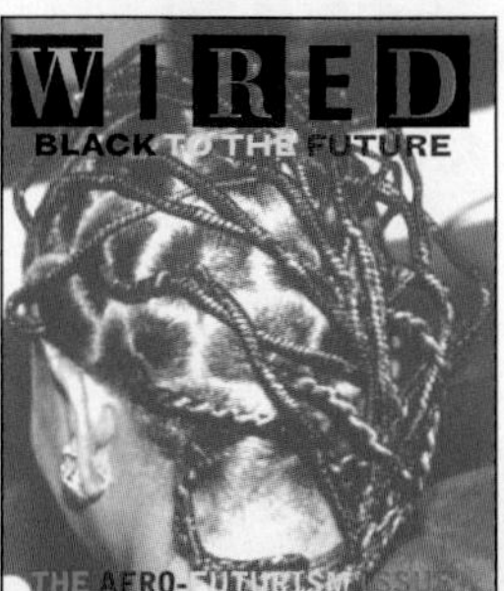

Wired's demographic profile is punctured with holes - as if the impact of technology had impacted the lives of only wealthy, white, middle-aged men. What would happen if *Wired* tailored its message to...women?... seniors?... teenagers?... blacks?

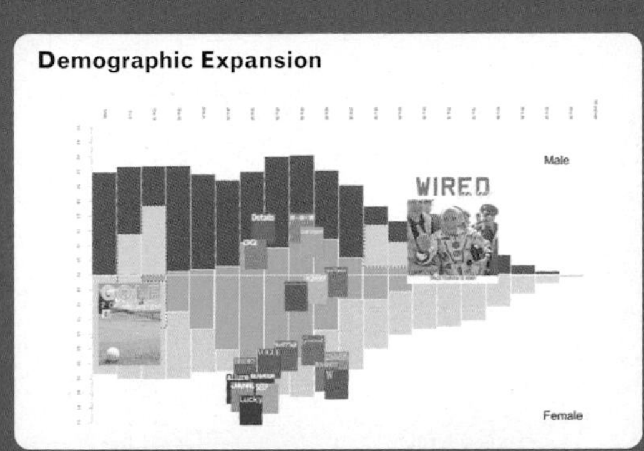

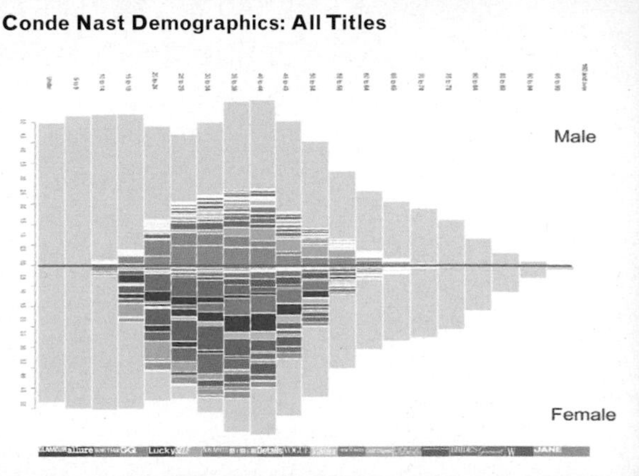

A Condé Nast matrix spawns theoretically unlimited offspring by intersecting individual identities: Golf-Brides, Car-Women, Men-Shoppers, etc.

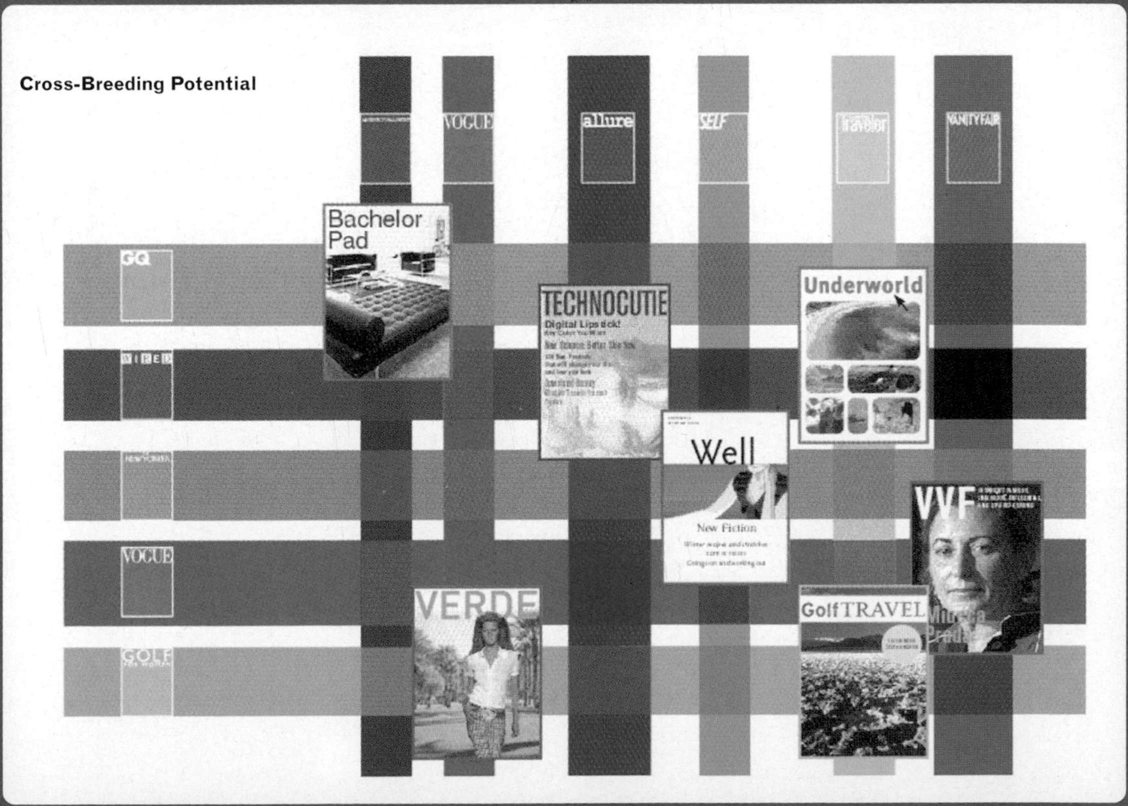

Cross-Breeding Potential

VOGUE
allure
SELF
Traveler
VANITY FAIR
GQ
WIRED
NEW YORKER
VOGUE
GOLF FOR WOMEN
Bachelor Pad
TECHNOCUTIE
Digital Lipstick!
Underworld
Well
New Fiction
VVF
VERDE
Golf TRAVEL

location 37°47'N122°26' W

P[illegible]a San Francisco

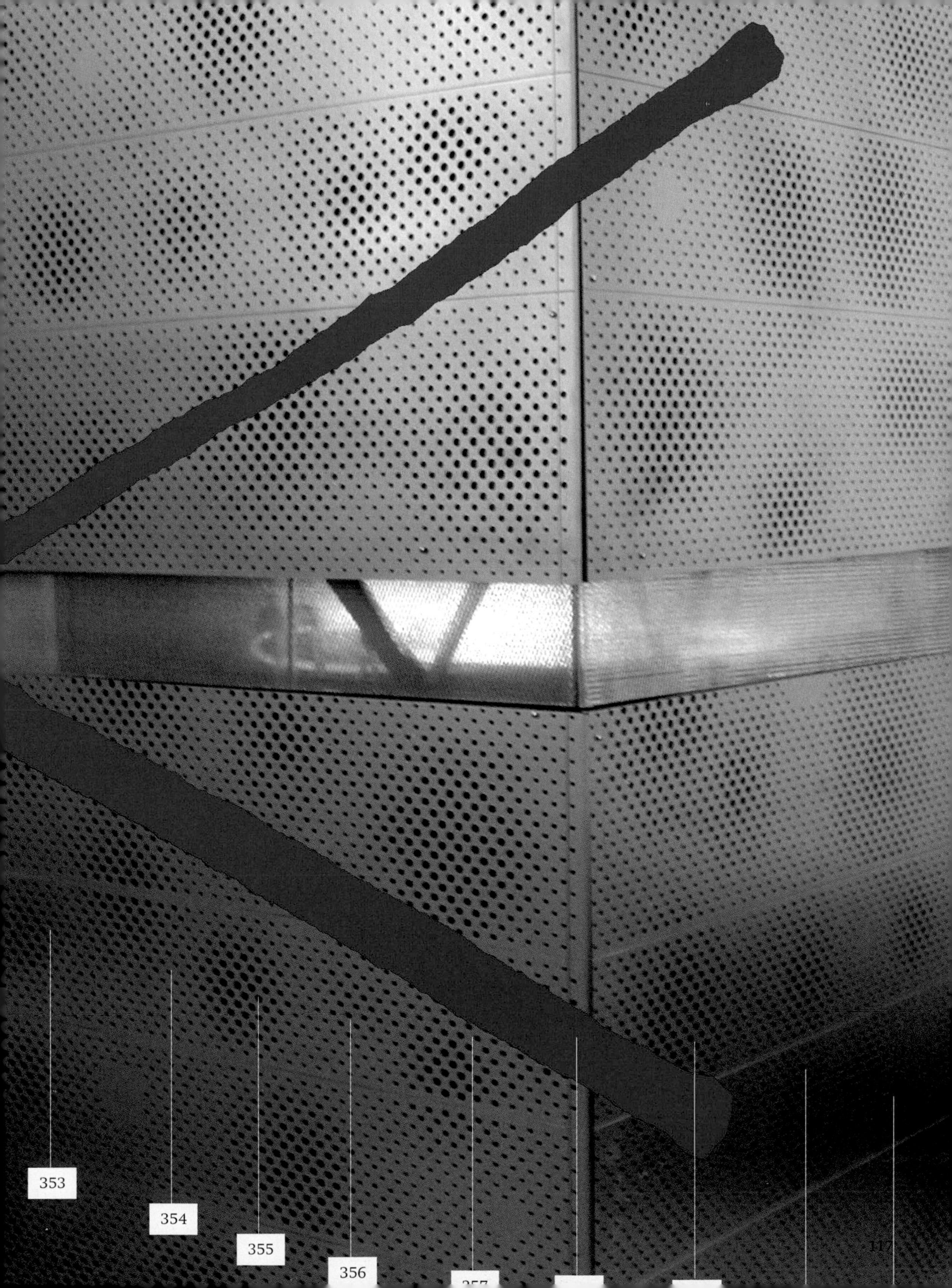
353
354
355
356

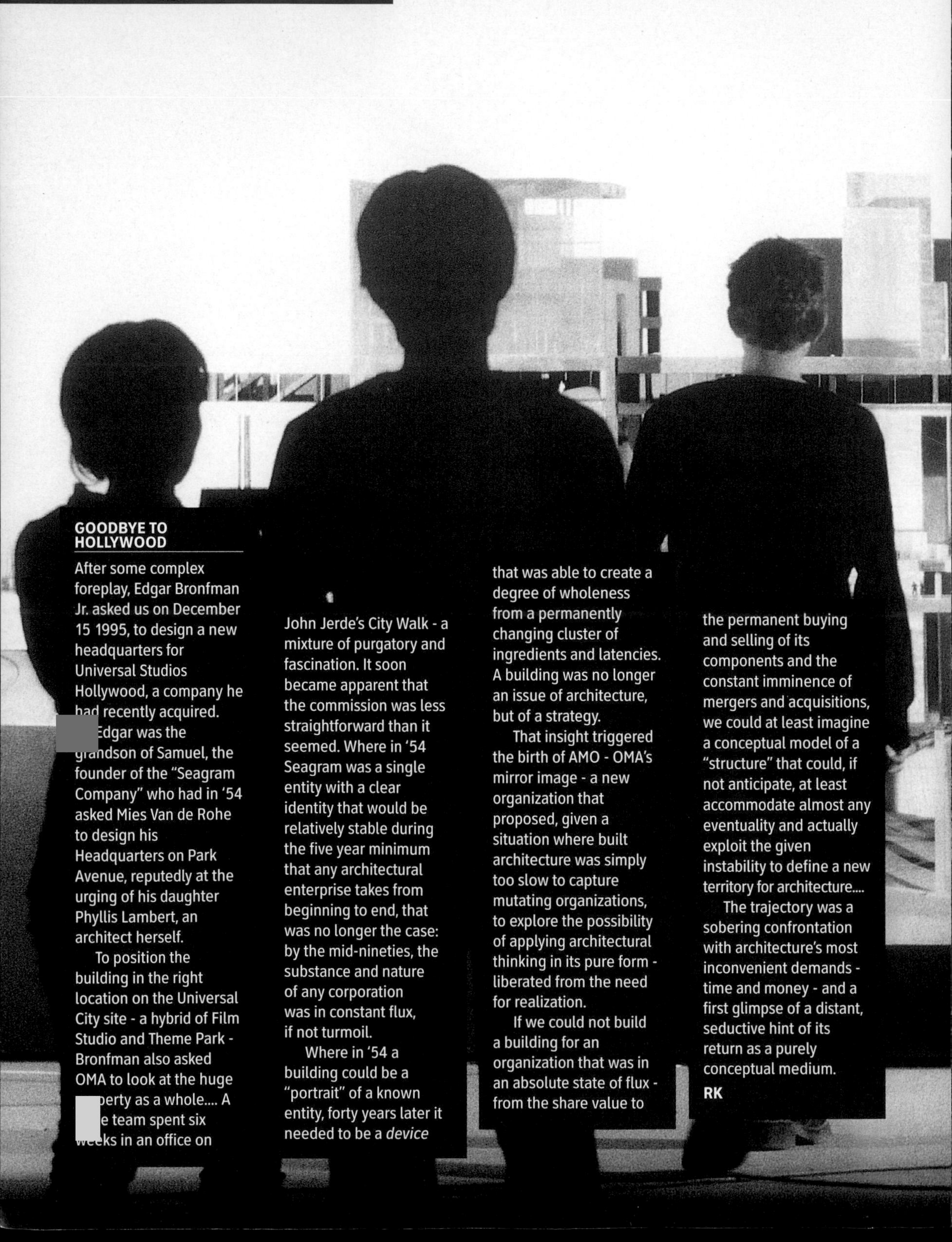

GOODBYE TO HOLLYWOOD

After some complex foreplay, Edgar Bronfman Jr. asked us on December 15 1995, to design a new headquarters for Universal Studios Hollywood, a company he had recently acquired.

Edgar was the grandson of Samuel, the founder of the "Seagram Company" who had in '54 asked Mies Van de Rohe to design his Headquarters on Park Avenue, reputedly at the urging of his daughter Phyllis Lambert, an architect herself.

To position the building in the right location on the Universal City site - a hybrid of Film Studio and Theme Park - Bronfman also asked OMA to look at the huge property as a whole.... A ...e team spent six weeks in an office on John Jerde's City Walk - a mixture of purgatory and fascination. It soon became apparent that the commission was less straightforward than it seemed. Where in '54 Seagram was a single entity with a clear identity that would be relatively stable during the five year minimum that any architectural enterprise takes from beginning to end, that was no longer the case: by the mid-nineties, the substance and nature of any corporation was in constant flux, if not turmoil.

Where in '54 a building could be a "portrait" of a known entity, forty years later it needed to be a *device* that was able to create a degree of wholeness from a permanently changing cluster of ingredients and latencies. A building was no longer an issue of architecture, but of a strategy.

That insight triggered the birth of AMO - OMA's mirror image - a new organization that proposed, given a situation where built architecture was simply too slow to capture mutating organizations, to explore the possibility of applying architectural thinking in its pure form - liberated from the need for realization.

If we could not build a building for an organization that was in an absolute state of flux - from the share value to the permanent buying and selling of its components and the constant imminence of mergers and acquisitions, we could at least imagine a conceptual model of a "structure" that could, if not anticipate, at least accommodate almost any eventuality and actually exploit the given instability to define a new territory for architecture....

The trajectory was a sobering confrontation with architecture's most inconvenient demands - time and money - and a first glimpse of a distant, seductive hint of its return as a purely conceptual medium.

RK

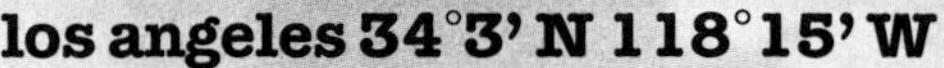

Universal HQ

Babylon falling

8 AM
10 AM
12 PM
2 PM
FILM
NEW MEDIA
RECREATION
FACILITIES
MUSIC

4 PM
6 PM
8 PM
10 PM

Almost Famous

The story of Universal HQ and all that could've been

BY DAN WOOD

BEGINNINGS

In June 1995, Seagram's Edgar Bronfman, Jr. - known throughout the compnay as EBJ - bought 80% of MCA, Inc. from Matsushita Electric. MCA was a multi-media company containing MCA music, Geffen Records, Universal Studios, Putnam publishing, Spencer Gifts, Universal Television, and Universal Recreation, which runs "Universal Studios Hollywood" theme parks in Los Angeles, California and Orlando, Florida.

In December 1995, OMA got word that they had received the commission for a new headquarters building in Universal City, Los Angeles. Rem Koolhaas and a group of collaborators were invited to Universal City to choose a site, write a program, and advise on any other improvements that OMA thought necessary in the reinvention of Seagram and MCA.

UNIVERSAL CITY

Universal City is a 400-acre piece of property on the border of Burbank, at the edge of the Valley and on the "wrong" side of the Hollywood hills. It is divided between the Top of the Hill, an amusement park that draws more than 5 million people per year, and the Lower Lot, combining an impressive grid of enormous studios, the back lot of outdoor sets representing specific locales ("western town," "little Europe," "New York," "suburbia"), and a group of SOM-designed Miesian office buildings.

REVOLUTIONARY

Through several stages of plans, presentations, and documents to coordinate OMA's work with an MCA Recreation Department Master Plan, a site choice emerged (an "unbuildable" steep slope between the Lower Lot and the Top of the Hill), and the Headquarters began to take shape. EBJ had requested a building that could capitalize on potential synergies between the different departments of Universal, which heretofore had been run as individual fiefdoms in strict competition with each other. OMA's concept was to take the most creative and productive elements of each of the five main departments and house them together in a single structure. The building would mirror its siting by being accessible to all disparate elements of the company, but itself firmly rooted in no one particular element.

INVESTIGATION

In August 1996 Koolhaas and eight OMA staff members forwent their summer vacations and moved to Los Angeles - specifically, to City Walk, an outdoor mall with urbanism as its theme (pseudo-urban retail, street performers, piped-in music, the world's largest collection of "historic neon") and designed to empty tourists' wallets both before and after a day at the theme park. With a Rotterdam-style late-night work ethic and eight individual rental cars for a two-minute Los Angeles-style commute, OMA spent a month studying and photographing the interiors and exteriors of Universal City, real and imagined.

The elements of the project fell into place surprisingly quickly, without anyone's exact knowledge how: a generic horizontal block of office space, articulated on the south façade with crenellations or "fingers" bringing light deep into the office floors (and providing corner offices for some 400 vice presidents), and penetrated vertically by four towers, each with a distinct identity and name. The Virtual Tower of double-height laboratory-like spaces would be the building's "loft district" where creative departments would develop new projects; the Circulation Tower's concentrated core functions including the main elevator bank; the Collective Tower acted as a vertical boulevard and social space for meetings, screenings, conferences, and amenities, bringing together people from different departments for productive chance interactions; the Executive Tower gathered more traditional isolated office spaces for each floor's management. A column-free Universal Floor, entirely supported by the four towers, extended the original Corporate Beam idea into a very large, highly visible canopy over the building's entrance court, with EBJ's office, the board room, and other important spaces cantilevered above the lobby. The façades would include a specially glazed transmitting/reflecting south face, changing appearance through the day with the sun, and a completely operable north face that could open in its entirety - essentially disappear - providing respite from hermetically sealed office air for an estimated 52% of the year.

TIMELESS

EBJ was always very direct in his comments on the work OMA had completed. Others would fawn or nervously express their concern about small details, but Edgar would wait until the end and present a precise reading of the project, his appreciation for the work, and his concerns. In February, he delivered the ultimate challenge to any architect: he wanted the building to be "timeless." His concern was that some of the preliminary material choices OMA presented were too contemporary and would become dated with time. "Timelessness" became the yardstick against which all material decisions were measured as the project developed. OMA was determined to combine seriousness of purpose, function, and material with a building in the most superficial of American cities, on a site facing directly on to Jurassic Park.

ENTERTAINMENT

Over the course of the next year, the concept was refined through a series of models, books, and presentations. The final schematic design presentation was in December 1997 in an empty movie studio on the Lower Lot. OMA had decided that entertainment executives needed to be entertained, and the rule for presentations was that each needed to be bigger than the last. Industrial designer Vincent De Rijk and OMA had created an illuminated 1:100 model designed to come apart, showing each tower, a generic floor, the Universal floor, the lobby, and the landscape. The Universal scenery department rigged a section of curtain, giving the executives their first glimpse of the building, fully lit and glowing, in complete darkness.

At the last minute, Koolhaas decided the slide room needed to be more intimate, and an OMA architect was asked to find an oriental rug for the space - ten minutes before the presentation was supposed to start. The props department had an entire sub-department of carpets, divided by size and rolled up. A carpet the right size was pulled down from the shelves and loaded onto OMA's golf cart, with the gaffer running behind to hold up the end off the street. With four minutes to spare, the chairs were cleared and three people unrolled the carpet into place. In the center of the exquisite Persian rug was an enormous painted swastika. Apparently the rug had last been used in a World War II movie - perhaps a little too much entertainment.

OMA quickly rolled it back up and held the presentation without intimacy. Regardless, the presentation was an unqualified success. The Universal executives seemed to really begin to understand the project and what the building could mean for the company. Edgar, however, was unsure about the timing. Universal's stock was at an all-time low. The press was continuously reminding people that the DuPont stock Seagram had unloaded to buy MCA was now worth more than ten times what they had sold it for three years before. The project went "on hold" until the company regained its financial footing.

At OMA, the models and drawings were packed away, and the team moved on to other projects.

REVIEW

We all realized that Universal's problem was not technical, but political. Over three years of work with Universal, OMA had noticed that the goal of seamless integration remained out of the company's reach; the more they saw, the more convinced they became that this building could actually help the company perform better. After almost a year's hiatus, OMA was contacted to work on the next phase - design development. Over ten months, the project was developed by the architects, engineers, cost estimators, and contractors to the point where construction could start within three months of giving the word to go. The final product of the DD phase was conceived as a portrait of Universal as it existed and how OMA imagined it could exist in the future. This final design development presentation included a 1:50 model of the building, as tall as a person and 14' (4.3 meters) long.

The nearly three-hour presentation oscillated between an architectural review of the vast amounts of work and detail that had gone into the project and OMA's criticisms and observations of Universal as a company. Following a tour of the studio and a review of the book, EBJ gave a succinct criticism of some of the material choices, expressed his deep gratitude for the work performed, and gave his reading of Universal's current situation. He said that many of the questions OMA raised in the final book, and in earlier observations, mirrored his own thinking about the direction of the company. He stated that the building had the potential to correct many of these problems, and he pledged his dedication to the project. In a replay of the Schematic Design presentation, however, he also said that Universal was not in a secure enough position to be able to build the project right away.

FUTURE

In early 1999, Rem Koolhaas and Dan Wood decided to found AMO to specifically address the larger questions of identity, culture, and organization that had emerged over the course of the Universal project. The gradual shift of OMA's focus, from strictly architectural issues to the status of Universal as a company, triggered the realization that this kind of thinking was, in the end, at least - if not more - important than the work done on the building itself. They became convinced that those issues that had informed the eventual design of the building could, freed from the pressure to generate an architectural solution, perhaps find more effective solutions in other, faster or more flexible, media; in the virtual age, architectural thinking was a resource that could be more generally applied in numerious situations, from pure research to website conception, independent of any investment in the physical.

THE END

At the end of 1999, the announcement of the America Online-Time Warner merger threw the entire entertainment industry into a state of shock. EBJ called Rem to say that the corporate landscape had - once again - changed; while Universal's acquisition of Polygram in early 1999 had created what at the time seemed like a media giant, in the current situation Universal was now too *small* to compete. EBJ had to find a partner and could not politically or financially afford to build the headquarters in the meantime. The Universal project would be put on hold, indefinitely - final confirmation, it seemed, of architecture's incapacity to respond to the new pressures of organization and instability. ■

> OMA was determined to combine seriousness of purpose, function, and material with a building on a site facing directly on to Jurassic Park.

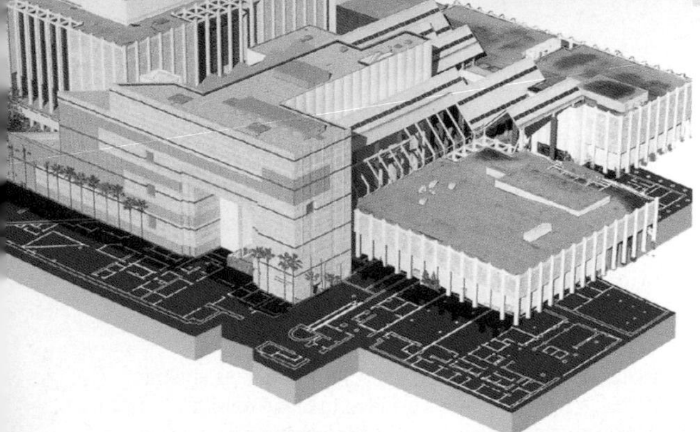

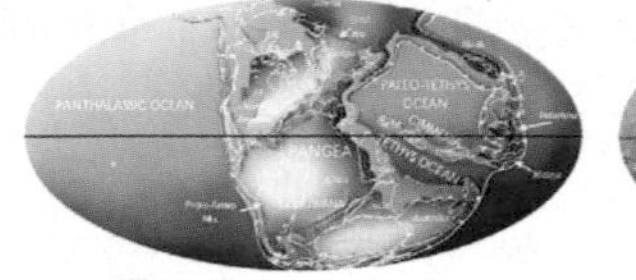

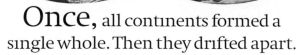

Once, all continents formed a single whole. Then they drifted apart. In LACMA we put them together again.

los angeles: 34°3'N 118°15'W

LACMA

Imagine an almost Utopian condition where the history of the arts can be told as a single and simultaneous narrative

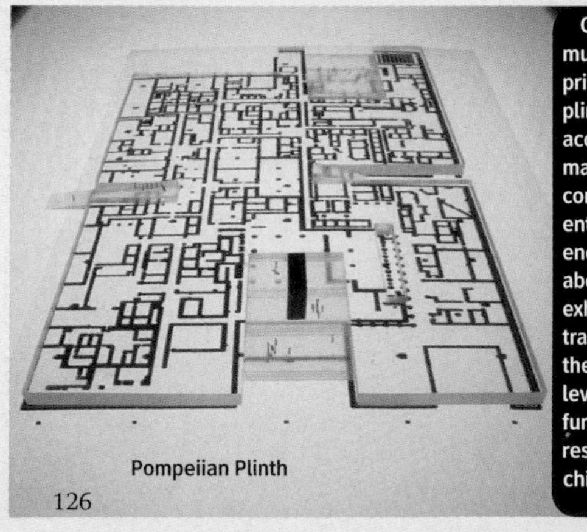

Pompeiian Plinth

On three distinct levels the museum accommodates its primary funtions: the re-used plinth of the existing buildings accomodates storage and maintenance, offices and conservatory functions - the entire "back of house." The encyclopedic plateau floats above to assemble and unite all exhibits underneath the transparent roof. In between, the public occupies the plaza level, with all its needs and functions, from stores to restaurants to auditoria and childrens' galleries.

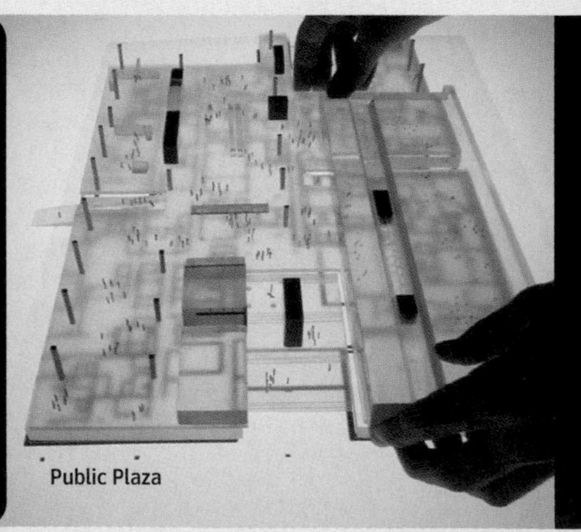

Public Plaza

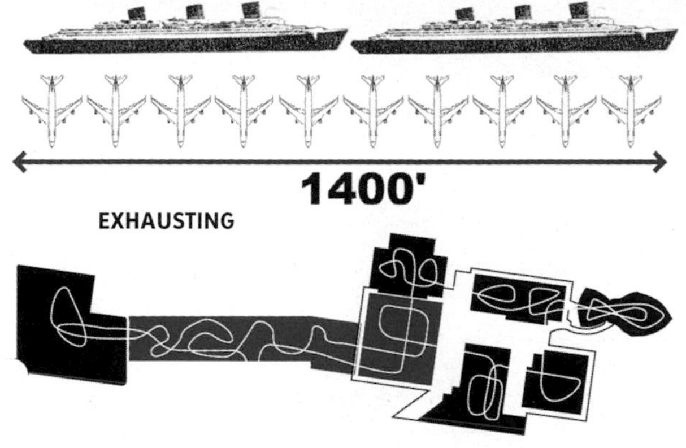

EXHAUSTING

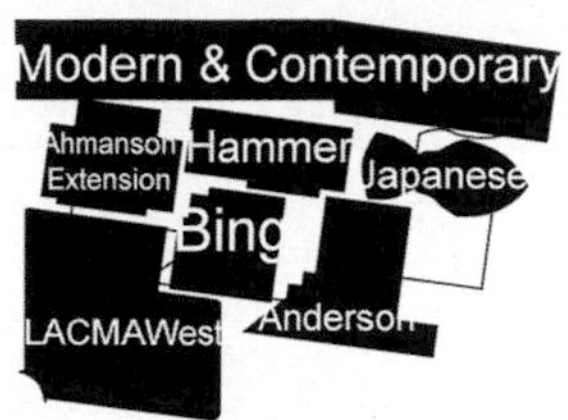

DIVIDE

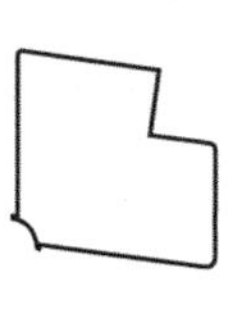

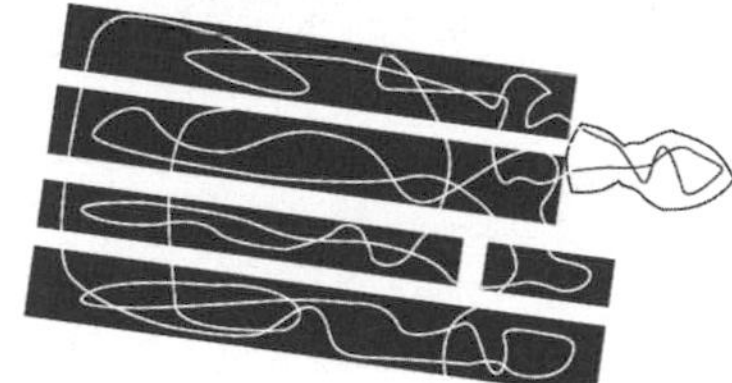

EXHAUSTIVE

CONSOLIDATE

LACMA is the only encyclopedic museum on the west coast. Its current proliferation is a microcosm of Los Angeles: distributed rather than focused, it inhibits the full unfolding of its potential, both as a museum and as an urban site.

LACMA organized a competition for its nth museum extension. The museum itself consisted of a motley collection of five pavilions standing on a plinth of storage and museum offices. Ten years earlier, LACMA had bought a defunct, listed department store; it wanted its extension to "bridge" between.

That would create a museum longer than the average airport terminal. One third of the money would have to be spent on renovating undeserving architecture. The collection would be permanently "put in its place" in the pavilions, frustrating a new interpretation of the encyclopedic. By reusing the plinth and proposing a single curatorial "field" to float above it, we discovered that the field could be divided in the four zones of the museum's collection. Sharing a single floor, new correspondences in time and new relations between the collections could be formed.

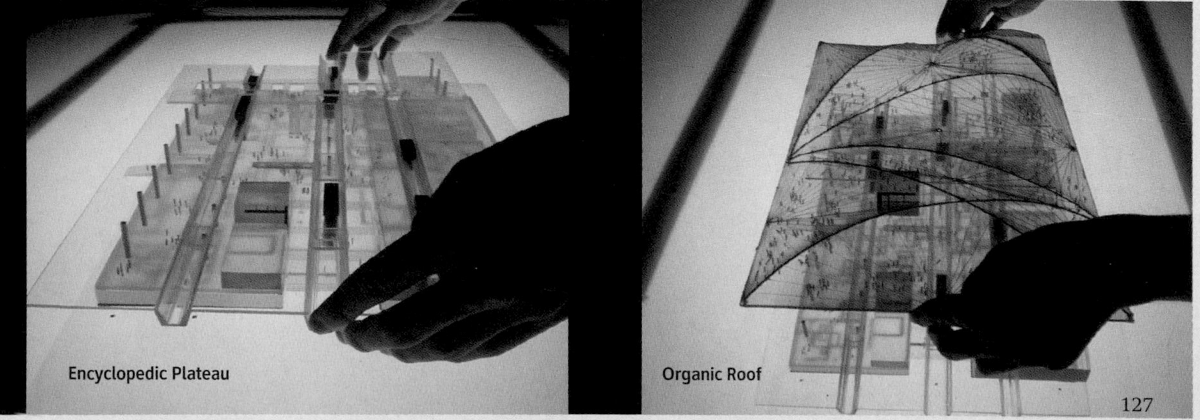

Encyclopedic Plateau

Organic Roof

COLLECTION ITEMS

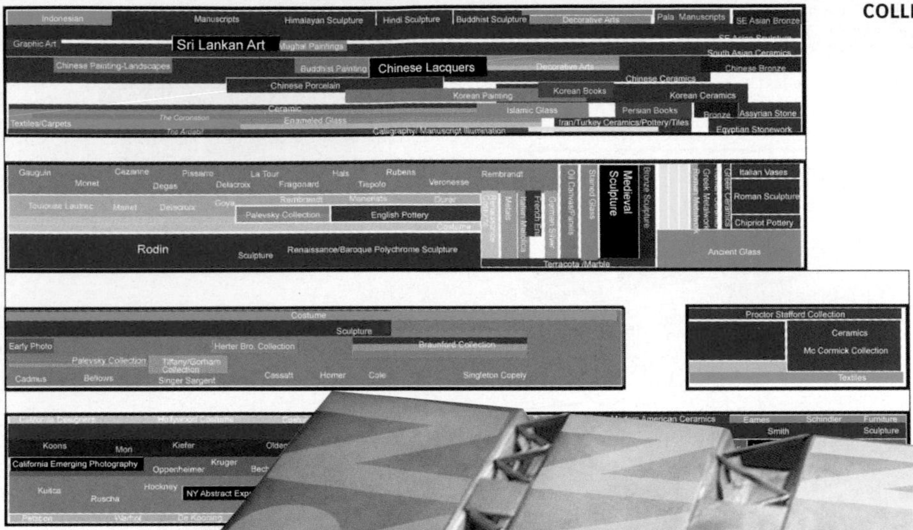

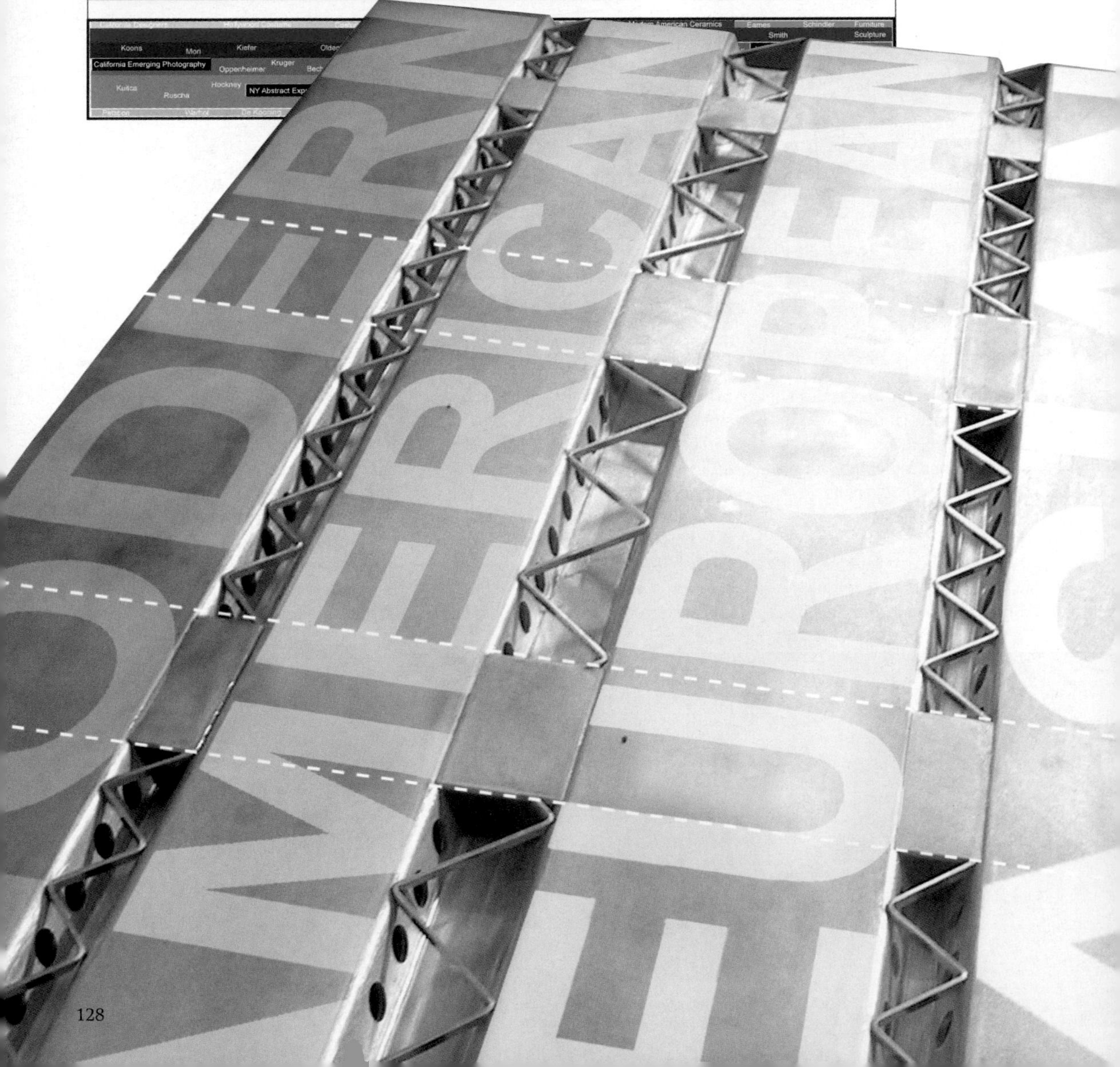

TIME CONNECTIONS

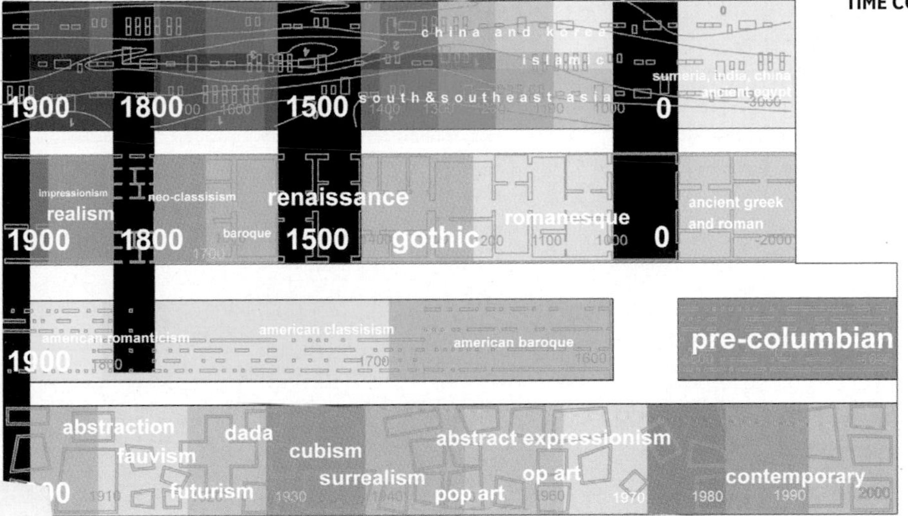

Our idea of time has become myopic: there is a hunger to experience historical depth, coincidence, the rising and waning of individual cultures and relationships. With our proposal, LACMA's collection can illustrate significant connections between cultures that have previously been presented as separate and independent.

The Asian, American, European, and Latin American Centers are arranged according to a chronological sequence on three plateaus.

Culminating in the 20th Century, and the beginning of globalization, the Modern/Contemporary Center doubles back on the fourth plateau to unite the continental streams.

In one direction, each center unfolds in complete independence; in the other, appropriate connections can be made, perspectives opened, vistas closed. The plateau allows for cross-curation and simultaneous reading: sections through time can be established to demonstrate historic convergence and rupture. Each collection can be accommodated according to its own typological character, but brought in contact with the other cultures.

Visits can be orchestrated following different logics, from slow to fast, from thorough to cursory - or simply focused on a specific continent or medium. The scale shifts from architecture to urbanism - the encyclopedic plateau becomes a museum of multiple exhibition typologies and techniques, a laboratory for the experience and (re)interpretation of history....

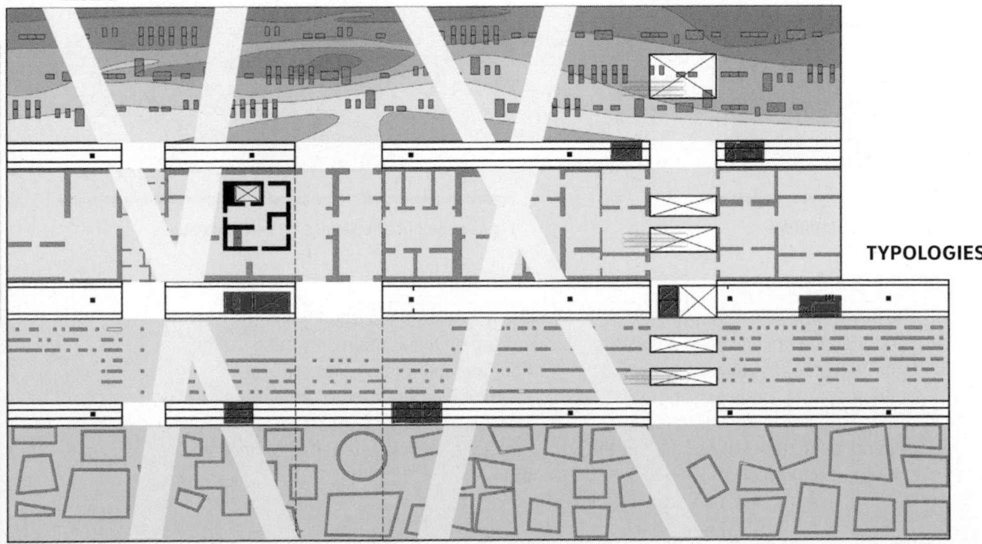

TYPOLOGIES

EXISTING

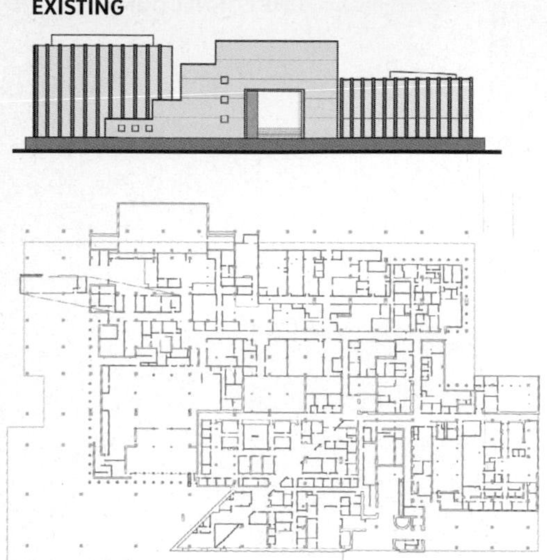

EXISTING WALLS

NEW

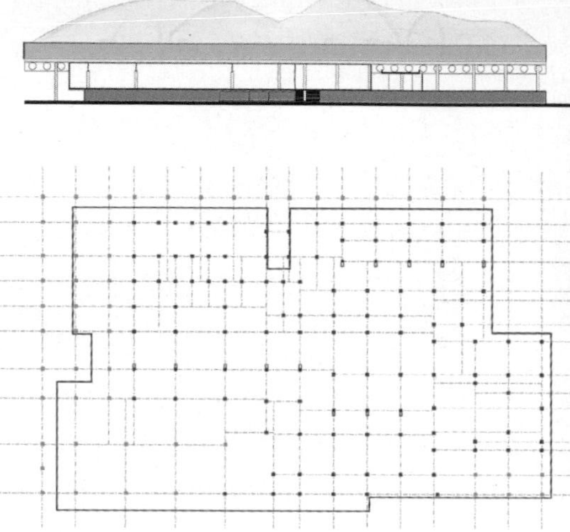

PROPOSED COLUMN GRID

We could (re)use the foundation of the plinth on the condition that the new plateau was lighter than the sum of the five pavilions that were eliminated.

Loads of existing buildings on mat foundations

Loads of proposed buildings on mat foundations

PLINTH

The newly built structure, with the curatorial plateau and the transparent light-weight roof, reduces the overall building weight of the existing situation. The new loads are delivered into the existing foundations through a carefully calibrated column grid.

The re-use of the existing buildings, shaved off to maintain only the ground floor and foundations, exploits the functional remains to accommodate storage, workshops, conservatory functions, and offices in its "Pompeiian" base.

ROOF

The roof is a partly translucent, partly transparent tensile structure supported by a cable net, spanning across seven large steel arches. Where the slopes were not steep enough for the material to stretch, we pulled it inward. The enclosure is composed of an outer PTFE membrane that provides weather protection and primary UV reduction, and an inner layer of inflated and self-supporting ETFE pillows, acting as thermal insulation.

I think in our museums we should really make sure that we do not just make spaces in order to contemplate the visual but that we create spaces where we are able to exchange and test our knowledge.

Cedric Price said that the annoying thing about art galleries is that they automatically distort time whether it is a distortion of place or whether it is a new place and not necessarily a distortion - as soon as someone looks at the painting, time is distorted.... I used to describe museums as a convenient distortion, but it must be more than that. It is nice on a wet Thursday to go to a rich museum and see 10,000 years of Egyptian history, but the second wet Thursday you are going to see it, it is different from the first - you distorted the contents of the museum through familiarity, which only occurs through going twice rather than once. So the distortion is two-fold, it is the combination of old bits of history in a convenient place for the receiver or consumer.

This whole idea is so essential to laboratories and experiments and the process itself being put forward is not so much about the selling of ideas but showing how experiments, ideas, and concepts work.

It would be nice to think about a museum architecture where you look for one thing and you find something else that you needed more.

We discussed the idea of involving all these new necessities such as retail zones but at the same time we very consciously injected laboratories

You also have in the MoMA project moments where you are in front of the work and then next you are entering the archive. So you have the virtual museum and the actual museum: in a very Deleuzian sense, what is virtual can at any moment be actualized.

When I look at LACMA, it is also about that distortion of time. The curators all accepted that the museum was time-based and thank God they never talked any more about "we have to find the best space for it."

Destabilized stability....

It really important in museums right now to rethink the museum as a laboratory of time. The exhibitions that most disturb the press and the public are the ones where you try out these anachronisms and diachronisms.

Which comes back to the laboratory.

But you are not only talking about time as an aspect of the collection or of the artwork but obviously also of the consumption of the artwork and therefore of the relationship the viewer can establish with the art work. There are spaces to experiment, there are spaces to contemplate or there is time to do all of these things, or there is no time to do any of these things.

And the responsibility towards the public is to explain to them that in the museum there is not an absence of time but a presence of time in all its contradictions.

Museums should not only be a space for paradox, contradiction, and confusion; above all, they should be spaces for time. Time for reflection and time for insecurity.

What we did for the Tate was to say that the conception of time is not always consistent - that, if you say to have time means to have a lot of time, it could also mean to have no time, to be quick....

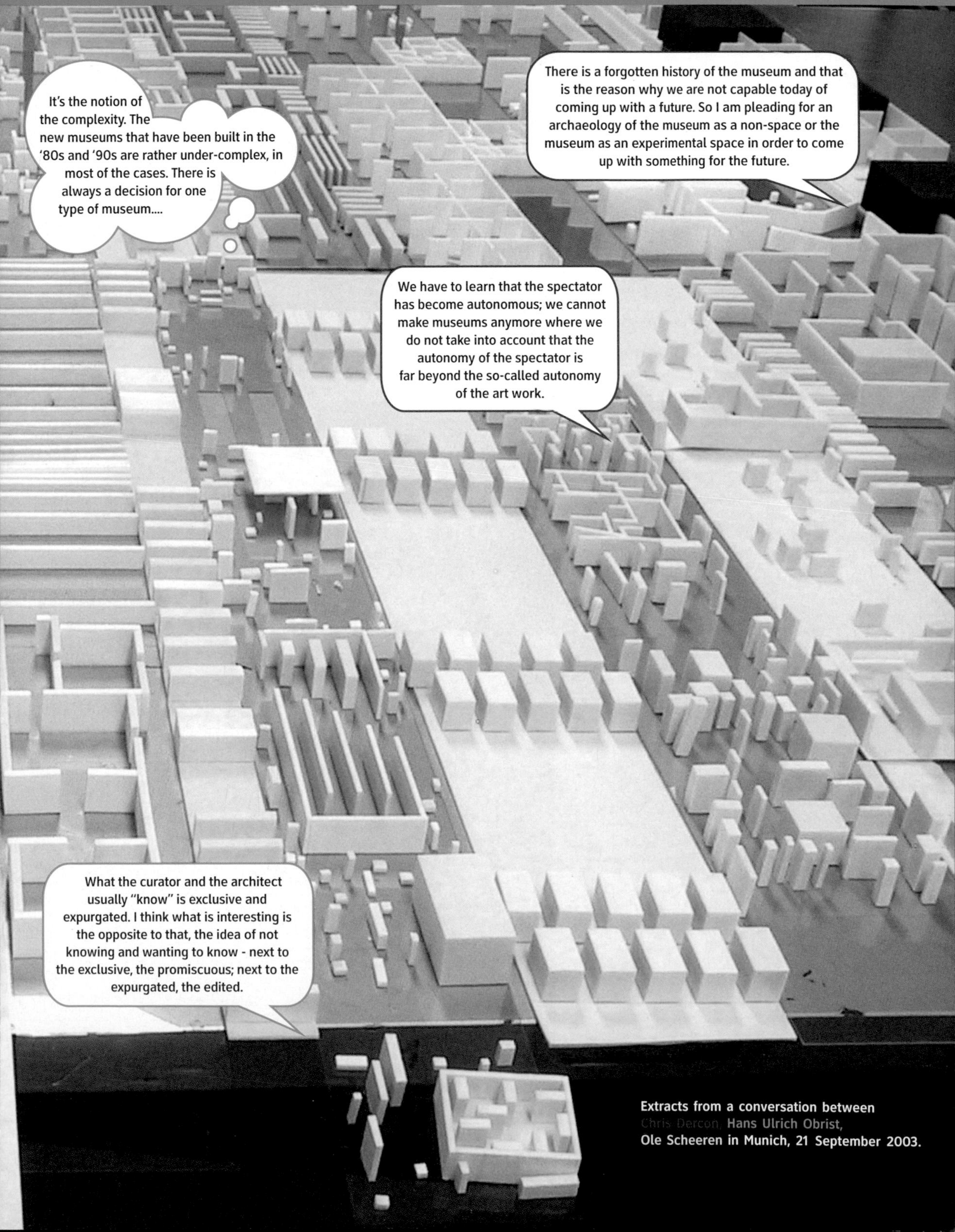

It's the notion of the complexity. The new museums that have been built in the '80s and '90s are rather under-complex, in most of the cases. There is always a decision for one type of museum....

There is a forgotten history of the museum and that is the reason why we are not capable today of coming up with a future. So I am pleading for an archaeology of the museum as a non-space or the museum as an experimental space in order to come up with something for the future.

We have to learn that the spectator has become autonomous; we cannot make museums anymore where we do not take into account that the autonomy of the spectator is far beyond the so-called autonomy of the art work.

What the curator and the architect usually "know" is exclusive and expurgated. I think what is interesting is the opposite to that, the idea of not knowing and wanting to know - next to the exclusive, the promiscuous; next to the expurgated, the edited.

Extracts from a conversation between Chris Dercon, Hans Ulrich Obrist, Ole Scheeren in Munich, 21 September 2003.

los angeles: 34°3'N 118°15'W

Taschen House

For the owner of a circular masterpiece, a guesthouse/sundeck that emerges from the lush Los Angeles hills like a monumental I-beam.

Prada Beverly Hills

Under Con

struction

los angeles 34°3'N 118°15'W

Seattle

The library represents, maybe with the prison, the last of th uncontested moral universes. The moral goodness of th library is intimately connected to the conceptual value of th book: the library is its fortress, librarians are its guardians..

BY JOSHUA RAMU

seattle: 37°47'N 122°26'W

Public

As new media emerge and gain currency, the library seems threatened, a fortress ready to be taken by a marauding hoard of technolgies. In this fairytale, the electronic becomes barbaric. Its intangible, ominous ubiquity, its uncontrollable accessibility seems to represent a loss of order, tradition, civilization. In response, the language of the library has become moralistic and defensive: its rhetoric proclaims a sense of superiority in mission, social responsibility, value...

The last decade has revealed an accelerated erosion of the Public Domain - replaced by increasingly sophisticated and entertaining forms of the Private.

The essence of the Public is that it is free.

Increasingly, public space has been replaced by accumulations of quasi-public substance that, while suggesting an open invite, actually make you pay. The library stands exposed as outdated and moralistic at the moment that it has become the last repository of the free and the public.

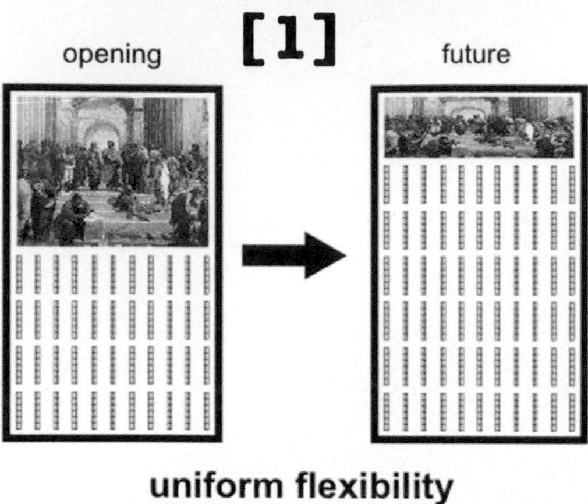

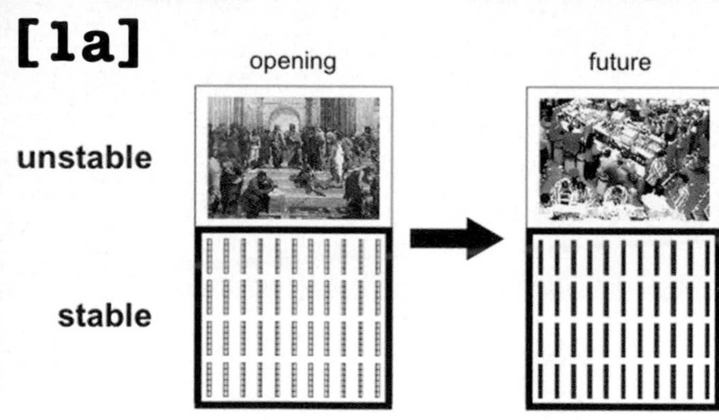

compartmentalized flexibility

[2]

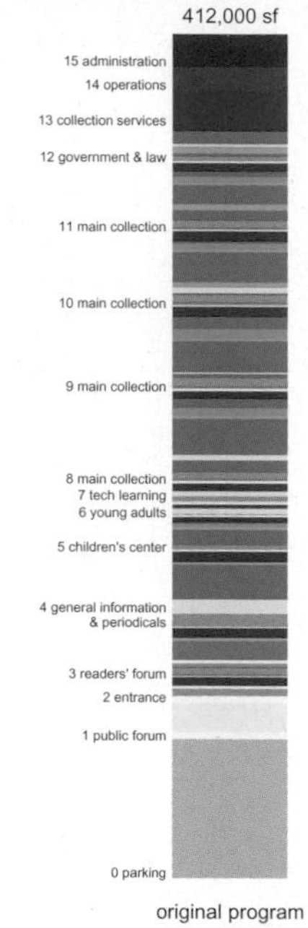

[1]

Flexibility in contemporary libraries is conceived as the creation of generic floors on which almost anything can happen. Programs are not separated, rooms or individual spaces not given unique characters. In practice, this means that bookcases define generous (though non-descript) reading areas on opening day, but, through the collection's relentless expansion, inevitably come to encroach on the public space. Ultimately, in this form of flexibility, the library strangles the very attractions that differentiate it from other information resources.

[1a]

Instead of its current ambiguous flexibility, the library could cultivate a more refined approach by organizing itself into spatial compartments, each dedicated to, and equipped for, specific duties. Tailored flexibility remains possible within each compartment, but without the threat of one section hindering the others.

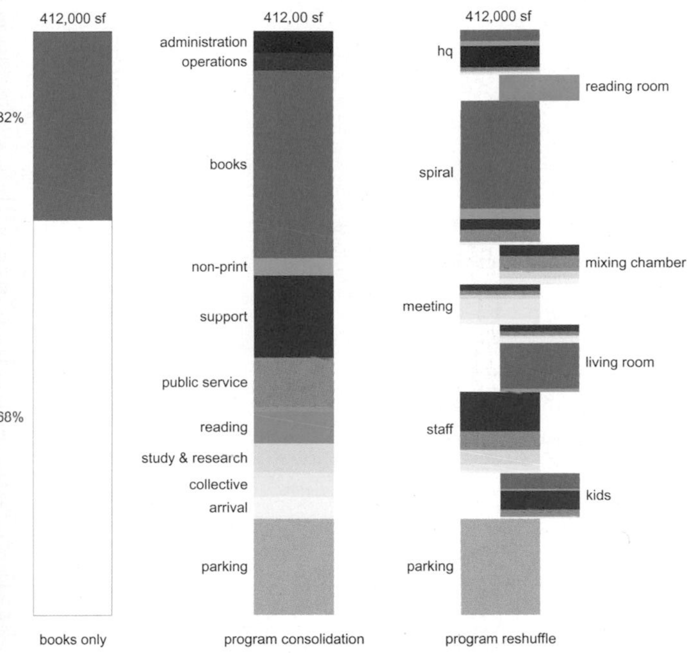

[2]

Our first operation was to "comb" and consolidate the library's apparently ungovernable proliferation of programs and media. By combining like with like, we identified programmatic clusters - five of stability, and four of instability.

[3]

Each platform is a programmatic cluster that is architecturally defined and equipped for maximum, dedicated performance. Because each platform is designed for a unique purpose, their size, flexibility, circulation, palette, structure, and MEP vary.

[3a]

The spaces in between the platforms function as trading floors where librarians inform and stimulate, where the interface between the different platforms is organized - spaces for work, interaction and play.

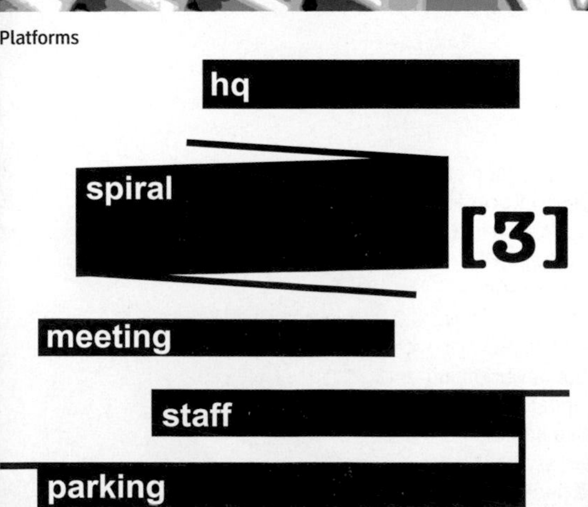

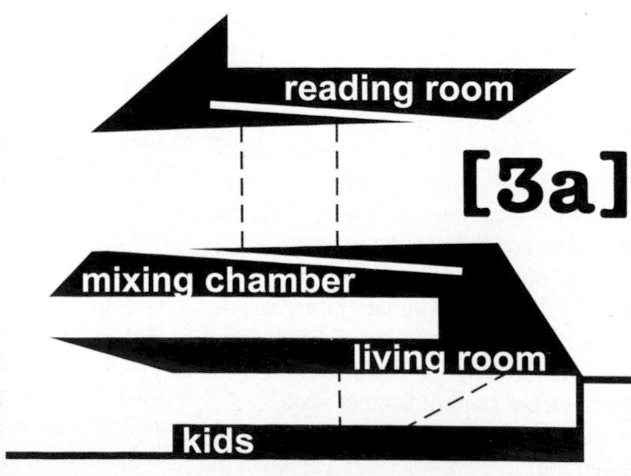

[4]

By genetically modifying the superposition of floors in the typical American high rise, a building emerges that is at the same time sensitive (the geometry provides shade or unusual quantities of daylight where desirable), contextual (each side reacts differently to specific urban conditions or desired views), iconic.

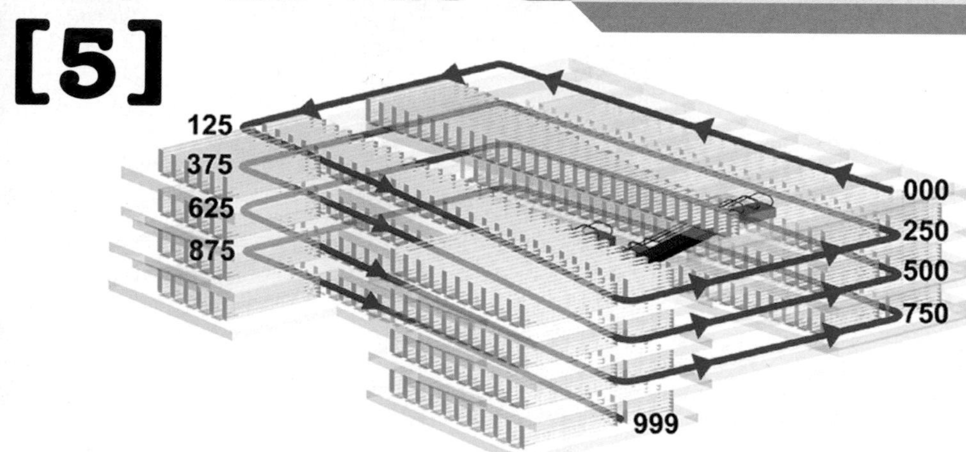

[5]

The problem of traditional library organization is flatness. Departments are organized according to floor plans. Each floor is discreet; the unpredictable fits of growth and contraction in certain sections are, theoretically, contained within a single floor.
In 1920, the Seattle Public Library had no classification for Computer Science - by 1990 the section had exploded.
As collections unpredictably swell, materials are dissociated from their categories. Excess materials are put in the basement, moved to off-site storage, or become squatters of another, totally unrelated department.
The Book Spiral implies a reclamation of the much-compromised Dewey Decimal System. By arranging the collection in a continuous ribbon - running from "000" to "999" - the subjects form a coexistence that approaches the organic; each evolves relative to the others, occupying more or less space on the ribbon, but never forcing a rupture. For Seattle, the Spiral's 6,233 bookcases are guaranteed to house 780,000 books upon opening, with the flexibility to add 1,450,000 books in the future (without adding another bookcase).

[6]

The traditional library presents the visitor with an infernal matrix of materials, technologies, "specialists." It is an often demoralizing process - a trail of tears through dead-end sections, ghost departments, and unexplained absences.

The Book Spiral liberates the librarians from the burden of managing ever-increasing masses of material. Newly freed, they reunite in a circle of concentrated expertise. The Mixing Chamber is an area of maximum librarian-patron interaction, a trading floor for information orchestrated to fulfill an essential (now neglected) need for expert interdisciplinary help.

The Mixing Chamber consolidates the library's cumulative human and technological intelligence: the visitor is surrounded by information sources.

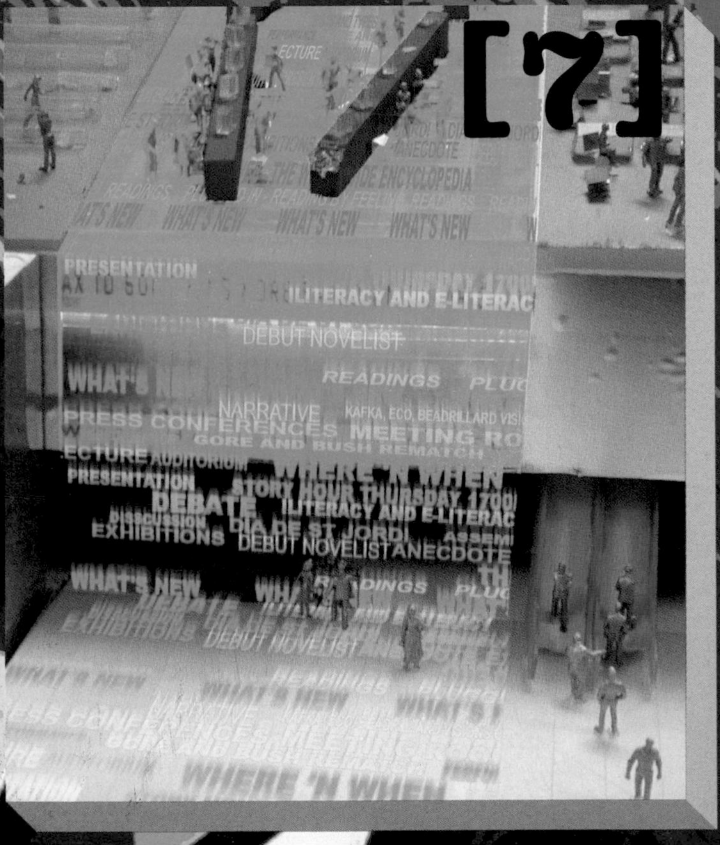

[7]

In the typical library, information remains concealed in opaque containers - librarians behind desks and rows of closed books. By releasing the librarians from their seated compounds, we open one of those containers. Their liberation is emphasized by foot haloes - a system that lights the floor beneath librarians within the Mixing Chamber.

An Information Flow reveals the otherwise hidden processes of the library and instigates new movements. Dynamic, billboard-sized screens show the latest books arriving in the building, the location of unused computer workstations, library member chat messages, event information (lectures, movies, films), local and international news, as well as custom content introduced by the librarians. Through the Information Flow, librarians become intellectual sports stars.

Contractors' drawing

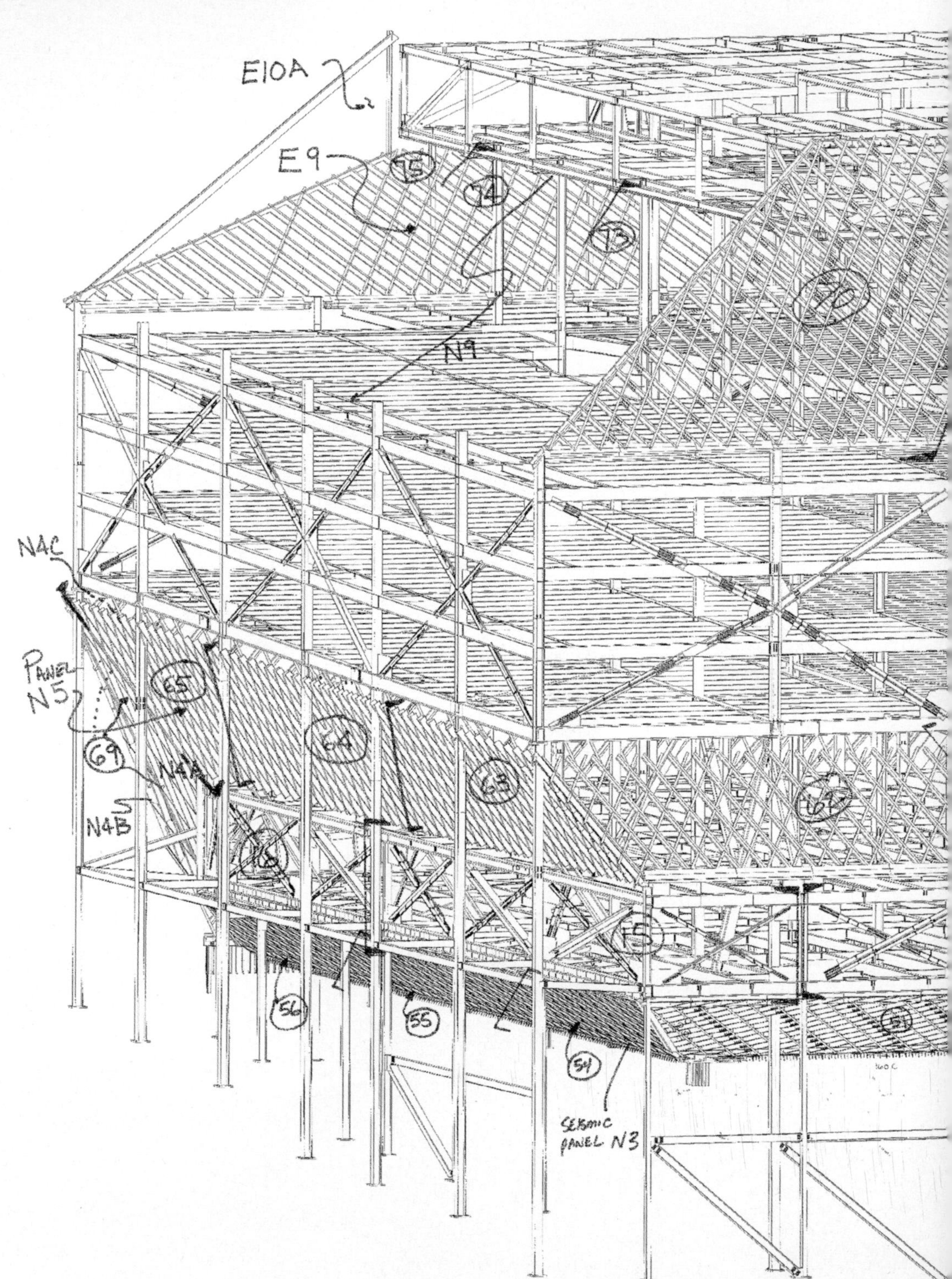

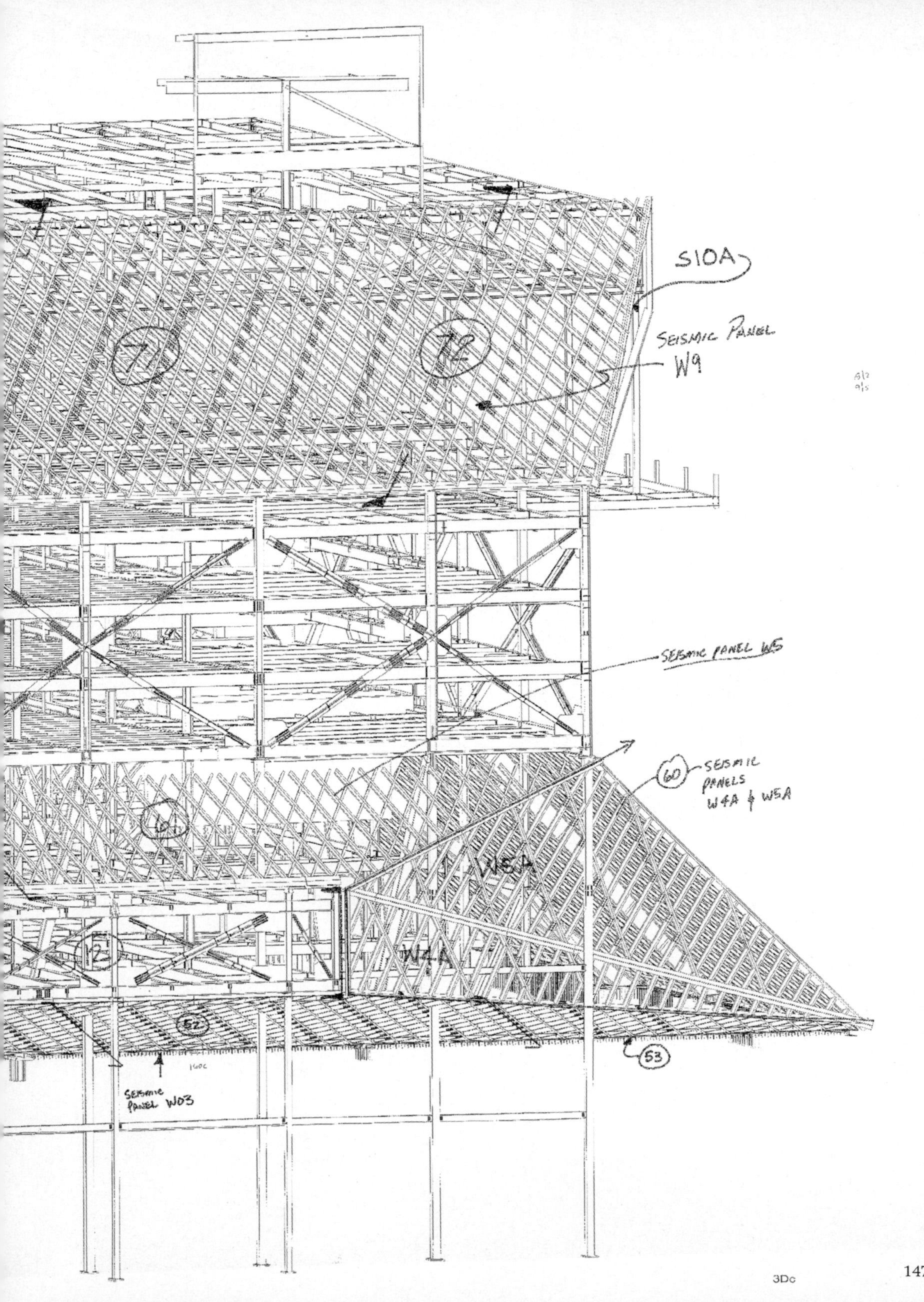
S10A
SEISMIC PANEL
W9
SEISMIC PANEL W5
60
SEISMIC
PANELS
W4A & W5A
W5A
W4A
52
53
SEISMIC
PANEL W03
3Dc

NESS CRANE

Seattle, exteriors

Seattle, interior of the reading room

Interview with Denise Scott Brown & Robert Venturi

Re-learning from Las Vegas

Learning from the existing landscape is a way of being revolutionary for an architect.- Learning from Las Vegas, 1972

INTERVIEW BY REM KOOLHAAS & HANS ULRICH OBRIST

: I discovered *Learning from Las Vegas* in 1972 as a Cornell student. For me, the book was both inspiration and threat: your work constituted a manifesto for the shift from substance to sign precisely at the moment that I was beginning, in what would become *Delirious New York*, to decipher the impact of substance on culture. Paradoxically, I sensed in your book a pair of architects who, in spite of their love of architecture, were horribly fascinated by its opposite - while I was becoming fascinated by architecture, coming *from* its opposite.

: On a related note, I was wondering about the fact that after your text, *Complexity and Contradiction in Architecture*, it's very difficult to find another manifesto about architecture. Rem was noticing that since then, most manifestoes were about the city.

RK: The point is not that the manifestoes are about the city, but that there are no manifestoes - only books about cities that *imply* manifestoes. So after *Complexity and Contradiction*, *Learning from Las Vegas* was the first of a trend: after your text there have been books about New York, Los Angeles, Singapore - we are currently doing one on Lagos, Nigeria - but nothing directly about architecture anymore. How do you interpret this? How have you, as the author of the "last" manifesto on architecture, operated in the 30-year interval since then?

: Our approach, currently, is one which really relates to what we have been saying all along, but says it in a different way. The essential element of architecture for our time is no longer space, it's no longer abstract form in industrial drag; the essential architectural element is iconography. But people today don't even know what iconography means. I wrote a book on iconography and, in America, it has been reviewed only once - by Martin Filler in the *New York Review of Books*.

Essentially, I say that it is time to learn from the architecture that preceded 20th century aesthetic abstraction. Last week we made a trip to the Villa Savoye; I adore it, but it's no longer relevant to me for its abstraction (though it *is* for its spatial layering). We are increasingly revisiting the iconographic tradition: Egyptian hieroglyphics on pylons are like billboards; early Byzantine or Christian basilicas, like those of Ravenna, have interiors teeming with signage-we call it high art, but really it's advertising art to teach the illiterate populace Christian theology; the great murals of the Baroque period are essentially counter-Reformation advertising by the Roman Catholic church, and so on.

Of course, another great example of iconographic architecture of today is the American commercial vernacular, which is just as relevant in the early 21st century as was the American industrial vernacular in the early 20th century. Le Corbusier was inspired by American Midwestern grain silos; Mies van der Rohe built buildings which were essentially industrial lofts via their vocabulary and their spatial systems. Then, the American industrial vernacular was the inspiration; today, the American commercial vernacular should be the inspiration. And therefore, signs are very important: they are the equivalent of the signs in the Byzantine and Counter-Reformation churches. That is what is relevant.

Otherwise, architecture to me is dead. *A bas* space-as-God with industrial iconography in the Post-Industrial Age: remember this is the Information Age (as well as the Electronic Age) and therefore signage is relevant, not industrial rocaille! Postmodernism was horrible, but the post-postmodernism of today, which revives a historical industrial vocabulary, is doing the equivalent of reviving a Renaissance historical style, because the Industrial Revolution is as historical now as is the Renaissance. Everyone else knows we are in the Post-Industrial Age,

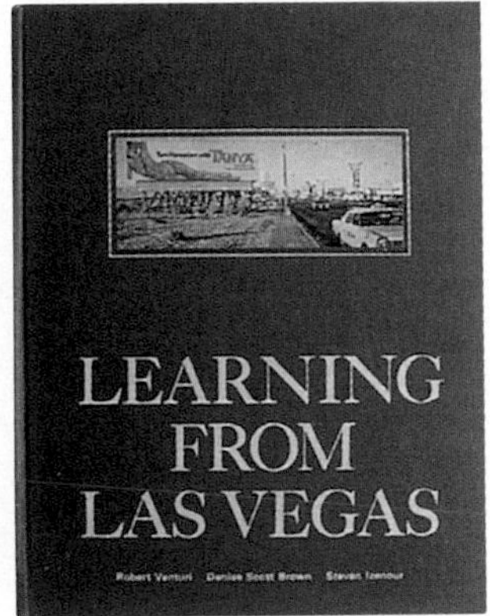

the Information Age - in an age when architecture should reject abstract form and promote electronic iconography! The pediment of a Greek temple has statues on it, which are artistically beautiful but also instructive. You can go on and on with examples of that sort; it was only in the 20th century that they got rid of iconographic communication - appropriately at the time. So I am saying that architecture stinks right now and that we have the answers!

LEARNING
FROM
LAS VEGAS
Robert Venturi Denise Scott Brown Steven Izenour

: There is an interesting issue here: in the name of what is happening and what is relevant, you are proclaiming the death of architecture: a shift from form to iconography which you say is totally recognizable. But how do you account for the enormous popular appeal of form-making, of architects who are putting entire cities on the map by doing sculpture?

: We're not proclaiming the death of architecture but its rebirth: we're proclaiming the death of sculpture as architecture. We're also saying: let's not forget that architecture, fundamentally, is shelter, and not sculpture. Abstract Expressionism in the mid-century was a wonderful and vital invention, but we think it's not relevant or significant now - especially as architecture.

: But are we not in a period in which a number of approaches that have "died" seem to have a surprisingly robust afterlife?

: Yes, but we forget that in the 1920s, the Ecole des Beaux Arts architecture and the Art Deco style were very popular. At the time of the Villa Savoye, at the time that Aalto, Gropius, *et. al.* were working, there were other architects who were doing what most schools in America were teaching: the architecture of the Ecole des Beaux Arts. What's thriving today as seen in the journals is perhaps the equivalent of the Ecole des Beaux Arts. The irony is amazing. And the Ecole des Beaux Arts represented the end of a period. I'm putting it rather strongly, but I think I'm right.

LAS VEGAS II

: Recently we have been comparing Las Vegas as it was in 1972 and as it is now in 2000, as a response to both the methods and conclusion of your book. When you look at the change in scale of the city between these two dates, not only in terms of area but in other categories like population, birth, marriages, personal income, hotel rooms, etc., the development is unbelievable: the archetype of unreality - the *city-as-mirage* you described in LFLV - has, through sheer mass, become a real city. So Las Vegas seems to be one of the few cities to become paradigmatic twice in thirty years: from a city at the point of becoming virtual in 1972 to an almost irrevocably substantial condition in 2000.

: Three times, if you start with desert and say forty years. Most cities change paradigms - many European cities began as Roman camps, then became Medieval towns, and eventually Modern cities.

: Yes, but that is over centuries, not in the course of decades. [But] when we were interested in Las Vegas twenty-five years ago, when it represented iconographic sprawl, our interest was clearly daring. This is hard to believe today because Las Vegas has become scenographic like Disneyland.

: But isn't it still daring? One of the paradoxes of Las Vegas is that in spite of its thirty years, it's still not taken seriously.

: Is it *still* a taboo to take Las Vegas seriously?

: The critics seem to take the present Las Vegas more seriously than they did the 1960s Las Vegas.

: How have you learned from Las Vegas in your own work?

: It's affected all our work: if we do a shingled beach cottage in Nantucket, it has learned from Las Vegas. In a life science complex we're designing right now, we call the place where three buildings meet the "meeting of the minds." Thinking of Las Vegas, we suggested that if you were to shine a >

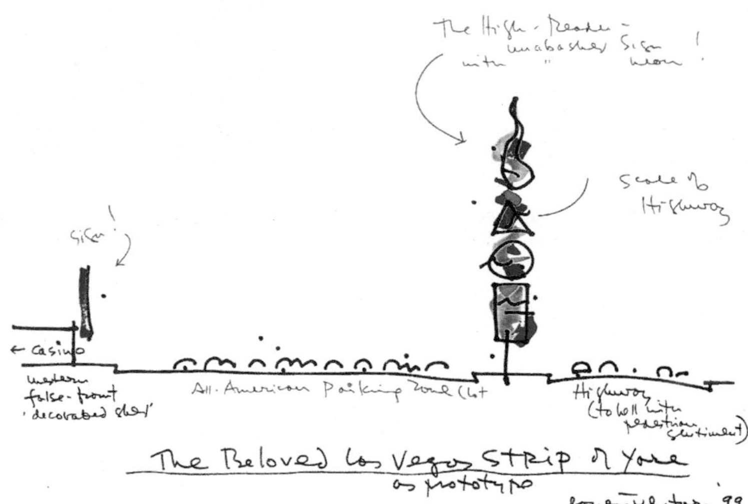

bright light full circle at that spot, the parts of the buildings it would hit should all be areas for communication with passersby - exhibition or expression sites of some type.

: But how much have you been able to engage directly with the commercial conditions you described in Las Vegas? Are you interested in doing commercial projects, in working with developers?

: It is sad we have seldom been able to get commercial work, even though we have been interested in it and respectful of it for a long time. We are considered highfalutin, having worked at Harvard, Yale, and Princeton, and for the governments of Britain, Japan, and France. That's an ironical sociological reason for our being excluded.

: Do you think that having formulated the manifesto for Las Vegas has disqualified you from participating in its elaboration?

: I think there are interesting aspects of developer psychology to be understood. Basically, I believe many developers are building to the glory of God. They have something beyond economics they're trying to achieve. This makes them not always rational. It's difficult to work with a client if you don't know where their logic lies, and doubly difficult if their intense passion and commitment makes them want to be the designer - if they want to do the best building in the world, they may want to be the architect themselves and may not really want you.

: You think that is the main point?

: I think, for some developers, that is the problem. Others are afraid that, because we are professors and have written books, we will not meet the budget. A third kind are afraid we may be brighter than they are. On the other hand, working with a bright developer can be great fun; compared with public institutions and government they are adventurous and their decision-making processes are refreshingly crisp.

: I remember a very ironic session in Paris over ten years ago, where we were both presenting hotels for Euro Disney. It was an incredibly painful moment: they had invited a number of architects to come back from their holidays at breakneck speed and put them all in one room - Gehry, Portzamparc, Nouvel, you, myself. There we realized that certain sites had two architectural projects: whoever came first could put their model in the overall model, while whoever came later had to find some other place for theirs-sometimes awkwardly on top, sometimes as neighbor.

You presented a hotel that was opposite our design, but we were both immediately disqualified, even though in that room we were probably the ones who best understood what Disney was about, what a theme park was about - the only people in the room who had actually looked at Disney and its real implications. But instinctively for the developers, and for Eisner (who was then supported by Michael Graves), we were out - the first sentence after the presentation was Bob Stern's immortal phrase: "I think the Europeans are endangering the idea of Disney." And it was not simply a matter of authority, but of our architectures: at that point, they could only see our work as an exhibition of modernism, and so (un)spectacular that it could not work, instead of an exhibition of form, and that was Gehry.

You were very strict in terms of the rules of Las Vegas: a casino is a huge wall with very little articulation except at the top and the bottom. For me this presented a very interesting moment, since your position was sandwiched between demonstrative modernism on the one side and demonstrative

"I believe that many developers are building to the glory of God. They have something beyond economics they're trying to achieve."

postmodern form on the other.

: Some architecture is easy to like. Ours frightens some people.

: We should mention an essay we recently wrote, called "Las Vegas After Its Classic Age," which evolved from the BBC's doing a program on Las Vegas and inviting Denise and me to be interviewed there. It's an analysis of the Las Vegas of now, the scenographic/Disneyland Las Vegas of now compared with the commercial strip Las Vegas of then. The comparative analysis of what was then and what is now is fascinating; the evolution is most significant.

: Do you still study commercial phenomena through your work?

: We do considerable research through our work, but it's applied research for projects. Bob and I have always done "basic" research by traveling around, looking and learning. And, of course, our studios were our research. Now that I do much of my shopping by mail order, I do "content analysis" of catalogues, viewing them as an anthropologist, watching for trends. I shop as a pedestrian on Main Street in Manayunk and in Geneva - otherwise, not at all.

An interesting recent development is airport shops. I am amused by how long it took airport programmers to work out that the best place to sell is where people are *waiting* for planes - not in the ticketing hall but along the concourse and as they wait at the embarkation gate. When you don't have architects around, it seems creativity takes a long time to blossom. But the notion of shopping while waiting for something else is developing rapidly now.

You also see what are called "profit centers." For example, hotel rooms today are full of things you pay extra money for: food in the refrigerator, phone calls, faxes... These amount to shopping in the room: goods pursue you into the bathroom, even into your bed. It's another aspect of the integration of shopping into life outside the store.

: You said something interesting: that if architects are not involved, creativity takes a longer time to develop. That's a very confident position. I would almost say the opposite: that it takes longer if architects are involved - or even that it may never happen if architects are involved.

: I am a great critic of architects. I feel many architects don't think broadly enough to design their projects well - that's a strong criticism. On the other hand, consider traffic lights: how long did it take before someone realized that you could go beyond plain red, yellow and green - that in the red light you could have an arrow to the right, that you may not need the yellow light? I think it took about fifty years from the invention of traffic lights to when they began to use different forms of communication through the lights. I suspect that, in focused problems of object design or space organization, architects are trained to be creative, to think beyond the box. However, they aren't educated to do that kind of innovative thinking for retail; that's an economist's job. In urban planning architects frequently lead the team because their training makes them good coordinators of things and ideas. But their lack of knowledge and their bias toward the physical may make them apply inappropriate ideas or coordinate the wrong things.

BACKGROUND

: Through your work on Las Vegas, as well as in *Complexity and Contradiction in Architecture*, you've created a conceptual space for a *possible* architecture: after those books, that space - the space in which architecture could be practiced - was different. How do you think that space has been exploited?

: What we have done has allowed many people to think differently, therefore to do things differently. Over and over, people have told us that suddenly they could be themselves....

: Or they could be yourselves.

: Well, the best ones thought it let them be *them*selves. And of course, it opened doors for us too, but other kinds than it did for many architects, because of where our interests lie. For example, our love of Pop Art. On first seeing the Las Vegas Strip, we felt an intense shiver - whether of hate or love, it was strongly affective and exciting.

: Which interest came first, Pop Art or Las Vegas?

: Pop Art; it was Denise who introduced me to Las Vegas but my work before that shows a love of the ordinary, the vernacular and signs.

: When Bob and I were teaching together in the early 1960s, I was busy photographing pedestrian retail strips in Philadelphia. In 1965 and 1966 I took hundreds of pictures of Los Angeles and Las Vegas roadside environments. But my interest in popular culture and everyday architecture goes back a lot further - I was interested in them in Africa in the 1940s and in England in the 1950s, before there was Pop Art.

: And were you aware in the fifties of the things people like Richard Hamilton were doing? >

"Many architects are afraid to acknowledge what they like; they like what they're supposed to like."

: Yes, I knew them when I was at the AA, and was part of a small group of students who were questioning 1950s architecture and heading towards ideas later defined as the New Brutalism. In America, as Pop Art developed, Bob felt the artists were leading, that they were ahead of the architects; but for me, given my English and European point of reference - Brutalism, the Independent Group, and later Team 10 and the demise of CIAM - the architects were leading.

: Did you know Lawrence Alloway?

: No, but I knew the Smithsons. My interest in their ideas derived in part from having grown up in Africa, where the culture that dominated, the high culture, came from a different country, almost a different planet. We had our local actuality and we had our rules from overseas. Much Southern African artistic thought and activity revolves around the gap between these two. I had a Dutch Jewish refugee art teacher in Johannesburg who told us: "you won't be creative unless you paint what you see around you." What she meant was the life of Africans in the streets of Johannesburg. So in my background, from childhood, was the idea that creativity depended on looking at what's around you.

: Which you applied to Las Vegas.

: Absolutely! Mine is an African view of Las Vegas.

: I have the impression of having been corrupted by Denise Scott Brown! It started for me with knowing Denise and being corrupted.

: In England in the early 1950s, the Smithsons and other members of the Independent Group were saying the same thing: look at the street life of the London East End. They referred to a sociological study of the East End, made shortly after WWII. In America in 1958, when I studied urban sociology with Herbert Gans, he had surveyed the West End of Boston and moved to Levittown, and he listed the London East End study as class reading. Our views on architecture derive as much from these social views, and their development during the 1960s social movements, as from Pop Art.

: And I was influenced by my Socialist mother - Socialists were rare in America at that time. My father was an immigrant who, I learned a while back from an architectural historian, at the age of 28 commissioned a fruit store for himself designed by a leading architect of Philadelphia of the time, then later had a famous architect design his warehouse. My father knew many of the architects in Philadelphia, but he had never finished high school, being too poor. My mother didn't either because her family was also poor, but she became a specialist in the works of Bernard Shaw and the Fabian Socialists. And I never went to a public school (that is, a state school) because you had to pledge allegiance to the American flag and my mother was a pacifist. So I had a very interesting childhood, both intellectual and ideological, in the good sense of that word.

: I was aware of African popular arts as contrasted with folk arts during my childhood; for example, the traditional African method of covering a gourd with beads whose colors and patterns convey messages, was applied to Coca-Cola bottles as well.

: Without Africa and socialism you might never have looked at Las Vegas! And were you also influenced by, or did you know personally, people like Warhol?

: No, we met him several times, but did not know him or the people around him personally. But we loved their art, Warhol, Ruscha,....

: That is interesting because, coming from an art context, I discovered *Learning from Las Vegas* through Dan Graham. And I saw a link to Ruscha's artist books - the gasoline stations, the streets....

: You're right - in fact we visited Ruscha while we were doing the Las Vegas studio. He invited the students to his studio in Los Angeles. Then we made films and photographs of the Las Vegas Strip based on his deadpan photography of Los Angeles architecture and urbanism. And I included his parking lots in an article on Pop Art and planning theory published in 1969.

: We have a Ruscha mural on one of our buildings in California, the museum in La Jolla. It's wonderful: it's a seascape with galleons and it says on it: "brave men run in our family!"

EVOLUTION

: To come back to the issue of conceptual space: how have you used the conceptual space you have opened in your own work?

: I'm not sure what you mean by conceptual space.

: I think you mean a metaphorical territory - and in our case, a broadened territory - in which thought and eventually action (design) can take place. I feel our interpretations have opened the way for thinking differently. Architects no longer needed to be intellectually or artistically constrained by modernism. Once the "way" was opened - and notice my metaphor contains movement - where did architects go? Some used the conceptual space to imitate us, or worse, to imitate their misunderstanding of us. How did we use it?

Las Vegas II (2000) according to Venturi and Scott Brown:
Iconography inflated to a new scale

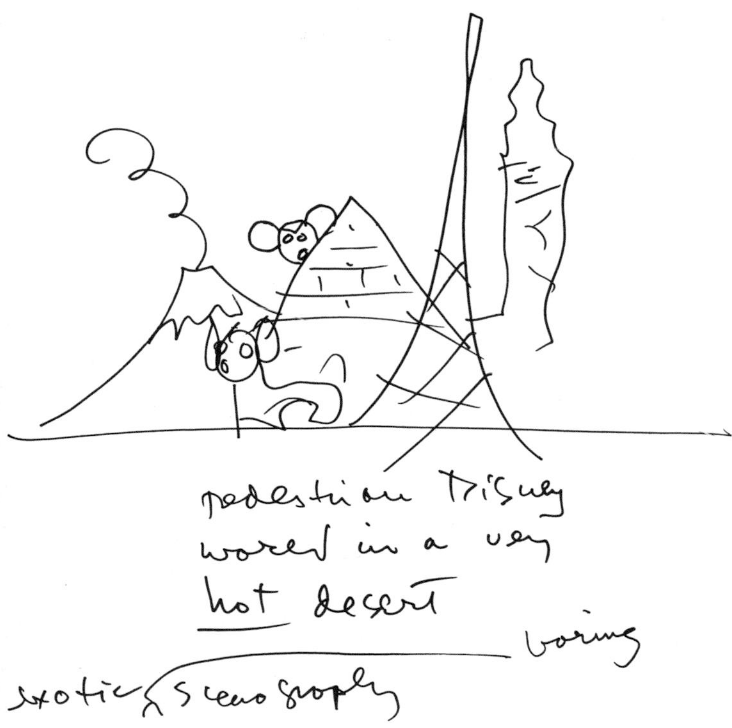

pedestrian Disney world in a very
hot desert
boring
exotic scenography

: Well, we used it to acknowledge architecture as shelter, to acknowledge the validity of the generic loft, and our belief that in architecture form need not follow function but must accommodate function: most buildings should not be designed like a glove that fits every finger exactly, but like a mitten that allows "wiggle-room" - flexibility - inside. So we're talking about the generic loft building, we're talking about iconographic, ornamental appliqué, we're talking about the American commercial vernacular as inspiration that we can learn from, as well as learning from the Byzantine, Ancient Egyptian, and other architectural traditions. And above all, because we're artists, we learn from what we like, what we find we like, or, as the expression goes, what turns us on. Many architects are afraid to acknowledge what they like; they like what they are supposed to like. But we enjoy analyzing what turns us on, because if we are sensitive to our time, what turns us on will be relevant.

Our approach is one of not trying to be heroic, not being necessarily revolutionary. It was often appropriate to be heroic and revolutionary in the early days of modernism, but there are also moments when evolutionary change makes sense. That is why we love starting from what's here, from the commercial vernacular of the American highway and such - from the ordinary and the conventional that can be relevant. So there are moments to be revolutionary and moments to be evolutionary. For instance, Le Corbusier was wrong - thank goodness it didn't happen - when he proposed and made drawings for the remaking of all Paris, except for the Ile de la Cité and the Ile Saint Louis, into a park with his slabs filtered through it. So, we are on the side of the non-heroic, evolutionary, because we love loving things. I have this statement which begins with "We love" and lists five hundred things: Beethoven, ketchup, Michelangelo, bungalows, billboards, craft art.... Loving a wide range of things in an unsnobbish way is something architects of today don't do. Viva tolerance concerning multicultures and multiple tastes. Viva pragmatism! *A bas* Utopia!

: In your advocacy of the American commercial vernacular, how do you distinguish yourself from simplistic American triumphalism? You are an immigrant, and the son of immigrants who were socialists and highly political, and yet your discourse - or so it can sound - is that everyone should be inspired by American commercialism. What have poor Europeans now to do with American commercialism? Or is there an equivalent source of inspiration - for instance Stalinist architecture, which I find fascinating, the Moscow metro being for me one of the absolute paradigms of public space?

: We are fascinated by the Stalin Allee and by its resemblance to certain parts of Miami Beach. But I don't think commercialism is only American. The dense aggregation of buildings around market places is typical of medieval towns as well as American cities. Rentable space huddles tightly up to European churches and town halls. Some of the most beautiful cities, Venice for example, were highly mercantile.

As for American triumphalism, doesn't every nation have a form of triumphalism? How many nations sincerely believe they invented democracy? But we don't have much connection with American triumphal commercialism. The large corporations pass us by, and they aren't the subject of our thinking about the everyday commercial landscape. European architects think Levittown is part of large-scale corporate America, but >

"Current Las Vegas is less relevent than old Las Vegas: it went from commercial strip to Disneyland."

Levitt was more a merchant builder than a global giant. Except for the gas station or the ad on the billboard, the urban phenomena we examine are not corporate. The Las Vegas that fascinated us was more local than global.

: But the larger issue is that your books now declare that iconography should be derived from a particular - American - source. In the absence of that source, what should be the inspiration?

: We were dismissing method not content. Perhaps it's not for the architect to designate the specifics of the content of architecture: that perhaps derives from societal culture in general. The architect of the Pantheon did not compose the graphic inscription on the pediment, the architect-builders of the Egyptian pylons did not specify the content of the hieroglyphics, etc., and in the Information Age the informational and decorative content that is to dominate form and space and compose architectural expression should not derive from the architect. It is also significant that the electronic iconography of our time is not permanent but flexible/changing: the architects decide the compositional position, shapes and scales of the signs that constitute the architecture, but the content, the evolving content, should be chosen by others. Also, when you make analogies, there are inevitable inconsistencies: most of the European architects of the modernist period who came to America - Gropius, Le Corbusier, Breuer, Mies van der Rohe - employed the American industrial vocabulary that derived from capitalist-oriented industry - while many of these architects were socially-oriented, if not Socialist, in their approach to architecture.

: But it's not these inconsistencies that I am remarking on. I am asking what a European could do if he or she were to adopt your theories.

: Many things: first, learn from your own environment. We learned from ours in America; I learned from mine in Africa (and applied the lessons in America). Yet, because some things are global and because we do face some similar problems, you may feel some American phenomena are precursors to things to happen in Europe and elsewhere; you may learn how to do them better, not to make the mistakes we've made. As for other sources of learning, we've found ours in Japan, ancient Egypt, and the whole history of Europe - remember "from Rome to Las Vegas"? We basically believe you can learn from everything.

: I would say that the influence we've had has generally been bad because of misunderstandings concerning our writings - especially *Complexity and Contradiction in Architecture*. It refers to history employed as an element for comparative analysis: it doesn't say design like Borromini, but learn from Borromini via the method of comparative analysis. The book does not advocate historical revivalism, but this is what postmodernism came to mean. I don't want to sound pretentious, but as people say Freud was not a Freudian, or Marx was not a Marxist, we are not postmodernists. We never called ourselves postmodernists or ever used the term in our writings. We feel we are modernists. So our influence, ironically, has been negative, involving misunderstandings and misapplications. But very often when people have good ideas, the ideas are subtle and complex, and therefore easily misunderstood.

Context was one of these. Postmodern ideas on context cause many design review boards to insist that new buildings look like the old building beside them, yet the Piazza San Marco is highly harmonious as a whole, although Byzantine, Gothic, and Renaissance buildings sit on it side by side. But of course, context is anti-universal, while the International style is universal: it wants to be the same in China as in Switzerland. Iconographic architecture can be universal and contextual - in terms of both the technology and the content of its signage.

: It's interesting to see how McDonald's ads are different in Europe. They use the big yellow arches, but they put them in a Roman forum. They're funny, and more sophisticated than the American ads.

SIGN VS. MASS

: If I were to caricature your position, I could say that signs are more important than substance....

: Rather, signs are more relevant/significant than buildings.

: Could we then say: signs are more important than mass? Since *Learning from Las Vegas*, the city has become more substantial, more massive: it is more built now than it ever was. Do you think the lesson of sign over building still applies?

: Yes: sign *is* more important than mass. Or, to put it another way, as someone wrote of our approach recently: building, sign, art - they're all one. And that's why we think current Las Vegas is ironically less relevant than old Las Vegas. It went from commercial strip to Disneyland. In "Las Vegas After Its Classic Age" we describe the following evolutions: from strip to boulevard, urban sprawl to urban density, parking lot to landscaped front yard, asphalt plain to Romantic garden, decorated shed to "duck," electric to electronic, neon to pixel, electrographic to scenographic, iconography to scenography, Vaughan Cannon to Walt Disney, pop culture to gentrification, pop taste to good taste,

Venturi and Scott Brown's Las Vegas II (2000) according to Rem Koolhaas:

Iconography overwhelmed by a new scale

perception as a driver to perception as a walker, strip to mall, mall to edge-city, vulgar to dramatique. To simplify, the main thing is that it went from the archetype of strip and sprawl to the scenography of Disneyland. Scenography is not necessarily bad - the Place des Vosges is scenographic, and architecture, in a sense, does involve making scenes. The danger is that it becomes an exotic theater rather than an actual place.

: But all the characterizations in this list are relatively dynamic; why do you end with a negative, "*dramatique*"?

: It's not necessarily negative and, as I said, a lot of good architecture has elements of scenography. The challenge would be to do it well - authentically - today.

: But how is it possible for a self-professed populist to declare the *par excellence* populist phenomenon inauthentic?

: It's not so simple as to say we are populist; we're very mixed, we're elitist as well as populist.

: Are you writing now?

: I'm always writing. I write mostly essays: since this book came out, I've written probably fifteen essays. A lot of manifestos and things like that....

: So are you undergoing a new period of stridency?

: Oh, I wouldn't put it that way! We're always working, in fact we work seven days a week, except on Christmas week when we work six and a half days.

: There is an interesting irony in the fact that you advocate the application of American commercialism and energy while right now, America is the worst country to apply it in, because there is a neurosis about context, about politeness, and about nostalgia....

: Yes, Americans are so ashamed of being commercial!

NOW

: So far, you have been discussing your career in terms of continuity and in terms of the development of themes which were there from the beginning. Are there also elements of discontinuity, of radical change?

: It's been evolutionary, mostly - but distinctly so - as in the evolution of *Complexity and Contradiction* as a manifestation of Mannerism - an explicit manifestation rather than as the implicit manifestation as described in the book. It is now what could be called the New Mannerism that Denise and I are currently writing about in our latest book.

: We've been lucky enough to have had a few good ideas - maybe only one - in our careers. Then we've built on our central theme, diversified it, and strengthened it, through our professional experience. But every ten years or so there has been a change in our work owing to the different projects we've been involved with. We ceased the practice of urban planning in the 1980s, because I couldn't have my firm lose as much money again as we did on planning projects during the Nixon and Reagan eras. But as we dropped urbanism, campus planning caught us unawares and we do indeed work as urbanists when we work on urban and small town campuses. Since 1980 we've built a succession of academic buildings and complexes from classrooms, to residences, labs, libraries, and campus centers. Our academic work led to urban institutional and civic work - mainly museums - and our Japanese and French government projects. And our lab work of the 1980s moved us toward medical precinct design in the 1990s. So there's been a change in subjects, but a continuity in philosophy. Our projects keep us continually learning.

: And there are no past insights that you now reject?

: No, I think not. There are two main philosophical changes. One is about *Complexity and Contradiction in Architecture*: when my old, wonderful teacher at Princeton, Donald Drew Egbert, read it, he said it should have been titled *Complexity and Contradiction in Architectural Form*, because it was essentially about form. Then, *Las Vegas* was essentially about symbolism, so there is this movement from form to symbolism - we are more into symbolism now. Viva signage! ■

Guggenheim Hermitage

las vegas 36°10'N 115°12'W

04 October 01/17:00

AGUSTA
750
ETIAN
Casino ~ Las Vegas

ARCHITECTURE THAT SOUNDS AS GOOD AS IT LOOKS

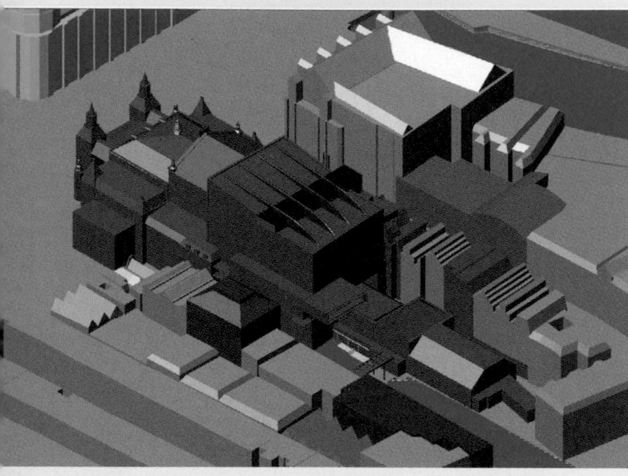

Municipal Theater, Amsterdam

Dancetheatre, The Hague
Bibliotheques de Jussieu, Paris
Municipal Theater, Amsterdam
Educatorium, Utrecht
McCormick Tribune Campus Center, Chicago
Dutch Embassy, Berlin
China Central Television, Beijing
Museum Kunsthal, Rotterdam
Casa de Musica, Porto
Millennium Dome, Londonderry (NI)
Royal National Theatre, London (UK)
Videopolis, Eurodisney, Paris (F)

dorsserblesgraaf

Renz van Luxemburg: Acoustical Engineer
Larixplein 1, Postbus 80007, 5600 JZ Eindhoven
Tel: 040 2509411, Mobile: 040 2509299
Email: renz.vanluxemburg@dorsserblesgraaf.nl
www.dorsserblesgraaf.nl

Universal (detail)
presentation model mixed
materials commissioned by OMA

Vincent de Rijk
Marconistraat 52
3029 AK Rotterdam
The Netherlands
+31 10 476 95 28

junk-

"Logan Airport : a world-class upgrade for the 21st century" (Late 20th century billboard)

BY REM KOOLHAAS

Rabbit is the new beef.... Because we abhor the utilitarian, we have condemned ourselves to a life-long immersion in the arbitrary.... LAX: welcoming - possibly flesh-eating - orchids at the check-in counter.... "Identity" is the new junk food for the dispossessed, globalization's fodder for the disenfranchised.... If space-junk is the human debris that litters the universe, junk-space is the residue mankind leaves on the planet. The built (more about that later) product of modernization is not modern architecture but Junkspace. Junkspace is what remains after modernization has run its course or, more precisely, what coagulates while modernization is in progress, its fallout. Modernization had a rational program: to share the blessings of science, universally. Junkspace is its apotheosis, or meltdown.... Although its individual parts are the outcome of brilliant inventions, lucidly planned by human intelligence, boosted by infinite computation, their sum spells the end of Enlightenment, its resurrection as farce, a low-grade purgatory.... Junkspace is the sum total of our current achievement; we have built more than all previous generations together, but somehow we do not register on the same scales. We do not leave pyramids. According to a new gospel of ugliness, there is already more Junkspace under construction in the 21st century than survived from the 20th.... It was a mistake to invent modern architecture for the 20th century. Architecture disappeared in the 20th century; we have been reading a footnote under a microscope hoping it would turn into a novel; our concern for the masses has blinded us to People's Architecture. Junkspace seems an aberration, but it is essence, the main thing... product of the encounter between escalator and air conditioning, conceived in an incubator of sheetrock (all three missing from the history books). Continuity is the essence of Junkspace; it exploits any invention that enables expansion, deploys the infrastructure of seamlessness: escalator, air conditioning, sprinkler, fire shutter, hot-air curtain.... It is always interior, so extensive that you rarely perceive limits; it promotes disorientation by any means (mirror, polish, echo).... Junkspace is sealed, held together not by structure, but by skin, like a bubble. Gravity has remained constant, resisted by the same arsenal since the beginning of time; but air conditioning - invisible medium, therefore unnoticed - has truly revolutionized architecture. Air conditioning has launched the endless building. If architecture separates buildings, air conditioning unites them. Air conditioning has dictated mutant regimes of organization and coexistence that leave architecture behind. A single shopping center now is the work of generations of space planners, repairmen and fixers, like in the Middle Ages; air conditioning sustains our cathedrals. (Unwittingly, all architects may be working on the same building, so far separate, but with hidden receptors that will eventually make it cohere.) Because it costs money, is no longer free, conditioned space inevitably becomes conditional space; sooner or later

space

all conditional space turns into Junkspace.... When we think about space, we have only looked at its containers. As if space itself is invisible, all theory for the production of space is based on an obsessive preoccupation with its opposite: substance and objects, i.e., architecture. Architects could never explain space; Junkspace is our punishment for their mystifications. OK, let's talk about space then. The beauty of airports, especially after each upgrade. The luster of renovations. The subtlety of the shopping center. Let's explore public space, discover casinos, spend time in theme parks.... Junkspace is the body double of space, a territory of impaired vision, limited expectation, reduced earnestness. Junkspace is a Bermuda triangle of concepts, a petri dish abandoned: it cancels distinctions, undermines resolve, confuses intention with realization. It replaces hierarchy with accumulation, composition with addition. More and more, more is more. Junkspace is overripe and undernourishing at the same time, a colossal security blanket that covers the earth in a stranglehold of care.... Junkspace is like being condemned to a perpetual Jacuzzi with millions of your best friends.... A fuzzy empire of blur, it fuses high and low, public and private, straight and bent, bloated and starved to offer a seamless patchwork of the permanently disjointed. Seemingly an apotheosis, spatially grandiose, the effect of its richness is a terminal hollowness, a vicious parody of ambition that systematically erodes the credibility of building, possibly forever.... Space was created by piling matter on top of matter, cemented to form a solid new whole. Junkspace is additive, layered and lightweight, not articulated in different parts but subdivided, quartered the way a carcass is torn apart - individual chunks severed from a universal condition. There are no walls, only partitions, shimmering membranes frequently covered in mirror or gold. Structure groans invisibly underneath decoration, or worse, has become ornamental; small shiny space frames support nominal loads, or huge beams deliver cyclopic burdens to unsuspecting destinations.... The arch, once the workhorse of structures, has become the depleted emblem of "community," welcoming an infinity of virtual populations to non-existent there's. Where it is absent, it is simply applied - mostly in stucco - as ornamental afterthought on hurriedly erected superblocks. Junkspace's iconography is 13% Roman, 8% Bauhaus, 7% Disney (neck and neck), 3% Art Nouveau, followed closely by Mayan.... Like a substance that could have condensed in any other form, Junkspace is a domain of feigned, simulated order, a kingdom of morphing. Its specific configuration is as fortuitous as the geometry of a snowflake. Patterns imply repetition or ultimately decipherable rules; Junkspace is beyond measure, beyond code.... Because it cannot be grasped, Junkspace cannot be remembered. It is flamboyant yet unmemorable, like a screensaver; its refusal to freeze ensures instant amnesia. Junkspace does not pretend to create perfection, only interest. Its geometries are unimaginable, only makeable. Although strictly non-architectural, it tends to the vaulted, to the Dome. Sections seem to be devoted to utter inertness, others in perpetual rhetorical turmoil: the deadest resides next to the most hysterical. Themes cast a pall of arrested development over interiors as big as the Pantheon, spawning stillbirths in every corner. The aesthetic is Byzantine, gorgeous and dark, splintered into thousands of shards, all visible at the same time: a quasi-panoptical universe in which all contents rearrange themselves in split-seconds around the dizzy eye of the beholder. Murals used to show idols; Junkspace's modules are dimensioned to carry brands; myths can be shared, brands husband aura at the mercy of focus groups. Brands in Junkspace perform the same role as black holes in the universe: essences through which meaning disappears.... The shiniest surfaces in the history of mankind reflect humanity at its most casual. The more we inhabit the palatial, the more we seem to dress down. A stringent dress code - last spasm of etiquette? - governs access to Junkspace: short, sneaker, sandal, shell suit, fleece, jean, parka, backpack. As if the People suddenly accessed the private quarters of a dictator, Junkspace is best enjoyed in a state of post-revolutionary gawking. Polarities have merged, there is nothing left between desolation and frenzy. Neon signifies both the old and the new; interiors refer to the Stone and the Space Age at the same time. Like the deactivated virus in an inoculation, Modern architecture remains essential, but only in its most sterile manifestation, High Tech (it seemed so dead only a decade ago!). It exposes what previous generations kept under wraps: structures emerge like springs from a mattress, exit stairs dangle in didactic trapeze, probes thrust into space to deliver laboriously what is in fact omnipresent, free air, acres of glass hang from spidery cables, tautly stretched skins enclose flaccid non-events. Transparency only reveals everything in which you cannot partake. At the sound of midnight it all may revert to Taiwanese Gothic, in three years segue into Nigerian Sixties, Norwegian Chalet or default Christian. Earthlings now live in a kindergarten grotesque.... Junkspace thrives on design, but design dies in Junkspace. There is no form, only proliferation.... Regurgitation is the new creativity; instead of creation, we honor, cherish and embrace manipulation.... Superstrings of graphics, transplanted emblems of franchise and sparkling infrastructures of light, LEDs, and video describe an authorless world beyond anyone's claim, always unique, utterly unpredictable, yet intensely familiar. Junkspace is hot (or suddenly arctic); fluorescent walls, folded like melting stained glass, generate additional heat to raise the temperature of Junkspace to levels where you could cultivate orchids. Pretending histories left and right, its contents are dynamic yet stagnant, recycled or multiplied as in cloning: forms search for function like hermit crabs for a vacant shell.... Junkspace sheds architectures like a reptile sheds skins, is reborn every Monday morning. In previous building, materiality was based on a final state that could only be modified at the expense of partial destruction. At the exact moment that our culture has abandoned repetition and regularity as repressive, building materials have become more and more modular, unitary and standardized; substance now comes predigitized.... As the module becomes smaller and smaller, its status become that of a crypto-pixel. With enormous difficulty - budget, argument, negotiation, deformation - irregularity and uniqueness are constructed from identical elements. Instead of trying to wrest order from chaos, the picturesque now is wrested from the homogenized, the singular liberated from the standardized.... Architects thought of Junkspace first and named it Megastructure, the final solution to transcend their huge impasse. Like multiple Babels, huge superstructures would last through eternity, teeming with impermanent subsystems that would mutate over time, beyond their control. In Junkspace, the tables are turned: it is subsystems only, without superstructure, orphaned particles in search of framework or pattern. All materialization is provisional: cutting, bending, tearing, coating: construction has acquired a new softness, like tailoring.... The joint is no longer a problem, an intellectual issue: transitional moments are defined by stapling and taping, wrinkly brown bands barely maintain the illusion of an unbroken surface; verbs unknown and unthinkable in architectural history - clamp, stick, fold, dump, glue, shoot, double, fuse - have become indispensable. Each element performs its task in negotiated isolation. Where once detailing suggested the coming together, possibly forever, of disparate materials, it is now a transient coupling, waiting to be undone, unscrewed, a temporary embrace with a high probability of separation; no longer the orchestrated encounter of difference, but the abrupt end of a system, a stalemate. Only the blind, reading its fault lines with their fingertips, will ever understand Junkspace's histories.... While whole millennia worked in favor of permanence, axialities, relationships and proportion, the program of Junkspace is escalation. Instead of development, it offers entropy. Because it is endless, it always leaks somewhere in Junkspace; in the worst case, monumental ashtrays catch intermittent drops in a gray broth.... When did time stop moving forward, begin to spool in every direction, like a tape spinning out of control? Since the introduction of Real Time™? Change has been divorced from the idea of improvement. There is no progress; like a crab on LSD, culture staggers endlessly sideways.... The average contemporary lunch box is a microcosm of Junkspace: a fervent semantics of health - slabs of eggplant, topped by thick layers of goat cheese - cancelled by a colossal cookie at the bottom.... Junkspace is draining and is drained in return. Everywhere in Junkspace there are seating arrangements, ranges of modular chairs, even couches, as if the experience Junkspace offers its consumers is significantly more exhausting than any previous spatial sensation; in its most abandoned stretches, you find buffets: utilitarian tables draped in white or black sheets, perfunctory assemblies of caffeine and calories - cottage cheese, muffins, unripe grapes - notional representations of plenty, without horn and without plenty. Each Junkspace is connected, sooner or later, to bodily functions: wedged between stainless-steel partitions sit rows of groaning Romans, denim togas bunched around their huge sneakers.... Because it is so intensely consumed, Junkspace is fanatically maintained, the night shift undoing the damage of the day shift in an endless Sisyphean replay. As you recover from Junkspace, Junkspace recovers from you: between 2 and 5 am, yet another population, this one heartlessly casual and appreciably darker, is mopping, hovering, sweeping, toweling, resupplying.... Junkspace does not inspire loyalty in its cleaners.... Dedicated to instant gratification, Junkspace accommodates seeds of future perfection; a language of apology is woven through its texture of canned euphoria; "pardon our appearance" signs or miniature yellow "sorry" billboards mark ongoing patches of wetness, announce momentary discomfort in return for imminent shine, the allure of improvement. Somewhere, workers sink on their knees to repair faded sections - as if in a prayer - or half-disappear in ceiling voids to negotiate elusive malfunction - as if in confession. All surfaces are archaeological, superpositions of different "periods" (what do you call the moment a particular type of wall-to-wall carpet was current?) - as you note when they're torn.... Traditionally, typology implies demarcation, the definition of a singular model that excludes other arrangements. Junkspace represents a reverse typology of cumulative, approximative identity, less about kind than about quantity. But formlessness is still form, the formless also a typology.... Take the dump, where successive trucks discharge their loads to form a heap, whole in spite of the randomness of its contents and its fundamental shapelessness, or that of the tent-envelope that assumes different shapes to accommodate variable interior volumes. Or the amorphous crotches of the new generation. Junkspace can either be absolutely chaotic or frighteningly aseptic - like a best-seller - overdetermined and indeterminate at the same time. There is something strange about ballrooms, for instance: huge wastelands kept column-free for ultimate flexibility. Because you've never been invited to that kind of event, you have never seen them in use, only being prepared with chilling precision: a relentless grid of circular tables, extending towards a distant horizon, their diameters preempting communication, a dais big enough for the politburo of a totalitarian state, wings announcing as yet unimagined surprises - acres of organization to support future drunkenness, disarray and disorder. Or car shows.... Junkspace is often described as a space of flows, but that is a misnomer; flows depend on disciplined movement, bodies that cohere. Junkspace is a web without spider; although it is an architecture of the masses, each trajectory is strictly unique. Its anarchy is one of the last tangible ways in which we experience freedom. It is a space of collision, a container of atoms, busy, not dense.... There is a special way of moving in Junkspace, at the same time aimless and purposeful. It is an acquired culture. Junkspace features the tyranny of the oblivious: sometimes an entire Junkspace comes unstuck through the non-conformity of one of its members; a single citizen of an another culture - a refugee, a mother - can destabilize an entire Junkspace, hold it to a rustic's ransom, leaving an invisible swath of obstruction in his/her wake, a deregulation eventually communicated to its furthest extremities. Where movement becomes synchronized, it curdles: on escalators, near exits, parking machines, automated tellers. Sometimes, under duress, individuals are channeled in a flow, pushed through a single door or forced to negotiate the gap between two temporary obstacles (an invalid's bleeping chariot and a Christmas tree): the manifest ill will such narrowing provokes, mocks the notion of flows. Flows in Junkspace lead to disaster: department stores at the beginning of sales, the stampedes triggered by warring compartments of soccer fans, dead bodies piling up in front of the locked emergency doors of a disco: evidence of the misfit between the portals of Junkspace and the narrow calibrations of the old world. The young instinctively avoid the Dantesque manipulations/containers to which Junkspace has condemned their elders in perpetuity. Within the meta-playground of Junkspace exist smaller playgrounds, Junkspace for children (usually in the least desirable square footage): sections of sudden miniaturization - often underneath staircases, always near dead ends - assemblies of under-dimensioned plastic structures - slides, seesaws, swings - shunned by their intended audience - kids - turned into junkniche for the old, the lost, the forgotten, the insane... last hiccup of humanism.... Traffic is Junkspace, from airspace to the subway; the entire highway system is Junkspace, a vast potential utopia clogged by its users, as you notice when they've finally disappeared on vacation.... Like radioactive waste, Junkspace has an insidious half-life. Aging in Junkspace is nonexistent or catastrophic; sometimes an entire Junkspace - a department store, a nightclub, a bachelor pad - turns into a slum overnight without warning: wattage diminishes imperceptibly, letters drop out of signs, air conditioning units start dripping, cracks appear as if from otherwise unregistered earthquakes; sections rot, are no longer viable, but remain joined to the flesh of the main body via gangrenous passages. Judging the built presumed a static condition; now each architecture embodies opposite conditions simultaneously: old and new, permanent and temporary, flourishing and at risk.... Sections undergo an Alzheimer-like deterioration as others are upgraded. Because Junkspace is endless, it is never closed.... Renovation and restoration were procedures that took place in your absence; now you're a witness, a reluctant participant.... Seeing Junkspace in conversion is like inspecting an unmade bed, someone else's. Say an airport needs more space. In the past new terminals were added, each more or less characteristic of its own age, leaving the old ones as a readable record, evidence of progress. Since passengers have definitively demonstrated their infinite malleability, the idea of rebuilding on the spot has gained currency. Travelators are thrown in reverse, signs taped, potted palms (or very large corpses) covered in body bags. Screens of taped sheetrock segregate two populations: one wet, one dry, one hard, one flabby, one cold, one overheated. Half the population produces new space, the more affluent half consumes old space. To accommodate a nether world of manual labor, the concourse suddenly turns into casbah: improvised locker rooms, coffee breaks, smoking, even real campfires.... The ceiling is a crumpled plate like the Alps; grids of unstable tiles alternate with monogrammed sheets of black plastic, improbably punctured by grids of crystal chandeliers.... Metal ducts are replaced by breathing textiles. Gaping joints reveal vast ceiling voids (former canyons of asbestos?), beams, ducting, rope, cable, insulation, fireproofing, string; tangled arrangements suddenly exposed to daylight. Impure, tortured and complex, they exist only because they were never consciously plotted. The floor is a patchwork: different textures - concrete, hairy, heavy, shiny, plastic, metallic, muddy - alternate randomly, as if dedicated to different species.... The ground is no more. There are too many raw needs to be realized on only one plane. The absolute horizontal has been abandoned. Transparency has disappeared, replaced by a dense crust of provisional occupation: kiosks, carts, strollers, palms, fountains, bars, sofas, trolleys.... Corridors no longer simply link A to B, but have become "destinations." Their tenant life tends to be short: the most stagnant windows, the most perfunctory dresses, the most implausible flowers. All perspective is gone, as in a rainforest (itself disappearing, they keep saying...). The formerly straight is coiled into ever more complex configurations. Only a perverse modernist choreography can explain the twists and turns, ascents and descents, sudden reversals that comprise the typical path from check-in (misleading name) to apron of the average contemporary airport. Because we never reconstruct or question the absurdity of these enforced dérives, we meekly submit to grotesque journeys past perfume, asylum seeker, building site, underwear, oysters, pornography, cell phone - incredible adventures for the brain, the eye, the nose, the tongue, the womb, the testicles.... There was once a polemic about the right angle and the straight line; now the 90th degree has become one among many. In fact, remnants of former geometries create ever new havoc, offering forlorn nodes of resistance that create unstable eddies in newly opportunistic flows.... Who would dare claim responsibility for this sequence? The idea that a profession once dictated, or at least presumed to predict, people's movements, now seems laughable, or worse: unthinkable. Instead of design, there is calculation: the more erratic the path, eccentric the loops, hidden the blueprint, the more efficient the exposure, inevitable the transaction. In this war, graphic designers are the great turncoats: where once signage promised to deliver you to where you wanted to be, it now obfuscates and entangles you in a thicket of cuteness that forces you past unwanted detours, turns you back when you're lost. Postmodernism adds a crumple-zone of viral *poché* that fractures and multiplies the endless frontline of display, a peristaltic shrink-wrap crucial to all commercial exchange. Trajectories are launched as ramp, turn horizontal without any warning, intersect, fold down, suddenly emerge on a vertiginous balcony above a large void. Fascism minus dictator. From the sudden dead end where you were dropped by a monumental, granite staircase, an escalator takes you to an invisible destination, facing a provisional vista of plaster, inspired by forgettable sources. (There is no datum level; you always inhabit a sandwich. "Space" is scooped out of Junkspace as from a soggy block of ice cream that has languished too long in the freezer: cylindrical, cone shaped, more or less spherical, whatever....) Toilet groups mutate into Disney Store then morph to become meditation center: successive transformations mock the word "plan." The plan is a radar screen where individual pulses survive for unpredictable periods of time in a Bacchanalian free-for-all.... In this standoff between the redundant and the inevitable, a plan would actually make matters worse, drive you to instant despair. Only the diagram gives a bearable version. There is zero loyalty - and zero tolerance - toward configuration, no "original" condition; architecture has turned into a time-lapse sequence to reveal a "permanent evolution".... The only certainty is conversion - continuous - followed, in rare cases, by "restoration," the process that claims ever new sections of history as extensions of Junkspace. History corrupts, absolute history corrupts absolutely. Color and matter are eliminated from these bloodless grafts: the bland has become the only meeting ground for the old and the new.... Can the bland be amplified? The featureless be exaggerated? Through height? Depth? Length? Variation? Repetition? Sometimes not overload but its opposite, an absolute absence of detail, generates Junkspace. A voided condition of frightening sparseness, shocking proof that so much can be organized by so little. Laughable emptiness infuses the respectful distance or tentative embrace that starchitects maintain in the presence of the past, authentic or not. Invariably, the primordial decision is to leave the original intact; the formerly residual is declared the new essence, focus of the intervention. As a first step, the substance to be preserved is wrapped in a thick pack of commerce and catering - like a reluctant skier pushed downhill by responsible minders. To show respect, symmetries are maintained and helplessly exaggerated; ancient building techniques are resurrected and honed to irrelevant shine, quarries reopened to excavate the "same" stone, indiscreet donor names chiseled prominently in the meekest of typefaces; the courtyard covered by a masterful, structural "filigree" - emphatically uncompetitive - so that continuity may be established with the "rest" of Junkspace (abandoned galleries, display slums, Jurassic concepts...). Conditioning is applied; filtered daylight reveals vast, antiseptic expanses of monumental reticence and makes them come alive, vibrant as a computer rendering.... The curse of public space: latent fascism safely smothered in signage, stools, sympathy.... Junkspace is post-existential; it makes you uncertain where you are, obscures where you go, undoes where you were. Who do you think you are? Who do you want to be? (Note to architects: you thought that you could ignore Junkspace, visit it surreptitiously, treat it with condescending contempt or enjoy it vicariously... because you could not understand it, you've thrown away the keys.... But now your own architecture is infected, has become equally smooth, all-inclusive, continuous, warped, busy, atrium-ridden....) JunkSignature™ is the new architecture: the former megalomania of a profession contracted to manageable size, Junkspace minus its saving vulgarity. Anything stretched - limousines, body parts, planes - turns into Junkspace, its original concept abused. Restore, rearrange, reassemble, revamp, renovate, revise, recover, redesign, return - the Parthenon marbles - redo, respect, rent: verbs that start with *re-* produce Junkspace.... Junkspace will be our tomb. Half of mankind pollutes to produce, the other pollutes to consume. The combined pollution of all Third World cars, motorbikes, trucks, buses, sweatshops pales into insignificance compared to the heat generated by Junkspace. Junkspace is political: it depends on the central removal of the critical faculty in the name of comfort and pleasure. Politics has become manifesto by Photoshop, seamless blueprints of the mutually exclusive, arbitrated by opaque NGOs. Comfort is the new Justice. Entire miniature states now adopt Junkspace as political program, establish regimes of engineered disorientation, instigate a politics of systematic disarray. Not exactly "anything goes"; in fact, the secret of Junkspace is that it is both promiscuous and repressive: as the formless proliferates, the formal withers, and with it all rules, regulations, recourse.... Babel has been misunderstood. Language is not the problem, just the new frontier of Junkspace. Mankind, torn by eternal dilemmas, the impasse of seemingly endless debates, has launched a new language that straddles unbridgeable divides like a fragile designer's footbridge... coined a proactive wave of new oxymorons to suspend former incompatibility: life/style, reality/TV, world/music, museum/store, food/court, health/care, waiting/lounge. Naming has replaced class struggle, sonorous amalgamations of status, high-concept and history. Through acronym, unusual importation, suppressing letters, or fabrication of non-existent plurals, they aim to shed meaning in return for a spacious new roominess.... Junkspace knows all your emotions, all your desires. It is the interior of Big Brother's belly. It preempts people's sensations. It comes with a soundtrack, smell, captions; it blatantly proclaims how it wants to be read: rich, stunning, cool, huge, abstract, "minimal," historical. It sponsors a collective of brooding consumers in surly anticipation of their next spend, a mass of refractory periods caught in a Thousand Year Reign of Razzmatazz, a paroxysm of prosperity. The subject is stripped of privacy in return for access to a credit nirvana. You are complicit in the tracing of the fingerprints each of your transactions leaves; they know everything about you, except who you are. Emissaries of Junkspace pursue you in the formerly impervious privacy of the bedroom: the minibar, private fax machines, pay TV offering compromised pornography, fresh plastic veils wrapping toilet seats, courtesy condoms: miniature profit centers coexist with your bedside bible.... Junkspace pretends to unite, but it actually splinters. It creates communities not of shared interest or free association, but of identical statistics and unavoidable demographics, an opportunistic weave of vested interests. Each man, woman and child is individually targeted, tracked, split off from the rest.... Fragments come together at "security" only, where a grid of video screens disappointingly reassembles individual frames into a banalized, utilitarian cubism that reveals Junkspace's overall coherence to the dispassionate glare of barely trained guards: videoethnography in its brute form. Just as Junkspace is unstable, its actual ownership is forever being passed on in parallel disloyalty. Junkspace happens spontaneously through natural corporate exuberance - the unfettered play of the market - or is generated through the combined actions of temporary 'czars' with long records of three-dimensional philanthropy, bureaucrats (often former leftists) that optimistically sell off vast tracks of waterfront, former hippodromes, military bases and abandoned airfields to developers or real estate moguls that can accommodate any deficit in futuristic balances, or through Default Preservation™ (the maintenance of historical complexes that nobody wants but the Zeitgeist has declared sacrosanct). As its scale mushrooms - rivals and even exceeds that of the Public - its economy becomes more inscrutable. Its financing is a deliberate haze, clouding opaque deals, dubious tax breaks, unusual incentives, exemptions, tenuous legalities, transferred air rights, joined properties, special zoning districts, public-private complicities. Funded by bonds, lottery, subsidy, charity, grant: an erratic flow of yen, euros and dollars (**¥€$**) creates financial envelopes that are as fragile as their contents. Because of a structural shortfall, a fundamental deficit, a contingent bankruptcy, each square inch becomes a grasping, needy surface dependent on covert or overt support, discount, compensation and fundraising. For culture, "engraved donor bricks"; for everything else: cash, rentals, leases, franchises, the underpinning of brands. Junkspace expands with the economy but its footprint cannot contract... when it is no longer needed, it thins. Because of its tenuous viability, Junkspace has to swallow more and more program to survive; soon, we will be able to do anything anywhere. We will have conquered place. At the end of Junkspace, the Universal? Through Junkspace old aura is transfused with new luster to spawn sudden commercial viability: Barcelona amalgamated with the Olympics, Bilbao with Guggenheim, 42nd with Disney. God is dead, the author is dead, history is dead, only the architect is left standing... an insulting evolutionary joke.... A shortage of masters has not stopped a proliferation of masterpieces. "Masterpiece" has become a definitive sanction, a semantic space that saves the object from criticism, leaves its qualities unproven, its performance untested, its motives unquestioned. Masterpiece is no longer an inexplicable fluke, a roll of the dice, but a consistent typology: its mission to intimidate, most of its exterior surfaces bent, huge percentages of its square footage dysfunctional, its centrifugal components barely held together by the pull of the atrium, dreading the imminent arrival of forensic accounting.... The more indeterminate the city, the more specific its Junkspace; all Junkspace's prototypes are urban - the Roman Forum, the Metropolis; it is only their reverse synergy that makes them suburban, simultaneously swollen and shrunk. Junkspace reduces what is urban to urbanity.... Instead of public life, Public Space™: what remains of the city once the unpredictable has been removed.... Space for "honoring," "sharing," "caring," "grieving" and "healing"... civility imposed by an overdose of serif.... In the third Millennium, Junkspace will assume responsibility for pleasure and religion, exposure and intimacy, public life and privacy. Inevitably, the death of God (and the author) has spawned orphaned space; Junkspace is authorless, yet surprisingly authoritarian.... At the moment of its greatest emancipation, humankind is subjected to the most dictatorial scripts: from the pushy oration of the waiter, to the answering gulags on the other end of the telephone, the safety instructions on the airplane, more and more insistent perfumes, mankind is browbeaten to submit to the most harshly engineered plotline.... The chosen theater of megalomania - the dictatorial - is no longer politics, but entertainment. Through Junkspace, entertainment organizes hermetic regimes of ultimate exclusion and concentration: concentration gambling, concentration golf, concentration convention, concentration movie, concentration culture, concentration holiday. Entertainment is like watching a once hot planet cool off; its major inventions are ancient: the moving image, the roller coaster, sound, cartoons, clowns, unicycles, dinosaurs, news, war. Except celebrities - of which there is a dramatic shortage - we have added nothing, just reconfigured. Corpotainment is a galaxy in contraction, forced to go through the motions by ruthless Copernican laws. The secret of corporate aesthetics was the power of elimination, the celebration of the efficient, the eradication of excess: abstraction as camouflage, the search for a Corporate Sublime. On popular demand, organized beauty has become warm, humanist, inclusivist, arbitrary, poetic and unthreatening: water is pressurized through very small holes, then forced into rigorous hoops; straight palms are bent into grotesque poses, air is burdened with added oxygen - as if only forcing malleable substances into the most drastic contortions maintains control, satisfies the drive to get rid of surprise. Not canned laughter, but canned euphoria.... Color has disappeared to dampen the resulting cacophony, is used only as cue: relax, enjoy, be well; we're united in sedation.... Why can't we tolerate stronger sensations? Dissonance? Awkwardness? Genius? Anarchy?.... Junkspace heals, or at least that is the assumption of many hospitals. We thought the hospital was unique - a universe identified by its smell - but now that we are used to universal conditioning we recognize it was merely a prototype; all Junkspace is defined by its odor. Often heroic in size, planned with the last adrenaline of modernism's grand inspiration, we have made them (too) human; life or death decisions are taken in spaces that are relentlessly friendly, littered with fading bouquets, empty coffee cups and yesterday's papers. You used to face death in appropriate cells, now your nearest are huddled together in atriums. A bold datum line is established on every vertical surface, dividing the infirmary in two: above an endless humanist scroll of "color," loved ones, children's sunsets, signage and art... below a utilitarian zone for defacement and disinfectant, anticipated collision, scratch, spill and smudge.... Junkspace is space as vacation; there once was a relationship between leisure and work, a biblical dictate that divided our weeks, organized public life. Now we work harder, marooned in a never-ending casual Friday.... The office is the next frontier of Junkspace. Since you can work at home, the office aspires to the domestic; because you still need a life, it simulates the city. Junkspace features the office as the urban home, a meeting-boudoir: desks become sculptures, the workfloor is lit by intimate downlights. Monumental partitions, kiosks, mini-Starbucks on interior plazas: a Post-it universe: 'team memory,' "information persistence"; futile hedges against the universal forgetting of the unmemorable, the oxymoron as mission statement. Witness corporate agit-prop: the CEO's suite becomes "leadership collective," wired to all the world's other Junkspace, real or imagined. *Espace* becomes e-space. The 21st century will bring "intelligent" Junkspace: on a big digital "dashboard": sales, CNNNYSENASDAQC-SPAN, anything that goes up or down, from good to bad, presented in real time like the automotive theory course that complements driving lessons.... Globalization turns language into Junkspace. We are stuck in a speech-doldrums. The ubiquity of English is Pyrrhic: now that we all speak it, nobody remembers its use. The collective bastardization of English is our most impressive achievement; we have broken its back with ignorance, accent, slang, jargon, tourism, outsourcing and multitasking... we can make it say anything we want, like a speech dummy.... Through the retrofitting of language, there are too few plausible words left; our most creative hypotheses will never be formulated, discoveries will remain unmade, concepts unlaunched, philosophies muffled, nuances miscarried.... We inhabit sumptuous Potemkin suburbs of weasel terminologies. Aberrant linguistic ecologies sustain virtual subjects in their claim to legitimacy, help them survive.... Language is no longer used to explore, define, express, or to confront but to fudge, blur, obfuscate, apologize and comfort... it stakes claims, assigns victimhood, preempts debate, admits guilt, fosters consensus. Entire organizations and/or professions impose a descent into the linguistic equivalent of hell: condemned to a word-limbo, inmates wrestle with words in ever-descending spirals of pleading, lying, bargaining, flattening... a Satanic orchestration of the meaningless.... Intended for the interior, Junkspace can easily engulf a whole city. First, it escapes from its containers - semantic orchids that needed hothouse protection emerging with surprising robustness - then the outdoors itself is converted: the street is paved more luxuriously, shelters proliferate carrying increasingly dictatorial messages, traffic is calmed, crime eliminated. Then Junkspace spreads like a forest fire in LA.... The global progress of Junkspace represents a final Manifest Destiny: the World as public space.... All the resurrected emblems and rekindled embers of the formerly public need new pastures. A new vegetal is corralled for its thematic efficiency. The outing of Junkspace has triggered the professionalization of denaturing, a benign eco-fascism that positions a rare surviving Siberian tiger in a forest of slot machines, near Armani, amidst a

twisted arboreal Baroque.... Outside, between the casinos, fountains project entire Stalinist buildings of liquid, ejaculated in a split-second, hovering momentarily, then withdrawn with an amnesiac competency.... Air, water, wood: all are enhanced to produce Hyperecology™ , a parallel Walden, a new rainforest. Landscape has become Junkspace, foliage as spoilage: trees are tortured, lawns cover human manipulations like thick pelts or even toupees, sprinklers water according to mathematical timetables.... Seemingly at the opposite end of Junkspace, the golf course is in fact its conceptual double; empty, serene, free of commercial debris. The relative evacuation of the golf course is achieved by the further charging of Junkspace. The methods of their design and realization are similar: erasure, tabula rasa, reconfiguration. Junkspace turns into biojunk; ecology into ecospace. Ecology and economy have bonded in Junkspace as ecolomy. The economy has become Faustian; hyperdevelopment depends on artificial underdevelopment; a huge global bureaucracy is in the making to settle, in a colossal yin/yang, the balance between Junkspace and golf, between the scraped and the scaped, trading the right to despoil for the obligation to create steroid rainforests in Costa Rica. Oxygen banks, Fort Knoxes of chlorophyll, eco-reserves as a blank check for further pollution. Junkspace is rewriting the apocalypse; we may die of oxygen poisoning.... In the past, the complexities of Junkspace were compensated by the stark rawness of its adjunct infrastructures: parking garages, filling stations, distribution centers that routinely displayed a monumental purity that was the original aim of modernism. Now, massive injections of lyricism have enabled infrastructure - the one domain previously immune to design, taste or the marketplace - to join the world of Junkspace, and for Junkspace to extend its manifestations under the sky. Railway stations unfold like iron butterflies, airports glisten like cyclopic dewdrops, bridges span often negligible banks like grotesquely enlarged versions of the harp. To each rivulet its own Calatrava. (Sometimes when there is a strong wind, this new generation of instruments shakes as if being played by a giant, or maybe a God, and mankind shudders....) Junkspace can be airborne, bring malaria to Sussex; 300 anopheline mosquitoes arrive each day at GDG and GTW with the theoretical ability to infect 8 to 20 locals in a 3 mile radius, a hazard exacerbated by the average passenger's reluctance, in a misplaced gasp of quasi-autonomy, to be disinfected once he or she has buckled up for the return journey from the dead end of the tourist destination. Airports, provisional accommodation for those going elsewhere, inhabited by assemblies united only by the imminence of their dissolution, have turned into consumption gulags, democratically distributed across the globe to give every citizen an equal chance of admission.... MXP looks as if all the leftovers of East Germany's reconstruction - whatever was needed to undo the deprivations of Communism - have been hurriedly bulldozed together according to a vaguely rectangular blueprint to form a botched sequence of deformed, inadequate spaces, apparently willed into being by the current rulers of Europe, extorting limitless euros from the community's regional funds, now causing endless delays for its duped taxpayers too busy on cell phones to notice. DFW is composed of three elements only, repeated ad infinitum, nothing else: one kind of beam, one kind of brick, one kind of tile, all coated in the same color - is it teal? Rust? Tobacco? Its symmetries scaled beyond any recognition, the endless curve of its terminals forces its users to enact relativity theory in their quest for the gate. Its drop-off is the seemingly harmless beginning of a journey to the heart of unmitigated nothingness, beyond animation by Pizza Hut, Dairy Queen.... Valley cultures were thought to be the most resistant to Junkspace: at GVZ you can still see a universe of rules, order, hierarchy, neatness, coordination, poised moments before its implosion, but at ZHR huge "timepieces" hover in front of interior waterfalls as an essay in Regionaljunk. Duty-free is Junkspace, Junkspace is duty-free space. Where culture was thinnest, will it be the first to run out? Is emptiness local? Do wide open spaces demand wide open Junkspace? Sunbelt: huge populations where there was nothing; PHX: warpaint on every terminal, dead Indian outlines on every surface - carpet, wallpaper, napkins - like frogs flattened by car tires. Public Art distributed across LAX: the fish that have disappeared from our rivers return as public art in the concourse; only what is dead can be resurrected. Memory itself may have turned into Junkspace; only those murdered will be remembered.... Deprivation can be caused by overdose or shortage; both conditions happen in Junkspace (often at the same time). Minimum is the ultimate ornament, a self-righteous crime, the contemporary Baroque. It does not signify beauty, but guilt. Its demonstrative earnestness drives whole civilizations into the welcoming arms of camp and kitsch. Ostensibly a relief from constant sensorial onslaught, minimum is maximum in drag, a stealth laundering of luxury: the stricter the lines, the more irresistible the seductions. Its role is not to approximate the sublime, but to minimize the shame of consumption, drain embarrassment, to lower the higher. Minimum now exists in a state of parasitic co-dependency with overdose: to have and not to have, craving and owning, finally collapsed in a single signifier.... Museums are sanctimonious Junkspace; no sturdier aura than holiness. To accommodate the converts they have attracted by default, museums massively turn "bad" space into "good" space; the more untreated the oak, the larger the profit center. Monasteries inflated to the scale of department stores: expansion is the third millennium's entropy, dilute or die. Dedicated to respect mostly the dead, no cemetery would dare to reshuffle corpses as casually in the name of current expediency; curators plot hangings and unexpected encounters in a donor-plate labyrinth with the finesse of the retailer: lingerie becomes "Nude, Action, Body," cosmetics "History, Memory, Society." All paintings based on black grids are herded together in a single white room. Large spiders in the humongous conversion offer delirium for the masses.... Narrative reflexes that have enabled us from the beginning of time to connect dots, fill in blanks, are now turned against us: we cannot stop noticing: no sequence too absurd, trivial, meaningless, insulting... through our ancient evolutionary equipment, our irrepressible attention span, we helplessly register, provide insight, squeeze meaning, read intention; we cannot stop making sense out of the utterly senseless.... On its triumphal march as content provider, art extends far beyond the museum's ever-increasing boundaries. Outside, in the real world, the "art planner" spreads Junkspace's fundamental incoherence by assigning defunct mythologies to residual surfaces and plotting three-dimensional works in leftover emptiness. Scouting for authenticity, their touch seals the fate of what was real, taps it for incorporation in Junkspace. Art galleries move en masse to where it is "edgy," then convert raw space into white cubes.... The only legitimate discourse is loss; art replenishes Junkspace in direct proportion to its own morbidity. We used to renew what was depleted, now we try to resurrect what is gone.... Outside, the architect's footbridge is rocked to the breaking point by a stampede of enthusiastic pedestrians; the designers' initial audacity now awaits the engineer's application of dampers. Junkspace is a look-no-hands world.... The constant threat of virtuality in Junkspace is no longer exorcized by petrochemical products, plastic, vinyl or rubber; the synthetic cheapens. Junkspace has to exaggerate its claims to the authentic. Junkspace is like a womb that organizes the transition of endless quantities of the Real - stone, trees, goods, daylight, people - into the unreal. Entire mountains are dismembered to provide ever-greater quantities of authenticity, suspended on precarious brackets, polished to a blinding state of flash that renders the intended earnestness instantly elusive. Stone only comes in light yellow, flesh, a violent beige, a soap-like green, the colors of Communist plastics in the 1950s. Forests are felled, their wood is all pale: maybe the origins of Junkspace go back to the Kindergarten... ("Origins" is a mint shampoo that stings the anal region). Color in the real world looks increasingly unreal, drained. Color in virtual space is luminous, therefore irresistible. A surfeit of reality TV has made us into amateur guards monitoring a Junkuniverse.... From the lively breasts of the classical violinist, to the designer stubble of the Big Brother outcast, the contextual pedophilia of the former revolutionary, the routine addictions of the stars, the runny makeup of the evangelist, the robotic body language of the conductor, the dubious benefits of the fundraising marathon, the futile explanations of the politician: the swooping movement of the TV camera suspended from its boom - an eagle without beak or claws, just an optical stomach - swallows images and confessions indiscriminately, like a trash bag, to propel them as cyber-vomit in space. TV studio sets - garishly monumental - are both the culmination and the end of perspectival space as we've known it: angular geometric remnants invading starry infinities; real space edited for smooth transmission in virtual space, crucial hinge in an infernal feedback loop... the vastness of Junkspace extended to the edges of the Big Bang. Because we spend our life indoors - like animals in a zoo - we are obsessed with the weather: 40% of all TV consists of presenters of lesser attractiveness gesturing helplessly in front of windswept formations, through which you recognize, sometimes, your own destination/current position. Conceptually, each monitor, each TV screen is a substitute for a window; real life is inside, cyberspace has become the great outdoors.... Mankind is always going on about architecture. What if space started looking at mankind? Will Junkspace invade the body? Through the vibes of the cell phone? Has it already? Botox injections? Collagen? Silicone implants? Liposuction? Penis enlargements? Does gene therapy announce a total reengineering according to Junkspace? Is each of us a mini-construction site? Mankind the sum of 3 to 5 billion individual upgrades? Is it a repertoire of reconfiguration that facilitates the intromission of a new species into its self-made Junksphere? The cosmetic is the new cosmic....

21 January 01/20:45

chicago 41°50'N 87°37'W

Black Metropol

Life and Death in Bronzeville

BY ELLEN GRIMES

PROLOGUE

1779 Jean DuSable, son of an African slave and a French trader, establishes a trading post at the mouth of the Chicago River.

1830 The city of Chicago is laid out by the Illinois-Michigan canal commission, a federal agency organized to build a canal between the Great Lakes-St. Lawrence waterway and the Mississippi River basin.There are 100 permanent citizens of the city.[1]

1837 The city is incorporated to enable the investment required to build the canal. A small African-American community exists near Harrision St., on the western and southern edges of the settlement. [2]

1848 The first railroad in the region, connecting Chicago with a lead mining town to the west, starts operation. The canal opens, the Chicago Board of Trade is founded, and the first telegraph line to the city is constructed. Europeans, mostly Germans displaced by the revolutions of 1848 and Irish escaping famine, begin to flood the city.

1850 As railroad infrastructure becomes concentrated south of the city, a residential area begins to grow around the railroad yards. At this point "more railroads [meet] at Chicago than at any other spot on the globe."[3] These railroads will define the city's social topography more rigidly than the grid that generated its street network. Of the nearly 30,000 people in Chicago, 750 are African-Americans; 80% live along the railroad yards south of the business district. >

Interior of a Chicago Public Housing high rise apartment, 1987: Linda, Latrice, and Mario pose beneath a photo of Harold Washington, Chicago's first African-American mayor

CREATING THE BLACK BELT

1861 The American civil war begins as a confederation of 11 southern states secede in an attempt to maintain their slave holding economies.

19 June 1865 A US Army General lands in Galveston, Texas and informs the people of Texas that "all slaves are free." In 1863, in the middle of the civil war, Abraham Lincoln, the American president had issued the Emancipation Proclamation, ending the legal basis for the institution of slavery. News of the proclamation was withheld from many confederate territories until after the rebel states surrendered in April of 1865.

1866 The Civil Rights Act grants citizenship to former slaves; three years later, voting rights will be granted to African-American men. In response, the Ku Klux Klan is founded in an effort to maintain white supremacy in the south.

1871 A fire starts on the west side of Chicago and destroys the central business district. The ethnic polyglot working class neighborhoods around city center are largely destroyed, but the city's industrial infrastructure - steel mills and stockyards - survives. A substantial number of German Jews and African-Americans, displaced by the fire, settle at the southern edge of the city. A "black belt" begins to emerge on the south of the central business district, occupying a narrow strip of land between State Street to the east and the CRI&P railroad tracks to the west.[4]

1882 A crowd of 300,000 (the city's population is 500,000) greets the first cable car in Chicago as it makes its inaugural run north from 21st St along State St. Financed by the merchant "king" Marshall Field, the line ends at the entrance to his department store. By the end of the year the convergence of new cable lines creates a loop of tracks near Field's State St. store. This "loop" would make the city's downtown one of the densest commercial cores in the world - by 1910, the half mile square loop area will contain 40% of the assessed land value in the 190 square mile city.[5] The development of rapid transit greatly accelerates the rate of urban development in the city and densifies the central business district. Patterns of land use become more sharply drawn.

1890 Chicago's population has doubled in the last decade, growing from 500,000 to one million.[6] It is the fastest growing city in the world.

1891 The Mecca, an apartment building, designed by Ed Brooke and F. P. Burnham, is built at 34th St. and State St., on the site that would become the location for Crown Hall; it is the first example of a low-rise courtyard apartment building in Chicago. The Armour Institute (a precursor to IIT) is opened. A non-denominational, co-educational, and racially integrated school, it is meant to provide instruction in industrial technologies to the children of Chicago's working class. Armour, the man who modernized meat, locates the school in a working class neighborhood, in the midst of the population it seeks to serve.[7]

1893 The World's Columbian Exposition opens. Orchestrated by Daniel Burnham, the Fair's "White City," built on a wasteland at the edge of the city's far southern lakeshore, will become a model for early 20th century American urbanism. Ida B. Wells, the anti-lynching activist and resident of the black belt, writes *The Reason Why the Colored American is Not in the World's Columbian Exhibition.*

1895 Chicago's first subsidized housing is built. Designed by Frank Lloyd Wright, the two-story courtyard building is rented to

A white "mob" chases a black man during the 1919 riot. Minutes later, he was caught and killed

CHICAGO HISTORICAL SOCIETY; PHOTOGRAPH BY JUN FUJITA

"Farewell, We're Good and Gone, Bound for the Promised Land."
-Message in chalk on railroad cars in Mississippi, bound for Chicago[9]

European immigrants. It is subsidized by a local business man who expects to earn a lower than market rate of return on his investment.

1897 The old downtown loop of cable car tracks is replaced by a ring of elevated trains, and the central business district becomes known as the "Loop."

1900 Chicago's "black belt" is well established, running along a narrow strip of land east of the Chicago Rock Island and Pacific Railroad line west of Wabash Ave. Virtually all of Chicago's African-American inhabitants live there.[10]

1905 *The Chicago Defender*, Chicago's first African-American owned and operated newspaper, is founded. *Defender* editorials urge African-Americans to leave the poverty of the south for new opportunities in the north. It stages events to encourage migration and provides names of churches and organizations in Chicago willing to help migrants settle in the city.

A METROPOLIS WITHIN A METROPOLIS

1910 At the beginning of what would become known as the "Great Migration," Chicago has a population of just over 2 million.[11] 2% of the city's population is African-American; over the course of the next decade, the African-American population in Chicago will increase by 148%, from 44,000 to 109,000.[12]

1915 The Association for the Study of Negro Life and History, one of the first groups devoted to African-American studies, is founded at the Bronzeville YMCA . The YMCA also provides housing and job training for new arrivals from the south.

1917 As the US enters World War I, the Army and Navy mobilize. One mobilization measure forces the closure of New Orlean's red light district, Storyville, despite appeals to the US Supreme Court. The musicians who had been employed in Storyville, known jazz players, move north to Chicago and work in clubs throughout the black belt, making Chicago the jazz capital for the next generation.

1919 The Chicago Race Riots take place over the course of 13 days; 38 die (23 blacks, 15 whites), 537 are injured and 1,000 African-Americans are left homeless. African-Americans are removed from integrated neighborhoods for "safety." Some of the most serious rioting occurs along State St. between 31st and 39th. This Chicago riot is one of 20 that occur across the US during the "red summer of 1919." The violence stems from massive demobilization and economic restructuring that occurs as a consequence of the war. Rural African-Americans flock to industrial centers to make up for the decline in immigration from Europe during war-time, and begin to compete with northern whites for housing and jobs. White fear and anger at the changing racial character of northern cities clashes with the rising militancy of returning African-American war veterans two generations removed >

"Well, it was a Black metropolis. And what made it a metropolis because it had everything that is necessary to survive in a metropolitan area. We had jobs; we had entertainment; although the housing was very over crowded, we had housing; we had a big park we could go to that we could enjoy ourselves in, Washington Park; and we had Douglas Playground; we had Forestville Playground. We had a lot of things that we could do and we could find jobs. Although most of the men worked in places like the steel mill and the stockyards, but once they came – once they left and came to the Black Metropolis, the South Side, they didn't have to go back out to enjoy themselves....

You see, in that period of time, we knew, without anybody writing it into law, that if we came on the east side of Cottage Grove, we might get arrested. Not doing anything, just being over there, they would ask you, what you doing over here. They wouldn't say, nigger, but 'What are you doing over here, boy?' or something. If we went to the west side of just west of Robert Taylor, then we might get into a fight, 'cuz then they would say, 'What are you doing over here, nigger?' So we had to adjust to that. If we went south of 67th Street, we might get into a fight and get arrested. And if we went north of 26th Street, we would be in a fight..."[13]

from slavery. After the riots, the Chicago Real Estate Board creates the Restrictive Covenant, a rider to property deeds which stipulates that certain properties can only be purchased and inhabited by whites. Primarily used as a tool to contain the growing population of African-Americans, the covenants can also be directed against Asians, Jews, and Eastern Europeans. The black belt becomes institutionalized by the force of law.

1920 Surrounded by the extended black belt, the Armour Institute begins plans to relocate.[14]

1927 The first city airport opens. Richard Wright moves to Chicago from Mississippi, and writes his first novel, *Native Son*, about African-American life in Chicago. The Harlem Globetrotters are formed by a group of basketball players who attended Phillips High School, the city's first predominantly African-American high school.

1928 Julius Rosenwald (creator of the Sears and Roebuck mercantile empire) builds the Michigan Boulevard Garden

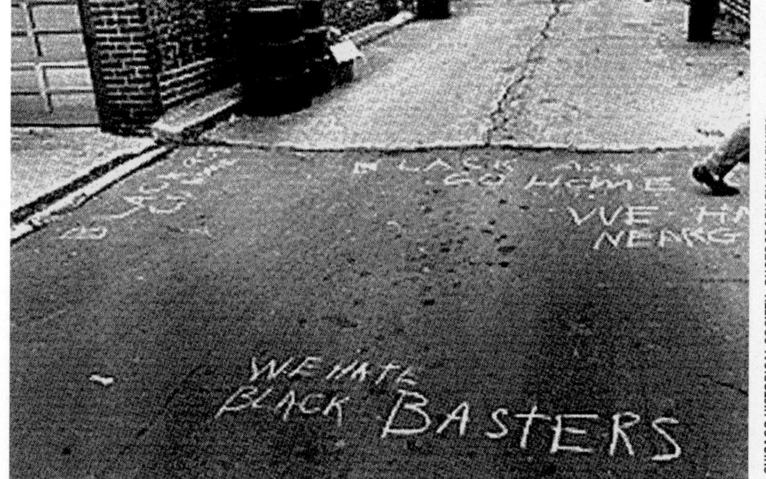

CHICAGO HISTORICAL SOCIETY: PHOTOGRAPH BY JUN FUJITA

Apartments in the southern end of the black belt. The 421 units are meant to attract private funding to subsidized housing for African-Americans. Marshall Field funds a similar project on the north side of the city, but both projects fail to stimulate further private investment in low cost housing, and definitively demonstrate the need for federal support.

1930 The intersection of 35th and State becomes the equivalent of the loop to the black belt, which is now "a narrow tongue of land, seven miles in length and one and one-half miles in width, where more than 300,000 Negroes are packed solidly."[15] A few blocks away, at the Pilgrim Baptist church, housed in a

Top: The basement at 3106 S. Wentworth, where ten families occupied cardboard cubicles, 1948

Left: An: alley in a white neighborhood on Chicago's South Side, 1962

Bottom: Map from the first sociological study of a black neighborhood in an American city. Drake and Cayton, the authors, were African-American graduate students at the University of Chicago

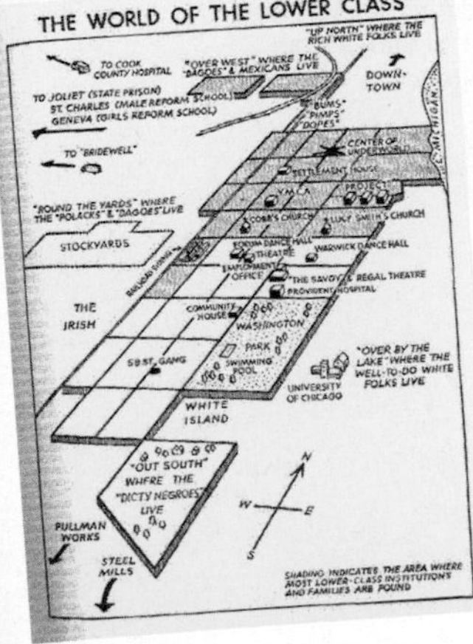

former synagogue designed by Louis Sullivan, Thomas Dorsey presides over the birth of gospel music.[17]

1931 The Depression exacerbates the housing shortage in Bronzeville. Eviction disturbances are increasingly common.[18]

1934 The Chicago Housing Authority begins building 5,000 units of public housing in response to increasing demands. Despite the extreme conditions in Bronzeville, the first developments are designed exclusively for whites.

ERASING BRONZEVILLE

1937 Constrained by finances, the Armour Institute decides to remain in its original location and starts acquiring land surrounding its site; Armour's president Willard Hotchkiss writes, "now is the time to move forward and possess the land."[19] The 1937 Federal Housing Act initiates federal assistance to cities for slum clearance. The Chicago Housing Authority is incorporated as a not-for-profit corporation supported by federal funds and managed by commissioners appointed by the mayor.

1940 Chicago's African-American population continues its steady increase: it grows by 77% between 1940 and 1950 - from 278,000 to 492,000.[20] The Illinois Institute of Technology is created as the Armour Institute merges with the Lewis Institute. The new school is consolidated on the Armour Institute's Bronzeville campus at 34th St. and Federal. Mies van der Rohe, displaced by the Nazi closure of the Bauhaus, is made director of the architecture school and is commissioned to design the first modern university campus in the US at the Bronzeville site.

1941 The Ida B. Wells housing project opens in Bronzeville; it is the first federally funded subsidized housing for African-Americans in the city. Federal policy (the Neighborhood Composition Rule) maintains that subsidized housing should be segregated by race. 18,000 families apply for 1,662 units in the Ida Bs.[21]

1942 The first controlled nuclear reaction occurs at the University of Chicago. Harvard holds its first conference on urbanism, "The Problem of Cities and >

"We moved to Chicago in 1948. It was our fourth state and our fifth city... We moved to a third floor, two-room, in-the-rear apartment at 1221 S. Sawyer, one of six two room-one way out apartments the building was converted into... In 1953 we move into a one-room community bath-and-kitchen apartment on the second floor of a two-story building with six other one-room apartments on south Lawndale.... At this 'apartment' we shared both the bathroom and the kitchen with our neighbors. People had to get along in sharing cooking time and using the bathroom... Space in the pantry and in the single refrigerator was assigned. Food and utensils would often disappear. As a result, we, as most families, kept everything we could inside our apartment. A schedule listing all the renters' bathroom and kitchen clean-up times was tacked on the wall. It was only adhered to by those who didn't want to live like slobs, or face the possibility of being put out..."[16]

Towns," signaling the beginning of a federal-state-municipal-corporate alliance that seeks to address the crisis of the postwar American city. Henry Held proposes to surround the Illinois Institute of Technology with a wall made of brick from demolished houses in Bronzeville.[22]

1947 The city develops a large-scale slum clearance and relocation program. Approximately 16,199 families will be displaced by 1963. The process begins on the south side with the Lake Meadows development sponsored by IIT and Michael Reese Hospital. Completed in 1953, the Lake Meadows project displaces 3,600 families to build 2,033 new units of integrated middle class housing. A state agency, the Land Clearance Commission had bought the land for $16 million and sold it to the developers for $3.4 million. Severe post-war housing shortages on the south side mean that 375,000 people live in an area meant to house 110,000.[23]

1948 Chicago's expressway development begins. The US Supreme Court outlaws restrictive covenants on home ownership. Lorraine Hansbury, daughter of one of the lawyers in the case, would dramatize the results of the ruling in *A Raisin in the Sun.* Chicago politicians sponsor the enactment of a state law which gives final approval of all sites for public housing to the Chicago City Council. This allows white communities to prevent the construction of public housing in or near their neighborhoods and ends the public housing authority's attempts to create racially integrated projects in white areas. Public housing is converted from a catalyst for social change to a new means of containing the city's African American population.

1950 For the first time, Chicago's population declines, having reached a peak of 3.6 million, but its African-American population continues to grow, increasing over the next ten years from 492,000 to 813,000, or by 65%.[24]

Gwendolyn Brooks becomes the first African American to win a Pulitzer Prize. At her home in Bronzeville, she gets the news in the dark because she cannot afford to pay her electric bill.

1956 Crown Hall opens on the former site of the Mecca apartment building. Brooks had once worked for a small business located in the Mecca.

March along State St., marking the dedication of the Ida B. Wells Homes, the first publicly funded housing development in Chicago to allow African American residents, 1941.

CHICAGO HISTORICAL SOCIETY

"We live stacked on top of one another with no elbow room. Danger is all around. There's little privacy or peace and no quiet. And the world looks on all of us as project rats, living on a reservation like untouchables."[29]

A resident of Robert Taylor Homes in 1965

Sit where the light corrupts your face.
Mies Van der Rohe retires from grace.
And the fair fables fall.[25]
-Gwendolyn Brooks, "In the Mecca"

1961 Elizabeth Wood, director of Chicago public housing from 1937 to 1954, writes that public housing super-blocks would establish "a new kind of urban residential neighborhood" to "compete with the suburbs for social desirability, especially for families with children. To abandon the large-scale planning that lies behind projects is to abandon one of the most important innovations in city development."[26]

1962 The Dan Ryan Expressway opens, clearing out a canyon on the west side of Bronzeville, creating a no-man's land between it and the Mayor's neighborhood to the west.

1964 IIT has grown from five buildings on seven acres in 1940 to 50 buildings on 110 acres in '64.

1966 Martin Luther King moves to Chicago to initiate the Poor Peoples Movement. With the completion of the major institutional reforms that would end legal segregation in the southern US, the next step in the civil rights movement would focus on the institutions and practices of racial prejudice in the north.

In the same year, the "State Street Corridor," the largest concentration of public housing in the world, is completed. "The projects stretch for 34 blocks (4 miles), with the only major break being the campus of the Illinois Institute of Technology from 30th to 35th streets."[27] Almost all of the projects along State St. are high-rise buildings housing large families. The housing authority claims that building high-rises minimizes construction costs and provides large areas of open space. However, public housing is 22% more expensive to build in Chicago than in New York City, even though market rate high-rise housing is >

> "The crew arrived at 9:15am with the heavy equipment. The ball was hoisted up and started to swing... I had my child right there on the 10th floor... I have mixed feelings about the projects... so, I think to myself, tear them all down. Well, I can't forget about all the good people who called them home.... No, no, leave them, cause so many people still need a place to live."[30]

17.8% more expensive to build in NYC.[28] The differential is produced in part by the choice of relatively expensive inner city sites that require substantial demolition, a result of the consolidation of power among white politicians who effectively prevent the construction of public housing outside the city's traditionally black neighborhoods. The "State Street Corridor," built on the ruins of Bronzeville is simultaneously an accident and a plan, both utopic and distopic in its intentions and results. Just as the emergence of the black belt at the turn of the 20th century materialized de facto racial segregation with such intensity that it eventually acquired the force of law, what began as a conflict between Utopian social reform and anxious white working class communities becomes a process with a momentum independent of particular decisions or a specific plan.

1968 Martin Luther King is assassinated in Atlanta. Rioting breaks out in Chicago and elsewhere. Large areas of the south side and west side of Chicago burn. The National Guard are called out to restore order; nine die.

1971 The stockyards close. Through the late '50s and early '60s, up to 80% of the stockyard workers were African-Americans. At its peak during World War I, the yards had employed 60,000 workers.

1975-85 Closures of south side steel plants; 11,000 jobs lost. The closings effectively end large scale industrial production within the city limits.

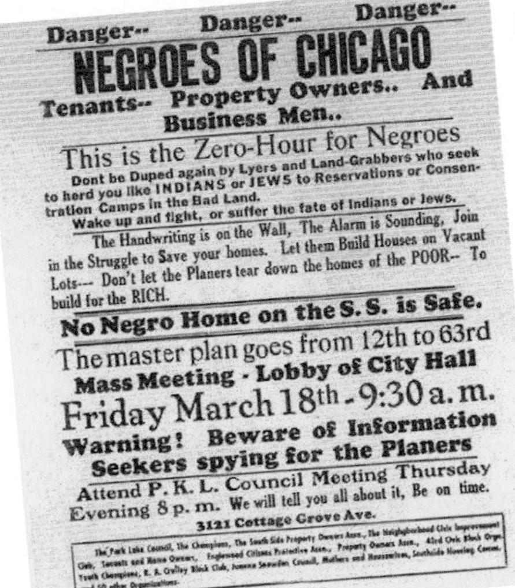

Danger-- Danger-- Danger--
NEGROES OF CHICAGO
Tenants-- Property Owners.. And Business Men..
This is the Zero-Hour for Negroes
Dont be Duped again by Lyers and Land-Grabbers who seek to herd you like INDIANS or JEWS to Reservations or Consentration Camps in the Bad Land.
Wake up and fight, or suffer the fate of Indians or Jews.
The Handwriting is on the Wall, The Alarm is Sounding, Join in the Struggle to Save your homes. Let them Build Houses on Vacant Lots--- Don't let the Planers tear down the homes of the POOR-- To build for the RICH.
No Negro Home on the S. S. is Safe.
The master plan goes from 12th to 63rd
Mass Meeting - Lobby of City Hall
Friday March 18th - 9:30 a. m.
Warning! Beware of Information Seekers spying for the Planers
Attend P. K. L. Council Meeting Thursday Evening 8 p. m. We will tell you all about it, Be on time.
3121 Cottage Grove Ave.

THEMING BRONZEVILLE

1992 The federal government announces HOPE VI, a program created to reconfigure U.S. housing policy. Vouchers for rent subsidies in private real estate markets will replace publicly owned and operated housing projects. Funding for building and maintaining publicly owned housing projects is virtually eliminated.

1995 The Chicago Housing Authority announces its plan to demolish most public housing high rises in the city.

1998 The "Black Metropolis-Bronzeville" historic district is created by the Chicago Landmarks Council. Only nine buildings are called out as historically significant. None of the housing projects are included.

1999 35,000 people live in CHA housing. Systematic teardowns of Chicago public housing have begun. At this point, HOPE VI has funded the demolition of over 90,000 public housing units in the US.

2001 The Chicago Housing Authority announces plans to rehabilitate 25,000 units and demolish 14,000, a total of 51 buildings will be lost. Most of the demolished units will be in Bronzeville. Citywide, the "Plan for Renewal" will require the relocation of as many as 14,000 families. The vacant land will be turned over to private developers at a substantial discount for the construction of new mixed-income neighborhoods. The money allocated to fund the program is about 50% of the funds needed to complete the project as planned.[31]

Some of this land I must own
Outta the city, they want us gone
Tearing down the 'jects creating plush homes
My circumstance is between Cabrini and Love Jones
Surrounded by hate, yet I love home

-Common, "Respiration"[32]

2003 IIT opens its new student center; the original design of the center included a basketball court embedded in the façade along State St. The court was one of a number of measures intended to invite inhabitants of Bronzeville into the center. The project, as built, breaks the line of its façade and leaves a grassy void were the court was meant to be.■

Miestakes

Left: Handbill protesting the demolition of African-American homes as part of the redevelopment of the black belt in the early 1950s.

LEFT: CHICAGO URBAN LEAGUE PAPERS, MANUSCRIPT COLLECTION, THE UNIVERSITY OF ILLINOIS AT CHICAGO, THE RICHARD J. DALEY LIBRARYCHICAGO HISTORICAL SOCIETY, NEGATIVE JCHI-17210

NOTES

1 HTTP://WWW.CHIPUBLIB.ORG/004CHICAGO /TIMELINE/POPULATION.HTML
2 DRAKE, S. C., CAYTON, H. *BLACK METROPOLIS.* (CHICAGO: UNIVERSITY OF CHICAGO PRESS. 1993): 32
3 MILLER, D. CITY OF THE CENTURY. (NEW YORK: SIMON & SCHUSTER. 1996): 91
4 DRAKE, S. C., CAYTON, H., IBID., 47
5 MILLER, D., IBID., 266
6 HTTP://WWW.CHIPUBLIB.ORG /004CHICAGO/TIMELINE/POPULATION.HTML
7 BLUESTONE, D., "CHICAGO'S MECCA FLAT BLUES." JOURNAL OF THE SOCIETY OF ARCHITECTURAL HISTORIANS (57:4, 382-403, DEC. 1998)
8 COOK COUNTY (ILL.). CORONER THE RACE RIOTS: BIENNIAL REPORT 1918-1919 AND OFFICIAL RECORD OF INQUESTS ON THE VICTIMS OF THE RACE RIOTS OF JULY AND AUGUST, 1919, WHEREBY FIFTEEN WHITE MEN AND TWENTY-THREE COLORED MEN LOST THEIR LIVES AND SEVERAL HUNDRED WERE INJURED. *WWW.CHIPUBLIB.ORG/004CHICAGO /DISASTERS/TEXT/CORONER/INTRO.HTML*
9 TURNER, B. C., A VIEW OF BRONZEVILLE (CHICAGO: HIGHLIGHTS OF CHICAGO PRESS): 8
10 DRAKE, S. C., CAYTON, H., IBID., 53
11 *WWW.CHIPUBLIB.ORG/ 004CHICAGO /TIMELINE/ POPULATION.HTML*
12 LEMANN, N., *THE PROMISED LAND* (NEW YORK: ALFRED A. KNOPF. 1991): 16
13 TIMUEL BLACK (INTERVIEW, HTTP://STREETLEVEL.IIT.EDU/YOUTHPROJECTS/CHS/DGB /TBLACK.HTML)
14 WHITING, S. "BAS RELIEF URBANISM: CHICAGO'S FIGURED FIELD." MIES IN AMERICA (HARRY N. ABRAMS, PUBLISHERS): 642-691
15 DRAKE, S. C., CAYTON, H., IBID. 12
16 VIRDAJEAN TOWNS-COLLINS. "LATERAL MOVES" (LOST IN DARKNESS, JOURNAL OF ORDINARY THOUGHT. SPRING 2002.): 6
17 IBID. 383
18 BOWLEY, D., JR., *THE POORHOUSE: SUBSIDIZED HOUSING IN CHICAGO, 1895-1976* (CARBONDALE: SOUTHERN UNIVERSITY PRESS): 17
19 WHITING, S., IBID., 655
20 LEMANN, IBID., 70
21 BOWLEY, IBID., 30
22 WHITING, S., IBID., 668
23 BOWLEY, IBID., 56
24 *WWW.CHIPUBLIB.ORG/ 004CHICAGO /TIMELINE/ POPULATION.HTML*
25 BROOKS, G. *IN THE MECCA*, (NEW YORK: HARPER & ROW.1964) 5
26 BOWLEY, IBID., 65
27 IBID., 130
28 IBID., 122
29 IBID., 124
30 PAT GUY, "3919: A SHORT STORY." (*SONGS OF OUR TIME, JOURNAL OF ORDINARY THOUGHT*. SUMMER 1997)
31 GROSSMAN, K. N., "CAN THE CITY SCRAPE UP MONEY FOR CHA'S PLAN?" *CHICAGO SUN-TIMES*: 28 MARCH 2001 (WWW.SUNTIMES.COM/SPECIAL_SECTIONS/CHA/CHA28.HTML)
32 COMMON. COMPOSERS: D. SMITH, T. GREENE, T. TROTTER, P. PHILLIPS "RESPIRATION" *MOS DEF AND TALIB KWELI ARE BLACKSTAR*. RAWKUS. 1999

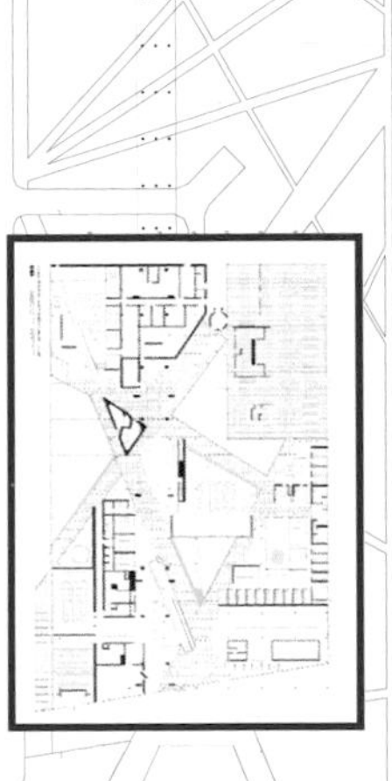

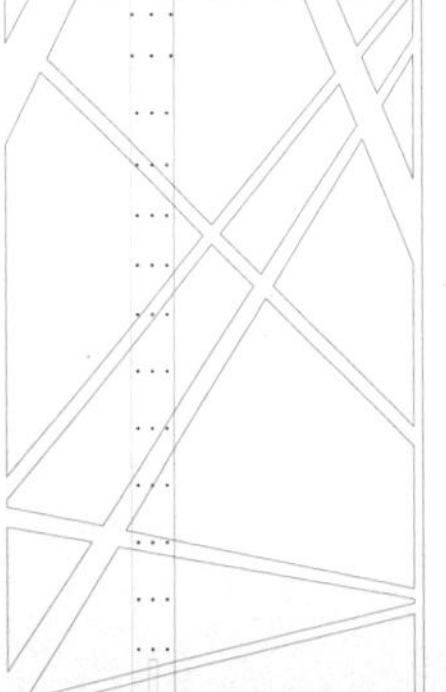

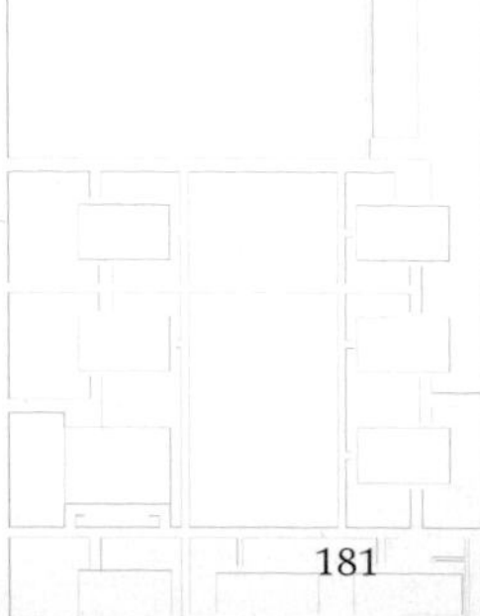

1: TROUBLE

According to statistics, a student and his or her parents decide, within five seconds of arrival, whether to apply to a given university or not. With that test, Mies van der Rohe's IIT Campus is in trouble. The IIT campus is a masterpiece invisible to the contemporary eye. Mies's work has become unnoticeable without explanation.

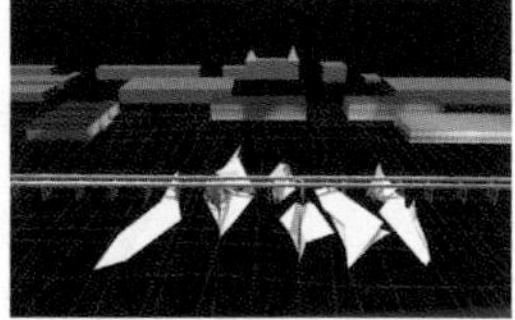

2: SIGNATURE

To reverse IIT's decline in popularity, a competition for a new Campus Center was organized in 1997. In their entries — shifted south from the Campus's center to face the more "unique" Crown Hall directly — Zaha Hadid and Peter Eisenman ignore Mies's meditation on the generic in favor of expressive architectures that propose a radical departure for the campus. Is Mies's greatness "sustainable" next to the average late 20th century masterpiece? Can the typical survive the signature, in the first five seconds even?

3: CLEANING

I do not respect Mies, I love Mies. I have studied Mies, excavated Mies, reassembled Mies. I have even cleaned Mies. Because I do not revere Mies I'm at odds with his admirers.

4: No one, especially in Chicago, talks about Mies's quality as an urbanist. It is the beautiful ambiguity of the IIT Campus that the status of its built substance oscillates between object and tissue, that its modules imply potential extension yet end emphatically, that its structures hover between recessive foreground and prominent background.

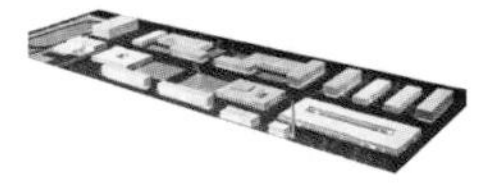

5: MAROONED

In its current form, Mies's IIT is marooned. The true crisis of IIT is not its relative neglect but the disappearance of the city around it, Chicago. This brutal cancellation has turned the campus into a metaphorical tabula rasa surrounded by a real tabula rasa; the disappearance of the city has pulled the rug out from underneath Mies.

6: MAROONED II

The Commons Building was intended as an object in a designed context. Now it inhabits a no-man's land. The encounter between the lone Mies box and the rocket of the passing EL trains is as absurd as Lautremont's encounter between the umbrella and the sewing machine - a surrealist pastiche. Without context, the Commons has become a nonevent.

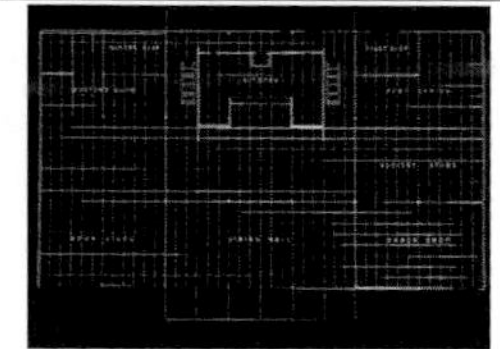

7: FUNDRAISING

Originally, the Commons was intended as an "amenities center" for the IIT campus, including a dining hall, grocery, barber shop, and a laundry. "[Due to] the inability of IIT to raise funds for the Student Union, a pendant to the library as one of the two buildings of a public character on campus, the Commons scavenged many of the functions allotted to the Student Union, and due to Mies's deep frustration... Crown Hall became the great symbolic presence on the Campus rather than the Student Union."[1] Uninterested in the Commons, Mies left its design to Gene Summers, the project architect, refusing to consider the project until Summers proposed creating an enclosed shopping mall.

[1] Phyllis Lambert, letter to the author.

8: LOYALTY

Can respect kill? Mies needs to be protected from his defenders. In 1986, the Barcelona Pavilion was reconstructed in color. (In architectural history, it remains stubbornly black and white.) Its resurrection killed its aura. The mid-80s coincided with the initial apotheosis of the market economy. Coincidence? Was Mies sacrificed by his defenders on the altar of city marketing? A large section of the Pavilion is now a souvenir shop.

CHICAGO TRIBUNE
MAR. 20, 2000

oice of the people

IT plans forget history

HICAGO—Although I applaud the Illinois In- ute of Technology's plans to revitalize its pus, I question the fact that its architect, Koolhaas, would be allowed to attach his ding to Mies van der Rohe's award-winning mons Building, altering it in such a way it no longer retains its pristine and elegant netry. I find it ironic that at a time when the ric and architectural monuments in this ave been for the most part protected, or at flagged for preservation, in this case no one aking out regarding this latest act of archi- al vandalism.

y is it that there is no word from the staff Chicago Architectural Landmark Com- n regarding this matter? Where does the ark Preservation Council of Illinois stand issue?

inly this building, now being ignored, in 1953 received the American Institute of ects highest award for architecture, is eli- r landmark status.

it be that too many sacred cows are in- r that too many toes would be stepped adverse opinion were stated?

y contributed to the Drelhaus Founda- ich initiated the architectural selection a foundation that supports landmark tion, has paradoxically fostered a bad ural precedent.

s we never learn from the past. I re- when Roosevelt University "remod- reat Auditorium Banquet Hall by tear- uis Sullivan's skylighted ceiling and it with fluorescent lighting, followed ration of the event with a banquet in the newly refurbished space. Now they are wisely seeking funds to restore the former Auditorium Banquet Room to its original splendor. There was a time when the Charnley House by Adler and Sullivan was about to be used as an entrance to a condominium complex that would have been an embarrassment for the city of Chicago.

Fortunately protests from preservationists prevented this from happening and today this landmark building is restored and safely in the hands of the Society of Architectural Historians.

It is not too late to save the Commons Building from wanton defacement. Why can't the university request that the Commons be reused in a more sympathetic manner? Does Koolhaas have to use the building as a loading dock with semi-trailers backing into it? Can't he let the interior of the building be restored to its original open symmetrical plan without his demonstrative interventions? And does he need to place a parking lot on its only remaining open corner elevation?

It would not take much to rethink this aspect of the project and still retain a dialog between Koolhaas' building, the "L" tracks and Mies' architecture. Are we so naïve as to think that it has to be done in such a destructive manner?

Are we so blinded by the glamour of hiring outside celebrity architects that we accept his novel ideas at the expense of diluting the profound architectural contributions made by a towering figure of our time and city?

John Vinci
Vinci/Hamp Architects Inc.
Adjunct professor
Illinois Institute of Technology

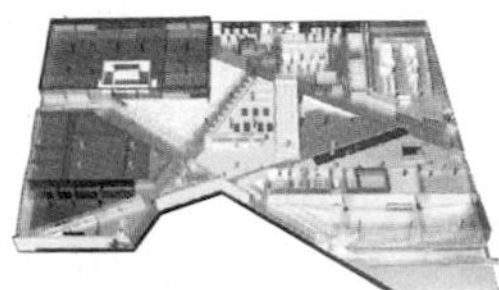

9: SOLUTION

Incorporating the Commons into the Student Center generated a context for it. The adjustments necessary for this new coexistence were a fraction of the abuse the building had already undergone. By planning it as one building, we could generate the dollars to restore it. The consolidated Student Center could reclaim its rightful place on the campus.

10: SOLUTION II

Years after its apparently indifferent conception and subsequent neglect, the Commons becomes a masterpiece overnight, simply through (the threat of) OMA's touch. "What about those of us who have to live with this kind of vandalism? What about the future of preservation?"[3] A preference for the embalmed over the authentic has fuelled American culture in the '90s. Instead of "using" the Center in a robust way, our critics proposed turning the Commons into a "visitors center" to enshrine its (retroactive) dignity. Final solution for the Miesian: to save from life, rescue by tourism. Vinci: "There are functions more compatible with the Commons that would not abuse its architecture.... Why not consider putting the University Club and Mies information Center in the Commons along with other compatible services? It would be a wonderful place to experience Mies's architecture."

[3] Vinci, open letter

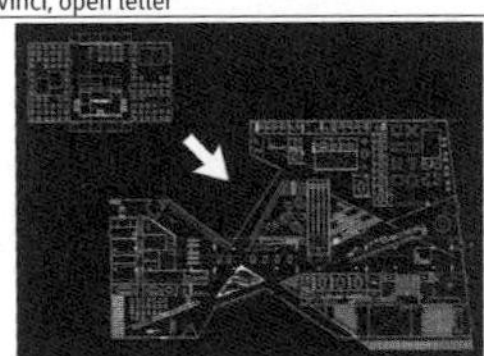

11: DISENGAGEMENT

Negotiations were launched, concerned with "minimizing" an engagement that could bring new vitality. Illinois Historic Preservation Agency: "The treatment of the immediate setting of the Commons Building is key to minimizing the effect of the new design on the historic building." Each breakfast with the Miesians brought new suggestions for disengagement, uncoupling, separation. And, from Vinci, "Please tell Koolhaas that I am not some monster trying to destroy him.... Some day I will have to face him... and I don't want to have to punch him in the nose.... Ask that Koolhaas move his building two bays of the Commons Building to the south. This will not change his plans or cost any more." [4]

[4] letter from Vinci, forwarded to author.

12: FOOD COURTSHIP

"Others" enjoy freedoms that are unavailable to the architect. As OMA was struggling with History, the IIT's client left the food consultant free range to speculate about reconfiguring Mies as a contemporary food court. Their sketches were breathtaking in their daring, energy, innocence. But they were unreadable on architects' radar. Only architects can defile architecture. CONTINUED ON PG195 >

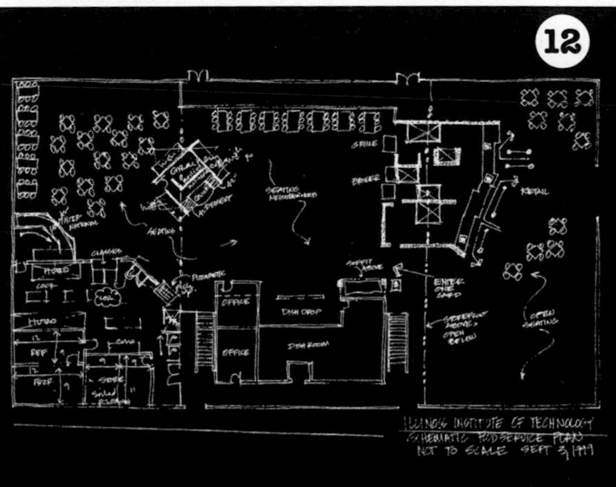

The Chicago School

McCormick Tribune Campus Center at IIT
Completed: October 2003

PHOTOS BY RICHARD BARNES

1941: 6000 students
57 acres

1998: 3200 students
120 acres

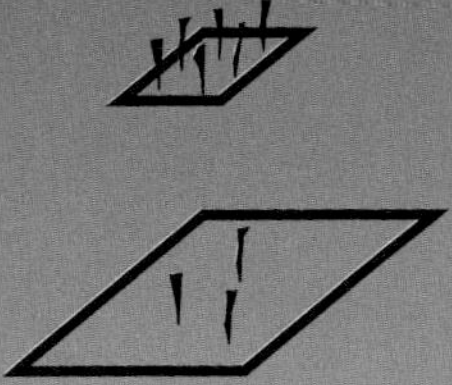

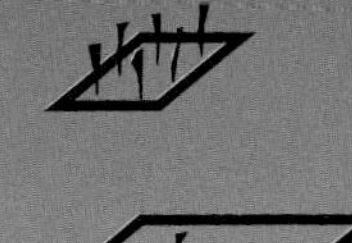

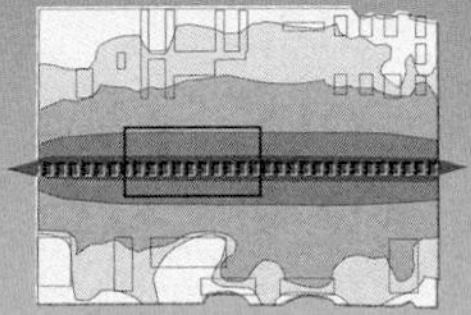

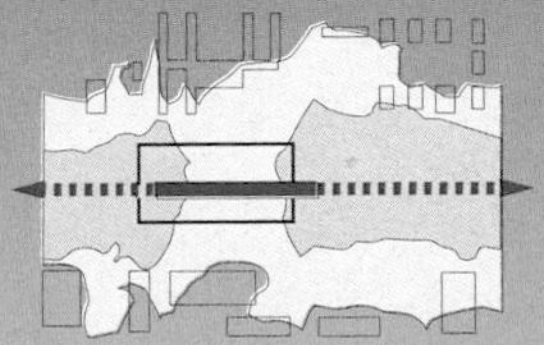

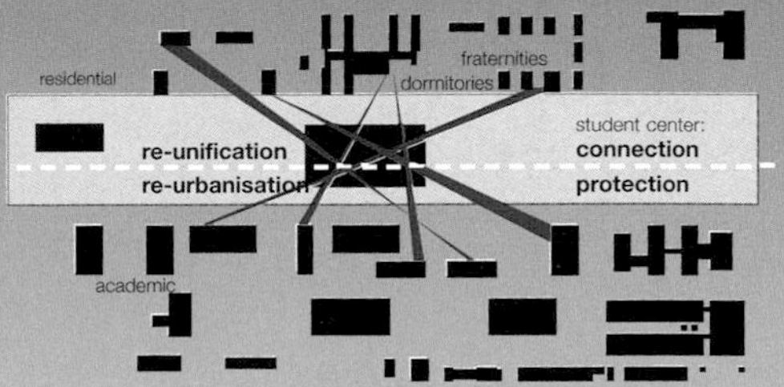

residential
fraternities
dormitories
re-unification
re-urbanisation
student center:
connection
protection
academic

13

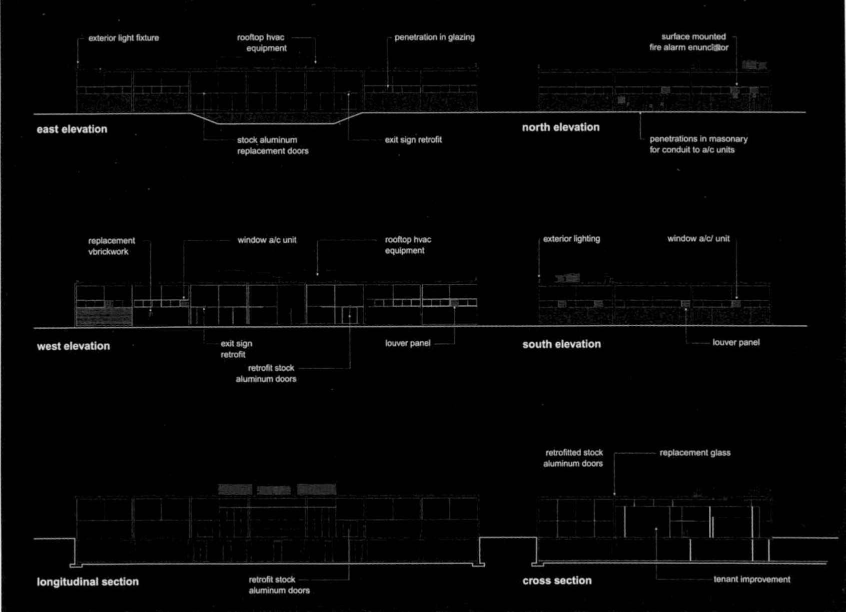

CONTINUED FROM PG183>

13: MIES WATCH

In the meantime, close scrutiny revealed that the Commons had undergone a shocking number of modifications without audible protest from the architectural community.

From 1953 to 1999, more than 30 interventions were undertaken in the "original" Commons: drain pipes, machinery plant room (on the roof), air conditioning boxes - an impressive record of abuse. The interior was completely unrecognizable. Glass had became sheetrock; a central pavilion acquired asymmetrical bulk to become a pizza parlor. The entire transformation took place on his acolytes' "Mies Watch." Their obliviousness allowed alterations by others ("food experts," electricians) to remain outside the meticulously policed borders of architectural consciousness. According to Vinci, "To this date... no successive architect has considered annexing or altering any of Mies's original architecture."

14: DEFACED

When is Mies more beautiful, defaced or rebuilt? As ruin, or reconstitution? The Commons could be read in two ways: a mere shed, intended by Mies to be common, to absorb whatever student life needs - even to undergo brutal retrofits, each improvization an addition to an ultimately aleatory, forever unfinished composition - or a pathetically martyred icon, full of wounds, scars, legible degradations.

Would that be the failure of Mies - defacement the only form of communication?

15: PROXIMITY

In all my visits to Chicago, I learned only one new thing from the Miesians, or actually two. One, Mies had received a letter from Hugh Hefner once, asking him to do the Playboy Headquarters - Mies had said no, for reasons no longer accessible. Two, Mies's model shop had a (frequently exploited) view of the photo studios of Playboy Magazine- all during the Fifties and Sixties, Mies's architecture and the first generation of playmates had been produced in voyeuristic proximity. It is exactly that kind of proximity we proposed for the Campus Center and the Commons, and which the Miesians wanted to undo.

16: LAPIDARY

Education can always be read as a plot: it may be that Mies at IIT was always a little too stimulating of the average, preferring to keep the sublime to himself.

"Less is More" is a smokescreen. Maybe it is a law that dogmas are defined by those that are most prone to violate them. Mies's work hides its formlessness, perversion, and anxiety behind a stealth shield of serenity. By never "explaining" himself except in the most lapidary terms, Mies condemned all of us - his intimates - to second guess his motives. Mies is (too) easily misread. Is Mies to blame for his own misreading?

Mies' fusion of the sublime and the generic/featureless into a new hybrid was a form of alchemy, a laboratory experiment that could never be duplicated by others.

Is the magician responsible for the lack of intelligence of his believers? Could Mies have avoided the endless reproduction of the Box that, in the 60s and 70s, threatened to take the essence of the original in an avalanche of reproduction, to give the original a bad name? Did he send us unknowingly to our mediocrity? ■ **RK**

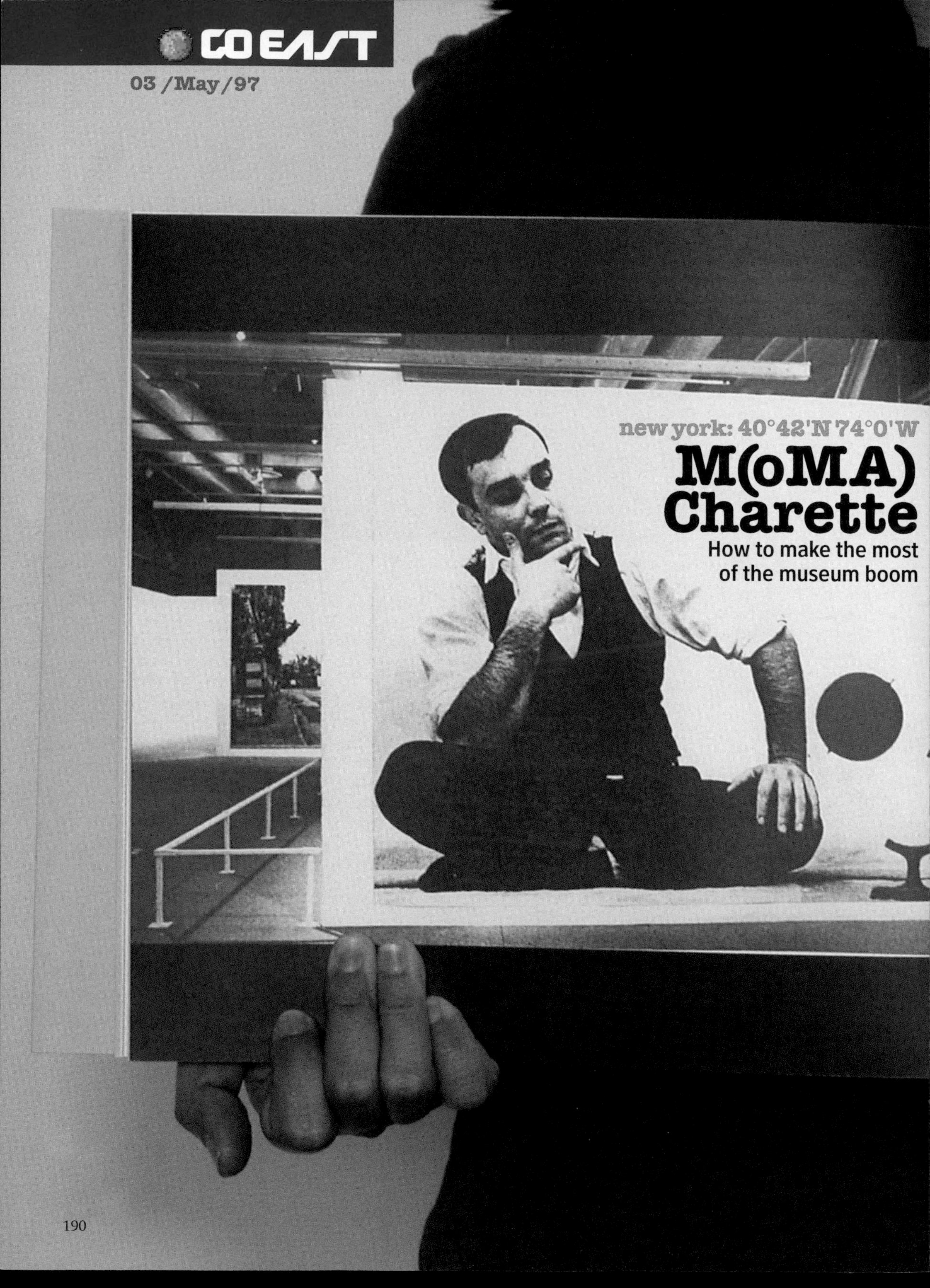

new york: 40°42'N 74°0'W

M(oMA) Charette

How to make the most of the museum boom

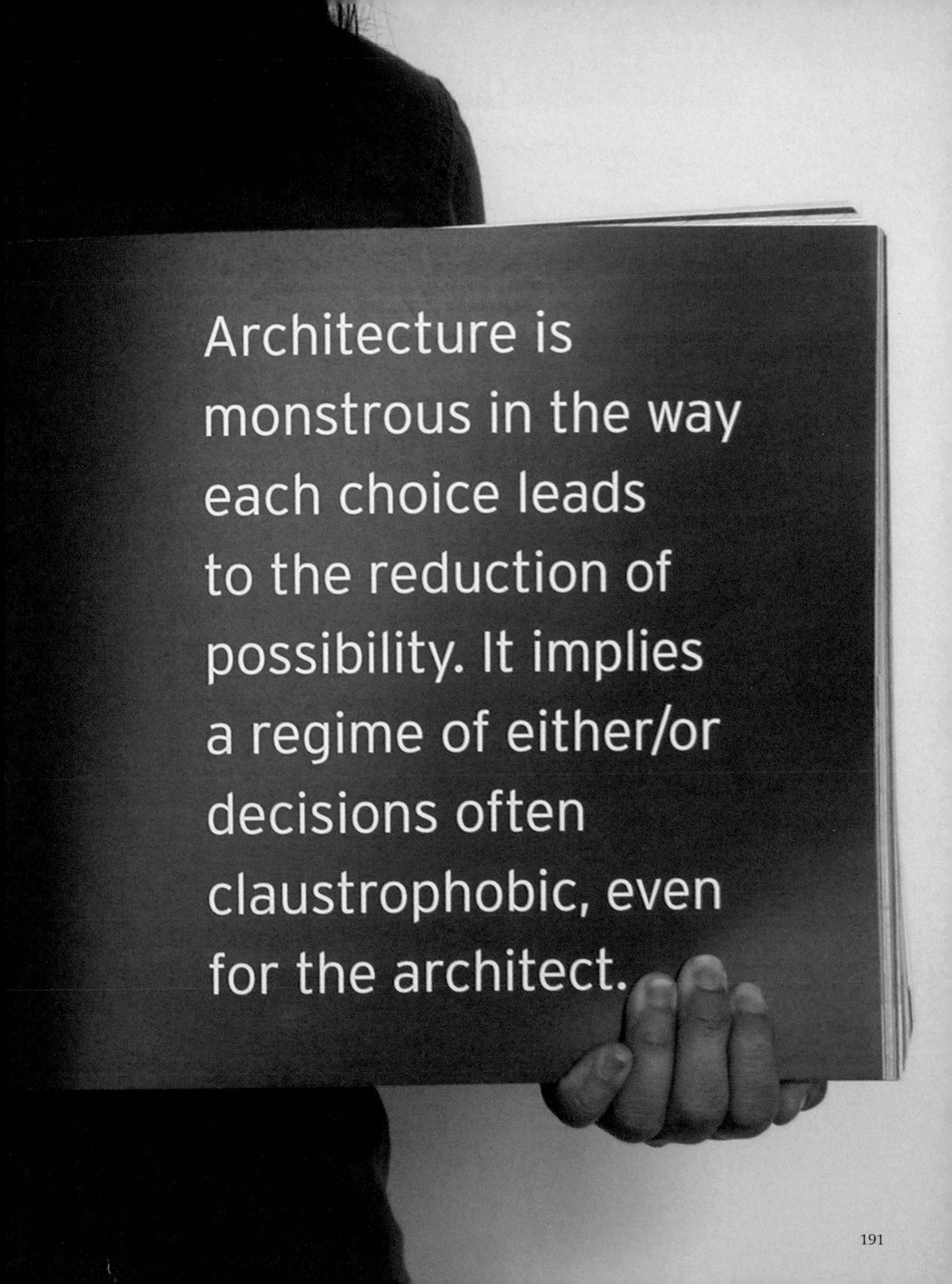

Architecture is monstrous in the way each choice leads to the reduction of possibility. It implies a regime of either/or decisions often claustrophobic, even for the architect.

You can be a Museum,
or you can be Modern,
but you can't be both.
Gertrude Stein

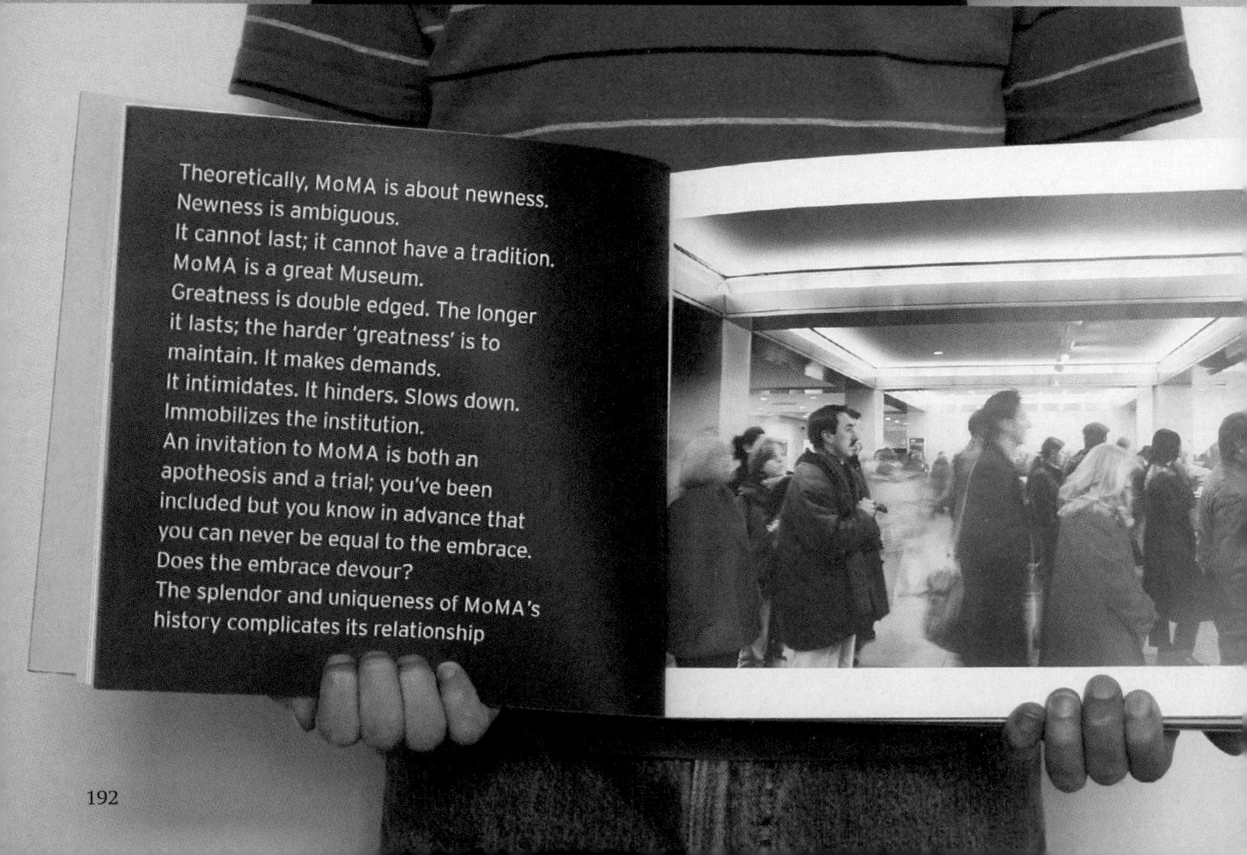

Theoretically, MoMA is about newness.
Newness is ambiguous.
It cannot last; it cannot have a tradition.
MoMA is a great Museum.
Greatness is double edged. The longer it lasts; the harder 'greatness' is to maintain. It makes demands.
It intimidates. It hinders. Slows down.
Immobilizes the institution.
An invitation to MoMA is both an apotheosis and a trial; you've been included but you know in advance that you can never be equal to the embrace.
Does the embrace devour?
The splendor and uniqueness of MoMA's history complicates its relationship

INTRO
- BOXES FOR MOMA
- TEXT I
- AHLGREN
- TEXT II
- URBANISM
SITUATION DERIVE INFLUENCES
RULES (ZONING)
- HANDS / I.E. BASIC ARGUMENTS
- PROCESS (MESSY RANDOM CREATIVITY)
- GROUND FLOOR - URBANISM 2
+ ODYSSEE COLLAGES AS EXT. OF GF.
- TRIANGLE
- 4 TYPES
- SCALE COMPARISONS
- FEASABILITY
- PHASING
- SUMMARY

with the present. The expectation of continuity penalizes what is 'other', what does not 'fit' , or the 'merely' contemporary. Beyond its power to intimidate, to set standards, to consecrate – an entire domain of exploration, experimentation has become problematic: its investment in a master narrative and the abundant evidence to support 'the line' make certain new shows seem like mere tokenism or simply impossible.

What can you challenge in a Temple ?

How do you cohabit with God(s)?

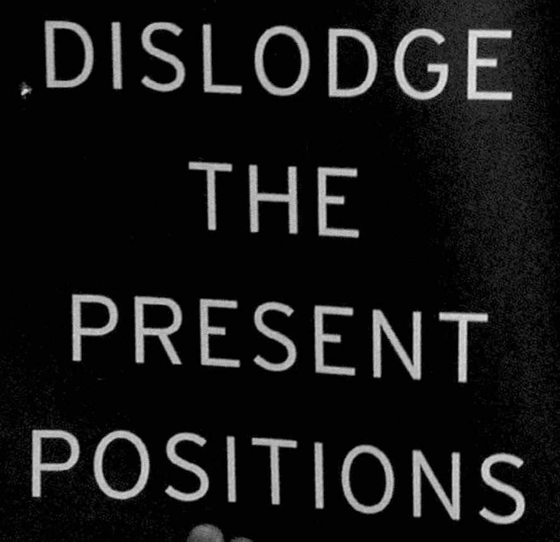
DISLODGE
THE
PRESENT
POSITIONS

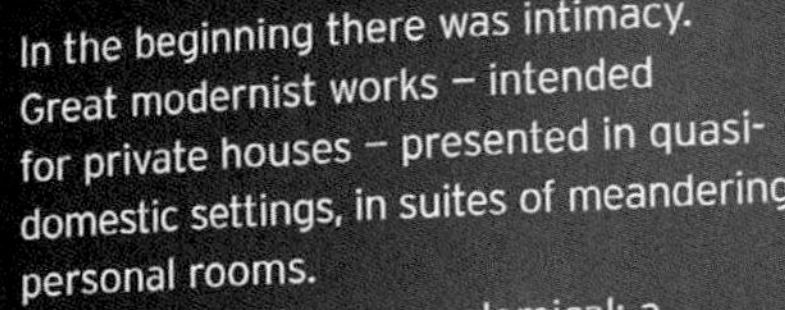
In the beginning there was intimacy.
Great modernist works – intended
for private houses – presented in quasi-
domestic settings, in suites of meandering,
personal rooms.
The presentation was polemical: a
parcours bonded to a narrative of linear
progress.
Forty years later, the Pelli extension
doubled MoMA's size. The author
of MoMA's initial polemic was no longer
present. World War II unleashed forces
both destructive and liberating, the
size of art exploded, new arts demanded
representation, visitors increased
exponentially, but the initial concept
was not revised.
51

Intimacy squared is no longer intimate, but oppressive, claustrophobic. MoMA now is an astonishing experience: the latent conservatism of its architectural configuration acts as a Procrustean bed that limits the potential of the entire institution.
Unintended reverse proof of the power of Architecture?

Ten architects come to Manhattan for a three day briefing.
They are treated to lectures. Like an existential mantra, the phrase 'best in the world' is routinely applied to MoMA by MoMA.
How confident is an institution that so insistently bestows such praise on itself? (Anyway, we already know. That's why we are there.)
During the three days, I look at MoMA for the first time as an architect and I am shocked. Shocked at the difference – I had never really 'seen' MoMA, only looked at its contents (or its machinery).
The old part of M[illegible]abby; the new

part of MoMA is tacky. While ingenious, the architectural quality of the 80's extension is dubious: its identity is blurred and compromised, its galleries have no particular qualities, the basement seems conceived as a corporate purgatory.

Never has such an important museum been accommodated in such mediocre surroundings. The present is constricted equally by reputation and configuration. All generations have been happily collaborating – in a process of expedient *bricollage* – on the systematic degradati[illegible]premises. MoMA has become a[illegible]y accident.

Will these spaces of infinitely malleable sheetrock ever regain relevance, dignity, or even character? Or has as an endless series of revisions, improvisations, and compromises squandered their aura forever?
How seriously can you plot the n-th version?
A mere reconfiguration is not going to resuscitate them. Only a new thinking can re-energize these thoroughly depleted conditions.

In this project, we have interpreted the Extension as a single operation that maintains what is good, undoes what is dysfunctional, creates new potentials, and leaves open what is undecidable.

A radical way out of the dilemma (the institution imprisoned by its own success, values, (hi)stories, plan) would have been separation: a bipolar MoMA – MoMA past and, somewhere else, MoMA present. In that case, each side could have achieved autonomy and pursued its own mission with unilateral vigor. But there could never have been influence, contrast, or confrontation.
That option has been discarded. The chosen model is coexistence.

Coexistence implies
RELATIONSHIPS.

Relationships imply
ENGAGEMENT.

Engagement implies
RISK.

Real coexistence implies the creation of *one single building*. A single building of multiple qualities, conditions, and environments equipped to deal with classical masterpieces in intimate spaces but also contemporary experiments and scales.
A building that can establish new equalities between various media and departments, a building entirely focused on the strategies, the qualities, the technologies, the architectures of display, the techniques of communication, and the organization of flows (of human beings, artifacts, information). The creation of a single display building – a

[illegible]ew MoMA – implies that it can be fully [illegible]quipped to generate unique conditions [illegible]or each segment of the collections and [illegible]ny of the exhibitions. It will have to [illegible]ccommodate drastically different scales. [illegible] will probably not be 'the seamless [illegible]hole' that Varnedoe suggested in [illegible]ocantico, but a *fin-de-siecle* Whole with [illegible]he capacity to establish relationships [illegible]hen wanted, isolation when needed, [illegible]onfrontation when desirable, short [illegible]ircuits when compelling...

Because an entirely new building will contain the entire Museum program, it will have the advantages of Bigness: "...programmatic hybridization, proximities/frictions/overlaps/superpositions, the entire apparatus of montage invented at the beginning of the century to organize the relationships between independent parts..."
It will not be a black box, but certain parts will be black boxes.
It will not be a sequence of rooms, but there will be such sequences.
Instead of fixed, it will be specific and varied; instead of flexible certain parts will be changeable and unstable.

GO EAST

After the sterile experiments with flexibility in the 60s and 70s, the threat of premature closure and pre-emptive definition in the eighties, a single, new Museum building can offer the performance of critical mass, the multiplicity of genuinely different conditions that can each accommodate art in unique ways.

72

Emancipate the Departments

Individual vs. Collective

It is a truism that museums are for the masses. The public. They are the temples of a late-20th-century collective. Their spaces, their circulation, their diagrams insist on the group, an abstract, undifferentiated client. Yet, more and more technologies provoke the splintering of the collective into an infinite number of individuals, each with their own interest. So far, the Museum has offered a single vision to the many. New techniques enable it to offer multiple visions/aspects to various individuals. Such a shift implies that an extension should not only contain new, bigger rooms, but begin to accommodate the individual visitor with a highly specific aim and to offer cellular accommodat

MoMA Inc.

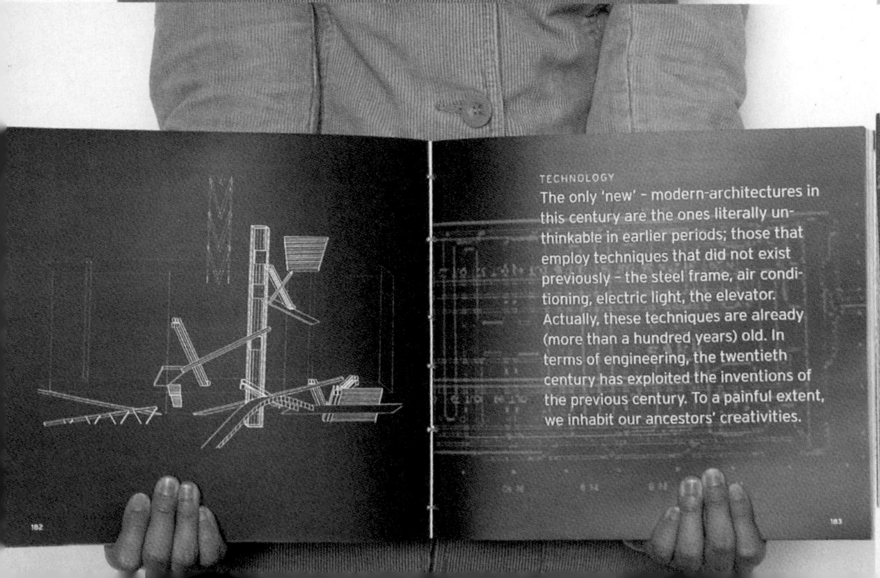

TECHNOLOGY

The only 'new' - modern-architectures in this century are the ones literally unthinkable in earlier periods; those that employ techniques that did not exist previously - the steel frame, air conditioning, electric light, the elevator. Actually, these techniques are already (more than a hundred years) old. In terms of engineering, the twentieth century has exploited the inventions of the previous century. To a painful extent, we inhabit our ancestors' creativities.

182 183

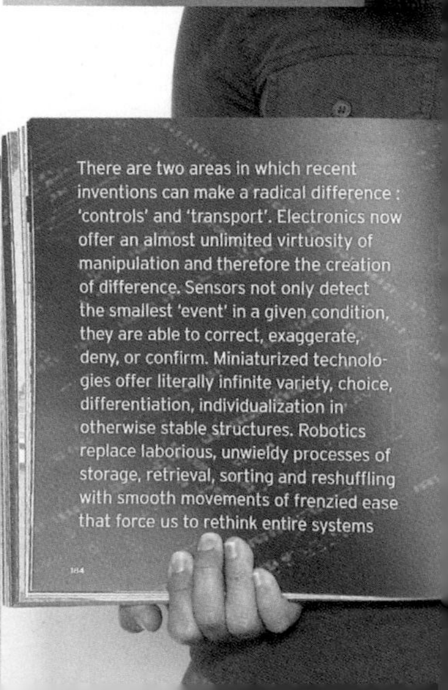

There are two areas in which recent inventions can make a radical difference : 'controls' and 'transport'. Electronics now offer an almost unlimited virtuosity of manipulation and therefore the creation of difference. Sensors not only detect the smallest 'event' in a given condition, they are able to correct, exaggerate, deny, or confirm. Miniaturized technologies offer literally infinite variety, choice, differentiation, individualization in otherwise stable structures. Robotics replace laborious, unwieldy processes of storage, retrieval, sorting and reshuffling with smooth movements of frenzied ease that force us to rethink entire systems

354

"MoMA is based on the coexistence of five departments."
But the real MoMA is not so blandly egalitarian.
On site, inequalities are glaring. The ideological model – with its connections to the Bauhaus, socialism, and labor – has been streamlined. Ironically, it is those departments – painting and sculpture – whose arts have been around 'always' and forever that dominate at the expense of the newer media, the ones that have defined modernity in this century.

75

Day

Night

More and more contemporary art needs spaces equipped for the interaction of human beings and technological implements, people and apparatus. Somehow, daylight is not conductive for this kind of interaction. The artificial withers under too much exposure. Video, computer, television, wiring, an entire panoply of virtual media takes real space. Where painting and sculpture are best revealed in conditions of (simulated) daylight; new arts need a darker, more artificial accommodation, an American night, illuminated by electronic haze, glowing and flickering. There is no escaping the inherent artificiality of the Museum.

77

It is an open secret that the presentation of art is not the only 'function' of the contemporary Museum. The very success of the institution has accrued additional interests and powers that require their own infrastructure. In addition, the way visual culture is now infinitely disseminated increases the value of access to real things. This allure makes it crucial for institutions to guard, exploit, and wherever possible enhance their aura. Paradoxically it raises the stakes for those who 'own' real things to play a role in their dissemination, if not to control it.

STORAGE VS. VIEWING

A Museum is an ambiguous treasure house of collections: part is on view and accessible, an often larger part is hidden in storage, aggressively inaccessible. The division inevitably corresponds to editing: in or out? The essential Museum experience is based on selection (by unseen hands, for unarticulated criteria, from unknowable quantities). The museum is the only institution that *systematically* freezes its assets away. Within the extension, the notion of storage should be emancipated. New forms of automated storage, visible storage, and ro[illegible]tic retrieval eliminate arguments of [illegible]t access, unwieldy

of classification and categorization. Electronic wiring enables the coexistence of authentic and virtual worlds with fundamental discretion.

When Victor Hugo announced more than hundred years ago that the 'book' would kill 'architecture,' he was wrong. For the same reason, the electronic is not necessarily the nemesis of the authentic. It could be its savior: every experience savored in cyberspace, 'uses' less of the Real. The New Museum will employ all of the new techniques – conditioning, representation, and communication – and will use them to create a new context for

185

10/January/02

Will Harvard reconcile its Janus-faced self-image by re-inventing its past through contemporary means, or by reinforcing its gentility through ...

Intellichintz

cambridge: 42°38'N 71°12'W

Breathing Space for the Bowtie

Where, until recently, modernity was compatible with Harvard's image - Sert and Le Corbusier's buildings have co-existed with the historical buildings on campus without special pleading – the university now has to proceed by stealth to realize the additional real estate needed for its expansion.

Harvard's dominant presence at the center of Cambridge – a city in the form of a bowtie - has put a stranglehold on its own and the city's future. It is nearing an impasse where increasingly greater cost and political effort are required to realize fewer square feet of new construction. A DMZ (DeMoralized Zone) now surrounds Harvard like a front line of gentility. To build along this zone, Harvard has been forced to adopt polite, if not invisible planning strategies involving underground facilities, neutered new construction, and the re-building of Georgian architecture. Its most widespread strategy is "mining" – gutting the insides of buildings and completely modernizing their interiors while preserving the "historicity" of their facades.

1. Exapansion within the confines of Cambridge has created a contested area, a DMZ (DeMoralized Zone), between the University and its neighbors.

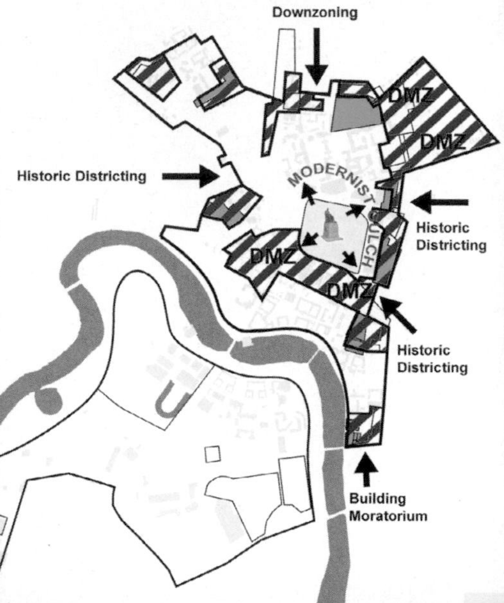

2. Life in the DMZ: political pressures force building costs to skyrocket as efficiency dwindles.

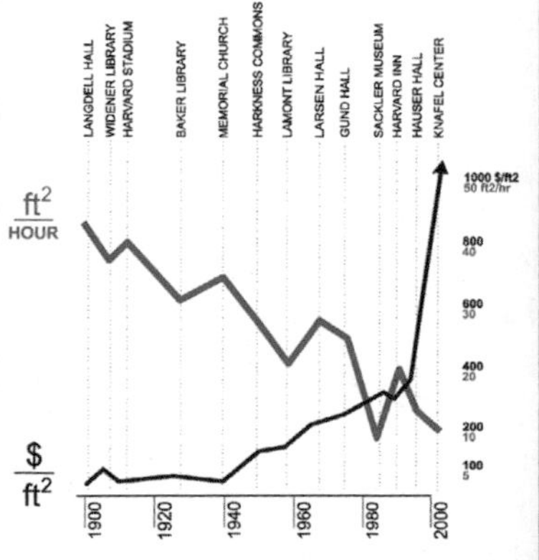

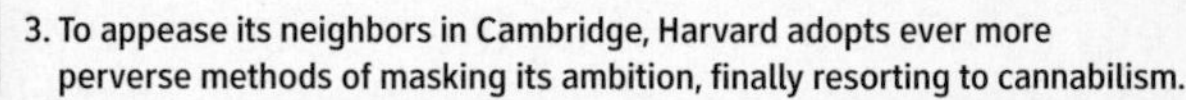
3. To appease its neighbors in Cambridge, Harvard adopts ever more perverse methods of masking its ambition, finally resorting to cannibalism.

As an escape clause, the University has accumulated large clumps of land across the Charles River to relieve the pressure in Cambridge and to offer Harvard the breathing space it requires. But the "TUBS," or faculties, don't want to move to the wrong side of the river. The only one to make a home there is the Business School, which has installed itself in the extravagant post-modern comfort of an Executive Arcadia to lure corporate part-timers.

To unlock the current impasse, one of AMO's proposals in a study of Harvard's current dilemmas involves radical surgery, not unlike its Cambridge rival MIT achieved in 1910, and is codenamed "Moses."
The Charles River is diverted to the south so that the current boomerang-shaped riverbed can be used for Harvard's extensions – the TUBS can move without crossing the river. The town of Allston suddenly faces the relocated river itself; its real estate values soar, and it can begin to (re)imagine itself as a New England Oxbridge.

Escalators penetrate the
pool to lead to a spa belov

In addition, recognizing and proclaiming power as its unique form of expertise, Harvard also announces the creation of Powerlab, the ultimate embodiment of its collective expertise – an institution that recognizes that we are currently passing through a moment of ideological confusion where there is no single ideal, but a series of equally threadbare - and questionable - systems that are interacting like tired gladiators. Clearly this is a moment to redefine the potential relationships between globalization, politics, religion, the economy – all elements that currently don't gel.

AMO

10 January 2002

Dear Larry Summers,

Thank you for meeting with us to discuss planning issues in Cambridge and Allston. At the end of our conversation, you asked us for some thoughts on a strategy for Harvard's future.

Compared to its peers, Harvard has not recently undertaken the creation of a new symbolic entity that both asserts its values and articulates an ambition to re-invent them. No one initiative or building emblematically expresses its overall vision. In contrast, MIT was able to claim the future through Media Lab, a building that has made it globally synonymous with technology. Media Lab functions not only as a center of digital innovation, but also as a symbolic condensation of all technological innovations occurring at the University.

Harvard's reputation has been based in significant part on its intimacy with governance. It has provided and taught leadership. It has engaged politics and been engaged by politicians. Yet its very familiarity with the corridors of power, its assumed closeness to players in Washington, Russia, at the World Bank and WTO, has slightly tarnished its aura and the credibility of its declared core mission. This, combined with the dynamics of current international affairs, constitutes an occasion for Harvard to re-define its aims and its role as a center of influence.As a strategy for its future, Harvard has the opportunity to launch a new era dedicated to the study of power. Because of the University's unique knowledge of governance, it alone can claim power as its field of expertise. The University has the chance to re-invent its relationship to politics by proposing to examine contemporary systems of influence. With its collective resources Harvard is able to analyze the heightened interaction among nations,the market, NGOs and religious bodies. Investigating these new tensions, potentials and values along with the more varied geo-political regimes they suggest will avail the University to explore politics with a renewed sense of responsibility. And by focusing on power as a subject of intellectual discourse, such an initiative will reinforce the University's commitment to scholarship.

Harvard can inaugurate development in Allston by constructing an entity for the study of power. Power Lab would declare politics as the subject of the future. It can bring together political thinkers from across the University making use of their knowledge of regions, be it Europe, the Middle East, Central Asia, China or Latin America. By hosting specialists in other fields, Power Lab can encourage debate leading to the creation of more currently relevant definitions of power as it relates to modernity, religion, planning, race, medicine,etc. Building Power Lab and at the same time relocating the President's Office across the river will prove Harvard's commitment to Allston. Only an initiative of this ambition will galvanize interest from the Tubs to move and the needed support for major infrastructure investment. It would also propose a clear vision for Harvard's two banks. Power Lab and the new 'White House' would help define Allston as a site of advanced scholarship and engagement with the political and professional world beyond Harvard, distinguishing Cambridge as the site of undergraduate instruction.

At AMO we are deeply interested in the function of power and have explored its representation through work with the European Community, NATO and in ongoing internal seminars with invited philosophers, political theorists and sociologists. We would be excited to discuss Harvard's future and its potential relationship with governance.

Best regards,

Rem Koolhaas

GO EAST
new york:
A
Protect us
BY FENNA HA
CHEESE 7 F
Alain almost
cheese-air
Herzog & d
office reek
outside St
stand che
I am glad it's all over. This joint venture between Rem and Jacques was doomed from the start.

This c
Almost e
hate: th
hierarc
the Ap
differe
dread
we h
Base
foo
and

he
pl
a
a

208

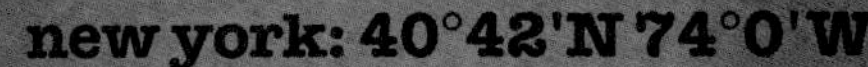

The Butterfly's Fate: In Praise of Oxymoron

A hundred reasons for why the OMA-Herzog & de Meuron marriage crumbled.

LUIS FERNANDEZ-GALIANO

You mean you were hoping it would fail. Mixing fire and water never appealed to you.

On the contrary! Rem thought that many were waiting to be disappointed, but some of us simply doubted a ship could sail with two captains. Architecture may be a choral business, and we may be sick and tired of the signature thing, but at the end of the day, a project needs someone in charge. Of course, there is this utopian strand, from Tatlin's collective artist to Rockefeller's design by committee, that tries to dissolve authorship, and look where it's taken us: bureaucratic town planning and corporate architecture. Do you think design by committee is going to produce a new Rockefeller Center at Ground Zero?

Now you're being unfair. The cohabitation of Daniel Libeskind and David Childs is not exactly a romantic one, and SOM has been put at the helm, so in any case, there's a CEO. As you know, the collaboration between OMA and H&deM was sparked by mutual admiration; it was no arranged marriage. And the fact that these are the two most influential firms of the past decade made their coming together even more exciting. I only miss a good picture of Rem and Jacques for the record, like the one taken of Le Corbusier and Mies at the Weissenhof!

The Weissenhof happened; Astor Place didn't. In Stuttgart, Mies was in charge of the Siedlung, and he and Corbu carried out their buildings independently. But who was Ian Schrager supposed to call to discuss details? Henry Kissinger once complained that he didn't know Europe's phone number; perhaps Schrager didn't know the number of his European architect. When he got fed up, the commission ended up in the predictable hands of Frank Gehry - a serial killer waiting for a victim in Manhattan!

That wasn't the case with Prada. Patrizio Bertelli knew exactly who to call for the New York store, and who to call for Tokyo.

And that's why the Prada jobs got done. For both OMA in Soho and H&deM in Omotesando, the brief was straightforward: sexing up a fashion brand with trophy architecture. Forget about Koolhaas trying to reinvent shopping or Herzog counterpoising with a store is a store is a store. In the end, both produced fine works, overflowing with intellectual sophistication and visual refinement, even if for a sadly trivial purpose. But was this a collaboration proper? Working for the same client, like building on neighboring sites in the same scheme, may account for closer contact, more intimate dialogue, and stronger mutual influence, but it's nothing like painting on the same canvas.

You know, Deyan Sudjic has described Jacques and Rem as the Picasso and Braque of contemporary architecture, roped together like mountaineers climbing for the summit. I think he's on to something. The joint-invention-of-cubism metaphor is somehow off the mark, but there's a scent of the Picasso-Braque story in their groundbreaking ambition and their close awareness of one another.

But even in such a carefully honed artistic partnership, each painter made his own works! Picasso and Matisse supply a better comparison, and one that accounts for the competitive aspect of their relationship. Watching those teams running back and forth between Rotterdam and Basel, I never had the feeling of a jam session, with the musicians effortlessly weaving a tune, but instead of one of those Colombian accordion contests in which two players start with different rhythms and each struggles to bring the rival into his own melody.

That wasn't the intention behind the Astor Place collaboration. As Rem has explained, it arose out of frustration with a competition system that pits architects against one another, and out of fatigue with the insistent demand for a characteristic style from each. Of course they also claimed to explore "strategic alliances in a globalized world," but this is the kind of management lingo Rem uses to place his projects in the XL-sphere of political economy. I believe that deep down, working together was about learning, friendship, and fun. Rem had suggested that the two firms collaborate on the Tate back in 1994, and five years later the Schrager hotel offered a second opportunity - this time leading to more than 18 months of close cooperation, abruptly halted by the client.

Maybe Ian Schrager is to blame. I remember the last revision of the project, undertaken at his demand: the haphazard pattern of holes of the outer envelope was transformed into camouflaged irregular windows that drew all the energy from the shape. But apparently, even this watered-down version was too risqué for him. Or perhaps Rem antagonized him with his dour attitude and brisk manners ... who knows? In any case, you clearly need a good client for a good project. Miuccia Prada has certainly been different, and who would not prefer working with her concetto than with Donatella Versace? Although I often wonder: why have all these haute couture clients become obligatory references for the finest talents in the profession?

Don't start moralizing now. You're probably right to describe Astor Place as an impossible job, but the experience was refreshingly innovative, brazenly political, and more than generous. And where do you find clients for this sort of laboratory, but in the upper tier of the luxury markets? Prada, Schrager, Guggenheim ... commerce as culture or culture as commerce, who cares? When boundaries blur, those on the borders are in the best position to shape the future. So don't lecture us on the frivolous nature of fashion architecture.

All right, touché. Now, be frank. Did you really buy Rem's enthusiasm about shopping, or his interest in fashion as a pure form of recreation that opens the door to the sublime? Weren't you disappointed by the Prada book, more a blown-up PR handout than the self-aware volume one expects from an accomplished writer and brilliant designer? Aren't you fed up with all this press coverage of Kool Rem as a fashion guru, the ultimate expert on the brand value of celebrity architecture? Because - full disclosure - I couldn't stand seeing the author of *Delirious New York* and *S, M, L, XL* sequestered by the junk world of advertising copy as a merchandising tie-in of a season campaign, to end up featured in the money shot of a gangbang!

Come on, hold it. Don't get carried away. How do you know he was not a fashion victim but, as some customers describe themselves, a happy victim of fashion? As consultant to Condé Nast, he's had opportunities to realize there is no real difference between custom magazines and custom architecture; and as an author for Taschen, he's at the core of a publishing mutation that's morphing art from middlebrow to cool, taking pornography from brown envelopes to supermarkets, and bringing design from cult books to coffee tables. The latest Koolhaas may be Rem Lite, but he is certainly a voluntary prisoner of the ¥€$ world of global logos and no-friction capital.

I hope you are aware of the irony of describing Koolhaas, the most abrasive of architects, as happily drifting in the no-friction amniotic fluid of global fashion! At any rate, I'm willing to admit that fashion is an interest he shares with Herzog, albeit with a different approach. In contrast with Rem's sociological, or even geopolitical vision, Jacques's perception is softer, subtler, closer to art proper and the textile as the ur-material of enclosure and protection - the Beuys-Semper connection. But if I was reluctant to see them working together, it was not because they there were doing it in a fashion-leisure context. Granted, after 9/11, wishful thinking predicted a blackout of the frivolous, and we're in a shifting intellectual ground that tinges the nineties retrospectively. My main contention with the OMA-H&deM collaboration was aesthetic, and dealt with authorship. Just as I can't imagine Picasso and Matisse fingering the same canvas, I simply can't picture Koolhaas and Herzog in concert! >

That's clearly contradicted by the many successful partnerships in the history of architecture, including that of Jacques Herzog and Pierre de Meuron. Their office is a good example of this shared approach to design, and one that can develop into a collective endeavor. I'm afraid that you're looking at the joint venture with Koolhaas as a friendly takeover bid to line up Jacques with Bruce Mau, Cecil Balmond, or Sanford Kwinter in Rem's galaxy.

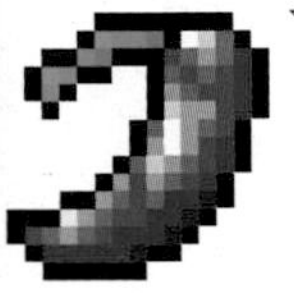

Well, companies may grow organically by taking on new partners, or merge fusing their corporate cultures, but they cannot survive without leadership, and it's always been pretty much the same way in the art world. Titian and Rubens, for instance, both had large ateliers, but it was ultimately the master who painted faces and hands, leaving drapery or landscapes to assistants. How do you bring together such different creatures? OMA is a top-heavy company, geared to Rem's mood, permanently reinventing itself, swift and unpredictable. H&deM is the product of gradual growth - cautious, conservative, and reliable in the Swiss tradition, slow-changing and competently run. Shortly after starting to work together, Rem felt they were partners, while for Jacques they were simply collaborating on a small commission. Both avoided the real issue: who is leading the art team?

You seem to think it's impossible to have two heavyweights in the same boat.

It's impossible to have two at the helm! Art is a solitary business. "Collaboration" stands for subordination or specialization more often than for dialogue. Some have suggested that OMA and H&deM could be complementary, with OMA at the XL scale of regional planning and H&deM at the XS end of building detail, thereby merging the territorial and the tactile; but Koolhaas is of course an extraordinary designer of small works and Herzog & de Meuron have produced several significant urban plans, so we can't get off the hook that way.

You still have one path to explore, one that might not make Jacques entirely happy. Following Rem's attachment to surrealism, you could present this ephemeral alliance - and indeed any artistic partnership - as a cadavre exquis, after the game in which Breton and his friends wrote poetry by adding words without knowing the preceding one.

An exquisite corpse indeed, and ultimately, a game: that's a good description of this collaboration! Koolhaas has used the method frequently in his own work, but the process demands slicing up the commission and designing parts independently, something that wasn't easy in Astor Place, where you could only segregate core and crust .

Would you deny that rubbing shoulders has made Koolhaas more materially aware and Herzog more graphically eloquent? Haven't they learned from each other? Haven't they moved closer? Look at their Beijing projects: with OMA's CCTV and H&deM's stadium, these two firms will provide the built symbols of the 2008 Olympic Games. Besides the obvious traces of the influence of engineer Cecil Balmond, one can perceive a visible convergence, which may be due to the very nature of the work - logo buildings for a world event - but that may also stem from this long period of frequent contact.

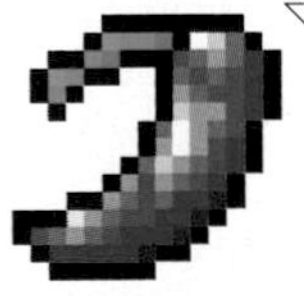

In Beijing, Koolhaas and Herzog are going to perform on the same stage - and a huge one at that! As close as their approaches have moved, Beijing is about emulation and competition. Of course, the convenient and slightly lazy confrontation between the artificially modern Dutch and the naturally archaic Swiss will be more than blurred by distance and scale, but loop and nest will remain as shorthand, ready-to-use metaphors for these neatly different interpretations of togetherness. >

Well, Jacques as a formalist I can still make out. But are you calling Rem - the archetypal cynical architect - a moralist?

So there's still some truth in the conventional critical use of Koolhaas and Herzog as opposed poles of contemporary architecture.

Less than before. I never strait-jacketed them into labels of journalist or cosmetician, as much as I admired the muscular writings of Koolhaas and the refined skins of Herzog. But I have often used the rhetorical opposition between the two as a pedagogical tool to describe the current landscape. Somehow, Rem and Jacques were the perfect representation of Vico's split between the intellect, dealing with truth, and the imagination, which belongs to the realm of poetic expression. Words versus images, but also life versus art, in a very fitting illustration of that early aesthetic divide between the effort to come to terms with the world and the will to create a world-in-itself, that artistic microcosm that Baumgarten would call "heterocosm." If you allow me the pedantry, I would add that Koolhaas's path is the one charted in Aristotle's *Poetics,* while Herzog's follows more closely that advocated in Plato's *Republic*.

The last thing I would expect is a case for an Aristotelic Rem and a Platonic Jacques! Realism versus idealism, or narrativity versus aestheticism, should be more than enough to describe the quite obvious tension between understanding and pleasure that distinguishes their respective attitudes.
As far as I can tell, Rem's literary rationalism makes him something of an honorary Frenchman, surrealist strand included, while Herzog's visual romanticism is firmly rooted in his Germanic humus; so their dialogue would seem to extend a time-honored conversation.

The conversation between the intellectual and the artist? Or the conversation between the moralist who thinks that art imitates life and the formalist who claims that, on the contrary, life imitates art?

A neo-realist, a social realist, a moralist, call him what you will. Or even a cynic in the Greek sense of the word. Think twice and you will see that this is not as outrageous as it seems. But what really interests me is that joining Rem and Jacques begets a philosophical monster and an artistic oxymoron. As an intellectual centaur or mermaid, it's an untenable chimera. But as an architectural oxymoron, it is an unstable relationship that, however brief the bond, splits releasing energy and changing the trajectory of both elementary particles. Rem has described both of them feeling trapped in their assigned stylistic spaces, pinned by needles on a board like butterflies, and how collaborating was a way of getting rid of those fixed identities. If one simply considers the fate of Astor Place, most would write it off in the debt column. But if you pull in the dazzling weight of the Beijing projects and their vanishing identity, one cannot but bow in praise of architectural oxymoron.

Perhaps our only hope of avoiding the butterfly's fate! ■

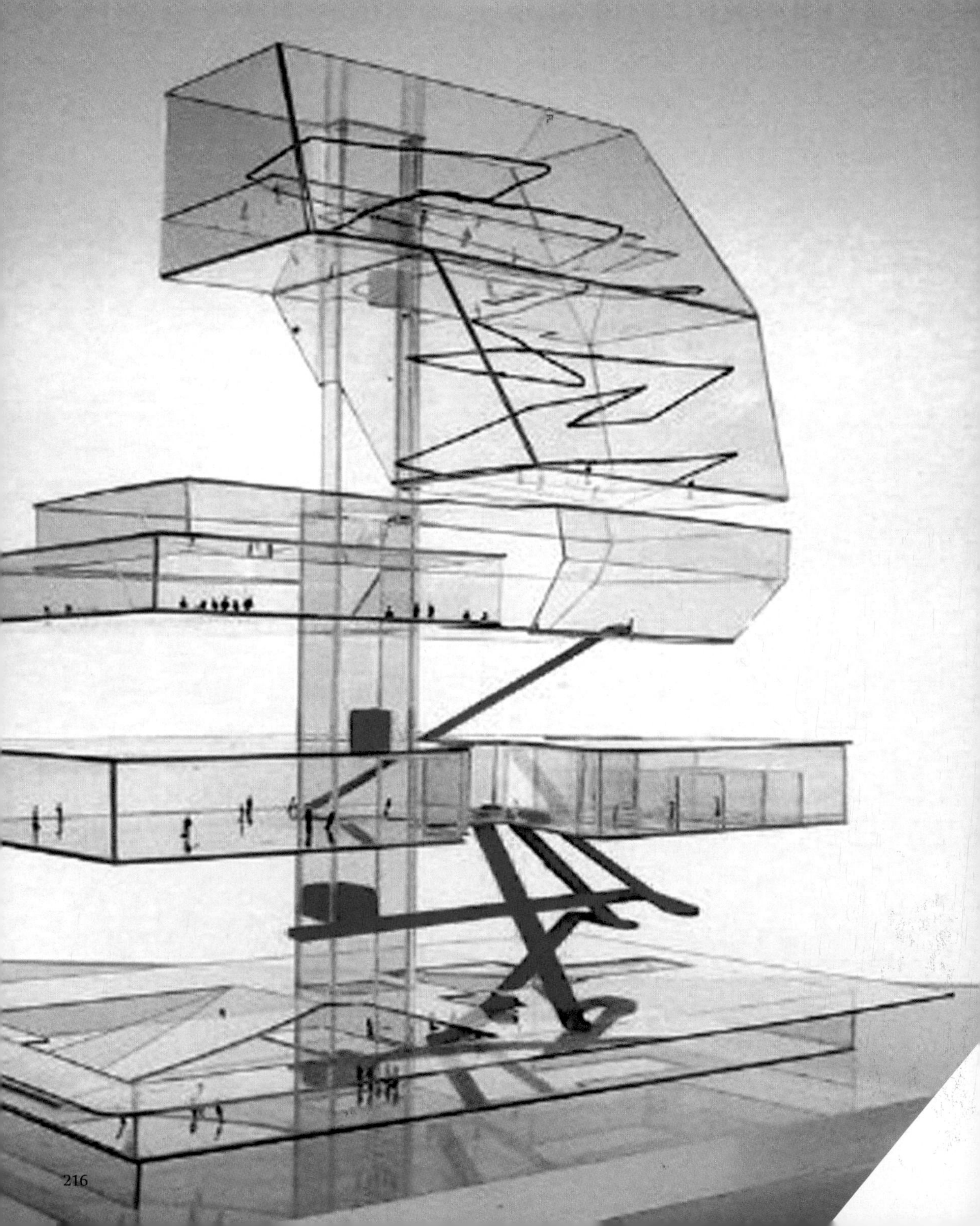

Experience
The permanent collection could infiltrate into areas other than the designated exhibition spaces, extending aesthetics into even the most prosaic of parts of the museum (commercial, circulation...), rendering art both auratic and ubiquitous.

Exhibition
Galleries are solely for the display of art. Flexibly generic, they allow for the reconfigurations necessary for changing exhibitions.

new york: 40°42'N 74°0'W

NeWhitney

Misidentified as an alien, the Whitney extension was a native New Yorker: shaped by zoning laws, surrounded by Landmarks, killed by conservatism.

Any architect aspiring to build in New York inevitably runs against the limitations of the city's zoning restrictions, an invisible, three-sided envelope that determines how high and wide a building is allowed to be. In the case of NeWhitney, an extension to Whitney Museum of American Art (WMAA) that OMA was commissioned to design in January 2001, the site - Madison Avenue, between 74th St. and 75th St. - was affected by both the residential district regulations and the Madison Avenue special preservation district regulations.

The main challenge to the NeWhitney was the existence of several historic brownstones that had been designated as Landmarks, therefore off-limits to destruction. Based on our initial conversations, we came to assume that WMAA was indirectly hoping that OMA would produce a masterpiece of such incontestable brilliance that everybody would beg for the Brownstones to be demolished. Should we leave them for political reasons, or instead make a masterpiece that will persuade everyone that they should be destroyed?

We struggled for weeks with the question of how to incorporate the Brownstones and the existing Whitney, designed by Marcel Breuer, with our extension. After a review session in which over 30 models were appraised placed in either a "promising" or "worthless" pile, we realized that the schemes that worked worst were those that either competed with the Breuer, independent buildings that >

NEWHITNEY

attempted to harmonize with it, or forms that entirely filled the zoning envelope. After scrutizing the models Koolhaas proclaimed, "The magic number is three." The difficulty with those schemes that either competed or harmonized with the Breuer is that they are a Breuer + 1 composition, and ultimately focused on a new-old dialogue. By preserving the Brownstones, the NeWhitney would comprise three buildings: Breuer + Brownstones + 1. Preservation of the Brownstones would be both interesting and politically advantageous.

There was another motive for preserving the Brownstones, the intimacy between artwork and the art appreciator. We had reservations about the increasing scale and homogenization of institutions such as MoMA, the Pompidou Center, the Bilbao Guggenheim, and Tate Modern; as the galleries had expanded, so had the art. We felt that, for NeWhitney, it might be possible to propose spaces that brought people and art into close proximity.

The domestic, living room-like spaces of the Brownstones seemed ideal for appreciating the comparatively small early 20th century paintings and sculptures owned by WMAA. The loft-like gallery of the Breuer, the more intimate galleries of the Brownstones, and the new gallery proposed by OMA would produce a variety that, in our view, would be help the WMAA distinguish itself from the increasing ostentation of other museums.

Preserving the Brownstones was, while conceptually beautiful, practically difficult. It was illegal to build on the roof, and we were opposed to the idea of preserving only the façade and placing a new gallery behind it. Touching the existing Whitney was, of course, taboo. At a particularly frustrating moment, Koolhaas suddenly asked, "What about a courtyard?" Although there was originally an irregularly-shaped residual space within the Brownstones, due to building alterations it had become illegible in the plans. Here, the Landmark designation didn't apply. The space was about 40x40 feet (12x12 meters). This hidden courtyard provided the spot from which the building could be launched.

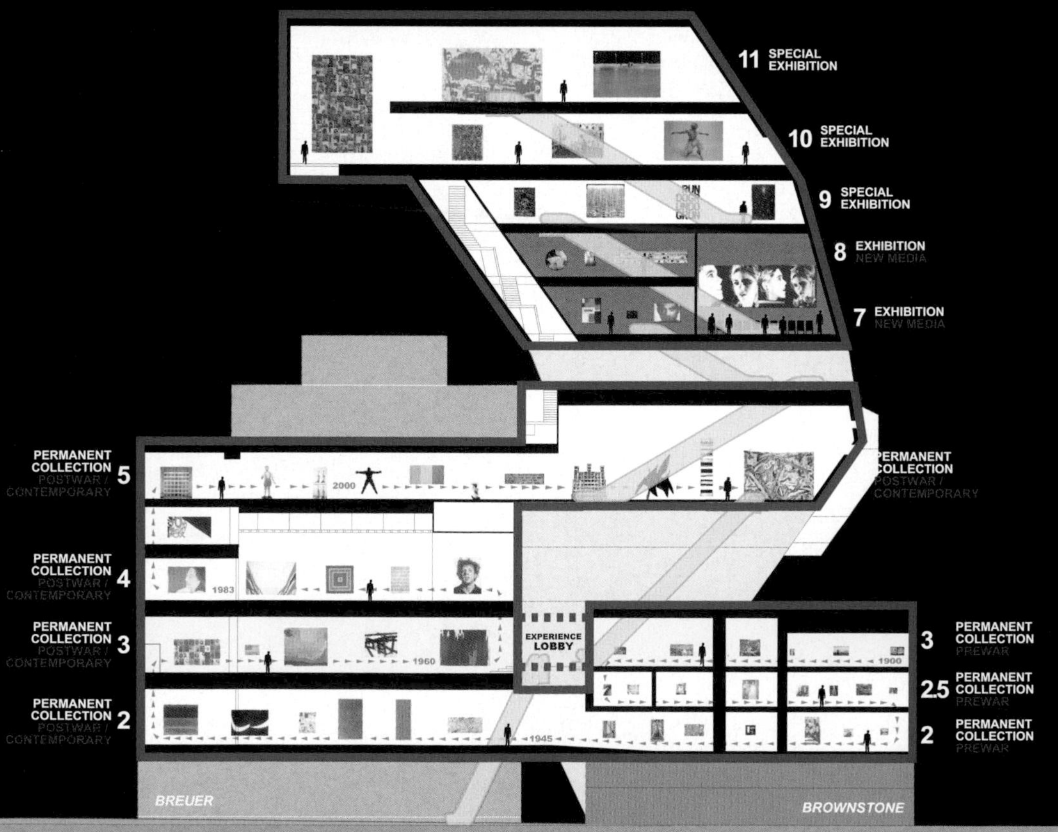

From the intersection of these decisions - the magic number 3, preserving the Brownstones, using the courtyard, pursuing verticality, filling the zoning envelope only partially - we made further study models, and at last a form, "the prototype," emerged.

The design then advanced rapidly through analysis of program. The extension scheme would approximately double the size of the existing program; we discovered that all of the new programmatic elements that were not contained in the existing museum - auditorium, shop, classroom, etc. - had no direct relationships with the exhibition spaces. From this we realized that the new program was the key to the scheme.

It is not easy to redefine the "white cube," the neutral exhibition space that has been cultivated over so many years. Instead, we thought that we could use the elements of the program without direct relationship to artworks to define new curatorial concepts. We immediately began researching the programs of museums in the USA, and learned that in present-day museums, the unprogrammed act of pure art appreciation totals about two thirds of the entire program. Dedicated exhibition spaces are about a third; storage, offices and other service spaces are about a third; and then there is a remaining third. In this remaining space we formed a strategy for escaping the "white cube." We thought it would be interesting to make the remaining third into spaces where art of any type may be presented. Koolhaas dubbed this space and function Experience©. By linking areas such as the shop, circulation, restaurant, auditorium, and library to the exhibition spaces, we thought that the experience of the museum would increase in novelty and variety. These miscellaneous spaces would be contained in the OMA annex, contrasted with the neutral exhibition spaces. By doing this, the Breuer, having previously been infiltrated by functions lacking a direct relationships to art appreciation, could be returned to its original pure loft-like gallery space. ■

GO EAST
20 January 03 15:00

new york: 40°42'N 74°0'W

No more surprises: Global Editing with Martha Stewart

The Queen of the American home talks of eastward expansion and the exhilaration of public life.

INTERVIEW BY BEATRIZ COLOMINA AND REM KOOLHAAS

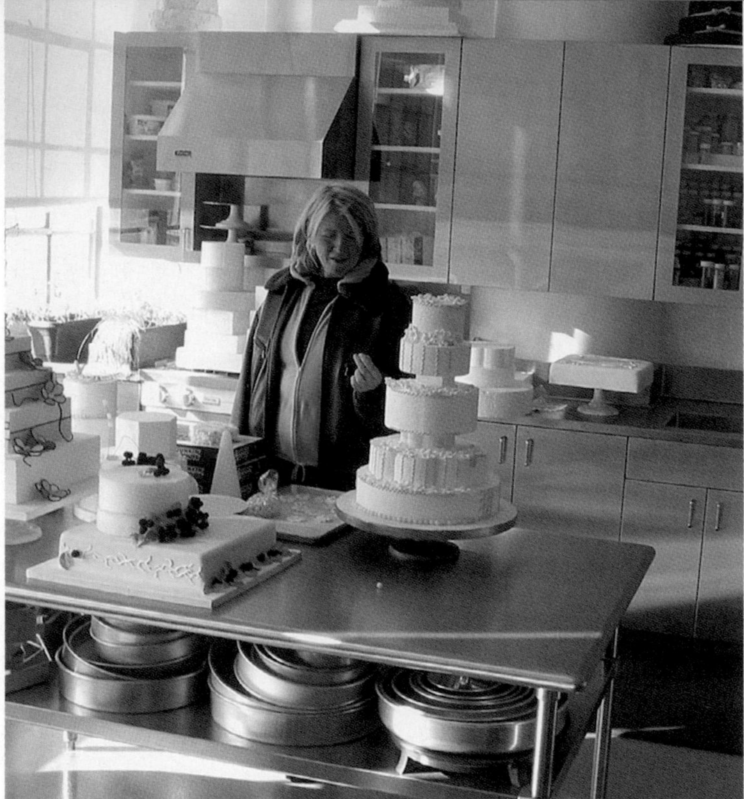

Martha Stewart: I just bought a new apartment. It's in the new Richard Meier building. I have the top two floors of the north tower.
Rem Koolhaas: That's going to be your main house?
Martha: One of my houses. I have a lot of houses.
Rem: Yes. That's what we want to talk about. In your article "Why I Left Westport," that appeared in the *New York Times Magazine*, you said: "the home is under-utilized." I think the word under-utilized is very interesting when used in relation to the house, because, in a way, the American suburb itself is under-utilized; there's a kind of thinning going on. What's the connection between the thinning of the home and your incredible success in homemaking? Are you, to some extent, a virtual answer to that thinness?
Martha: The homes I like best are completely occupied, busy, and useful. I find smaller spaces - comfy spaces - better than great big houses that are hardly used. By comfy I mean full of books and things that people are doing. In my sister's kitchen, there are three computers on the table, the sewing machine, all the threads, the complicated patterns, the animals, the stove, and the smells of cooking. That's my favorite kind of room.
Beatriz Colomina: So comfort, for you, is actually fullness.
Martha: Right.
Rem: Mixing.
Martha: Yes. That's probably why I like the kitchen; it's not just for cooking; it's for everything; it's that lively hub. At my new farm I've designed a three-room house: bedroom on top, living room in the middle, and kitchen on the ground. My new apartment in New York has only two rooms - two floors, really - but two rooms. The Gordon Bunschaft house that I'm restoring has three rooms. A three-room house - that's all I want. It fits me; it fits my lifestyle.
Rem: But you've already mentioned eight rooms. Each house is small, but you inhabit eight rooms.
Martha: But my houses, Rem, are my laboratories; I have to have them! And they're all different styles, so I can experiment with the modern way of living in an 1800 house, a 1925 house, a 1960 house, and a 2001 house. Bill Gates's house, for example, is totally out of date now; he built it right before wireless happened. He doesn't need those big tunnels for all his wires anymore.
Beatriz: So it's aging faster than houses that are more traditional.
Rem: What would you say has changed in the experience of the home in the last 20 years?
Martha: The biggest challenge in the last 20 years has been incorporating technology into the contemporary home - in any style. It's very hard, in an old home, to become wired.
Rem: I'm interested not only in the way you live, but also in why so many people want to learn from you.
Martha: We've been editing, and editing, and editing - rooms and living spaces. That's what we do. And now these famous decorators and interior designers say: "We want the Martha Look!" We take out the unnecessary, the excessive, the voluminous curtains.
Beatriz: It's a kind of streamlining.
Martha: You can call it streamlining; I prefer to call it editing.
Beatriz: There's an efficiency; that's what makes your work modern.

"My private life, my business life, my job, my thinking time - they're all public. People learn from seeing something great happening in front of them."

Martha: It's modern, but it can be any period. It can be Swedish-19th-century, French, early-American, but it isn't cluttered, busy, or overly decorated. We want every object to be important. I can go in a room and just take out, take away.
Rem: Yes, but living, traditionally, was un-edited. In fact, liveliness has been defined as an un-edited condition. And you describe your sister's kitchen as a prototype of completely un-edited living. Yet you're a huge editor, and you're hugely successful, in a situation where the American home - the American lifestyle - is getting thinner and thinner.
Martha: People realize that within that edited space there can be... life. The rooms that appear on my television show don't look empty; there are always people, or signs of people. We build the sets as real rooms, with real animals, real plants, real things, and the water works when you turn on the faucet. The sets work; they are enlarged copies of my real spaces - the spaces I live in.
Rem: What happens to your sense of privacy when your publications give access, in these numbers, to some of your most inner environments?
Martha: My private life, my business life, my job, my thinking time - they're all public. People learn from seeing something great happening in front of them. My new farm in Bedford is a good example of that: it's going to be a 150-acre compound. It's a village, for me, but also for lots of other people. There are two streets, with a mile-long frontage, and six houses, all on the road where everybody can see. Everyone was telling me to knock them all down, and put my house in the middle of the property. Instead I restored every single one of them, because they belong in the neighborhood - one of them has been there since 1770. But the doorways used to all face the road. Well, I reversed them; I put all the doorways facing inside. This made all the sense in the world, because now you can ride along and look at all these beautiful places, and the huge fields behind them; it's still pretty for the neighbors to look at. That's my way of teaching people that you don't need an 8-foot wall....
Beatriz: So you are broadcasting your own image. But how do you see yourself? Are you an architect? An interior designer?
Martha: I would never say I'm an architect in Rem's presence, but I am. I am!
Beatriz: Do you think people turn their houses into the Martha Stewart houses?
Martha: No! I don't go into people's houses and see me everywhere, not at all.
Beatriz: But the audience that watches you so carefully, that is so interested in everything you do - what do they do with your advice?
Martha: Instead of starting with the products and then trying to inspire the audience, we try to inspire first and then provide. We inspire through the magazine, the TV show, and then we provide kits through our catalogs. But the kit doesn't do it for you. We try to turn "dreamers" into "doers."
Rem: Is it your role to defend the last bastion of hominess?
Martha: I don't think hominess needs much defending anymore. We've already turned the tide. When I started writing books 21 years ago, busy women, who had forgotten about the home for a while, were already starting to turn back and look at the house as a very important place.
Beatriz: So you're not advocating that women leave their work?
Martha: No. Many women are realizing that a balance has to be struck between homemaking, business, and family.
Beatriz: I think you're a role model for modern women - extremely successful, busy, and ever-expanding. In many ways, what you teach is necessary. In America, many people of the last generation didn't learn from their mothers how to cook, to arrange flowers, or to sew. You're offering some direction.
Rem: Are you like a surrogate mother?
Martha: Definitely. Last week, I went to Nashville and there was a huge storm. On the way from the airport to the hotel, while we were stuck in the snow, I saw these gangs of kids, mostly black, walking home from school. So I opened the window and said, "Hey, are you having fun in the snow?" They all looked at me >

BETTER LIVING

Martha Stewart is the founder of Martha Stewart Omnimedia Inc., a multimedia empire that spans books, magazines, mail order, endorsements, and television.

and started to scream; they were thrilled! These 16-year-old black kids from poor neighborhoods all knew exactly who I was! They watch the show. And because they learn from me, I treat them like students.
Beatriz: Where are the geographical borders of your work?
Martha: I don't think there are any.
Beatriz: Is there anything you wouldn't want to export?
Martha: No. The world has become a smaller place. The Internet has enabled every culture to relate to every other culture. There are no more secrets, nothing surprising anymore, and I think that is very valuable.
Rem: Why is "nothing surprising anymore" a good thing? Don't you like surprises?
Martha: I like surprises, but what's valuable is constant edification, revelation. I have China, the largest country in the world, yet to conquer - and I don't mean conquer egomaniacally. I would love for them to know about transfer-ware, because, in fact, they started it.
Rem: How do you feel about disseminating your message in environments where it might cause upheaval? Or are you thinking that, for instance, you could also import Chineseness to America?
Martha: I'm fascinated with their intelligent solutions. A Chinese friend who works for me taught me how to keep my chickens from pecking one another: I hang a huge cabbage from a long wire so they peck at the cabbage instead of at each other. This is how I learn! I love the decorating techniques of the Japanese, the furniture of the Chinese; we'll be appropriating all that. Have you seen the Japanese issue of our magazine with Valentine's Day on the cover?

"Of course Americans are hated; but mostly for our politics, not for our lifestyle."

Beatriz: Do the Japanese celebrate Valentine's Day?
Martha: They do now! Rem, do you know what quilling is?
Rem: No.
Martha: It's an early American craft; the Japanese love it. You twirl paper strips on a little needle. Look how cute!
Rem: Cute and complicated.
Beatriz: Do you think that taste is exportable?
Martha: You bet. We've proven it.
Rem: But you must realize that the unhindered progress of American civilization is beginning to encounter some resistance. Do you feel that?
Martha: Of course Americans are hated; but mostly for our politics, not for our lifestyle. They don't hate the way we cook; they hate the way we behave. I can't take responsibility for that. All I can do is help everybody, everywhere, to live a little better.
Rem: Is there anything that you think ought to be invented to make us all happier?
Martha: I have a dream: a computer screen that can be anywhere. It would be voice-activated; I'd like to be able to talk to a screen on my refrigerator, or on my wall. I'm always running around, so I want instant on/off. I don't have time to sit and wait for the stupid thing to turn on. I don't want to wait. The homemaker doesn't want to wait. She wants to save time. She wants to make time to do other things.
Rem: Have you talked to anybody about this?
Martha: I've talked to Steve Jobs, and to Bill Gates's crew, about developing technology for the homemaker, but they're not interested. So I'm developing my own software for the homemaker right now. It tells you what kind of shade of curtain you can make. It gives you a yardage, a pattern. It also tells you how much water your house used last August - so you wouldn't have to go back to the paper file. I want my hydraulic company and my insurance company to send me everything via computer. I call it "living by synopsis."
Rem: So who are you working with?
Martha: Me!
Rem: It's going to be big?
Martha: Very big.
Rem: Do you have a name for it?
Martha: Yes I do, but I don't want to tell you. It's a funny name.... ■

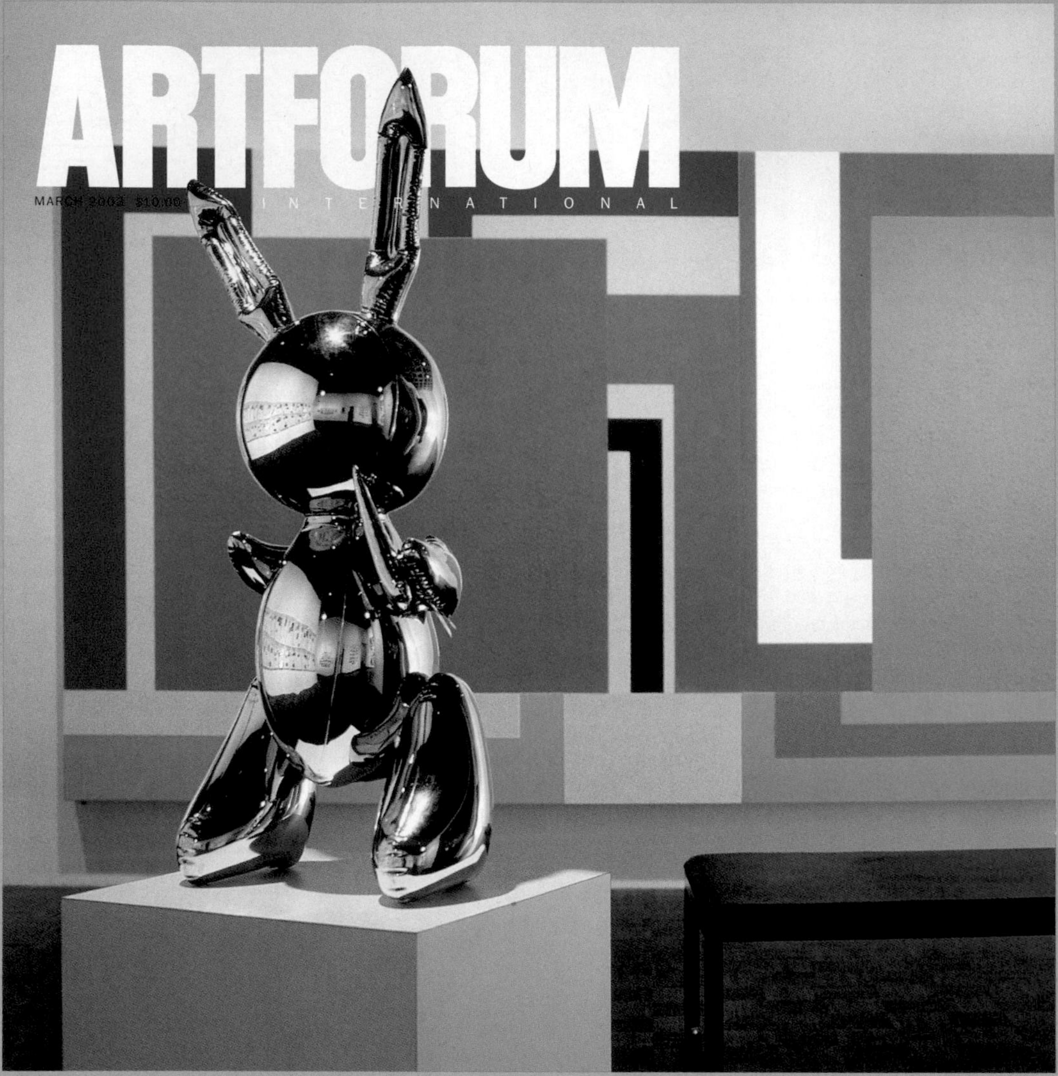

Crib Death

BY REM KOOLHAAS

You suddenly sense that some kind of planetary realignment - political/economic/personal - has started to erode the viability of a project.... Because you are more sensitive, have better antennae, inevitably you sense it first, even before "they" have allowed the fatal message to become fully conscious, a convenient delay that enables them to stay just this side of outright dishonesty in their further transactions. Now the possible death of a project stares you in the face - against the weaselly rhetoric of reassurance proffered by powerless proxies. You double your efforts - wax more eloquent, convince every skeptic, invest in the most peripheral contact, but you have seen the cold, cloudy eyes of waning commitment. Each handshake reinforces the imminence of separation. You notice it in the way he smiles goodbye to continue talking to his once unanimous board; you know it's over, another dream you dreamt for them....

But now they woke up. And proceed with business as usual: cancellation. The reptilian lack of engagement on the part of the real power is exacerbated by the jaunty, elaborate efforts launched by his underlings to make it work. "Campaigns" - mayors that vouch their "support," critics that speak of a "masterpiece" - continue on like a headless chicken, while the leaders withdraw. Canceling you, for one delicious second, suspends their dread of imminent death; sometimes they die not long afterwards.

One thing is certain: like a mistress who gave him a dose of the clap, you will never hear from him again. They won't say "it's over." And they won't pay the last bill; deep down they never thought that you were worth that amount of money....

He was not alive enough to want it, but strong enough to kill it.

Prada NY

(from HBO's Sex and the City)

"In every relationship there comes a time when you take that next important step.

For some couples that step is meeting the parents, for me its meeting the Prada.

ron livingston

Do I look all right?

Don't worry. They'll love you.

I just want to make the right impression.

They'll love you because I love you. Here we are.

Holy shit! You know, on my planet
the clothing stores have clothes.

Carry!

Hi!!

If only all my customers were this beautiful....

Tony, this is my boyfriend, Jack Berger....
This is his first time at Prada.

location 40°42'N 70°0'W

White briefs against filth

The Waning Power of New York

BY REM KOOLHAAS

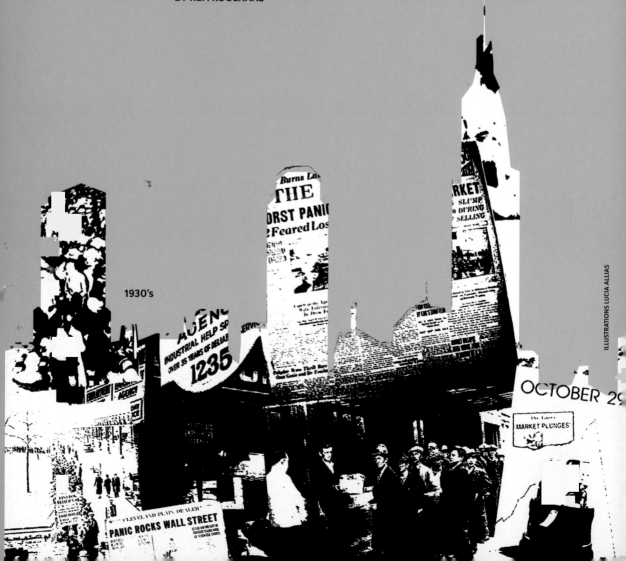

1930's

ILLUSTRATIONS LUCIA ALLIAS

1850-1933

New York is built, from 1850 to 1933, in a single spurt of imagination and energy. The first prototype of the modern metropolis, Manhattan is turned into a laboratory to test the potential of modern life in a radical, collective experiment. A free-form coalition of developers, visionaries, writers, architects, and journalists intersects with popular expectations to make the city an extreme and exhilarating democratic machine, one that is able to process all newcomers into New Yorkers. Its genius is to create a universe parallel to sober and abstract European modernism - to imagine life in the metropolis as a deeply irrational experience that uses sparkling-new technologies to exacerbate desire.

From 1900 to 1932, the speed of building is convulsive: Flatiron, Chrysler, Empire State, and finally Rockefeller Center. New York's instruments are not necessarily architectural masterpieces, but apparatuses for reinventing city life. They create both a density that astronomically expands the repertoire of programs, events, and overlappings and a smoothness that urban life has never known before.

The Depression slows this regime of architectural delirium. In 1933, King Kong's agony on top of the Empire State Building is a provisional climax: New York's revolutionary moment is over by the time of the talkies.

1950s-'60s

After World War II, buildings become "important." Each is the work of an individual architect rather than a collective. In the next 20 years, only a handful are realized: Lever ('52), UN ('53), Seagram ('58), Pan Am ('63). At the same time, Robert Moses's highways, bridges, and tunnels allow the populations accumulated by previous generations to escape to the burbs. He also organizes the 1964 World's Fair. The results appear lackluster, like a fair that could have been held anywhere.

1970s

In 1972 (president: Nixon; mayor: Lindsay), the World TradeCenter is finished. No one likes it. The towers are abstract and structurally daring; their interiors entirely column-free, 10 million square feet of real estate carried on two cores and two envelopes. The towers dominate Manhattan's skyline but don't really participate in it - twinning is their only genius. 1972 is a turning point: the towers are delivered at the exact moment New York's passion for the new is spent. Along with the Concorde, they are modernism's apotheosis and its letdown at the same time - unreal perfection that can never be equaled. >

1950's-'60's

1970's

New York is not doing well. It is old now. It has a long past; it doesn't want to be a machine anymore. It worries about context and humanism. Hung over from the '60s - Malcolm X killed in '65, Andy Warhol shot in '68 - the city is basking in an aura of danger.

It can no longer be governed; only the forbidden is well organized. Its repertoire is reduced to extremes. New York becomes a hunting ground. Separate crises - financial, social, drugs - merge into a cocktail that only hedonists enjoy. In 1973, Governor Rockefeller introduces draconian drug laws, and McDonald's opens its first Manhattan franchise. 1974 sees the first Gap. Plato's Retreat opens in '75; Studio 54 follows in '77 and acts as Manhattan's epicenter - the splendors and miseries of a metropolis compressed to the scale of a disco. Also, the city almost goes bankrupt.

1977 (presidents: Ford/Carter; mayor: Beame) is New York's annus horribilis: the blackout, the Son of Sam summer, a rotor blade from a helicopter crashes into the streets from the top of the Pan Am. But it is also the year of its definitive comeback: a blast of self-love pulls the city out of its doldrums. New York is rescued by a double whammy of denial, a heroic non sequitur: the "I ♥ NY" campaign (created by Well, Rich, and Green with Milton Glaser) and Liza Minnelli's "New York, New York" (composed by Kander and Ebb). The campaign mobilizes disbelief to fight disbelief; the song overpowers urban anxiety through loudness, introduces the high kick as a euphoric goose step.

"I ♥ NY" is a prison. Its logo, like a brand, diminishes the virtual space of the city, trivializing what it can mean. New York's shriveling is reinforced by the regime of Ed Koch, its new mayor. His "How'm I doin'?" reflects a city that obsessively measures its own pulse. Danger becomes vibrancy. A global city turns "world class."

In this state of narcissism, Manhattan's architects and developers begin to clone and rip off the most obvious features of the city's pre-WWII architecture. Boxes sprout spires; art deco becomes the new new. They perform a tectonic pornography - over-dimensioned displays of excitement, each relentlessly pursuing its own climax, an architecture of money shots.

An ecology of lawyers, dealmakers, zoning experts, and enablers grotesquely inflate the arcane complexities of "getting things done" in Manhattan and intimidate any outsider into helpless surrender to their intricate cynicism. "Union or nonunion?" That is the question, as in a Mafia Hamlet.

1980s-'90s

Now, the popular press and the US government turn against the United Nations - depicted as a conspiracy of shady foreign diplomats running up millions in unpaid parking tickets, molesting call girls with impunity, protesting innocence behind dark glasses. In 1984, like a slumlord, Washington stops paying the UN's maintenance fees; the cornerstone of New York cosmopolitanism becomes a political punching bag. In a neat lockstep with Reaganomics, what is not brutalized from the outside is eroded from the inside. The art system, with its voracious appetite for authenticity (and, later, "edginess") consumes whole districts, leaving acres of gallery space that can effortlessly morph into shopping districts or university precincts.

What determines art's size? If the average painting was 6 square feet in 1940, by the '80s it has expanded to 40.

1980's

Sculptures inflate at the same rate. Installations are measured in rooms, even entire buildings. What already exists is inherently more sexy than what is recently made. The greater the (New York) architect, the smaller the conversion. Architects' fragile egos are boosted by a corpocultural axis that intimately unites the art world's sincerity with the corporate world's integrity in a very contemporary marriage.

In 1982, the world's first billboard-sized crotch shot proclaims the emasculation of Times Square: white briefs against filth. The idea of the first cleanup is hatched. The 42nd Street Development Project follows in 1985. A master plan by Philip Johnson lingers, but in 1993 (president: Clinton; mayor: Dinkins), four years after the fall of the Berlin Wall, the idea returns as "42nd Street Now!" Disney announces the restoration of the New Amsterdam Theater.

Giuliani becomes mayor in 1994. He presides over the Wall Street bubble, the media bubble, the Internet bubble, the art bubble, and instigates his own law bubble. Giuliani's is a regime of enforced quality of life. The police become a gang of roving, computerized flaneur, ridding the streets of surprise to deny criminals access to victims. The city becomes safer for some, more dangerous for many others. "Zero tolerance" is a deadly mantra for a metropolis: what is a city if not a space of maximum license?

In 1996, a new zoning law orders the removal of sex-related businesses from Times Square. Comfort has become the final human right, security a Faustian gambit - surrender freedoms to gain an illusion of certainty. Liberals condone the suburbanization of New York.

9/11

From now on, the most important city in the world is dominated by the tower from which once dangled an ape. What is the connection between zero tolerance and the cult of Ground Zero? In any case, the disaster resurrects Giuliani's depleted persona.

New Yorkers surrender to empathy. The tragedy of 9/11 inspires a mood of collective tenderness that is almost exhilarating, almost a relief: hype's spell has been broken and the city can recover its own reality principle, emerge with new thinking from the unthinkable. But politics interfere. In spite of Bloomberg's pragmatic sobriety, the transnational metropolis is enlisted in a national crusade. New York becomes a city (re)captured by Washington. Through the alchemy of 9/11, the authoritarian morphs imperceptibly into the totalitarian. A competition for rebuilding Ground Zero is held, not to restore the city's vitality or shift its center of gravity, but to create a monument at a scale that monuments have never existed (except under Stalin).

The winning architect, an immigrant, movingly recounts his first encounter with liberty but avoids what he left behind: Stalinist Poland, in '57. Instead of the two towers - the sublime - the city will live with five towers, wounded by a single scything movement of the architect, surrounding two black holes. New York will be marked by a massive representation of hurt that projects only the overbearing self-pity of the powerful. Instead of the confident beginning of the next chapter, it captures the stumped fundamentalism of the superpower.
Call it closure. ■

Previously published in *Wired* 11.06 (June 2003)

9/11

An Autopsy. For fans of turmoil, the past 14 years were a great decade. How many revolutions – why did nobody call it that? - can you handle at the same time? Bookended by the end of the "wall" and the ongoing construction of the "security fence" – we witnessed the life and death of the dot-com, "Yeltsin," oligarchs, Rwanda, and the return of the Crusade – an accordion of interlocking crises – predictable, surprising, and avoidable - held together by a baseline of dumbness. Architecture contributed a surprising sequence of masterpieces to this drunken party....

BY THEO DEUTINGER WITH MAJA BORCHERS, MATTHEW MURPHY, NANNE DE RU, MAX SCHWITALLA, SEBASTIAN THOMAS

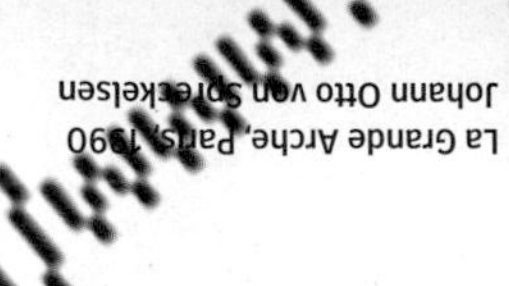

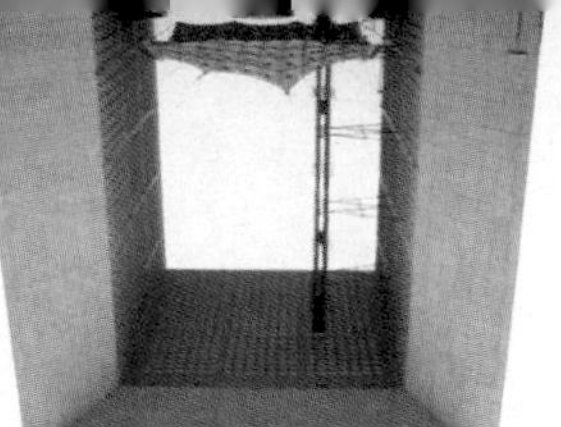

La Grande Arche, Paris, 1990
Johann Otto von Spreckelsen

Haas Haus, Vienna, 1990
Hans Hollein

¥ € $

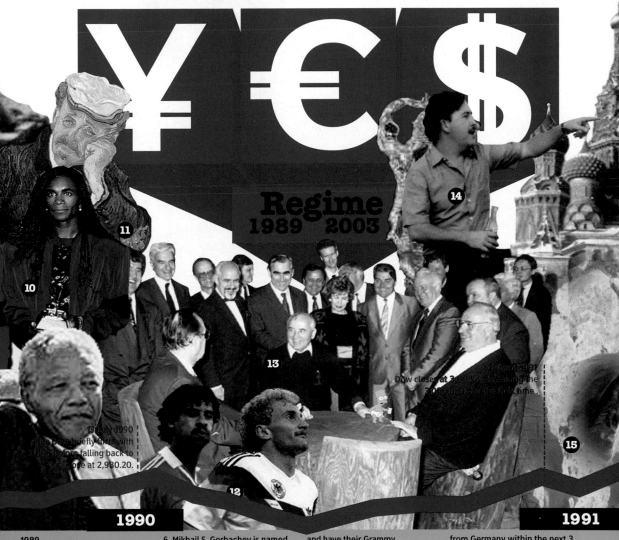

Regime 1989 2003

13 July 1990
The Dow briefly flirts with 3,000 before falling back to close at 2,980.20.

17 April 1991
Dow closes at 3,004.46, breaking the 3,000 mark for the first time.

1990

1991

1989

1. Demonstrators frolic on the newly "fallen" Berlin Wall.
2. Supertanker Exxon Valdez sinks off the coast of Alaska, spilling almost 11 mil. gallons of oil.
3. The Dalai Lama wins the Nobel Peace Prize.
4. A Beijing man stares down a tank convoy during the Tiananmen Square protests.
5. The Hubble space telescope is launched.
6. Mikhail S. Gorbachev is named President of the Soviet Union.
7. Army Gen. Colin R. Powell becomes the first black Chairman of the Joint Chiefs of Staff.

1990

8. The Internet goes public.
9. After 27 years behind bars, Nelson Mandela is released from prison in Cape Town, SA.
10. Euro dance sensation Milli Vanilli admit to lip-synching and have their Grammy awards revoked.
11. Vincent van Gogh's portrait of Dr. Gachet is sold to Ryoei Saito for a record $ 82.5 million.
12. Dutch player Frank Rijkaard spits on German striker Rudi Voeller at a WC match in Italy.
13. At an informal meeting in the Kaukasus, Mikhail Gorbachev agrees to remove Soviet troops from Germany within the next 3 years. The same year, Gorbachev receives the Nobel Peace Prize.

1991

14. Drug overlord Pablo Escobar turns himself in to the authorities. He would be incarcerated for just a year, in a prison that he had built for himself.
15. "Operation Desert Storm" - Gulf War I - is launched. >

16. A soldier patrolling Red Square during an attempted coup by opponents of Gorbachev.
17. George Soros, the Hungarian born philanthropist, releases Underwriting Democracy, a guide for communist states seeking a gentle transition to capitalism.

1992

18. Rioting erupts in Los Angeles after four LAPD officers are acquitted of the beating of African-American motorist Rodney King.
19. US President George Bush presents Russian President Boris Yeltsin with a pair of cowboy boots as a birthday present. On the same day, both officially declare the end of the Cold War.
20. Referred to by its employees as "Mouseschwitz" for the company's disregard of French labor laws, EuroDisney opens outside Paris with a price tag of over $4 billion.
21. Pascal Lissouba becomes the Republic of Congo's first democratically elected president.
22. The world's largest McDonald's opens in Beijing - a two-story facility that seats 700+ and employs 1000.

1993

23. A terrorist bombing of the World Trade Center in New York kills six people and injures at least 1,040.
24. The bridge at Mostar, built during the Ottoman Empire and recognized as an invaluable piece of historical heritage by UNESCO, is destroyed during armed conflict between Croats and Muslims.
25. Sumner Redstone, owner of

Viacom, takes over Paramount in a merger worth $10bn. Viacom would follow a year later with an $8 bn merger with Blockbuster Video.
26. A botched, ATF-led assault on the Branch Davidian compound near Waco, Texas results in the deaths of four federal agents and eighty Branch Davidians, including seventeen children.

27. The Spice Girls are formed by a British tabloid. They soon become worldwide icons for the "Girl Power" movement.
28. The Treaty of Maastricht is signed, setting the European Union's ambitious program: monetary union by 1999, new common policies, European citizenship, a common foreign and security policy, and improved internal security.

29. Opponents of Russian President Boris Yeltsin, led by ousted vice president Alexander Rutskoy and Congress of People's Deputies speaker Ruslan Khasbulatov, take over the Kremlin, urging citizens to attack the Moscow mayor's office and television center.

30. The North American Free Trade Agreement (NAFTA) between Canada, the US, and Mexico goes into effect.
31. Yitzak Rabin and Yassir Arafat shake hands upon signing the peace accord between Israel and the PLO at the White House. >

TGV Station, Lyon, 1994
Santiago Calatrava

SBB Stellwerk 4, Basel, 1995
Herzog & de Meuron

1994

32. A small plane crashes into the White House.The pilot, Frank E. Corder dies in the crash.
33. Olympic figure skater Nancy Kerrigan is attacked by a rival skater's husband just before the US championships.
34. Over 100 days, starting in April 1994, an estimated 1 million Tutsis, an ethinic minority in Rwanda, are massacred by Hutus. An estimated 2 Million refugees flee Rwanda to neighboring countries.
35. Kurt Donald Cobain is found dead from a shotgun wound in his home. His death is ruled a suicide.
36. The opening of the Channel Tunnel turns the centuries old dream of a fixed link between the UK and mainland Europe into a reality.
37. The World Trade Organization is created; it is to be the only global body overseeing the rules of trade between nations.
38. Yitzhak Rabin is assassinated by a Jewish right-wing extremist. Aged 73 at his death, he is laid to rest before a shocked and grieving nation on Mt. Herzl in Jerusalem.

1995

39. 168 people are killed in a car bomb explosion outside a federal office building in Oklahoma City. Over 220 buildings sustain damage.
40. A nerve gas attack in Tokyo kills eight and injures thousands. Aum Shinrikyo ("Supreme Truth") is deemed responsible.
41. European budget carrier Easy Jet debuts: it offers two routes, from Luton to Glasgow

and Edinburgh.

42. Ken Saro-Wiwa and eight other leaders of the Movement for the Survival of the Ogoni People (MOSOP) are executed by Nigeria's military government.

43. Laurence Tisch, CEO of CBS, shakes hands with Michael Jordan, CEO of Westinghouse, at the occasion of CBS's takeover of the electronics giant.

44. An estimated 150 million people watch as O. J. Simpson is pronounced not guilty of the murder of his ex-wife and her associate.

45. Serbian President Slobodan Milosevic, Croat President Franjo Tudjman, and Bosnian President Alija Izetbegovic sign multiple copies of the Dayton Peace Agreement in the Palais de l'Elysee. Six other world leaders look on as witnesses.

1996

46. French President Jacques Chirac announces an early end to his country's controversial nuclear weapons tests.

47. A truck bomb containing 2.5 tons of explosives explodes outside of a US military compound in Saudi Arabia in one of the first al Qaeda attacks. 19 Americans are killed and nearly 300 people injured.

48. Rapper Tupac Shakur is killed in a drive-by shooting in Las Vegas.His killer is never apprehended; conspiracy theories abound. >

Therme Vals, Vals, 1996
Peter Zumthor
Guggenheim Museum,
Bilbao, 1997
Frank O. Gehry
14 October 1996
The Dow breaks through the 6,000 points level for the first time and closes at 6,010.00, double where it stood just five-and-a-half years earlier. NYSE volume routinely exceeds 2bn shares per week.
50
56
55
57
58
51
49
54
52
53
60
DIANA OF LOVE
REPUBLICAN NATIONAL CONVENTION
1996
1997

49. A report in the Jewish Chronicle claims that, through Swiss misappropriation of Jewish funds during World War II, $4 billion ($65 billion in 1996 dollars) was looted by the Nazis.
50. The UN General Assembly appoints Kofi Annan of Ghana the seventh United Nations Secretary-General.
51. Under pressure from proponents of Newt Gingrich's "Contract with America," Bill Clinton urges US citizens to say farewell to welfare " as we know it."
52. With his "Some Comfort Gained From the Acceptance of the Inherent Lies in Everything," Damien Hirst shocks the art world in his first exhibition in New York.

1997

53. British scientists clone Dolly the sheep, sparking widespread debate over the implications of genetic engineering.
54. WorldCom merges with MCI corp., forming MCI WorldCom. The deal creates an enterprise value of $32.3bn, the biggest corporate merger in US history. The merger is made possible by the passage of a bill that deregulates the American telecommunications industry.
55. After the announcement by the British government that all cattle over 30 months old are to be slaughtered, the cull of more than 100,000 cattle in the UK begins.
56. The United Kingdom hands over control of Hong Kong to the Chinese after 156 years of British rule.
57. Lady Diana, "the Queen of Hearts," dies in an car "accident."
58. "Titanic," the most expensive

Commerzbank Tower,
Frankfut am Main, 1997
Norman Foster
Jin Mao Tower, Shanghai, 1998
Skidmore, Owings & Merrill
3 April 1998
The Dow rises above
9,000 points early in the
session as surprisingly
high unemployment
figures send interest
rates lower.
61
62
VIEWERS ARE CAUTIONED THAT
THIS BROADCAST CONTAINS STRONG
LANGUAGE AND SEXUAL CONTENT
63
64
65
66
1998

movie ever made ($260 million), is released. It is a world wide smash, eventually grossing $1.6 billion.
59. In Zaire, Tutis and other anti-Mobutu rebels stage a coup and remove Josheph Désiré Mobuto from power. Mobuto had been in power for 32 years and was thought to have embezzled $4bn.

60. The so-called "tiger" states of the Far East suffer a precipitous decline following a currency crisis brought on by the collapse of the Thai baht.

1998

61. Microsoft and Bill Gates are taken to court by the US government on charges of antitrust.

62. Bill Clinton confesses on television to the American people that he did indeed have sexual relations with "that woman," Monica Lewinsky.
63. Prescription anti-impotence drug VIAGRA is released.
64 A German high-speed train (ICE) derails, hitting a bridge at over 200 km/h, killing over 100 people.
65. In May, India conducts five underground nuclear tests, and declares itself a nuclear state. In reaction, Pakistan initiates its own atomic testing four weeks later.
66. On August 7th, US embassies in Nairobi, Kenya and Dar es Salaam, Tanzania are bombed, killing 258 people and injuring over 5,000. >

Jewish Museum, Berlin, 1999
Daniel Liebeskind
Lords Cricket Ground Media Center, London, 1999
Future Systems
29 March 1999
"Dow 10,000" - after a surge of 170 points the Dow Jones closes at 10,006.78 - breaking 10,000 for the first time
14 January 2000
The Dow peaks at 11,722.98 points, an all-time high.
14 April 2
Dow suffers its big
loss in history, shed
617.78 points or 5.66
close at 10,30
Sydney 2000
67
68
69
70
71
72
73
74
75
76
红旗
POLICE
AOL
Google
1999

67. Nigerian Cardinal Francis Arinze is identified as a popular candidate to replace John II.

68. A WTO conference in Seattle is thrown into turmoil by the protests of over 10,000 anti-globalists.

69. A train on the Paddington line crashes near Ladbroke Grove in West London. The accident provides an early sign of the dire situation of the British railway following privatization.

70. Larry Page and Sergey Brin launch the search engine Google.

71. To fight against the hegemony of the American software giant Microsoft, China develops a local brand of the open-source Linux operating system, "Red Flag Linux."

72. Priest Sean Fortune, commits suicide after being accused of molesting 66 children.

73. 14 students and one teacher are killed, 23 others wounded, at Columbine High School in Littleton, Colorado in the US's deadliest school shooting.

74. On the night before the final vote, the Australian Olympic chief dines with two African IOC members at a swank resort on the Riviera. He offers his two guests $70,000 in inducements to vote for Sydney, which defeats Beijing by two votes the next morning.

2000

75. All 109 passengers and crew, and four people on the ground, are killed when a New York-bound Concord jet crashs into a hotel in Gonesse, on the outskirts of Paris.

76. The Japanese merger between the Fuji Bank, Dai-Ichi Kangyo

bank and the Industrial bank of Japan results in the creation of the world's largest financial institution with $1.1 trillion in assets.

77. The creation of AOL-Time Warner, a multimedia Goliath with a value of $140bn, is announced.

78. Dennis Tito, a California billionaire and former NASA employee becomes the first ever space tourist, paying $20mn. for his trip.

79. George W. Bush is elected President of the United States. The election is the closest in history: it is finally decided by Florida, where Jeb Bush (George's brother) serves there as Governor.

2001

80. On April 14th, the tech-heavy Nasdaq drops 355 points and the DJIA drops 617.78 points, signaling the beginning of the dot-com crash.

81. Hundreds of thousands of Californians lose power, the consequence of a poorly executed plan to deregulate California's energy industry.

82. Afghanistan's Taliban destroys the Buddha statues of Bamiyan.

83. After having successfully escaped capture for over 31 years, the "Great Train Robber" Ronnie Biggs is discovered in Rio.

84. Former Yugoslav president Slobodan Milosevic is delivered to the UN tribunal in The Hague where he is to stand trial for war crimes. >

Bellevue Art Museum,
Washington, 2001
Steven Holl
23 July 2002
Accounting scandals
involving energy gia
Enron and telecom
firm WorldCom -
shake investor
confidence to the
core. The Dow falls t
7,702 points
21 September 2001
Fears over the attacks and the impact on the world
economy send the Dow plummeting
11 September 2001
The terrorist attacks on New York halt
trading for an unprecedented four days,
with the index frozen at 9,605.
VOODOO DOLL
POLO
OBRERO
2001
2002

85. Terrorists attack the World Trade Center killing an estimated 2,750.
86. In response, New York's fire fighters, noted for exceptional bravery during the rescue efforts, become America's newest heroes.
87. "$1 from every Osama bin Laden voodoo doll sold will be donated to the Red Cross Relief Fund."

88. The Guggenheim museum opens a new outlet in Las Vegas.
89. A month after September 11, a US led military invasion of Afghanistan begins.

2002

90. On 2 January, Europe's new currency, the euro, is put into use by the 12 countries comprising the "euro zone."
91. Weighed down by debt, Argentina's economy collapses. Amid massive social upheaval, the former South American powerhouse sees five presidents come and go within a single month.
92. Hu Jintao is elected President of China by the National People's Congress.
93. A 41-year-old computer systems expert confesses to killing and eating Bernard Jurgen after the two men met in an internet chat room.
94. Professor Gunther von Hagens of Germany performs Britain's first public autopsy in 170 years as part of an exhibition that attempts to continue the anatomical fetishism established by Britart.
95. Ten former employees of the disgraced energy behemoth pose for Playboy in the June 2002 "Women of Enron" edition.

2003

96. On the 15th of February (F15)

anti-war protests are held across the globe in protest of the looming US-led attack on Iraq.
97. On the 19th of March, America, together with a "coalition of the willing," commences "Operation Iraqi Freedom" - Gulf War II.
98. American soldiers enjoy a 4th of July barbeque at the recently vacated Saddam Hussein Presidential Palace in Baghdad.
99. Looters raid museums in Iraq pillaging and destroying items ranging from prehistoric tools to 4,000-year-old pottery, to contemporary Islamic art.
100. SARS, a pneumonia-like disease, spreads to Canada. Emanating in China, its appearance outside of Asia sparks global panic.
101. New York Stock Exchange Chairman Richard Grasso resigns amid criticism of his $160 million pay package.
102. Zimbabwe President Robert Mugabe orders the forced eviction of all white farmers, sparking international criticism and decimating the country's economy.
103. 150,000 people protest WTO talks in Cancun, Mexico.
104. China sends its first Taikonaut, Yan Liwei, into outer space.
105. Arnold Schwarzenegger wins the California recall election, becoming the first foreign-born governor of a US state.
106. Facing up to 15 years in prison for allegedly sexing a 14 year old girl, R&B superstar R. Kelly explains, "Osama bin Laden is the only one who knows exactly what I'm going through."
107. Israel begins the second phase of construction on its "security fence." When completed, the concrete wall will stand 8m high and 360km long. ■

Museum: Economy

The overwhelming success of the museum - in purely quantitative terms - has ultimately transformed its role and operations....

BY OLE SCHEEREN

Greenspan, who warned in December 1996 that investors could be in the grips of "irrational exuberance," said, "The notion that a well-timed incremental tightening could have been calibrated to prevent the late-1990s bubble is almost surely an illusion."
The Gazette (Montreal) August 31 2002

Louvre
880 156,000 m2
Hermitage
1801 Sommerset 200 m2
1852 Hermitage 127,478 m2
Metropolitan
1880 106,200 m2
1897 Tate Britain : 10,000 m2
1959 NYC: 11,176 m2
LACMA
Guggenheim
Tate
MoMA
Whitney

MARKET Amid rising economic pressures and shrinking government subsidies, the museum - like the entire public - has been subjected to market-driven privatization. The models range from "straight forward" sponsorship to new hybrids of corporate promotion - franchising, branding, and bartering the museum's name and knowledge for fees and donations.

INSTITUTION Trapped between its responsibility to serve the public and new (largely privatized) financial mechanisms, the museum has established a machinery - partly cultural, partly political, partly economical, fuelled and maintained by shifting combinations of directors, boards, donors, governmental bodies, and curatorial and operational staff all endeavoring to navigate a web of vested interests. Subject to the judgmental verdict of critics and media (supposedly qualitative) and the ebb and flow of visitor numbers (purely quantitative), museums must now balance an ever more complex set of ambitions. The result is often confused, a product tailored to please, succeed, conserve, value, renew, sustain....

INFLATION The nineties introduced increasing need to "perform," to compete on the basis of economic growth and an associated idea of size and "presence," concerns that had theretofore existed only on the periphery of the cultural sphere. The motto became: the bigger, the better. The culture business was growing faster than many other domains, and bucks could be made with stock market-like speeds of speculation and capital gain. Those who didn't participate were doomed to obsolescence; those who didn't generate attention were threatened to disappear.

EXPANSION With budget figures far exceeding the range of millions, more and more museums began to plot strategies of territorial expansion, identifying potential venues across the globe, and developing new strategies to accomplish and sustain their (often

speculative) enlargements. New kinds of couplings, alliances, and joint ventures were instigated to address the increasing range of demands; content-providers, the owners of the actual "material" (artworks) joined with leading figures in the world of business to orchestrate new symphonies of cultural celebration, this time charging admission.

CONVERSION While museums in America constructed a fleet of shiny new buildings and additions to expand their corpo-cultural presence (in and outside of the US), Europe adopted an alternative strategy - part camouflage, part compromise - to satisfy its own need for cultural representation, namely the re-use of derelict industrial structures. While this approach didn't satisfy the American thirst for glamour (for the most part fuelled by private money) , it was appropriate for its intended context: derived from the European sense of "democracy" (with its attendant public funding), it was the "best possible compromise," ensuring the rehabilitation of listed buildings, and providing everything "modern" (and contemporary) a context of "historical background." Half historical, half progressive, conversion lent itself to the construction of European identity.

ENTERPRISE The increasing size of museums, and the monstrosity of the budgets needed to run, maintain, and theoretically improve the operation - without even speaking of the actual value of artworks and their acquisition - has transformed the institutional structure into something more of an economic enterprise. The commercial activities have spread beyond selling trinkets at the museum store into hosting events, licensing products, and running publishing houses.... Already experienced in financial speculation and endowments, corporate franchising techniques, and selling its know-how on the free market, it may only be a matter of time until the concept of "no-nonsense" management enters and re-scripts the operations of the museum.

HARVARD PROJECT ON THE CITY
1.GREAT LEAP FORWARD

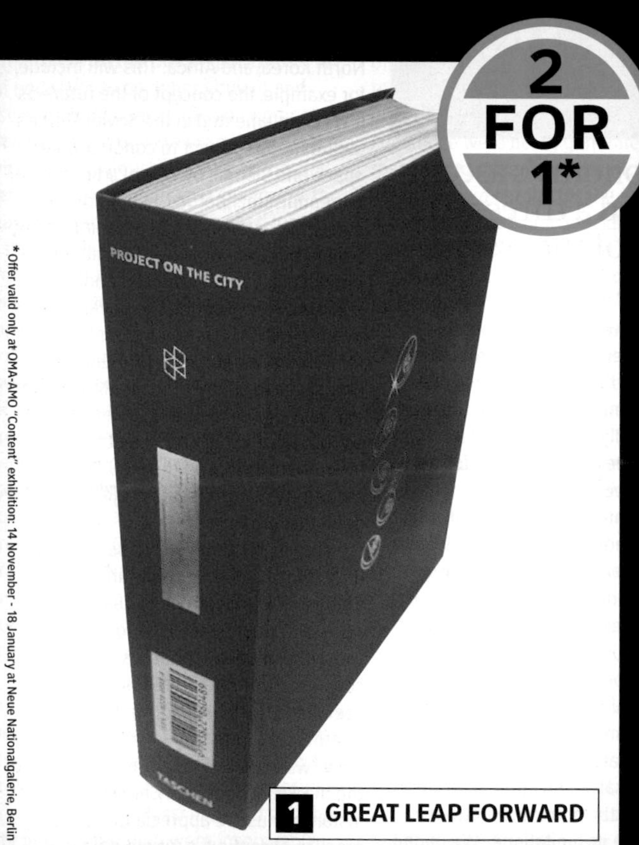

1 GREAT LEAP FORWARD

*Offer valid only at OMA-AMO "Content" exhibition: 14 November - 18 January at Neue Nationalgalerie, Berlin

1 Destined to become a crucial presence in the twenty-first century through sheer size alone, the Pearl River Delta region of the People's Republic of China - a cluster of five cities with a population of 12 million that will become a megalopolis of 36 million inhabitants by the year 2020 - has been gripped by a relentless pursuit of development at a scale and velocity previously unseen in the world. This maelstrom of modernization has been hastened by the presence of two Special Economic Zones in the Pear River Delta - laboratories for the combined experimentation of communism and capitalism that have produced an entirely new urban substance. Great Leap Forward is based on field work conducted in 1996 and consists of a series of interrelated studies investigating a complex urban condition that has resulted from a uniquely transformed political environment.

TASCHEN
www.taschen.com

architecture art classics design digital fashion film interiors photography pop-culture sex travel

New conceptual framework included

IN ONE OF THE WORLD'S FASTEST GROWING AREAS...

...A MAELSTROM OF MODERNIZATION...

...IS REWRITING THE CONTEMPORARY CITY

The dump is the lowest form of spatial organization. Pure accumulation, it is formless, has an uncertain perimeter and location. The surface of the dump reveals only part of its contents; the dump is fundamentally inconsistent and unpredictable. But it has potential; it attracts scavengers.

Things and people that are dumped have somehow lost their previous usefulness - once they were something, now they are waste. They don't work; they are empty; they are beyond resuscitation (or love or respect), no matter how modest.

Fresh foods and things that still work are stored with care, kept in special climatic conditions, assembled with a degree of formal precision - with premeditation and organization - in piles, mountains, racks, shelves. Only the worthless is dumped. The worthless no longer has any right to geometry, to order. To be dumped is to be condemned to the world of disorder.

But in an overorganized world - a groaning, decrepit universe of systems - the shapeless and the worthless have a new value, a new allure. The dump is free from constraints, from selection, from the tyranny of style.

Ein Italiener in Brügge

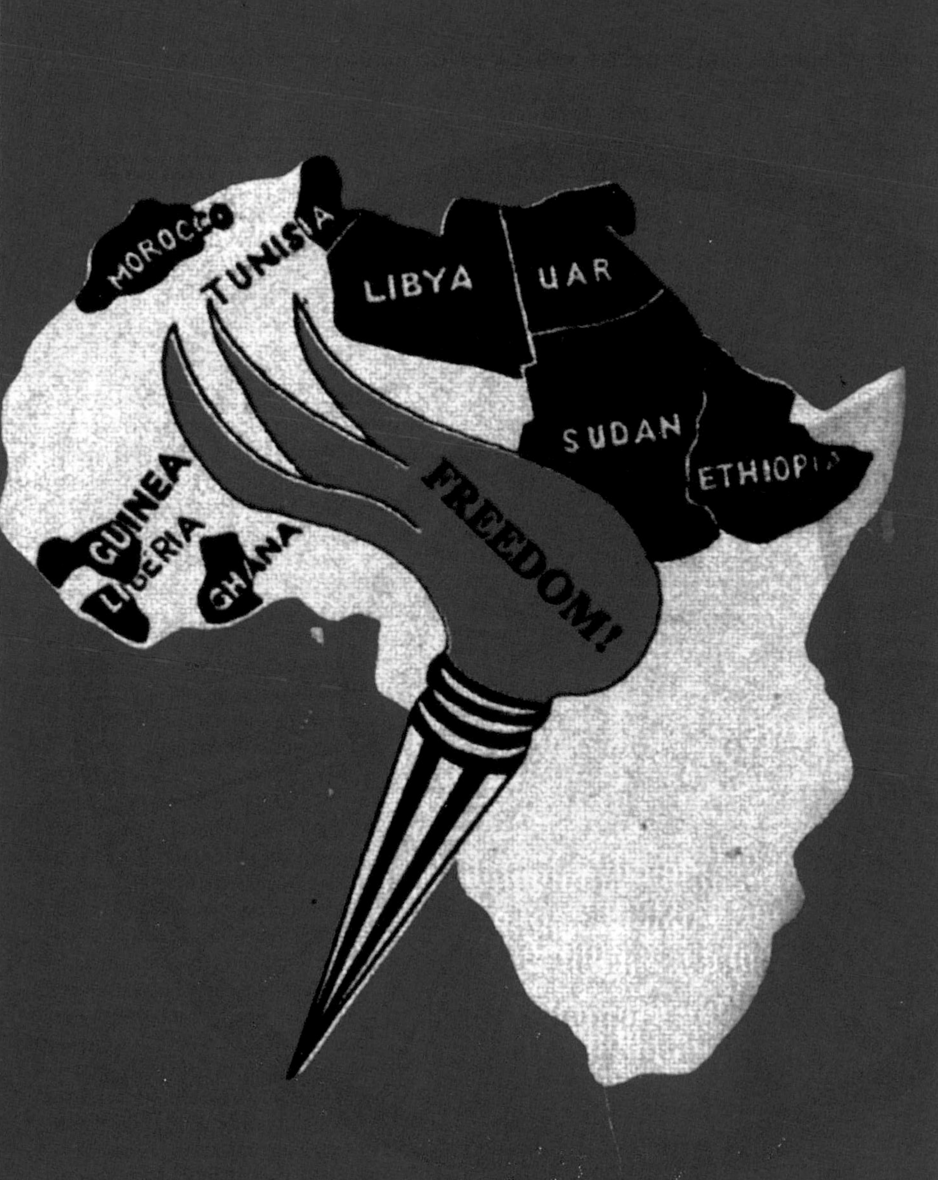

INDEPENDENCE TIMELINE

Ethiopia never colonized
Liberia 26.7.1847
South Africa 31.5.1910
Egypt 28.2.1922
Libya 24.12.1951
The Sudan 1.1.1956
Morocco 2.3.1956
Tunisia 20.3.1956
Ghana 6.3.1957
Guinea 2.10.1958
Cameroon 1.1.1960
Togo 27.4.1960
Senegal 20.8.1960
Madagascar 26.6.1960
The Democratic Republic of Congo 30.6.1960
Mali 22.9.1960
Somalia 1.7.1960
Benin 1.8.1960
Niger 3.8.1960
Burkina Faso 5.8.1960
Ivory Coast 7.8.1960
Chad 11.8.1960
Central African Republic 13.8.1960
The Republic of Congo 15.8.1960
Gabon 17.8.1960
Nigeria 1.10.1960
Mauritania 28.11.1960
Sierra Leone 27.4.1961
Burundi 1.7.1962
Rwanda 1.7.1962
Algeria 5.7.1962
Uganda 9.10.1962
Kenya 12.12.1963
Tanzania 26.4.1964
Malawi 6.7.1964
Zambia 24.10.1964
The Gambia 18.2.1965
Botswana 30.9.1966
Lesotho 4.10.1966
Mauritius 12.3.1968
Swaziland 6.9.1968
Equatorial Guinea 12.10.1968
Guinea Bissau 24.9.1973
Mozambique 25.6.1975
Cape Verde 5.7.1975
Comoros 6.7.1975
São Tomé and Principe 12.7.1975
Angola 11.11.1975
Seychelles 29.6.1976
Djibouti 27.6.1977
Zimbabwe 18.4.1980
Namibia 21.3.1990
Eritrea 24.5.1993

africa in the '60s

Red Radio

The story of the Cold War fight for Africa's airwaves

BY ADEMIDE ADELUSI-ADELUYI *RESEARCH BY ANAND KRISHNAN*

Interview with His Excellency Bola Ahmed Tinubu, Governor of Lagos State

05/November/03/16:15

RK: I have been in Lagos a number of times and have noticed improvement and a large amount of activities that engage situations in Lagos that are not perfect; can you say something about your program and the sequence of improvements that you are aiming for, especially regarding the newly launched Kick Against Indiscipline?

BT: The KAI has 3-dimensional ramifications, the first is a clean up of the Lagos environment - getting rid of the filth through refuse management, discipling people who litter the streets and fill the drains and gutters with refuse. Second is the anti-flooding program, which attempts to get the community involved in drain clearing to help address Lagos's chronic problem of flooding - because the water table in Lagos is higher than normal, like in Holland.

Third, we are continuing to discipline the road users to encourage them to be more organized and more obedient, to obey the traffic rules. That's it.

Generally, the ambition is to transform Lagos *radically* into a city state that is progressing and is under control as to its environment. To this end, we are now pursuing a number of new urban developments that will transform the shanties into low, medium, and high income areas. We continue to work on creating new roads and creating new avenues. We want to have an inner-city road network that can be tolled, and therefore give the opportunity for self-maintenance. We are supplementing that with LASTMA the Lagos State Traffic Management Authority. We are using LASTMA to supplement the efforts of the traffic wardens, and we are working hard to upgrade our various assignments and improve our presence in that respect.

RK: Is "self-maintenance" a new concept? I never heard it before.

BT: It is a new concept, because if we can have some of the roads tolled, we will generate enough revenue to cover the expense. Lack of adequate revenue allocation from the Federal to the State has deterred our progress signifiantly, and international aid and grants are not coming in as expected to help counter the decay of Lagos state, particularly its infrastructure and the high rate of pollution being caused by diesel generated emissions from buses. In place of the bus network, we want to be able to establish a light rail system that will allow for mass movements of people.

RK: And would that be above ground or underground?

BT: That's above ground.

RK: And these new roadways will be self-supporting?

BT: Yes, self supporting. We are also encouraging private investment whenever possible. If necessary, we will be able to use taxes to supplement any short fall; this makes the propositon more attractive to investors....

RK: Is there a great interest on the part of international investors in Lagos at this moment?

BT: Oh yes, they are showing some interest in the 4th mainland bridge and some other toll roads being planned.

RK: And from which nations particularly?

BT: The World Bank is on the light rail, but we've not gotten substantial help from Europe or America.

RK: Is Europe taking more responsibility?

BT: At the moment, the over-centralization of European Union grants is adversely affecting the progressive plans of Lagos....

RK: Can you give more detail about that?

BT: For example, if any grant - for instance, for the flooding program, as I've said, the road network gets spoiled because it is flooded easily - any grant for addressing the floods or the environment goes to the Nigerian Central Bank, as a bilateral grant or whatever. Despite the fact that it is intended for Lagos solely, the grant then becomes a discretionary disbursement from the federal level. It starts into the bureaucratic process; each step dips in and spends the money for its own purposes. With the money that remains, the original goal is hardly realizable. So the efficiency is gone. Often, of course, the grants are highly politicized: they are used for political patronage, rather than for effective, realistic programs.

RK: Are you implying that the current support methods in Europe are ineffective or unrealistic?

SATURDAY PUNCH

THE MOST WIDELY READ NEWSPAPER

THE PUNCH

Miliki in London

An uncertain future

GSM operators get December deadline for seamless interconnection

NSE cancels 7.1m shares of Afribank

Kupolokun gets order to clean up NNPC

• Why FG removed Obaseki

House panel wants payment of N303.6bn to varsities

• FG, ASUU meet on 2001 pact

Anger, condemnation over missing Okigbo report

Gateway SESA

Gatewaybank

Bola Ahmed Tinubu was elected governor of Lagos State in 1999, shortly after democracy was restored to Nigeria.

> "At the moment, the over-centralization of European Union grants is adversely affecting the progressive plans of Lagos."

BT: It is old fashioned; it is weak....

RK: And how do you explain that apart from over-centralization? Is it also about a fundamental misunderstanding of Africa?

BT: Yes, fundamental. The dynamics of African politics are not even taken into account. They hold on to the old perceptions and old values, and, unfortunately, such a position does not help promote the stability of the economy and democracy.

RK: And do you think that that misunderstanding is worse in Europe or America right now?

BT: It is present in both, but worse in Europe. The Chinese are more flexible: in fact, although their own system appears more rigid, they are actually more flexible and more aggressive.

RK: Is there increased participation of the Chinese in any enterprise in Lagos?

BT: Oh yes, they are taking an active role in planning the Export Processing Zone, the free trade zone in Lagos, and they are ready to work on the light rail as well.

RK: So far in the things you have mentioned, you mention things that would make Lagos more like other cities. Are there also particular aspects of Lagos that you want to keep, so that you maintain some of what is unique about Lagos?

BT: Ah, well, there are of course some that we want to keep. We want to be able to keep some of the key areas, in terms of monuments, and improve upon them, for instance our Idumota Market, Tinubu Square, and various shrines of the old city. We want to keep all of that and from that move to develop new towns around Lagos, so that we can soon have a decongested Lagos.

RK: So how optimistic are you that Lagos within 5 or 10 years will take its rightful place among the major cities of the world?

BT: Ah well, I am optimistic that the world will realize the danger to quality of life that a population of this size creates, and hopefully they will come to realize that a mega-city that is at about 15 million people right now, with a growth rate of about 6 to 8 %, could become a danger to all of us in the world - particularly in Africa and the West African sub-region - if its problems are not addressed. The population explosion is potentially unmanageable.

RK: Unmanageable unless there are interventions now.

BT: Yes.

RK: But are you optimistic about the outcome of that, or do you think that, with the current plans, this unmanageable state can be avoided?

BT: It is a highly critical issue. I strongly believe that, if attention is not given to it immediately, it can bring a serious epidemic to humanity. ■

Modernity in the 1970's

Fueled by oil money, in a frenzy of building, Lagos's major landmarks and infrastructure were established.

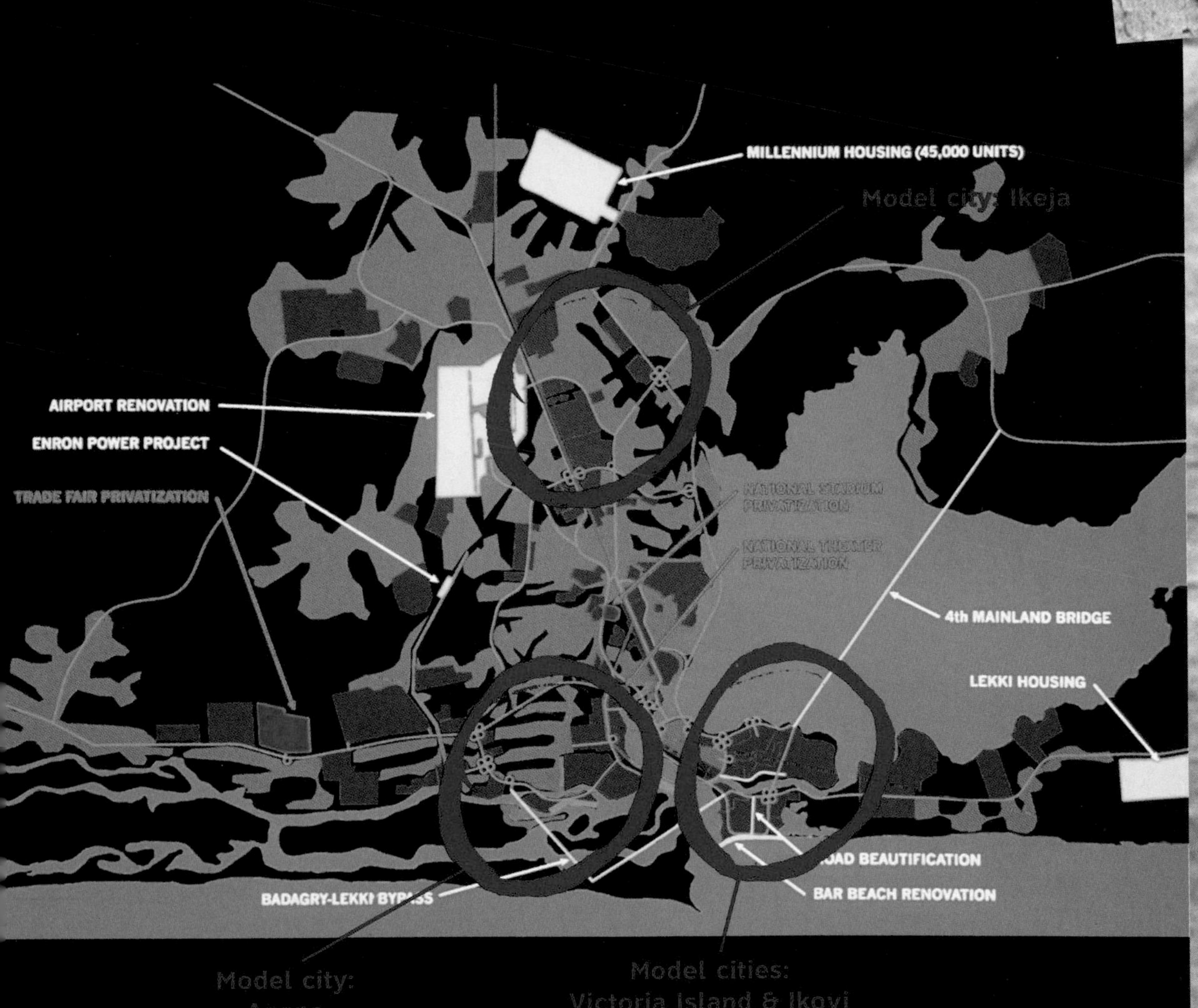

Modernity in the 2000's

On 3 November 2003, Gov. Tinubu initiated an executive order declaring Ikoyi, Victoria Island, Ikeja, and Apapa "model cities," making them zero tolerance zones for refuse, traffic, and planning violations.

BY A ROADSIDE BILLBOARD

AT THE LAGOS STOCK EXCHANGE

MISS NIGERIA AT A FASHION BOOK LAUNCH

AWOLOWO ROAD, IKOYI

"he primary objective of
his administration is to
rovide potable water for all"

- Senator Bola Ahmed Tinubu
Governor, Lagos State

BAR AT AKIN ADESHOLA

21 January 01/20:45

lagos 6°27'N 3°24'E

Prada yada

W3:...because you work for them?
M5: No no no no....
General laughter
M5: No, no, I really work with them very intimately, and the way their brain works is really interesting.
M4: Hmm.
W3: Sometimes, I don't understand....
M4: Hey. The way their brain works? Toyin, mama, zero in.
W3: But how does their...? What is their...
M5: So, what's your, what is ur criticism?
I just think that they're o expensive. I like what but I mean es, I wonder, why that a little osts $2000? ?
rada!
W3: Yes, because it's Prada. But I don't understand why they.... And now they want to make a mobile phone out of wood.
Laughter
W3: Next thing, it'll be out of....
W3: Wo, you're worried that they are going to start cutting down our trees here?
M4: Ah, no....
Laughter
W3: Anyway, you know what, all that I am trying to say is that maybe you should pass the message.
M5: I could probably get you a discount.
W3: That is what I am trying to say; if I criticize enough, maybe you'll tell them that there's one lady unhappy in Africa, maybe you could give her a bag, and she'll keep quiet.
General laughter
W3: You are not soliciting, ehn?
M4: So that is what the noise is about? So that's what your noise...? That's all?
W3: That's what my noise is for o.
M4: It is campaigning for a bag.
M4: Only for a bag?
W3: I know they are good!
M5: Which one do you like? The small one, the...?
W3: Yes, the one...you know those ones that Jackie Onassis (laughter intensifies) used to have, the nice long ones... Yes, the box kind, yeah.
More laughter
M1: You are a disgrace...
M4: So keep it in mind.
Background: Prada o!!
M5: So why don't you come to Europe and I'll introduce you?
LAUGHTER
W3: Ah, I am going to take you up on that.
M4: Ah, taking over....
W3: I am going to....Listen, you are not busy when I come; you better not be busy.
M5: Actually Miuccia Prada wants to come here.
W3: Please, Rem say it!
M4: To Lagos?
W3: Rem, say it.
M5: Yes, to Lagos.
M4: Let's make a deal and set up a Prada shop here now.
W3: Yes, let them make me.... Let me start up a franchise.
M4: Exactly. We are really good people.
More Laughter
M5: Yes.... Say this is the first Prada store in Nigeria.
W3: And then you could come do some nice architectural design, and make me the head of it, I don't mind.
M1: Well done, kuu se....
M5: Yeah, yeah, this
Yeah ok....

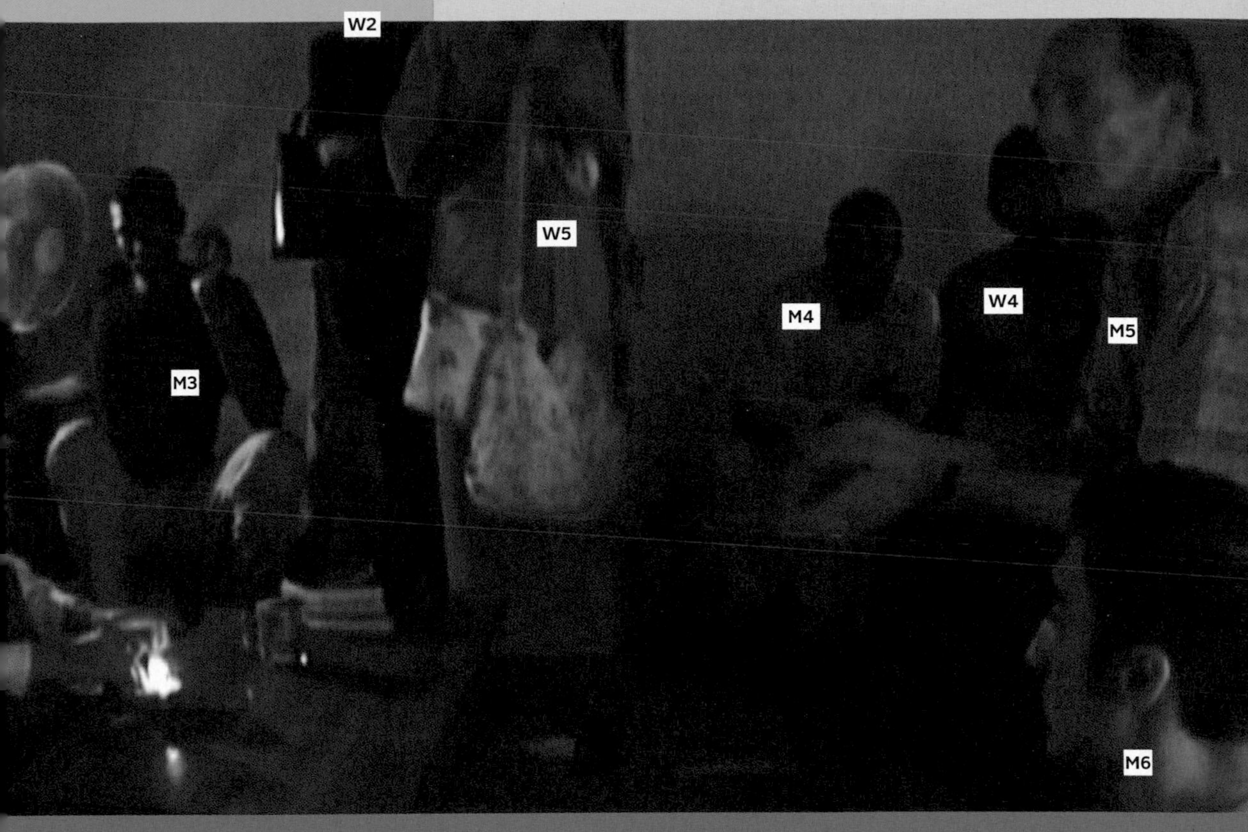

Protracted general laughter, slight awkward silence

W3: Ah, nice.

Baby starts crying

W1: But Rem, what would, what do you think would happen if Prada would rapidly cut the price?

W2: I don't understand o....

W1: What would happen to the product?

Background: You are not recognizing any number four hundred and *kini, omo ti do* [number four hundred & something, the child has become number one, the most important] *E leyi naa n ke.* [This one too is crying]

M5: They would sell four times as much. They would sell four times as much is my guess. I don't know.

W1: But by increasing....

M5: I think it is nothing really to do with the price. It would become too.... It would become like jeans. But they are already selling more than they can produce, so it is a totally theoretical thing.

Background: *Ko fe lo o le mon, Pampers wa, o ti di nnkan mii.* [He doesn't want to go home anymore. These Pampers are so expensive. They've really become something else] *Se ko jo le e lori?* [It didn't leak on you did it?] *O ga o*, meeting of the babies

W2: This is serious, a meeting of the babies.

M2: Rem, I was reading about you in *Time* or *Newsweek*, about ah...

M4: The Guggenheim.

M2: How you set up the Guggenheim, yes, the museum.

M5: Yes.

M2: And then, em, three of you....

M5: Well, no I actually didn't go, but Frank Gehry is making plans. But then that's another serious thing I want to do: I really want to start a Guggenheim here.... I really want to make sure that there are some real projects here.

M2: What about the other guy you mentioned last time, the Microsoft chap?

M5: Yes, he is still coming, but probably in the later part of the year.

Pause.

M5: And because all those people lost unbelievable amounts of money.... I mean like they had four billion,and now they have one billion.

M2: But you were saying the last time that the whole thing is a bit shaky?

M5: Well I am not sure how shaky it is, but in terms of the stock market....

M2: Yeah, the stock market.

M5: It's kind of very strange now that we know these people that are incredibly rich, but they lose incredible sums overnight.

M4: Overnight. Hn.

M5: So you go to a party, and everybody has a certain expression that, because most of the people in the room have lost two billion between the day before and now. And it is always a fund raising party so....

M4: How do they react?

M5: They have this kind of pained expression on their face. They smile with a face kind of like "aaaarrh..."

M2: Paper money.

Intense silence.

Departures: *Odaro, ok o, ese gaa n.* You guys are off, toodles *[Good night. OK, thank you very much...]* ■

BBA

For its third incarnation in Africa, the "Big Brother" series expanded beyond South Africa to include contestants from twelve different countries across the sub-Saharan region. MNET, the South African company responsible for BBA, made the decision to expand based primarily on financial concerns: with MNET's market expanding faster outside South Africa than within it, the pool of participants was expanded to countries where the satellite providers' customers were. The show, presenting Big Brother's now standard cocktail of sex, pain, and drunkenness with an African twist, was wildly popular - watched by an estimated 30million in 46 countries.

Criticism followed predictable lines, as the show's trademarked "cultural diversity" - celebrated by most on the continent – was seized by purist politicians and media personalities who argued that African = black, thereby questioning how "African" a white or multiracial contestant could be. Others argued that, by arranging the first-ever transcontinental cast and allowing Africans to, for the first time, observe one another in intimate detail, BBA may be an instigator of neo-Pan-African sentiments, and a crucial indicator of unity within a continent so frequently presented as torn apart by ethnic conflict.

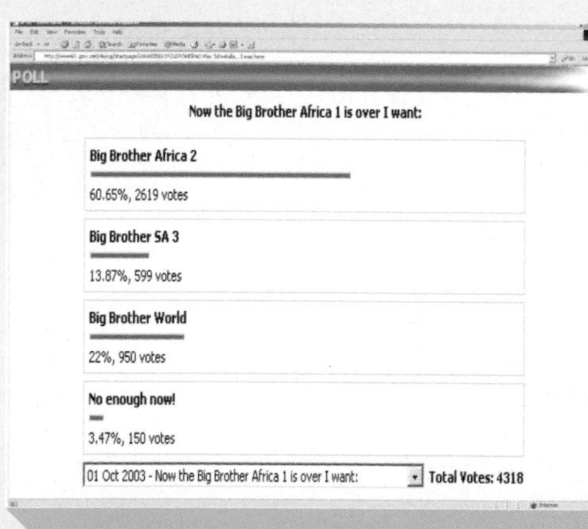

POLL

Now the Big Brother Africa 1 is over I want:

Big Brother Africa 2	60.65%, 2619 votes
Big Brother SA 3	13.87%, 599 votes
Big Brother World	22%, 950 votes
No enough now!	3.47%, 150 votes

01 Oct 2003 - Now the Big Brother Africa 1 is over I want: Total Votes: 4318

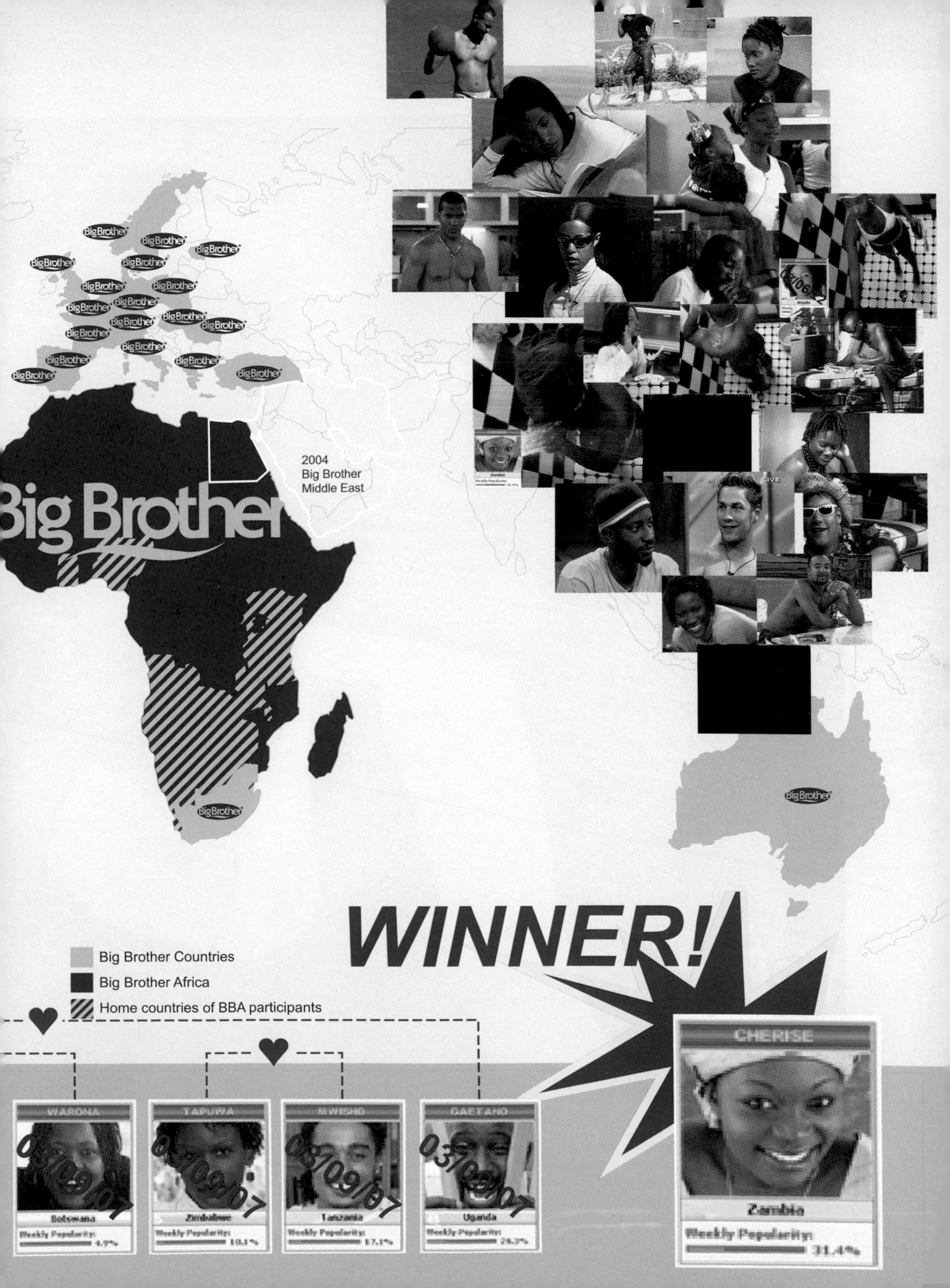

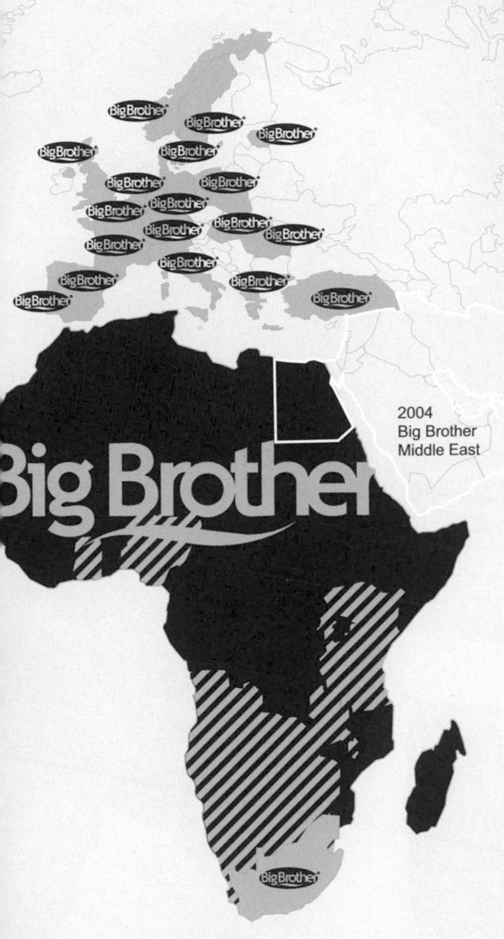

WINNER!

Big Brother Countries

Big Brother Africa

Home countries of BBA participants

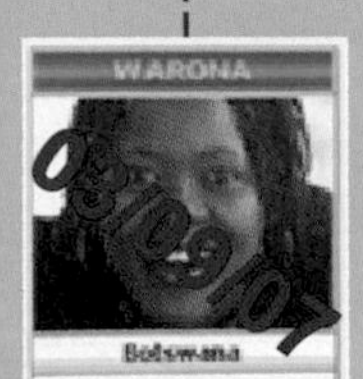

almere 5°15'N 52°37'W

17 September 99/20:30

Big Vermeer

Through an alchemy of transparency and daylight, Dutch painters like Vermeer turned, in the 17th century, the everyday into a Low Countries sublime; a world with nothing to hide - inside and outside separated by mere sheets of glass - its only intolerance for what is hidden.

Three centuries later, the Dutch still trade on intimacy - perhaps their last resource after agriculture has become ornamental, the seas over-fished, the waters tamed, industry disappeared to the sweat shops.... - when they unleash Holland's contribution to the tail end of the nineties - *Big Brother* - ruthlessly engineering exposure to industrial-strength exhibitionism - the only boom not yet deflated - a terminal footnote to Andy Warhol's fifteen minutes....

A SAD WOMAN - 2001
A woman sits in front of a dark curtain; she has a sad expression on her face and is holding her hand up to emphasize the subject she is discussing. She is fashionably dressed in a white blouse with a dark, skirt-like dress over it and a sober necklace. She complains about the competitive atmosphere in the Big Brother house and is considering leaving. It is a very serious situation.

A WOMAN WRITING A LETTER - 1667

A woman is writing a letter, looking quite concentrated. She is fashionably dressed in a white blouse with a dark, skirt-like dress ove… pearl jewelry. On a table covered by a Persian carpet, we see a seal and a crumpled piece of paper, which is probably a draft o… letter certainly concerns a serious matter, as she has a maid waiting for her to finish the letter. >

ALLEGORY OF THE DIGITAL CAMERA - 2000

...en are working with a digital camera, trying to film their daily routine. The inhabitants of the Big Brother house have recorded a song ... the melody of George Bakers' 'Big City' with new lyrics: "Big Brother, don't bother." Now they have been ordered by Big Brother to ... matching video clip. Despite their efforts, the material produced by the two men will not be used for the video, since it is not ... in quality to the 24 cameras that have been installed in the house to record their daily routine for the Dutch audie...

THE ALLEGORY OF PAINTING - 1656
A painter in fashionable clothes is painting a scene of a young woman posing as Clio, muse of history. The map of Holland [illegible] background symbolizes the political situation: the United Netherlands has only recently been formed, and the map [illegible] the period in which the Habsburg empire still occupied the Netherlands. The chandelier in front of the map [illegible] eagle on it, symbol of the Habsburg family; there are no candles in it, however, to symbolize the lack of [illegible]

COUCH - 2000

men and two women are engaged in a lively discussion with various others. The subject of the discussion ranges from relationships to
d descriptions of sexual activities. The blonde man in the middle is heavily engaged in the discussion, and is clearly the most
d in the subject. The woman next to him tries to stay outside the conversation, but she is interested to listen to the opini
turally, since she is having an affair with another inhabitant. The discussion deals with topics that directly conce

THE PROCURESS - 1656
Two men stand behind a woman; one of them has his hand on her breast, another woman watches with a quiet smile on her face. The first woman is probably a prostitute, and the other woman could very well be her madam, trying to set her up with a customer. This is Vermeer's most provocative painting. The woman on the right has been said to be Vermeer's wife, although it is difficult to believe he used his own wife as a model for a prostitute. The young man on the left has often been identified as Vermeer himself, though there is no direct evidence to support this. ■

Information is a differen
Who ever saw a communication?
If there is no difference
Europe is a network of monads
Architecture needs to b
Informat fference me

location 54°56'N 30°18'E

09 Oct 2003: 11:00

Intensity generators

Scott Lash and Arjen Mulder in conversation

Scott Lash: Content was a funny word up until five years ago. I remember going to multimedia days for various kinds of European bodies, and the whole idea then was "the Americans might have the technology, but we Europeans are going to get the content." For broadcasting, the idea was to have 45% of French content in France, and 70% of German content in Germany. Content was so boring, at that point it had nothing to do with what we now call "intensivity." We didn't understand how content too was informational. We saw content as more extensive, content was connected to national territory. People stopped talking about national content in the last three years or so. Now we see content differently. In the publishing industry they used to speak about books or texts or magazines or poems, but now all this has turned into "content."

Arjen Mulder: You're talking about content as an experiential thing, and not so much as an amount of information that you put in your media, as in the notion of national content?

SL: Yes, we're looking at something experiential, something that's experienced but not directly perceived. Who ever saw a communication? Who ever saw a bit of information? You see stuff that is volumetric. You could argue that OMA's kind of architecture and urbanism, and also AMO's material, is intensive and not extensive. It plays off of surfaces of communication and flow and intensity, and it's often non-linear.

AM: But isn't all architecture about creating intensities?

SL: No, not at all. Van der Rohe's architecture is volumetric. Architects make the distinction between tectonic and stereotonic, but I think that, whether it's Van der Rohe's tectonic or Corbusier's stereotonic, both tectonic and stereotonic are territorial and extensive. I think that Koolhaas's and Virilio's idea of breaking with the fixity of architecture for the movement of urbanism is a question of intensity, and not directly perceivable. Volumes are perceivable, intensities are not. It's like the shift from the manufacturing to the information society: the movement from the volumetric solids of manufacturing to the intensivity of the information society. In that sense architecture is becoming intensive. But it didn't use to be and most of it still isn't.

It's like the distinction between the old archive and the new digital or informational archives. The old archive was territorial; it was a national archive, a *Stadt* archive or a *Staat* archive. It worked off of extensivities, of bits of paper, of deeds of property, of volumes. And it had to do with the symbolic structures of a nation. The new archive is intensive, you can't see it, but you experience it. What we are talking about is more an architecture of experience than an architecture of direct perception. This is what I would describe as intensive architecture, and it's clearly part of the work of Koolhaas and Lars Spuybroek and Greg Lynn.

I'm thinking now of Gregory Bateson's idea of information as difference: of informational ontology as an ontology of difference.

AM: Information is a difference that makes a difference.

SL: If there's no difference there's no information. Information as difference means information not as identity. Information then has to be not atomistic, as in Descartes, Hobbes, because that works with the principle of identity. The atom is the fundamental unit of an ontology of identity, the monad of an ontology of difference. Information is monadological, because from Leibniz to Deleuze the monad is a self-organizing system - it's always generating difference. The monad belongs to life, the atom to mechanism. Information has, by definition, something to do with the monad. It has to do with "the virtual" as people understand it nowadays. It has to

that makes a difference.
ho ever saw a bit of information?
here is no information.
urope is a lattice of differences.
an experience-machine.
s information not as identity
vities. Europe is like information.

do with the event, which is also not perceivable, because where is it? It comes and it goes, it happens in time and space.... Europe has to work from a collection of differences; it has 15 or 18 countries that are different as collectivities. America is not; it's identical. It has a lot of different people coming in, but look how American they get. Look at Schwarzenegger. For all the American multiculturalism, I think the US is much more a melting pot, it doesn't preserve differences, it melts them into this one nation or hypernation.

Robert Kagan is very influential among the neo-conservatives and the Bush administration. He sees Europe in terms of a nexus of treaties. But that's not such a bad idea. Here in contrast to America, which is made of homogenities, Europe is a network of monads. Europe is a nexus of connected singularities. Europe is a lattice of differences. These singularities connect through a set of linked "treaties," which are to be understood in terms of informal modes of connection and communication that could form a wonderful pluralistic self-designing chain or nexus of differences. This for me is Stefano Boeri's Unstable States of Europe. Europe is a combinatoire of intensivities. Europe is like information.

AM: It seems to me that the interesting artists and architects of today are not so much into ideas or concepts, but into organizing differences, organizing information, organizing ideas and interesting people. They are creating structure out of other people's content. For me this is connected with the computer and digitalization. The organizational principal of the computer consists basically of looking for the intensities, and then organizing these intensities. If you are into architecture, like OMA, you organize them into a building, or an urbanistic project.

SL: Content becomes a matter of patterning and organizing intensities of information and communication.

AM: It is about organizing intensities or letting intensities self-organize, and creating new intensities. That's the goal. In architecture, the intensity is the building: the building is an intensity in the city, and it also creates intensities inside itself, which is different from the classical modernist architecture. Mies van der Rohe wanted to create neutral spaces.

SL: It's hard for me to know what the intensity is, though. Sometimes the intensities seem to be in the virtual, in the open, self-organizing systems or rhizomes that are creating the intensities; sometimes intensities seem to be in the actualizations, in the ways that they actualize into the creation of differences. The intensity might be in the interface of the virtual and the actual. But it only can work with actualisations. A pure virtual gives you nothing.

Look at the way that the towers bend in the model of OMA's CCTV building, and lean on each other. That's not classical boxes and rectangular corners at all. And it's incredibly tectonic, because it's all load bearing. Open, non-linear systems are intensity generators - but is the intensity the event, is it the building, is it the interface, or all of the above? I'd say that it's both the intense experience and some sort of technological or prosthetic device, some kind of vision-machine or some kind of intensity machine that's yielding these intensities in its own self-modification. Architecture needs to be an experience-machine: though not an operationally closed self-organizing system, as in Niklas Luhmann's or Varela's autopoesis. And even the classical monad was closed, like Leibniz said: no doors, no windows. To be open, there's got to be this machine that generates intensities. Maybe Europe can be this kind of machine, to the extent that it can be a nexus of singularities. Maybe Europe can be an event generator, an intensity generator. To be that, Europe needs to be not just unstable, but also open. ■

rotterdam: 51°55'N 4°29'E

Copy and Paste

How to turn a Dutch house into a Portugese concert hall in under 2 weeks.

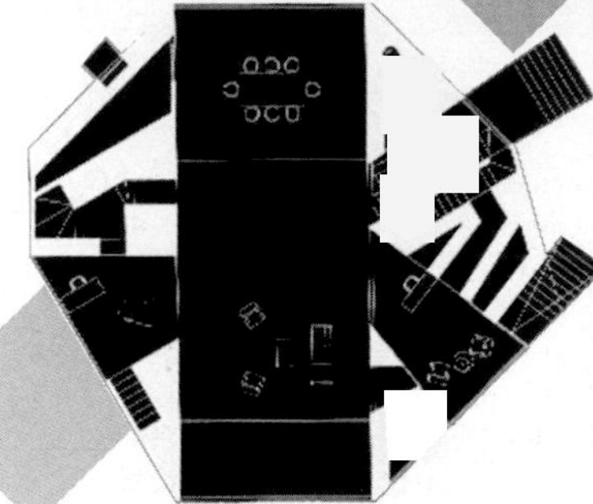

Casa da Musica began its life as a house for a Dutchman. Its "recycling" is an allegory for the unstable relationship between form and use, a mixture of psychology, scientific investigation, and naked opportunism.

After completing the house in Bordeaux, we were approached to design another house. The client asked us to design according to his three dominant neuroses - a hatred for all clutter and mess, a dread fear of the year 2000 and the Y2K bug, and a certain ambiguity about the status of the family. We would have to design a house that would hide all clutter, guarantee autonomy to each family member, yet enable their voluntary assembly.

To address the mess-phobia we proposed that the client imagine the entire volume of the house as a single container that could absorb any amount of organizational chaos. Individual spaces - for him, for her, for their children - would be excavated from the storage. The theater of their community would be a tunnel - completely free of furniture, drilled through the form from end to end. To exorcise the Y2K phobia, the entire house stood on a disk that enabled it to rotate to exploit particular moments, views, weather, etc.

The client was always enthusiastic, but never completely convinced. Sober, hand-written faxes would systematically undo initial verbal agreement.

The first trip to Nigeria was welcome relief in this process-as-therapy. Expecting distress, we were stunned by energy, intelligence, creativity, and - to survive - hyper-efficiency.

Back in the office, there were two weeks left to finish a competition for a concert hall in Porto. We had been wrestling with the myth of the shoebox - acoustically perfect, architecturally deadly. In a Nigerian afterglow, a blinding flash suggested that the house enlarged offered a way out: the family's tunnel could become the detested shoebox; because we took it out rather than built it, there was no danger of boredom. The switch abruptly ended the therapy.

The office was shocked at the cynicism. There was disbelief that what had been tailored for one very specific condition could be suddenly used for a completely different purpose. ■RK

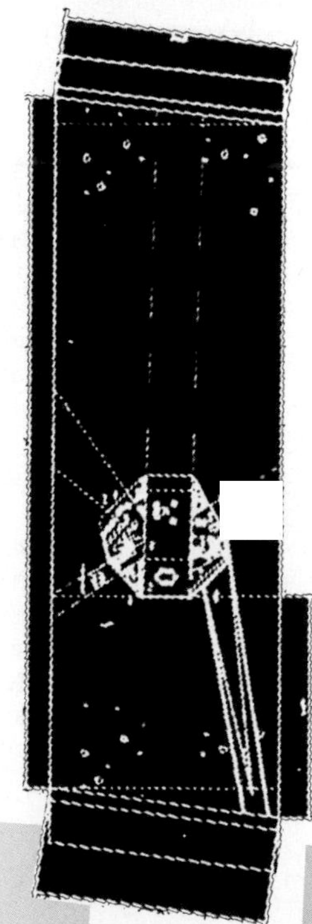

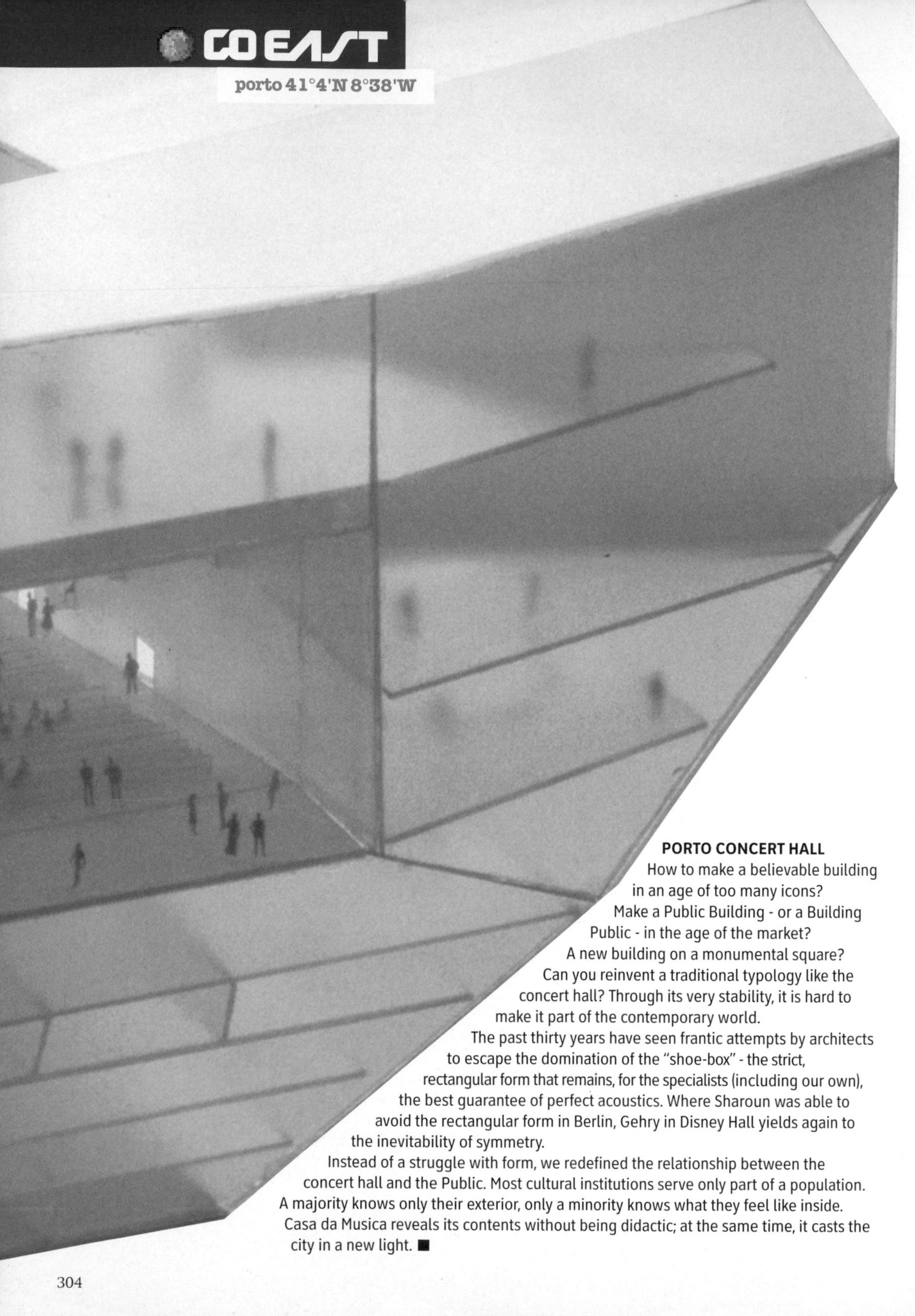

PORTO CONCERT HALL

How to make a believable building in an age of too many icons? Make a Public Building - or a Building Public - in the age of the market? A new building on a monumental square? Can you reinvent a traditional typology like the concert hall? Through its very stability, it is hard to make it part of the contemporary world.

The past thirty years have seen frantic attempts by architects to escape the domination of the "shoe-box" - the strict, rectangular form that remains, for the specialists (including our own), the best guarantee of perfect acoustics. Where Sharoun was able to avoid the rectangular form in Berlin, Gehry in Disney Hall yields again to the inevitability of symmetry.

Instead of a struggle with form, we redefined the relationship between the concert hall and the Public. Most cultural institutions serve only part of a population. A majority knows only their exterior, only a minority knows what they feel like inside. Casa da Musica reveals its contents without being didactic; at the same time, it casts the city in a new light. ■

Casa da Musica

Completed: Summer, 2004

ROOMS

1. Dressing Rooms 2. Musicians' Restaurant 3. Offices 4. Rehearsal Rooms 5. Soloist Rooms 6. Foyer 7. Ticket Office, Cloakrooms 8. Large Auditorium 9. Cyber Music 10. Bar 11. Small Auditorium 12. Educational Rooms 13. Restaurant 14. Terrace

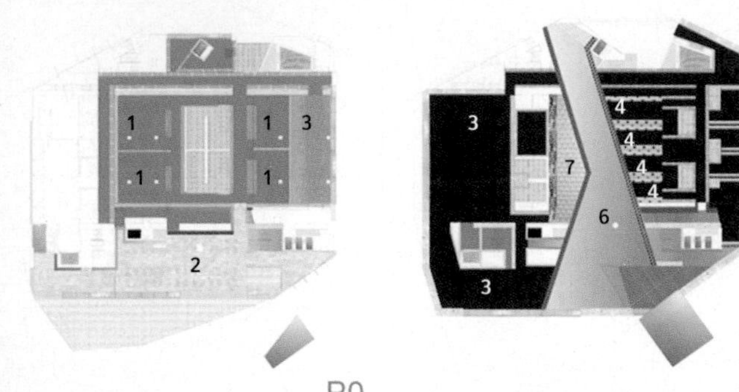

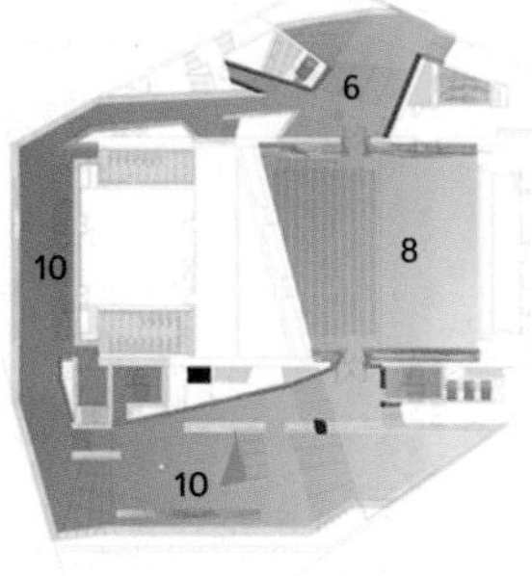

6

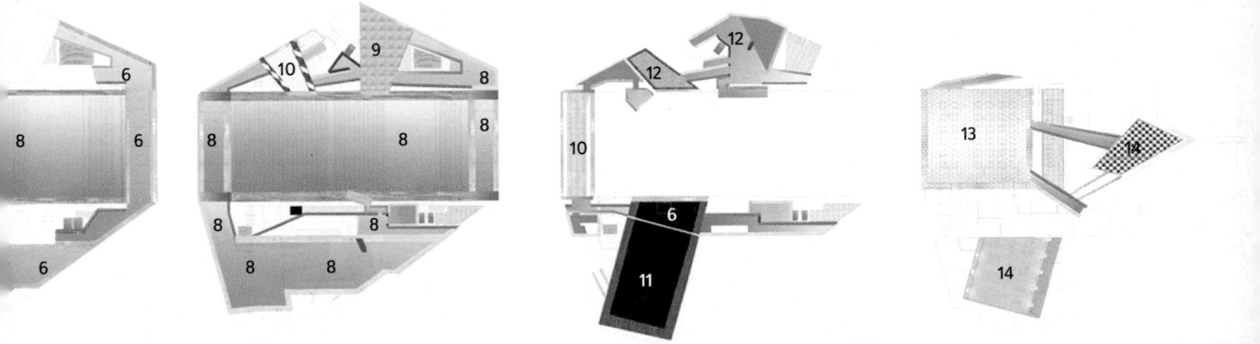

P3

P4

P5

P8

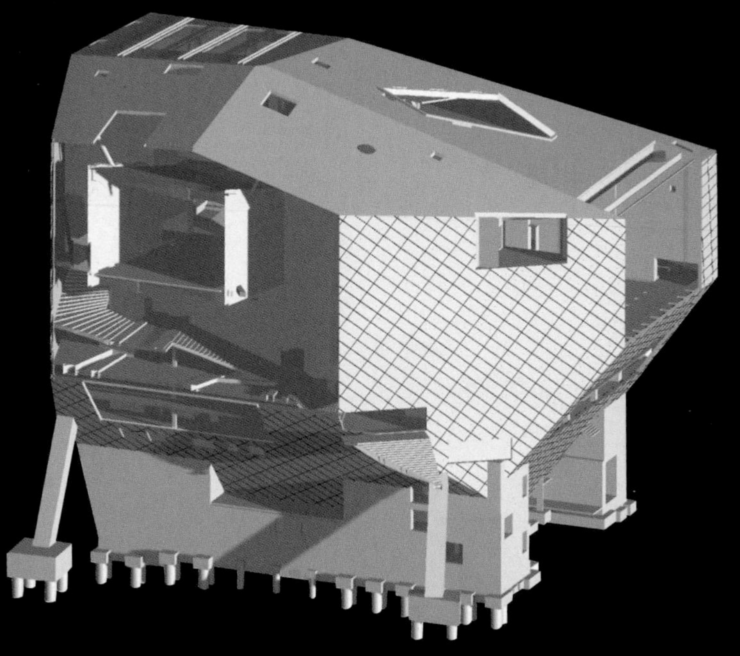

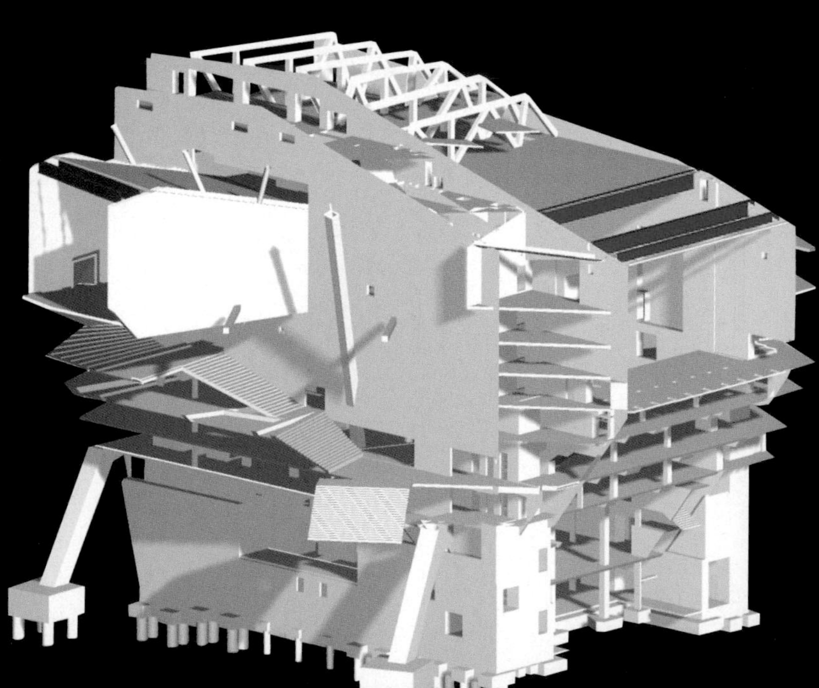

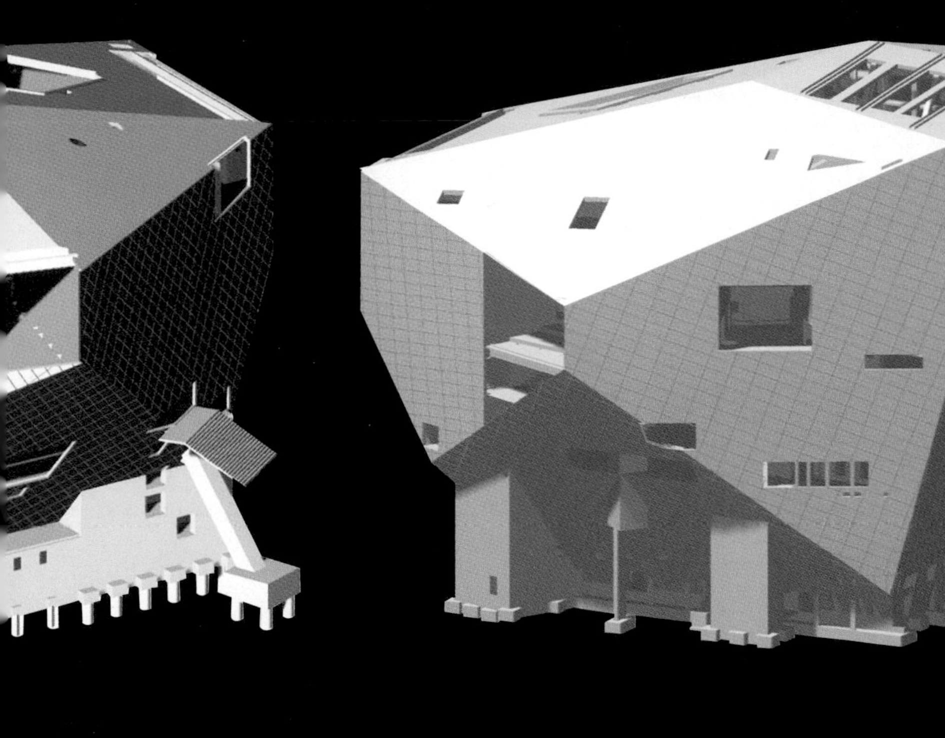
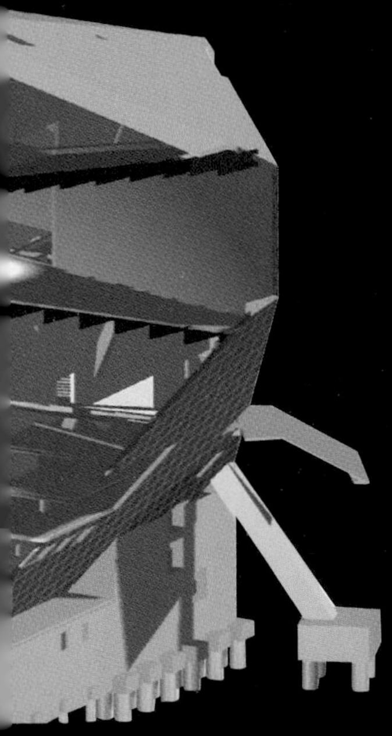
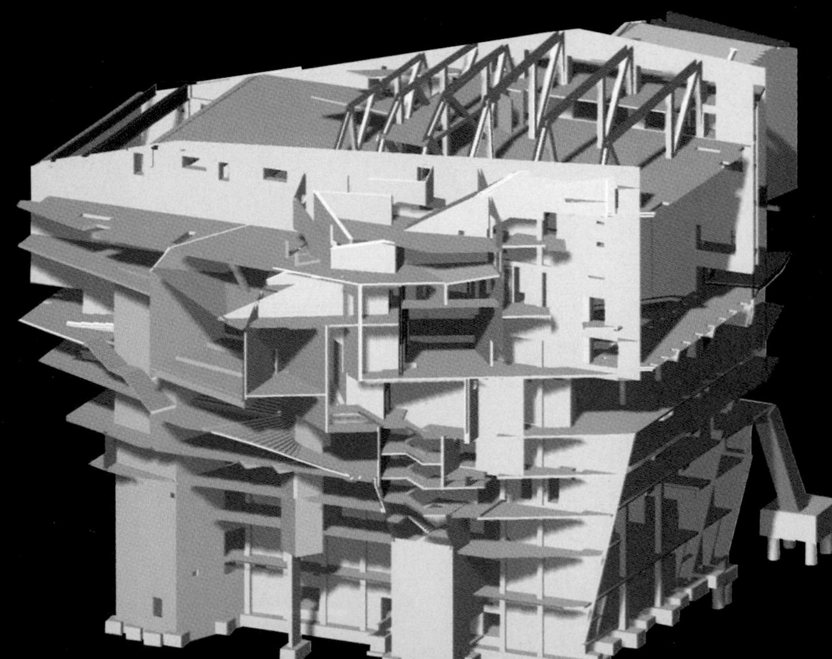

GO EAST

GO EAST
milan 45°27'N9°17' E
Aura

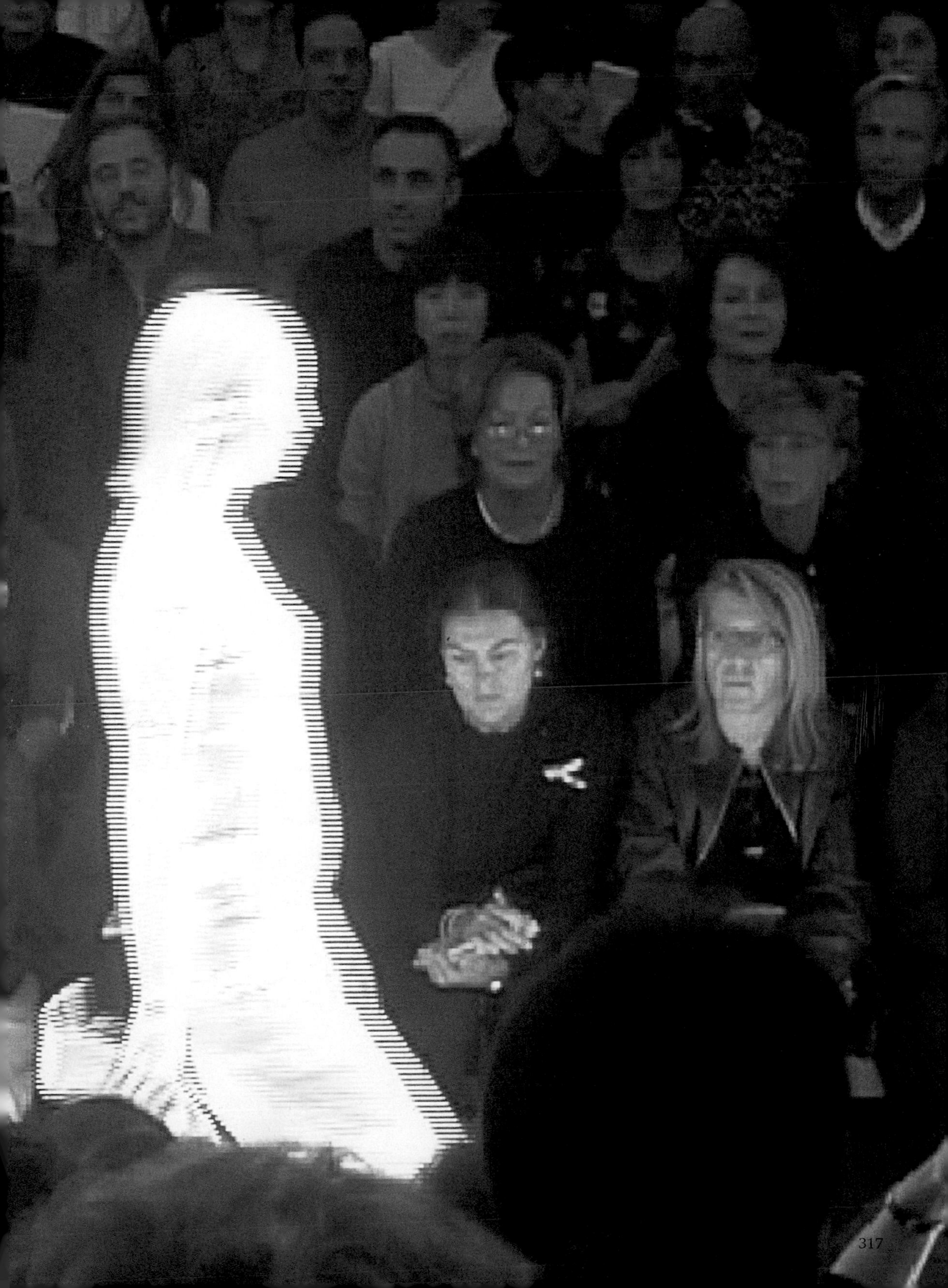

BEAUTIFUL PRADA SLINGBACKS W/LOGO SZ 10
Item #431904257

Currently **$150.00** First bid $150.00
Quantity 1 # of bids 0 bid history | with emails
Time left 10 hours, 48 mins + Location NY
Country/Region USA/New York
Started Sep-07-00 17:22:50 PDT mail this auction to a friend
Ends Sep-17-00 17:22:50 PDT watch this item

Seller (Rating) pookiee23 (112)

This is an authentic pair of Prada shoes. These shoes are a size 40 or US 10. They are made out of a material Prada is calling canvas tech in grey. They are brand new and never worn. These fabulous shoes are made in Italy. They will come to you in a Prada box. Please e-mail me with any questions for this is a final sale. There is no returns or exchanges. Buyer pays $5.00 priority shipping. Will ship internationally but pricing varies. I accept money orders or checks. You may also use X.COM and PAYPAL.COM if you wish to use a credit card. Good luck bidding.

PeRbAaDAY™

Presentation is everything.

PeRbAaDAY

brand new PRADA shirt size 40 black
Item #435046570

Currently $66.00 First bid $34.99
Quantity 1 # of bids 2 bid history | with emails
Time left 3 days, 11 hours + Location new york
Country/Region USA/New York
Started Sep-10-00 21:14:28 PDT mail this auction to a friend
Ends Sep-20-00 21:14:28 PDT watch this item

Seller (Rating) skitrip (39)
High bid dawnse (15)

This is a beautiful brand new, 100% guaranteed authentic Prada tank top style shirt. Never ever worn. Size 40. This shirt has a unique closed back with a more open front in the neck area. Perfect for accesorizing. Black charcoal colour. If you have any questions about this item, just email and I'll be glad to answer them. Bidding will start at an incredibly low $34.99, tons lower than you'd pay for this in any Prada retail store. High bidder will pay actual shipping charges. I accept money orders and credit card payments through www.PayPal.com

perbaaday

PRADA AUTHENTIC CHANGE WALLET BROWN PURSE
Item #433469401

Currently $49.99 First bid $49.99
Quantity 1 # of bids 1 bid history | with emails
Time left Auction has ended Location DELTASTEWS HOUSE
Country/Region USA/Miami
Started Sep-09-00 13:35:23 PDT mail this auction to a friend
Ends Sep-16-00 13:35:23 PDT request a gift alert

Seller (Rating) deltastew (454)
High bid pazzane (1)

PRADA AUTHENTIC CHANGE WALLET BROWN PURSE

AUTHENTIC AND 100% GUARANTEED PRADA THIS IS A BROWN PRADA MICROFIBER CHANGE PURSE AND IT IS REAL NEW AND 100% AUTHENTIC I GUARANTEE IT OUR YOUR MONEY BACK. CHECK MY FEEDBACK. ZIPS ALL THE WAY AND OPENS TO A CHANGE PURSE WITH LEATHER LINED. RETAILED FOR 282.00. ALL SALES FINAL AND DUE IN 7 DAYS WITH PAYPAY.COM MONEY ORDERS OR CHECKS OR BIDPAY FOR MY INTERNATIONAL FRIENDS. 6.00 S +H I DO NOT SELL FAKES ON THE OUTSIDE IT READS PRADA MILANO DAL 1913. I GUARANTEE ITS AUTHENTIC EMAIL ME FOR ANY QUESTIONS. GREAT FOR CHANGE AND CREDIT CARDS AND A WONDERFUL PRADA STYLE

perbaaday

AUTH. PRADA MOHAIR SPECTACULAR BLOUSE! NWT!!
Item #439342792

Currently $37.00 First bid $24.99
Quantity 1 # of bids 4 bid history | with emails
Time left 22 hours, 27 mins + Location USA
Country USA
Started Sep-16-00 13:06:32 PDT mail this auction to a friend
Ends Sep-16-00 13:06:32 PDT watch this item

Seller (Rating) 2 sweetstylz4u (201)
High bid pikocute (44)

~Sweetstylz4u~ visit us now by clicking our link

A beauty of a blouse. this Burgundy and red velvet blouse is a nice sexy design. it's not itchy to have against your skin. the materials are that soft! 3/4 sleeve design with a scooping neckline.
this blouse is featured in a size LARGE. (36 INCH BUST)

Presentation
We present our items to you in the best manner possible, using live modeling so you can actually see what the item looks like. We find that using a mannequin or "dummy" takes away from the aspect of the item, which is critical in your satisfaction of our products.

Images and Photography
We use the newest and most innovative programs and peripherals, bringing to you true-life and true color photographs. You'll never have to worry about wrong coloring or shading, as we make sure the true coloring can be seen on our items. ~Exactly~ what you see is what you get.

Products
We have on staff a Product buyer who is a graduate from the City school of Fashion Design. She assures our customers and potential buyers that our items are the newest in fashion trends, allowing us to bring it to you "first" before it falls to the "discount hunters"

Quality
We have another staff member, strictly in charge of quality assurance-- he sees to it that no item slips by us with a flaw. Each item is inspected and logged before we even place it up for sale. If the item does have any rips, tears or markings you WILL be told in the auction. Extensive pictures of each item are taken and kept on file to assure both us and the buyer of this

perbaaday

Fab Hologram Mules by Miu Miu*NEW*6.5-7
Item #435946671

Currently $66.00 (reserve not yet met) First bid $59.99
Quantity 1 # of bids 3 bid history | with emails
Time left 1 days, 11 hours + Location Fabulous Las Vegas
Country/Region USA/Las Vegas
Started Sep-11-00 20:30:30 PDT mail this auction to a friend
Ends Sep-18-00 20:30:30 PDT watch this item

Seller (Rating) rey95 (032)
High bid ountides (-1)

Fab Hologram Mules by Miu Miu*NEW*6.5-7

Fabulous leather and techno mules by the ultra hot Miu Miu by Prada These are dark brown with a great funky hologram pattern in hot pink canary and brown and the heel is a super rounded kitten heel They are a 7B/37 and are 10 1/4 inches long if your foot is a bit wide a 6.5 may work better They are Brand New and Retail for $270.00 but the best designer finds are less here

Please email me with any questions These are Final Sale items

Buyer to pay 4.50 priority shipping and insurance if desired Items can be combined to save on shipping Outside US extra
There is a 10 banking day HOLD for personel checks Please send Money Order for quick shipping or for Credit Card users Bidpay(Great for International Bidders!) OR PayPal
Please Only Serious Bidders!

All items are guaranteed 100% authentic or double your money back!

perbaaday

NEW! Classic PRADA MUI MUI Purse $595 +Chanel
Item #426695581

Currently $162.50 (reserve not yet met) First bid $89.99
Quantity 1 # of bids 3 bid history | with emails
Time left 4 hours, 44 mins + Location PALM BEACH, FL
Country/Region USA/Miami
Started Sep-02-00 09:29:17 PDT mail this auction to a friend
Ends Sep-12-00 09:29:17 PDT watch this item
Seller (Rating) hollygolly (82)
High bid evi13 (24)

TEN DAY AUCTION!
MAGNIFICENT MUI MUI Classic Handbag from PRADA~
GORGEOUS BLACK AND CAMEL Leather ~ EXCLUSIVE!
BRAND NEW ~ MINT ~ Est. RETAIL VALUE $695!
GUARANTEED AUTHENTIC and Made in Italy~
Elegant and Stunning in EVERY WAY!!
Pair this beauty up with any outfit this FALL and you will be ~ a complete KO (KNOCK OUT!!)
LOW RESERVE!
This auction is for the Feminine MUI MUI two-tone camel and black handbag purse(HOT trend for FALL!) The colors and workmanship are exquisite and truly a masterpiece! Style MB1729. Bag is 9 1/4" wide X 5 3/4" tall X 2" deep. Beautifully appointed with silver accents. Black fabric lined. Shoulder strap is black calfskin with bow on one side ~ CLASSIC CHIC!
In August/Sept. magazines there is a big trend toward two-tone. And CAMEL is very big this season. You must see these pictures! Wow!! This bag sells for $595. You pay less!
This handbag is so Classic~ could be worn daytime or evening and be perfect! Comes with a BONUS CHANEL CHRISTALLE Fragrance valued at $15!
A fine PRADA MUI MUI MASTERPIECE!
totally PALM BEACH Chic!
This handbag is a current COUTURE style found in SAKS Fifth Avenue, Nieman Marcus and Bergdorf Goodman. ~if you can find it ~ Est. Retail $590!
You simply must have this bag. You will not be disappointed. EMail us with any questions you might have.

perbaaday

$250 NWT STUNNING MIU MIU PRADA SHOES 6
Item #438313903

Currently $115.00 First bid $115.00
Quantity 1 # of bids 0 bid history | with emails
Time left 1 days, 21 hours + Location BRENTWOOD, CA
Country/Region USA/Los Angeles
Started Sep-14-00 12:24:20 PDT mail this auction to a friend
Ends Sep-19-00 12:24:20 PDT watch this item

Seller (Rating) littlebubble2000 (35)

$250 NWT STUNNING MIU MIU PRADA SHOES 6

*LET EVERYONE KNOW YOUR FABULOUS TASTE IN SHOES WITH THESE STUNNING MIU MIU FLATS *SIZE 6 *LUSCIOUS LIME GREEN COLOR *BRAND NEW AND IN BOX *ADORABLE FRONT TIES *NO RESERVE!!!

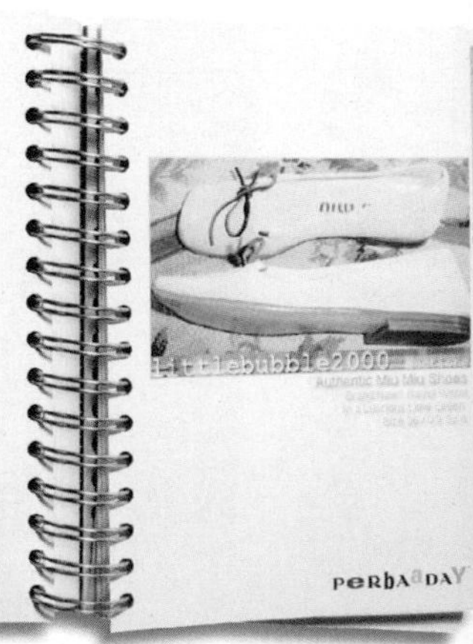

perbaaday

New Prada Sport Nylon Jacket 44

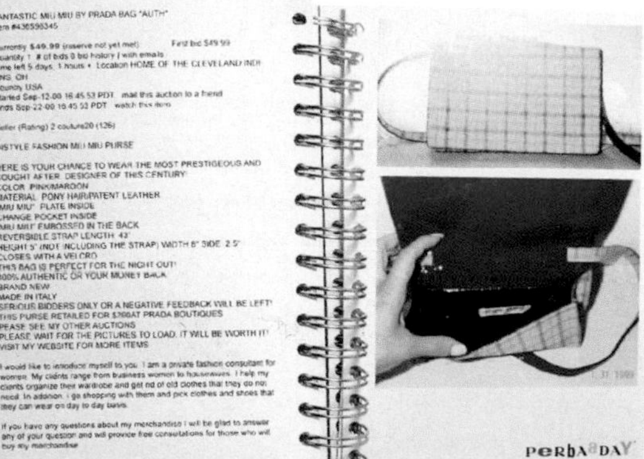
FANTASTIC MIU MIU BY PRADA BAG "AUTH"

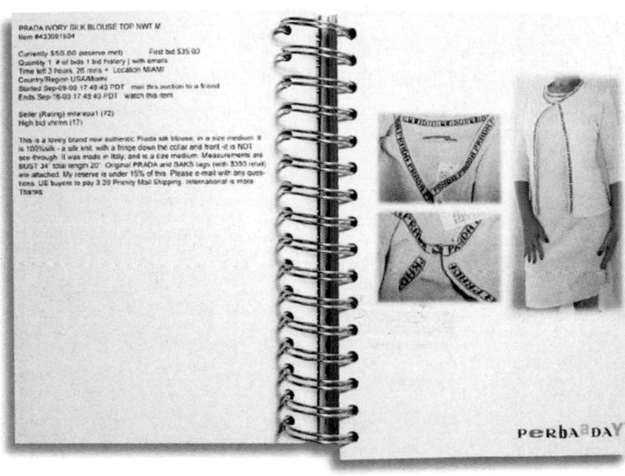
PRADA IVORY SILK BLOUSE TOP NWT M

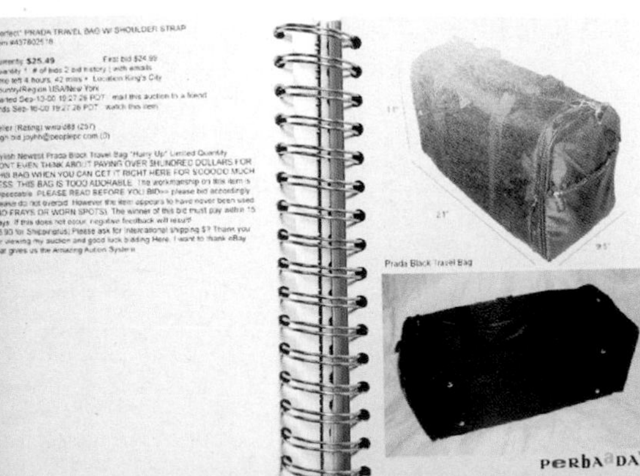
Prada Black Travel Bag

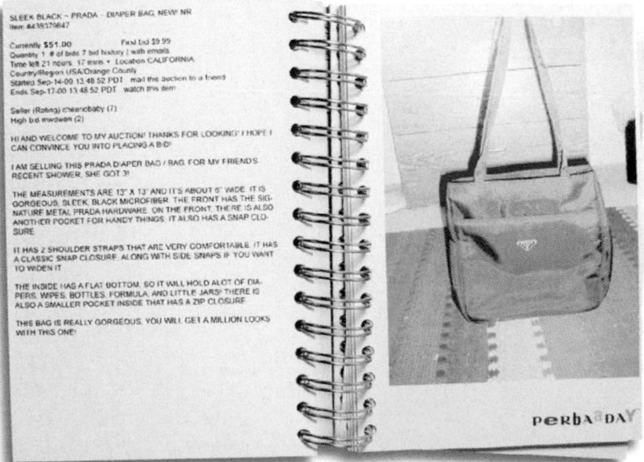
SLEEK BLACK ~ PRADA ~ DIAPER BAG, NEW! NR

Sexy NWT PRADA Cotton/Linen Suit Skirt Top 8
Item #433574390

Currently **$149.00** (reserve not yet met) First bid $149.00
Quantity 1 # of bids 0 bid history | with emails
Time left 1 hours, 50 mins + Location U.S.A./Arizona
Country/Region USA/Phoenix
Started Sep-09-00 15:43:42 PDT mail this auction to a friend
Ends Sep-16-00 15:43:42 PDT watch this item

Seller (Rating) wyattsmom7*27 (383)

BRAND NEW AUTHENTIC PRADA DRESS, SIZE 8/42
Very unique style
Sexy and quite comfortable
Versitile style, great for work or partying
Gorgeous fitted tayloring
Funky fringe hem
Color is Ivory or White
The original retail price is $1,040.00
Never worn, in perfect condition
Top measures 22" in length, chest 34"
Skirt measures 30" waist, length measures 16 1/4"
Payment within 7 days by cashier's check/money order/personal check(must wait for clearance before shipment), or BY Visa/Mastercard through PAYPAL
High bidder pays $7.00 for U.S. shipping + insurance
Intl rate will vary
All sales are final so please mail me if you have any questions
Please check out my "Me" page for cute photos and auction rules
Good Luck!

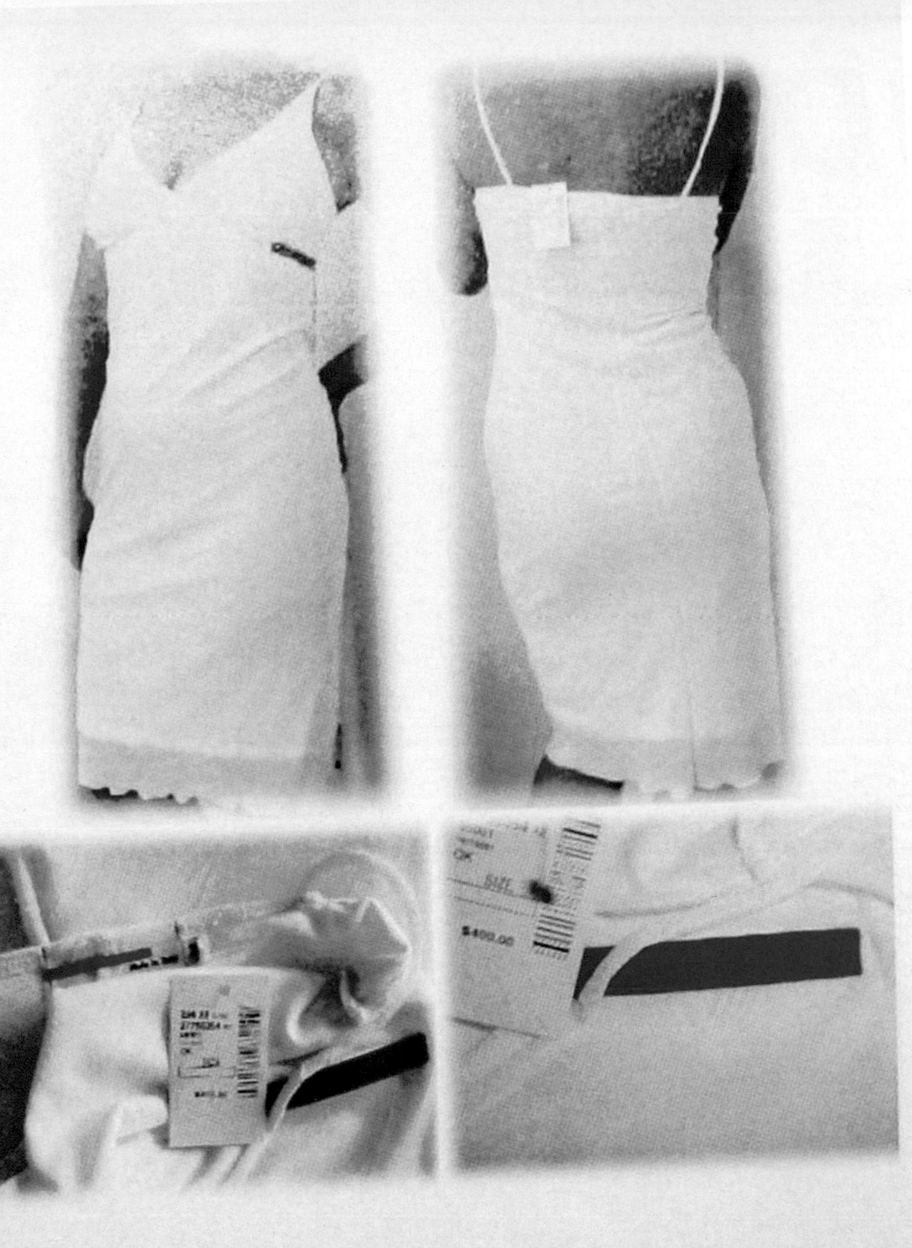

PERBAaDAY

BID ON

ebay®

Available on e-bay from
24/12/03 - 31/12/03

MUST HAVE

NEW WHITNEY
NEW YORK

EXCLUSIVE OMA-AMO T-SHIRTS

STAR BUY

AVAILABLE WHILE SUPPLIES LAST!!

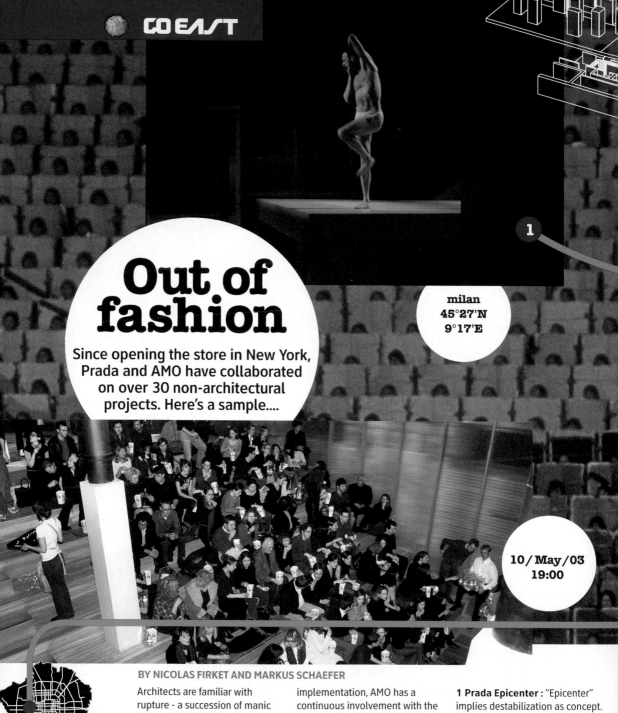

1

Out of fashion

Since opening the store in New York, Prada and AMO have collaborated on over 30 non-architectural projects. Here's a sample....

milan
45°27'N
9°17'E

10/May/03
19:00

BY NICOLAS FIRKET AND MARKUS SCHAEFER

Architects are familiar with rupture - a succession of manic labor and post-delivery abandonment. With Prada, OMA-AMO has left architecture's wild mood swings and entered (unwittingly) the state of an eternal jogger's high. Instead of disengaging after implementation, AMO has a continuous involvement with the store and its displays. Prada SoHo is not about architecture anymore, but about a timeline of events and media production. Prada is not a client, but collaborator and source of content.

1 Prada Epicenter : "Epicenter" implies destabilization as concept. The store should not be a shrine to a brand, but an ongoing experiment. In New York, it hosts events to re-inject public space into the commercialized desert of SoHo, then exploits the events as potential content sources.

2 Ubiquitous Information: The store has layers of changeability, of which media is the most flexible. Information technology aims to permeate space with information - at once digital ornament and roving window into the stock and customer databases. Digital information offers a parallel reality and an opportunity to instigate new scenarios that unfold in space. Technology extends the store to the web and grounds the web site in the reality of the store.

3 Media Content: Within the overlapping intuitions of AMO and Prada are shared fascinations with patterns, Asian moods, the derouting of modern icons, and a common reading of actuality. Moments of resonance are perhaps due to an analogous approach to modernity as a repertoire, or to a shared sense of opportunity.

4 Parallel Universe: Producing media is a way of seeing, recording and recontextualizing. What the web does in the digital realm - creating the >

potential to juxtapose anything with anything like a surrealist machine - media can do with real space. For the "Parallel Universe" installation, scenes from a Chinese shopping mall were transplanted into the Soho store.
5 Duty Free: Since there it has no real need for the web site, Prada's can become a space for experimentation. E-commerce product proposals include Prada mobile phones, fur palm, shoe-phone, laptop-bag, augmented reality sunglasses, Prada SM, headline t-shirt, and an alliance of Prada and Ebay.
6 Prada Friend: Prada's web site is linked to its stores and acts as a local service and fulfillment center by which customers are incorporated. "Prada Friend" is the link to the sales staff, "Prada Closet" the link to interactive dressing room and to staff recommendations.
7 Fragrance mixer: A perfume flask for the entire gender spectrum. Male and female fragances are mixed on demand, and can be adjusted to suit the wearer'schanges in mood.

8 Backdrop: The fashion show is the heartbeat of Prada, an unrelenting mechanical rhythm and source of 75% of Prada content.
9 Sport Stripe: Continuous involvement with Prada's visual approach led to work on advertisement proposals. The first published ad campaign done by AMO was based on re-branding pictures of the Mexico Olympics (by Magnum).
10 Plywood Minimalism: Furniture at once rough and refined
11 Sponge: A display system without a systematic nature
12 Ad Porn: Desire revisited
13 Tokyo Content: AMO's first collaboration with another architectural firm - content produced for the Snorkels designed by Herzog & de Meuron for their Tokyo Aoyama store
14 Sports Guide: A "Falk" city map turned into a collection guide
15 Fashion Show Wallpaper: Prada beats the fear of flying
16 Prince Trust: Fashion Rocks: Mila Jovovich + Prada + AMO + Prince Charles = "Fashion Rocks," as seen on Channel 4. >

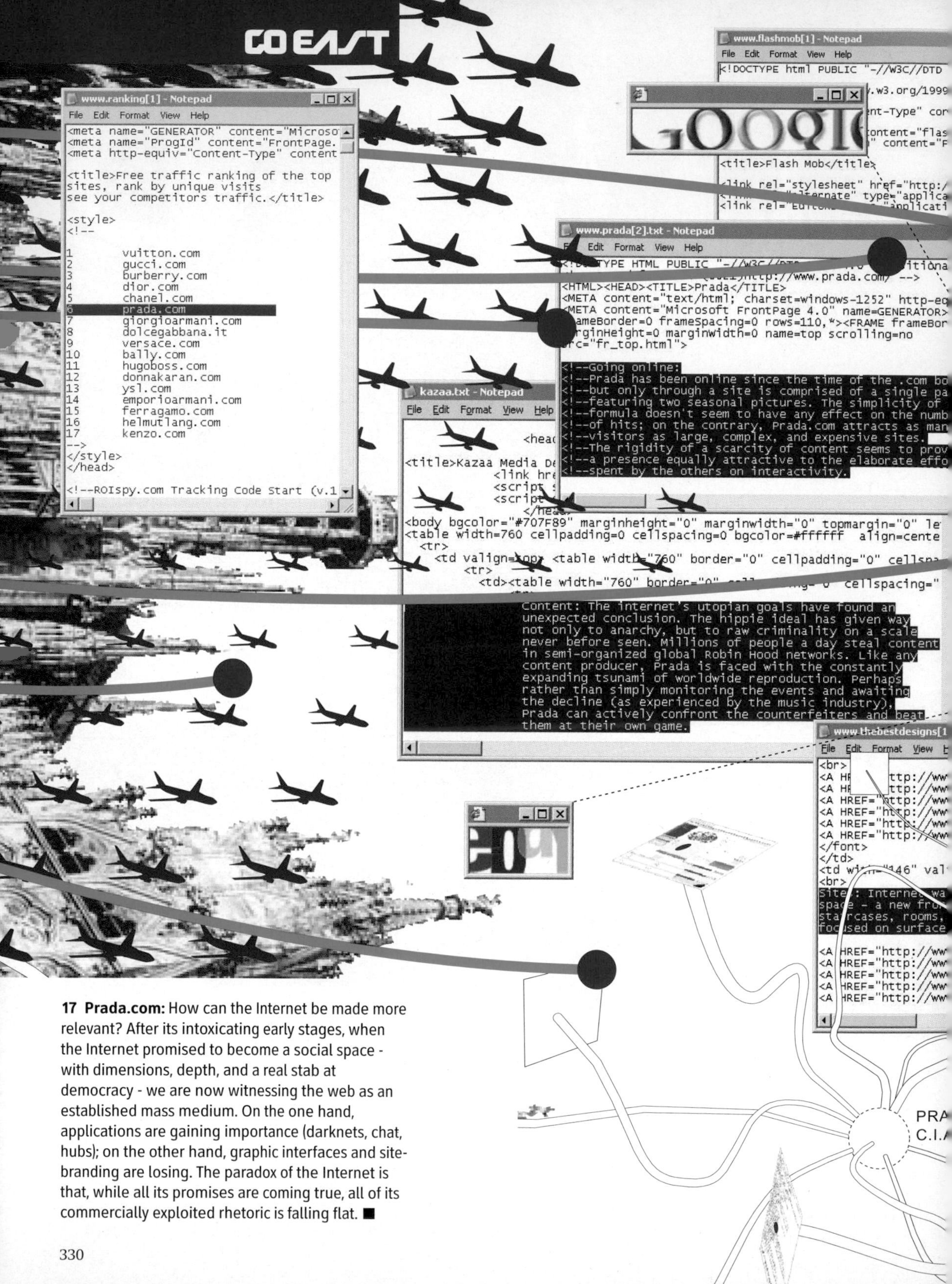

17 Prada.com: How can the Internet be made more relevant? After its intoxicating early stages, when the Internet promised to become a social space - with dimensions, depth, and a real stab at democracy - we are now witnessing the web as an established mass medium. On the one hand, applications are gaining importance (darknets, chat, hubs); on the other hand, graphic interfaces and site-branding are losing. The paradox of the Internet is that, while all its promises are coming true, all of its commercially exploited rhetoric is falling flat. ■

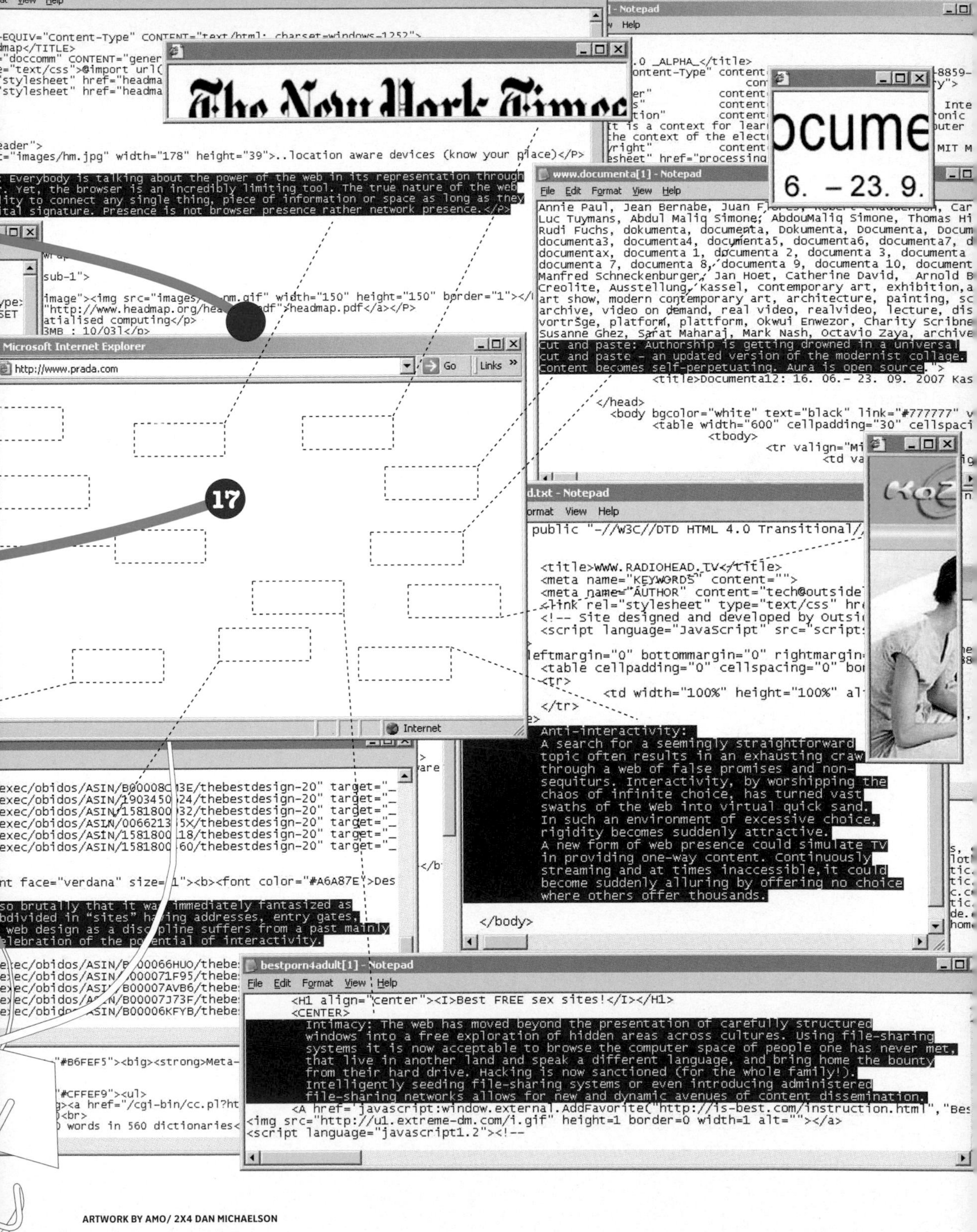

The New York Times
ocume
6. – 23. 9.
: Everybody is talking about the power of the web in its representation through
. Yet, the browser is an incredibly limiting tool. The true nature of the web
lity to connect any single thing, piece of information or space as long as they
ital signature. Presence is not browser presence rather network presence.</P>
www.documenta[1] - Notepad
Cut and paste: Authorship is getting drowned in a universal
cut and paste - an updated version of the modernist collage.
Content becomes self-perpetuating. Aura is open source.
Microsoft Internet Explorer
http://www.prada.com
17
<title>WWW.RADIOHEAD.TV</title>
Anti-interactivity:
A search for a seemingly straightforward
topic often results in an exhausting craw
through a web of false promises and non-
sequiturs. Interactivity, by worshipping the
chaos of infinite choice, has turned vast
swaths of the web into virtual quick sand.
In such an environment of excessive choice,
rigidity becomes suddenly attractive.
A new form of web presence could simulate TV
in providing one-way content. Continuously
streaming and at times inaccessible, it could
become suddenly alluring by offering no choice
where others offer thousands.
so brutally that it was immediately fantasized as
bdivided in "sites" having addresses, entry gates,
web design as a discipline suffers from a past mainly
elebration of the potential of interactivity.
bestporn4adult[1] - Notepad
<H1 align="center"><I>Best FREE sex sites!</I></H1>
Intimacy: The web has moved beyond the presentation of carefully structured
windows into a free exploration of hidden areas across cultures. Using file-sharing
systems it is now acceptable to browse the computer space of people one has never met,
that live in another land and speak a different language, and bring home the bounty
from their hard drive. Hacking is now sanctioned (for the whole family!).
Intelligently seeding file-sharing systems or even introducing administered
file-sharing networks allows for new and dynamic avenues of content dissemination.

ARTWORK BY AMO/ 2X4 DAN MICHAELSON

GRABARZ & PARTNER
PRADA

DRUM

africa's leading magazine

AUGUST 1966 1/-

Registered at G.P.O. as a Newspaper

Two who have jumped on London's fashion roundabo

Picture story inside

General China Shot! Captured! Brought to trial!

Last instalment of his book

Uganda Crisis

The plot and the palace

Kabaka's own story 'How I escaped'

Exclusive pictures of battle scene

DRUM EAST AFRICA

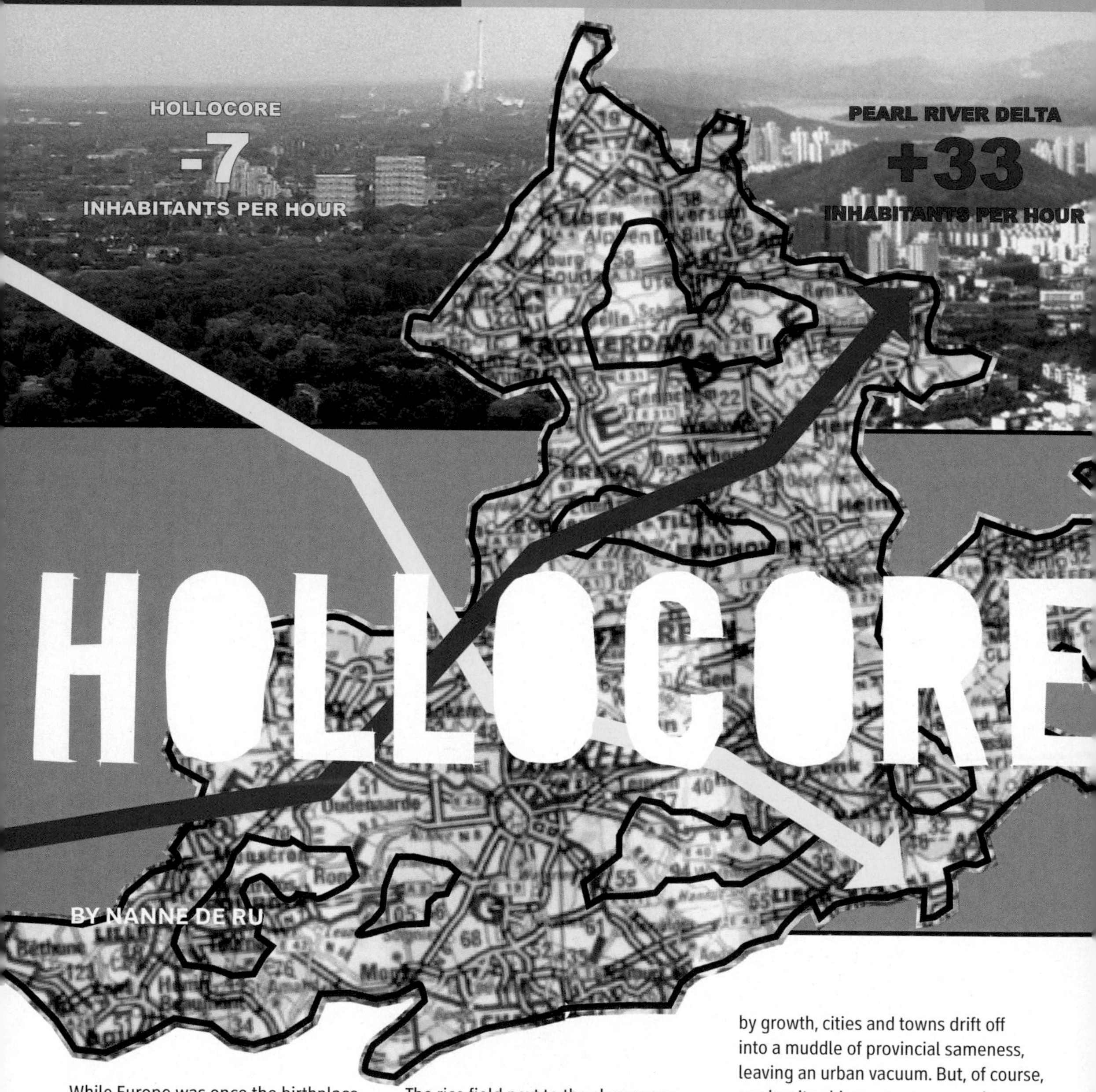

HOLLOCORE -7 INHABITANTS PER HOUR

PEARL RIVER DELTA +33 INHABITANTS PER HOUR

HOLLOCORE

BY NANNE DE RU

While Europe was once the birthplace of the metropolis, the future of the modern city is now being defined in the developing world. According to a recent United Nations report, Europe's population will decline in the coming fifty years. Where the Asian population is expected to rise by 41%, Europe's population will decrease by 13%.[1] Ironically, the urban substance of Europe in decline intersects China in ascension. The rice field next to the skyscraper in China's Pearl River Delta finds its counterpart in the derelict industrial estate surrounded by urban fabric in the German Ruhr Valley: in both cases the metropolis has become a field condition of dispersed moments of concentration. Where the cities in the developing world explode into bigger, less containable metropolitan areas, urban Europe is in a state of entropy. No longer energized by growth, cities and towns drift off into a muddle of provincial sameness, leaving an urban vacuum. But, of course, modernity abhors a vacuum, and an infinite multiplicity of new forms of urbanity emerges to take the place of what has become redundant.

The HOLLOCORE© is emblematic of Europe's new urbanity – the amorphous super-region that links Brussels, Amsterdam, and the Ruhr Valley is urban Europe's non-event: it houses 32 Million inhabitants or 9% of Europe's population, yet has no city larger than one million >

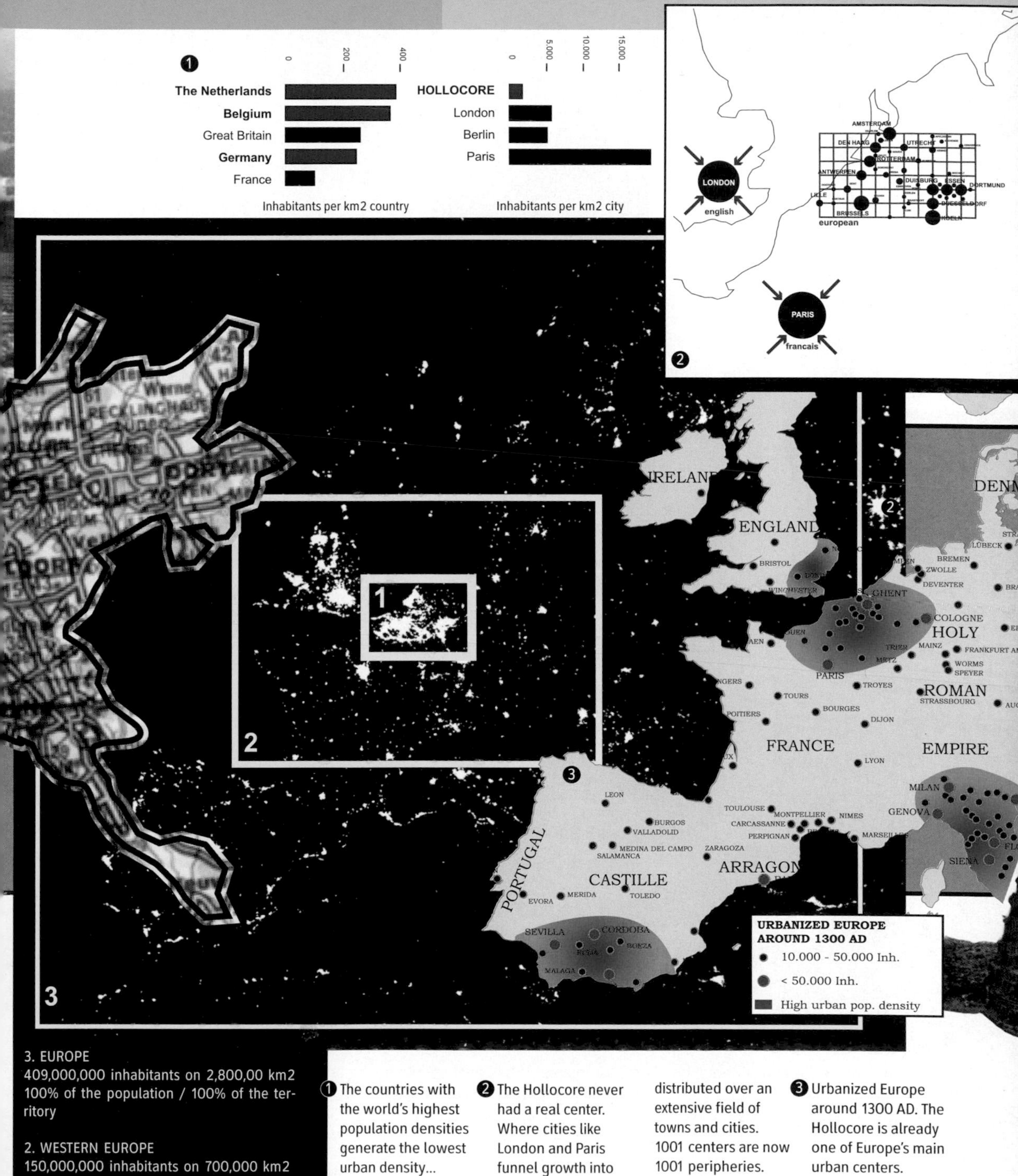

3. EUROPE
409,000,000 inhabitants on 2,800,00 km2
100% of the population / 100% of the territory

2. WESTERN EUROPE
150,000,000 inhabitants on 700,000 km2
37% of the population / 25% of the territory

1. EUROCORE©
32,000.000 inhabitants on 42,700 km2
9% of the population / 1% of the territory

1 The countries with the world's highest population densities generate the lowest urban density...

2 The Hollocore never had a real center. Where cities like London and Paris funnel growth into suburban rings that are dependent on the pull of the city center, in the Hollocore massive growth is distributed over an extensive field of towns and cities. 1001 centers are now 1001 peripheries. 1001 cities, each with its own hospital, public transport network, and art museum.

3 Urbanized Europe around 1300 AD. The Hollocore is already one of Europe's main urban centers.

1 In the three cultures of the Hollocore, realism and surrealism have always been very close – from Durer's realism to Vermeer's hyperrealism to Bosch's visionary surrealism.

inhabitants. Two thirds of its population lives in cities smaller then 200,000 inhabitants – in places no one has ever heard of.

The Hollocore has had one of the highest concentrations of cities and towns in Europe since the Middle Ages. Despite explosive population growth during the industrial revolutions, the Hollocore is not dominated by a single center. Instead, it has swelled into a cloud of atomized sub-centers and peripheries. Every center claims its own identity, history, and centrality, while numerous peripheries offer space for new cultures and identities to unfold.

In the Hollocore, all that is urban is losing ground. Over the last decades overall population growth has dropped to -0,2%.[2] Within this static condition, mercurial movements of the population ensure that metropolitan density recedes: established cities lose residents while thinly populated areas gain. In the name of identity, city centers are stripped down to their historic pedestrian shopping streets, and appear more village-like than ever – frozen in a time that never was. Meanwhile, the

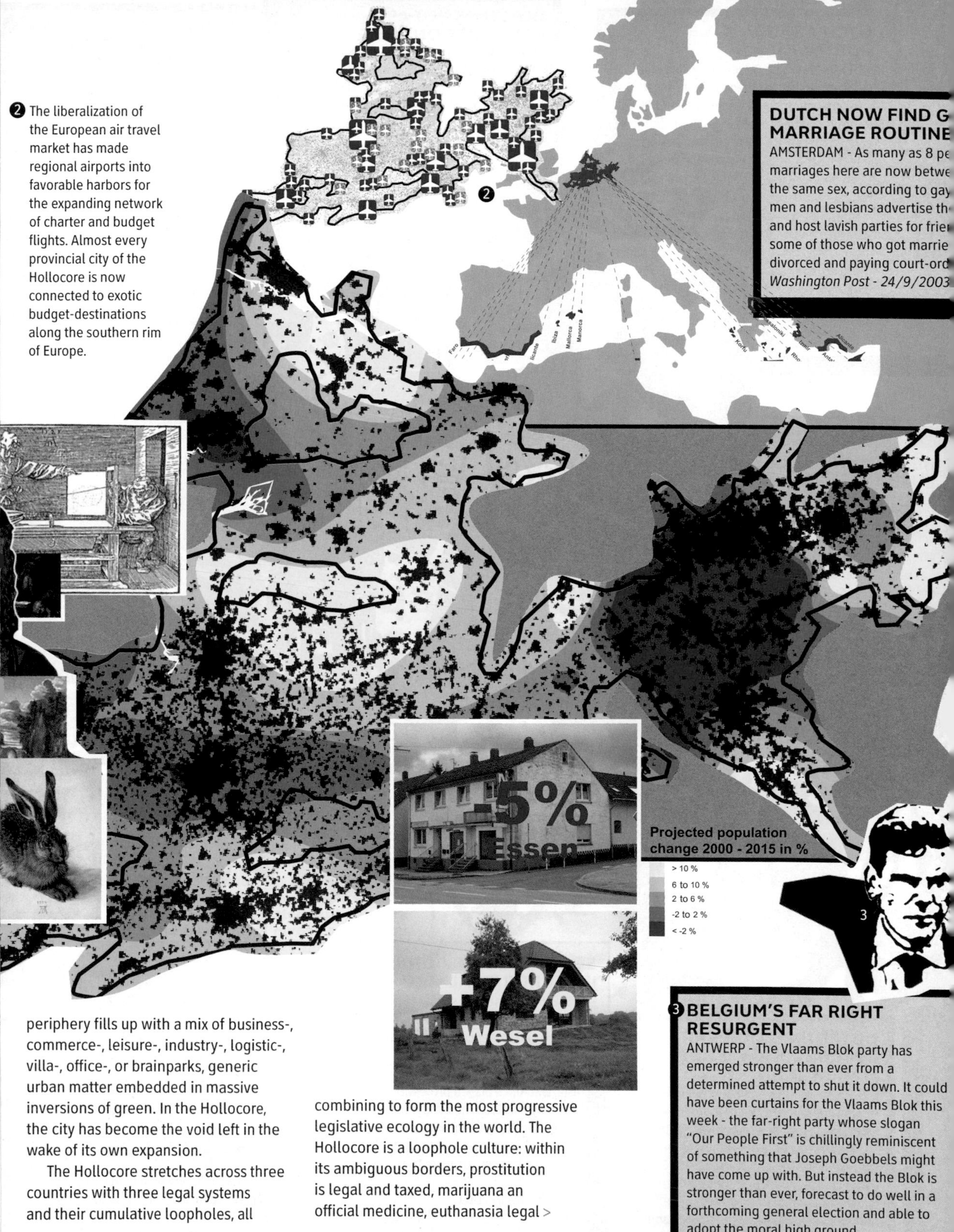

❷ The liberalization of the European air travel market has made regional airports into favorable harbors for the expanding network of charter and budget flights. Almost every provincial city of the Hollocore is now connected to exotic budget-destinations along the southern rim of Europe.

DUTCH NOW FIND G
MARRIAGE ROUTINE

AMSTERDAM - As many as 8 pe
marriages here are now betwe
the same sex, according to gay
men and lesbians advertise th
and host lavish parties for frie
some of those who got marrie
divorced and paying court-ord
Washington Post - 24/9/2003

periphery fills up with a mix of business-, commerce-, leisure-, industry-, logistic-, villa-, office-, or brainparks, generic urban matter embedded in massive inversions of green. In the Hollocore, the city has become the void left in the wake of its own expansion.

The Hollocore stretches across three countries with three legal systems and their cumulative loopholes, all combining to form the most progressive legislative ecology in the world. The Hollocore is a loophole culture: within its ambiguous borders, prostitution is legal and taxed, marijuana an official medicine, euthanasia legal >

❸ BELGIUM'S FAR RIGHT RESURGENT

ANTWERP - The Vlaams Blok party has emerged stronger than ever from a determined attempt to shut it down. It could have been curtains for the Vlaams Blok this week - the far-right party whose slogan "Our People First" is chillingly reminiscent of something that Joseph Goebbels might have come up with. But instead the Blok is stronger than ever, forecast to do well in a forthcoming general election and able to adopt the moral high ground.
The Guardian - 28/2/2003

Trauma

Over the last century Brussels has been battered by a relentless campaign of modernization projects. Its climax was the construction of the European Quarter, an architectural wasteland that has mobilized an army of pressure groups determined to oppose any plan.

Since the sixties, under the influence of deregulation, the average height of construction in the Netherlands – the country with the highest number of people/km2 – has steadily diminished.

GOLDEN AGE **WELFARE STATE** **IKEA HEIGHT**

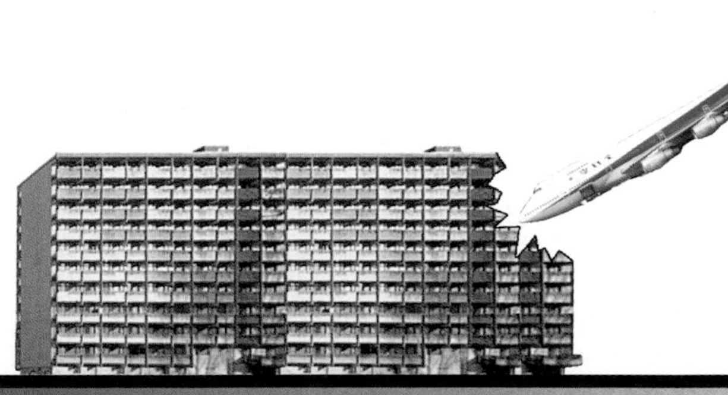

®UR: cleaning the Ruhr Valley's identity to make room for new insertions

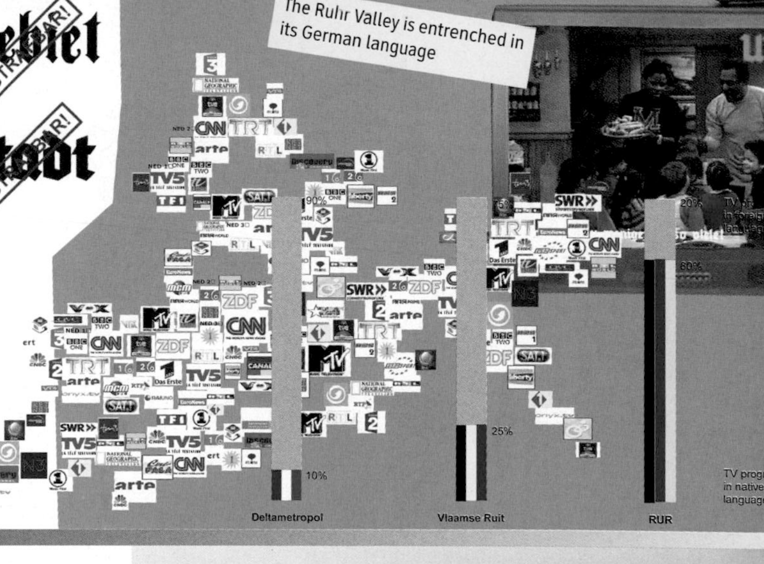

The Ruhr Valley is entrenched in its German language

Meanwhile, the European Union has retreated into a bastion of non-descript buildings.

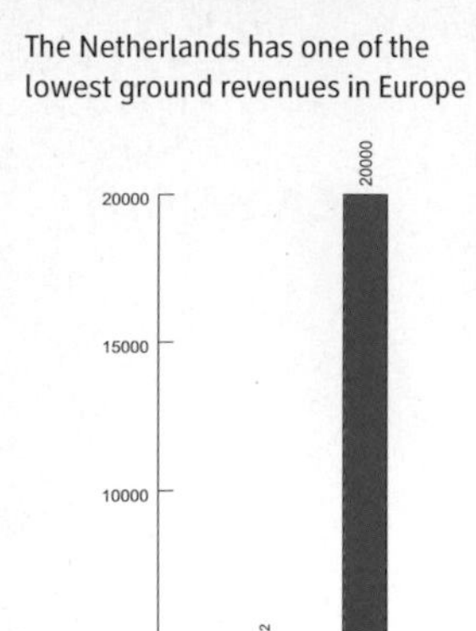

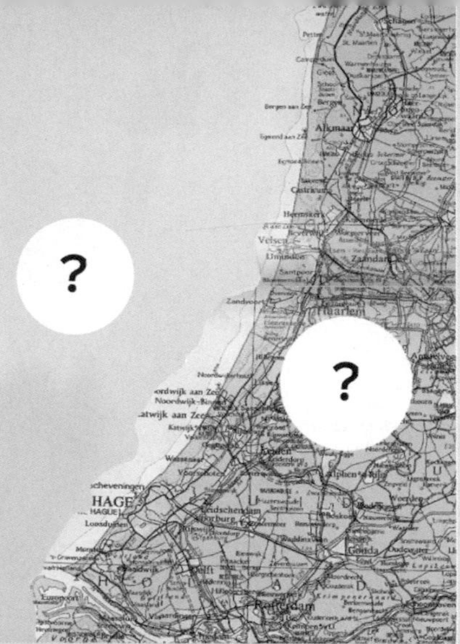

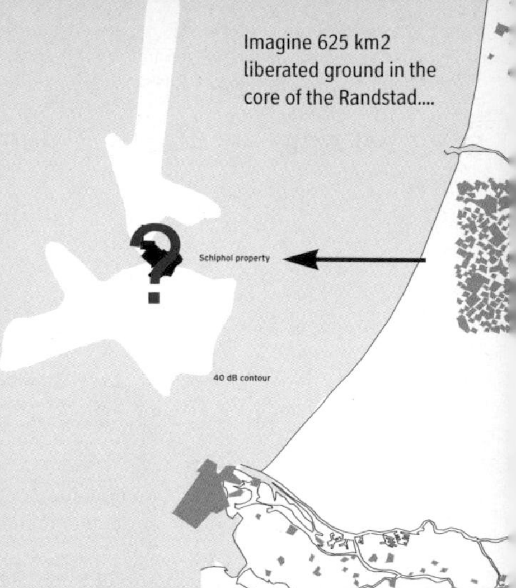

Reconstruction

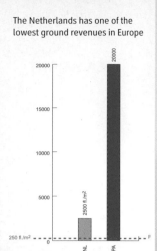

In 1982, post-modernist architects gathered in Brussels for the formulation of a "Declaration of Brussels," a manifesto against the project of a modern Europe and in support of the "reconstruction of the European city." With Brussels as its epicenter, European city centers were reconstructed into village squares.

LA RECONSTRUCTION DE LA VILLE EUROPÉENNE :

DÉCLARATION DE BRUXELLES

Les participants du colloque international qui s'est tenu à Bruxelles les 15, 16 et 17 novembre sous l'égide de la Commission Française de la Culture de l'Agglomération de Bruxelles ont décidé, au terme de leurs travaux, de formuler la déclaration suivante :

— ils soulignent la valeur des actions engagées par l'ensemble des Comités d'habitants de Bruxelles pour la défense et la réparation de leur ville directement touchée par les transformations brutales et aberrantes de sa structure; ils condamnent spécialement la politique irresponsable de la C.E.E. dont l'action destructrice en matière d'implantation de ses propres bâtiments touche, tout aussi gravement, des villes comme Luxembourg, Strasbourg et Bruxelles; ils exigent la formation au sein des Institutions Européennes d'une Commission qui prendrait enfin en compte les objectifs de reconstruction de la Ville Européenne voulue par les habitants;

— ils demandent à toutes les écoles d'architecture d'orienter leur enseignement et leur recherche vers les tâches de la réparation des villes européennes;

— ils demandent que soit orientée dans ce sens la formation technique et professionnelle des métiers de la construction;

— ils entendent par réparation de la Ville Européenne, l'intégration de l'histoire dans la pratique urbaine : tout le patrimoine doit être sauvegardé et pas seulement quelques centres prétendument historiques.

Toute intervention sur la Ville Européenne doit obligatoirement réaliser ce qui toujours fut la ville, à savoir : des rues.

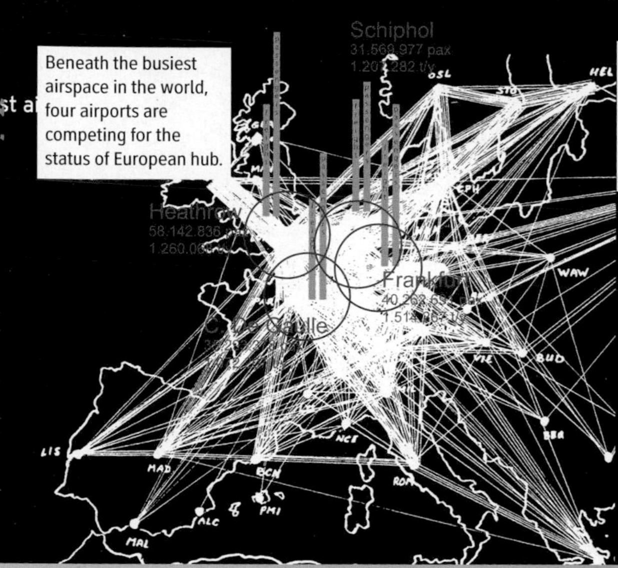

Beneath the busiest airspace in the world, four airports are competing for the status of European hub.

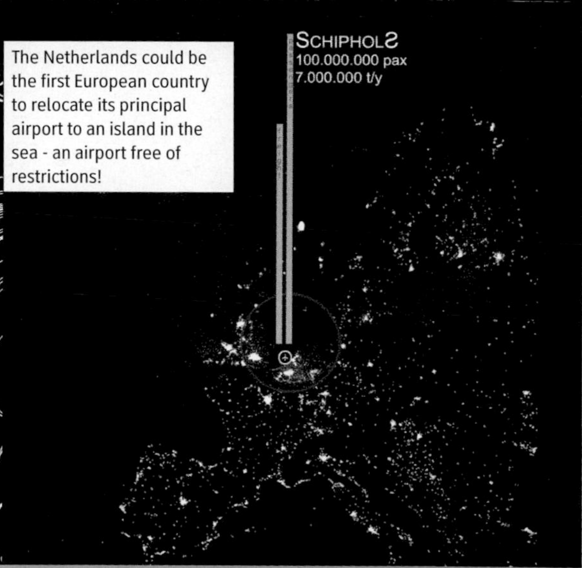

The Netherlands could be the first European country to relocate its principal airport to an island in the sea - an airport free of restrictions!

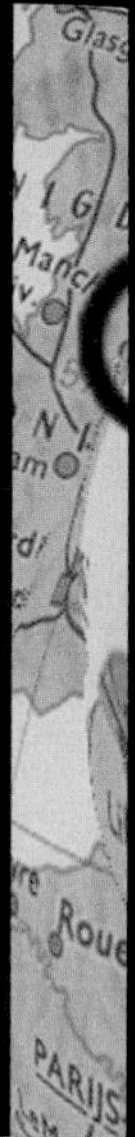

Illegal immigration grows, the shadow economy flourishes

Easy ®UR: the strategic relaxation of the Ruhr Valley's most inflexible regulations

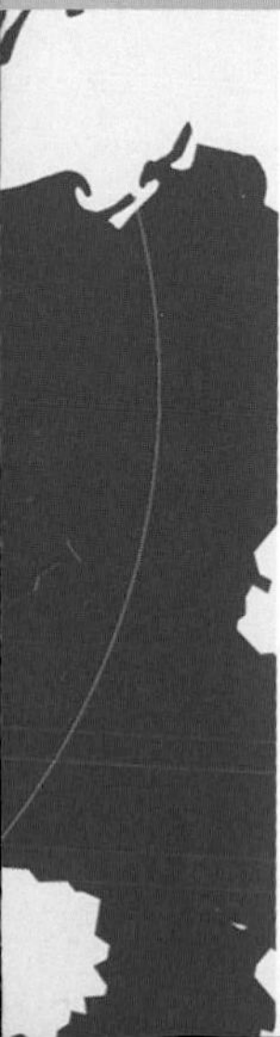

Mini-Europe
Anticipating the coming status of capital of Europe, the former Brussels Expo site in 1989 became home to *Mini Europe*, an amusement park featuring models of Europe's architectural highlights. Its mascot is a turtle.

Trimcity
Recently, the mayor of Brussels, François-Xavier de Donnea initiated the trimming of "a number of towers from the fifties and sixties that ruin the view (on the city), because they tower above their surroundings." After 100 years of traumatic attempts at modernization, Brussels is to regain its medieval city skyline.

Ground Zero
Europe's coming capital will be devoid of modern icons towering above the city. Brussels has created its own voluntary ground-zero.

Antifasc
ANTIFA Ge
Gelsenkirch
evening, ch
the cozy ba
code is enf
ripped sec
suits.

Animal
3607 1001
tests agains
testing reg

CASINO
RED LIGHT
ENTERTAINMENT SPORTS
TRANSFER LAS VEGAS
BLUE LIGHT SHIPPING
FORMULA 1 RACING BELLAGIO
EURO TERMINAL
FAIR MALL OF EUROPE
VALUE ADDED LOGISTICS GOLF
FLOWERFIELDS BEACH
EUROLAND STADIUM
TULIPS SHOPPING
MUSEUM
TAX FREE

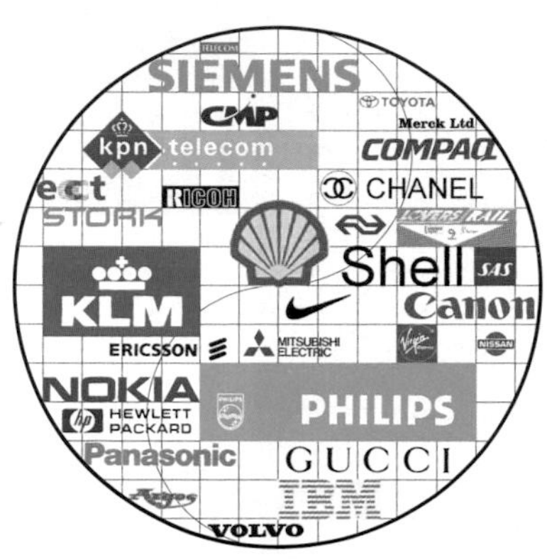

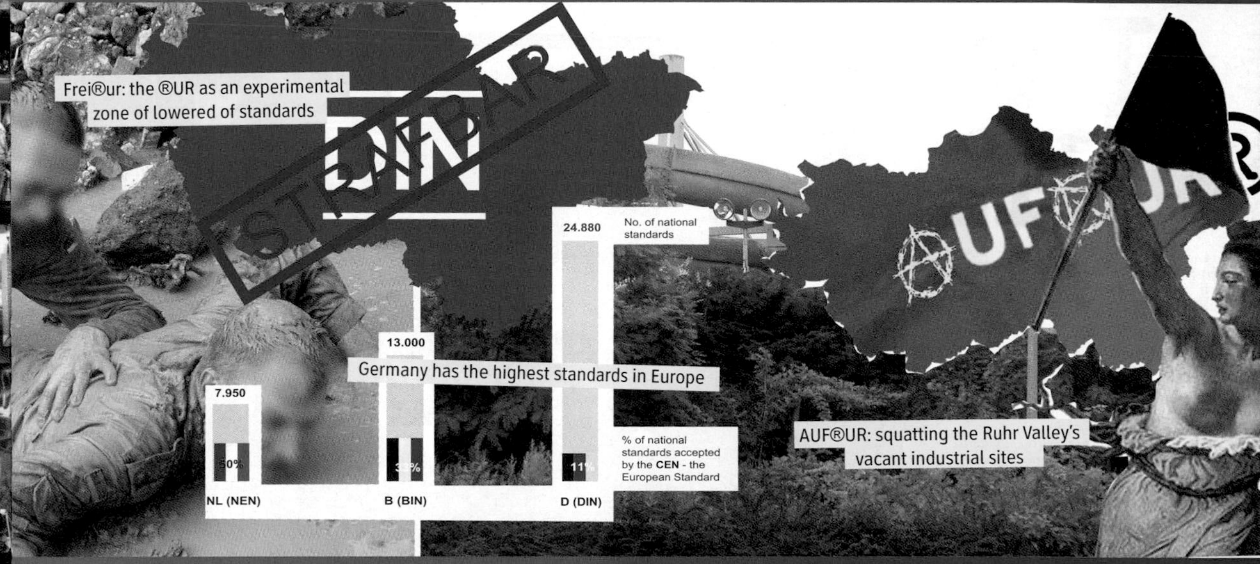

brand-
dedica
shares
3B. Or
vacant
ized ca
Hollar
the m

CO EAST

berlin 54°56'N 30°18'E

OMA-AMO exhibition

14 November 03 – 18 January 2004

Content has been created on the occasion of the exhibition of Rem Koolhaas/OMA-AMO held at Neue Nationalgalerie in Berlin from 14 November 2003 to 18 January 2004.

WE WOULD LIKE TO THANK THE FOLLOWING INSTITUTIONS AND CORPORATIONS FOR THEIR GENEROUS SUPPORT:
THE NETHERLANDS CULTURE FUND
THE NETHERLANDS ARCHITECTURE FUND
THE NETHERLANDS FOUNDATION FOR VISUAL ARTS, DESIGN AND ARCHITECTURE
THE SAMSUNG FOUNDATION OF CULTURE
THE PRINCE BERNHARD CULTUURFONDS

SEELE GMBH & CO. KG

CURATORS
OMAMO: KAYOKO OTA
STAATLICHE MUSEEN ZU BERLIN: DR. ANDRES LEPIK, DR. CRISTINA STEINGRÄBER

DESIGN
JENS HOMMERT

PRODUCTION
GÜNTHER KRÜGER

MANAGEMENT
IZABEL MELLINGHOFF

ASSISTANTS
CHRISTOPH HELMUS
MARIEKE KUMS
TILLMAN SCHMIDT
IM SIK CHO
NICK ALBERS
JEREMY GODENIR
JOSSE POPMA
EREZ ELLA
OLGA ALEXAKOVA

WALLS
AMOMA WITH 2X4/MICHAEL ROCK
IRMA BOOM
CECIL BALMOND, RORY MCGOWAN, CAROLINA BARTRAM/ ARUP
INSIDE-OUTSIDE/ PETRA BLAISSE
LUCIA ALLAIS
HOSOYA-SCHAEFER ARCHITECTS
C.W.I.D.

EXHIBITION TITLE DESIGN
&&&

COLLABORATORS
VINCENT DE RIJK (SUPERVISOR OF MODEL RESTORATION; CCTV RESIN MODEL)
MARC HEUMER (TOGOK TOWERS, CCTV-TVCC PLAQUES)
CLAUDI CORNAZ (TELEPHONE BOOTH SYSTEM)

COOPERATION
JOAKIM DAHLQVIST
ANDREAS HUHN
PHOTOGRAPHS
HANS WERLEMANN
WERNER VAN DERMEERSCH
RICHARD BARNES
PUBLIC RELATIONS
JAN KNIKKER
CHANTAL DEFESCHE
ARTISTS
TONY OURSLER
JEFF PREISS
CANDIDA HÖFER
FILMS
ALISON MACLEAN
JENS HOMMERT
CONTENT
EDITOR: BRENDAN MCGETRICK
DESIGNERS:
&&& - JON LINK / SIMON BROWN
PUBLISHER:
TASCHEN VERLAG, KÖLN
SPECIAL THANKS
HIEU DAM
MARIJ DE BRABANDERE
FRANCESCO GARDFALO
SCARLETT HOOFT GRAAFLAND
RALF MÜLLER
HÉLÈNE LEMOINE
LOUISE LEMOINE
JOSHUA THORSON
WERNER VAN DERMEERSCH
DONALD VAN DANSIK
ALEXANDER VON VEGESACK
ATELIER VAN LIESHOUT
content
REM KOOLHAAS
OMA AMO
BAUTEN, PROJEKTE UND KONZEPTE SEIT 1996
access to downstairs

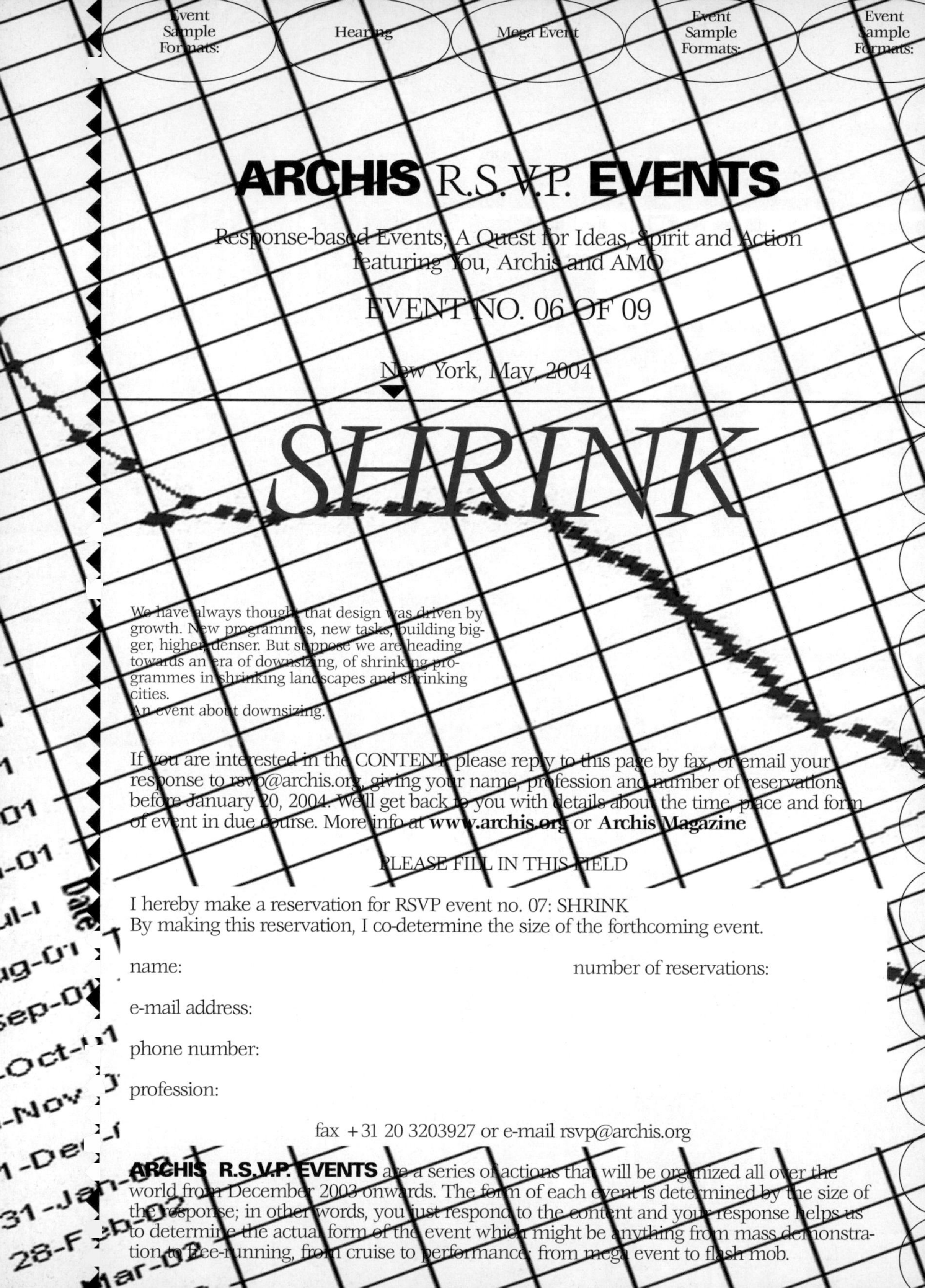

Event Sample Formats: | Hearing | Mega Event | Event Sample Formats: | Event Sample Formats:

ARCHIS R.S.V.P. EVENTS

Response-based Events; A Quest for Ideas, Spirit and Action featuring You, Archis and AMO

EVENT NO. 06 OF 09

New York, May, 2004

SHRINK

We have always thought that design was driven by growth. New programmes, new tasks, building bigger, higher, denser. But suppose we are heading towards an era of downsizing, of shrinking programmes in shrinking landscapes and shrinking cities.
An event about downsizing.

If you are interested in the CONTENT please reply to this page by fax, or email your response to rsvp@archis.org, giving your name, profession and number of reservations before January 20, 2004. We'll get back to you with details about the time, place and form of event in due course. More info at **www.archis.org** or **Archis Magazine**

PLEASE FILL IN THIS FIELD

I hereby make a reservation for RSVP event no. 07: SHRINK
By making this reservation, I co-determine the size of the forthcoming event.

name: number of reservations:

e-mail address:

phone number:

profession:

fax +31 20 3203927 or e-mail rsvp@archis.org

ARCHIS R.S.V.P. EVENTS are a series of actions that will be organized all over the world from December 2003 onwards. The form of each event is determined by the size of the response; in other words, you just respond to the content and your response helps us to determine the actual form of the event which might be anything from mass demonstration to free-running, from cruise to performance: from mega event to flash mob.

Salon

Event Sample Formats:

Chat Session

Election

Tribunal

ARCHIS R.S.V.P. EVENTS

Response-based Events; A Quest for Ideas, Spirit and Action featuring You, Archis and AMO

EVENT NO. 07 OF 09

Moscow, November, 2004

GOING EAST

According to the investment bank Goldman Sachs, the Chinese economy will be the second largest in the world in 2016 and by 2041 the largest. In 2023 the Indian economy will be bigger than the German economy. By 2032 it will be the world's third largest economy.

And as of today, Russia is proclaimed a safe investment area. Capital, resources, talent and markets are shifting east. Are you?
An event about new geo-economic realities and your place in it.

If you are interested in the CONTENT, please reply to this page by fax, or email your response to rsvp@archis.org, giving your name, profession and number of reservations before July 15, 2004. We'll get back to you with details about the time, place and form of event in due course. More info at **www.archis.org** or **Archis Magazine**

PLEASE FILL IN THIS FIELD

I hereby make a reservation for RSVP event no. 08: GOING EAST
By making this reservation, I co-determine the size of the forthcoming event.

name: number of reservations:

e-mail address:

phone number:

profession:

fax +31 20 3203927 or e-mail rsvp@archis.org

ARCHIS R.S.V.P. EVENTS are a series of actions that will be organized all over the world from December 2003 onwards. The form of each event is determined by the size of the response; in other words, you just respond to the content and your response helps us to determine the actual form of the event which might be anything from mass demonstration to free-running, from cruise to performance; from mega event to flash mob.

GO EAST
EMPFANG
SCHLEUSE
FOYER
MEHRZWECKRAUM
WARTEN
INTERNET
PRESSE
BESPRECHUNG
ADMIN.
VERKEHR
BESPRECHUNG

POLITIK
FITNESS
CAFE
TEEKUECHE
KODIFIZIERUNG
STELLVERTRETER
BOTSCHAFTER
DACHTERASSE

GO EAST
Receptie

+7.230
+7.230
+7.230

GO EAST
+6.650
+6.650

The project carves the single structure implied by Berlin's regulations in two parts - a wall and a cube. The carving continues inside the building, creating an erratic path from bottom to top, surrounded by regular office accommodation. The trajectory captures salient elements of Berlin's architectures outside - 19th century, Nazi, communist....

GO EAST
21 January 01/20:45

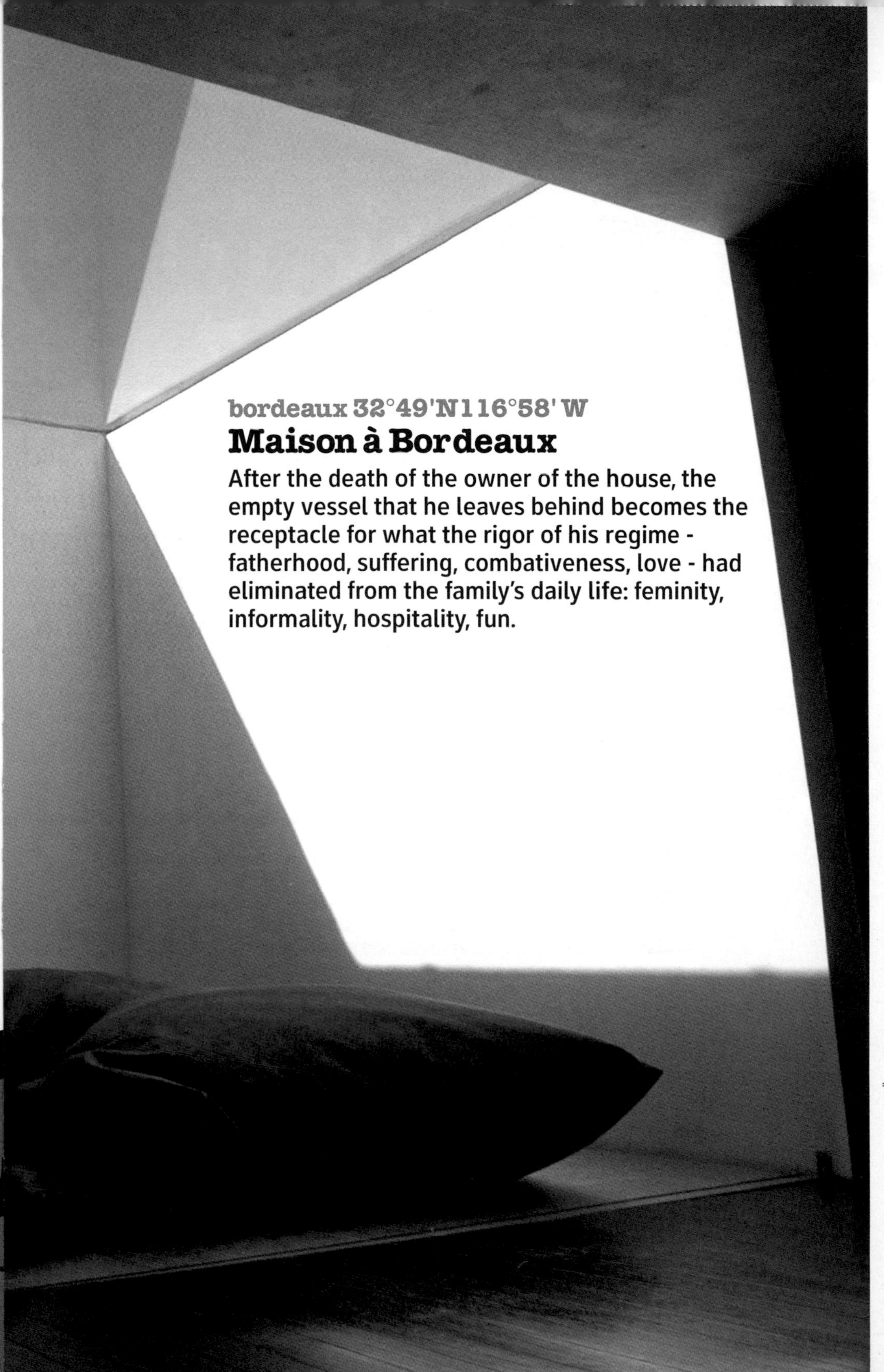

bordeaux 32°49'N116°58' W

Maison à Bordeaux

After the death of the owner of the house, the empty vessel that he leaves behind becomes the receptacle for what the rigor of his regime - fatherhood, suffering, combativeness, love - had eliminated from the family's daily life: feminity, informality, hospitality, fun.

MODIFICATIONS: REM KOOLHAAS AND OLIVER SCHÜTTE. SEAT: WENER VAN DERMEERSCH

In a systematic schizophrenia, while its leaders hammered out the details of its integration, "Europe" internally served as a political scapegoat that could be saddled with any amount of blame. In this climate, Europe could only gather strength by stealth: its most impressive achievement is the "acquis," an impenetrable stack of 80,000 pages that together define the practices it stands for, rather than the promises it will deliver. It is a document that, slowly but surely, infiltrates the consciousness of nations in Africa and South America as "syndicated (i.e. borrowed) legislation," theoretically enabling anyone to become "one of us," or at least improve interaction with us.

Europe's largely invisible legislative virtuosity has triggered a huge crisis in representation. Perhaps traumatized by the efficiency of Nazi and Soviet propaganda, Europe prefers inhibited displays of authenticity to orchestrated political theater. Because our union is voluntary, we can only be united when we are leaderless.

Incapable of asserting its own identity - how do you represent a stack of 80,000 pages? - Europe has designated Brussels as its headquarters - the only city that was part of each of Europe's earlier incarnations, now drained of its last traces of authenticity.... >

EARLY CLARITY
Somehow an illustration from 1948 surpassed all subsequent efforts in clarity.
Europe: ship propelled forward by the sails of its individual members.

CURRENT MUDDLE
In spite of Europe's achievements, its visual manifestations systematically undermine any sense of "European pride."
Is there a connection between the blandness of Europe's symbols and its inability to arouse popular appeal for its causes?

NATO members

Euro-atlantic partnership council

EUROZONE

EUROPEAN UNION

SCHENGEN

EXTENDED EU

UEFA

EUROVISION

...reduced to Blueurope.

AMERICA UNDER ATTACK
CHIRAC PLEDGES SUPPORT
IN FIGHT AGAINST TERRORISM
CNN

Instead of suggesting an unwanted homogeneity, Europe should insist on the richness of its persistent diversity.... Instead of national identity usurped by Euro-bureaucracy, "the European" should be presented as an extended identity, additional space that enables each culture to reinvent itself in a new framework.>

THE BARCODE

New symbolism for a new coalition: Europe shown as the sum of the cultural identities of its current and future members. Whereas the number of stars on the current EU flag is fixed, the barcode can accommodate newcomers and gain impact.

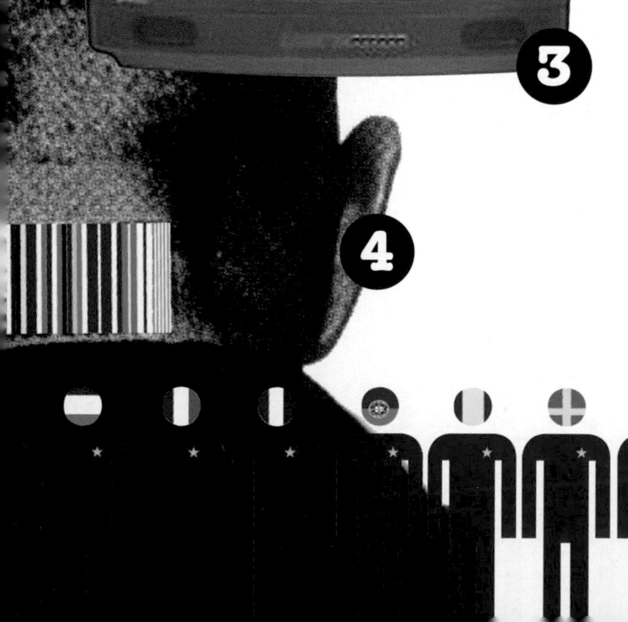

1 Euro-pass
2 Euro website
3 Euro TV
4 Euro tattoo

Improving Europe's image: Look beyond Europe's current symbols (the flag, passport, and the euro); develop a visual language for all Europe's appearances (advertisements, commercials, publications, websites, etc....); make Europe invade daily life; boost Europe's media presence; look at youth culture, create a Europe especially aimed at children and teenagers.... Insist on a high caliber architecture for the European institutions. Use Europe to set examples.... >

BRUXELLES

Léopold | L'architecte Rem Koolhaas a présenté ses idées pour casser l'image bureaucratique de l'Union

Coup de fun européen dans la capitale

REPÈRES

THE INDEPENDENT

THE BROADER VIEW

IN THE NEW REVIEW

When Matisse met Picasso: a tale of two geniuses

Health – the surprising truth about low-fat diets

DEBORAH ORR

The hate tearing Europe apart

EDITORIAL AND COMMENT THIS SECTION, PAGE 11

Goodbye stars, hello stripes: The new symbol of the EU

Business

EUROPEAN EDITION / NOVEMBER 18, 2002

ITALY

SCHEMING AGAINST MEDIOBANCA

FRANCE

BEHIND THE MESSIER PROBE

BUSH'S BIG WIN

WHAT IT MEANS FOR U.S. POLICY

IBM

A TALK WITH LOU GERSTNER

CHINA

WHAT IT IS BUYING ABROAD

25 states, 450 mill

challenge both

EU

HYPE

Following the publication of the barcode as the "new European flag" on the *Independent*'s front page, the combined attention of European press, radio, and TV kept the office from work for more than a week. No work of AMO-OMA ever came close to receiving so much attention. The hype that ensued testified to the urgency of the issue of Europe and its representation. Apparently the "flag" had hit a nerve of pent up Euro-sentiment throughout Europe. In a reaction to the barcode, Britain, the EU's staunchest anti-Europe member, emphatically professed its loyalty to the old European flag, symbol of everything it had loved to hate.

Jan Knikker

From: Jennifer Hackney [Hackney@euroscript-ls.de]

Sent: Friday, May 10, 2002 11:08 AM

To: pr@oma.nl

Subject: Flag

Dear Mr Koolhaas,

your design for the new EU logo is totally hideous and a complete fucking joke. It will make the EU a laughing stock, just because you feel the need to be post modern and show off. Please withdraw it and try to thing of something that makes sense, IS an actual logo not a foul giftwrap design, and has a chance of lasting.

Yours,

J Hackney

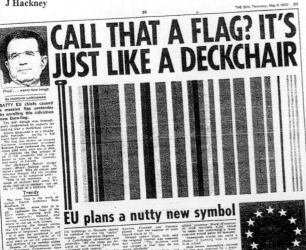

THE SUN, Thursday, May 9, 2002 23

CALL THAT A FLAG? IT'S JUST LIKE A DECKCHAIR

Prodi . . . wants new image

By DUNCAN LARCOMBE

BATTY EU chiefs caused a massive flap yesterday by unveiling this ridiculous new Euro-flag.

Trendy

EU plans a nutty new symbol

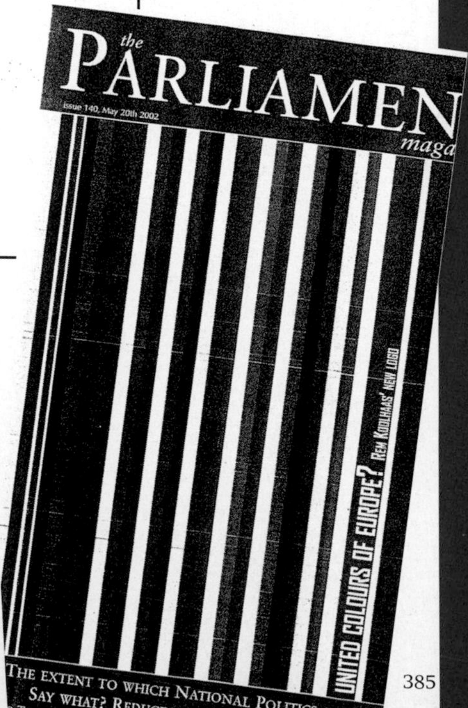

the PARLIAMEN

maga

Issue 140, May 20th 2002

UNITED COLOURS OF EUROPE? REM KOOLHAAS' NEW LOGO

THE EXTENT TO WHICH NATIONAL POLITICS SET THE

SAY WHAT? REDUCING THE NUMBER OF LANGUA

-TOURISM, CORPORATE SOCIAL RESPONSIBILITY

EU	USA
Venus	Mars
Kant	Hobbes
Divided	United
Multilateral	Unilateral
Washing Up	Cooking
Spent	High handed
Weak	Belligerent
Indecisive	Can-do
Wimps	Alpha male

The helplessness of Europe's branding in the age of the MTV sound bite has become a humiliating vulnerability to the muscular rhetoric of others. Europe's division will look weak as long as it is not claimed as its greatest virtue.

Because we have made little effort to articulate our ideals to the outside world, others write Europe's script.

The axis of reflexive Atlanticism: USA-GB-NL

When AMO first presented its work on September 18th, 2001, the momentous events of the week before seemed to make it irrelevant. Now, two years later, the drastically altered landscape of global politics has given new urgency to the articulation of European positions and values. The leaders' disarray was in stark contrast to the anti-war demonstrations that provided overwhelming proof of a shared European sensibility, cohesion that its leaders had never been able to capture. ■

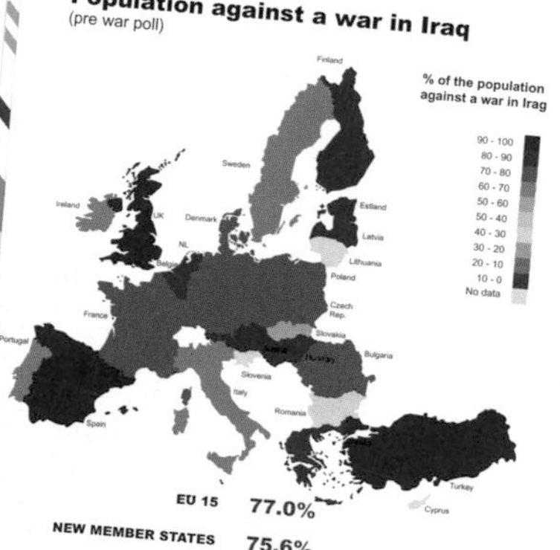

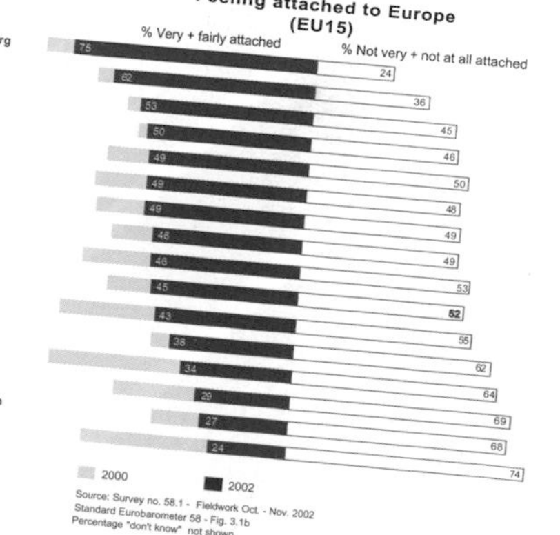

The Union paid dearly for the disconnection between the official and the "lived" project of Europe. While Europeans spontaneously asserted their common identity, their identification with the "official Europe" nose-dived.

Euroformula: predicting enthusiasm for Europe.

$$EU_{d}(€) = \lim_{t \to \infty} \int_{30°}^{75°} \frac{c(€)\, s(e + €) T°}{p(€)\, h(A + €) R}$$

T° = local temperature
p = population density
€ = local price level
A = Alcohol consuption
h = historical values
c = local cuisine
s = social values (fashion, design, clubs, music)
e = economical infrastructure
R = amount of rain

Value of € vs $

$ = €

05 Jan 01 · 20 Apr 01 · 03 Aug 01 · 16 Nov 01 · 01 Mar 02 · 14 Jun 02 · 27 Sep 03

The Narkomfin rooftop, post celebration

ROOF OF NARKOMFIN

On the roof, there had recently been a great party, to launch a new line of furniture.... Empty bottles of Italian wine were stacked up in neat piles and filled every cavity.

It could be that the residue of this celebration would cause the small collapse of the Socialist ruin....

ROOF OF NARKOMFIN 2

"There is also a penthouse," said our hosts... . They took us to two tiny rooms. Milutin, the inventor of the linear city, lived here. The paint is still original.

Covered in mold we discovered flakes of bright blue on ceilings and walls - the other room had an "inverted" scheme simply in white. There was a time when Utopias could be established with paint.

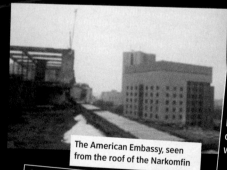

The American Embassy, seen from the roof of the Narkomfin

AMERICAN EMBASSY

The American embassy is housed in a comfortable Stalinist palazzo on Novinskiy Boulevard. In spite of its architecture, simply because it represented the "free world" it became an emblem. When it became too small, a new, vaguely Eisenmanesque structure - a tortured cube - was built. It took very long and when it was completed, the Americans discovered such a proliferation of listening devices integrated into its structure - they were omnipresent and almost undistinguishable from the reinforcement of concrete - that after the futility of debugging became apparent, the Americans abandoned it. In the meantime a new residential compound - quasi-Scandinavian housing - was erected behind the embassy. The personnel lived there in a slightly isolated way - not really part of Moscow. After September 11, the security issues became more compelling and the compound was reinforced. Rolls of barbed wire now surround it, watch towers inspect the environment. It looks like the Berlin wall, on a smaller scale. From the surrounding city, it looked like a caricature of the past, before the fall of communism. "Freedom" defended by entirely discredited means.

PLANETARIUM 1

The Moscow planetarium was also one of the masterpieces we had to see. One of the reasons, its experimental construction. Its dome was made from a thin concrete shell - as if, for once, the construction method itself was Utopian. In it stood a German machine, which regardless of revolution or regime, projected the movement of heavenly bodies on the thin shell with the same certainty with which, outside, history went through its motions.

It also stood in the park - closed, but ready to be renovated. It was already dark, but we could visit it. A small crowd waited for us, among them the architect of the conversion - he looked in his 80s or even 90s - but very well preserved, as if he had used the same embalmment facilities that took care of Lenin; under his arm he had a traditional portfolio.

We tried to gain entry to the old structure. There was no light. Nobody knew the entrance. Suddenly appeared the "custodian." Does every building have a human counterpart? Someone not quite incarcerated but whose life seems to have been spent in maintaining its viability against incredible odds. They know the DNA of the structure and wiring, were present at some weird moments of its history.

He let us in. The dome was still dark. We "saw" it with our ears, as our feet crushed the flakes that had fallen off the ceiling. Suddenly light was restored. The German projector still stood in the center, a giant dysfunctional ant. It would soon be replaced by wall-to-wall, more like ... experience.

The Planterium, post-Market

PLANETARIUM 2

In the harsh light, the embalmed architect unveiled his plan for the restoration: the entire planetarium would be lifted by seven meters; each column would be individually jacked, their movement computer-coordinated not to crack the thin shell.... Then an entirely new sockle would be built like a table underneath a small egg. Within it: museum store, restaurants, meeting center, educational center, all the paraphernalia of the market economy. Finally, the access road from the old gate would be widened, and a ramp of almost Brazilian flamboyance would deliver people by car. The roof of the plinth would serve as the parking.

Underground Utopias

Residential high rise in Kudrinskaya Square

The attic of the Generals' Apartments

GENERALS' APARTMENT BUILDING
When the architects came from the war, they mostly were homeless. One of their first projects was a huge apartment building for returning generals along Stalin's new boulevard. Because all buildings now were classical, it had to have an attic, a mansard. A space too humble for generals. The architects realized that it could be subdivided and serve as their homes. On top of the generals lived, anonymously, the elite of the Russian architects. They worked at one end of the building; each morning, they had to move from one building to the other, conveniently at attic level. Each morning, the architects' children witnessed a procession of professionals trekking from apartment to apartment through an internal connection, on the way to work - a living history. In the apartments themselves, the doorknobs had been produced by German slave labor - the only esthetic they knew, Fascist. From scraps of tin they had laboriously crafted knobs as if they had been designed for the Führer by Albert Speer. An unusually high proportion of the children - almost 90% - became architects. The emergency housing acted as an architects' incubator. Even though/because they had witnessed their parents' hard times.

BARRIKADNAJA
In the twenties, in architectural school, it was assumed that gravity would soon be conquered, become a thing of the past. Entire floating cities were designed, colonies of different spaceships, and entire new planets were conceived by Malevitch. After WWII, gravity was one of the survivors. Soviet architecture was now emphatically monumental. Moscow planners conceived its future as a city ringed by colossal towers - each an enlargement of one of the Kremlin gates - a virtual Kremlin. One was Barrikadnaja. It was popular with test-flyers - experimenting with the low-tech-gravity-defying products of Soviet airplane ingenuity - matching American know-how by sheer improvisation. One inhabitant was Yuri Gagarin, the first man in space. If you see the desolate congregations of skyscrapers in the contemporary city - formless and uninspired - this metaphorical stretch and the comforting ring were not that bad, in retrospect.

METRO
After all this time, the subway station was still astonishing. In fact more. It was almost unthinkable anywhere else that public space would be so stark, so free of commercial overlay - the steep accelerated descent - Soviet esca move faster and at a steeper angle, to inspire awe, a simulation of a free fall? In the west, crowds collect at the beginning of escalators, here they are drained so fast that the crowds thin at the point where they are sucked down stairs to other layers - disgorged in the metallic foyer underground, its walls suddenly splitting to reveal a new train. The ceiling is a sequence of 24 vaults, each topped by its own mosaic medallion. The cosmic disguised as decoration, the theme is weight and weightlessness - all seen from a worm's perspective - airplanes against blue skies, parachutes landing, gliders launched by strong arms, but also fruit hanging bulbous and overripe fr branches. The camera looks up at strong legs of young men and women, ending in indeterminate darkness. The sequence suggests that we are all being pulled down by gravity, but all potentially able to escape. At the end of the station a man stands with the bouquet of roses. The light is steel-gray. The entire architecture is a mis-en-scène of a future encounter.
State sponsored romanticism and sensuality. Caring?

Proposal for a floating city by Georgi Krutikov

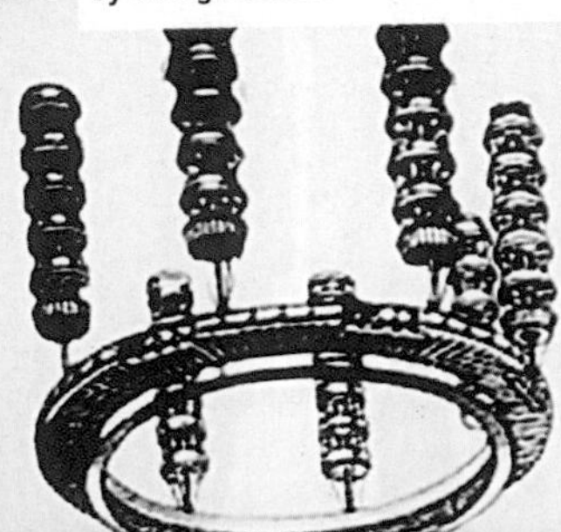

When we celebrated Leonidov's 100th birthday, one of his friends, an architect told us that Leonidov had once stopped him when they were walking here on the new boulevard, looked at the looming enormity of Stalin's new buildings, and whispered, "What would happen if they invested the same might into kindness...?" ■

After the October Revolution, Hermitage officials boycotted the new authorities and refused to acknowledge the Bolshevist government. The Louvre personnel behaved in exactly the same way during the Commune of Paris.

During the 1930s, the Germans secretly acquired paintings at the Hermitage and treated the museum's staff to cigarettes. Those who accepted were arrested and deported.

The Hermitage's designer Von Klenze, recommended using redwood boxes - in which sugar had been imported from Brazil - as museum furniture.

After his arrest, the figure of Professor Troinitsky - the former director of the Hermitage - was cut out of all staff group photos with scissors.

The director of the Hermitage A. Orbeli, famous primarily for his black beard, was familiar with the craft of stonemason. By night, he loved to build new walls in the museum, to brick up passages and doorways. Stories of secret rooms he personally constructed circulate to this day.

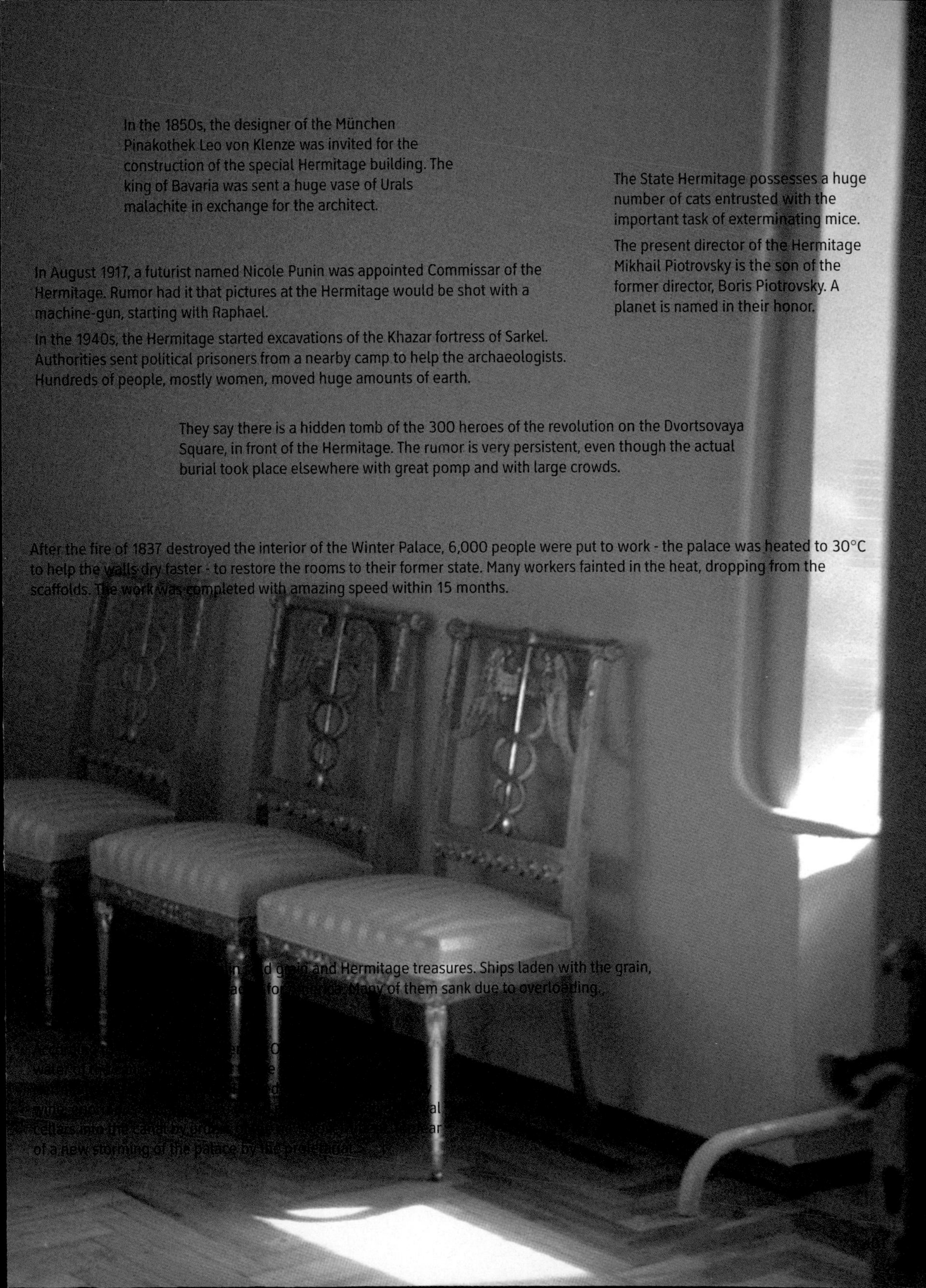

In the 1850s, the designer of the München Pinakothek Leo von Klenze was invited for the construction of the special Hermitage building. The king of Bavaria was sent a huge vase of Urals malachite in exchange for the architect.

The State Hermitage possesses a huge number of cats entrusted with the important task of exterminating mice.

The present director of the Hermitage Mikhail Piotrovsky is the son of the former director, Boris Piotrovsky. A planet is named in their honor.

In August 1917, a futurist named Nicole Punin was appointed Commissar of the Hermitage. Rumor had it that pictures at the Hermitage would be shot with a machine-gun, starting with Raphael.

In the 1940s, the Hermitage started excavations of the Khazar fortress of Sarkel. Authorities sent political prisoners from a nearby camp to help the archaeologists. Hundreds of people, mostly women, moved huge amounts of earth.

They say there is a hidden tomb of the 300 heroes of the revolution on the Dvortsovaya Square, in front of the Hermitage. The rumor is very persistent, even though the actual burial took place elsewhere with great pomp and with large crowds.

After the fire of 1837 destroyed the interior of the Winter Palace, 6,000 people were put to work - the palace was heated to 30°C to help the walls dry faster - to restore the rooms to their former state. Many workers fainted in the heat, dropping from the scaffolds. The work was completed with amazing speed within 15 months.

[illegible] d grain and Hermitage treasures. Ships laden with the grain, [illegible] Many of them sank due to overloading.

[illegible] cellars into the canal by pro[illegible] of a new storming of the palace by the proletariat [illegible]

Everything that the staff of the Palace of Arts (which functioned in the building of the Winter Palace after the revolution) considered of little value - for example, furniture and other items from rooms of maids of honor - was heaped into great stacks on Dvortsovaya Square. In the 1920s, you could get palace furniture, cutlery, and clothes there, almost for free.

After 1945, trains carried the exhibits confiscated as trophies from German museums from Berlin to Leningrad. The treasures of the Egyptian Museum in Berlin, the Pergamon Altar, and the French paintings from Krebs's private collection were all heaped neglectfully in the Hermitage cellars, where mice inflicted serious harm to artistic objects.

In 1914, the Hermitage bought Leonardo Da Vinci's Madonna with a Flower from the family of the artist Benoit. The family had acquired it from an itinerant Italian musician for a trifling sum.

There are several legends concerning secret passages leading from the Winter Palace to exits in various parts of the city. According to one of them, Prime Minister [illegible] Kerensky used one of those passages (it leads to the apartment of the [illegible] [illegible]hese lines) on the night of the October Revolution. Having dressed up a[illegible] [illegible] fled from the revolting proletariat, in the hope of gathering remnants of [illegible]rmy together and stamping out the revolution.

The imposing assault at the Winter Palace, shown by the director Eisenstein in his famous movie October, never took place. The palace was taken in 1917, noiselessly and without any serious opposition.

Emperor Nikolai I ordered the removal of Voltaire's statue by Goudon from the Hermitage room containing libraries of the French Enlightenment figures in order to "exterminate that old ape."

In March 2001, the canvas of the *Swimming Pool at the Seraglio* (1824) by J.L. Jérome was cut from its frame during an exhibition of French 19th-century painting. The robbery is rumored to have been ordered by a mad Arab billionaire with a penchant for Western stylizations of Oriental motifs.

The rule prescribed to the visitors of the Hermitage, which included the personal apartments of Catherine II and her picture gallery, was as follows: "Make merry, but break and gnaw nothing."

In 1985, a monomaniac splashed Danaë by Rembrandt with concentrated hydrochloric acid and stabbed the canvas twice with a knife to protest the depiction of a naked female body. The restoration took 12 years.

In the 1930s, it was planned to put a huge figure of Stalin atop the Petropavloskaya Fortress spire. The project was never put into practice due to academician Orbeli, then the director of the Hermitage, who said: "Comrades, the Petropavlovsk spire is reflected in the Neva. Do you really want comrade Stalin to be seen upside down?" >

During the first half of the 19th century, the heads of Hermitage departments wore sumptuous uniforms and were equal in rank to top-level officials of the state. It was then that tickets and special permits enabling the bearer to enter the museum were introduced. Such a pass was humorously labeled "ticket to eternity." An additional regulation prohibited entry to those who wore furs and bore umbrellas and walking sticks.

The tsar questioned the leaders of the 1825 aristocratic uprising (the "Decembrists") in the Hermitage picture gallery.

During the 900-day Nazi blockade of Leningrad, 2000-odd people made their makeshift quarters in the cellars of the Hermitage. It was rumored among the famished Leningrad citizens that the secret storage facilities of the museum contained - along with works of art - food supplies sufficient to feed the city.

After World War II, the Hermitage staff began excavating the ancient city of Penjikent, Tajikistan. Secret nuclear tests were being conducted in a neighboring valley and many scholars of that expedition subsequently died of radiation. During the 1950s, the sequence of deaths was attributed to the vengeance of disturbed ancient spirits.

After the German attack of 1941, Hermitage exhibits were evacuated by train to Sverdlovsk. Pictures were placed at the local picture gallery, a church, and in the cellar of the famous Ipatiev house, where the last tsar and his family were shot after the revolution.

Andrew Mellon, the United States Treasury Secretary, secretly acquired paintings from the Hermitage such as The Adoration of the Magi by Botticelli, Venus with a Mirror by Titian, The Annunciation by Jan van Eyck, as well as works by Perugino, Veronese, Van Dijk, Hals, Velasquez, Rembrandt. The 21 paintings he purchased from the Hermitage formed the core of the newly established National Gallery in Washington. Galouste Gulbenkian, the head of Iraq Petroleum, helped the Soviet Union sell Baku oil on the Western market and was allowed to buy Rembrandt's portrait of Titus and pictures by Watteau and Ter Borch. The sold works were packed at night, by candlelight.

In 1928, the Hermitage was headed by Pavel Clark, a professional revolutionary who had been sentenced to death in 1906 for participating in the armed revolt at Chita. The death penalty was replaced by 15 years of punitive labour in Siberia, from where he escaped to Japan and then later to Australia. He returned to Siberia under the alias of P. Gray. In 1918, after the defeat of the revolutionary movement in the Far East, he fled to Australia once more. Later he returned to receive the post as director of the largest museum in the USSR.

To transport one exhibit of the "Mexican Art" exhibition - a six-ton head of an Olmec deity - through the Hermitage, special railway tracks were laid in its rooms.

Guests and hosts often left their signatures on the glass panes at the Winter Palace, scratching windows with the diamonds of their rings. This practice was prohibited at the Hermitage.

In 1837 an enormous fire broke out at the Winter Palace and lasted a fortnight. It occurred by fault of Montferrand the architect, who had miscalculated the chimney's layout. The Hermitage was saved through expediency: the gallery that connected the palace to the museum was cut in two. Hundreds of soldiers died in the process. >

Mostly through economic conditions, the Hermitage did not participate in the late-twentieth-century museum boom. While this once seemed to be a disadvantage, it turned into an opportunity with the burst of the museum bubble in the late nineties. Where other cultural institutions became economically vulnerable, the Hermitage managed to avoid turning itself into a commercial enterprise. Where other museums became overstretched and bloated by additional programs that do not directly contribute to the core role of the museum - to show art - the Hermitage retained its original purpose.

With its reputation untainted, the Hermitage can now focus on its strengths - its virtually priceless and limitless collection, its scale, and its non-commercial character. With this unique history, it can be the first major museum to proclaim a renewed focus on art. ■

General Staff Building in the context of the Greater Hermitage

GO EAST
western painting 600,000 pieces
russian culture
archeology 500,000 pieces

The Hermitage Collections

The enormity of the collection combined with its extensive collection of rooms has created a scale and complexity and organization that approaches urbanism. It now becomes possible to exhibit the almost endless amount of artifacts across a vast array of different conditions, allowing a large extension of the repertoire of installation and curatorial concepts.

Rooms of the Hermitage (629 out of 1928 rooms)

The vast reservoir of all rooms of the combined Hermitage presents an endless variety of spaces in typology and quality. Some interiors are protected, others practically derelict.

- ■ palace and museum rooms with historical decoration fully preserved
- ■ rooms with historical decoration maintained
- ■ rooms with historical decoration not maintained
- □ rooms newly built

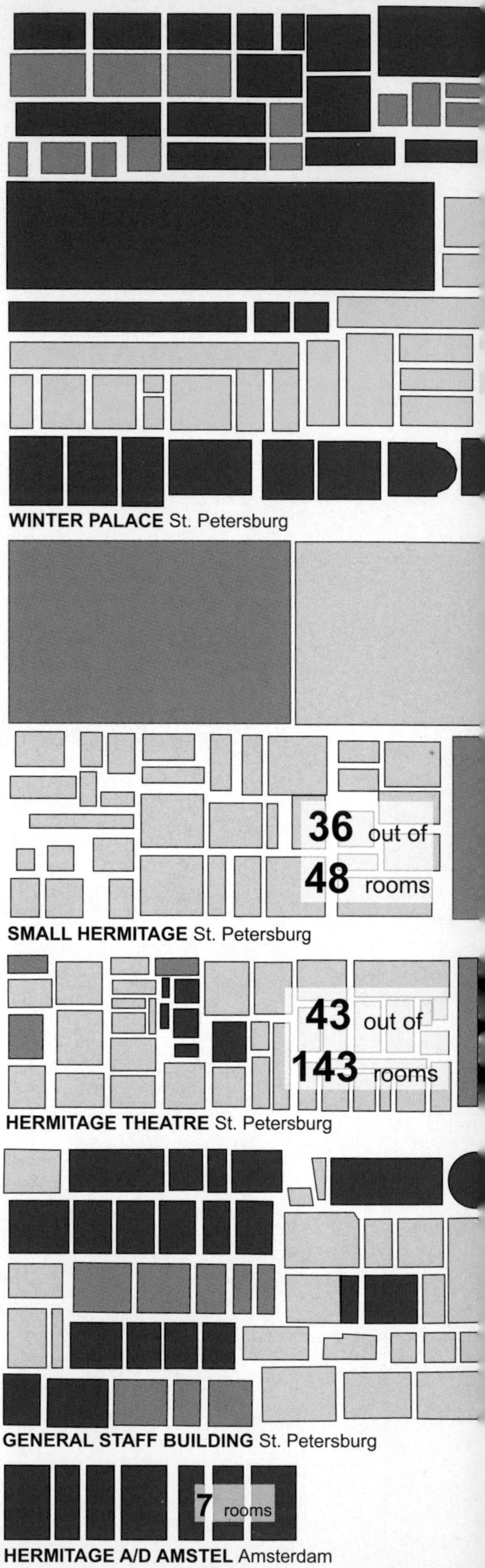

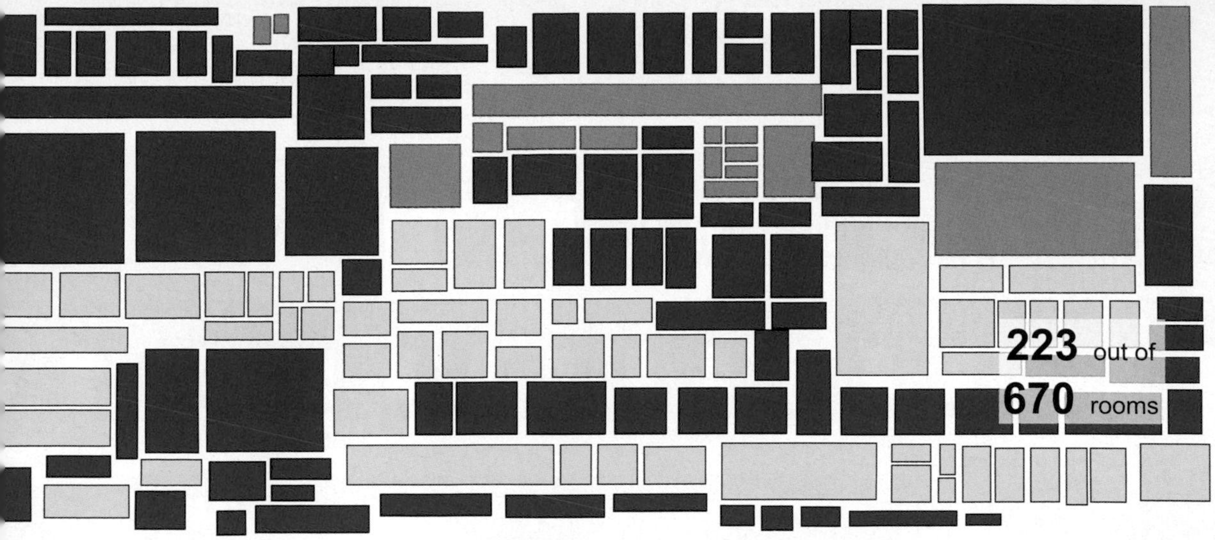

223 out of
670 rooms

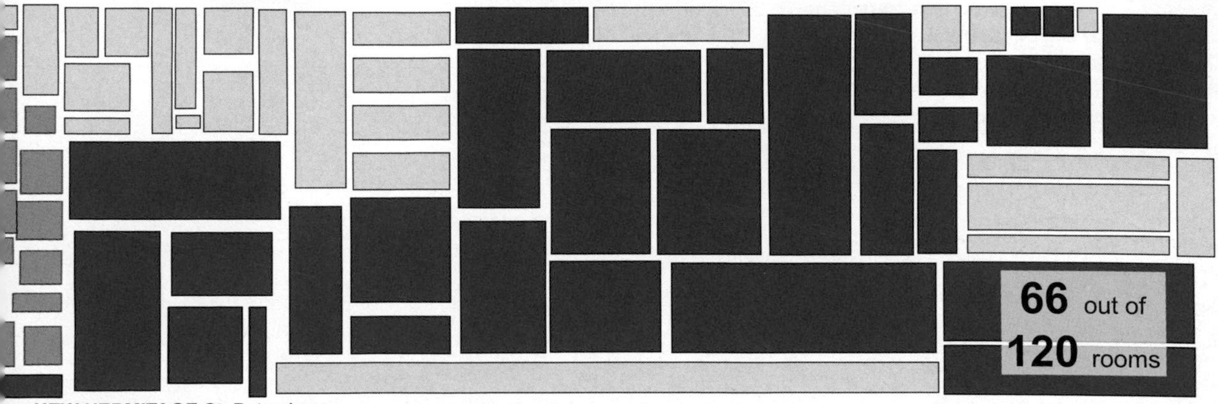

66 out of
120 rooms

NEW HERMITAGE St. Petersburg

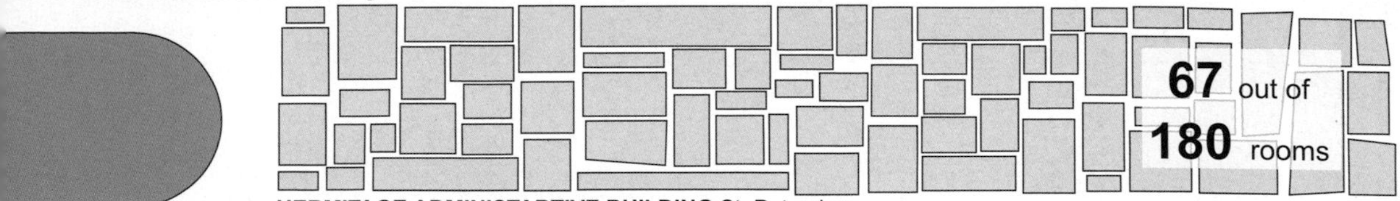

67 out of
180 rooms

HERMITAGE ADMINISTARTIVE BUILDING St. Petersburg

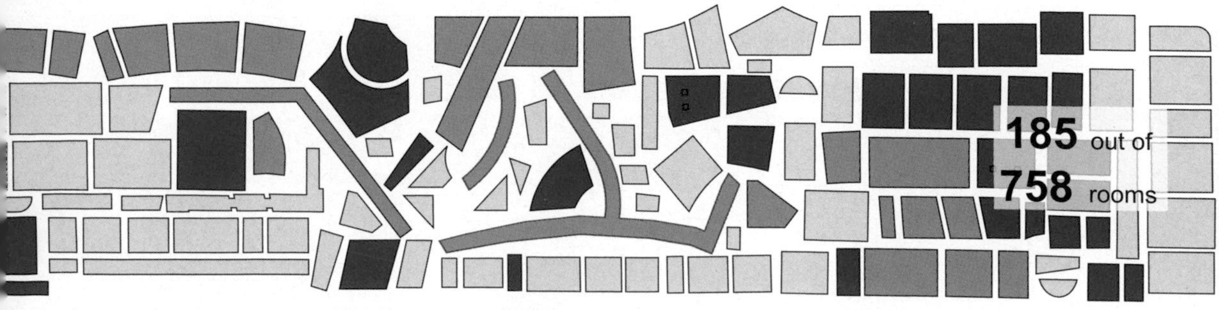

185 out of
758 rooms

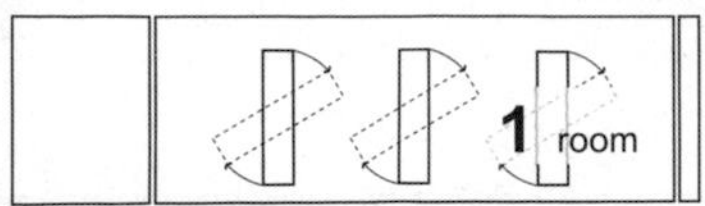

1 room

SOMMERSET HOUSE London

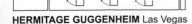

HERMITAGE GUGGENHEIM Las Vegas

Winter Palace, St. Petersburg

Total wall-space of the Hermitage (327 out of 7850 walls)
Unfolded interior elevations of the rooms of the combined Hermitage

- palace and museum rooms with historical decoration fully preserved
- rooms with historical decoration maintained
- rooms with historical decoration not maintained
- rooms newly built

General Staff Building, St.Petersburg

8 out of 12 walls

Hermitage-Guggenheim, Las Vegas

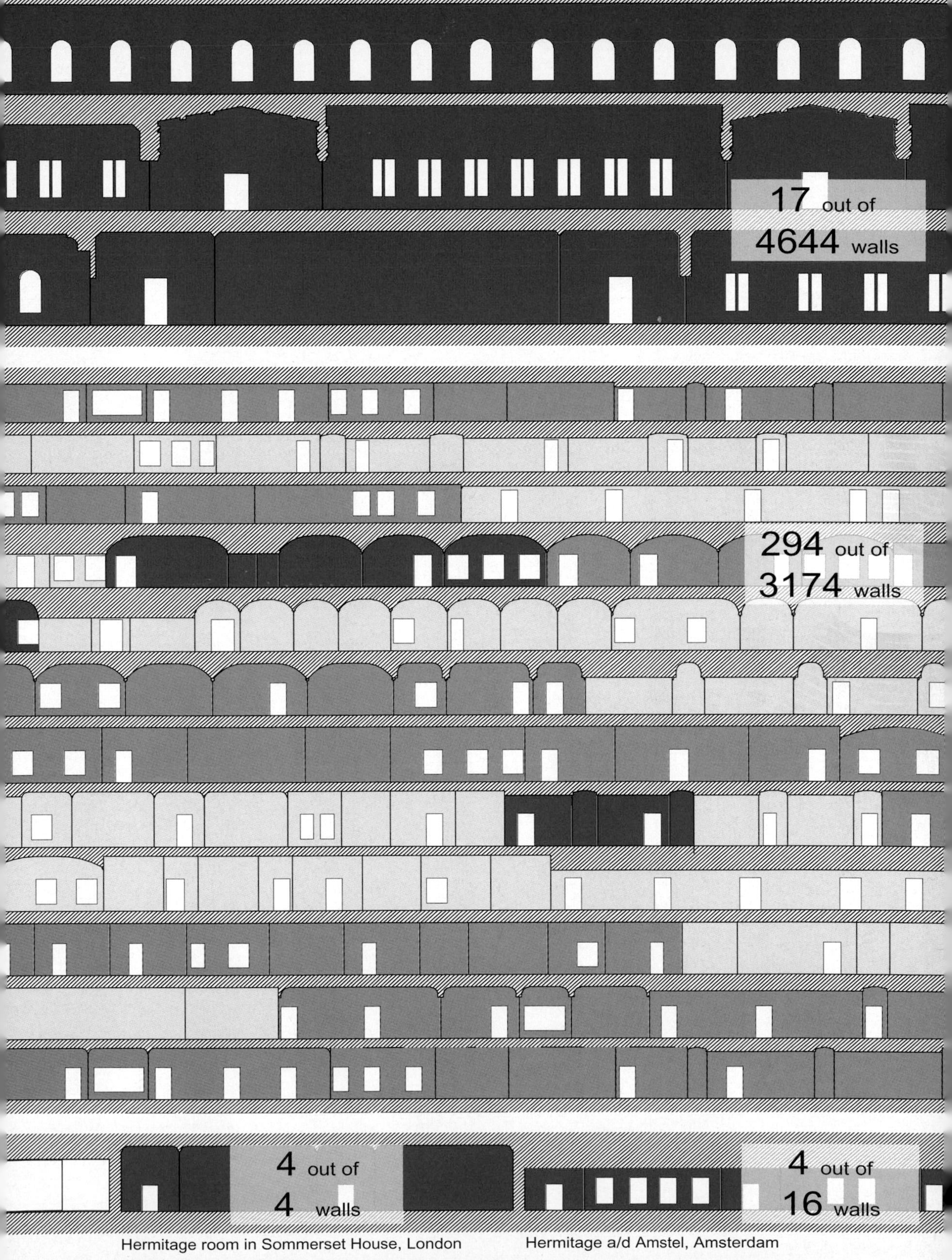

Hermitage room in Sommerset House, London

Hermitage a/d Amstel, Amsterdam

jerusalem 31°47'N 35°13'E

THE SITE: the politician walked there four months later and triggered the second intifada
THE SPEAKER: the mayor, who later, as Minister of Communication, would announce that Arafat "might have to be killed"
THE WINNER: the architect regretted "that political obliviousness is now assumed to be part of the architect's equipment," and was subsequently declared the most ungrateful winner in the history of the prize by its PR person

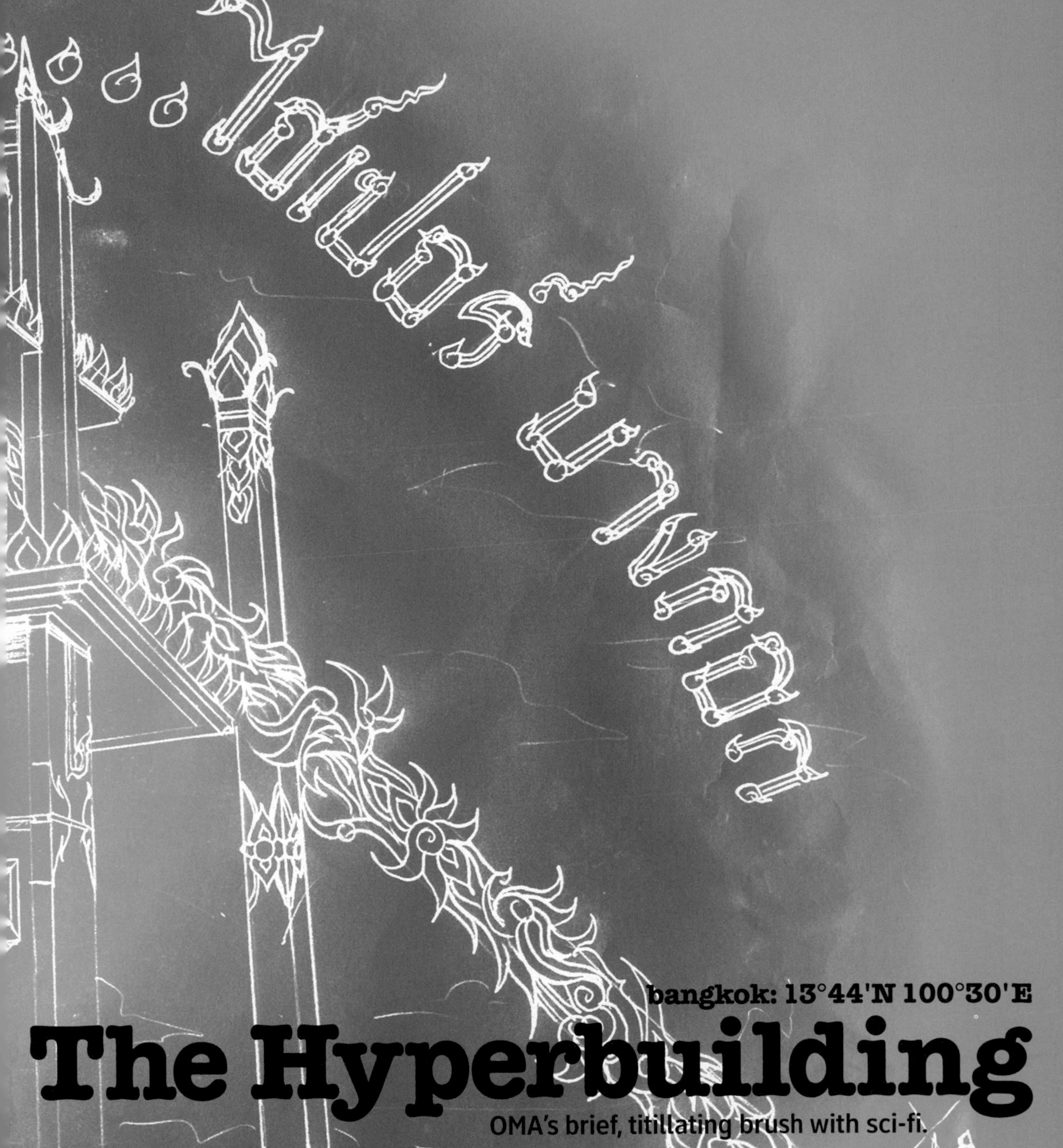

bangkok: 13°44'N 100°30'E

The Hyperbuilding

OMA's brief, titillating brush with sci-fi.

Bangkok is a city on the edge of the tolerable... a city ripe for experimentation.

Instigated by the Japanese government - increasingly nervous about the vulnerability of Tokyo - the Hyperbuilding is a city-in-a-building, a self-sustaining indoor metropolis for a population of 120,000. Sure that the project would spark paranoia at home, the organizers stipulated that the architects situate their proposal anywhere in the world, except Japan.

THEORY I: A self-contained city would be less credible in the almost "completed" urban conditions of Japan, Europe, and America, than in a society undergoing the drastic upheaval of modernization at full force, where the virtues of providing an enormous, controllable critical mass could be of demonstrable advantage.

THEORY II: In the context of a developing nation, it is better to play down rather than play up, the technical aspect of the Hyperbuilding. Although it is a "next step," Hyperbuilding should not be confused with high-tech. It works only if the visionary ambition of the hyper-scale is combined with a degree of elementary simplicity.

Bangkok - a city on the edge of the tolerable - offers the perfect context in which to test these theories. From its traffic to its haphazard development to its politics, it is a city of many crises - a city ripe for experimentation.

STRUCTURE

In order to accommodate so huge a population, the building requires a height of over 1000 meters. To avoid the core of darkness inevitably present in very large pyramidal skyscrapers, we propose a mass of thin towers and blocks of program.

Composite stability is achieved through an orchestration of mutual dependence: several buildings are integrated into a single mass - there are no soloists - the different elements support each other in every sense. The vertical elements connect through horizontal plates; the diagonals work as braces; the volumes are lodged in spatial knots. It is an organization in which no component is conceived as essential, and any element can be rebuilt independently.

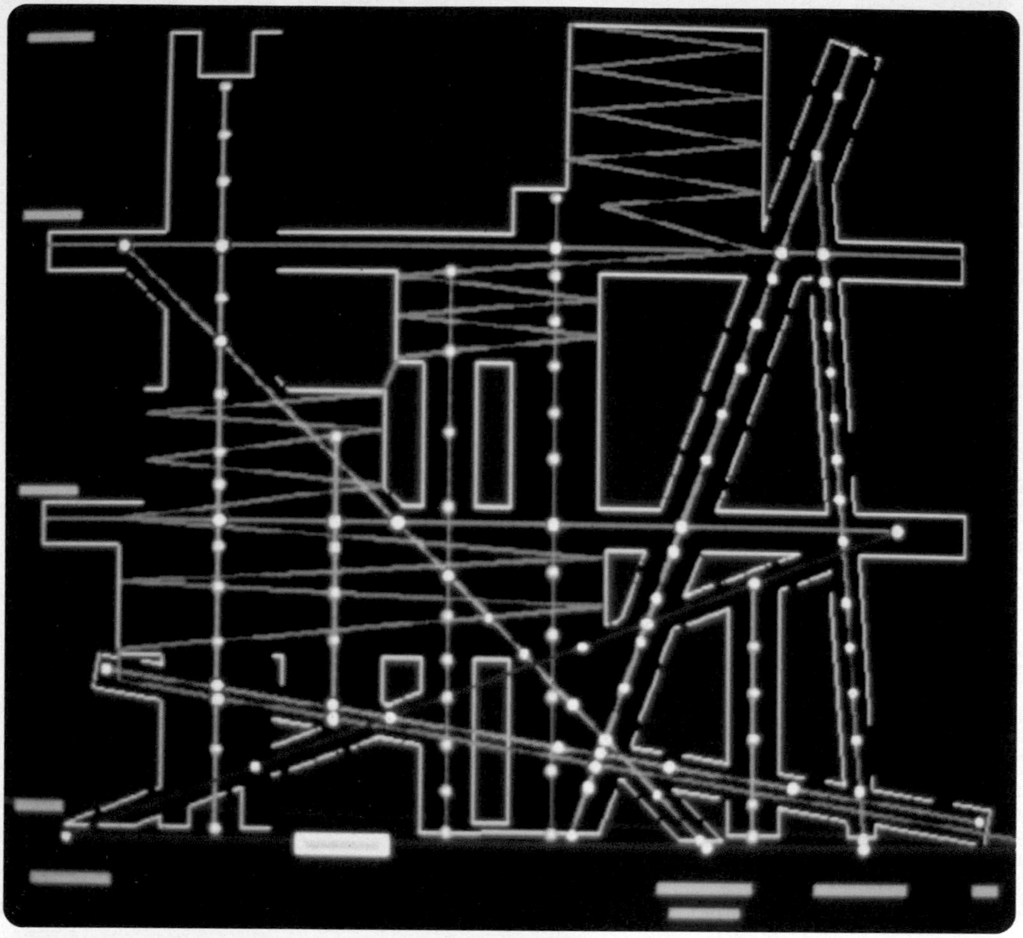

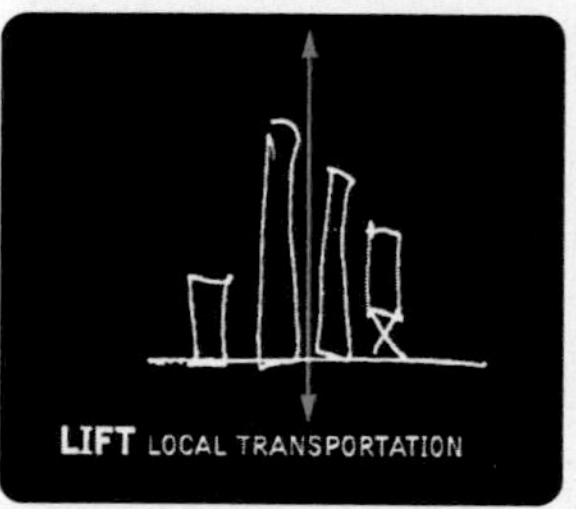

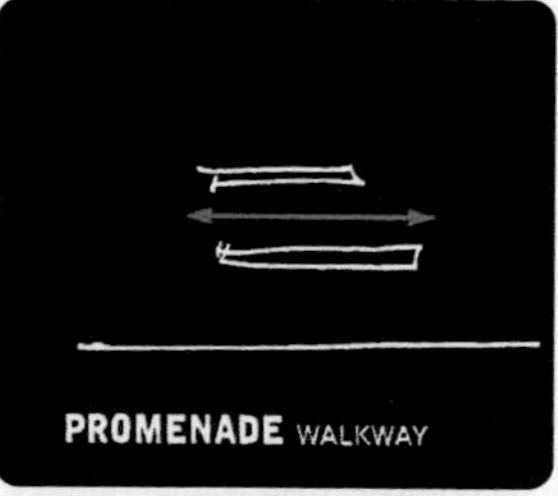

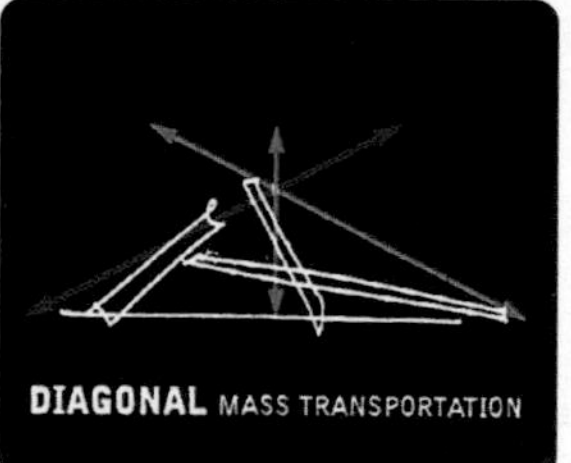

CIRCULATION

Four diagonal "boulevards" with mass transportation cable cars, gondolas, and train elevators connect the Hyperbuilding to the city below. Six "streets," each equipped with high and low speed elevators, provide the main vertical connections. A walkable "promenade" allows a resident to go from ground level to the top via a 12 km pedestrian path. Snaking through most of the programs on the way, the path leads through stores, gardens, schools, factories, while lazily reaching 1000 m above the ground. ■

Asia New Towns

Despite daily forecasts of the region's impending financial ruin, in the last decade Asian cities have expanded at unprecedented rates. In Asia, the city is being reinvented both by design and by default.

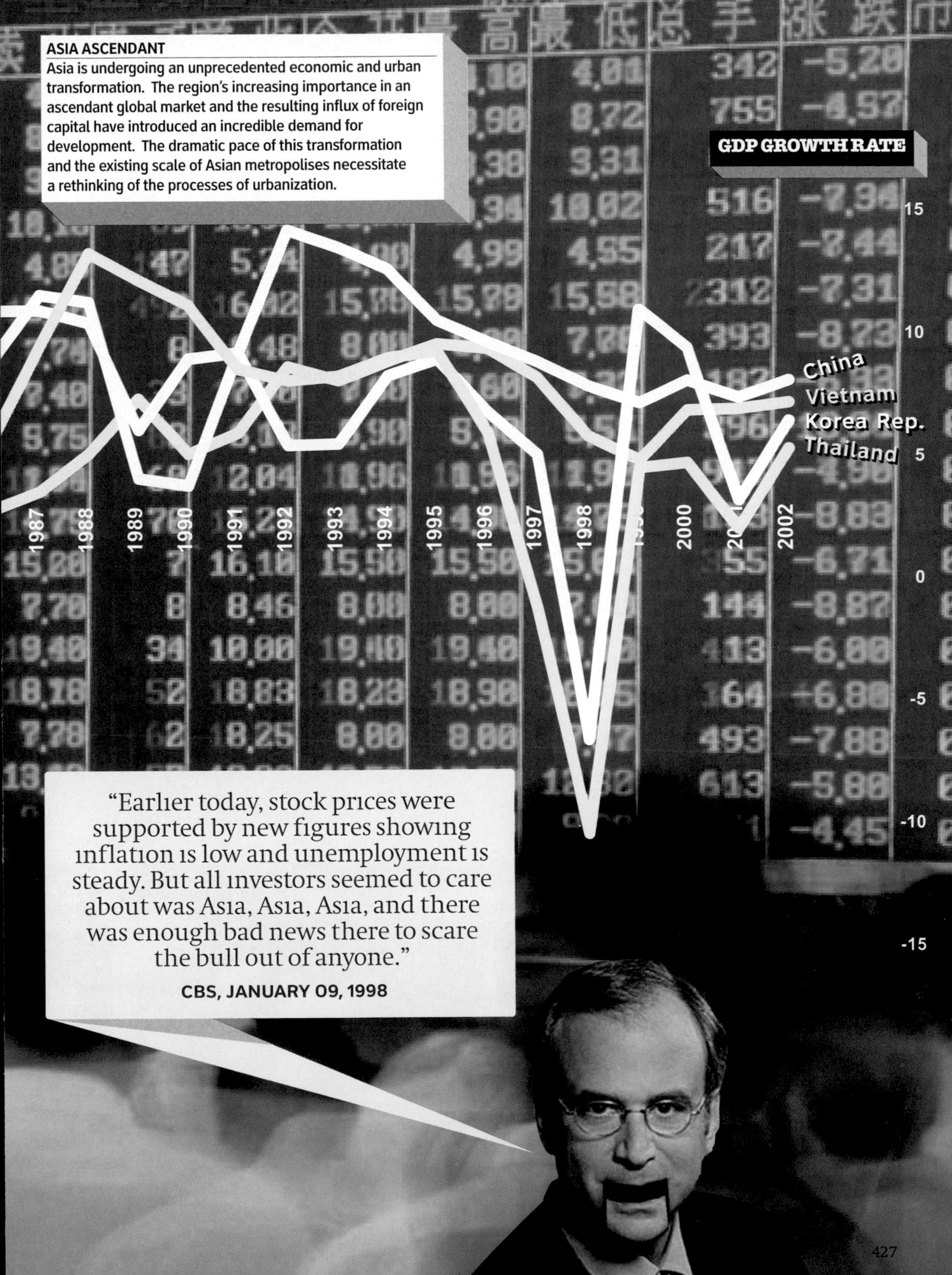
ASIA ASCENDANT
Asia is undergoing an unprecedented economic and urban transformation. The region's increasing importance in an ascendant global market and the resulting influx of foreign capital have introduced an incredible demand for development. The dramatic pace of this transformation and the existing scale of Asian metropolises necessitate a rethinking of the processes of urbanization.
GDP GROWTH RATE
China
Vietnam
Korea Rep.
Thailand
15
10
5
0
-5
-10
-15
1987
1988
1989
1990
1991
1992
1993
1994
1995
1996
1997
1998
2000
2002
"Earlier today, stock prices were supported by new figures showing inflation is low and unemployment is steady. But all investors seemed to care about was Asia, Asia, Asia, and there was enough bad news there to scare the bull out of anyone."
CBS, JANUARY 09, 1998

1

1997

Hanoi New Town

Unchecked, Hanoi's modernization would demand the wholesale destruction of the old as its price. Rather than ravaging the old city, Hanoi's future growth can be organized and realized by projecting a twin city north of the Red River. Hanoi New Town has both its own CBD and, in and on the river, a number of special districts for government research and entertainment for the use and benefit of both the new and the old cities. (We presented the project to the Vietnamese government. We later heard that Bechtel had won the competition.)

Hanoi New Town

Old Hanoi

> "Vietnam has come from nowhere to one of those economies clearly showing the most signs of sustainable Asian type growth."
>
> CNNFN, APRIL 30 1997

Hanoi - "Water City"
The integration of landscape, water, and cityscape is present throughout the new town. The diverse programs of a modern city are linked through the presence of the natural within the urban.

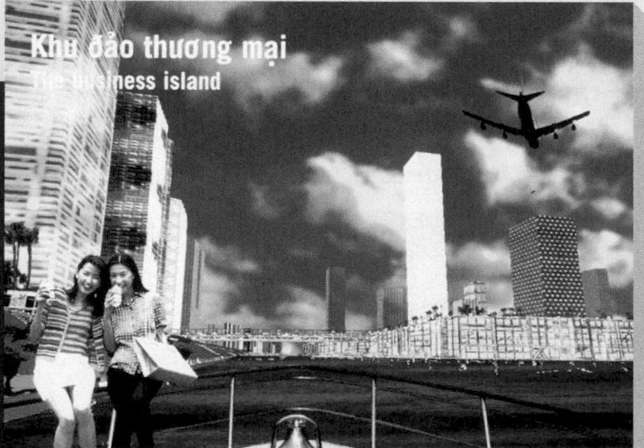

Thành phố Hà Nội mới

Hanoi New Town

Proximity

The site is part of a beautiful agricultural region north of Hanoi. This landscape, rich with water, recalls the polder systems in the Netherlands. Organized by a series of East/West strips, the new town is an alternating landscape of built and unbuilt, urban and green. These strips react to site conditions like the dike and existing water systems and vary in width to accommodate different urban conditions. They ensure the proximity of urban and green and allow a gradual transformation and urbanization of the site, comparable to the aging rings of a tree.

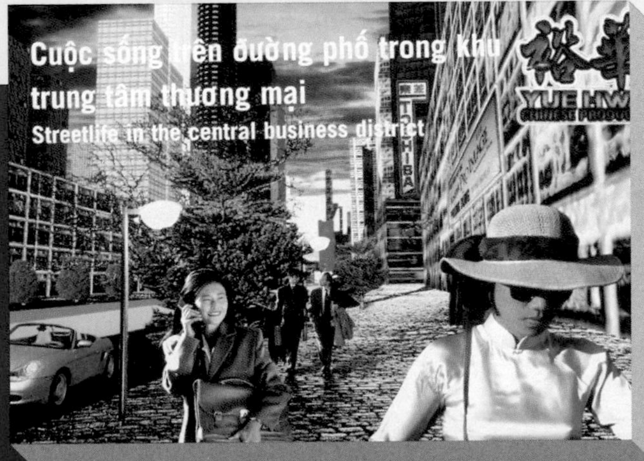

Cuộc sống trên đường phố trong khu trung tâm thương mại

Streetlife in the central business district

SONG DO NEW TOWN

Inchon, located between Seoul, Kimpo Airport, New Seoul International Airport and the harbor, is poised to become the IT and logistics hub of Northeast Asia. On an area of reclaimed land on Inchon's coast, a polder condition similar to much of Netherlands, Song Do New Town is planned to become a central part of this new metropolis. Compared to the chaotic and compromised conditions that now prevail in Seoul - where the pressure of development constantly outstrips planning - the 'new' regions on the Yellow Sea offer ambitions and opportunities to start from scratch and create new communities where architecture, landscape and infrastructure form an integrated whole.

2
Inchon
NSIA
Seoul
SDNT
URBAN UNCERTAINTY
Planning new urban territories typically requires nearly delusional optimism, a blind faith that current trajectories will continue unabated. The economic turmoil that spread throughout Asia in the late 1990's heightened the difficulty of anticipating future developments, needs, or potentials with any form of precision. Under these circumstances, new wholes have to be created from unknown and unknowable elements. Strategies that accommodate - even exploit - uncertainties must be devised.
"With the financial turmoil in Asia, a lot of potential buyers are thinking 1998 could be a good time to get a deal on a Asian made car, and they might be right."
CNN, DECEMBER 30 1997
Just-In-Time Planning
Large-scale urban operations are the ones most subject to instability; business enterprises and cultural institutions may contribute substantially to a city's identity, but their cost makes them particularly sensitive to financial uncertainty. The smallest operations are the most stable; housing is the generic urban substance that you can plan. The zoning strategy for SDNT addresses this split between known and less intense program and unknown and intense program that will develop over time. A network of programatic bands is set within a field of highly structured generic fabric (housing, services, public open space).

BUSINESS ZONE
Takes the form of the highway

RESIDENTIAL ZONE
Absorbs hilltop and seaside into bar

RESEARCH & DEVELOPMENT ZONE
Ring encircling the city

HIGH TECH ZONE
Edge of the city

INTERNATIONAL ZONE
Winds from airport east

CULTURAL ZONE
Occupies interstices between dense programs

ENVIRONMENTAL ZONE
Winds from hills to seaside

WORLD UNIVERSITY
Transgresses and transforms all zones

UTOPIAN POINTS
Points of special programs linked thematically

Overlap
Bands of urban typologies are partly overlapped to create, artificially, a thickness of urban conditions.

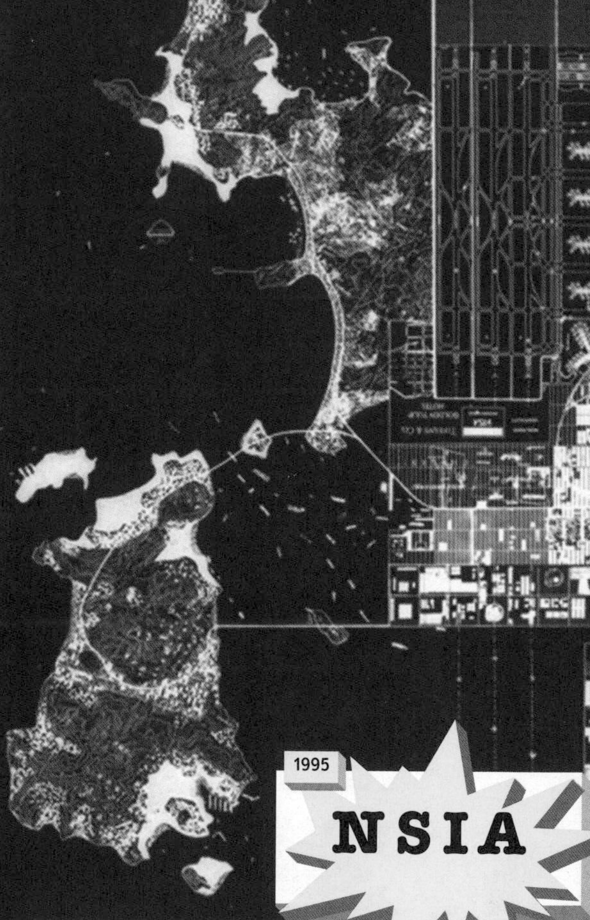

1995

NSIA

NEW SEOUL INTERNATIONAL AIRPORT

Between 1990 and 2000, the number of international air passengers carried to and from the Republic of Korea more than doubled to just under 20 million. The creation a new airport to accommodate this increase represents a massive infrastructural effort: access roads, connections to the city center, and in the case of New Seoul International Airport a vast area of landfill in the sea. Only a part of this effort is exploited by the airport itself, another segment is always redundant - if only because the entire infrastructure is dimensioned for "peaks." At NSIA, a single effort sustains two major ambitions - simultaneously creating the most modern airport and the most modern city.

SPOILED AND UNSPOILED

The coastline between Seoul and Inchon is a combination of exisiting harbor infrastructure and unspoiled seascape. NSIA is a dialogue between these two conditions in which a number of incidents - the islands, the mountains, the sea, but also the sound profiles of airplanes - are used to enrich an urban diagram of extreme efficiency.

Natural and Artificial

A rectangle of artificial land is divided into programatic bands, then deformed and made complex by engaging exceptional natural conditions, so that they disturb the bands to create difference - the universal becomes specific.

城市，让生活更美好
Better City, Better Life

Better City Better Life:
The theme for Shanghai's 2010 Expo.
Shanghai Planning Musuem, April 2003

Shanghai Expon

BY JASON LONG

In the last 15 years, development has transformed Shanghai's center and exploded in its sister city Pudong. In contrast to dispersed developments in the Pearl River Delta, Shanghai has constructed a new image for a compact urban center, a postcard that reads "City of the Future" and "Gateway to China." In 2010, in the wake of this transformation, Shanghai will host China's first World Expo.

COMPACT GATEWAY

Shanghai has long been the least Chinese city in China. In 1842 the Treaty of Nanjing split the city into separate concession zones for the colonial powers and opened the way for an influx of foreign imports, not the least of which were urbanism and architecture. Suppressed during Mao's time, this history has been resurrected as the foundational myth for a new global city. Despite its recent transformation, the city has remained remarkably compact even as its population has grown nearly 50% in the last 20 years.

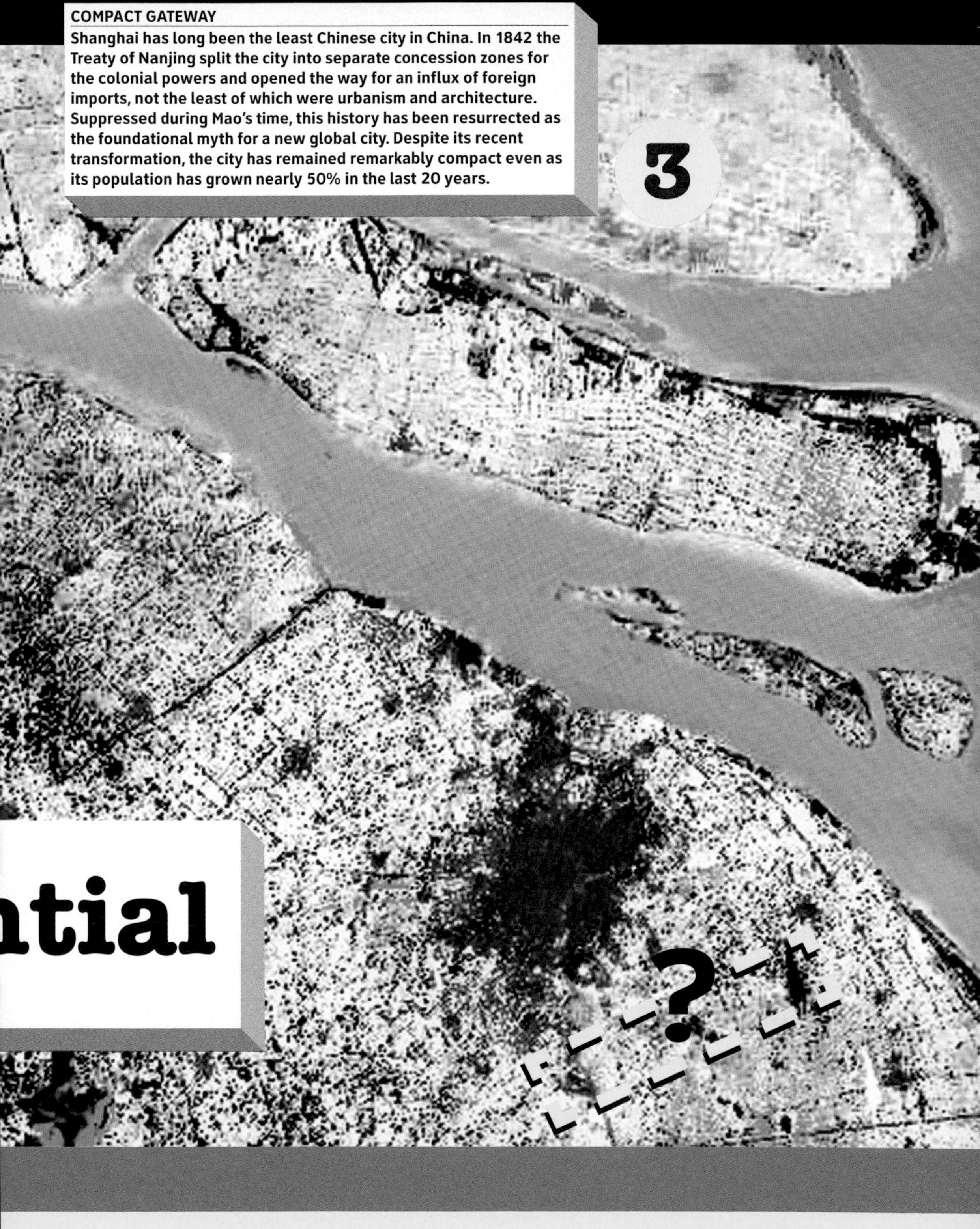

SUCCESS AND FAILURE

Historically, an Expo's success and impact has been linked to both its message and its context. Successful Expo's have always been held in cities with rising GDP growth undergoing radical urbanization. Embracing the potential of modernization and the promise of progress, these Expo's have been catalysts for the development of the city. Given its current trajectory, Shanghai's 2010 World Expo appears doomed to success, but unless Shanghai takes on the responsibility to rethink the current form of the Expo and its role in the city, 2010 will be remembered as yet another wasted opportunity.

EXPO THEME

URBANIZATION

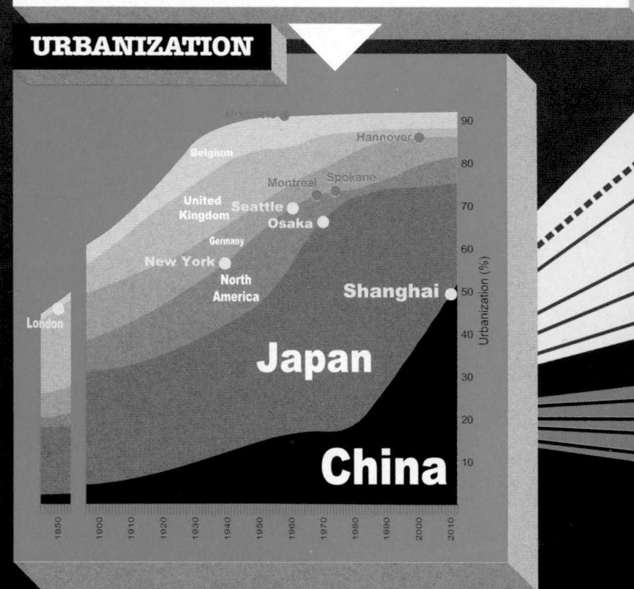

AN EMPTY SHOWCASE

Halfway through the 19th century, the World Expo emerged alongside the city as a showcase for the developments of the industrial revolution. Pavilions on a field housed the technological and urban achievements of newly defined and increasingly competitive nation-states. Today, in the wake of globalization, Expo's have become increasingly irrelevant. The 2000 Hanover Expo, like its logo, became nothing but a blur when it passed. Once linked to the development of city planning and emerging political realities, World Expos have become mere excuses for empty architectural masterpieces.

London 1851

Philadelphia 1876

Paris 1898

Barcelona 1929

1840 | 1851 | 1860 | 1870 | 1880 | 1890 | 1900 | 1910 | 1920

Propeller
Telegraph
Underground railway
Refrigirator
Elevator
Tungsten steel
Telephone
Phonograph
Electric light
Car
Escalator
Air conditioner
Neon light
Synthetic plastic
Color photography
Stainless steel

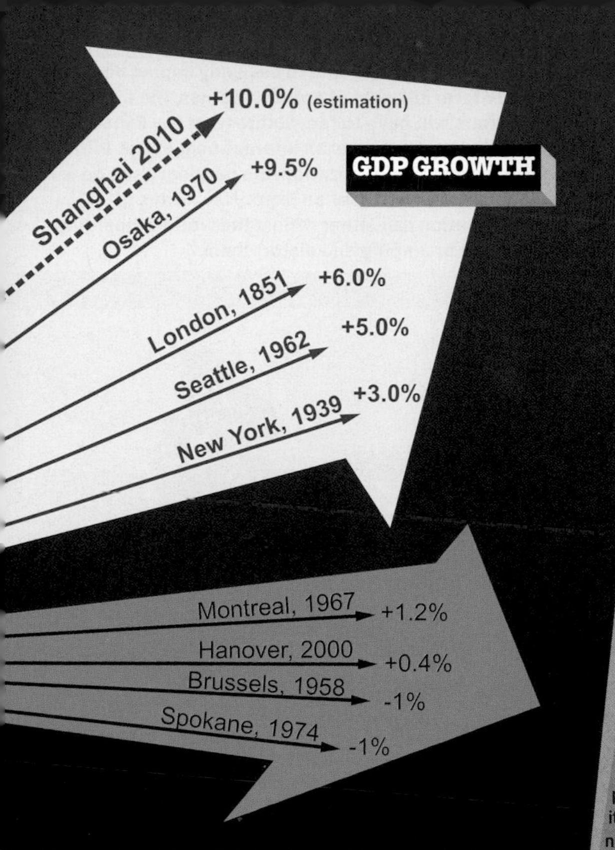

The 1970 Expo in Osaka was the first Asian expo and perhaps the last to have a lasting impact on the popular imagination. Japan's situation was not unlike China today: rapid modernization, an unbelievable urban expansion, and a society undergoing incredible social transformation. Following a masterplan by Kenzo Tange, the Osaka Expo was embedded within the efforts of Japan's architects and planners to theorize these changes. Arata Isozaki's Festival Plaza was conceived as an urban space within the Expo grounds, a place for cultural events and chance meetings. His space-frame acted as an armature for mobile stairs, platforms and screens that could be reconfigured by the events taking place beneath it. In contrast to the point pavillions surrounding it, it presented a new model for architecture's place within the city.

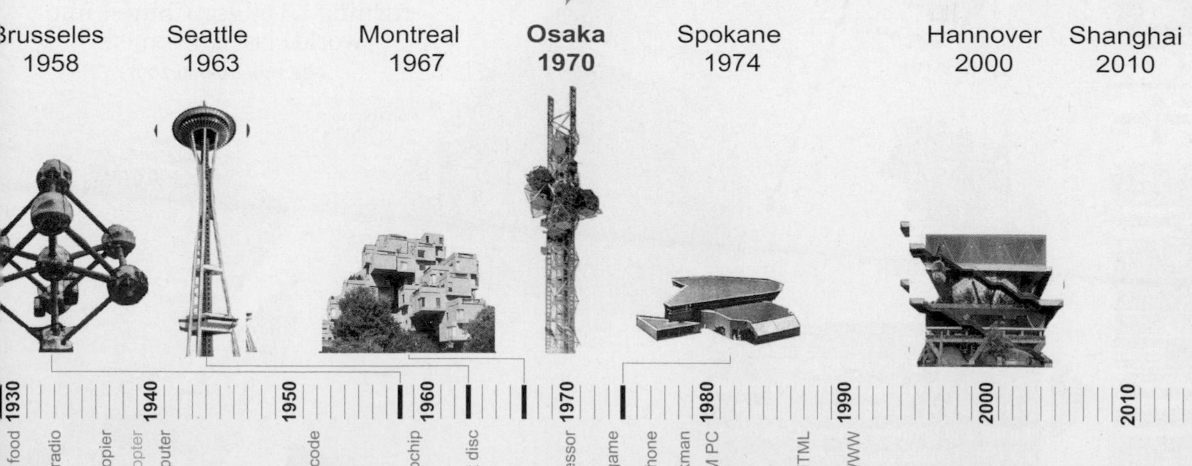

EXPO SITE

The 5.4km2 Expo site can be unfurled throughout the city in strategic configurations that would allow for engagement with Shanghai's future urban development. The Expo becomes a planning tool rather than merely a trope, an active investigation of the city's potential rather than a passive display of its ambitions.

AMO EXPO

If the 2010 Expo is going to have any impact beyond a short-term inflation of property values, the event's planners will have to reevaluate what the Expo means both to the city and as an international event. Within the context of globalization, the national pavilion is no longer a valid form for an Expo. New forms of organization can either reflect the world's emerging realities or amplify and distort them.

single site

linear ring

point expo

exurban expo

consolidated bands

It's impossible to predict how dramatically entry into WTO will change China. But American companies have high hopes of turning 1.3 billion Chinese into world-class consumers.

CBS, November 10, 2001

COLORCODE EXPO

Grouped through seemingly arbitrary relations such as flag color, nations would find themselves in unexpected alliances: the U.S. and North Korea bound together in a feat of architectural fantasy.

GEO-EXPO

G8 summits and IMF meetings have become the de facto expositions of the contemporary world. They are perhaps the only moment of public engagement with the political and economic forces that shape the contemporary city. The turmoil that inevitably surrounds them could be elevated to the status of global celebration. Rather than national pavilions, the arbiters of international capital and global interconnections are given pavilions alongside the anti-globalists that work against them. The emerging alliances and transnational economic agencies that shape the world would for once be put on display.

RICH/POOR EXPO

The economic disparities that have become crucial to the workings of the global economy could be showcased in an Expo battle-royal: poor countries cultivate landscape within the city, while rich countries build pavilions in the periphery.

seoul: 37°30'N 127°0'E

Togok

Slim is beautiful.

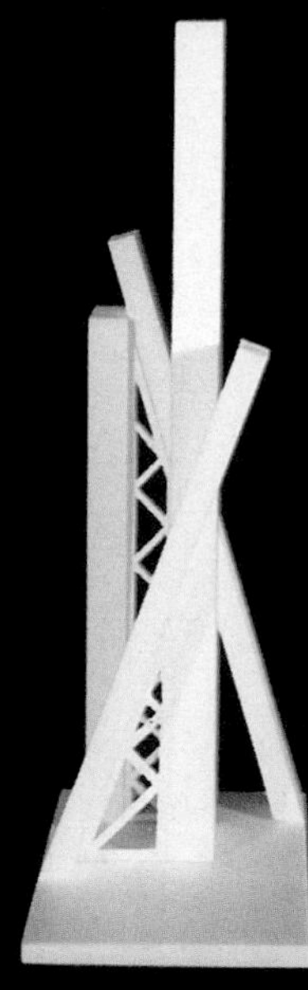

Togok Towers

There has been no real "invention" in the skyscraper since the '70s. Their structural principles have remained stagnant - the Tower as Tube: the taller, the deeper its plan, the further removed its floor space from daylight and Tower as Pyramid: the taller, the broader its base, the vast majority of its accommodation in its dark lower half, an elitist fraction at the top.

What if the inevitable structural diagram of the triangle is configured by individual members? Instead of the obvious stability of narrow top and wide base, a composite stability of slender members that combines accommodation with structure. Instead of the blatancy of the bloated, the mutual support of the slender. In such configurations, the self-evidence of the single core could be replaced by distributed cores that connect at points where individual towers intersect. In Togok - intended as HQ for Samsung Electronics in Seoul, victim of the "Asian Crisis" - the composite model is conceived for a super-high rise of implausible slenderness that is launched from a stable base - 200 meters in the air - formed by the convergence in space of three separate structures, locked together by a single structural strap.

The entire 400 meters of the tower complex consists of spaces free of the gloom that the deep plan of the contemporary super-high rise implies. The distributed core enables innovations on the ground - towers floating in space without touching the earth, unexpected transparencies, a skyscraper with a light touch....

hEUMER@WXS.NL

hEUMER

Irma Boom Office
irmaboom@xs4all.nl

12/November/03

Below 30% urbanization, the balance between city and country feels organic - two mutually reinforcing identities. Above that percentage, the advance of the city triggers alarm: as its growth accelerates, it becomes artificial; modernization takes hold. The city is now an artifact that has to be questioned, thought, planned.

Between 1900 and 1980, when their cities more than doubled, Europe and America produced their key manifestos, always along two axes - the vertical of maximum concentration (Corbusier's "Voisin"), the horizontal of maximum distribution (Wright's "Broadacre") - in an avalanche of arguments, alternatives, dogmas, and Utopias. The stream stopped abruptly exactly at the moment where urbanization on both continents reached a plateau, around the '70s: now tracts were written not about how the city *should* be constructed, but based on interpretations of the city as it *existed*. Still the categories remained - Las Vegas as a form of distribution to the point of virtuality (Venturi), and New York as the archetype of concentration (RK). In this stagnant phase, America and Europe mostly produce doubt about the contemporary city and nostalgia for the past (New Urbanism, Krier, Prince of Wales).

Asia is modernizing at three times the speed of its predecessors - urbanization doubling every 20-30 years, but Europe and America are no longer thinking - not for themselves, not for others. We export the two most sterile outcomes of the vertical and the horizontal - the skyscraper and the "themed" (often gated) suburb - and witness Asia's urbanization with cruel smugness. The final chapter of modernization is taking place in an intellectual void partly of our making....

Urbanization (%)

80
70
60
50
40
30
20
10

North America

Eu

Howard, *Garden Cities of Tomorrow* - 1900
Otto Wagner, *The Megacity* - 1911
T. Garnier, *Une cite industriele* - 1917
Taut, *Die Aufloesung der Staedte* - 1920
Corbusier, Ville Contemporaine - 1922
Corbusier, Plan Voisin - 1925
CIAM, *Athens Charter* - 1933
Wright, Broadacre City - 1935
Saarinen, *The City* - 1943
Bolz, *Die sechzehn Grundsaetze des Staedtebaus* - 1950
Liang, *Beijing: A Masterpiece of Urban Planning* - 1951
Bolotnikov, Beijing Masterplan - 1953
Constant, New Babylon - 1956
Lynch, *Image of the City* - 1960
Kikutake, et. al., *Metabolism* - 1960

1900
1910
1920
1930
1940
1950
1960

 Because the west stopped thinking about what the Metropolis - the Olympics, the World's Fair -

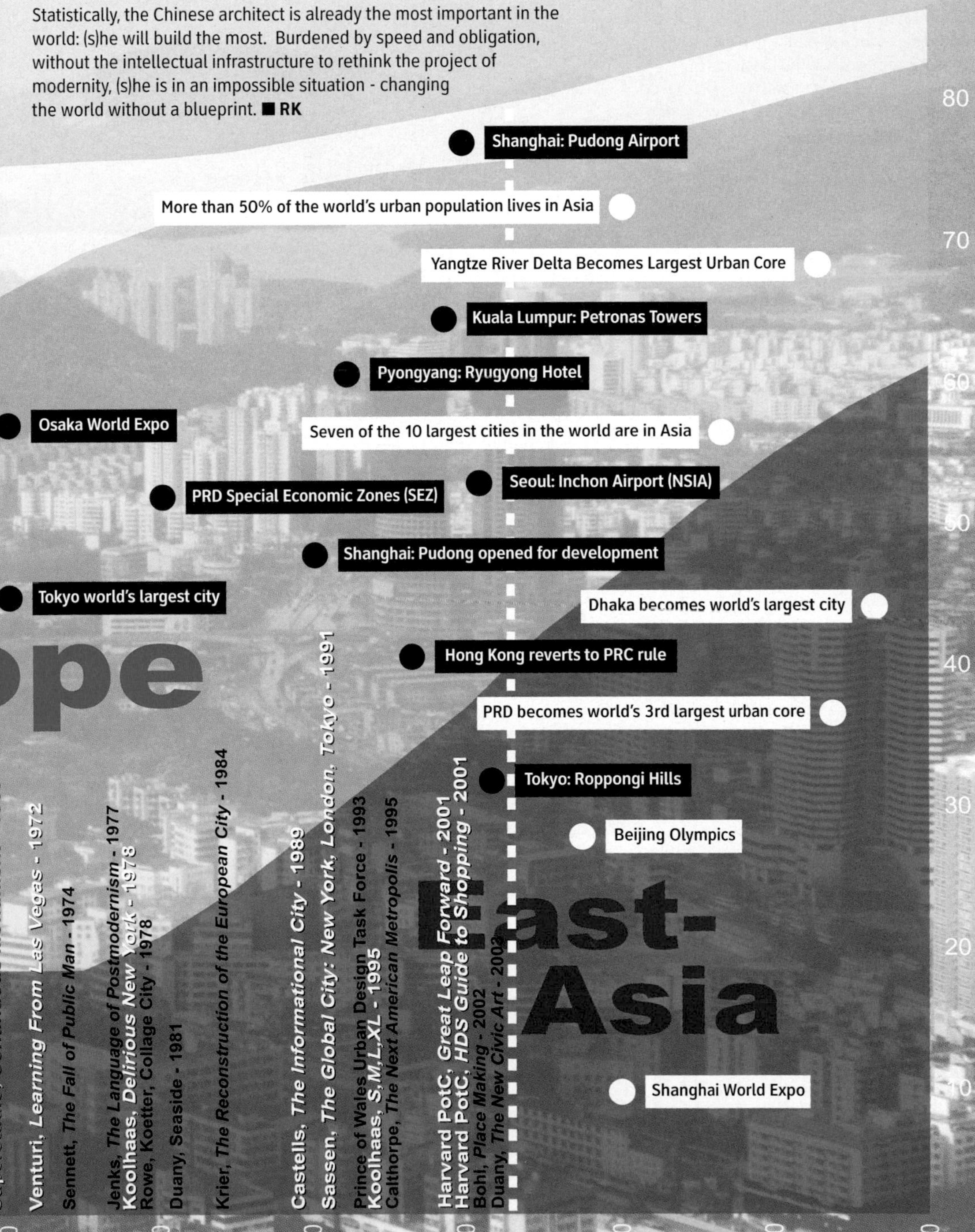
Statistically, the Chinese architect is already the most important in the world: (s)he will build the most. Burdened by speed and obligation, without the intellectual infrastructure to rethink the project of modernity, (s)he is in an impossible situation - changing the world without a blueprint. ■ RK
Shanghai: Pudong Airport
More than 50% of the world's urban population lives in Asia
Yangtze River Delta Becomes Largest Urban Core
Kuala Lumpur: Petronas Towers
Pyongyang: Ryugyong Hotel
Osaka World Expo
Seven of the 10 largest cities in the world are in Asia
Seoul: Inchon Airport (NSIA)
PRD Special Economic Zones (SEZ)
Shanghai: Pudong opened for development
Tokyo world's largest city
Dhaka becomes world's largest city
Hong Kong reverts to PRC rule
PRD becomes world's 3rd largest urban core
Tokyo: Roppongi Hills
Beijing Olympics
Shanghai World Expo
ope
East-Asia
Superstudio, Continuous Monument - 1969
Venturi, Learning From Las Vegas - 1972
Sennett, The Fall of Public Man - 1974
Jenks, The Language of Postmodernism - 1977
Koolhaas, Delirious New York - 1978
Rowe, Koetter, Collage City - 1978
Duany, Seaside - 1981
Krier, The Reconstruction of the European City - 1984
Castells, The Informational City - 1989
Sassen, The Global City: New York, London, Tokyo - 1991
Prince of Wales Urban Design Task Force - 1993
Koolhaas, S,M,L,XL - 1995
Calthorpe, The Next American Metropolis - 1995
Harvard PotC, Great Leap Forward - 2001
Harvard PotC, HDS Guide to Shopping - 2001
Bohl, Place Making - 2002
Duany, The New Civic Art - 2002
80
70
60
50
40
30
20
10
1970
1980
1990
2000
2010
2020
2030
Sources: United Nations, World Urbanization Prospects; Bairoch, Cities and Economic Development

could be, it offers no further alternatives for its ultimate dissemination in Asia.

Conservation Planning of 25 Historic Areas in Beijing Old C
Beijing Municipal Planning Commision, 2002

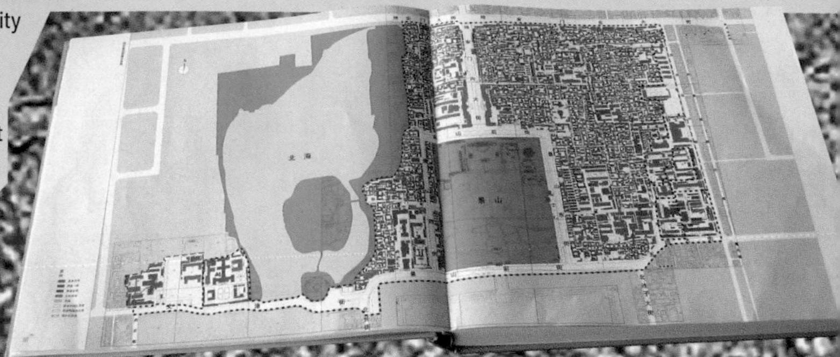

The traditional substance of the Chinese city is the hutong – a mat of courtyards impressive for its intimacy and versatility, but often casual in its construction. In a society that is modernizing with passion, it is perhaps hard to share the passionate defense of the past that characterizes societies that have their modernization behind them. But responding to internal and foreign criticism, the issue is now taken very seriously by Beijing's planners.

"All the News That's Fit to Print"

The New Yor

NEW YORK, SUNDAY, MARCH

CUNY
On Stu

Plan Wou

A Burst of Renewal Sweeps Old Beijing Into the Dumpsters

New York Times, 01/March/98

197

 Is there a way to avoid the apparently inevitable conflict between preservation and modernization

Beijing Preservation

Beijing Planning Office model showing the 6.6 x 8.8 km low rise area surrounding the Forbidden City

991

Does the growth of Beijing automatically imply the destruction of its past?

Beijing Now

BY HOU HANRU

Beijing is going through the most drastic mutation in its history, and perhaps the most radical process of urban transformation in Chinese history. In the last decade, Beijing has shifted from a typically Chinese capital city with all the trademarks of traditional Chinese urbanism, to become a truly global city. Originally more conservative than other cities in China, such as Shanghai or Shenzhen, today it is becoming one of the most extreme examples of an entirely new form of urbanity. For the next decade, spurred by the increasing euphoria of development and the 2008 Olympic games, this process will accelerate still further.

Traditionally, Beijing had been an enclosed city, typically represented by its gridded streets, based on square courtyards, or *Sihe Yuan*. This particular kind of grid, an expression of the ideology of the imperial Chinese political system, was based on clusters of defined family units rather than typical, informal urban communities.

The culture of Beijing is something between urban and rural. This has resulted in a local orientation that is considerably more conservative and stable than those of the cities along the east coast of China, such as Guangzhou and Shanghai. Today, Beijing's citizens are faced with a dramatic challenge: to remove themselves from tradition and build an open, "global" society.

Beijing's particular historical conditions make it a unique city. The question is how to re-interpret its imperial and communist past - a legacy embodied in the urban forms of the forbidden city, the immense avenues, the monumental Soviet-nationalist architectures - with emblems of the new liberal capitalism, exemplified by commercial centers, hotels, office buildings, and luxury residential towers.

By consensus, the hutongs – the generic substance of the Chinese city – are most characteristic of Beijing's "past." The dilemma: "building" is less permanent in Asia; restoration often leads to a harsh reconstruction from zero that removes all traces of authenticity in favor of a rigid, bloated rebuilding. In the name of preservation, the past is made unrecognizable.

Rapid modernization demands new labor forces. Hundreds of thousands of migrant workers from different parts of the country, both urban and rural, are streaming into the capital, while the international population continues to grow. Their coming has not only considerably increased the city's population, but has also altered the very structure of its social life and culture.

Vertically, the city is increasingly dominated by commercial high rises. They form a semi-private territory throughout the city. How can new forms of public space be developed at a time when space is becoming increasingly privatized? The answer is perhaps found in the least spectacular actions: re-introducing informal urban fragments - self-organizing, constantly transforming, "dark" communes, or *quartiers* - to inform and deconstruct the "highly efficient," linear structure embodied by the flamboyantly lit ring roads and skyscrapers. In order to grasp this moment of radical transition, urban life should get back to the street level. It should negotiate with the problem of security and control in a more "unsecured," "uncontrolled" way to absorb the tension of urban urgency.

Beijing should encourage an urbanism of maximized flexibility, openness, spontaneity, and interaction between people and their environment; it should sponsor "disorder" as a form of compensation for the market's fanatical search for efficiency and "brightness." This is also to encourage the mutual movements and dynamic negotiations between different social groups, communities, and classes - encouraging self-organization and the complication of social structures through informal, DIY actions. Ultimately, it is urgent to search for alternative forms of existence and urban (re)organization - self-organization and social/ communal independence against the overwhelmingly hegemonic, market-driven political system. ■

and "restorations" contaminate the object of our desire. Then we don't like the old anymore.

EAST # The Invention of

Piranesi, Self Portrait

1877: Society for the Protection of Ancient Buildings (England)

1851: Ruskin - *Stones of Venice*

1844: Viollet-le-Duc - Carcassonne Restoration

1790: Commission for Art and Monuments (France)

1742: Piranesi - *The Sights of Rome*

ZIPPER 1910
COMBUSTION ENGINE 1876
OIL 1859 MOVING PICTURES 1877
RAYON 1855 DEISEL ENGINE 1892
MICROPHONE 1827 NEON LIGHT 1901
TIN CAN 1810 PASTEURISATION 1856 TRACTOR 1904
GAS LIGHTING 1804 PLASTIC 1862 ZEPPELIN 1900 TANK 1
LITHOGRAPHY 1798 ELECTROMAGNET 1825 MODEL T 1908
SMALLPOX VACCINATION 1796 MACHINE GUN 1862 ROBOT
BICYCLE 1791 RAILROAD 1830 TYPEWRITER 1867 HELICOPTER
STEEL ROLLER 1783 BLUEPRINT 1840 TELEPHONE 1876 SONAR
BIFOCAL EYEGLASSES 1780 MORSE CODE 1838 ESCALATOR 1900
SPINNING JENNY 1764 STETHOSCOPE 1819 LIGHT BULB 1879 PYREX 19
POWER LOOM 1764 SPECTROSCOPE 1814 DYNAMITE 1866 VACUUM 1899
THERMOMETER 1724 HOT-AIR BALLOON 1783 ANASTHESIA 1846 RADAR 1887 INSULIN
STEAM ENGINE 1712 SPINNING FRAME 1768 PORTLAND CEMENT 1824 MAIL ORDER 1872
LIGHTNING ROD 1701 CHROMATIC LENS 1758 PHOTOGRAPH 1814 GLIDER 1853 AC MOTOR 1888
SLIDE RULE 1614 TELESCOPE 1668 TUNING FORK 1711 SEXTANT 1758 COTTON GIN 1793 REFRIGERATOR 1834 FLIGHT 1903

1650 1700 1750 1800 1850 1900

There are two key dates to the invention of preservation - the first in 1790 just after the French Revolution in France and the second in 1877 in the middle of the Victorian Age in England. From 1600 to 1900 the quantity of modern inventions escalated. Preservation was invented at the moment that modernization gained speed....

Re-reading Preservation

BY EMILIE GOMART

The two founding documents of the modern preservation movement, the *Athens Charter* of 1931 and the *Venice Charter* of 1964, define preservation as inaction, the inverse of architectural production. The 1931 Charter describes historical monuments as "entails" to be "passed on" without transformation. The 1964 Charter prohibits creative intervention: "no new constructions," "no demolition or modification," "no alteration of mass or colour," do not "separate," do not "move." Both texts established an oppositional logic that continues to operate today. Despite the absolutist tone of their directives, each relies upon a set of concepts that arose within a particular historical moment. The concept of "heritage," an invention of the French Revolution, forms the basis of the first; John Ruskin's *Stones of Venice*, the mythological underpinnings of the second. Upon closer examination, these origins reveal a more complex reality behind the motives and operations of preservation.

The French Revolution, 1789

During the French Revolution, huge numbers of objects were labeled "insults" and "offences" to Republicanism; entire towns could be denied the right to existence: "In the name of the Sovereignty of the People...we strike to death this abode of crime whose royal magnificence was an insult to the poverty of the people and the simplicity of republican morals."[1] Time itself was represented as a young woman smashing the symbols of monarchy.[2] Within this tumult, selections were made between objects that would be melted, pulverized, or burnt and those that might continue to endure.

Piranesi, Etching: Roman Ruins
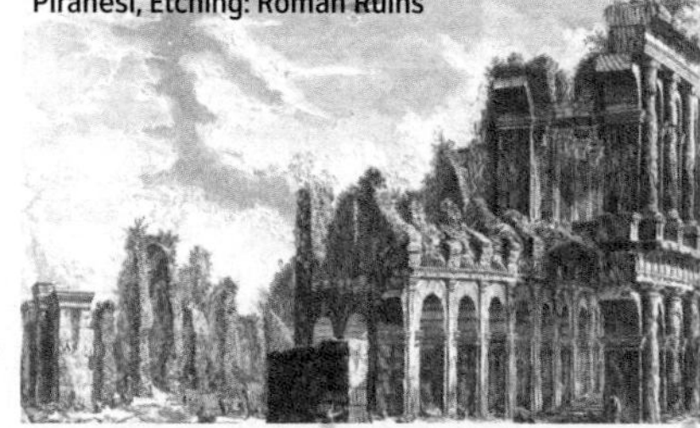

The term "heritage" (*patrimoine*) was introduced as a juridical instrument in 1790 to ward off the degradations and destruction of revolutionary "vandals." Objects and structures came to be appraised for their "historical and artistic value," a value which "resides in the fact that it represents a particular stage, in some sense unique, of the development of a domain of the creation of man."[3] The concept of heritage implied that the value of an object was made all the greater if it had remained unchanged since its (supposed) moment of completion. Though it is extremely difficult to date the Chateau de Versailles or its gardens, promoters of "heritage" sought to stall any further degradation and put into motion techniques for "freezing" objects.

By distinguishing between sign and signified, it became possible to say that the Porte St. Denis, originally dedicated to Louis XIV, "deserves the hatred of free citizens... but it is a masterpiece," and that

Like the steam engine, preservation is an "invention," in fact it is part of the repertoire of invention
The apparent collision between preservation and modernity has disrupted our discourse on the city

"a sceptre is not a sceptre," but "a piece of 14th century goldsmith art."[4] The object or structure was reduced to the status of a text, narrating a history (of "art" or of "France") and staged alongside other texts, catalogues, and *bons mots*.[5] Preservation of "historical and artistic heritage" was an aggressive act of selection, de-contextualization, and exhibition: for the first time, movable objects were transported into museums, churches closed to worship but opened to amateurs of art, mansions and castles gutted of their inhabitants and opened to non-aristocratic visitors.[6]

"Heritage" thus referred not to inaction but to an enormous transformation of objects and forms. Heritage was not only what was done to objects to avoid catastrophe, it was the physical trace in the object of historical catastrophe. The object's material transformation (de-contextualisation, musealization, publicization, narratization) was achieved by a particular architect, the French Revolution, a large-scale and catastrophic force outside any creative hand's control.

Ruskin's *Stones of Venice*, 1851

Implicitly referring to Ruskin's *The Stones of Venice*, the 1964 Venice Charter invokes a 19th century art and society critic who, 50 years after the French Revolution, argued for a passive preservation of buildings against Viollet-le-Duc's active, artistic "restoration." Ruskin was motivated by what he saw as the discoloring or "graying" effects of industrialization on buildings, and his distrust of the 19th century architect's capacity to ever invent a "new style" that would be "worthy of our engines and telegraphs; as expansive as steam, and as sparkling as electricity."[7]

"A building cannot be considered in its prime until four or five centuries have passed over it."

JOHN RUSKIN

{Authenticity}

Ruskin's ruins, depicted in his numerous watercolors, looked nothing like the destructions of historical violence or the musealized objects of the French Revolution's aftermath.[8] Ruins represented not destruction, but gradual decline. A building, Ruskin wrote, should not be appreciated merely for the architectural elements designed by men. "[The] greatest glory of a building is not in its stones, nor is it in its gold, its glory is in its Age, and in that deep sense of voicefulness, of stern watching, of mysterious sympathy, nay, even of approval or condemnation, which we feel in walls that have long been washed by the passing waves of humanity."[9] Ruskin

Viollet Le Duc:
Resoration of Carcassonne, France

was fascinated by a building's patina, the impact of accidents that came after the human act of architectural creation: "[In] architecture... accidental beauty[10]... consists in the mere sublimity of the rents, or fractures, or stains, or vegetation, which assimilate the architecture with the work of Nature."[11]

For Ruskin, value was everywhere in the building where traces of the creator's hand were washed and worn away. This "timely decay" was not a simple abandonment of the object to wind, humidity, frost, and vegetation: it required an active selection and guidance of forces that exerted themselves in a slow, predictable, rhythmic[12] manner and the exclusion of the catastrophic or staccato forces, natural and human, which might accelerate decline, hack into or disintegrate the object in un-picturesque ways. For Ruskin, "building to age" is a creative act which gives itself over to but also anticipates a series of destructive physical forces.

When Ruskin's writing is interpreted as recommending "neutral," "photographic," observation, then preservation leads to a un-inventive, "neutral," "passive" form of protection. But if we consider that Ruskin's favorite painter was Turner, and that the reason for this appreciation was the "accuracy" of his eye, it becomes possible to say that a fateful mistake is made when Ruskin is equated with defensive, minimal preservation rather than with artful, creative preservation. The nature of "creation," however, has been significantly re-defined. It is not the wilful, conceptual activity that Viollet-Le-Duc describes in his *Entretiens*. For Ruskin, the creative artist commits himself to the strict observation of phenomena "outside" himself. Only under these conditions of subjection to external phenomena does true creativity emerge.[13] In a similar way, preservation can be re-read as a rigorous attentiveness to the phenomena "outside," in an effort not to cancel out but to foster creativity. Re-reading Ruskin, preservation becomes a specific architectural endeavor, a series of techniques for creatively orchestrating the external forces of "timely decay."

Notes

1. Dario Gamboni, *The Destruction of Art*, Yale University Press, New Haven, 1997, p.32.
2. Gamboni, op.cit., Chapter 11 'Embellishing Vandalism'.
3. Alois Riegl, *Le Culte moderne des monuments : son essence et sa genese*, Seuil, Paris, 1984 (1903), p.73-5.
4. Ibid, p.35.
5. This was of course the product of a much longer history, see Pommier, op.cit.
6. See Edouard Pommier, 'Naissance des Musees de Province' and Dominique Poulot 'Alexandre Lenoir et les musees des monuments francais' reprinted in Nora (op.cit.), respectively p.1471-1514 and 1515-1544.
7. Ruskin, cited in Kristine Garrigan, *Ruskin on Architecture*, University of Wisconsin Press, Madison, 1973, p.17.
8. Dario Gamboni, (op. cit.), p.33.
9. Ruskin, John, *Seven lamps*, London, 1849, p.339-340
10. Ruskin also uses the term picturesque. On the emergence of the Picturesque in 18th century England, see Woodward, , Christopher In Ruins, Vintage, London, 2001, p.120-121.
11. Ruskin, p.351-352.
12. Ruins, as Georg Simmel later wrote, are works of men "subjected to the inexorable laws of nature." Georg Simmel, "The Ruin," in *Essays on Sociology, philosophy and aesthetics*, ed. Kurt Wolf, New York, Harder, 1965.
13. See P. Ball (op. cit.)

"Reestablish in finshed state."

Eugene-Emmanuel Viollet-Le-Duc, 1954

{Restoration}

that define modernization. The past is only an issue when the future is being constructed. Preservation is an integral part of modernization.

EAST The Onward Mar

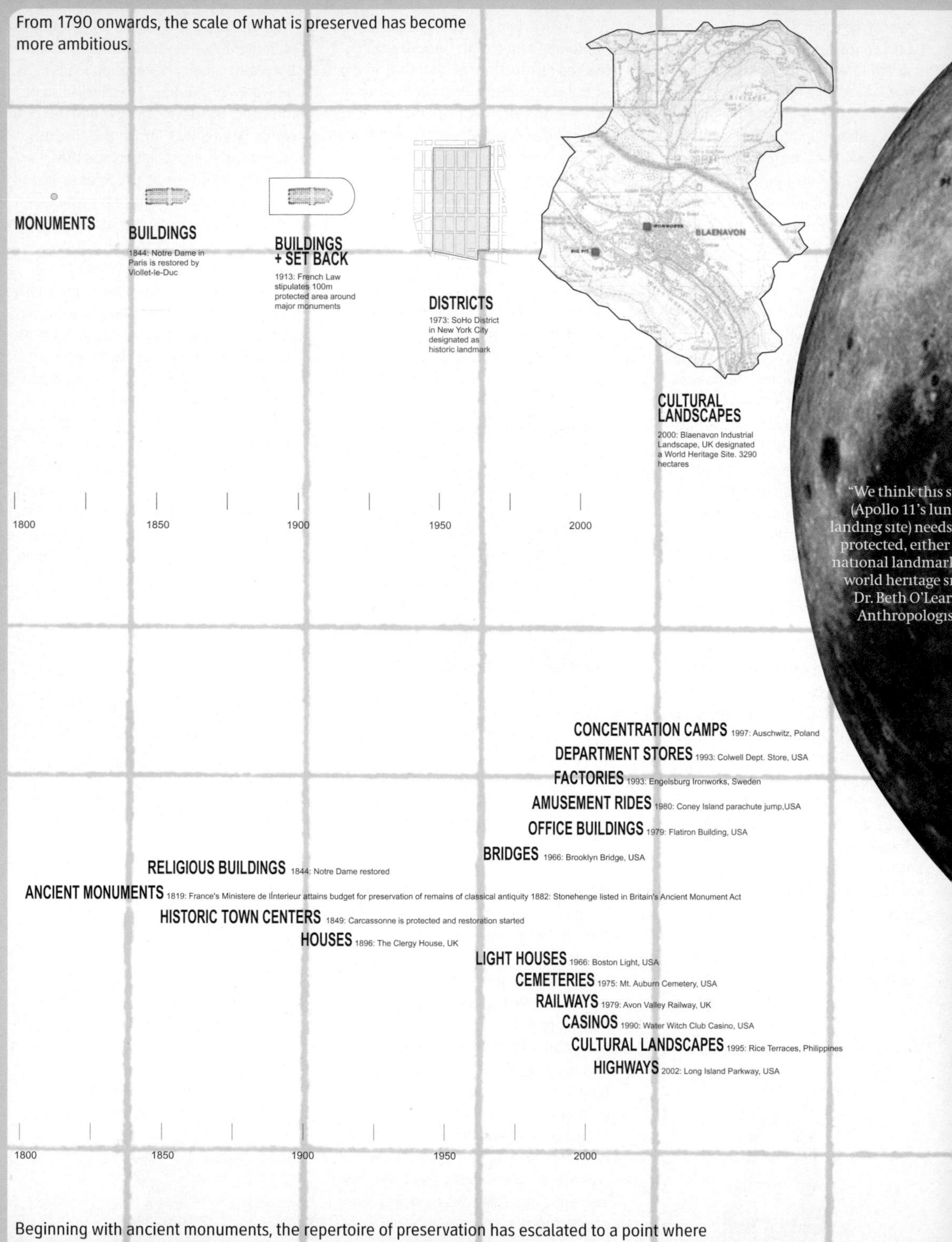
From 1790 onwards, the scale of what is preserved has become more ambitious.
MONUMENTS
BUILDINGS
1844: Notre Dame in Paris is restored by Viollet-le-Duc
BUILDINGS + SET BACK
1913: French Law stipulates 100m protected area around major monuments
DISTRICTS
1973: SoHo District in New York City designated as historic landmark
BLAENAVON
CULTURAL LANDSCAPES
2000: Blaenavon Industrial Landscape, UK designated a World Heritage Site. 3290 hectares
1800
1850
1900
1950
2000
"We think this s
(Apollo 11's lun
landing site) needs
protected, either
national landmar
world heritage si
Dr. Beth O'Lear
Anthropologis
CONCENTRATION CAMPS 1997: Auschwitz, Poland
DEPARTMENT STORES 1993: Colwell Dept. Store, USA
FACTORIES 1993: Engelsburg Ironworks, Sweden
AMUSEMENT RIDES 1980: Coney Island parachute jump,USA
OFFICE BUILDINGS 1979: Flatiron Building, USA
BRIDGES 1966: Brooklyn Bridge, USA
RELIGIOUS BUILDINGS 1844: Notre Dame restored
ANCIENT MONUMENTS 1819: France's Ministere de lÍnterieur attains budget for preservation of remains of classical antiquity 1882: Stonehenge listed in Britain's Ancient Monument Act
HISTORIC TOWN CENTERS 1849: Carcassonne is protected and restoration started
HOUSES 1896: The Clergy House, UK
LIGHT HOUSES 1966: Boston Light, USA
CEMETERIES 1975: Mt. Auburn Cemetery, USA
RAILWAYS 1979: Avon Valley Railway, UK
CASINOS 1990: Water Witch Club Casino, USA
CULTURAL LANDSCAPES 1995: Rice Terraces, Philippines
HIGHWAYS 2002: Long Island Parkway, USA
1800
1850
1900
1950
2000
Beginning with ancient monuments, the repertoire of preservation has escalated to a point where it includes practically all typologies that make up the current environment.

 Seemingly in opposition to development, the current scale and thrust of the combined preservation construction are in fact twin phenomena, not opposites. They could be part of a single "planning"

# of Preservation

The arguments for preservation have become steadily more political over time, expressed now in the language of cultural correctness.

HISTORICAL MONUMENTS ARE TO BE GIVEN STRICT CUSTODIAL PROTECTION
ANCIENT MONUMENTS
WARDENS OF CIVILIZATION
PROPERTY OF MANKIND
EXPERTS UNANIMOUSLY AGREED

RESPECT FOR ORIGINAL MATERIAL
HAND ON IN FULL AUTHENTICITY
MAINTAIN PERMANENTLY
EVALUATION
SAFEGUARDING

GLOBAL RESPECT AND UNDERSTANDING
LEGITIMACY OF THE CULTURAL VALUES OF ALL
HERITAGE DIVERSITY
FUNDAMENTAL CULTURAL VALUES
AUTHENTICITY IS A VALUE JUDGEMENT

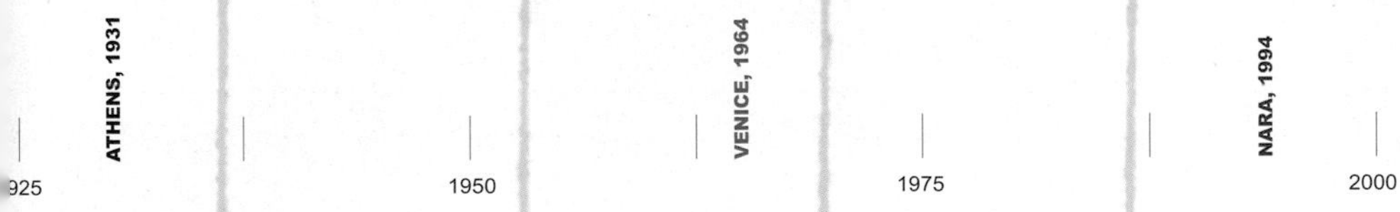

Preservation charters and declarations

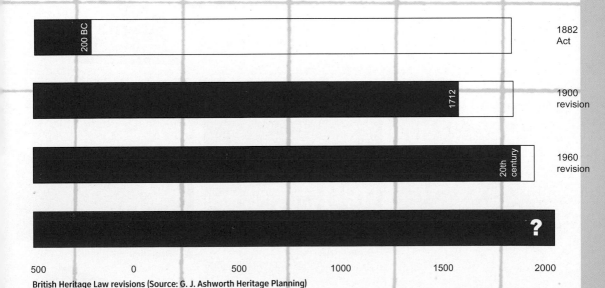

British Heritage Law revisions (Source: G. J. Ashworth Heritage Planning)

The interval between the object and the moment of its "preservation" has decreased from about two millennia in 1882 to mere decades today. Soon, the interval will disappear. In a radical shift from the retrospective to the prospective, we will then have to decide what to preserve before we build. Some structures will be conceived to last, others to have a limited life span. Preservation will introduce a deliberate phase difference in the texture of the city. We will invest ourselves more in long lasting construction - and perhaps have more fun with short-term architecture.

effort in fact suggests a parallel universe of alternative planning. Preservation and discipline that ultimately decides the duration of any construction...

AMO Preservatio

Beijing could reinvent preservation by expanding its agenda and introducing it as a parallel planning of the city, rather than depending on existing practices and approaches.

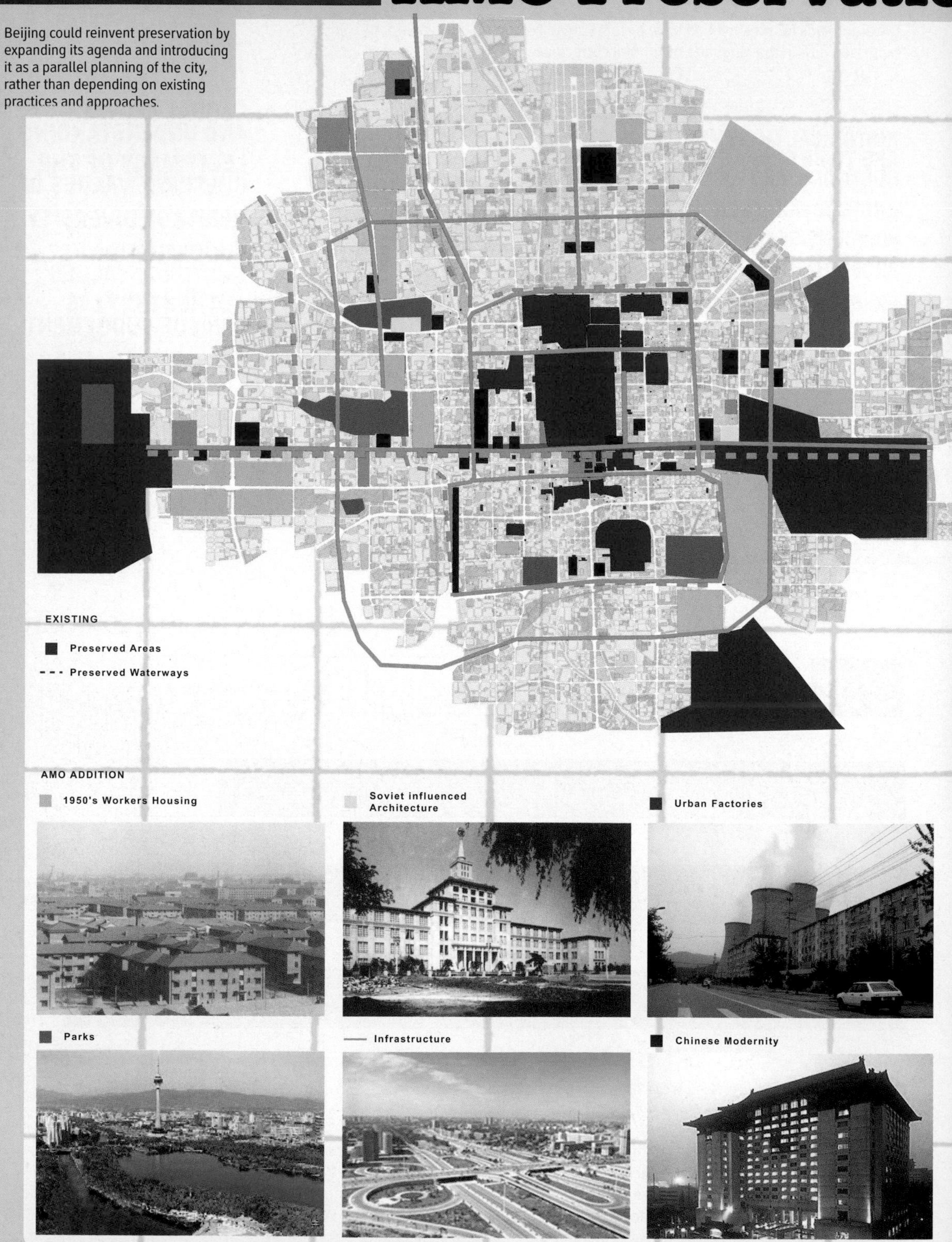

 If the point of preservation is to identify and keep the elements that make a given city unique, urban situations that deserves the same consideration as the "old" center.

Instead of a seemingly inevitable focus on the center - the oldest, the most beautiful, the most historic part - different models of preservation can be imagined: an infinite wedge could record, systematically and without esthetic bias, all the developments that have occurred in an urban system over time; a point grid could act as a form of sampling, a "statistical" preservation model where every condition is captured in the form of samples.

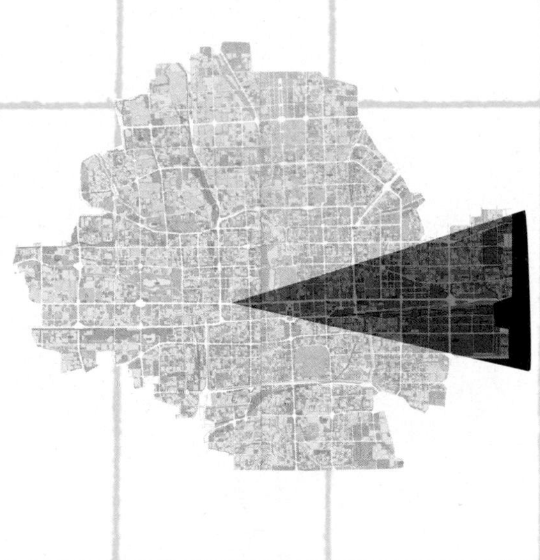

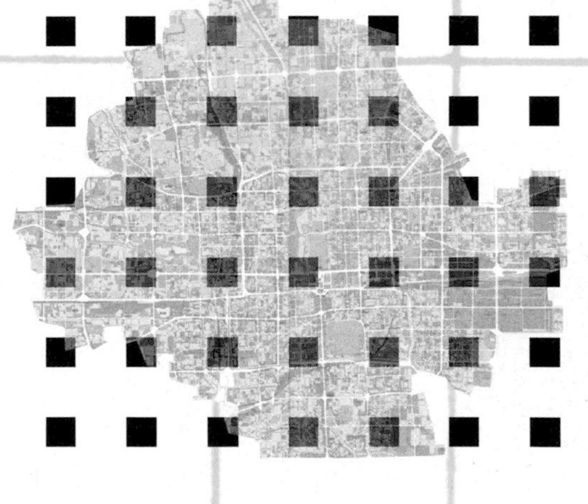

Political Space

Beijing, through its recent history contains a vast arsenal of relatively new architecture and

Preservation as C

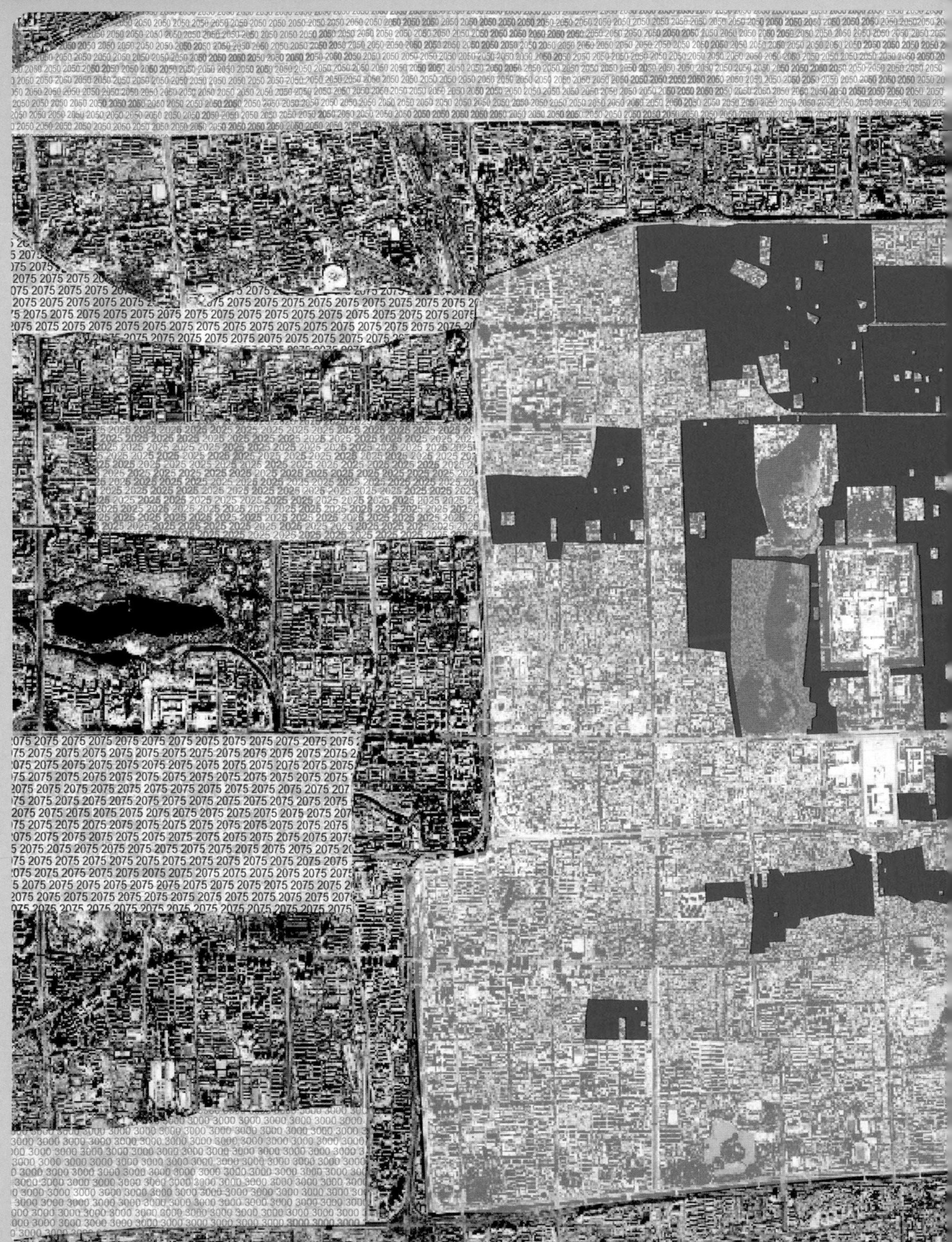

 By adopting a forward-looking interpretation of preservation, Beijing can be the first to experimen

p Rotation

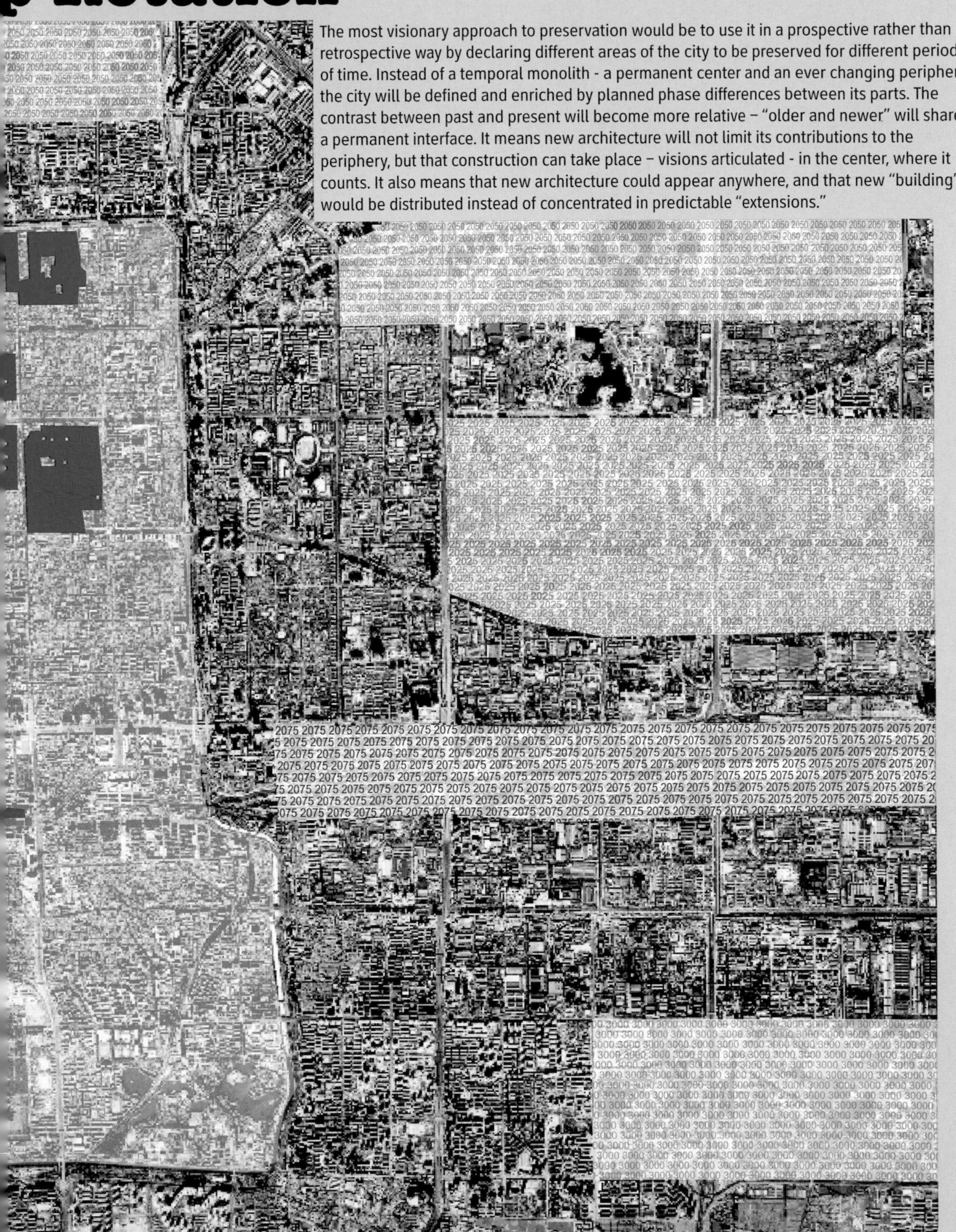

The most visionary approach to preservation would be to use it in a prospective rather than retrospective way by declaring different areas of the city to be preserved for different periods of time. Instead of a temporal monolith - a permanent center and an ever changing periphery, the city will be defined and enriched by planned phase differences between its parts. The contrast between past and present will become more relative – "older and newer" will share a permanent interface. It means new architecture will not limit its contributions to the periphery, but that construction can take place – visions articulated - in the center, where it counts. It also means that new architecture could appear anywhere, and that new "building" would be distributed instead of concentrated in predictable "extensions."

vith a comprehensive, time-based ecology of historical substance.

20
中国中

电视台

Virtual Meeting | Street Parade | Event Sample Formats: | Sound Scape | Fashion Show

ARCHIS R.S.V.P. EVENTS

Response-based Events; A Quest for Ideas, Spirit and Action
featuring You, Archis and AMO

EVENT NO. 08 OF 09

Bejing, December 2004

TIME

Often, all too often, architecture denies time. It challenges eternity and aspires to permanence. It poses for the photographer as a frozen tableau, unsullied by mortality. The question is what happens when we approach architecture from the opposite direction, not from a longing for perfection, but from the viewpoint of the ravages of time. Can there be an architecture that gives, rather than takes time?
An event about making things happen, about not standing still.

If you are interested in the CONTENT, please reply to this page by fax, or email your response to rsvp@archis.org, giving your name, profession and number of reservations before August 15 2004. We'll get back to you with details about the time, place and form of event in due course. More info at **www.archis.org** or **Archis Magazine**

PLEASE FILL IN THIS FIELD

I hereby make a reservation for RSVP event no. 09: TIME
By making this reservation, I co-determine the size of the forthcoming event.

name: number of reservations:

e-mail address:

phone number:

profession:

fax +31 20 3203927 or e-mail rsvp@archis.org

ARCHIS R.S.V.P. EVENTS are a series of actions that will be organized all over the world from December 2003 onwards. The form of each event is determined by the size of the response; in other words, you just respond to the content and your response helps us to determine the actual form of the event which might be anything from mass demonstration to free-running, from cruise to performance; from mega event to flash mob.

Event Sample Formats: | Event Sample Formats: | Happening | Event Sample Formats: | Rave

ARCHIS R.S.V.P. EVENTS

Response-based Events; A Quest for Ideas, Spirit and Action featuring You, Archis and AMO

EVENT NO. 09 OF 09

Shanghai, November 2004

HERITAGE

Ancient sculptures of Buddha destroyed; Korans in flames; decaying monuments of Western civilization. In the light of looting and destruction, of amnesia and total indifference, an important issue has arisen. We may start to wonder whether history represent any value.

In a climate of colossal forgetting the fundamental question is no longer which history counts, but whether history counts at all.
An event about the art of memory.

If you are interested in the CONTENT, please reply to this page by fax, or email your response to rsvp@archis.org, giving your name, profession and number of reservations before August 15 2004. We'll get back to you with details about the time, place and form of event in due course. More info at **www.archis.org** or **Archis Magazine**

PLEASE FILL IN THIS FIELD

I hereby make a reservation for RSVP event no. 10: HERITAGE
By making this reservation, I co-determine the size of the forthcoming event.

name: number of reservations:

e-mail address:

phone number:

profession:

fax +31 20 3203927 or e-mail rsvp@archis.org

ARCHIS R.S.V.P. EVENTS are a series of actions that will be organized all over the world from December 2003 onwards. The form of each event is determined by the size of the response; in other words, you just respond to the content and your response helps us to determine the actual form of the event which might be anything from mass demonstration to free-running, from cruise to performance; from mega event to flash mob.

HIGH-RISE

On the last day of August 2003, the number of Asian high rise buildings surpassed that of North America for the first time.

In recent years, Asia has hosted a race to the sky, with several rapidly-developing countries scrambling to erect the tallest skyscraper. On 17 October 2003, the final structural beam on the Taipei 101 building was raised into place, making it the world's tallest building - more than 50 meters taller than the former world #1, the Petronas Towers in Kuala Lumpur, Malaysia.

In the west, pundits continue to debate the viability of the skyscraper post 9-11, apparently unaware that in most of the world the high-rise has become a pre-requisite.

Source: www.worldskyscrapers.com

Woolworth Building - Cass Gilbert

Chrysler Building William van Alen

Empire State Building - Shreve, Lamb & Harmon Associates

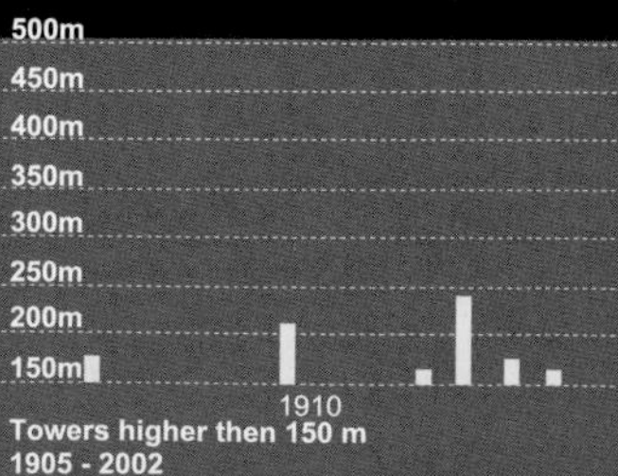

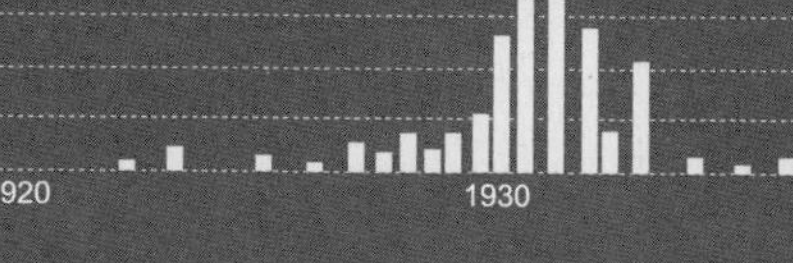

Towers higher then 150 m
1905 - 2002

Taipei 101
Urbanized Population
< 20 %
20 - 40 %
40 - 60 %
60 - 80 %
> 80 %
Toronto Dominion Bank Tower - Ludwig Mies van der Rohe
Sears Tower - S.O.M.
Menara Maybank - Hijjas Kasturi
Central Plaza HK - DLN Architects
Petronas Tower - Cesar Pelli
Commerzbank Tower - Sir Norman Foster
Taipei 101 - C.Y. Lee & Partners
1960
1970
1980
1990
2000

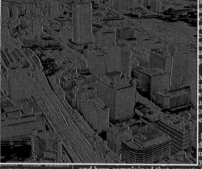

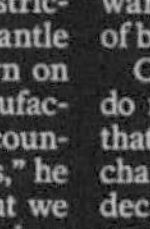

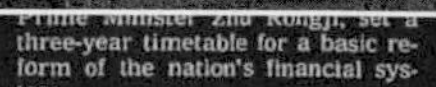
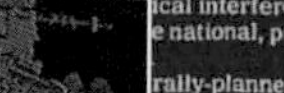

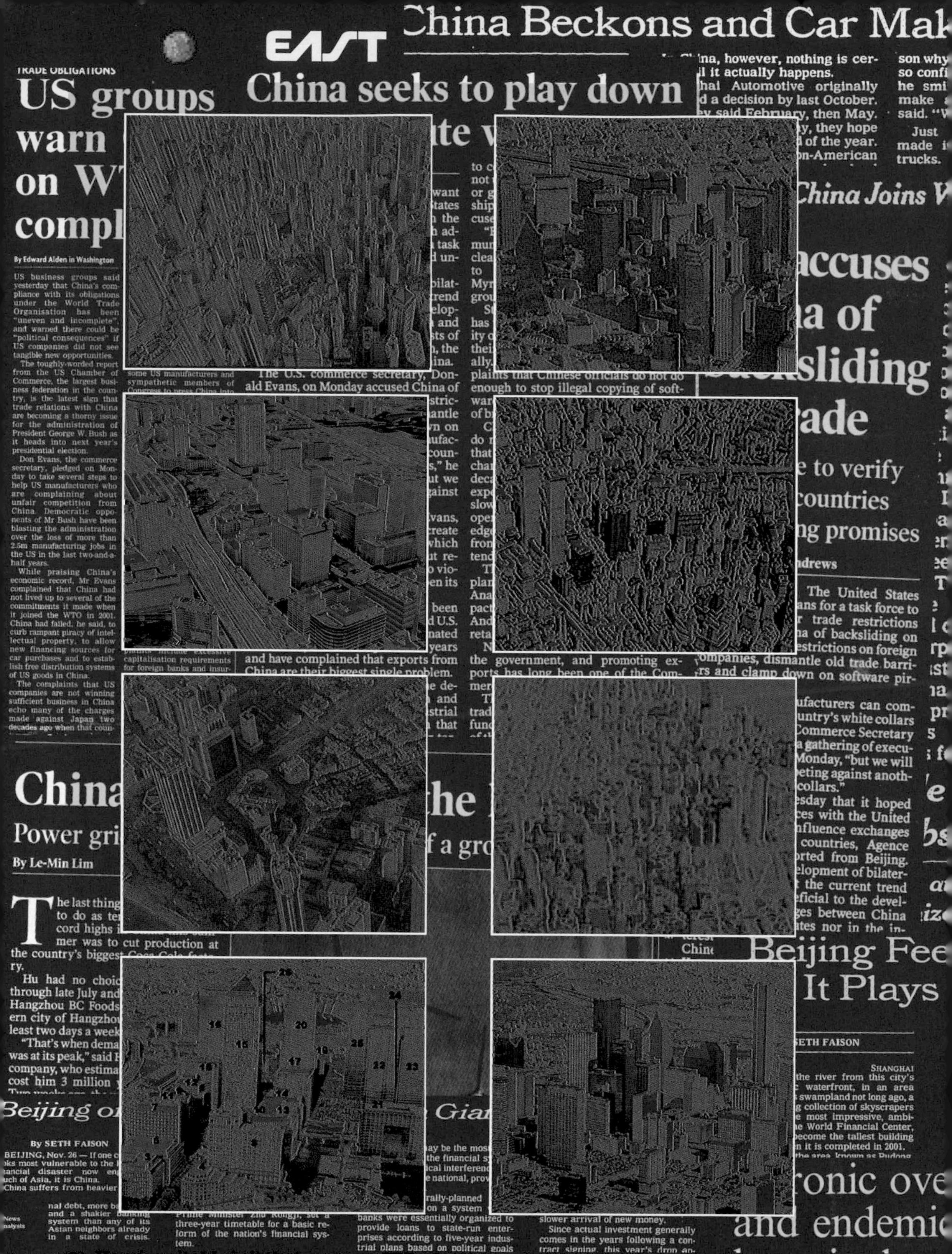

**How inevitable is it that any new CBD adopts a model – the CBD as a collection of free-standing
remain the symbol of business? Why is the skyscraper the symbol of business?**

Kill the Skyscraper

Beijing CBD Core

The skyscraper is a bizarre typology. Almost perfect at its invention - and more than any other more evolutionary type, it is an invention - the skyscraper has become less interesting in inverse proportion to its success. It has not been refined, but corrupted; the promise it once held - an organization of excessive difference, the installation of surprise as a guiding principle - has been negated by repetitive banality. The intensification of density it initially delivered has been replaced by carefully-spaced isolation.

For Beijing's new CBD, more than 300 new towers are planned. Asia has adopted the skyscraper as the symbol of its modernity, almost to the exclusion of all other typologies, at precisely the moment that the type's possibilities seem exhausted.

Condescendingly assuming the worst about their clients' values and taste, major architecture firms are prolonging the life of a type that has not been invested with new thinking or ambition since the World Trade Center's completion in 1972.

Having made New York City an unbearable demonstration of architectural mediocrity, they continue their mission on a new continent.

towers - that has erased the features of hundreds of cities before? How long will the skyscraper

EAST

Neglected Typolo

In the Sixties, Leslie Martin showed the irrationality of the skyscraper as an urban type. The same amount of urban substance can be configured in many different ways, from a compact Monolith to a dispersed Network. It is a tragedy that at the beginning of the 21st century, the tower typology is the remaining survivor, while almost all other forms have more potential for organizing urban life.

Seperate Towers

CBD Core Program

Monolith

Seperate Medium Rise

Seperate Low Rise

Network

It is a myth that the skyscraper is the only typology that generates urban density. More and more interaction and communication.

Instead of the isolated cores of the typical skyscraper...

The typical skyscraper, a tall building standing in a degree of isolation, attracts its own inhabitants but limits direct communication with others.

Two typologies offer promising alternatives. The first is the hyperbuilding - a building which has such an enormous population that it generates an urban condition within itself. The other is an expanse of disperse cores in a low rise condition that performs as an extended field of interaction.

Concentrated hyper-core...

...or a field condition of distributed cores.

examples of autarkic towers demonstrate how the skyscraper can deny instead of promote

EAST CBD Core: 2002

China gets scapegoat role in U.S. election theater

Third Ring

Chang'an Avenue

Instead of the typical CBD, a combination of two new typologies is employed: a hyperbuilding and a business courtyard carpet, both more sympathetic to the interactions of contemporary business and urban life than the skyscraper. The site of the new CBD core sits at the intersection of two ideological bands: the emerging market axis along the Third Ring Road and the socialist axis of Chang'an Avenue. The hyperbuilding sits on top of this intersection, marking a new monumentality within the city. The low-rise courtyard typology consists of a series of office rings connected by an intermediate cartilage of meeting spaces and multipurpose rooms. Three lines are cut through the structure, preserving paths already defined on the site and defining new trajectories. Together these two conditions provide for twice the given program on the same site, while simultaneously enabling heightened direct physical interchange.

With its ancient power and new prominence, Beijing could be more ambitious in planning its future apparatus should experiment with new configurations of the contemporary metropolis.

For a Taste of China's Free-Market Woes, Try Tsingtao

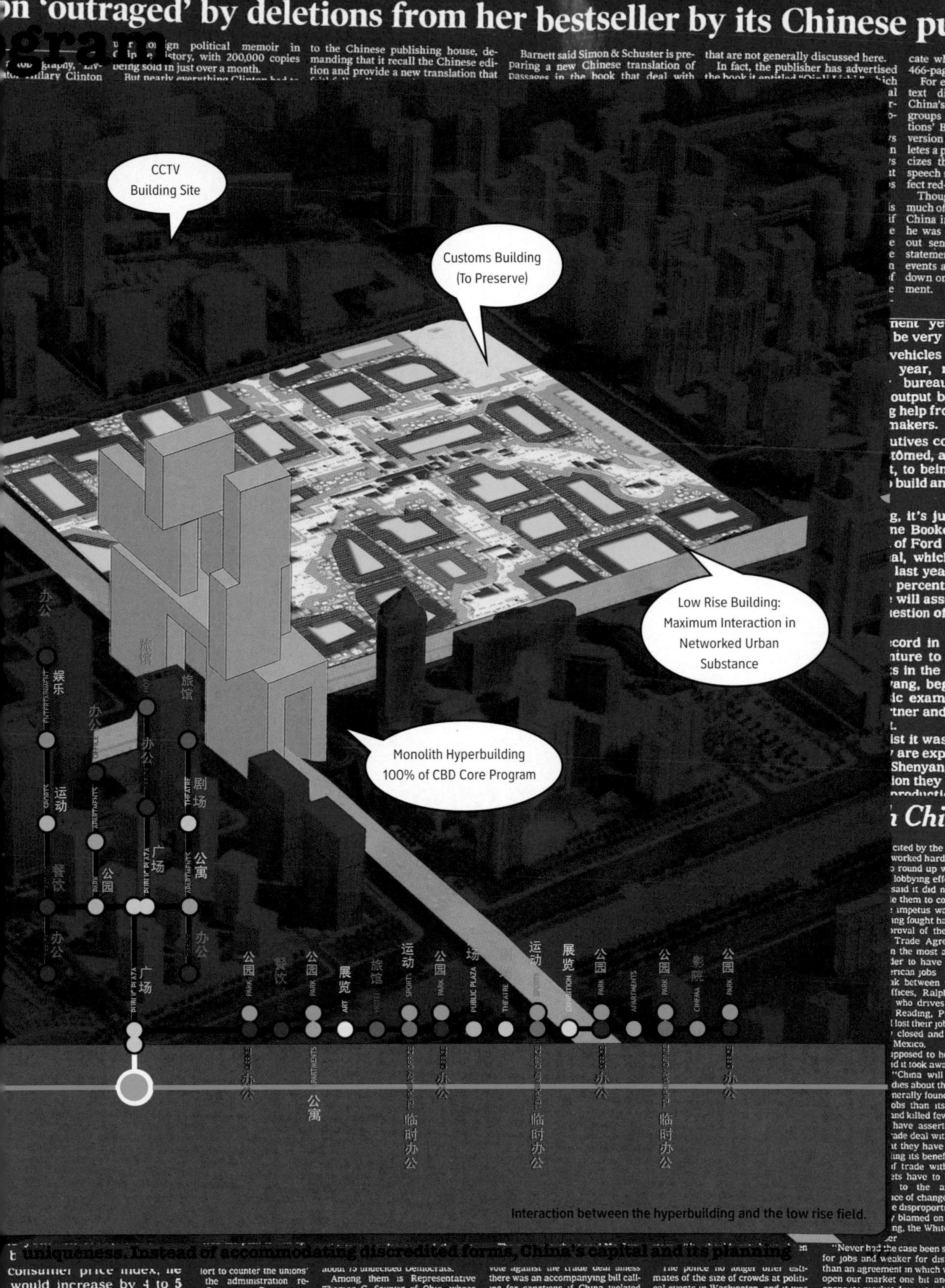

Interaction between the hyperbuilding and the low rise field.

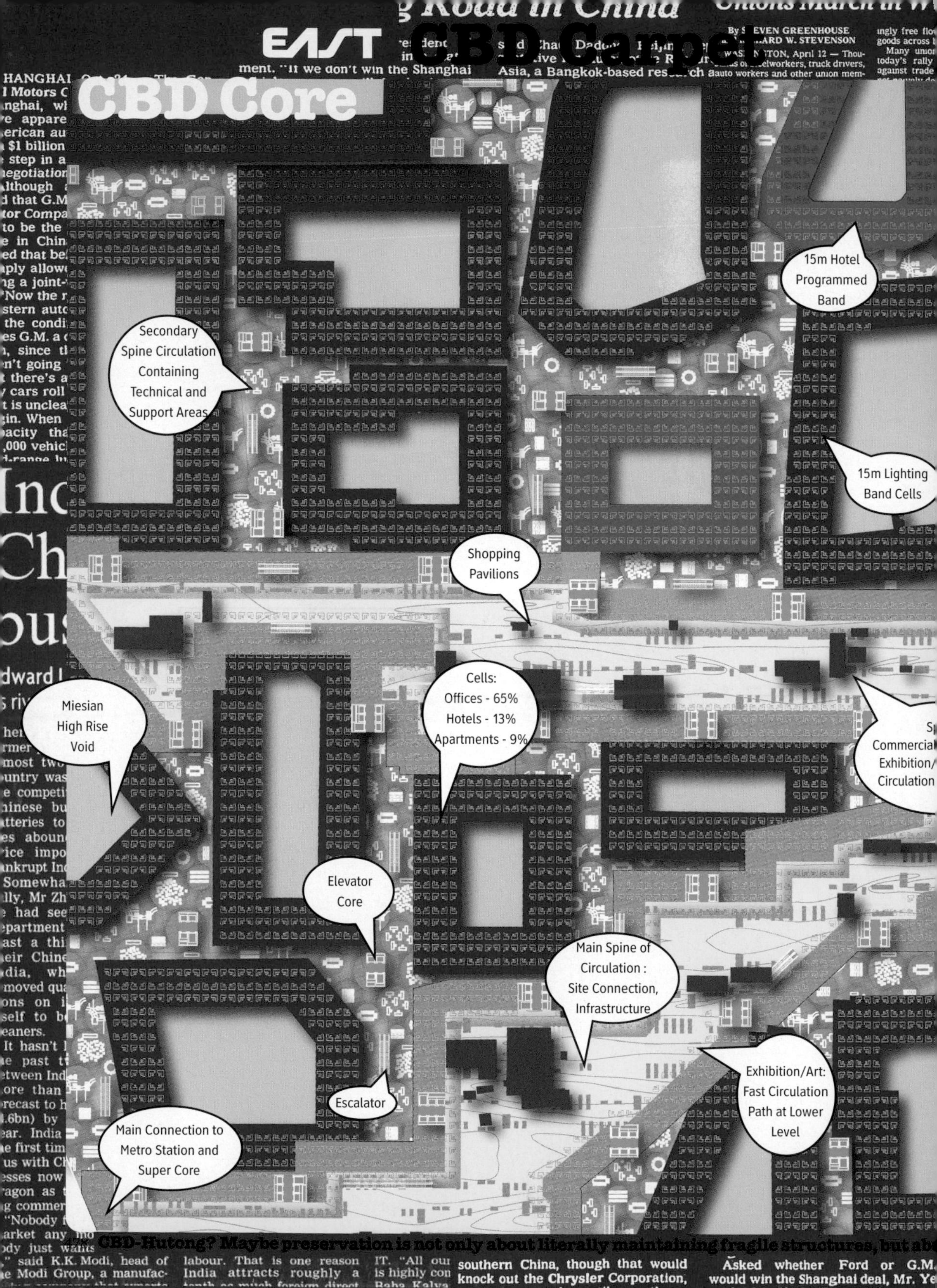

EAST
CBD Carpet
CBD Core
Secondary Spine Circulation Containing Technical and Support Areas
15m Hotel Programmed Band
15m Lighting Band Cells
Shopping Pavilions
Miesian High Rise Void
Cells: Offices - 65% Hotels - 13% Apartments - 9%
Commercial Exhibition/ Circulation
Elevator Core
Main Spine of Circulation : Site Connection, Infrastructure
Exhibition/Art: Fast Circulation Path at Lower Level
Escalator
Main Connection to Metro Station and Super Core
CBD-Hutong? Maybe preservation is not only about literally maintaining fragile structures, but abo

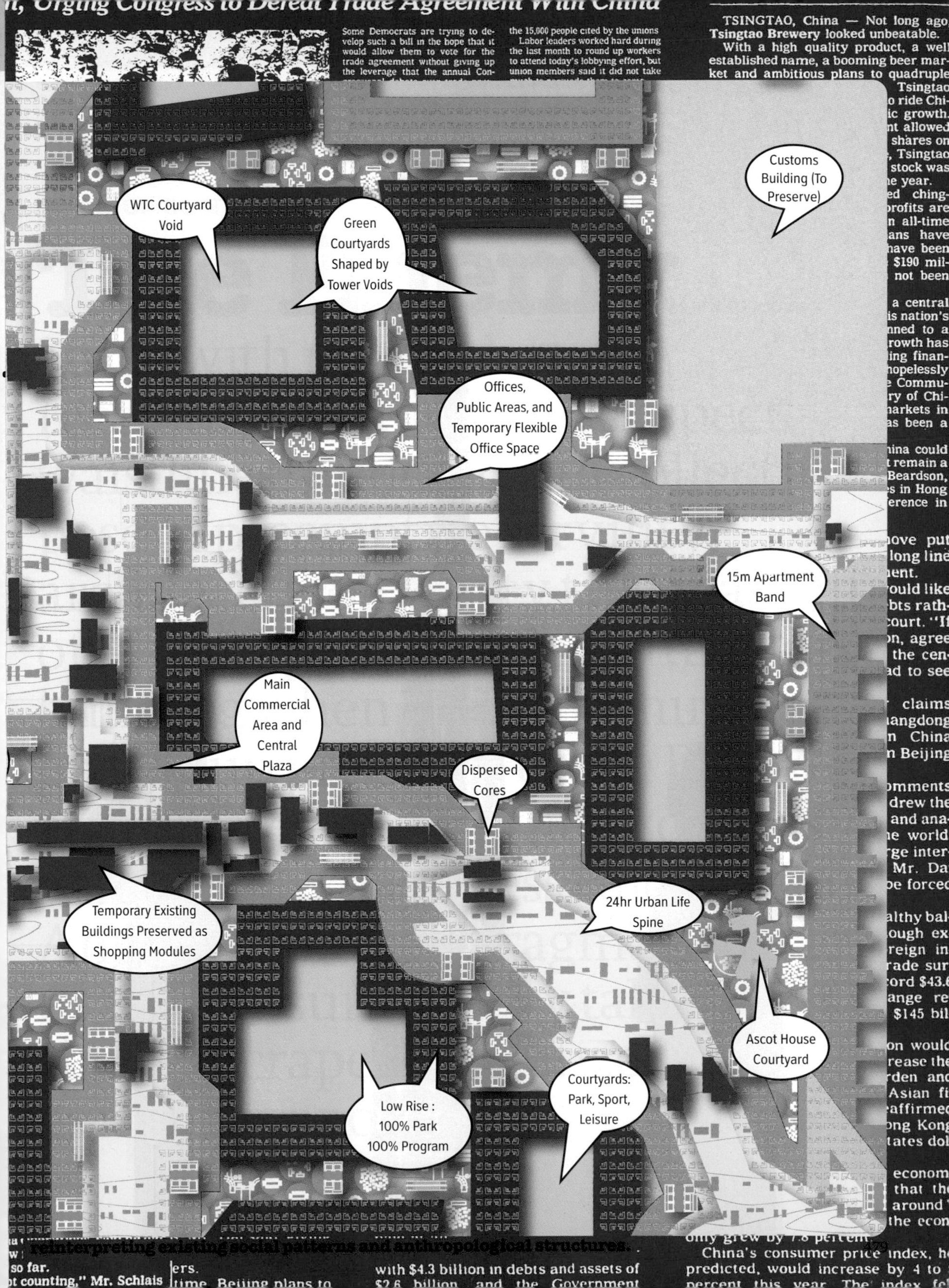

reinterpreting existing social patterns and anthropological structures.

 In the sixties, the Metabolists were the first to think beyond the skyscraper; they imagined

CCTV

Saved by a Fortune Cookie

Early 2002 –We received two invitations, one to apply to consider what should happen at Ground Zero, the other for the headquarters of China Central Television in Beijing. We discussed the choice over a Chinese meal. The life of the architect is so fraught with uncertainty and dilemmas that any clarification of the future, including astrology, is disproportionately welcome. My fortune cookie read, "Stunningly Omnipresent Masters make minced meat of memory.">

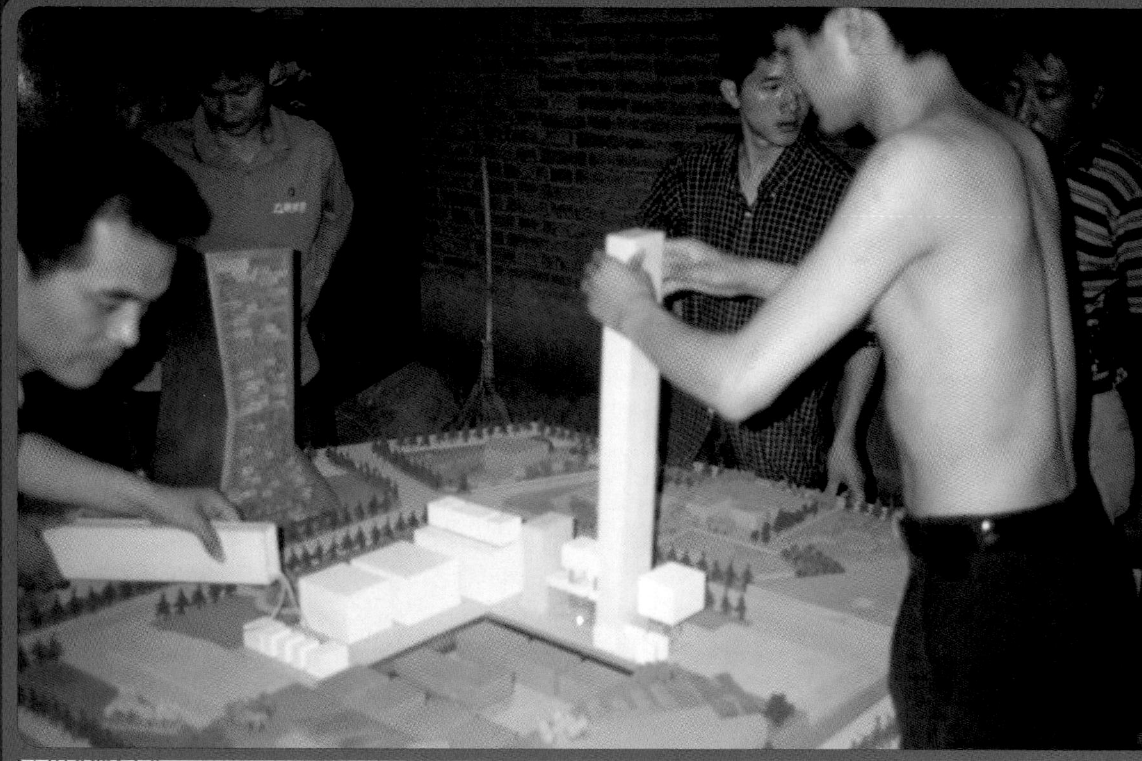

Revised July 29, 2003: Version 05

2002

2003

CCTV EXTENDED PRELIMINARY DESIGN SCHEDULE
CCTV SCHEDULE

JULY (backgrounds) | AUGUST (development) | SEPTEMBER (devel...

DEADLINES & SUBMISSIONS
OMA To CCTV (ECADI)
OMA To ECADI
OMA To ARUP - Consultants
ECADI To OMA
ECADI To CCTV
ARUP To OMA
ARUP To ECADI
Consultants To OMA
CCTV To OMA
POLITBURO MEETINGS
WORKSHOPS ROTTERDAM - CCTV-OMA-
ECADI - Mr. Wang in Rotterdam
CCTV Team in Rotterdam
CCTV Board In Meeting in Beijing
WORKSHOP BEIJING - CCTV-OMA-ECADI
ECADI - Mr. Wang in Beijing
Structural Expert Panel Review
Fire & Lifesafety Expert Panel Review
APPROVAL PERIOD
HOTEL OPERATOR Collaboration

 One of architecture's great virtues is its complete immersion in a totally unpredictable sequence

中央电视台新台址建设工程
CCTV New Site Construction & Development Program

设计合同签字仪式

To a layman, we were told, the plaster model that had apparently seduced the jury would seem just a sculpture. In four days – in a computerized sweatshop, with ample child labor, by half-naked workers, partly in alleyways – we made a new one, transparent and modern, that was apparently put in a van that would visit leaders at their holiday resorts – a journey that culminated somehow in a contract signing at the state guest house in December, for a building to be completed before the Beijing Olympics (2008).

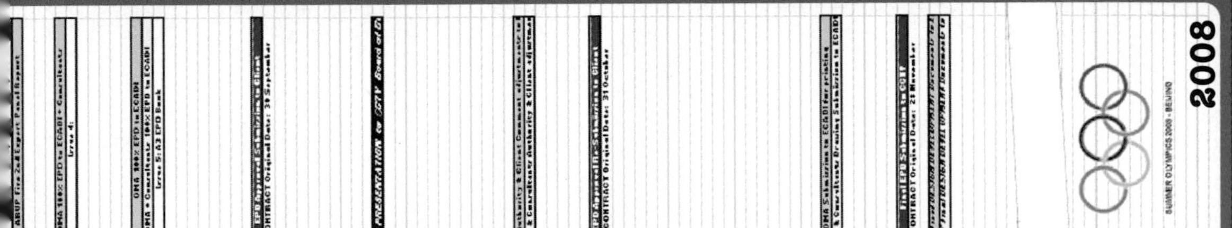

2008

SUMMER OLYMPICS 2008 - BEIJING

OCTOBER (final submittal)

November (1st Approvals Period)

December (2nd Approval Period)

EPD Approvals & Preparation for CD Phase

CD and Construction phase

ARUP fire 2nd Expert Panel Report

OMA 100% EPD to ECADI + Consultants

OMA 100% EPD to ECADI

EPD Approved Submission to Client
CONTRACT Original Date: 30 September

OMA PRESENTATION to CCTV Board of Di...

OMA Authority & Client Comment adjustments

EPD Approved Re-Submission to Client
CONTRACT Original Date: 31 October

OMA Submission to ECADI for printing

Final EPD Submission to CCTV
CONTRACT Original Date: 21 November

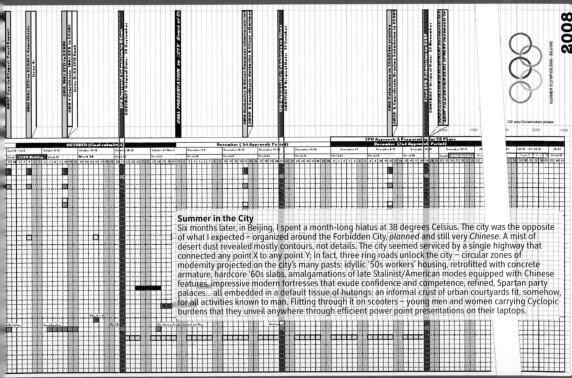

Summer in the City

Six months later, in Beijing, I spent a month-long hiatus at 38 degrees Celsius. The city was the opposite of what I expected – organized around the Forbidden City, *planned* and still very *Chinese*. A mist of desert dust revealed mostly contours, not details. The city seemed serviced by a single highway that connected any point X to any point Y; in fact, three ring roads unlock the city – circular zones of modernity projected on the city's many pasts: idyllic '50s workers' housing, retrofitted with concrete armature, hardcore '60s slabs, amalgamations of late Stalinist/American modes equipped with Chinese features, impressive modern fortresses that exude confidence and competence, refined, Spartan party palaces... all embedded in a default tissue of hutongs: an informal crust of urban courtyards fit, somehow, for all activities known to man. Flitting through it on scooters – young men and women carrying Cyclopic burdens that they unveil anywhere through efficient power point presentations on their laptops.

of radically different subcultures.

Saved by a Fortu

The new China Central Television Station will be located in Beijing's new Central Business District, close to the intersection of Chang'an Avenue and the Third Ring Road, and will be completed for the Olympic Games in 2008.

The project is located in the north of the Central Business District on a site of four blocks with a total area of 180,000 m^2. The 558,000 m^2 of program are distributed in two major buildings and a series of secondary and underground facilities – CCTV, which accommodates aspects of TV making, and TVCC, a theater-hospitality center with a hotel. On the block in the south-east, the Media Park is conceived as an extension of the proposed green axis of the CBD. It is open to the public for events and entertainment, or closed, so that it can be used for outdoor filming.

In the market, architecture = real estate. Any complex organization is dismantled – each part put in its place for the least amount of money. All media companies suffer the subsequent paranoia: each sector talks about the others as "them," distrust is rife, motives questioned. There is no whole.

In China, money does not have the last word (yet). There is a conceptual space that could accommodate the construction of CCTV as a whole – a single entity in which all parts are housed permanently – aware of each others presence. A collective.

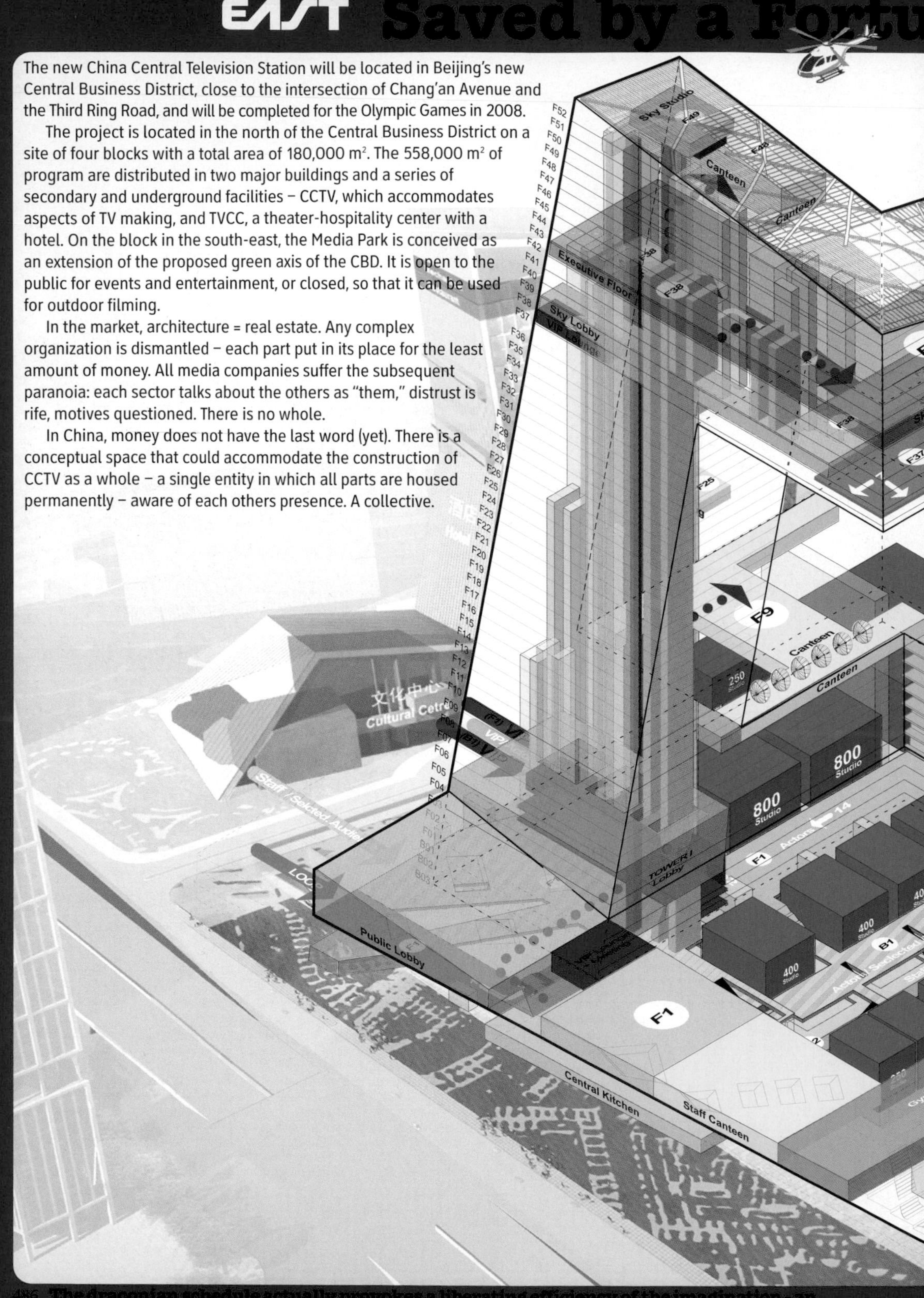

 The draconian schedule actually provokes a liberating efficiency of the imagination - an

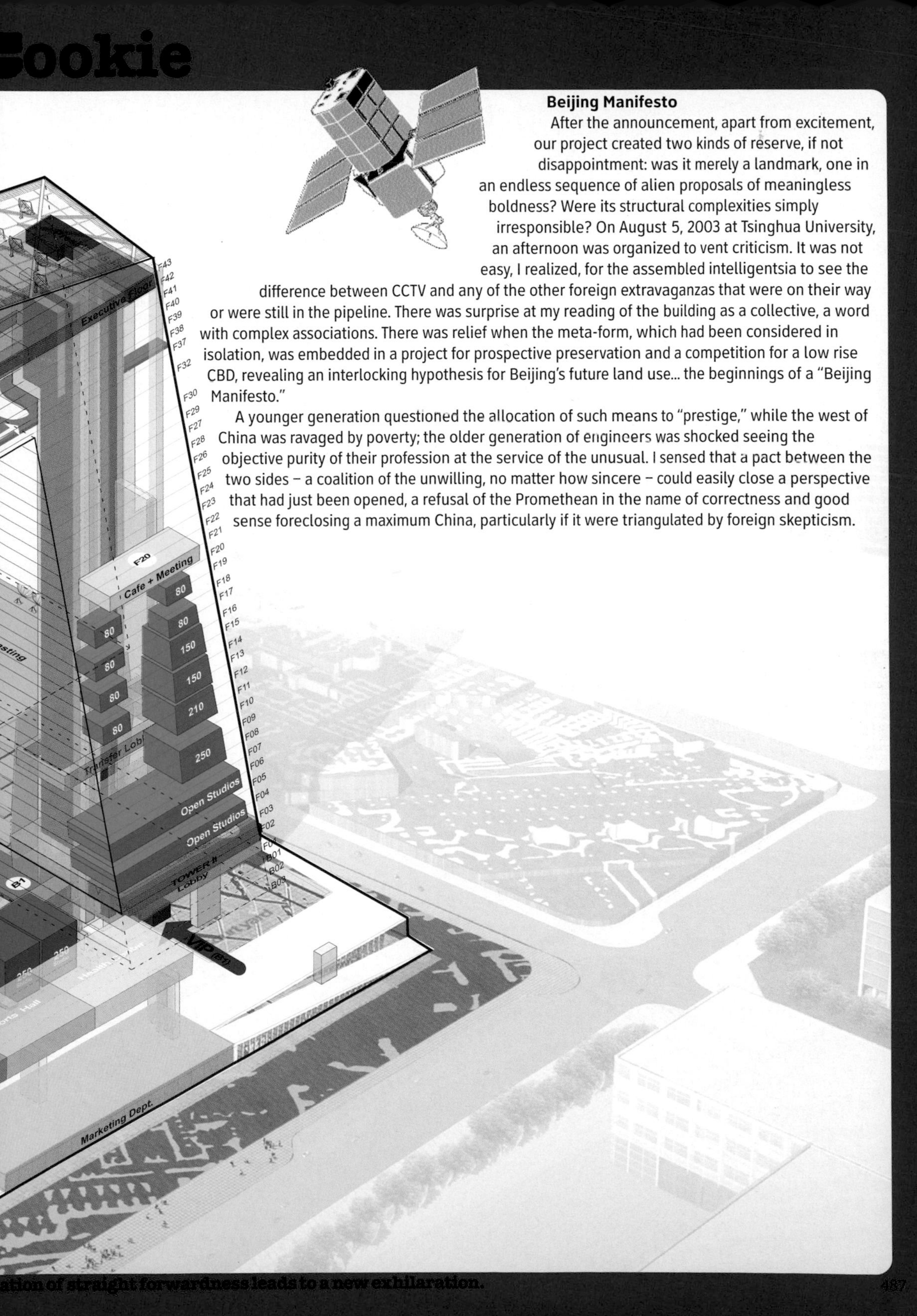

Beijing Manifesto

After the announcement, apart from excitement, our project created two kinds of reserve, if not disappointment: was it merely a landmark, one in an endless sequence of alien proposals of meaningless boldness? Were its structural complexities simply irresponsible? On August 5, 2003 at Tsinghua University, an afternoon was organized to vent criticism. It was not easy, I realized, for the assembled intelligentsia to see the difference between CCTV and any of the other foreign extravaganzas that were on their way or were still in the pipeline. There was surprise at my reading of the building as a collective, a word with complex associations. There was relief when the meta-form, which had been considered in isolation, was embedded in a project for prospective preservation and a competition for a low rise CBD, revealing an interlocking hypothesis for Beijing's future land use... the beginnings of a "Beijing Manifesto."

A younger generation questioned the allocation of such means to "prestige," while the west of China was ravaged by poverty; the older generation of engineers was shocked seeing the objective purity of their profession at the service of the unusual. I sensed that a pact between the two sides – a coalition of the unwilling, no matter how sincere – could easily close a perspective that had just been opened, a refusal of the Promethean in the name of correctness and good sense foreclosing a maximum China, particularly if it were triangulated by foreign skepticism.

EAST Loop

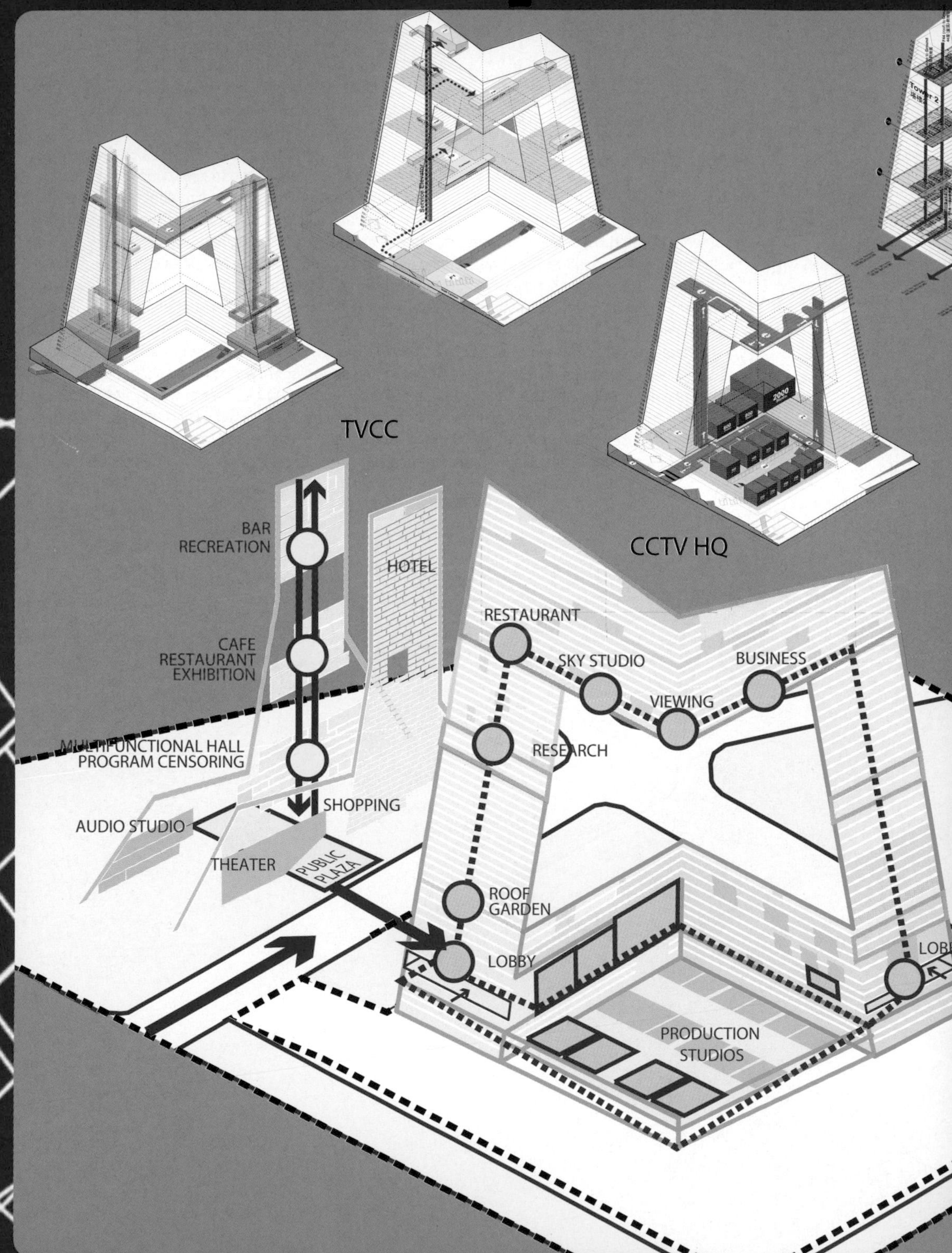

 All technical aspects are mobilized to reinforce the metaphor / reality of the loop....

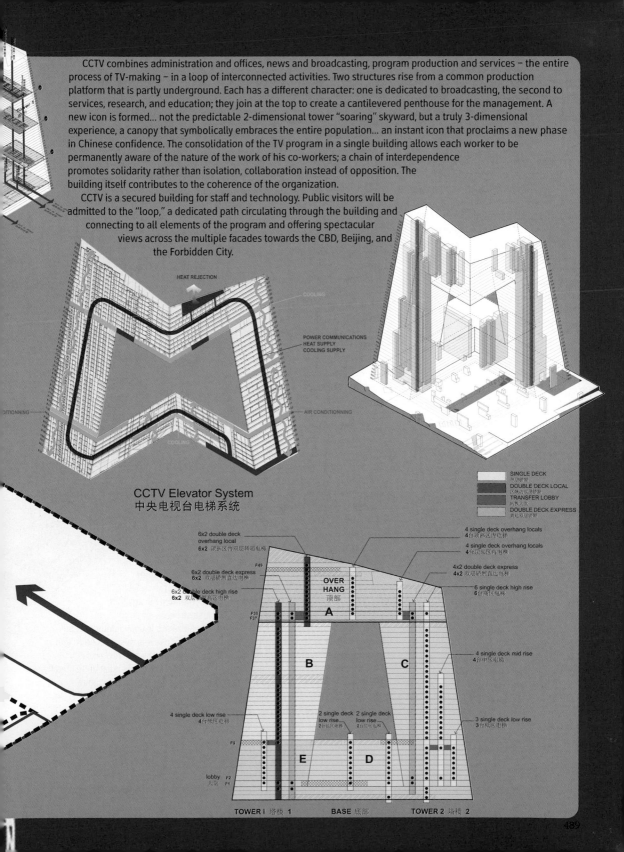

CCTV combines administration and offices, news and broadcasting, program production and services – the entire process of TV-making – in a loop of interconnected activities. Two structures rise from a common production platform that is partly underground. Each has a different character: one is dedicated to broadcasting, the second to services, research, and education; they join at the top to create a cantilevered penthouse for the management. A new icon is formed… not the predictable 2-dimensional tower "soaring" skyward, but a truly 3-dimensional experience, a canopy that symbolically embraces the entire population… an instant icon that proclaims a new phase in Chinese confidence. The consolidation of the TV program in a single building allows each worker to be permanently aware of the nature of the work of his co-workers; a chain of interdependence promotes solidarity rather than isolation, collaboration instead of opposition. The building itself contributes to the coherence of the organization.

CCTV is a secured building for staff and technology. Public visitors will be admitted to the "loop," a dedicated path circulating through the building and connecting to all elements of the program and offering spectacular views across the multiple facades towards the CBD, Beijing, and the Forbidden City.

CCTV Elevator System
中央电视台电梯系统

Dissecting the Iconic Exosymbiont: The CCTV Headquarters, Beijing, as Built Organism By William B. Millard

Gross anatomy: defiance of disaster

The procedure of characterizing the CCTV begins with gross or macro-scale observation before advancing to dissection. The apparent simplicity of the structure, combining symmetries and asymmetries, suggests that a substantial amount of this initial level of observation will be useful.

To the naked eye, the entity consists of six approximately rectangular or rhomboidal blocks (two at the base, two vertical, two forming an overhang) arranged in L-shaped pairs to suggest a superimposition of geometric forms. The CCTV-structure is a single irregular rhomboid hollowed out at the center, a cornered loop. When viewed from the northeast and above, it displays a rough radial symmetry, while containing no actual circles or arcs. It is none of the common geometric forms, while gesturing toward many of them; it appears, like so many ostensibly haphazard natural phenomena, to mock the simplistic precision of ideal forms by approximating them. Composed entirely of straight lines, it nonetheless generates sinuous motion. Right angles exist only in its horizontal dimension, and externally only in the plane where it touches the Earth; above that plane, deviations of a few degrees from plumb imply a relativistic warping of space.

The CCTV-body is both dense (horizontal and bricklike when viewed from afar) and ethereal, with pervasive plate glass, substantial exposure of internal features to the external view, and panoramic views from every level within. Its macrostructure is tubular and ouroboric. Moreover, its salient feature is a visually intuitive instability. Its cantilevered overhang section casts an impressive and ominous shadow; this weighty component appears poised to pitch the entire structure over onto its southwestern point at the slightest provocation by wind, seismic force, or any other form of shock. Flagrantly centerless, the CCTV implies a center of gravity that bears no reassuring relation to its center of mass.

That a structure should pose such a basic problem for itself (if not an apocalyptic collapse, then a steady entropic retreat into structural fatigue and eventual insupportability) and proceed elegantly to solve it – defying not only common gravity but a set of expectations so commonly held that they are as transparent as air to most observers – marks the CCTV as an exceptionally perceptive and adaptive organism. To stave off the tipping-point topple that overimaginative eyes cannot resist projecting, the CCTV-system offers a strategy familiar to many biologists. Immediately beneath the CCTV's deceptive facade lies a visible rigid exoskeleton, an adaptation borrowed from the arthropod phylum, that strengthens structural resistance to either the acute or the chronic form of collapse, dramatic shear or gradual Pisan decline.

Due to its unusual form, certain areas of the CCTV's surface (generally joints between major block units, and particularly the overhang segment compressed by the weight of the inwardly leaning towers) appear to bear dangerously disproportionate loads, while others remain relatively spared. The adjustment that apparently evolved in response was to discard uniform density of diagonal members and embrace irregularity. The CCTV's visible and tangible framework in its final form features a varying scale of density in the arrangement of angular struts, so that more bracing appears in areas subject to greater stress. This "Adapted Pattern" guarantees that the *prima facie* collapsibility of the entire organism remains an optical illusion, a gesture toward impracticality on the part of a structure that is both unconventional and surprisingly practical.

The CCTV's gross shape is the physical expression of a set of interlocking ideas (and, broadly, of the idea of interlocking): counterpoise, complementarity, reciprocality. Its rhetorical trope is chiasmus, the reversal of an initial form in the next iteration by an inversion of that form. Weight distribution appears based on a dynamic interdependence: of the six component blocks, four can maintain structural integrity only in the presence of all four; only the two contiguous with the Earth, forming the L-shaped base, are stable in isolation. The towers press their over-hanging heads together, as if each were wearied by the effort to remain upright. Neither would stand if the other gave way.

Hierarchy in any high-rise structure or large organization is unavoidable, yet the CCTV-loop levels this perception and bends hierarchy into reciprocality: everything that rises must quite literally converge. The skyscraper genre's relentless vertical thrust becomes an archaism, an icon of one-dimensionality, a plaintive assertion that only one direction, Up, ultimately matters. The CCTV brings other dimensions into view and requires the horizontal and the vertical to negotiate a treaty of mutual recognition and interdependence.

Surface inspection and histology: texture, mutability, attraction

After studying the gross appearance, one proceeds with invasive investigations: incision, removal of epithelial layers, microscopic tissue examination, and correlation of structures with functions. The CCTV's epithelium has assumed a form resembling that of certain aquatic vertebrates whose skin contains little pigmentation and reveals more about internal organs than would be possible above sea level. Apparently the atmosphere of Beijing imposes no need to armor the internal processes of Chinese Central Television against either ultraviolet light or visual inquiry.

Translucent from some angles and in certain forms of light, opaque at others, and bearing a combination of permanent and temporary images and projections, the CCTV's facade combines protective and communicative functions in ways not customarily found in comparable built organisms. The surface is a complex laminate of tempered glass and finely woven metal; light passes through both glass and mesh to reveal the exoskeleton on which the laminated panels are mounted, but the texture is only partially transparent. The icons can be internally lit, making the surface function as body armor, weatherproofing, and thermal insulation.

Skin has obvious and nonobvious functions in the animal kingdom: thermal regulation, conveyance of moisture, containment of internal organs, enhancement of sexual attraction. In the built-organism kingdom, skin has analogues of most of these properties. A glass skin cannot transmit moisture but readily conveys light, heat, and information. A laminated glass-mesh skin that admits evanescent images from internal and external sources tells both its endosymbionts and its external observers that it can be controlled, that it is not a monolith, that it will adjust to their interests, that it is friendly.

Internal exploration: layering, flow, cascade

Investigating further beneath the glass and fine mesh, probing past the coarser mesh of the visible framework, one finds the inescapably regular grid of functional floors and vertical supports for the external panels. The looping structure around an absent center creates patterns that organize the behavior of individual human occupants as well as the collective functions of the CCTV-community. Some of the adaptations sustaining these patterns have been observed in only small segments of the built-organism kingdom, or in the CCTV-species alone.

The base-block and subterranean levels, the two vertical tower-blocks, and the conjoined overhanging section form organic zones of related activity that complicate, though they do not invert or deconstruct, the hierarchies inherent in any large institution. In the case of Chinese Central Television, the major functions of a national-scale media firm (news reporting, broadcasting, program production, new-media production, research, training, auxiliary services, and management), in most other cases distributed across disparate and sometimes physically separated structures, can be integrated within the CCTV-organism and connected by a common infrastructure – the combined circulatory, ventilatory, internal transportation, alimentary, and communicative organs of the overall system. Individuals can traverse the entire structure, and conceivably observe every facet of news production, decision-making, and dissemination, in a single long walk. Executives high in the overhang operate with the constant visible reminder that they are supported by, and are literally dependent on, layer upon layer of laborers.

The final penetration of an observer's instruments finds a core of practical infrastructure. The CCTV's services loop has a serial rather than parallel structure, but multiple mechanical rooms are regularly distributed, and modules of each system are detachable and replaceable, allowing critical heating, cooling, ventilation, and plumbing functions to continue uninterrupted when components are under repair, blocking cascading system failures. This design resembles the modularity and redundancy of "primitive" organisms adapted for difficult environments such as the subterranean (segmented worms) or the aquatic (coral and other marine colony-organisms).

In a structure where over 50 percent of the floors (stories 11 through 38, or 28 of the total of 55) are discontinuous pairs, efficient internal transportation is a challenge. The elevator system has evolved to solve this problem, not only through the conventional strategies of combining local and express elevator banks, dedicating certain spaces to transfer lobbies, and limiting the vertical span of most elevators, but also through double-deck elevator design, a relatively recent adaptation among built organisms. Making fewer stops on alternate floors during peak use periods, the double-deck cars help conserve both usable floor space and human transportation time.

Inferences from multimodal observations

The CCTV-entity simultaneously calls for definitions and resists them. Its materials appear inorganic, yet it displays characteristics of life, chiefly forms of change and changes of form. It has clearly evolved; it shows traces of adaptation in response to external conditions and pressures. It performs myriad functions, responds to its environment, changes that environment, and processes the information resulting from that dialogue. It appears to be still evolving as it grows; its features reflect processes improvised in response to experience, not theories imposed *a priori*. It appears capable of defending itself. We will know whether it is alive only if it eventually reproduces. ■

The weaker build

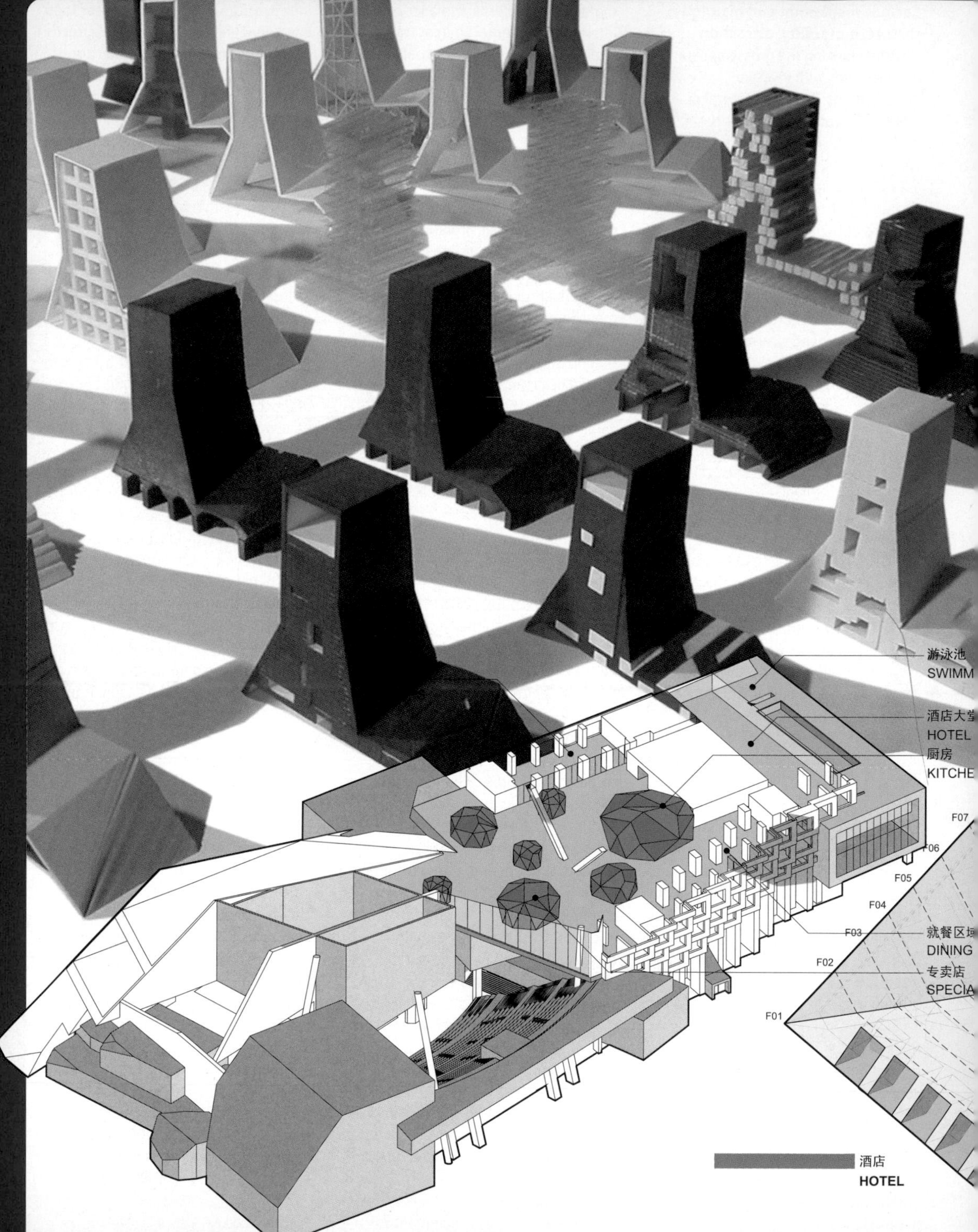

 Against the rigor of CCTV, we needed a "fuzzy" counterpart – a hospitality building that "welcomes"

TVCC

The Television Cultural Center (TVCC) is an open, inviting structure. It accommodates visitors and guests, and will be freely accessible to the public. On the ground floor, two different lobbies provide access to the 1500-seat theater and a large ballroom. The hotel guests enter at a dedicated drop-off from the east of the building and ascend to the second floor, housing the check-in as well as restaurants, lounges, and conference rooms. The hotel rooms occupy both sides of the tower, forming a spectacular atrium above the landscape of public facilities.

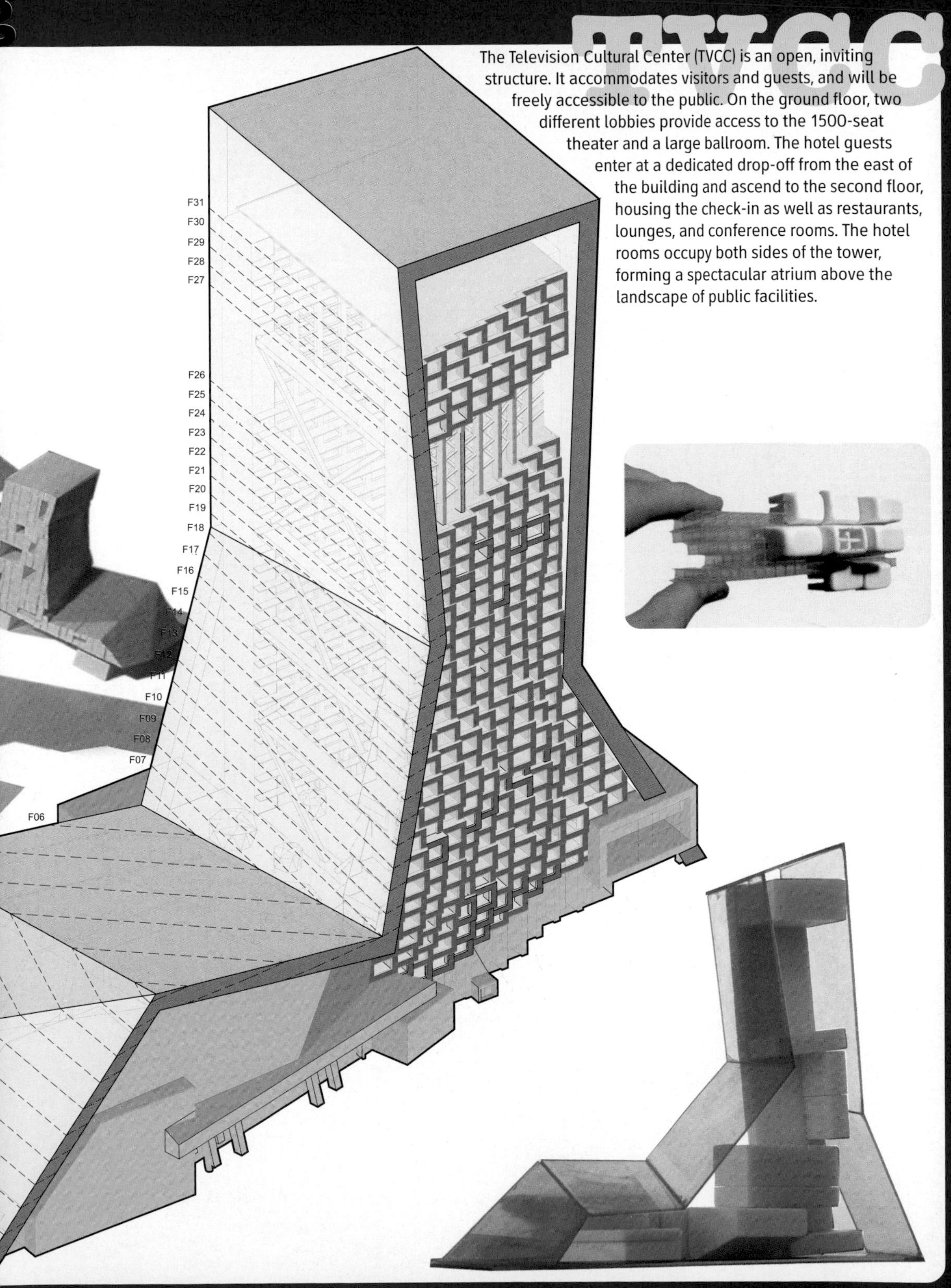

visitors, in a way we never dared before.

 High pressure work in a low pressure city – OMA could never exist without Rotterdam, a city that

has no scene, makes no demands, offers no distractions—a laboratory of indifference....

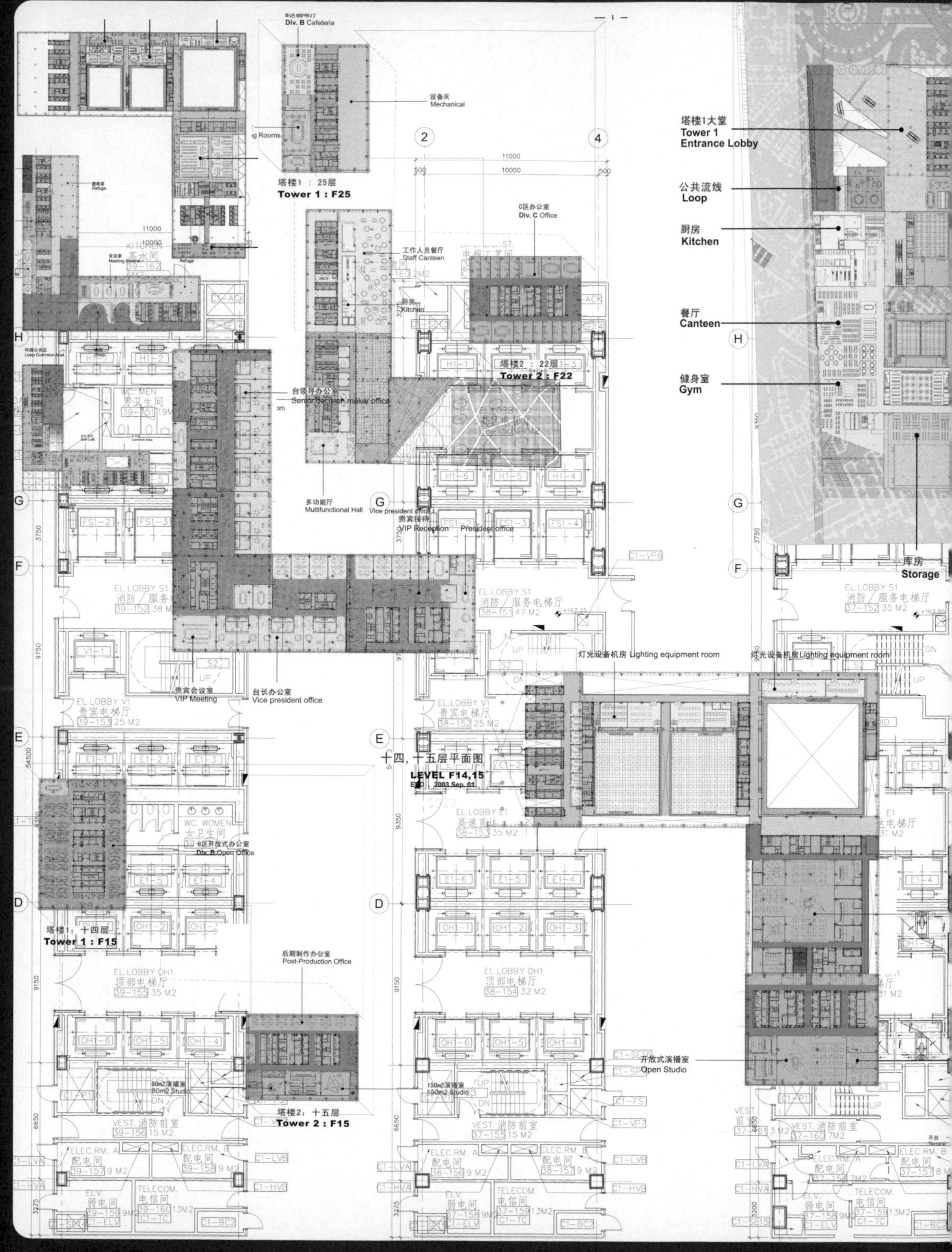

In the age of the Blob, a paroxysm of the orthogonal; last stand or, inevitably, the future?
top of each other (and were making subtle compromises to the spherical to make it work).

in 1825 days

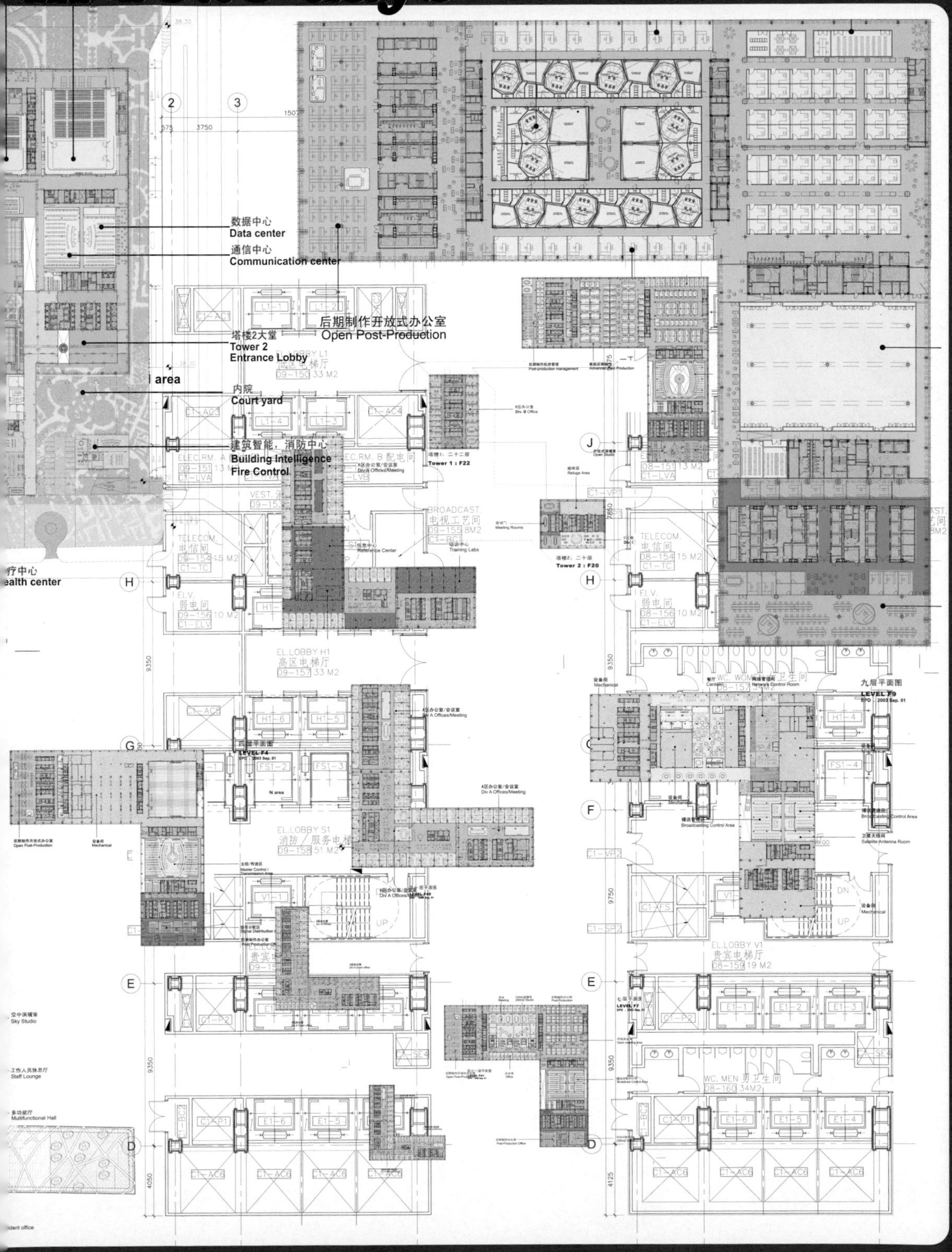

数据中心
Data center

通信中心
Communication center

后期制作开放式办公室
Open Post-Production

塔楼2大堂
Tower 2
Entrance Lobby

l area

内院
Court yard

建筑智能，消防中心
Building Intelligence
Fire Control

疗中心
ealth center

塔楼1：二十二层
Tower 1 : F22

塔楼2：二十层
Tower 2 : F20

九层平面图
LEVEL F9

空中演播室
Sky Studio

工作人员休息厅
Staff Lounge

多功能厅
Multifunctional Hall

ident office

As some of our best friends were struggling with the issue of how to stack two blobs on working on an almost Roman model of scale and planning feels both ancient and new.

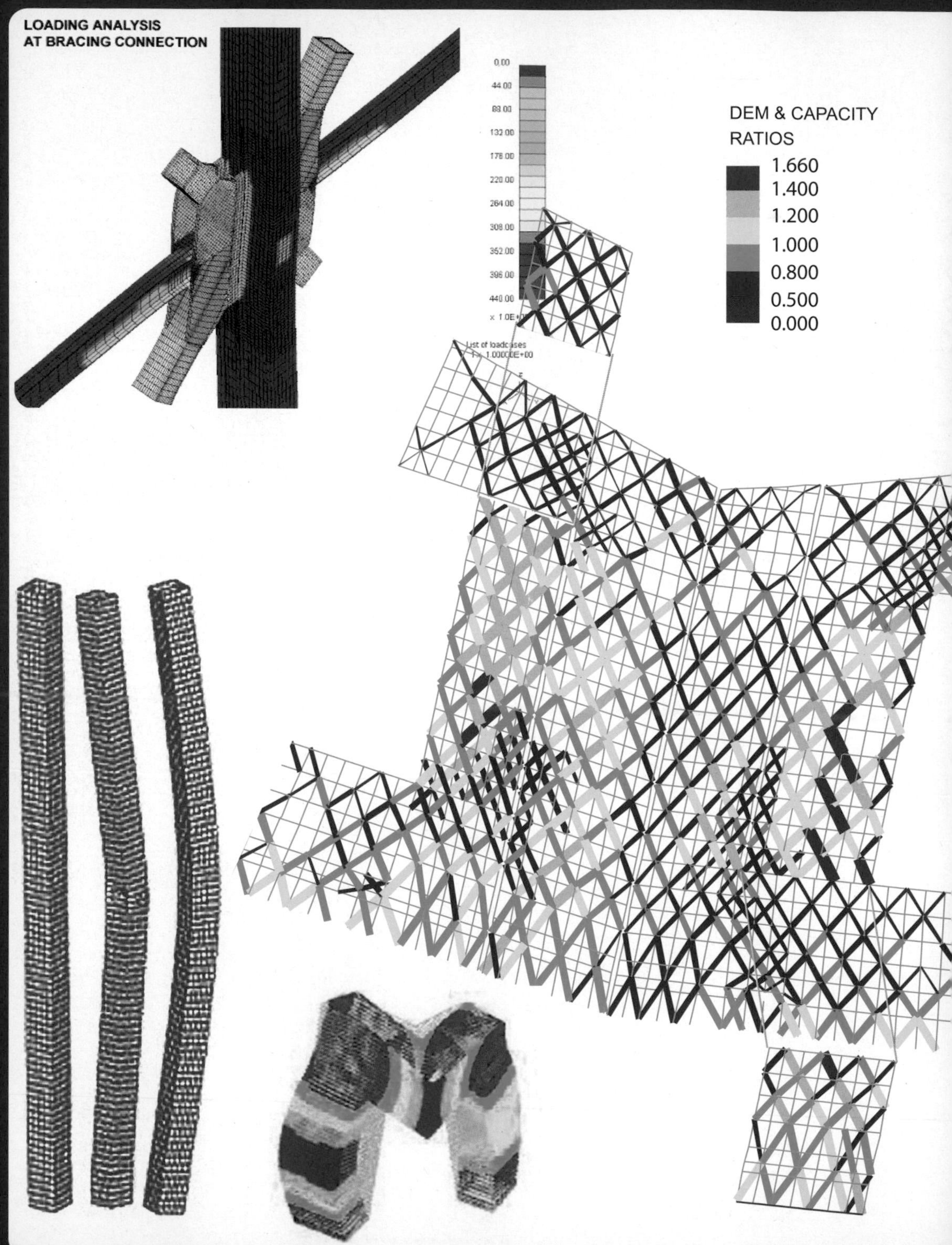

 Contrary to architecture, which promiscuously embraces uncertainty and risk, engineering is

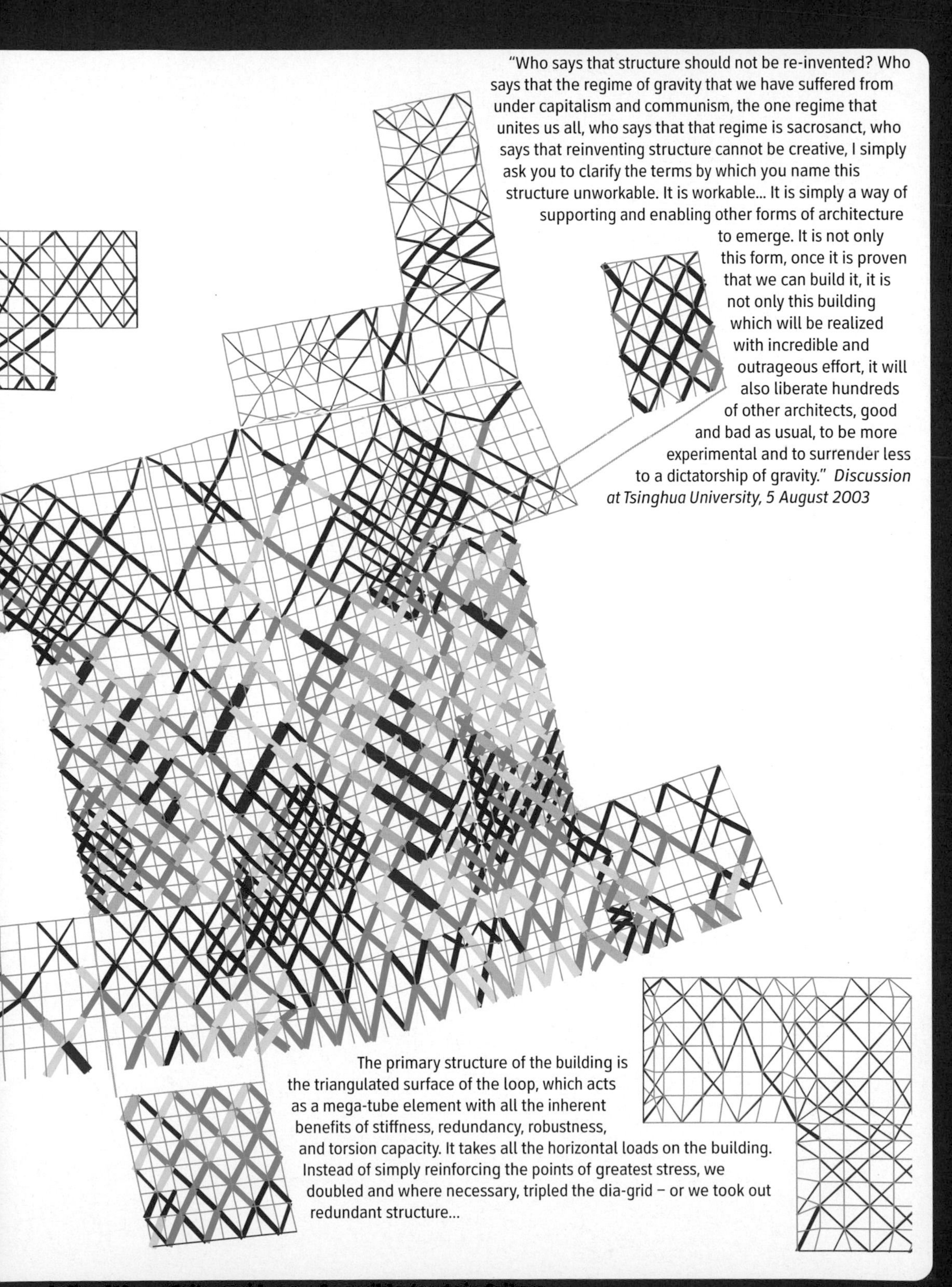

"Who says that structure should not be re-invented? Who says that the regime of gravity that we have suffered from under capitalism and communism, the one regime that unites us all, who says that that regime is sacrosanct, who says that reinventing structure cannot be creative, I simply ask you to clarify the terms by which you name this structure unworkable. It is workable... It is simply a way of supporting and enabling other forms of architecture to emerge. It is not only this form, once it is proven that we can build it, it is not only this building which will be realized with incredible and outrageous effort, it will also liberate hundreds of other architects, good and bad as usual, to be more experimental and to surrender less to a dictatorship of gravity." *Discussion at Tsinghua University, 5 August 2003*

The primary structure of the building is the triangulated surface of the loop, which acts as a mega-tube element with all the inherent benefits of stiffness, redundancy, robustness, and torsion capacity. It takes all the horizontal loads on the building. Instead of simply reinforcing the points of greatest stress, we doubled and where necessary, tripled the dia-grid – or we took out redundant structure...

EAST Iconography

While television is a medium that reaches everybody,
television buildings all over the world are mute.
They fail to achieve their public and urban potential, remaining lifeless both day and night.
CCTV will be one of the most influential TV stations worldwide.
An active façade will launch a contemporary iconography for the city and the world....
It will bring invaluable business potential for CCTV,
and further integrate CCTV'S headquarters with the city.

 In New York, entire buildings glow incandescent with the movement of the stock markets: what is

302 Does the Dutch embassy in Berlin fit in the lobby of CCTV?

10 000 people lobby

WTC III, Bin Laden II

In September 2000, the Spanish critic Galiano compared me to the writer Houellebecq. "It is not easy," he writes, "to feel sympathy for either of these bitter heroes... impossible not to feel admiration for their toxic talent." In October 2001, when I had just been acquitted of a charge of plagiarism in London High Court, my accuser compared me to "the third World Trade Tower," and vowed to bring me down, yet. Two years later, Galiano, in a terrifying escalation of metaphor, admitted that he felt "the same genre of fascination and repulsion provoked in many of us by Osama bin Laden, a charismatic figure whose lure cannot be abstracted from his ominous audacity...." If I'm bin Laden, what is my America? Will he put a price on our heads in future issues? Should we look out for the "Dead or Alive" cover? Personally, what most strikes me about Houellebecq is his humor. And the indiscriminate tenderness he extends to all his protagonists, as they scrape a minimum of pleasure from our flattened, uncivil society....

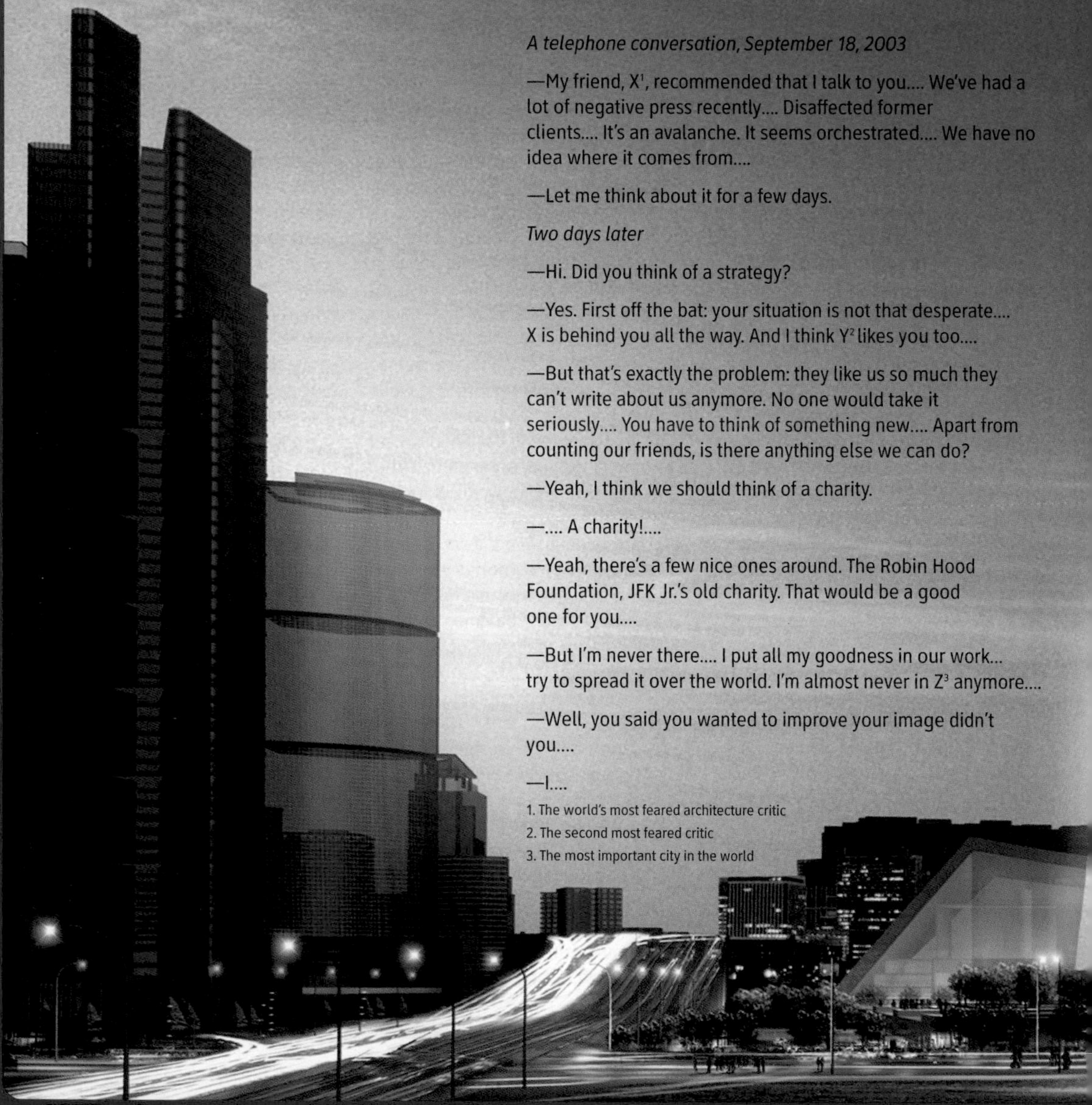

A telephone conversation, September 18, 2003

—My friend, X[1], recommended that I talk to you.... We've had a lot of negative press recently.... Disaffected former clients.... It's an avalanche. It seems orchestrated.... We have no idea where it comes from....

—Let me think about it for a few days.

Two days later

—Hi. Did you think of a strategy?

—Yes. First off the bat: your situation is not that desperate.... X is behind you all the way. And I think Y[2] likes you too....

—But that's exactly the problem: they like us so much they can't write about us anymore. No one would take it seriously.... You have to think of something new.... Apart from counting our friends, is there anything else we can do?

—Yeah, I think we should think of a charity.

—.... A charity!....

—Yeah, there's a few nice ones around. The Robin Hood Foundation, JFK Jr.'s old charity. That would be a good one for you....

—But I'm never there.... I put all my goodness in our work... try to spread it over the world. I'm almost never in Z[3] anymore....

—Well, you said you wanted to improve your image didn't you....

—I....

1. The world's most feared architecture critic
2. The second most feared critic
3. The most important city in the world

EAST

tokyo 35°40'N 139°45'E

Roppongi Hills

It is a terrifying thought that, at the dawn of the 21st century, is realized - at enormous expense, by the international elite of corporate architecture, under the auspices of a celebrity board that reads like an international who's who of personalities known for their gravitas - Nick Serota, Glenn Lowry, Wenzel Jacob, Alfred Pacquement....- a building named after the idyllic urban patch that its presence obliterates - a project of unmitigated awfulness that embodies, with seeming deliberation, a recapitulation of everything bad about 20th century architecture.

It contains zero intent executed with crushing competence: it is tall and fat, crowned by a tempieto that represents the exact moment where a formerly specific condition - museum space - has become generic, a new spatial category defined by large minimalist slabs of uneven sheetrock, no longer even pretending to be a container of treasures, just a cynical entrapment of hopefuls. It has been years in the planning, in an elaborate war-room, where mobile cameras overhead swoop down on the microscopic details of a megalomaniac model of the entire city – developers' target practice - and the where the future impact of any new structure is recorded from every angle in real time - a guaranteed bulls-eye.

Its appearance is significant for several reasons. It shows that amnesia is a critical part of our repertoire of distraction that enables us to efficiently recycle each mistake, each crime, each stupidity that we imagined safely disposed of. We thought we hammered stakes through them, but now they seem to be resurrected. We are facing an army of architectural zombies, in a kind of night-of-the-living dead apotheosis.

How could so much evil premeditation, pursued with the same persistence that Pakistan looks for Uranium, not only "emerge" without obstacle, but actually arise from hoarding conceived and decorated by the world's foremost artists and thinkers?

It also shows with dazzling clarity how the perfection of construction itself has become a nihilist tool that facilitates exploitation and masks a complete absence of generosity.

Where, in more extreme circumstances, we marvel at the weakness of victims that barely resist incarceration or even extermination, here we allow ourselves to be led past cute colors and smooth details - luxury - by elevators seemingly based on teleportation to the heart, no the pinnacle of nothingness, to watch, pathetically, from the top of this battering ram - acoustically isolated from any bleating - a city on its way to the slaughterhouse. Is this the apotheosis of globalization? Is this the west? Is this our best? Are we, from this decadent pulpit, skeptical about China?

But this tower is only a miniscule part of a vast presence - more and more of the world's ground floor is handed over to Jerde - at first a harmless alternative to the flawed geometries of exhausted planners or the poetic straightjackets of landscape architecture, scripting entertainment on the least promising surfaces in accidental, but evermore captivating configurations, but now his slack doodles are chiseled by our best brains into sky-high extrusions of antiform, in a kind of desperate Situationism gone corporate.

Japan, trying to spend itself out of its lingering somnolence, has succeeded in cementing the once charmingly chaotic and provisional into a definitive and immutable formlessness set in granite - embalmed in luxury and money. Jerde & Co.'s universal blueprint seamlessly closes off all horizons, blocks all the exits, eliminates all perspective.... A permanent house of horror for all. ■ **RK**

TCS NETHERLANDS / CORBIS

continued from p. 83 **Patent Office**

UNIVERSAL MODERNIZATION PATENT [14]

TALL & SLENDER (1996)

Patent Number: 9,346, 587

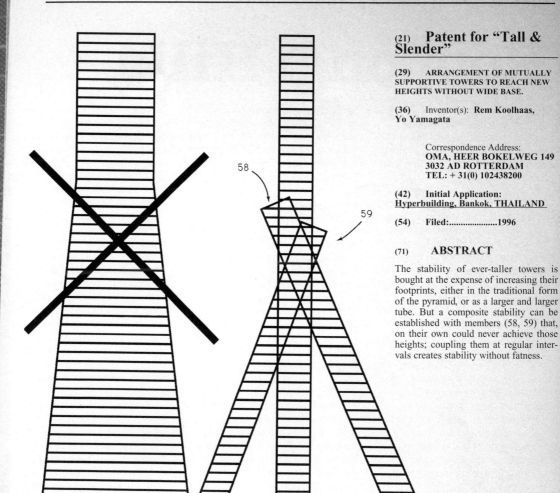

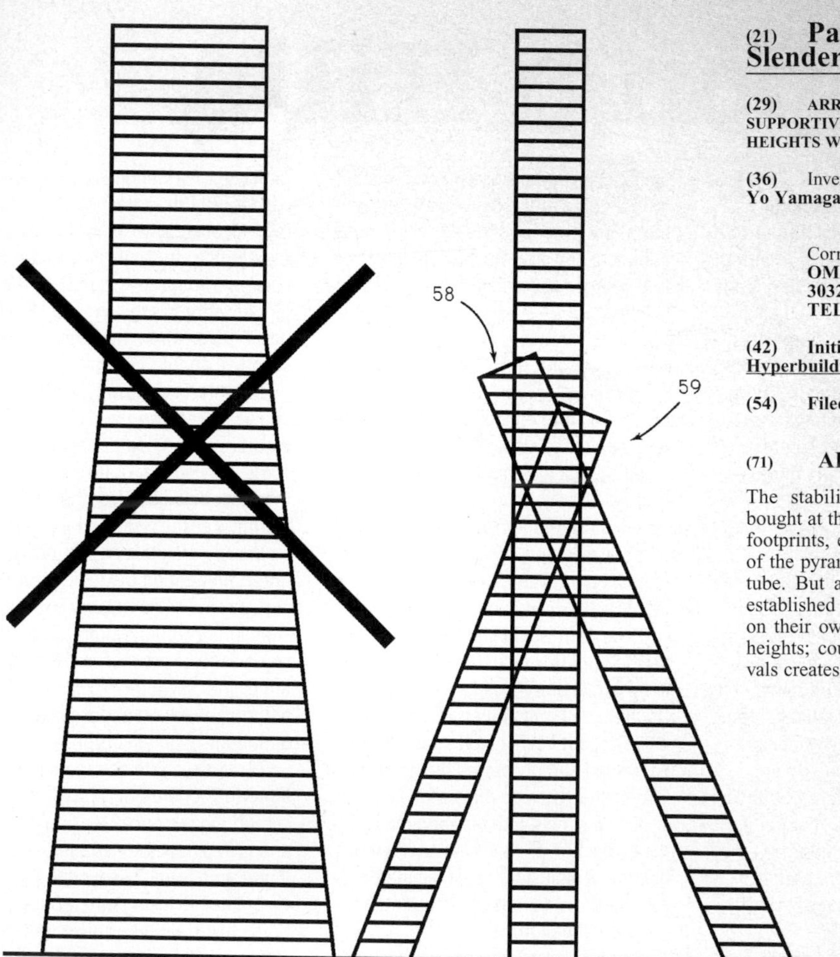

(21) **Patent for "Tall & Slender"**

(29) **ARRANGEMENT OF MUTUALLY SUPPORTIVE TOWERS TO REACH NEW HEIGHTS WITHOUT WIDE BASE.**

(36) Inventor(s): **Rem Koolhaas, Yo Yamagata**

Correspondence Address:
OMA, HEER BOKELWEG 149
3032 AD ROTTERDAM
TEL: + 31(0) 102438200

(42) **Initial Application:**
Hyperbuilding, Bankok, THAILAND

(54) **Filed:....................1996**

(71) **ABSTRACT**

The stability of ever-taller towers is bought at the expense of increasing their footprints, either in the traditional form of the pyramid, or as a larger and larger tube. But a composite stability can be established with members (58, 59) that, on their own could never achieve those heights; coupling them at regular intervals creates stability without fatness.

UNIVERSAL MODERNIZATION PATENT [14]

SKYSCRAPER LOOP(2002)

Patent Number: 2, 565, 267

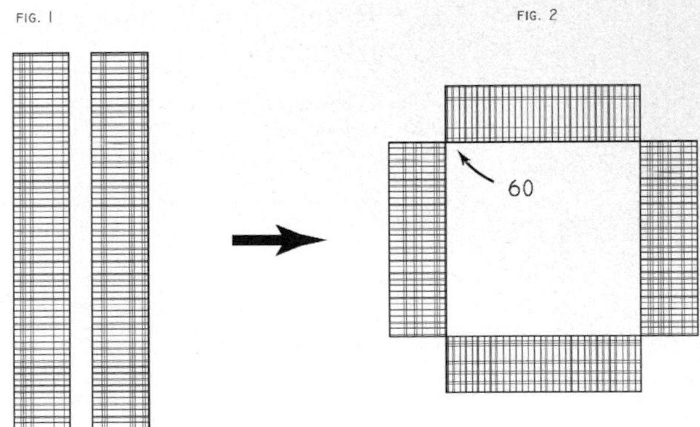

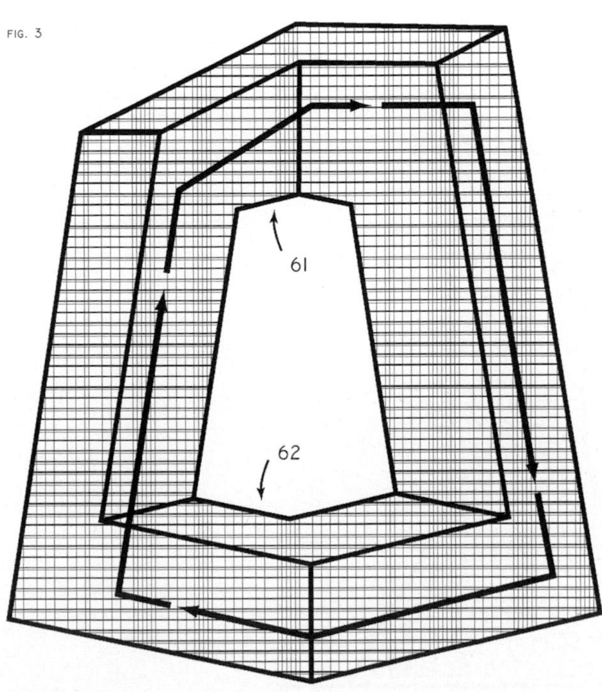

(54) Patent for "Bent Skyscraper"

(54) METHOD OF AVOIDING THE ISOLATION OF THE TRADITIONAL HIGH RISE BY TURNING FOUR SEGMENTS INTO A LOOP

(76) Inventors: **Rem Koolhaas, Ole Scheeren, Shohei Shigematsu, Fernando Donis, Alain Fouraux**

Correspondence Address:

OMA, HEER BOKELWEG 149
3032 AD ROTTERDAM
TEL: + 31(0) 102438200

(21) Initial Application: CCTV, Beijing, CHINA

(22) Filed:......................2002

(23) ABSTRACT

By breaking (60) the traditional tower that merely goes up and down at four points, a loop of building can be generated that unites and confronts (61, 62) its population in a single whole and cements a coherence of elements, isolating and separating them.,

UNIVERSAL MODERNIZATION PATENT [14]

"CAKE-TIN ARCHITECTURE" (2002)

Patent Number: 11, 428, 187

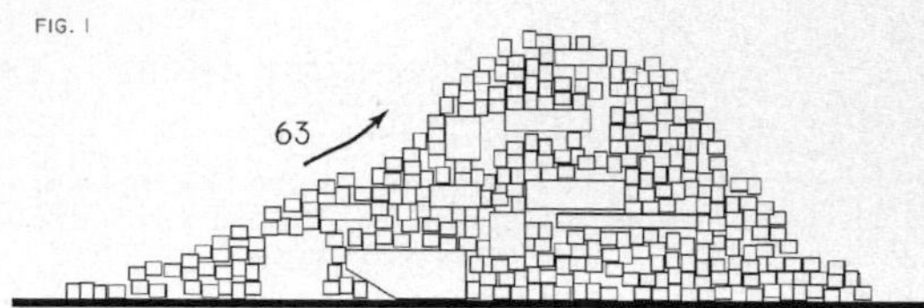

(21) **Patent for "Cake-Tin Architecture"**

(29) **ACCOMODATION OF THE RESIDUALS OF A DOMINANT PROGRAM IN A NOUVELLE CUISINE MOLD**

(36) Inventors: **Rem Koolhaas, Ole Scheeren, Shohei Shigematsu, Fernando Donis, Alain Fouraux**

Correspondence Address:
OMA, HEER BOKELWEG 149
3032 AD ROTTERDAM
TEL: + 31(0) 102438200

(42) **Initial Application: <u>TVCC, Beijing, CHINA</u>**

(54) **Filed:......................2002**

(71) **ABSTRACT**

By collecting all the contradictory demands of a complex program without attempting to resolve them and casting them in a totally arbitrary, pleasing form, charm can be generated on a big scale from heterogeneous elements.

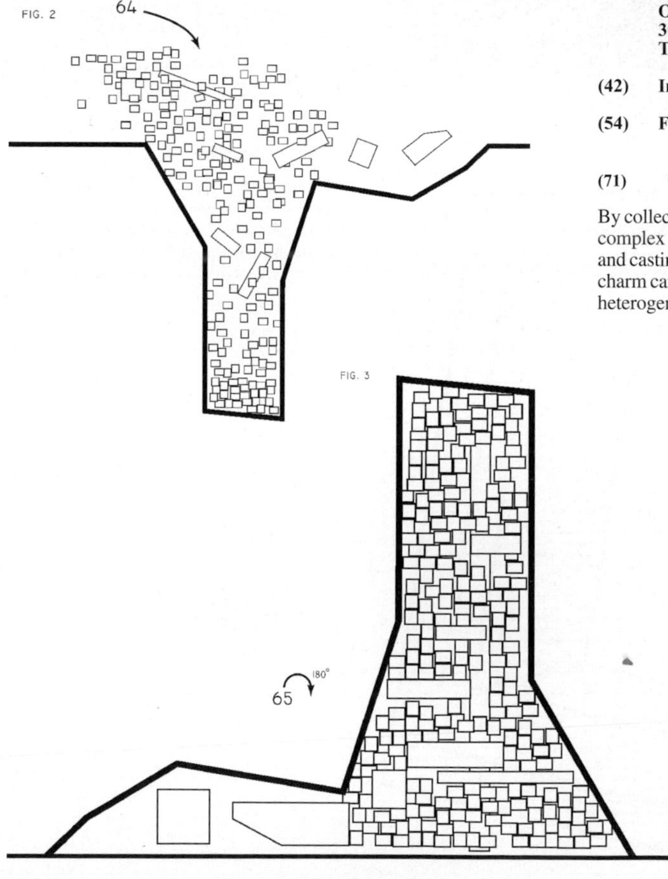

UNIVERSAL MODERNIZATION PATENT

"THE END OF THE ROAD" (2003)

Patent Number: 12, 175, 276

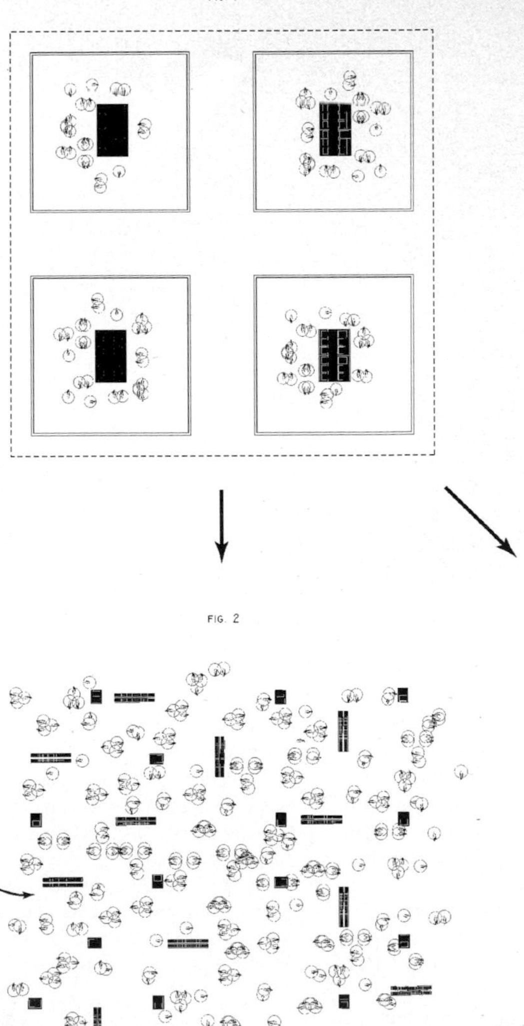

(54) Patent for "The End of the Road"

(54) ACTIVATION OF THE CENTRAL BUSINESS DISTRICT ARCHETYPE BY EITHER CONCENTRATING OR DIFFUSING THE CORES OVER A SINGLE URBAN CARPET

(76) Inventors: **Rem Koolhaas, Ma Qingyun, Fernando Donis**

Correspondence Address:

OMA, HEER BOKELWEG 149
3032 AD ROTTERDAM
TEL: + 31(0) 102438200

(21) **Initial Application: CBD, Beijing, CHINA**

(22) **Filed:.....................2003**

(23) **ABSTRACT**

Take the distributed cores of the typical Central Business District (Fig.1); lower the buildings and distribute the cores even further so that they create a field condition of pervasive insulation (Fig.2) or consolidate them in a single mega core (Fig.3), so that the same urban area can support two times the program in typologies that both promote interdependence instead of creating the clusters of stand-alone entities - the so-called skyscraper - of the typical CBD.

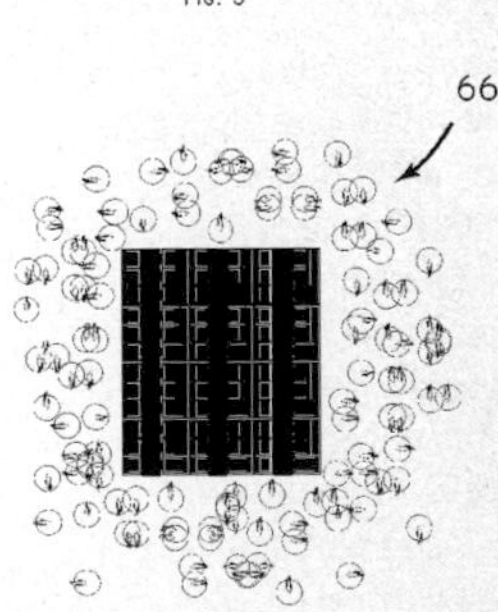

01/November/03

11/Sept/2001

Post-modern engineering?

With our current sophistication, the collapsed WTC – the trade center as ruin – seems almost more plausible than the building in its original state, as if its destruction was a mere adjustment to the Zeitgeist.

With our current apparatus – both our own shock-proof tolerance and the facile virtuosity of the computer - we can read the ruin, not as an irreversible tragedy, but almost as a phase difference, a unique moment in a long chain of possible states, that you could erase with a simple "undo."

Two of "our" engineers were involved in 9-11's aftermath: one the inheritor of the original firm that had engineered it as a masterpiece of modernism pushed to its ultimate conclusion - i.e. the absolute rationality of a predictable universe where, in a ruthless reduction of detail and a focus on essence, all structure between core and load-bearing wall was eliminated, the horizontal and the vertical connected in one ultimate coupling, repeated everywhere in the tower, *ad infinitum*.

For the second, his firm's computer simulation of the infernal heat that the WTC ruin retained and the predicted pattern of its eventual cooling off, which dictated the sequence in which its remnants could be dumped in New Jersey, was almost as exciting as that of its erection, an intellectual challenge of the same, if not superior, order. We can think construction and destruction in the same breath....

He had an ability to engage the arbitrary demands of an ever-extending stable of architects, each with his or her own "tics," none of them interested, anymore, in claiming reason either as an argument or ally. On the contrary, together - without knowing it - their individual demands constituted a campaign to kill off all the sacred cows of structural precedent and good practice. For them, he had calculated walls out of kilter, sloping floor plates, pushed columns in all directions, created tenuous houses of cards, put together absurd Humpty Dumpties. Like a Samson by proxy, he had destroyed the Temple of Cartesianism almost single-handedly (he could not help thinking sometimes). His firm, once avid supporters of High Tech, modernism's moment of decadence, were - in a form of emancipation - now exploring a kind of science fiction, meta-engineering as a total answer to everything.

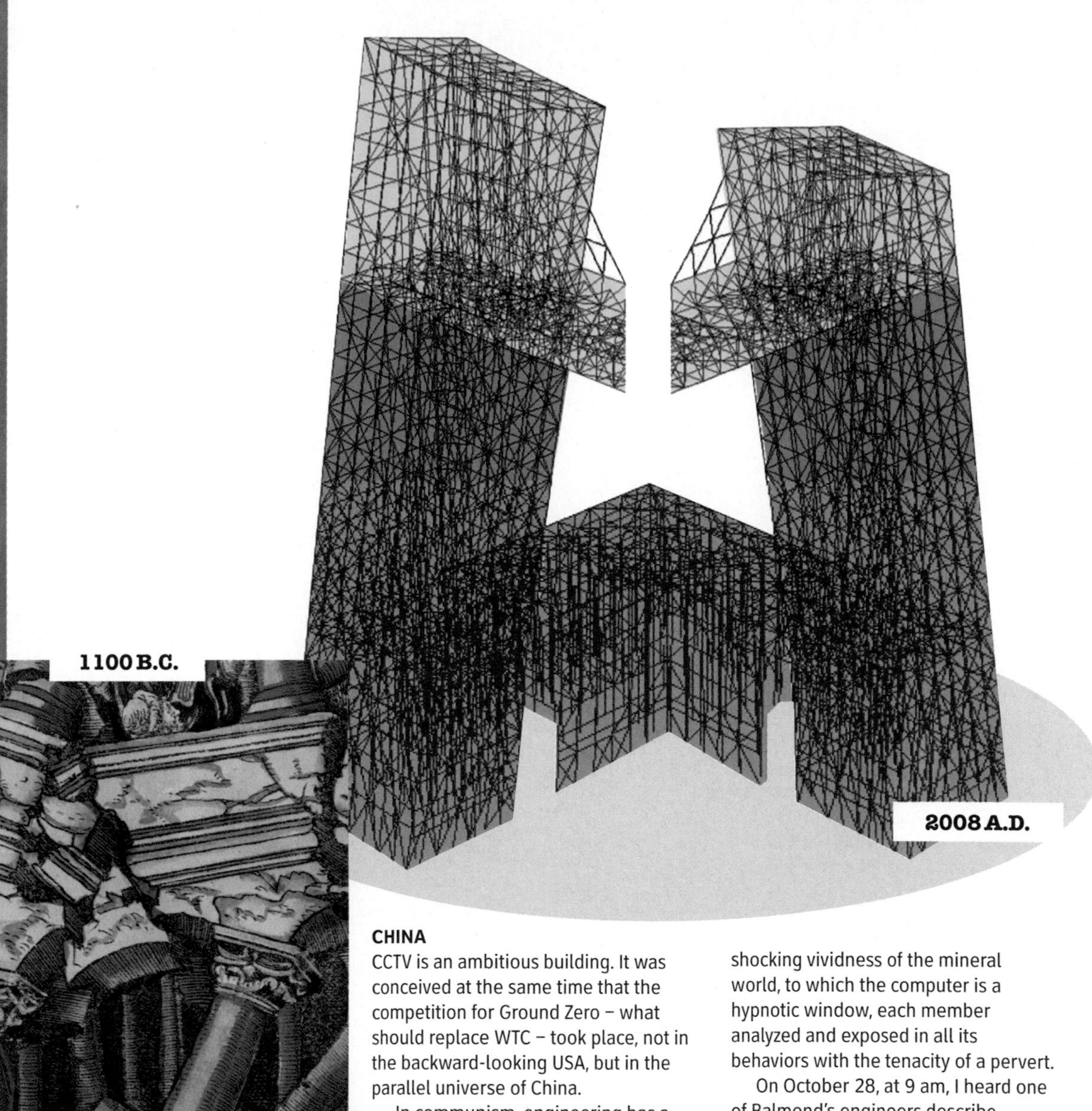

JUDGES, FOL.LV: SAMSON TEARING DOWN THE HOUSE OF THE PHILISTINES

CHINA

CCTV is an ambitious building. It was conceived at the same time that the competition for Ground Zero – what should replace WTC – took place, not in the backward-looking USA, but in the parallel universe of China.

In communism, engineering has a very high status, its laws resonating with Marxian wheels of history. To prove the stability of a structure that violated some of the most sincerely held convictions about logic and beauty, ARUP had to dissect every issue in extreme degrees of detail. The effort to reassure only reveals the scary aliveness of every structure – its continuous elasticity, creep, shrinkage, sagging, bending, buckling, the shocking vividness of the mineral world, to which the computer is a hypnotic window, each member analyzed and exposed in all its behaviors with the tenacity of a pervert.

On October 28, at 9 am, I heard one of Balmond's engineers describe, without irony or noticeable wavering, how the encounter and eventual joining, at 200 meters, of sloping steel structures that, through their relative positions on the ground were exposed to different amounts of solar heat-gain, could only take place at dawn, when both had cooled off during the night and were most likely to share the same temperature. I was elated and horrified by the sheer outrage of the problem that we had set them. Why do they never say NO? ■ **RK**

OMA / AMO SINCE SMLXL

UNITED STATES OF AMERICA

Project: Metro Dade Performing Arts Center. Status: Competition 1994. Client: Metropolitan Dade County, Performing Arts Center Trust, Florida. Location: Miami, USA. Site: Biscayne Boulevard, Miami. Program: 2480 seat Opera Hall, 2200 seat Concert Hall, supporting facilities. Team: Rem Koolhaas, Floris Alkemade, Hernando Arrazola, Gary Bates, Petra Blaisse, Gro Bonesmo, John Dehart. Structure: Arup. Acoustics: Artac.Theater Consultant: Fisher Dachs

Project: MCA Master Plan and Headquarters Building Concept Design. Status: Commission and Design Development 1996. Client: Universal Studios. Location: Los Angeles, California. Site: Universal City, Los Angeles. Program: Re-develop Universal City 1,000,000m2: City Walks including amphitheatre, cinema, cafés, retail, theme parks, hotels, studios and parking. Team: Rem Koolhaas, Dan Wood, with Floris Alkemade, Mathias Bauer, Frans Blok, Gro Bonesmo, Emanuelle Champalle, Minsuk Cho, Christophe Cornubert, Hans Cool, Vincent Coste, Otto Driesden, Chris van Duijn, Sarah Dunn, Anthony Fontenot, Bill Gaskins, Wilfried Hackenbroich, Machteld Hendricks, Reiner Hermes, Matthias Hollwich, Andreas Huhn, Alex Karcher, Anna Kling, Niko Knebel, Christine Machynia, Jose Molmans, Sophie Morgense, Simone Nagel, Oleg Nikolaevski, Philip Oswalt, Rinske van Ramshorst, Joshua Ramus, Ole Scheeren, Sandra Schneider-Marfels, Charlotte Senly. Structure: Arup. Cost: Donnel Consultants inc.

Project: Universal Headquarters Building. Status: Commission 1996. Client: Seagram. Location: Los Angeles, United States. Site: Universal City, Los Angeles. Program: 600,000sf Offices; 50,000sf health club, cafeteria, screening room, etc. 200 parking spaces. Schematic Design Team: Rem Koolhaas, Dan Wood, Sarah Dunn, Mark McVay, Adrianne Fisher, with Xavier Calderon, Pedro Costa, Bert Karel Deuten, Chris van Duijn, Keith Donnelley, Robert Donnelly, Piet Eckert, Roger van Est, Mark Guinand, Wilfried Hackenroich, Reinier Hermes, Matthias Hollwich, Andreas Huhn, Kohei Kashimoto, Rob de Maat, Beth Margulis, Oleg Nikolaevski, Bill Price, Joshua Ramus, Erik Schotte, Florian Seidel, Isabel da Silva. Design Development Team: Rem Koolhaas, Dan Wood, Ellen van Loon, Adrianne Fisher, with Olga Aleksakova, Eliot Bu, Robert Choeff, Chris van Duijn, Mark Eacott,Erez Ella, Keren Englman, Anne Filson, Bruce Fisher, Jens Holm, Anna Jacinto, Annt Lassila, Anna Little, Shawn Mulligan, Oliver Michell, Christian Muller, Daan Ooievaar, Ala Pratt, Bill Price, Markus Randler, Gerald Rogers, Fernando Romero Havaux, Shohei Shigematsu, Ann Shih, Peer Sievers, Isabel da Silva, Galia Solomonoff, Ilkka Tarkkanen, Lucien Tinga, Olivier Touraine, Jan Vermeulen, Leonhard Weil, Bernard Wolff, Marco Zurn. Associate Architect: House and Robertson Associates, USA. Structure: Arup. Landscape: Inside Outside / Mia Lehrer & Associates. Curtain Wall Consultant: Robert Jan Van Santen, Germany. Curtain Wall Sub-Contractors: Benson Industries, USA. Geo-technical Consultant: Converse Consultants West, USA

Project: McCormick-Tribune Campus Center. Status: Competition 1997, 1st Prize. Completion 2003. Client: Illinois Institute of Technology. Budget: $35m (US). Location: Chicago, USA. Site: In the center of historic Mies van der Rohe campus, underneath the metro, neighboring a Mies pavilion. Program: 10,690 m2: campus center. Principal: Rem Koolhaas. Project Director: Dan Wood. Project Architects: Kristina Manis, Jonilla Dorsten, Anne Filson, Sarah Dunn. Site Architects: Jeffrey Johnson, Mark Schendel (SGA). Team: Gary Bates, Frans Blok, Gro Bonesmo, Eliot Bu, Becca Dudley, Martin Felsen, Adrianne Fisher, Bruce Fisher, Christina Fuchs, Laura Gilmore, Uwe Herlyn, Matthias Hollwich, Fernando Romero Havaux, Krystyan Keck, Adam Kurdahl, Vanessa de Assis Lamounier, Julien Monfort, Christian Müller, Matteo Poli, Julien de Smedt, Tuomas Toibonen, Angela van der Zee. R+D: Erik Schotte, Bill Price. Associate Architect: Holabird & Root. Site: Studio Gang Architects (SGA). Structure: Arup London. Services: Huygen Elwako. Graphics: 2x4. Acoustics: TNO Center for Building Research. Landscape: Inside Outside / Schaudt Landscape Architecture. Curtains and Interiors: Inside Outside. Models: Vincent de Rijk, Bert Karel Deuten, Marc Guinand, Gaspar Libedinsky

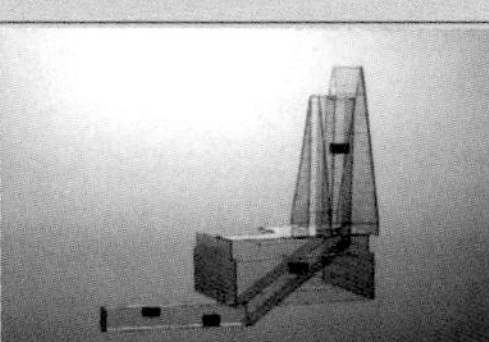

Project: M(oMA) Charrette. Status: Competition 1997. Client: Museum of Modern Art, New York. Location: New York, USA. Site: 53rd and 54th street, Manhattan, New York. Program: 470,120sf: Exhibition space, curatorial department, education facility, film/performance space, book store, workspaces, restaurant, garden lobby, lobby, storage. Team: Rem Koolhaas, Dan Wood, with Vincent Coste, Roijer van Est, Wilfried Hackenbroich, Matthias Hollwich, Kohei Kashimoto, Joshua Ramus, Ole Scheeren, Isabel da Silva. Model: Werkplaats de Rijk/Parthesius. Research: Stijn Rademakers, Jeff Hardwick, Bill Price, Eric Schotte. Graphic Design: 2x4. Photography: Hectic Pictures.

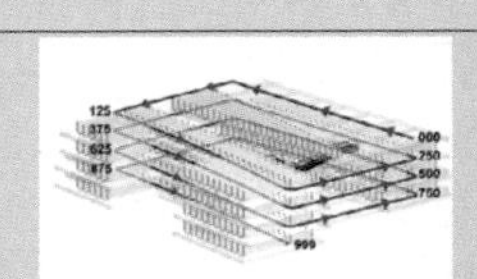

Project: Seattle Central Library. Status: Commission 1999. Completion 2004. Client: The Seattle Public Library. Budget: $111.9m (US). Location: Seattle, USA. Site: City block located at 1000 Fourth Avenue, Seattle, WA 98104, USA. Program: 412,000sf: Central library including HQ, reading room, book spiral, mixing chamber, meeting platform, living room, staff floor, children's collection, and auditorium 363,000sf; parking 49,000sf. Partners-in-Charge: Rem Koolhaas and Joshua Ramus. Project Architects: Meghan Corwin, Mark von Hof-Zogrotzki, Bjarke Ingels, Carol Patterson, Natasha Sandmeier, Dan Wood. Team : Keely Colcleugh, Rachel Doherty, Sarah Gibson, Laura Gilmore, Anna Little, John McMorrough, Kate Orff, Beat Schenk, Saskia Simon, Anna Sutor, Victoria Willocks with Florence Clausel, Thomas Dubuisson, Chris van Duijn, Erez Ella, Achim Gergen, Eveline Jürgens, Antti Lassila, Hannes Peer, Jao Costa Ribeiro, Kristina Skoogh, Sybille Wätli, Leonard Weil. Joint Venture Architect: LMN. Structure: Arup London, Los Angeles / Magnusson Klemencic Associates. Services: Arup London, Los Angeles. Fire: Arup London, Los Angeles. IT & A/V: Arup London, Los Angeles. Civil: Magnusson Klemencic Associates. Acoustics: Michael Yantis Associates. Environmental Graphics: Bruce Mau Design. Facades: Dewhurst Macfarlane & Partners. Interiors: OMA, LMN / Inside Outside. Landscape: Inside Oustide / Jones & Jones / Greenlee Nursery. Lighting: Kugler Tillotson Associates.

See pg 517. Project: Astor Place Hotel. Status: Commission 2000. Client: Ian Schrager Hotels. Location:New York, USA. Site: Empty lot at Astor Place, Manhattan,. Program: 150,000sf: Hotel with 260 rooms, lobby, health club, lounge, restaurant, bar, urban plaza. Principals: Jacques Herzog(H&dM), Rem Koolhaas, Pierre de Meuron(H&dM). Project Managers: Harry Guger (H&dM), Dan Wood. Team: François Charbonnet (H&dM), Anja Ehrenfeld (H&dM), Hans Focketyn, Alain Fouraux, Fenna Haakma Wagenaar, David Moore, Christopher Pannett (H&dM), Stephan Segessenmann (H&dM), Stan Vandriessche (H&dM), Adrien Verschuere (H&dM). Joint Venture: Herzog & de Meuron (H&dM)

Project: Brooklyn Academy of Music Cultural District Master Plan. Status: Commission 2000. Client: BAM Local Development Corporation. Location: Brooklyn, New York, USA. Site: 1.5 million SF mixed-use development on four sites adjacent to BAM Center in

Bel +31(0)102438200

Astor Place Hotel. Could mankind's love for prismatic form be one of the losses of 9/11? Are we condemned by neo-caveman to regress to the level of the cave dweller? Our addiction to comfort can only terminate at the cave. In retrospect, the history of Astor Place is spooky. Begun as an effort by two European architects to conceive a boutique hotel in Manhattan for the inventor of the type - Ian Schrager. It turned, through the combined effects of the client's insecurity, financial considerations, and the architects' uncanny premonition, from an initial proliferation of miniature WTCs into, finally, a vertical piece of Afghanistan rock, perforated by inhabited caves, fifteen months before 9/11.

Lehman Maupin. Second incarnation of a Manhattan gallery that had to move from SoHo to Chelsea to avoid commercialization and to respond to artists demands....

historic Downtown Brooklyn. Program: 1,500,000sf: commercial 500,000sf; mixed-income residential 500,000sf; cultural 450,000sf; retail 50,000sf. Principal: Rem Koolhaas. Project Director: Dan Wood. Team: Eric Chang, Matthias Hollwich, Casey Mack. Associate Architect: Dillier + Scofidio, New York. Zoning: Michael Kwartler and Associates. Parking: Philip Habib & Associates

Project: Guggenheim Las Vegas and Hermitage Guggenheim. Status: Commission 2000. Completed 2001. Client: The Venetian Casino Resort and the Solomon R. Guggenheim Foundation. Location: The Venetian Casino Resort, Las Vegas, USA. Site: Guggenheim Hermitage: small strip between entrance and lobby of The Venetian; Las Vegas Guggenheim: space between hotel and parking garage. Program: 7,660sf: Guggenheim Hermitage: flexible exhibition space and Museum store; 63,700sf: the Las Vegas Guggenheim: flexible exhibition space and Museum store. Principal: Rem Koolhaas. Project Director: Joshua Ramus. Project Architect: Christian Bandi. Team: Lotte Adolf, Bina Bhattacharya, Alexandra Bub, Brandon Cook, Mark Frohn, Christian Kronaus, Peter Müller, Sebastian Reusch, Natasha Sandmeir, Sibylle Wältly, Mark Watanabe, Victoria Willocks. Associate Architect: Stubbins Associates. Consultants: Martin & Martin/Martin & Peltyn/Arup/MSA Engineering/Syska & Hennessz/Rolf Jensen Associates. Contractor: Taylor International.

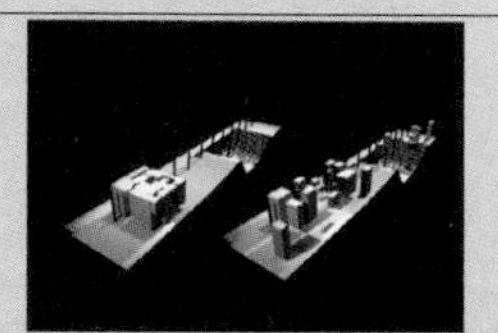

Project: Prada New York Epicenter. Status: Commission 2000. Completed 2001. Client: Prada (I.P.I. USA Corp.). Location: 575 Broadway, New York. Site: Space of former Broadway Guggenheim, Ground Floor and Basement. Program: 2,190 m2: New Epicenter store. Partners-in-Charge: Rem Koolhaas and Ole Scheeren. Project Architects: Timothy Archambault, Eric Chang. Team: Ergian Alberg, Amale Andraos, Benjamin Beckers, Christina Chang, Chris van Duijn, Alain Fouraux, Jennifer Jones, Julia Lewis, Christiane Sauer, Markus Schaefer, Oliver von Spreckelsen. Associate Architect: ARO. Structure: Leslie E. Robertson Associates (LERA). Services: Arup New York. Lighting: Kugler Tillotson Associates. Material R&D: Panelite/Werkplaats de Rijk. Acoustics: Shen Milsom & Wilke. Curtains: Inside Outside. Wall Paper: 2x4. Movable Furniture: Seufert.

Project: Prada Los Angeles Epicenter. Status: Commission 2000. Completion 2004. Client: Prada (I.P.I. USA Corp.). Location: 343 Rodeo Drive, Beverly Hills. Site: Lot on Rodeo Drive. Program: 1,900m2: New Epicenter store. Partners-in-Charge: Rem Koolhaas and Ole Scheeren. Project Architects: Jessica Rothschild, Eric Chang. Team: Amale Andraos, Christian Bandi, Catarina Canas, Chris van Duijn, Keren Englman, Ali Kops, Jocelyn Low, David Moore, Torsten Schroder, Mark Watanabe. Associate Architect: Brand+Allen Architects. Structure, Services: Arup Los Angeles. Lighting: Kugler Tillotson Associates. Material R&D: Panelite/Werkplaats de Rijk/RAM Contract/Chris van Duijn. Curtains: Inside Outside. Façades: Dewhurst McFarlane. Hydraulic Wall: Hamilton Engineering.

Project: Prada San Francisco Epicenter. Status: Commission 2000. Client: Prada (I.P.I. USA Corp.). Location: Kearny Market Mason Sutter District, San Francisco, USA. Site: On the corner of Post Street and Grant Avenue, San Francisco. Program: 4,000 m2: Store, Prada west coast headquarters and penthouse. Partners-in-Charge: Rem Koolhaas and Ole Scheeren. Project Architects: Kelly Ishida, Hilary Sample. Team: Evan Bennet, Chris van Duijn, Laszlo Fecske, Joao Ferrao, Alain Fouraux, Jens Hommert, Anttie Lassila, Kees Lemmens, Kit Lewis, Karolina Machalica, Jao Costa Ribeiro, Pim van Wylik, Yumiko Yamada, Hiroshi Yoshino . Associated Architect: Brand+Allen Architects, San Francisco. Structure, Services: Arup USA. Material R&D: Panelite/Werkplaats de Rijk/Parthesius / Chris van Duijn

Project: Taschen House. Status: Commission 2000. Client: Benedikt and Angelika Taschen. Location: Los Angeles, USA. Site: Hollywood Hills, Los Angeles. Program: Extension to Chemosphere house. Principal: Rem Koolhaas. Project Architect: Jeffrey Inaba. Team: Dorte Boerresen, Shiro Ogata, Henning Stueben

See pg 518. Project: Lehmann Maupin Gallery. Status: Commission 2001. Completed 2002. Client: Rachel Lehmann and David Maupin. Location: New York, USA. Site: Two-storey industrial building in New York's Chelsea neighborhood. Program: 5,700sf: art exhibition 3,200sf; administration 1,000sf; art storage 500sf. Principals: Rem Koolhaas, Dan Wood. Project Architects: Tim Archambault, Jeffrey Johnson. Team: Amale Andraos, Eric Chang. Associate Architect: Jacobson, Shinoda & Middleton Architects. Structure, Services: Guy Nordenson & Associates. Lighting Designers: Light & Space/Kugler Tillotson Associates. Curtain Design: Inside Outside

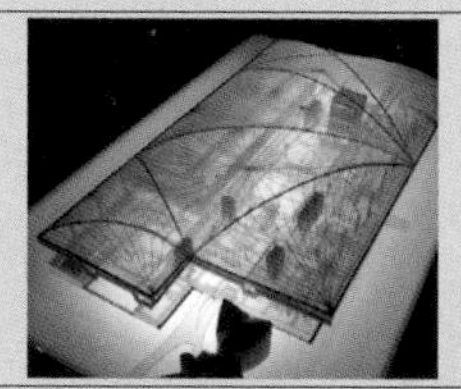

Project: Los Angeles County Museum of Art. Status: Competition 2001, 1st Prize, Pre-Schematic Design 2002. Client: Los Angeles County Museum of Art. Budget: $200m (US). Location: Los Angeles, USA. Site: located in Hancock Park at the site of the existing museum. Program: 175,410sf plinth, service & support; 199,973sf plaza, public facilities & temporary galleries; 18,000sf study center; 228,399sf Plateau, permanent collections. Partners-in-Charge: Rem Koolhaas and Ole Scheeren. Project Manager: Carol Patterson. Project Architects: Christian Bandi, Saskia Simon. Team: Charles Berman, Gabriela Bojalil, Selva Gurdogan, Jens Hommert (AMO), Stuart Maddocks, Shiro Ogata, Torsten Schröder. Competition Team: Olga

UN City. South of the United Nations building on the East River, three towers by three firms - Japanese, American, European - explore mutual dependencies and support.

Aleksakova, Christian Bandi, Meghan Corwin, Markus Dettling, Fernando Donis, Erez Ella, Alain Fouraux, Sharon Goren, Jens Holm, Jeffrey Johnson, Matthew Murphy, Shiro Ogata, Roberto Otero, Will Prince, Joshua Ramus, Deborah Richmond, Jonas Sandberg, Shohei Shigematsu, Joris Voorn, Fenna Haakma Wagenaar, Dan Wood, Yumiko Yamada. Structure, Services: Arup. Cost: DLA. Curatorial: Hans Ulrich Obrist, Chris Dercon.

See pg 519.Project: UN City. Status: Competition 2001. Location: New York, USA. Site: Former ConEd site at the East River between 42 Street and 34 Street, Manhattan. Program: Large scale entertainment, shopping, housing and office complex with a large public and infrastructural program. Team: Rem Koolhaas, Dan Wood, with Amale Andraos, Alisa Andrasek, Evan Bennet, Meghan Corwin, Erez Ella, Shohei Shigematsu, Henning Stuben, Yumiko Yamada. Joint Venture with: Kohn Pedersen Fox / Davis Brody Bond / Toyo Ito & Associates / The Onlin Partnership / DIRT Studio / 2x4 Incorporated

Project: Whitney Museum Extension, Scheme A. Status: Commission 2001, Concept Design. Client: Whitney Museum. Location: New York, USA. Site: Whitney Museum of American Art, 945 Madison Avenue, New York. Program: 60,000sf: lobby, new galleries, auditorium, new restaurant, library expansion, education, new museum store, art storage. Principal: Rem Koolhaas. Project Director: Dan Wood. Project Manager: Carol Patterson. Project Architect: Shohei Shigematsu. Team: Olga Aleksakova, Ali Arvanaghi-Jadid, Brandon Cook, Markus Dettling, Erez Ella, Marissa Fort, Alain Fouraux, Sarah Gibson, Laura Gilmore, Fenna Haakma-Wagenaar, Caya Loeper, John McMorrough (AMO), Shiro Ogata, Natasha Sandmeier, Tuomas Toivonen, Sybille Waltly, Dan Wood, Yumiko Yamada. Associate Architects: DBB. Structure: Arup

Project: Whitney Museum Extension, Scheme B. Status: Commission 2002, Concept Design. Client: Whitney Museum. Location: New York, USA. Site: Whitney Museum of American Art, 945 Madison Avenue, New York. Program: 3,212m2: lobby, new galleries, auditorium, new restaurant, library expansion, education, new museum store, art storage. Partner-in-Charge: Rem Koolhaas. Project Manager: Carol Patterson. Project Architect: Erez Ella. Team: Kunle Adeyemi, Sarah Gibson, Narjis Lemrin, Victoria Willocks. Associate Architects: DBB. Structure: Arup

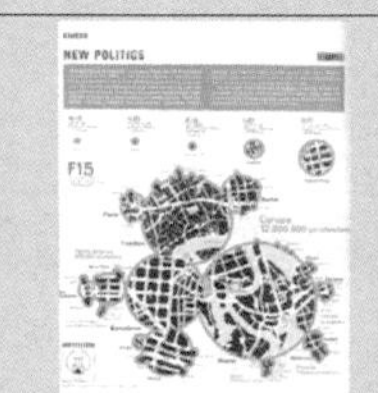

Project: Wired, AMO. Status: Commission 2002. Client: Wired. Program: Editing special issue of wired magazine. Team AMO: Rem Koolhaas, with Lucia Allais, Michael Rock and Theo Deutinger, Reinier de Graaf, Jeffrey Inaba, Brendan McGetrick, Hans Ulrich Obrist, Nanne de Ru, Markus Schaefer.

BAHAMAS

See pg 520.Project: The Distributed House. Status: Commission 2000. Client: Withheld. Location: Harbor Island, the Bahamas. Site: Allotment 17, between Nesbitt road and the Atlantic Ocean, North of Dunmore town, Harbor Island. Program: Private residence: master bedroom, kids tower, dining room, guesthouse and staff house are distributed across the site plan . Principal: Rem Koolhaas . Project Director: Dan Wood. Project Architects: Andreas Huhn, Jeffrey Johnson . Team: Olga Aleksakova, Catarina Canas, Thomas Duda, Chris Van Duijn, Sharon Goren, Thorsten Kiefer, Will Prince, Karen Shanski, Shohei Shigematsu, Pim van Wylick. Associate Architect: Bruce LaFleur & Associates ltd. Bahamas. Structure: Advicebureau voor. Bouwtechniek BV. Services: Arup .Interior/Landscape: Inside Outside

PORTUGAL

Project: Casa da Musica. Status: Competition 1999, 1st Prize. Completion 2004. Client: Porto 2001, The City of Porto. Location: Porto, Portugal. Site: Rotunda da Boavista, a round square not far from the city center. Program: 30,000 m2: Concert hall with 1,200 seats, concert hall with 350 seats, restaurant, music shop, café, roof terrace, car park for 600 cars, educational and cybermusic facilities. Partners-in-Charge: Rem Koolhaas and Ellen van Loon. Project Architects: Adrianne Fisher, Michelle Howard. Team: Fernando Romero Havaux, Isabel da Silva, Robert Choeff, Barbara Wolff, Saskia Simon, Christian von der Muelde, Rita Armando, Philip Koenen, Peter Mueller, Krystian Keck, Eduarda Lima, Christoff Scholl, Alex de Long, Nuno Rosado, Alois Zierl, Uwe Herlijn, Olaf Hotz, Lorge Toscana, Duarte

1993-2003 Architectural adventures?

The Distributed House. As the endless boom flourished and with the Hamptons as a test-bed, the American Home inflated to reach morbid proportions where any relationship with anything - nature, or even the suburb - became delusional. On a delicate site of small dunes, hills, and valleys, covered by a semi-accessible jungle on Harbor Island in the Bahamas, all the separate elements of a house are distributed so that each captures a particular feature of the landscape. The dining room dominates the center like a mini acropolis; the master bedroom is poised on the dunes like a Temple of Venus; the guesthouse is relentlessly focused on the ocean; the kids inhabit an Atelier van Lieshout (AVL) container assembly; the pool is a connector, and the servants discreetly guard the entrance.

Santos, Nelson Carvahlo, Stefanie Wandinger, Catarina Canaas, Shadi Rahbaran. Structure: Arup London/ AFA Lda. Services: Arup London/AFA Lda/RGA. Fire Consultancy: Ohm/Gerisco. Acoustics: Dorsser Blesgraaf. Interiors, Curtains: Inside Outside. Scenography: Ducks Scèno. Facade: van Santen. Auditorium Chairs: Martin van Severen.

SPAIN

Project: Santa Cruz de Tenerife. Status: Competition 1998. Location: Tenerife, Spain. Program: Urban Strategy, consolidate the port to the north allowing Santa Cruz to reach the water as it develops southward. Team: Rem Koolhaas, Joshua Ramus, Gary Bates, Donald van Dansik, Chris van Duijn, Walter Hoogerwerf, Bjarke Ingels, Isabel da Silva, Galia Solomonoff, Hanna Svensson. Port Consultant: de Weger Engineers.

Project: Barcelona Airport - Espacio Pasatiempo. Status: Competition 2001. Client: AENA. Location: Barcelona, Spain. Program: New terminal for Barcelona Airport. Team: Rem Koolhaas, Reinier de Graaf, Alain Fouraux, Carolina Ligtenberg, Paz Martin, Shohei Shigematsu, Johan De Wachter.

See pg 523.Project : Cordoba Congess Center. Status: Competition 2001, 1st Prize. Design Development 2002. Client: City of Cordoba. Budget: €50m. Location: Cordoba, Spain. Site: Strip between Miraflores Park and Miraflores neighborhood on the South Bank of the Guadalquivir River. It is adjacent to the UNESCO protected Historic Center of Cordoba. Program: 35,500m2: visitor's center, auditorium, conference center, exhibition hall, five-star hotel, retail lobby, and public rooftop activities. Principal: Rem Koolhaas. Project Director: Ellen Van Loon.Team: Christian Bandi, Fernando Donis, Saskia Simon, Gregers Thomsen, Johan de Wachter Competiton Team: Rem Koolhaas, Erik Schotte, Fernando Donis, Roberto Otero with Catarina Canas, Thorsten Kiefer, Sibylle Wältly

UNITED KINGDOM

See pg 522.Project: Cardiff Bay Opera House .Status: Competition 1994 .Client: Cardiff Bay Opera House Trust, Cardiff. Budget: £25m. Location: Cardiff, Wales, United Kingdom. Program: 1500 seat auditorium. Team: Rem Koolhaas, Gary Bates, Gro Bonesmo, Jeanne Gang, Udo Garritzmann, Xaveer de Geyter, Fumi Hoshino, Barend Koolhaas, Mark Schendel, Andy Woodcock, Yo Yamagata . Structure: Arup

Project: Tate Modern. Status: Competition 1994, 2nd Prize. Client: Tate Gallery, Millbank, London SW1P 4RG. Budget: $63 (US). Location: London, England. Site: Former Electric Facility in Southwark, London. Program: Extension of Tate gallery in a former electric facility including; experimental exhibition space 7695m; classic exhibition space 7725m2; themed exhibition space 5995m2; pavilions 2930m2; lecture halls 2370m2; large exhibition space 3360m2; temporary exhibition space 2990m2; auditorium, café/bar 945m2. Team: Rem Koolhaas, Floris Alkemade, Gro Bonesmo, Frans Blok, Dan Wood. Associate Architect: Richard Gluckman Architects, New York. Structure: Arup. Models: Werkplaats de Rijk/Parthesius. Graphic Design: 2x4. Cost: Davis Landon & Everest.

Project: Cities on the Move. Status: Exhibition Design 1999. Client: Hayward Gallery, London. Location: South Bank, London. Site: Hayward Gallery and public terraces along the Thames. Program: Travelling exhibition on Southeast Asian cities, art and architecture with more than 100 participants. Team: Rem Koolhaas and Ole Scheeren. Curators: Hans Ulrich Obrist and Hou Hanru

Bel +31(0)102438200

Project: South Bank Master Plan. Status: Competition 1999. Client: SBC. Location: London, United Kingdom. Site: South bank of the Thames, city center. Program: Re-organize surroundings of existing cultural facilities. Additional buildings: film school, music auditoria, commercial facilities. Team: Rem Koolhaas, Ole Scheeren, Donald van Dansik

Project: Ascot Residence. Status: Competition 2003. Client: anonymous. Location: Ascot, United Kingdom. Program: Residence for anonymous Russian client. Team: Rem Koolhaas, Floris Alkemade, Olga Aleksakova, Georg Bucher, Paz Martin, Florian Pucher, Sebastian Thomas, Johan De Wachter

FRANCE

Project: Maison à Bordeaux. Status: Commission 1994. Completed 1998. Location: Bordeaux, France. Site: 5km from Bordeaux centre on a cape-like hill. 180° view on the city and the river. Program: 500m2: 5 bedrooms, 3 bathrooms (main house); 100m2: 2 bedrooms, 2 bathrooms (guard/guesthouse). Team: Rem Koolhaas, with Maarten van Severen and: Jeanne Gang, Julien Monfort, Bill Price, Jeroen Thomas, Vincent Costes, Chris Dondorp, Erik Schotte, Yo Yamagata. Structure: Arup London. Fitted Furnishing and Mobile Platform: Maarten van Severen, Raf de Preter. Bookcase: Vincent de Rijk, Chris van Duijn. Coordination and Technical Assistance: Michel Règaud, Bordeaux. Facades: Robert-Jan van Santen. Hydraulics: Gerard Couillandeau. Interior: Inside Outside.

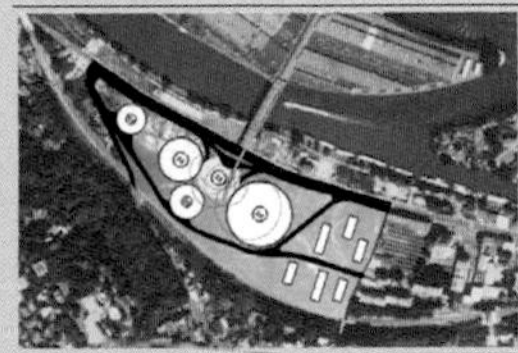

Project: Havas Seige Sociale. Status : Competition 2000. Client: Havas. Location: Paris, France. Program: Havas advertising 42,000 m2; lodgements 15 000m2; gymnasium 20,000 m2; public park. Team: Rem Koolhaas, Andreas Huhn, Annemie Depuydt (UAPS), with Frans Blok, Erik van Daele (UAPS), Hans Focketyn, Govert Gerritsen, Ben Jacquemet, Emanuele Mattutini, Shohei Shigematsu, Ron Southwick, Beatrice Timm, Kiki Verbeeck (UAPS). Associate Architect: UAPS.

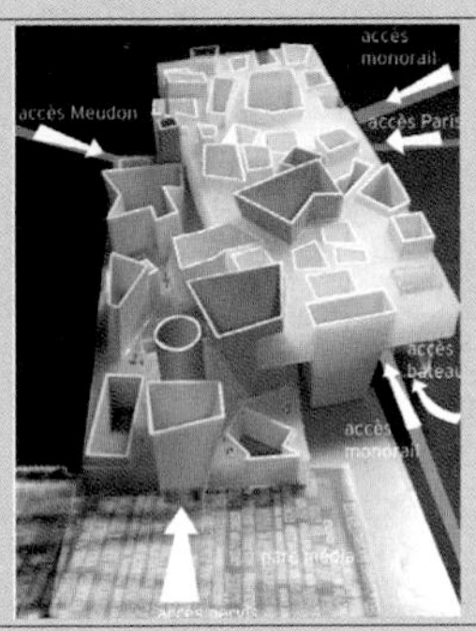

Project: Fondation Pinault. Status: Competition 2001. Location: Paris, France. Site: Ile Seguin, Paris. Program: Museum for a private collection. Team: Rem Koolhaas, Floris Alkemade, Toma Damish, Claudia Dische, Fernando Donis, Meghan Gorwin, Reinier de Graaf, Fenna Haakma Wagenaar, Beatriz Izquierdo, Alex de Jong, Paz Martin, Julien Montfort, David Moore, Shiro Ogata, Roberto Otero, Katayoun Parssanedjad, Matthieu Puyaubreau, Saskia Simon, Johan De Wachter, Sybille Waelty with Thorsten Kiefer, Cornelia Locke. Structure: Arup. Services: Arup. Acoustics: Dorsser Blessgraaf. Curatorial: Hans Ulrich Obrist. Model: Werkplaats de Rijk/Parthesius.

Project: Mutations. Status: Exhibition 2000-2001. Client: Arc en reve centre d'architecture. Location: Bordeaux, France. Site: Arc en reve centre d'architecture, Bordeaux. Program: Exhibition and book studying the acceleratod urbanization of the planet. Contributors: Rem Koolhaas and the Harvard Project on the City, Stefano Boeri Multiplicity, Sandford Kwinter, Nadia Tazi, Hans Ulrich Obrist. Directors: Francine Fort, Michel Jacques.

Project: Les Halles. Status: Competition 2003. Client: SEM Centre. Location: Paris, France. Site: Les Halles, Paris. Program: Masterplan for Les Halles. Team: Rem Koolhaas, Floris Alkemade, Benjamin Clarens, Nicolas Firket (AMO), Natacha Fricout, Michael Smith, Johan De Wachter. Associate Architects: XDGA/One Architecture/Agence Ter/ Partennaire Development.

BELGIUM

Project: Mercator Bank. Status: Competition 2001. Client: Mercator Bank. Location: Antwerp, Belgium. Site: Between Karel Coggestraat and Roderveltlaan, Antwerp. Program: Offices, auditorium, garden, library, shops, fitness, creche. Team: Rem Koolhaas, Erik Schotte, Roberto Otero, with Patrick Bruhn, Chris van Duijn, Paz Martin, Tammo Prinz, Johan de Wachter Associated Architect: MVS.

Project: European Identity Study, AMO. Status: Study 2001. Client: European Commission. Program: Examination of Brussels's role as "The Capital of Europe." Team AMO: Rem Koolhaas, Reinier de Graaf, with Catarina Canas, Fernando Donis, Nicolas Firket, Roberto Otero, Markus Schaefer, Saskia Simon, Johan de Wachter.

See pg 526.Project: New NATO Headquarters. Status: Competition 2002. Client: North Atlantic Treaty Organization. Location: Brussels, Belgium. Site: Leopold III Lane, Brussels. Program: Fully integrated NATO Headquarters: office space, conference center, connection square, press facilities, restaurants, retail, staff center; sports complex, creche, brasserie. Team: Rem Koolhaas, Carol Patterson, Reinier de Graaf, with Erez Ella, Alain Fouraux, Nicolas Firket, Sarah Gibson, Fenna Haakma Wagenaar, Matthew Murphy, Roberto Otero, Tammo Prinz, Shohei Shigematsu.

THE NETHERLANDS

See pg 525. Project: Educatorium, multifunctional university building. Status: Commission 1993. Completed 1997. Client: University of Utrecht. Budget: €12m. Location: Utrecht, Netherlands. Site: Utrecht University campus, based on masterplan by OMA (master plan second phase under construction and guided by Art Zaaijer Architects, Amsterdam). Program: University building 11,000m2: canteen (900 seats), 2 auditoria (400 and 500 seats), 3 examination rooms, lobby and connection to two existing campus buildings and parking for some 1100 bicycles. Team: Rem Koolhaas, Cristophe Cornubert, with Gary Bates, Frans Blok, Richard Eelman, Clement Gillet, Gaudi Houdaya, Michel Melenhorst, Enno Stemerding, Boukje Trenning, Henrik Valeur, Luc Veeger, Jacques Vink. Technical Support: Christian Müller, Erik Schotte.

Project: C3 - Towers on the Maas. Status: Feasibility Study 1994. Client: Geerlings Vastgoed. Location: Rotterdam, Netherlands. Program:

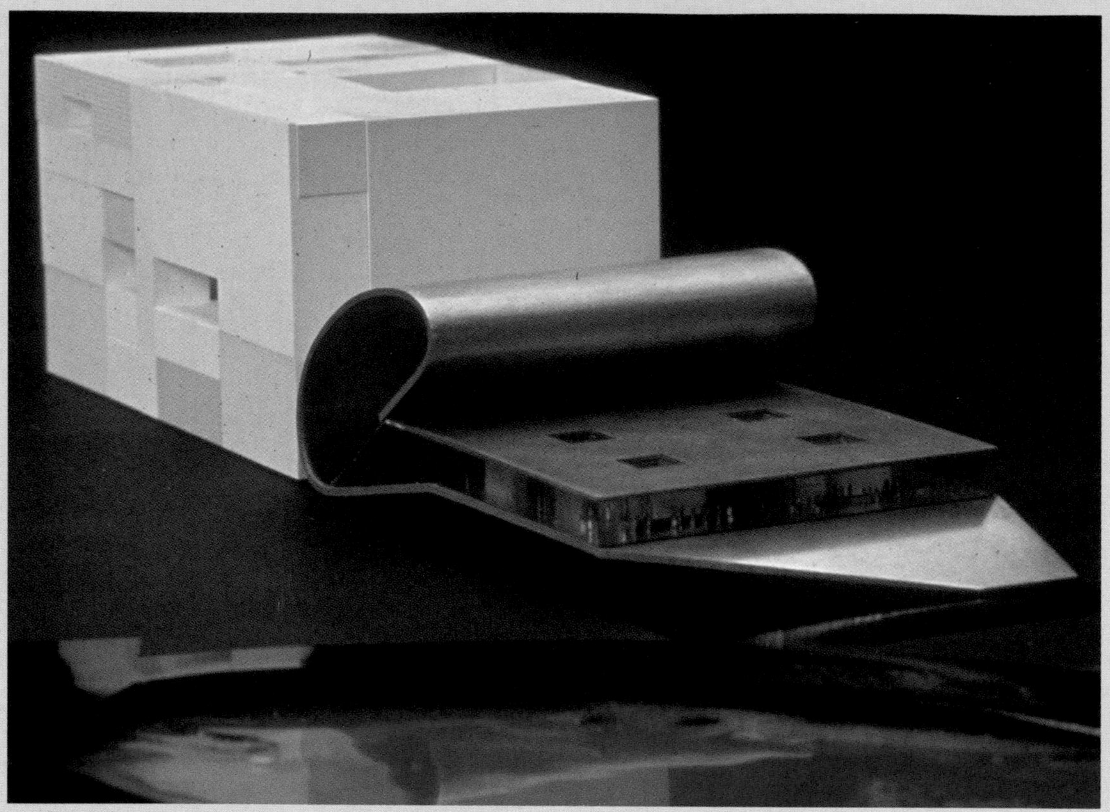

Cardiff Bay Opera House. For the opera in Cardiff, stage and auditorium are radically separated to enable both to perform as efficiently as possible; stage, rehearsal rooms, ateliers, form a single block; for the public, a broad stair turns into foyer, becomes stalls, turns up, becomes proscenium to meet the factory - the stage opening the only contact between the two volumes - to turn around as ceiling, to end as balcony.

Bel +31(0)102438200

CCC. Not obliged to put our building on the allocated site, we preferred to escape from the box and use it as a bridge toward Cordoba's main attractor, the Guadalquivir River, so that the sequence from the confrence center to the exhibition hall becomes a portico along the river bend, allowing the city to make money on the abandoned site.

500,000sf Offices; 200,000sf mixed use - residential, cinema, retail, offices; 450 parking spaces. Team: Rem Koolhaas, Esther Dekhuiyzen, Jeroen Thomas. Structure: Arup.

Project: A Star is Born. Status: Commission 1994. Completed 1995. Client: City of Groningen. Location: Groningen, Netherlands. Program: Public Toilet. Team: Rem Koolhaas, Gro Bonesmo, Jeroen Thomas. Design Associate: Erwin Olaf, Photo Artist.

Project: Souterrain The Hague. Status: Competition 1994. Completion 2004. Client: The City of The Hague, project team Souterrain. Budget: €130m. Location: Center of The Hague, The Netherlands. Program: Tram tunnel (1200 m), 2 tram stations, parking garage for 500 cars, poster museum. Team: Rem Koolhaas, Renè Heijnen, with Hernando Arrazola, Juliette Bekkering, Frans Blok, Rients Dijkstra, Odo Garritzmann, Jeanne Gang, Douglas Grieco, Fuminori Hoshino, Winy Maas. Site: Floris Alkemade. Advisor: S.A.T. (construction, installations).

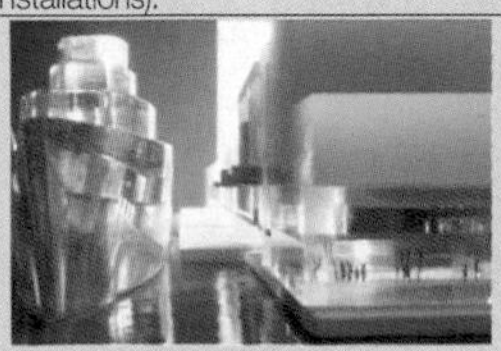

Project: Oostelijke Handelskade. Status: Commission 1995. Client: City of Amsterdam. Location: Amsterdam, Netherlands. Program: Urban master plan for former port site, design of cruise terminal. Team: Rem Koolhaas, Udo Garritzman, Ole Scheeren, Domenico Raimondo, Catherine Lassen.

Project: t'Paard.Status: Commission 1995. Completed 2003. Client: Ingenieursbureau Den Haag. Budget: €11.8m. Location: The Hague, Netherlands. Site: 2 classic former residences at major axis in center of The Hague. Program: 4,000 m2: 2 concert halls (300 and 1100 people), lobby, offices, café, backstage area, expedition space and technical facilities. Principal: Rem Koolhaas. Project Director: Floris Alkemade. Team: Bart Cardinaal, Jan Kooijman. Team 1995: Rem Koolhaas, Frans Blok, Rob Hilz, Christos Marcopoulos, Fokke Moerel, Don Weber. Project Management: Ingenieursbureau Den Haag / Bureau Bouwkunde Rotterdam. Monument Consultant: Rappange & Partners. Acoustics: Prinssen en Bus. Construction: Haskoning. Installations Consultant: Technisch Adviesbureau Galjema. Contractor: HBG Utiliteitsbouw. Theatre Installations: Stakebrand.

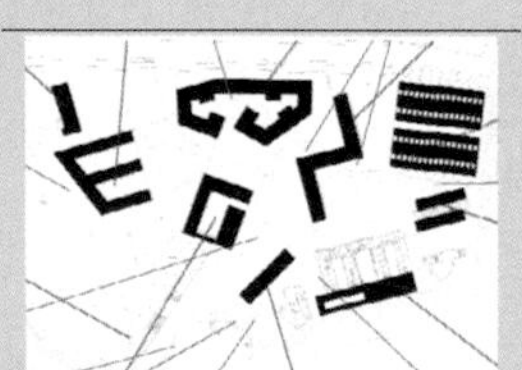

Project: Masterplan Chassè Terrein Breda. Status: Commission 1996. Completed 2000. Client: City of Breda. Budget: 200m NLG. Location: Breda, Netherlands. Site: In the Center of Breda, on a former military terrain. Program: 100,000 m2 housing; 18,500 m2 parking; 20,000 m2 other. 730 rental and owner-occupied houses. Patio houses, apartments, maisonettes, and ground-bound houses. Team: Rem Koolhaas, Xaveer de Geyter with Piet Eckert, Udo Garritzmann, Govert Garritsen, Christina Machynia, Michel Melenhorst, Sanna Schuiling, Enno Stemerdink, Catherine Thiebaut, Jeroen Thomas. Buildings: Kuiper Compagnons / Architecten Werkgroep / Van Sambeek en Van Veen / MAP Architects / Kollhoff + Rapp. Landscape: West 8. Model: Albert Bouwman.

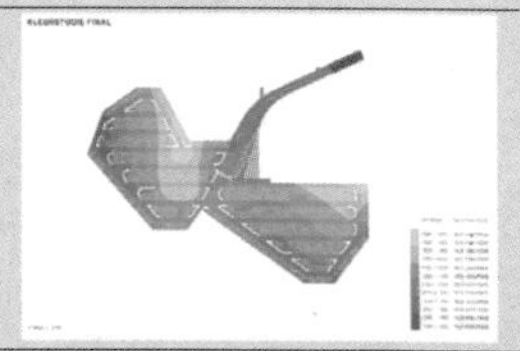

Project: Chassè Parking. Status: Commission 1996. Client: City of Breda. Location: Breda, Netherlands. Site: In the center of Breda, on a former military terrain. Program: 18,500 m2 for 670 parking spaces. Team: Rem Koolhaas, Bart Cardinaal, Bob Choeff, Richard Eelman, Udo Garritzman, Govert Gerritsen, Ana Almeida Jacinto, Jenny Jones, Philip Koenen, Jan Kooijman, Rob de Maat, Michel Melenhorst, Oliver Schütte, Shohei Shigematsu, Enno Stemerdink, Jeroen Thomas. Structure: Snellen Meulemans van Schaick. Services: Huisman en van Muijen BV. Site Supervision and Technical Support: Royal Haskoning BV. Cost: Peutz.

Project: Luxor Theater, Rotterdam. Status: Competition 1996, 2nd prize. Client: Municipality Rotterdam. Budget: 55m NLG. Location: Rotterdam, the Netherlands. Site: Kop van Zuid, Wilhelminapier, Rotterdam. Program:

1993-2003 Architectural adventures?

Theater 1500 seats: Public space 2,965m2; Auditorium 3,246m2; Backstage spaces 3,454m2; Facilities horeca spaces 536m2; Offices 590m2; General supporting spaces 300m2; Theatercafé 600,0m2. Team: Rem Koolhaas, Floris Alkemade, Christos Marcopoulos, Ole Scheeren, Frans Blok, Tom Bergevoet with Gro Bonesmo, Catherine Lassen, Sanna Schuiling, Enno Stemerding. Structure: Arup. Services: Arup. Acoustics: TNO Center for Building Research. Stage Design: Stakebrand bv. Model: Dan Wood, Vincent de Rijke. Cost: De Blaay-Van den Boogaard Raadgevende Ingenieurs bv.

Project: Netherlands 2030, Study . Status: Study Commission 1996. Client: Rijksplanologische Dienst. Location: Netherlands. Program: Study on the future planning of the Netherlands. Team: Rem Koolhaas, Donald van Dansik, Reinier de Graaf, Stijn Rademakers, Enno Stemerding.

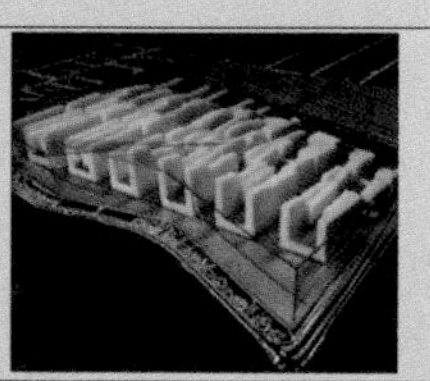

Project: Schiphol Logistics park. Status: Urban Study 1996. Client: Schiphol Area Development Company. Location: Schiphol, the Netherlands. Site: Kruisweg Zuid, south perimeter of Schiphol Airport, close to main cargo handling. Program: 200 ha site for value added logistics facilities. Team: Rem Koolhaas, Seong Lok Bae, Reinier de Graaf, Neville Mars. Consultants: de Weger Engineers / WACO Rotterdam

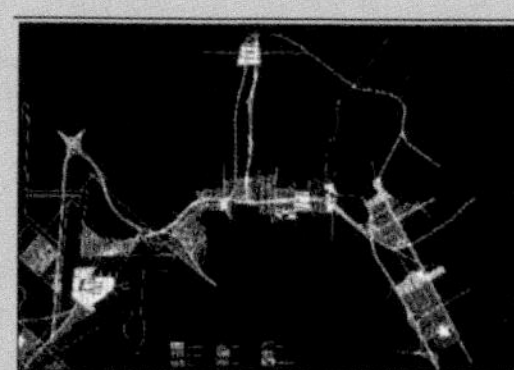

Project: Zuid As. Status: Study Commission 1996. Client: NS Vastgoed. Location: Amsterdam, Netherlands. Program: Study. Development of infrastructure of area in the south of Amsterdam into A-location for future office. Team: Rem Koolhaas, Mitchel Alonso, Minsuk Cho, Donald van Dansik, Reinier de Graaf, Rob Hilz, Sanna Schuiling, Enno Stemerding.

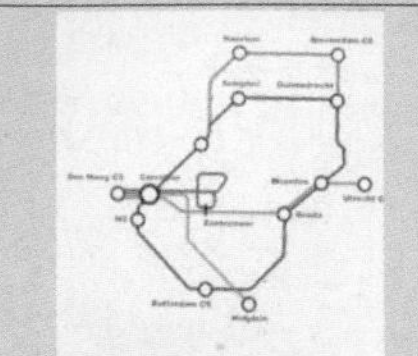

Project: Carre-Four. Status: Study Commission 1997. Location: The Hague, Netherlands. Program: Study of the railway station area in The Hague. Team: Rem Koolhaas, Donald van Dansik, Reinier de Graaf, Jens Hommert.

Project: Lensvelt. status: Competition 1997. Completed 1999. Location: Rotterdam, Netherlands. Site: 36-40 Van Vollenhovenstraat, Rotterdam. Program: Conversion and extension of classic residence. Commercial and public space, showroom, offices, housing, live/work loft, penthouse. Team: Rem Koolhaas, Gary Bates, Minsuk Cho, Govert Gerritsen, Reinier de Graaf, Aziza Jardaoui, Jan Kooijman, Sanna Sihviling, Jeroen Thomas.

Project: Papendorp, Holland Network City. Status: Commission 1997 . Client: Projectbureau Leidse Rijn, City of Utrecht. Location: Utrecht, Leidse Rijn, The Netherlands.Program: 600,000m2: business park, 1500 residential units, school, sports facilities (5 soccer fields, tennis, squash and indoor sports hall under bridge ramp), transferium - intermodal facility to change from private to mass transit, and mass transit system. Team: Rem Koolhaas, Donald van Dansik, Richard Eelman, Sanna Schuiling with Gary Bates, Jaakko van 't Spijker. Structure: De Weger Engineers

See pg 527.Project: Almere, Masterplan Urban Redevelopment. Status: Competition 1998. Completion 2005. Client: City of Almere. Budget: €1.2b . Location: Almere, Netherlands. Site: Centre of new town on regained land. Program: 1000 housing units; retail 53,000m2; 4300 constructed parking spaces; leisure 9,000m2; theater 8,000m2; concert hall 2,000m2; library 8,000m2; arts school 7,000m2; extension hospital with 32,000m2 and 600 parking spaces; offices 130,000m2; extension Almere Central Station, hotel 100 rooms, waterfront of 1km and infrastructure. Principal: Rem Koolhaas. Project Director: Floris Alkemade. Project Architect: Rob de Maat. Team: Olga Aleksakova, Bina Bhattacharya, Bart Cardinaal, Kees van Casteren, Markus Detteling, Philip Koenen, Karen Shanski, Shohei Shigematsu , Mark Watanabe

See pg 526.Project: Blok 6. Status: Commission 1998. Client: MAB. Budget: €22.6m. Location: Almere, Netherlands. Site: In the future City Center on top of large scale parking garage. Program: 19,135m2: Cinema - 7,680m2, 10 Auditoria, 2028 seats, 3.3 m2 per seat, lobby 1615m2; Commercial - mega store 3,260m2, small retails 1,100m2, restaurant 1280m2, supermarket 3230 m2, loading dock 1,120m2; storage 585m2. Principal: Rem Koolhaas. Project Director: Floris Alkemade. Team: Olga Aleksakova, Bina Bhattacharya, Bart Cardinaal, Kees van Casteren, Rob de Maat, Laszlo Fecske, Sharon Goren, Philip Koenen, Antti Lassila, Paz Martin, Markus Schaefer, Karen Shanski, Shohei Shigematsu, Mark Watanabe with Christina Beaumont, Tobias Reinhardt, Lutz Ring.

Project: COB. Status: Study 1998. Client: Centrum Ondergronds Bouwen. Location: Netherlands. Program: Study on subterranean Architecture. Team: Rem Koolhaas, Floris Alkemade, Rob de Maat. Advice: de Weger Engineers/ TNO Human Factors Research Institute.

See pg 528.Project: De Rotterdam, Multi-Use Building, 'Vertical City'. Status: Commission 1998. Client: MAB, The Hague. Location: Rotterdam, Netherlands. Site: Former harbor waterfront between KPN tower and Café Rotterdam at Kop van Zuid. Program: 125,750m2: offices 42,000m2; hotel and congress center with 196 rooms 14,000m2; housing with 197 apartments 40,000m2; 7 cinemas 1,500 seats 4,000m2; stores 250m2; restaurants 1,500m2; fitness 2,000m2; garage 750 spaces 22,000m2. Principal: Rem Koolhaas. Project Directors: Reinier de Graaf, Ellen van Loon. Team: Floris Alkemade, Robert Cheoff, Bert-Karel Deuten, Juan Guardatti, Jens Holm, Alex de Jong, Adam Kurdahl, Anna Little, Barbara Wolff, Sharon Goren. Associate Architect: ABT Bouwkunde. Structure: Arup, London/Corsmit. Services: Deerns bv. Photography: Hectic Pictures

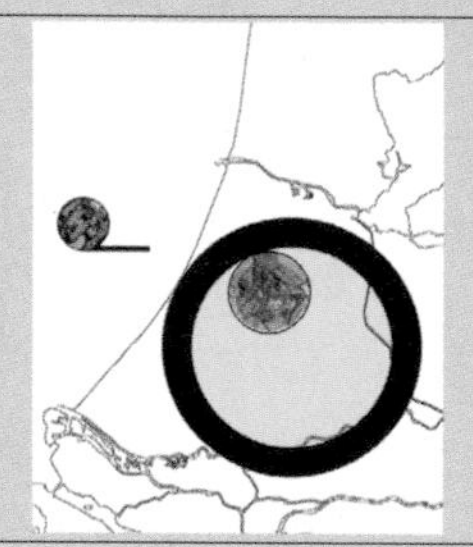

Project: Schiphol City, AMO. Status: Study Commission 1998. Client: Schiphol Airport. Location: The Netherlands. Program: To find a new concept for the Schiphol-site under the premise that the airport itself would be relocated off-shore. To investigate what implications this could have on the Netherlands. Team AMO: Rem Koolhaas, Reinier de Graaf, with Bert Karel Deuten, Jens Hommert, Adam Kurdahl, Anna Little, Mateo Poli. Associate Architect: ONE Architecture. Graphic Design: Graphic Language, Rotterdam.

Project: Y2K. Status: Conceptual Design 1998. Location: Rotterdam, The Netherlands. Program: Private Residence, Rotterdam. Team: Rem Koolhaas, Fernando Romero Havaux, with Uwe Herlyn, Erik Schotte.

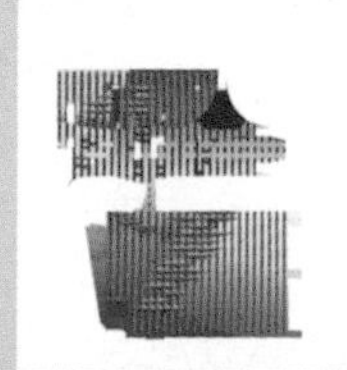

Project: Almere Terminal. Status: Commission 1999. Client: City of Almere. Location: Almere, Netherlands.

Site: Center of new town on regained land. Program: Garage Station. Principal: Rem Koolhaas. Project Director: Floris Alkemade. Team: Olga Aleksakova, Bina Battacharyya, Bart Cardinal, Markus Dettling, Kees van Casteren, Philip Koenen, Rob de Maat, Karen Shanski, Shohei Shigematsu, Mark Watanabe.

Project: Philips Masterplan. Status: Competition 1999. Client: Philips. Location: Eindhoven, Netherlands. Site: Evoluon Terrain, Noord Brabantlaan, Eindhoven. Program: Offices, Meeting Rooms, Storage and Reproduction. Team: Rem Koolhaas, Krystyan Keck, Kristina Manis, Natasha Sandmeier, Erik Schotte, with Frans Blok, Bob Choeff, Pauline van Gulik, Matthias Hollwich, Jenny Jones, Rombout Lohman, Oliver Schutte.

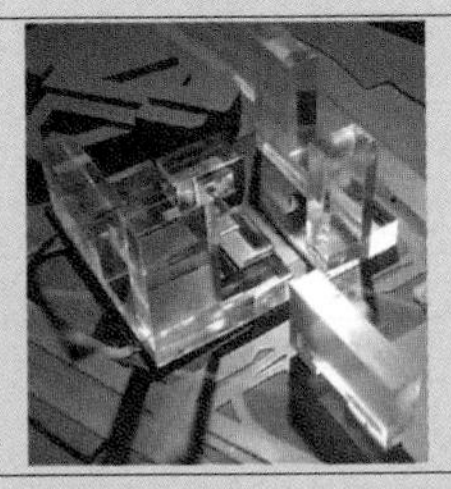

Project: Zoetermeer Centrum West. Status: Commission 1999. Location: Zoetemeer, Netherlands. Site: Nederlandlaan, Zoetemeer. Program: Urban design study: housing 24,270m2; offices 15,000m2; facilities 1,500m2; shops 14,500m2; parking 18,750m2. Team: Rem Koolhaas, Donald van Dansik, Reinier de Graaf, Jens Hommert, Tom Kolbasenko, Neville Mars, Markus Schaefer.

Project: Mahler 4. Status: Study Commission 2000. Client: Mahler 4 Consortium. Location: Amsterdam, Netherlands. Program: 30,186m2: offices, retail, parking. Team: Rem Koolhaas, Reinier de Graaf, with Christina Beaumont, Carolina Ligtenberg, Lutz Ring.

Educatorium. By coupling an orthogonal box and a folded plane generate all the specificities the program demands on a site in Utrecht where they also connect two previously isolated emblems of late-sixties modernity, tower and slab.

NATO HQ. In Brussels, the new capital of Europe, the uneasy coexistence of past, current, and future members of a once unquestioned security organization is staged in separate wings, offices that converge at a huge, political town square, under a massive cloud of suspended meeting rooms on top of a sockle of lavish health club facilities.

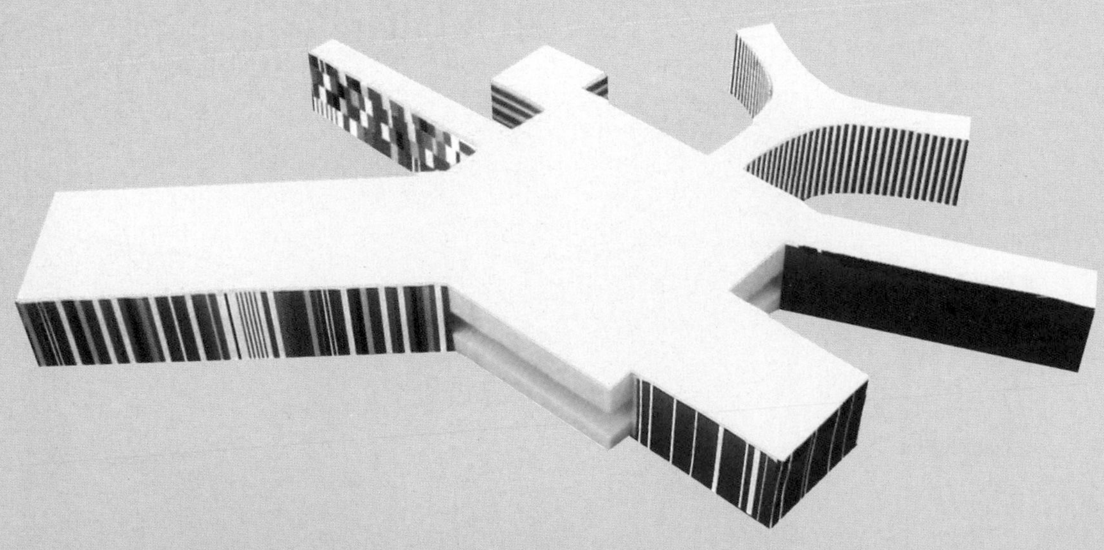

Bel +31(0)102438200

Almere. To create a center, assume the counter geometry of the immediate environment and double the density. To temper the domination of the commercial and the profit motive, assemble as much stability subsidies to support what, in the past, somehow paid for itself - life.

As if undoing the lamination of a shopping layer - bottom - and a carpet of six cinemas - top - public space is generarted by tearing the two halves apart.

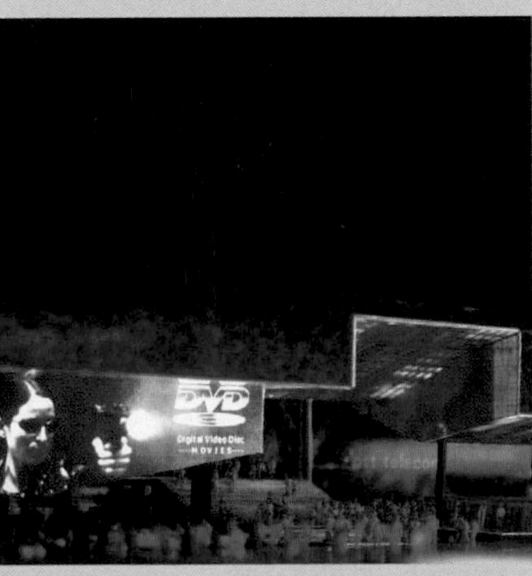

Project: C-Project. Status: Commission 2001. Location: Archives located in Rotterdam and Vlaardingen. Program: Organising and documentation of the OMA archive collection. Principal: Rem Koolhaas. Project Director: Donald van Dansik. Team: Talitha van Dijk, Robin van 't Haar, Jan Knikker, Sanden van Wees

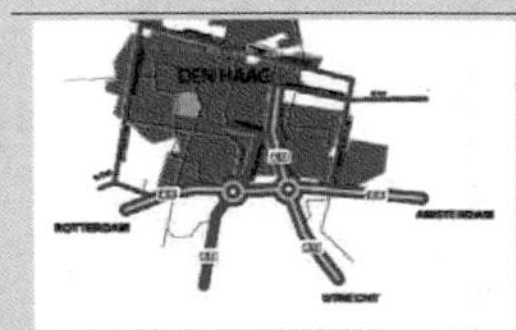

Project: Prins Claus Plein. Status: Study Commission 2001. Client: City of The Hague. Budget: €610m. Location: The Hague, Netherlands. Site: Prins Clausplein, The Hague. Program: Study, urban master plan for infrastructural area around The Hague. Principal: Rem Koolhaas. Project Director: Floris Alkemade. Team: Stefan Bendiks, Catarina Canas, Bart Cardinaal, Claudia Dische, Reinier de Graaf, Alex de Jong, Jan Knikker, Carolin van Lightenberg, Matthieu Puyanbreau, Orri Steinorsson

Project: FNWI - Faculty for Natural Sciences and Computer Technology. Status: Competition 2002. Client: University of Amsterdam. Location: Amsterdam, The Netherlands. Site: Watergraafsmeer, Amsterdam. Program: 56,000m2: hotel 150 rooms 3,750m2; congress center 400 people 2,652m2. Team: Rem Koolhaas, Olga Aleksakova, Kunle Adeyemi, Alain Fouraux, Reinier de Graaf, Roberto Otero, Tammo Prinz, Ole Scheeren, Hiromasa Shirai, Victoria Willocks.

MAB Towers. Along the Maas in Rotterdam, the footprints of a group of generic towers are shifted back and forth at ground level and midway, to liberate complex latencies from apparent banality, displayed on a podium of urban collectivity.

Project: Schiphol Airport Navigator, AMO. Status: Study Commission 2002. Client: Schiphol Airport. Location: Schiphol Airport. Program: Study into possibilities for future development of the Schiphol airport site. Team AMO: Rem Koolhaas, Reinier de Graaf, Matthew Murphy, Roberto Otero, Johan De Wachter.

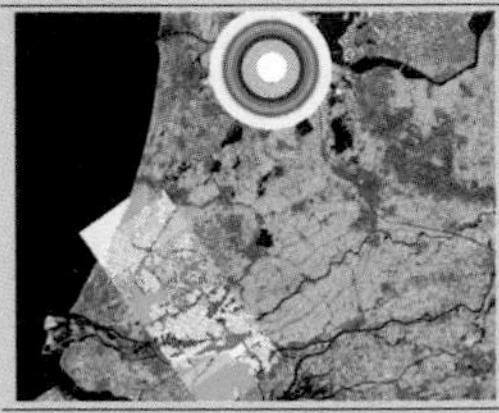

Project: Deltametropool. Status: Study Commission 2002. Client: Stuurgroep Ontwerpatelier Deltametropool. Location: Randstad, Netherlands. Program: Study, large scale urban master plan for urbanized region of the Netherlands. Prartner-in-Charge: Rem Koolhaas. Project Director: Floris Alkemade. Project Architects: Johan de Wachter, Paz Martin. Team: Paul Burgstaller, Stephane Derveaux, Melissa Dowler, Tim O'Callaghan, Orri Steinarsson, Gregers Thomsen, Gerd Wetzel.

See pg 529. Project: Koningin Julianaplein. Status: Competition 2002. Client: City of The Hague. Location: The Hague, Netherlands. Site: square in front of Central Station. Program: 100,000 m2: offices, housing and commerce. Team: Rem Koolhaas, Floris Alkemade, Paz Martin, Erik Schotte, Shohei Shigematsu, Johan De Wachter, with Gabriela Bojalil, Patrick Bruhn, Erez Ella, Sarah Gibson, Jan Roters, Hiromasa. Shirai, Michael Smith. Advice: Arup London

Project: Rotterdam CS. Status: Competition 2003. Client: City of Rotterdam. Location: Rotterdam, The Netherlands. Site: Rotterdam Central Station. Program: Re-development of Rotterdam CS: fast food/catering 2,060m2; retail 1,565m2; offices 60,000m2; services 1,700m2. Team: Rem Koolhaas, Reninier de Graaf, Ellen van Loon, with Benjamin Clarens, Haiko Cornelissen, Selva Gurdogan, Oriol Hostench, Jeff Ludlow, Neville Mars, Roberto Otero, Michael Smith, Gregers Thomsen, Jasper Tonk, Johan De Wachter. Structure, Services: ABT Adviesbureau voor Bouwtechniek bv. Video Presentation: Vincent van Duin.

SWITZERLAND

See pg 530. Project: Schauspielhaus Zurich. Status: Study Commission 1995 . Client: Schauspielhaus Zurich. Budget: 45m SFr. Location: Zurich, Switzerland. Site: Zeltweg 5, CH-8032, Zurich. Program: Extension to a former shipyard with theater, rehearsal stages, workshops, administration, artists' residences, jazz club, restaurant and museum. Team: Rem Koolhaas, Ole Scheeren, with Albert-Jan Berman, Gro Bonesmo, Grisha Bourbouze, Piet Ekert, Wim Eckert, Wilfried Hackenbroich, Catherine Lassen, Domenico Raimondo, Juta Raith, Jeroen Thomas. Structure: de Weger Engineers. Services: de Blaay-Van den Bogaard Radgevende Igenieurs bv. Acoustics: D.G.M.R. consulting engineers Den Haag. Cost: de Weger Engineers

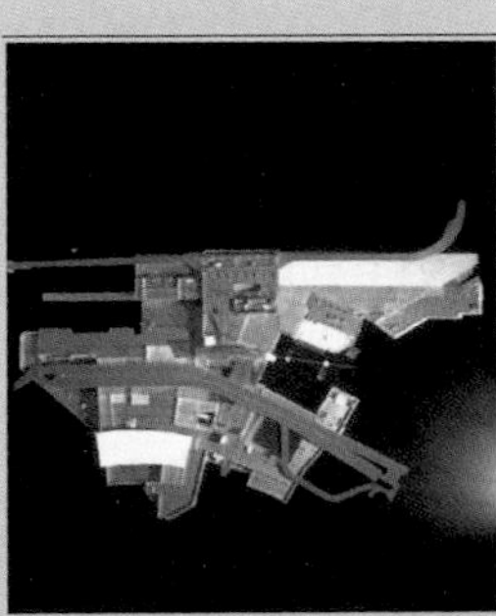

Project: Extension of the International Airport Zurich. Status: Competition 1995. Client: Flughafen Immobilien Gesellschaft. Budget: 365m SFr. Total infrastructure: 2.3b SFr. Location: Zurich, Switzerland. Program: 941,000m2: Extension of land and airside. Team: Rem Koolhaas, Piet Eckert, Wim Eckert, with Tom Bergvoet, Reinier de Graaf, Wilfried Hackenbroich, Julien Monfort, Jeroen Thomas. Associate Architect: Sulzer GmbH.

Koningen Julianaplein. So many styles have been assembled in such a small part of the former center of the Hague that a cheerleader building that declares a carnival-like suspension of serious identity seems the only possible strategy.

Project: Maison des droits de l'homme. Status: Competition 1996, 1st Prize. Client: Dèpartement des Travaux Publics et de l'Energie, Canton de Genève. Budget: 22m SFr. Location: Place des Nations, Genève, Switzerland. Program: 7,975m2: administration building, exhibition space, public visitors center, parking. Team: Rem Koolhaas, Xavier Calderon, Piet Eckert, Beth Margules, Jeroen Thomas. Structure: Arup.

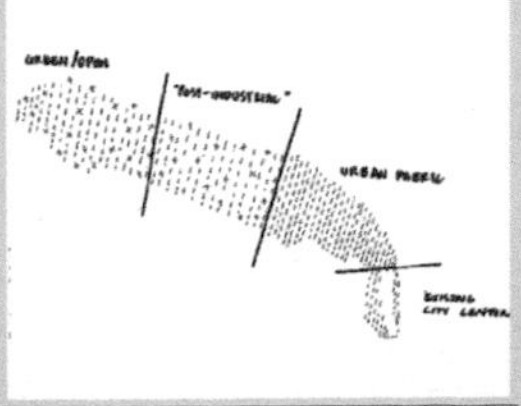

Project: Zurich West. Status: Study Commission 1998. Client: City of Zurich, MDC Project Development. Location: Zurich, Switzerland. Program: 2,000,000m2: Master plan for former industrial area. Team: Rem Koolhaas, Donald van Dansik, Bert Karel Deuten, Anu Leionen, Evert van der Zee, with Schaetz Florian Benjamin, Donald van Dansik, Christian Fuchs, Walter Hoogerwerf, Philip Koenen, Christian Müller, Joshua Ramus, Stijn Rademakers, Erik Schotte, Colin Seah, Isabel da Silva, Wim Steutel. Consulting Engineer: Arup.

Project: Zurich Stadium. Status: Competition 1999, First Prize. Client: City of Zurich, MDC Project Development. Location: Zurich, Switzerland. Program: Master plan for new stadium and quarter: stadium 49,500 m2; commercial 48,600 m2; offices and housing 103,700 m2; convention center 14,400 m2; hotel 6,700 m2; educational 15,300 m2; casino 5,100 m2; sport and cinema 17,600 m2; parking 62,500 m2. Team: Rem Koolhaas, Donald van Dansik,

Schauspielhaus. In Zurich, each component of the program is accommodated in its own hermetic box. The residual between the assembled boxes accomodates a museum and public space.

Evert van der Zee, with Eliot Bu, Christian Müller, Shohei Shigematsu, Leonhard Weil with Floris Alkemade, Mary Ellen Cooper, Bruce Fisher, Alexander Moreno, Ronald Southwick. Associate Architects: T&T Design bv. Structure: Arup. Moveable Roof Structure: Baily Technogroup.

Project: Flick House, Private Museum. Status: Commission 2001. Client: Dr. Friederich Christian Flick. Location: Zurich-West, Switzerland. Site: Hardturmstrasse, Sulzer-Escher-Wyss estate. Program: Museum for private collection and apartment. Principal: Rem Koolhaas. Project Director: Erik Schotte. Project Architect: Olga Aleksakova. Team: Thomas Duda, Stan van den Driesche, Jens Holm, Katy Parsa, Florian Speier, Sygil Walty, with Paul Burgstaller and: Mellisa Dowler, Stephane Derveaux, Tim O'Callaghan.

NORWAY

Project: Oslo Vestbanen. Status: Competition 2002, 1st Prize. Client: Statsbygg. Site: Defunct central train station lot bounded by Oslo City Hall, Akershus Castle and Aker Brygge Waterfront Development. Program: 121,600m2: library 18,000m2; museum 3,000m2; cineplex 10,500m2; conference center 2,700m2; hotel 6,200m2; housing 27,000m2; offices 26,300m2; commercial 11,000m2; additional culture 5,000m2; parking 8,200m2; services 3,700m2. Team: Rem Koolhaas, Joshua Ramus, Olga Aleksakova, Gro Bonesmo (SG), with Kunle Adeyemi, Floris Alkemade, Gary Bates (SG), Johannes Bucholz, Patrik Buhn, Erez Ella, Nicolas Firket, Ellen Hellsten (SG), Jens Holm, Erhard Kinzelbach, Adam Kurdahl (SG), Ena Lloret, Casey Mack, Paz Martin, Roberto Otero, Tammo Prinz, Gregers Thomsen, Mark Watanabe. Associate Architect: SPACE Group (SG), Oslo . Structure: Arup: Rory McGowan, Stephen Jolly. Model: Werkplaats de Rijk/Parthesius.

GERMANY

Project: Breuninger, Department Store . Status: Competition 1995, 1st Prize. Commission 1996. Client: F. Breuninger GmbH + Co, Herr van Agtmael, Marktstrasse 1-3, 70173 Stuttgart. Budget: 12m DM. Location: Stuttgart, Germany. Site: on the Marktplatz in the city center of Stuttgart. Program: 2600m2: new façade and vertical circulation for existing building. Team: Rem Koolhaas, Matthias Bauer, with Stephanie Bender, Minsuk Cho, Vincent Coste, Chris van Duijn, Tobias Fehr, Rob Hilz, Jan-Willem van Kuilenberg, Catherine Lassen, Christos Marcopoulos, Sabine Schaaf, Ole Scheeren, Erik Schotte, Don Weber. Competition Team: Rem Koolhaas, Matthias Bauer, Ole Scheeren, Christos Marcopoulos. Structure: Weidleplan, Stuttgart. Façade: van Santen, Lille. Climate: Transsolar, Stuttgart.

See pg 533. Project: Hypo-Bank. Status: Competition and Design Development 1995. Client: Bayerische. Hypothek und Wechselbank. Location: city center Munich, Germany. Program: 10,000m2: Existing building fabric to be replaced but monuments on site to be preserved. Team: Rem Koolhaas, Udo Garritzmann, Matthias Bauer, Ole Scheeren, Jeroen Thomas. Competition Team: Rem Koolhaas, Udo Garritzmann, Gro Bonesmo, Xaveer de Geyter, Fuminori Hoshino, Luc Veeger, with Arjen de Groot, Tom Hage, Bas Suijkerbuijk, Tom Tullock

Project: Netherlands Embassy Berlin. Status: Commission 1997. Completion 2003. Client: Netherlands Ministry of Foreign Affairs - Dienst Gebouwen Buitenland, The Hague. Location: Berlin-Mitte, Rolandufer / Klosterstraße. Site: Facing street corner, park and riverfront. Program: 8,500m2: offices 4,800m2; housing 1,500m2; parking 2,200m2. Principal: Rem Koolhaas. Project Directors: Ellen van Loon, Erik Schotte. Project Architect: Michelle Howard, Gro Bonesmo. Team: Beth Margulis, Anu Leinonen, Daan Oievaar, Robert Choeff, Christian Müller, Adrianne Fisher, Oliver Schütte, Fernando Romero Havaux, Matthias Hollwich, Katrin Thornhauer, Barbara Wolff, Bruce Fisher, Anne Filson, Udo Garritzman, Jenny Jones, Mette Bos, Adam Kuhrdahl, Stan Aarts, Jlien Desmedt, Annick Hess, Rombout Loman, Antti Lassila, Thomas Kolbasenko, Moritz von Voss, Paolo Costa, Carolus Traenkner, Susanne Manthey, Christiane Sauer, Tammo Prinz, Nils Lindhorst, Felix Thoma, Shadi Rahbaran. Research: Bill Price, Marc Guinand. Structure: Royal Haskoning/ Arup Berlin. Services: Huygen Elwako / Arup Berlin. Project Management: Royal Haskoning. Fire: Hosser Hass + Partner, Berlin. Lighting: OVI, Washington DC, Berlin. Curtains: Inside Outside.

Project: Haus um die Schenkung, Berlin, Germany. Status: Study 1998. Client: Haus um die Schenkung GmbH, Berlin, Germany. Location: Berlin - Mitte: Stralauerstrafle / Klosterstraße, Berlin, Germany. Site: Situated behind the Netherlands Embassy. Program: 9,000m2: culture 1,100m2; offices 2,400m2; commercial 2,400m2; housing 1,500m2; parking 1,600m2. Team: Rem Koolhaas, Frans Blok, Robert Choeff, Julien DeSmedt, Fernando Romero Havaux, Matthias Hollwich, Krystyan Keck, Rombout Loman, Erik Schotte, Oliver Schütte, Barbara Wolff. Structure, Services: de Weger Engineers.

See pg 533. Project: Museum Ludwig. Status: Commission 2001. Client: Museum Ludwig, Cologne. Budget: 6.5m DM. Location: Cologne, Germany. Program: 2,500m2: renovation and conversion of museum entrance and bookstore. Team: Rem Koolhaas and Ole Scheeren. With: Dorte Borresen, Catarina Canas, Claudia Discher, Chris van Duijn, Jens Holm, Thorsten Kiefer, Anu Leinonen, Cornelia Locke, Tammo Prinz, Saskia Simon, Barbara Wolff. Associated Architect: Busmann+ Haberer GmbH. Structure: Büro Naumann, Cologne. Services: RCI GmbH, Mühlheim an der Ruhr. Typography: Yvonne Quirmbach, Cologne. Lighting: Lichtplan, Cologne.

Project: Essen Kohlenwasche. Status: Commission 2002. Client: Ministry for Culture, Sports and Housing of Nordrhein-Westfalen (NRW) and development company Zech Zollverein. Location: Essen, Germany. Program: Museum and visitors center in Zeche Zollverein master plan, conversion. Partner-in-Charge: Rem Koolhaas. Project Director: Floris Alkemade. Team: Bart Cardinaal, Alex de Jong, Paz Martin, Johan De Wachter. Associate Architect: Heinrich Böll Architekt BDA DWB Hans Krabel.

Project: Ruhr Study, AMO. Status: Study Commission 2002. Client: EGZ Entwicklungs Gesellschaft Zollverein. Location: Ruhr, Germany. Program: Study of identity and spatial development of the Ruhr area. Team AMO: Rem Koolhaas, Reinier de Graaf, with Daniel Dendra, Theo Deutinger, Mamen Escorihuela, Nanne de Ru, Markus Schaefer, Kerstin Vogel.

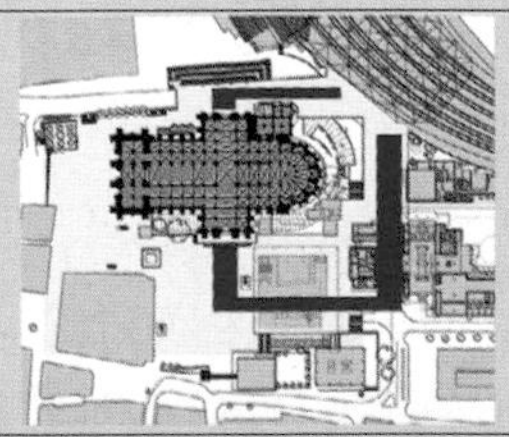

Project: Workshop Domplatte. Status: Competition 2002, 2nd Prize. Client: City of Cologne. Location: Cologne, Germany. Site: Area around the Cathedral in the city center.. Program: Establish a new urban configuration including pedestrian and vehicular traffic around the cathedral and major cultural institutions. Team: Rem Koolhaas, Ole Scheeren, with Catarina Canas, Anu Leinonen, Gabriela Bojalil Rebora, Yvonne Quirmbach, Jan Roters

Property

1993-2003 Architectural adventures?

Project: Master Plan Zeche Zollverein Essen - Germany. Status: Commission 2002, Completion 2008. Client: Ministry for Culture, Sports and Housing of Nordrhrhein-Westfalen (NRW) and development company Zeche Zollverein. Budget: €200m. Location: Essen, Germany. Site: 100 ha former industrial site. Classified UNESCO World Heritage site. Program: Business Parks of 160,000 m2: Attractors and other new programs of 100,000m2. Master plan for former mining and coal refinery area. Partner-in-Charge: Rem Koolhaas. Project Director: Floris Alkemade. Project Advisor: Ole Scheeren. Team: Kees van Casteren, Olv Klein, Patrick Kuhn, Ena Lloret, Paz Martin, Katy Parssanedjad, Tammo Prinz, Jonas Sandberg, Erik Schotte, Johan De Wachter.

Project: European Central Bank Headquarters. Status: Competition 2003. Client: European Central Bank. Location: Frankfurt, Germany. Site: on the site of the Grossmarkthalle in Frankfurt. Program: 150,000m2: offices, library, restaurant, social/sports facilities, conference & press facilities, plant, parking. Team: Rem Koolhaas, Reinier de Graaf, Olga Aleksakova, Roberto Otero, with Georg Bucher, Rodrigo Nunèz, Sebastian Thomas, Daniela Zimmer

ITALY

Project: Port of Genova. Status: Competition 1997. Client: The City of Genova. Location: Genova, Italy. Site: Genova Harbor, Ponte Parodi, San Beningo, Fiumare, Seafront. Program: Urban masterplan for port, connection between harbor and inner city, redefinition of former industrial sites and renovation of the embankments. Team: Rem Koolhaas, Floris Alkemade, Donald van Dansik, with Vincent Coste, Adrianne Fisher, Matthias Hollowich, Adam Kurdahl, Isabel da Silva, Julien de Smedt, Hanna Svensson. Structure: de Weger Engineers.

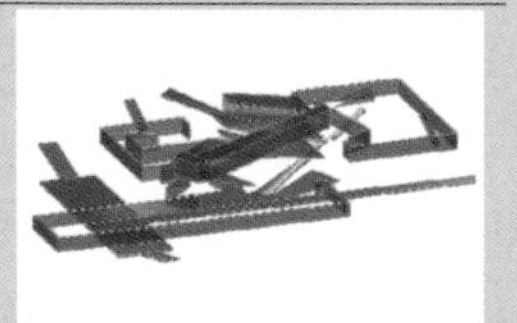

Project: Museum of Contemporary Arts Roma. Status: Competition 1999. Client: MoCA, Rome. Location: Rome, Italy. Program: Exhibition spaces, shops, private art galleries, restaurant/cafè, auditorium, institute for advanced studies, library, resident fellows living space, offices. Team: Rem Koolhaas, Seong Lok Bae, Gary Bates, Donald van Dansik, Gianmaria Sforza Fogliani, Fernando Romero Havaux, Matteo Poli, with Robert Choeff, Uwe Herlyn, Krystan Keck, Barbara Wolff, Marco Zurn. Structure: Arup.

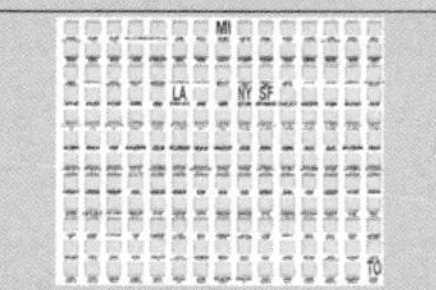

Project: Prada Research, AMO. Status: Commission 1999. Client: Prada (I.P.I USA Corp.). Program: Research into Prada Identity to examine different ways to reinvent the retail experience..Project Team: Rem Koolhaas, Dan Wood, Ole Scheeren, Markus Schaefer, Jens Hommert, Michael Rock, Jeffrey Inaba, Bruce Mau, Reed Kram. Research Team: Rem Koolhaas, Markus Schaefer, Ole Scheeren, Jens Hommert, Amale Andraos, Sze Tsung Leong, Chuihua Judy Chung, Jeffrey Inaba, Alain Fouraux, Laszlo Feckse, Matteo Poli, with Sandford Kwinter

Project: Prada In-Store Technology, AMO-OMA. Status: Commission 2000. Client: Prada (I.P.I. USA Corp.). Location: Prada Epicenter New York, Los Angeles and San Francisco. Program: In-Store Technology. Team AMO: Rem Koolhaas, Markus Schaefer with Gergely Agoston, Lucia Allais, Stefan Bendiks, Chiuhua Judy Chung, Joakim Dahlqvist, Laszlo Fecske, Jens Hommert, Alex de Jong, David Lemoine, Michael Kubo, Dirk Roosenburg, Samuel Spitzer, Francesco Tiribelli, Sze Tsung Leong , Victoria Willocks, OMA: Ole Scheeren, with Ergian Alberg, Amale Andraos, Evan Bennet, Eric Chang, Olivier Guenin, Kit Lewis, Taiji Miyasaka, David Moore. Industrial Design: Weisshaar Industrial Design. Interaction Design: IDEO Europe. Computational Design: Kramdesign. Systems Integration: IconNicholson. Aurau Content Production: 2x4. IT Implementation: Scharff Weisberg Inc.

Project: Prada Sponge. Status: Commission 2000. Client: Prada (I.P.I. USA Corp.). Program: Material research and development, production. Team: Rem Koolhaas, Ole Scheeren, Chris van Duijn, Eric Chang. Conceptual Development: Werkplaats de Rijk/Parthesius. Detailed Development: Panelite. Production: RAM Contract.

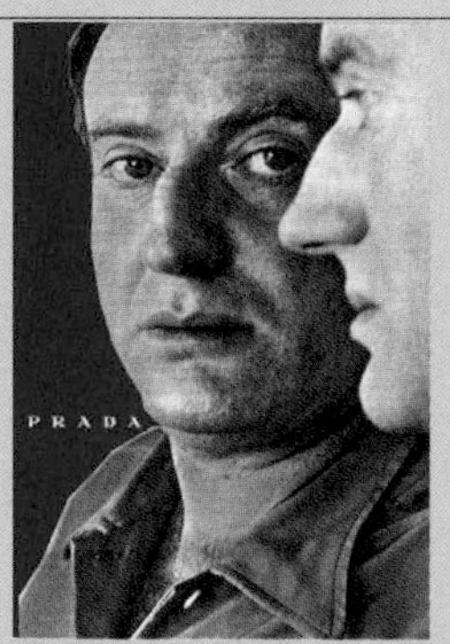

Project: Prada Advertising, AMO. Status Commission 2001. Client: Prada (I.P.I. USA Corp). Program: Development of the Prada Advertising Campaign. Team AMO: Rem Koolhaas, Markus Schaefer, Jens Hommert, Nicolas Firket, Remco van de Krapats.

Project: Prada Content (Parallel Universe), AMO. Status: 2003. Client: Prada (I.P.I. USA Corp.). Location: New York and Tokyo. Program: Store content production and curatorial work for Prada Epicenters in New York and Tokyo. Team AMO: Rem Koolhaas, Markus Schaefer, Joakim Dahlqvist, Jens Hommert, Nicolas Firket, Rachel Meyrick, Michael Rock, Francesco Tiribelli.

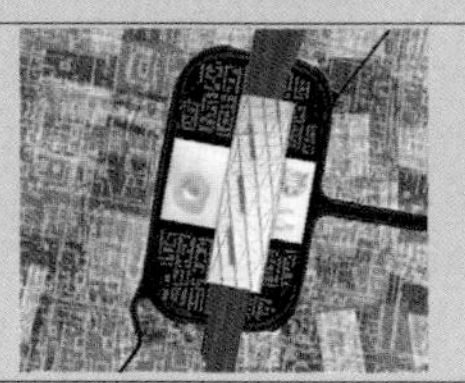

Project: Naples High Speed Train Terminal. Status: Competition 2003. Client: TAV. Location: Napoli, Italy. Program: Train station interchange. Team: Rem Koolhaas, Ole Scheeren, with Floris Alkemade, Benjamin Clarens, Reinier de Graaf, Paz Martin, Roberto Otero, Michael Smith, Sebastian Thomas, Ellen van Loon and: Olga Aleksakova, George Bucher, Joao Bravo da Costa, Chris van Duijn, Gaspard Estourgie, Natacha Fricout, Christophe Helmns, Jens Hommert, Jason Long, Alexander Sverdlov, Steffi Wedde. Associate Architect: Boeri Studio. Structure, Services: Arup. Model: Werkplaats de Rijk/Parthesius.

SWEDEN

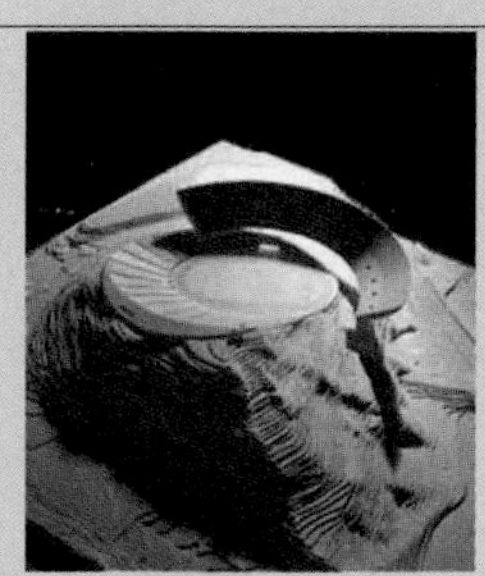

Project: Stockholm Olympic Stadium. Status: Competition 1995. Location: Stockholm, Sweden. Program: Olympic Stadium with service facilities and ecological program. Team: Rem Koolhaas, Rob Hilz, Christos Marcopoulos, Eric Schall, Yo Yamagata with Catharina Lundeberg. Structure: de Weger Engineers. Olympic Buildings Advice: Francesco Gnecchi-Ruscone.

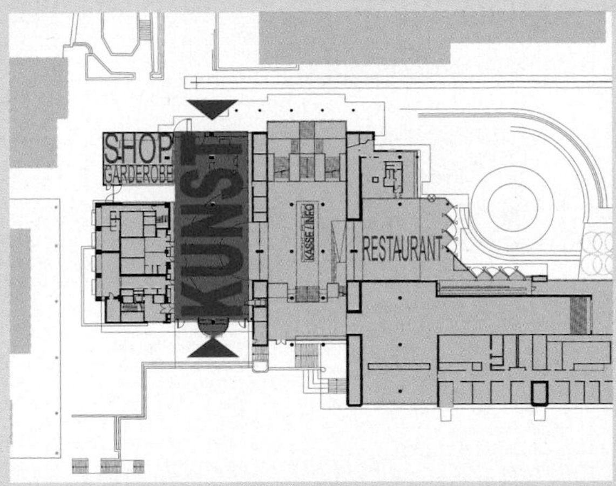

Cologne. In other museums you have to fight your way through shops, wardrobes, cafes and counters. In Museum Ludwig you would have to fight your way through art.

Hypobank. The restrictive zoning laws that grudgingly dictate the nature of new architecture that may be imposed on given sites in old and rich European cities represented, in Munich, as maximum built volumes that take their place among the classical architecture.

1993-2003 Architectural adventures?

GREECE

Project: Nea Krini - Pier Project. Status: Competition 1996. Location: Thessaloniki, Greece. Program: Public square in open sea at the end of a pier housing boarding passengers, culture and leisure facilities. Team: Rem Koolhaas, Simon van Amerongen, Paul Kroese, Christos Marcopoulos, Jeroen Thomas.

RUSSIA

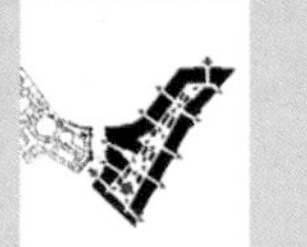

Project: Hermitage Extension. Status: Study Commission 2003. Client: Hermitage Guggenheim Foundation. Location: St. Petersburg, Russia. Site: Dvortzovaja Square, St. Petersburg. Program: Redefinition and curatorial strategy of Hermitage Museum. Team OMA-AMO: Rem Koolhaas, Olga Aleksakova, Fernando Donis, Alexey Levchuk, Paz Martin, Markus Schaefer, Alexandr Sverdlov, Johan De Wachter, Nanne de Ru.

SAUDI ARABIA

Project: Makkah Western Gateway. Status: Competition 2002. Client: Makkah Construction and Development Company. Location: Makkah, Saudi Arabia. Site: Stretch of land between the third ring road interchange and Makkah's central area. Program: New Western highway-boulevard into Makkah; reinforce the city's identity, develop a new access corridor to the city, provide a direct connection to the central area, provide the city with a multi-modular corridor serving the central area, increased mixed land-use and housing capacity, upgrade the physical environment and services offered. Team: Dan Wood, Amale Andraos, Jens Holm, with Rem Koolhas, Casey Mack Erhard An-He Kinzelbach, Jill Leckner, Leonard Weil, Robert Zeiner, Casey Mack. Model: Cassandra Thornburg, Clementina Ruggieri. Graphics: Omnivore . Traffic: Arup US . Consulting: L.E.F.T.

CHINA

Project: CCTV Television Station and Headquarters. Status: Competition 2002, 1st Prize. Completion 2008. Client: China Central Television (CCTV). Budget: €600m. Location: Beijing, China. Site: 18ha in new central business district. Program: Total 575,000 m2: CCTV building 400,000m2; TVCC building 75,000m2; service building 15,000m2; parking 85,000m2. CCTV: administration 75,000m2; program offices 65,000m2; news production 70,000m2; broadcasting 40,000m2; program production 120,000m2; staff facilities 30,000m2; parking 65,000m2. TVCC: hotel 52,000m2; public facilities 23,000m2 including 1500 seat theatre; parking 20,000m2. Partners-in-Charge: Rem Koolhaas and Ole Scheeren. Project Architects: Shohei Shigematsu, Adrianne Fisher, Erez Ella, David Chacon, Anu Leinonen, Charles Berman, Hiromasa Shirai, Chris van Duijn, Bruce Toman (DMJM). Project Coordinator: Dongmei Yao. Technical Advisor: Ellen van Loon. Team: Jia Bo (ECADI), Gabriela Bojalil, Catarina Canas, Holly Chacon, Jane Chen (DMJM), Gaspard Estourgie, Lin Feng (ECADI), Yang Guang (ECADI), John Hess (DMJM), Ling Ji (ECADI), Xu Jialong (ECADI), Abhijit Kapade, Michel van der Kar, Peter Lee, Chen Li (ECADI), Stuart Maddocks, Xiang Ming (ECADI), Joseph Monteleone, Cristina Murphy, Xu Nuo (ECADI), Daan Ooievaar, Andre Schmidt, Torsten Schröeder, Zhang Sheng (ECADI), Wenchian Shi, Faustina Tsai, Tian Tian Xu, Zhao Weiliang (ECADI), Dai Wenwei (ECADI) Jiang Wenwei (ECADI), Jiang Xinhua (ECADI), Li Yao (ECADI), Fan Yifei (ECADI), Dai Yiming (ECADI), Guo Yiming (ECADI), Sun Yu (ECADI), Wu Zheng (ECADI), with Joao Bravo da Costa, Shangwen Chiu, Stephane Derveaux, Xiaodong Liu, Manuel Shvartzberg; Interns: Antonio Branco, Max Burianek, Melissa Dowler, Rodney Eggleston, Stefan Ell, Keren Englman, Joris Fach, Antonis Karides, Suse Koch, Andreas Lyckefors, Tim O'Callaghan, Tae Hoon Oh, Florian Pucher, Max Schwitalla. Competition Team: Rem Koolhaas, Ole Scheeren, Shohei Shigematsu, Alain Fouraux, Fernando Donis with Johannes Buchholz, Catarina Canas, Guillaume Colboc, Erez Ella, Mamen Escorihuela, Adrianne Fisher, Sarah Gibson, Anu Leinonen, Shiro Ogata, Tammo Prinz, Torsten Schröder, Hiromasa Shirai, L. E. Tsao, Victoria Willocks, Zhaohui Wu, Yimin Zhu. Associate Architect and Engineer: ECADI (East China Architecture & Design Institute), Shanghai. Structure, Services: Arup London, Hong Kong. Strategic Advisor: Qingyun Ma, Shanghai. High Rise Consultant: DMJMH+N, Los Angeles. Curtain Wall: Front, New York. Broadcast Design: ECADI, Shanghai/Sandy Brown Associates, London. Acoustics: Dorsser Blesgraaf, Eindhoven. Scenography: DuckS Scéno, France. Vertical Transportation: Lerch Bates & Associates, London. Lighting: LPA, Tokyo.

See pg 535. Project: Guangzhou Opera House. Status: Competition 2002. Budget: 850m RMB. Location: Guangzhou, China. Site: On a plot surrounded by Huyai road, Huajiu road, Zhujiang boulevard and Linjiang boulevard, Zhujiang new town, Guangzhou. Program: 24,380m2: 1,800 seat Grand Theater, entrance lobby + lounge, multi-function hall. . Team: Rem Koolhaas, Fernando Donis, Erez Ella with Gabriela Bojalil, Selva Gurdogan, Kerem Piker, Victoria Stewart, Gregers Thomsen. Structure, Services: Arup. Acoustics: TNO Center for Building Research. Model: Werkplaats de Rijk/Parthesius

Project: Multi-Media Building. Status: Competition 2002. Client: City University of Hong Kong. Budget: €60m. Location: Shep Kip Mei, Kowloon, Hong Kong. Site: "Site A", City University of Hong Kong Campus. Program: 32,000 m2: Gross Floor Area of Multi-Media and Institutional Program including 13,400 m2 net of 1000 person theatre, sound stages, performance theaters, exhibition spaces, media research, library, computer laboratories, virtual reality research, and cave, classrooms, administration offices, visiting scholars accommodations, art studio, media shop, workshops, cafeteria/restaurant. Team: Rem Koolhaas, Ole Scheeren, Ellen van Loon, Markus Schaefer (AMO), with Guillaume Colboc, Roberto Otero, Tammo Prinz, Hiromasa Shirai, Gregers Thomsen. Structure: Arup London, Hong Kong. Services: Aedas / RMJM Check. Geotechnical Engineer: Arup Hong Kong, SAR. Traffic/Transport: Arup. Mechanical/Electrical: Arup . Scenography/Lighting: DuckS Sceno. Acoustics: Dorsser Blesgraaf. Interiors, Landscape: Inside Outside

Project: BJBB, Beijing Books Building. Status: Competition 2003. Client: Beijing Xinha Books Co., Ltd. Location: Beijing, China. Site: ChangAn Boulevard, Beijing. Program: 100,000m2: new building integrated with conversion of existing structure; conversion 52,000 m2; new construction 48,000 m2. Team: Rem Koolhaas, Ole Scheeren, Ellen van Loon, Fernando Donis, Alain Fouraux, with Georg Bucher, Selva Gurdogan, Oriol Hostench Ruiz, Michelle Liu, Jeff Ludlow, Nuno Rosado, Hiromasa Shirai, Sebastian Thomas, Gregers Thomsen, Camia Young. Associate Architect: Mada Spam, Shanghai. Structure, Services: Arup.

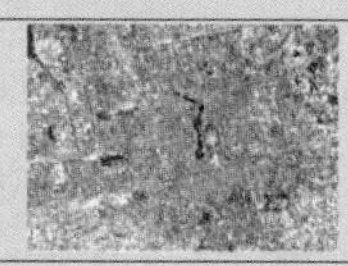

Project: Beijing Preservation Study, AMO. Status: Commission 2003. Client: Beijing Planning Bureau. Location: Beijing, China. Program: Research and analysis of historic preservation. Team AMO: Rem Koolhaas, Emilie Gomart, Markus Schaefer, with Jason Long, Matthew Soules, Liang Zhao. Strategic Advisor: Qingyun Ma, Shanghai. .

Project: Beijing Olympic Conference Center.Status: Competition 2003. Location: Beijing, China. Program: 178,236m2: Olympics: IBC International broadcasting center 83,500m2; MPC media press center 58,400m2; fencing court 27,150m2; modern pentathlon 4,900m2; security 4,286m2. Post Olympics: Conference Center. Team: Rem Koolhaas, Alain Fouraux, Roberto Otero, Nanne de Ru, Ole Scheeren, with Georg Bucher, Fernando Donis, Teman Evans, Teran Evans, Nicolas Firket, Selva Gurdogan, Tobias Labarque, Mee Michelle Liu, Max Schwitalla, Gregers Thomsen.

See pg 536 .Project: CBD Core. Status: Competition 2003. Client: Beijing Municipal Institute of City Planning and Design. Beijing CBD Development and Construction Co. Ltd.. Location: Beijing, China. Program: 38.28ha: Detailed planning to provide facilities and

Guangzhou Opera House. Illusion producers - technical, intellectual, and artistic - deserve their own factory; illusion consumers need to be transported to another world by sensuous architecture; for the factory, the cube remains the most appropriate shape - the public spaces are generated by a plate that curls increasingly as its program becomes more theatrical.

CBD. In a rapidly modernizing city - Beijing - take the now distributed cores of the typical CBD, lower the buildings and distribute the cores even further so that they create a field condition of pervasive insulation, or consolidate them in a single mega core, so that the same urban area can support two times the program in typologies that both promote interaction instead of creating the parallel universes of the typical CBD.

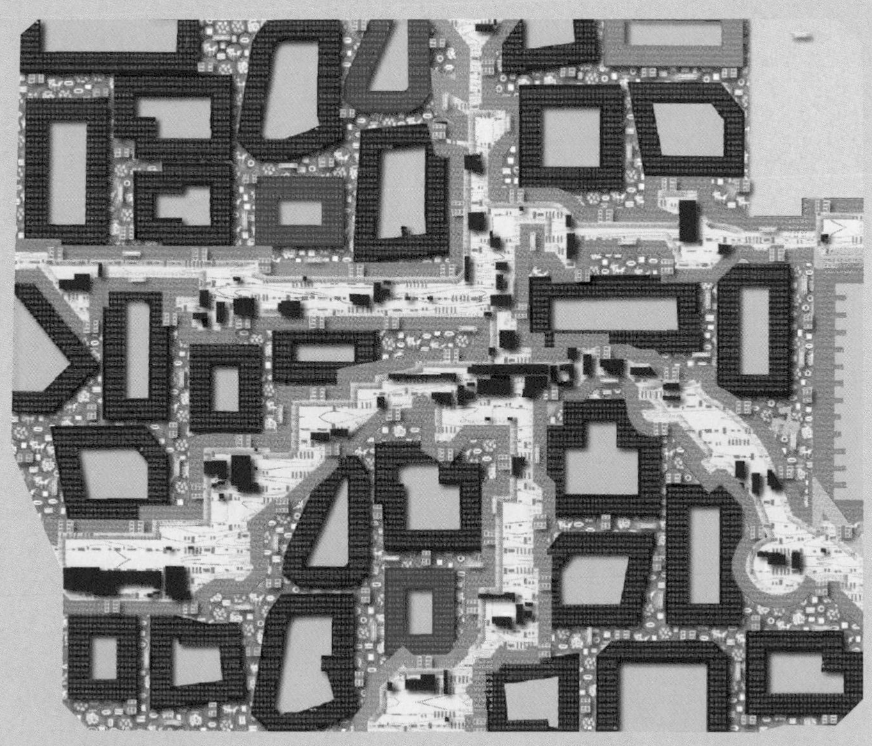

SNU. In Seoul, on the mountainous campus of the National University, a hollow library tower supports a wedge whose top is an art space and whose belly an auditorium.

services for modern business enterprises, accompanied by hotels, exhibition and conference spaces, commercial services and space for cultural recreation. Team: Rem Koolhaas, Christian Bandi, Georg Bucher, Paul Burgstaller, Jin Chong, Fernando Donis, Teman Evans, Teran Evans, Emilie Gomart, Selva Gurdogan, James Harper, Peter Knutson (Mada S), Michelle Liu, Qingyun Ma (Mada S), Florian Pucher, Nanne de Ru, Gregers Thomsen, Victoria Willocks Associate Architect: Mada Spam, ShanghaiStructure, Services: Arup

Project: Shanghai Planning and EXPO 2010 Strategy Study, AMO. Status: Commission 2003. Client: Shanghai City Planning Bureau. Budget: €40,000. Location: Shanghai, China. Program: Strategic planning for Shanghai urban spatial development. Team AMO: Rem Koolhaas, Markus Schaefer, Theo Deutinger, Emilie Gomart, Nanne de Ru, with Margaret Arbanas, Teman Evans, Teran Evans, Jason Long, Matthew Soules, Kerstin Vogel Liang Zhao. Strategic Advisor: Qingyun Ma, Shanghai

INDONESIA

Project: Netherlands Embassy, Jakarta. Status: Study Commission 1999. Client: Ministerie van Buitenlandse Zaken. Location: Jakarta, Indonesia. Site: Jalan Rankayo Rasuna Said, Jakarta. Program: entrance, offices, social program; restaurant, conference center, visiting delegation, Portuguese section. Team: Rem Koolhaas, Rob Hilz, with Laszlo Fecske, Stephen Griek, Jenny Jones, Tom van Kats, Ron Southwick, Beatrice Timm. Associate Architects: de Weger Engineers / P.T. Triweger International

THAILAND

Project: Hyperbuilding. Status: Study Commission 1996. Client: Hyper Building Research Committee Office. Location: Bangkok, Thailand. Site: Phra Pradaeng, a peninsula on the west bank of the Chao Phraya River. Program: 5,000,000 m2: A self-contained city for 120,000 inhabitants with housing/education, culture, welfare, medical, amusement/industry, economy, urban society/environment, resources, others. Team: Rem Koolhaas, Yo Yamagata, with Xavier Calderon, Donald van Dansik, Luc Lèvesque, Kohei Kashimoto. Structure, Services: Arup London

VIETNAM

Project: Hanoi New Town masterplan. Status: Commission 1997. Client: Daewoo Corporation. Location: Hanoi, Vietnam. Site: 700ha in the City of Hanoi. Program: Integration of District B in the existing masterplan by Bechtel Civil Company. Team: Rem Koolhaas, Donald van Dansik, Udo Garritzmann, Young-Joon Kim, with Floris Alkemade, Stephanie Bender, Frans Blok, Xavier CalderÙn, Grace SukChing Cheung, Claudia Dias, Chris van Duijn, Tobias Fehr, Verena Haydin, Reiner Hermes, Andrea Marlia, Philip Oswalt, Jaakko van't Spijker, Dong Ky Than. Model: Werkplaats de Rijk/Parthesius. Hydrological Advice: IWACO. Model Photography: Hectic Pictures.

KOREA

Project: H-Project - I. Status: Commission 1995. Client: Samsung Cultural Foundation. Location: Seoul, Korea. Site: In the city centre, at a steep hill in a living area. Program: 9,900m2: social studies/physical education center. Team: Rem Koolhaas, Gary Bates with Frans Blok, Sarah Dunn, Wilfred Hackenbroich, Fokke Moerel, Eric Schall, Heidi van der Wardt, Dan Wood. Associate Architect: Samoo, Seoul. Structure: Arup. Model: Werkplaats de Rijk / Parthesius.

H Project. Originally conceived as a base for a Botta-Nouvel skyline (against Seoul's densely encrusted hills), on a slope that makes one section disappear and the other emerge from the granite rock, the project resumed after the Asian Crisis has morphed into a black box suspended between a deep excavation and a floating roof - a section offering all the eventualities of a Kunsthalle.

Kansai Kan. Folding the spread-out accommodation of Japan's national library in Kansai - like a cardboard model cut-out - creates a colossal, book-lined interior, lit by a huge fireplace like the library in an English country house.

1993-2003 Architectural adventures?

Project : New Seoul International Airport City & Regional Development Plan. Status: Commission 1995 . Client: Organiser: ESPRI, Environmental Studies and Policy Research Institute, Hwan Kyung Group, Inc. Sponsor: Koaca, Korean Airport Construction Authority. Location: On the Youngyou and Mui islands and on the reclaimed land of the coast of Korea, west of Inchon. Site: 14,5 km long and 4 km wide reclaimed land on the islands and reclaimed land on the coastline creating a new face for Korea. Program: Design of a new city + humanities and infrastructure for 300,000 - 1 million inhabitants, next to a new airport where in 2020 100 million passengers are expected. Residential / Research / Hi-tech / University / Cultural / International. Team: Rem Koolhaas, Gary Bates, Piet Eckert, Jeroen Thomas, Dan Wood, with Simon van Amerongen, Vincent Coste, Bobby Fogel, Kwang Soo Kim, Paul Kroese, Margaret Muller, Greetje van den Nouweland, Fanny Smelik.

Project Name: SNU Museum - I. Status: Commission 1996. Client: Seoul National University, Samoo, Seoul, South Korea. Budget: $10m (US). Location: Seoul, Korea. Site: Hilly forest site, next to the main entrance gate of Seoul National University Campus. Program: 4300m2: museum; exhibition; education; research. Team: Rem Koolhaas, Minsuk Cho, Piet Eckert, Wim Eckert, Young Joon Kim with Mike Magner, Andreas Huhn, Jutta Raith. Associate Architect: Samoo, Seoul . Structure: Arup

Project: Togok. Status: Schematic Design 1996. Client: Samsung Corporation. Location: Seoul, Korea. Program: 8,250,000sf: offices 4,000,000sf; retail 1,450,000sf; hotel 1,000,000sf; other 1,800,000sf. Team: Rem Koolhaas, Gary Bates, with Floris Alkemade, Frans Blok, Gro Bonesmo, Xavier Calderon, Minsuk Cho, Thorsten Deckler, Sarah Dunn, Wilfried Hackenbroich, Kohei Kashimoto, Mike Magner, Oleg Nikolaeuski, Domenico Raimondo. Structure: Arup. Models: Vincent de Rijk, Bert Simons.

Photography: Hectic Pictures

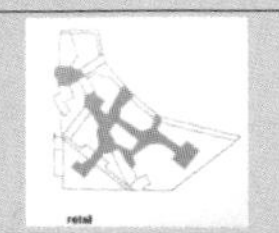

Project: Song Do New Town Masterplan. Status: Commission 1998. Client: Daewoo Corporation. Location: Inchon, Korea. Program: 42km2: new town for estimated 200,000 inhabitants, informative. technology based industry, research and development. Team: Rem Koolhaas, Donald van Dansik, Gary Bates, Minsuk Cho, Eliot Bu,Adrianne Fisher, Richard Eelman, Bert Karel Deuten, Adam Kurdahl, Floris Alkemade. Structure: Arup. Water Management: Haskoning / De Weger Engineers. Environment: Iwaco.

See pg 538 .Project: H-project - II. Status: Commission 2002, Completion 2004. Client: Samsung Cultural Foundation. Location: Seoul, Korea. Site: in the city centre, at a steep hill in a living area. Program: 13,500m2: exhibition, offices, children's center. Partners-in-Charge: Rem Koolhaas and Ole Scheeren. Project Architect: Kunle Adeyemi. Team: Shiro Ogata, Torsten Schroder, Mark Watanabe, Victoria Willocks with Charles Berman. Associate Architect: Samoo, Seoul. Structure: Chunglym Engineers. Landscape: Inside-Outside

See pg 537.Project: SNU - II. Status: Commission 2002, Completion 2004. Client: Seoul National University, Samoo, Seoul, South Korea. Budget: $8.5m (US). Location: Seoul, Korea. Site: Hilly forest site, next to the main entrance gate of Seoul National University Campus. Program: 4,300m2: museum, exhibition, education, research. Partner in Charge: Rem Koolhaas . Project Architect: Kunle Adeyemi. Team: Natacha Fricout, Roberto Otero, Rodrigo Nunez, Steffi Wedde, Camia Young, Daniela Zimmer, with Paul Burgstaller, Shiro Ogata

JAPAN

See pg 539.Project: Kansai-Kan, National Diet Library. Status: Competition 1996. Client: Ministry of Construction, Japan . Location: Kansai science city, Japan. Site: Kyoto prefecture, Seika-Nishikizu district, Kansai science city, Japan. Program: 60,000m2: modelled on US library of congress, to hold one of every book published in Japan, 150 parking spaces. Team: Rem Koolhaas, Kamiel Klaasse, with Gricha Bourbouze, Paul de Graaf, Kohei Kashimoto, Barend Koolhaas, Gijs Pyckevet . Structure: Arup. Acoustics: TNO Human Factors Research Institute. Day lighting: TNO Human Factors Research Institute

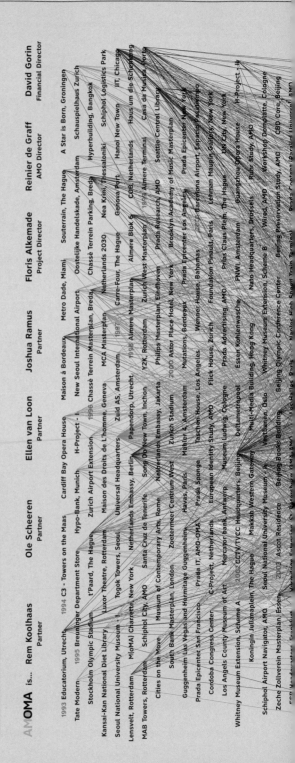

Bel +31(0)102438200

Aarts
Kunle Adeyemi
Lotte Adolf
Gregerly Agoston
Ergian Alberg
Olga Aleksakova
Floris Alkemade
Lucia Allais
Anna Almeida Jacinto
Mitchel Alonso
Simon van Amerongen
Alisa Andasek
Amale Andraos
Margaret Arbanas
Timothy Archambault
Rita Armando
Hernando Arrazola
Ali Arvanagh-Jadid
anessa de Assis Lamounier
Christian Bandi
Gary Bates
Mattijs Bauer
Christina Beaumont
Benjamin Beckers
Juliette Bekkering
Stephanie Bender
Stefan Bendiks
etz Florian Benjamin
Evan Bennet
Tom Bergevoet
Albert-Jan Berman
Charles Berman
Bina Bhattacharyya
Petra Blaisse
Frans Blok
Dorte Boerresen
Gabriela Bojalil
Bonesmo
Mette Bos
Gricha Bourbouze
Antonio Branco
Patrick Bruhn
Elliot Bu
Alexander Bub
Georg Bucher
Johannes Bucholz
Paul Burgstaller
Max Burianek
Xavier Calderon
Catarina Canas
Bart Cardinaal
Nelson Carvahlo
Kees van Casteren
David Chacon
Holly Chacon
Emanuelle Champalle
Eric Chang
Christina Chang
Grace SukChing Cheung
Shangwen Chiu
Minsuk Cho
Robert Choeff
Jin Chong
Benjamin Clarens
Florence Clausel
Guillaume Colboc
Keel Colcleugh
Brandon Cook
Hans Cool
Haiko Cornelissen
Cristophe Cornubert
Meghan Corwin
Pedro Costa
Paolo Costa
Joao Bravo da Costa
Jao Costa Ribeiro
Vincent Coste
Joakim Dahlqvist
Toma Damish
Donald van Dansik
Thorsten Deckler
John Dehart
Esther Dekhuiyzen
Daniel Dendra
Stephane Derveaux
Julien DeSmedt
Markus Dettling
Theo Deutinger
Claudia Dias
Rients Dijkstra
Claudia Dische
Rachel Doherty
Chris Dondorp
Fernando Donis
Keith Donnelley
Robert Donnelly
Jonilla Dorsten
Melissa Dowler
Stan van den Dreische
Otto Dreisden
Thomas Dubuisson
Thomas Duda
Becca Dudley
Chris van Duijn
Sarah Dunn
Mark Eacott
Piet Eckert
Wim Eckert
Richard Eelman
Rodney Eggleston
Stefan Ell
Erez Ella
Mary Ellen Cooper
Keren Englman
Mamen Escorihuela
Roger van Est
Gaspard Etourgie
Teman Evans
Teran Evans
Joris Fach
Laszlo Fecske
Tobias Fehr
Martin Felsen
Joao Ferraro
Anne Filson
Nicolas Firket
Adrianne Fisher
Bruce Fisher
Hans Focketyn
Bobby Fogel
Anthony Fontenot
Marissa Fort
Alain Fouraux
Natacha Fricout
Mark Frohn
Christian Fuchs
Jeanne Gang
Udo Garritzman
Bill Gaskins
Achim Gergen
Govert Gerritsen
Xaveer de Geyter
Sarah Gibson
Clement Gillet
Laura Gilmore
Emilie Gomart
Sharon Goren
Reinier de Graaf
Paul de Graaf
Douglas Grieco
Stephen Griek
Arjen de Groot
Juan Guardatti
Olivier Guenen
Marc Guinand
Paul van Gulik
Selva Gurdogan
Fenna Haakma Wagenaar
Wilfried Hackenbroich
Tom Hage
Jeff Hardwick
James Harper
Verena Haydin
Rene Heijnen
Christoph Helmus
Machteld Hendricks
Uwe Herlijn
Reinier Hermes
Annick Hess
Rob Hilz
Mark von Hof-Zogrotzki
Matthias Hollowich
Jens Holm
Jens Hommert
Walter Hoogerwerf
Tae Hoon Oh
Fuminori Hoshino
Oriol Hostench
Olaf Hotz
Gaudi Houdaya
Michelle Howard
Andreas Huhn
Nahyung Hwang
Jeffrey Inaba
Bjarke Ingels
Kelly Ishida
Beatriz Izquierdo
Ben Jacquemet
Aziza Jardaoui
Jeffrey Johnston
Jenny Jones
Alex de Jong
Chuihua Judy Chung
Eveline Jürgens
Anja Kalusche
Abhijit Kapade
Michel van der Kar
Alex Karcher
Bert Karel Deuten
Antonis Karides
Kohei Kashimoto
Tom van Kats
Krystan Keck
Thorsten Kiefer
Young-Joon Kim
Erhard Kinzelbach
Kamiel Klaasse
Olv Klein
Anna Kling
Niko Knebel
Suse Koch
Philip Koenen
Thomas Kolbasenko
Jan Kooijman
Rem Koolhaas
Barend Koolhaas
Ali Kops
Remco van de Kraats
Paul Kroese
Christian Kronaus
Michael Kubo
Patrick Kuhn
Adam Kurdahl
Jan-Willem van Kuilenberg
Sandford Kwinter
Dong Ky Than
Catherine Lassen
Antti Lassila
Peter Lee
Anu Leionen
Kees Lemmens
David Lemoine
Narjis Lemrin
Alexey Levchuk
Luc Levesque
Julia Lewis
Kit Lewis
Jill Leckner
Carolina Ligtenberg
Eduarda Lima
Nils Lindhorst
Anna Little
Xiaodong Liu
Mi Michelle Liu
Ena Lloret
Cornelia Locke
Caya Loeper
Rombout Lohman
Seong Lok Bae
Robert Loman
Alex de Long
Jason Long
Ellen van Loon
Jocelyn Low
Jeff Ludlow
Catharina Lundberg
Andreas Lyckefors
Winy Maas
Rob de Maat
Karolina Machalica
Christina Machynia
Casey Mack
Stuart Maddocks
Mike Magner
Kristina Manis
Susanne Manthey
Christos Marcopoulos
Beth Margulis
Neville Mars
Paz Martin
Emanuele Mattutini
Brendan McGetrick
John McMorrough
Mark McVay
Michel Melenhorst
Rachel Meyrick
Oliver Michell
Xiang Ming
Taiji Miyasaka
Fokke Moerel
Jose Molmans
Julien Montfort
David Moore
Alexander Moreno
Sophie Morgense
Christian von der Muelde
Peter Müller
Christian Müller
Margaret Müller
Shawn Mulligan
Matthew Murphy
Cristina Murphy
Simone Nagel
Oleg Nikolaevski
Greetje van den Nouweland
Rodrigo Nunez
Hans Ulrich Obrist
Tim O'Callaghan
Shiro Ogata
Daan Ooievaar
Kate Orff
Philip Oswalt
Roberto Otero
Katayoun Parssanedjad
Carol Patterson
Hannes Peer
Kerem Piker
Matteo Poli
Ala Pratt
Bill Price
Will Prince
Tammo Prinz
Florian Pucher
Matthieu Puyaubreau
Gijs Pyckevet
Yvonne Quirmbach
Stijn Rademakers
Shadi Rahbaran
Domenico Raimondo
Juta Raith
Rinske van Ramshorst
Joshua Ramus
Markus Randler
Tobias Reinhardt
Sebastian Reusch
Deborah Richmond
Lutz Ring
Michael Rock
Gerald Rogers
Fernando Romero Hauvax
Dirk Roosenburg
Nuno Rosado
Jan Roters
Jessica Rothschild
Nanne de Ru
Hilary Sample
Jonas Sandberg
Natasha Sandmeier
Duarte Santos
Christiane Sauer
Sabine Schaaf
Markus Schaefer
Eric Schall
Ole Scheeren
Mark Schendel
Beat Schenk
Andre Schmidt
Sandra Schneider-Marfels
Christoff Scholl
Eric Schotte
Torsten Schröeder
Sanna Schuiling
Oliver Schütte
Manuel Schvartzberg
Max Schwitalla
Colin Seah
Florian Seidel
Sandra Senly
Martin van Severen
Gianmaria Sforza Fogliani
Karen Shanski
Wenchian Shi
Shohei Shigematsu
Ann Shih
Hiromasa Shirai
Peer Sievers
Sanna Sihviling
Isabel da Silva
Saskia Simon
Kristina Skoogh
Fanny Smelik
Michael Smith
Galia Solomonoff
Kwang Soo Kim
Matthew Soules
Ron Southwick
Florian Speier
Jaakko van't Spijker
Samuel Spitzer
Oliver von Spreckelsen
Orri Steinorsson
Enno Stemerdink
Wim Steutel
Victoria Stewart
Henning Stueben
Bas Suijkerbuijk
Anna Sutor
Hanna Svensson
Alexander Sverdlov
Ikka Tarkkanen
Catherine Thiebaut
Felix Thoma
Jeroen Thomas
Sebastian Thomas
Gregers Thomsen
Katrin Thornhauer
Beatrice Timm
Lucien Tinga
Francesco Tiribelli
TuomasToibonen
Bruce Toman
Jasper Tonk
Lorge Toscana
Olivier Touraine
Carlos Traekner
Boukje Trenning
Faustina Tsai
L.E .Tsao
Sze Tsung Leon
Tom Tullock
Henrik Valeur
Luc Veeger
Jan Vermeulen
Jacques Vink
Kerstin Vogel
Joris Voorn
Moritz von Voss
Johan De Wachter
Sybille Wältly
Stefanie Wandinger
Heidi van der Wardt
Mark Watanabe
Don Weber
Steffi Wedde
Leonard Weil
Gerd Wetzel
Victoria Willocks
Bernard Wolff
Barbara Wolff
Dan Wood
Andy Woodcock
Zhaohui Wu
Pim van Wylik
Tian Tian Xu
Yumiko Yamada
Yo Yamagata
Dongmei Yao
Hiroshi Yoshino
Camia Young
Angela van der Zee
Evert van der Zee
Robert Zeiner
Liang Zhao
Yimin Zhu
Alois Zierl
Robert Zimmer
Daniela Zimmer
Marco Zurn

1993-2003 Architectural adventures?

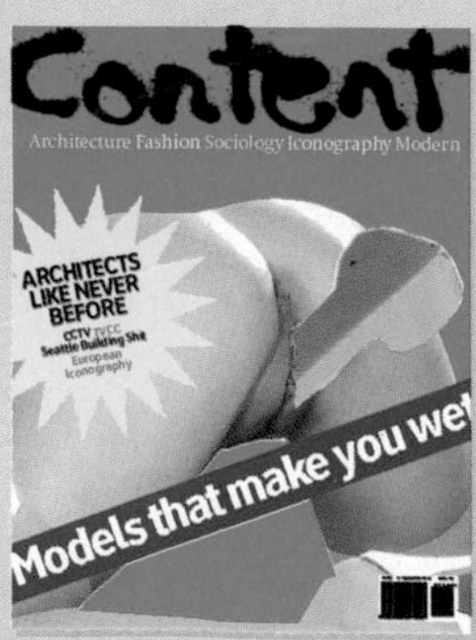

Content

New release from OMA *Rem Koolhaas*

Published by *Taschen*

Worldwide circulation: 100,000

chitecture Fashion Politics Technology Economics

Estimated readership: 300,000

'The most talked-about builder on the planet' *LA Times*

Bel +31(0)102438200

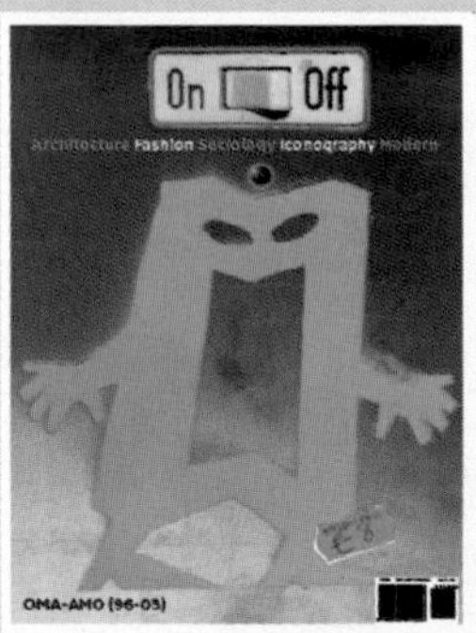

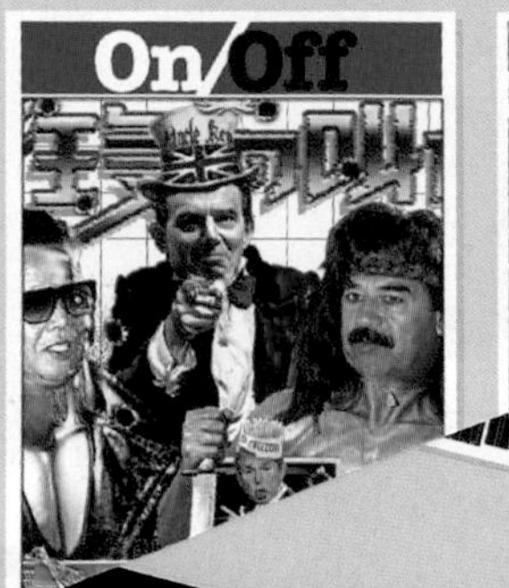

WHEN BUILDINGS ATTACK

TVCC, China ✔
CCTV, China ✔
Maison a Bordeaux, France ✔
NATO HQ, Belgium ✕
NeWhitney, USA ✕
Koningen Julianaplein, The Netherlands ✔
Prada Epicenter, USA ✔
Guangzhou Opera House, China ✕
Astor Place Hotel, USA ✕
Seattle Public Library, USA ✔
Porto Casa da Musica, Portugal ✔
Hyperbuilding, Thailand ✕